# Africana Critical Theory

D1518844

# Africana Critical Theory

## Reconstructing the Black Radical Tradition, from W. E. B. Du Bois and C. L. R. James to Frantz Fanon and Amilcar Cabral

Reiland Rabaka

LEXINGTON BOOKS
A division of
ROWMAN & LITTLEFIELD PUBLISHERS, INC.
*Lanham • Boulder • New York • Toronto • Plymouth, UK*

LEXINGTON BOOKS

A division of Rowman & Littlefield Publishers, Inc.
A wholly owned subsidary of The Rowman & Littlefield Publishing Group, Inc.
4501 Forbes Boulevard, Suite 200
Lanham, MD 20706

Estover Road
Plymouth PL6 7PY
United Kingdom

Copyright © 2009 by Lexington Books
First paperback edition 2010

*All rights reserved.* No part of this publication may be reproduced,
stored in a retrieval system, or transmitted in any form or by any
means, electronic, mechanical, photocopying, recording, or otherwise,
without the prior permission of the publisher.

British Library Cataloguing in Publication Information Available

**Library of Congress Cataloging-in-Publication Data**

The hardback edition of this book was previously cataloged by the Library of Congress as
follows:

Rabaka, Reiland, 1972–
  Africana critical theory : reconstructing the black radical tradition, from W.E.B. Du Bois
and C.L.R. James to Frantz Fanon and Amilcar Cabral / Reiland Rabaka.
    p. cm.
  Includes bibliographical references and index.
  1. African Americans—Study and teaching. 2. Critical theory. 3. African American
philosophy. I. Title.
  E184.7.R33 2009
  305.896′073—dc22                                                          2008038341

ISBN: 978-0-7391-2885-5 (cloth : alk. paper)
ISBN: 978-0-7391-2886-2 (pbk. : alk. paper)
ISBN: 978-0-7391-3309-5 (electronic)

Printed in the United States of America

♾™ The paper used in this publication meets the minimum requirements of
American National Standard for Information Sciences—Permanence of Paper
for Printed Library Materials, ANSI/NISO Z39.48-1992.

*For my nieces and nephews*
Robert Smith III, Ryan Smith, Kalyn Smith, Remington Smith,
Dominique Clewis, and Journey Clewis


*And, as with all of my work,*
*for my mother, grandmothers, and great aunt*
Marilyn Jean Giles, Lizzie Mae Davis, Elva Rita Warren,
and Arcressia Charlene Connor


*Nkosi Sikelel' iAfrika . . .*

# Contents

Prelude to a Conceptual Kiss: Preface and Acknowledgements ix

1 (Re)Introducing the Africana Tradition of Critical Theory: Posing
   Problems and Searching for Solutions 1

2 W. E. B. Du Bois: The Soul of a Pan-African Marxist Male-Feminist 37

3 C. L. R. James: Pan-African Marxism Beyond All Boundaries 89

4 Aimé Césaire and Léopold Senghor: Revolutionary Negritude and
   Radical New Negroes 111

5 Frantz Fanon: Revolutionizing the Wretched of the Earth, Radicalizing
   the Discourse on Decolonization 165

6 Amilcar Cabral: Using the Weapon of Theory to Return to the
   Source(s) of Revolutionary Decolonization and Revolutionary
   Re-Africanization 227

7 Africana Critical Theory: Overcoming the Aversion to New Theory
   and New Praxis in Africana Studies and Critical Social Theory 285

Bibliography 307

Index 415

About the Author 431

# Preface and Acknowledgements

## Prelude to a Conceptual Kiss

> Critics have their purposes, and they're supposed to do what they do, but sometimes they get a little carried away with what they think someone should have done, rather than concerning themselves with what they did.
>
> —Duke Ellington, *Music Is My Mistress*

For more than a decade my primary intellectual preoccupation has been to widen the world of ideas of critical theory. Although critical theory has long been associated with the Frankfurt School, and specifically the intellectual lives and legacies of Theodor Adorno, Walter Benjamin, Erich Fromm, Jurgen Habermas, Max Horkheimer, and Herbert Marcuse, the names and contributions of several other significant critical social theorists have been recently raised. For instances, my first book, *W. E. B. Du Bois and the Problems of the Twenty-First Century* (2007), explored Du Bois and Africana Studies' contributions to critical theory. It endeavored to innovatively demonstrate the ways in which Du Bois's *transdisciplinary* discourse contributes to the deconstruction and reconstruction of the intellectual history and history of ideas of "conventional" or "classical" critical theory, by bringing "classical" critical theory into deep discursive dialogue with Du Bois's distinct contributions to: philosophy of race, sociology of race, psychology of race, anthropology of race, history of race, and critical race theory; Pan-Africanism, anti-colonialism, decolonization theory, and critical postcolonial theory; black Marxism, black nationalism, and other brands of black radicalism; and, black feminism, womanism, and the Black Women's Club Movement (specifically the National Association of Colored Women and, later, the National Council of Negro Women).

My second book, *Du Bois's Dialectics: Black Radical Politics and the Reconstruction of Critical Social Theory* (2008), shifted the focus from extending and expanding the intellectual and political discourse(s) of classical critical theory, by accenting and analyzing Du Bois and Africana Studies' often-overlooked contributions, to broadening the base of contemporary or "new" critical theory, by bringing it into dialogue with Du Bois and Africana Studies discourse. In both of my previous books, therefore,

Du Bois's seminal work as a *transdisciplinary* social theorist and radical political activist was shown to be of immense importance to contemporary critical theorists interested in intellectually overhauling the foundations of critical theory, making it more multicultural, transethnic, transgender, transgenerational, sexual orientation-sensitive, and non-Western European philosophy-focused by placing it into deep dialogue with theory and phenomena it has heretofore woefully neglected. As the urgent issues of racism, sexism, capitalism, and colonialism were scrutinized in *Du Bois and the Problems of the Twenty-First Century*, boldly blurring and unmistakably moving the critical theoretical margins even further, *Du Bois's Dialectics* endeavored ideological critiques of education, religion, the politics of reparations, and the problematics of black radical politics in contemporary culture and society. Similar to *Du Bois and the Problems of the Twenty-First Century*, *Du Bois's Dialectics* employed Du Bois as its critical theoretical point of departure and primary paradigmatic intellectual-activist ancestor, decidedly demonstrating his (and Africana Studies') contributions to, as well contemporary critical theory's connections to: philosophy of education, sociology of education, critical pedagogy, and critical educational theory; philosophy of religion, sociology of religion, liberation theology, and womanist theology; reparations theory and revolutionary humanism; and, it ingeniously offered the first critical theoretical treatment of the infamous W. E. B. Du Bois–Booker T. Washington debate, which lucidly highlights Du Bois's transition from a bourgeois black liberal touting a "Talented Tenth," to a bona-fide black radical and revolutionary democratic socialist advocating a "Guiding Hundredth."

## CRITICAL THEORY GOT IT BAD (AND THAT AIN'T GOOD): ON CRITICAL THEORY'S AVERSION TO BLACK RADICALISM AND EMBRACE OF THE INTRICACIES OF EUROCENTRISM

Where *Du Bois and the Problems of the Twenty-First Century* exhibited a preoccupation with the philosophical foundations and intellectual and political agendas of classical critical theory (demonstrating that many of the problems of the past remain problems in the present because many classical critical theorists quarantined their discourses along racial and gender lines), *Du Bois's Dialectics* was intellectually obsessed with broadening the base of contemporary or new critical theory (demonstrating that many contemporary critical theorists are unwittingly weakening the critical potency and radical potential of their theories by limiting their intellectual lenses to "traditional," single-subject disciplines, Eurocentric theorists and theories, and, ironically, "ivory tower," white-washed [as opposed to multicultural neo-Marxist and/or transethnic anti-imperialist] discourse). Contemporary critical theory, as I envision and expatiate it, should not only challenge "conventional" critical theory to be more race and racism conscious, develop a deeper commitment to gender justice and women's liberation, compassionately concern itself with colonialism (especially racial colonialism) and its interconnections with capitalism (especially racist capitalism), and unequivocally dialogue with cutting-edge anti-heterosexist and queer theory, but it should also unapologetically and generously draw from the work of W. E. B. Du Bois, C. L. R. James, Aime Cesaire, Leopold Senghor, Frantz Fanon, and Amilcar Cabral, as well as innumerable other non-European/non-white critical theorists, who collectively emphasize(d): the importance of avoiding the ob-sessive economism of many mainstream modern and postmodern Marxists; the power of ideology critique; the primacy of politics; the political economy of race (es-pecially "the black race") in a white supremacist world; the racist nature of colo-nialism *and* capitalism; the political economy of patriarchy and the need for women's decolonization and women's liberation; the politics of leadership and lib-eration; the politics of religion in a racialized and unjustly gendered world; and, the need to constantly deconstruct and reconstruct critical social theory to speak to the special needs of "the new times," to borrow one of Stuart Hall's favorite phrases (S. Hall, 1996a).

Surviving in the jungles of Europe's ivory towers and quarantined to racially col-onized and ghettoized spaces in the European and American academies, often qui-etly combating the constantly "on safari" attitudes (or, stuck-on-stupid stances!, if you will) of well-meaning whites' unrepentant refusal to acknowledge their power and privilege in a white supremacist world, and amid the current intellectual trepi-dation and word-wizardry of many of the long-lauded "conventional" (read: white, unmistakably Marxist, and male) critical theorists, the distinct discourse(s) of the Africana tradition of critical theory exists furtively in the insurgent intellectual-activist imagination, seemingly stripped of its critical potency, and even mocked by postmodernists, postcolonialists, and post-Marxists (among many others) who ar-gue that black radicalism is outdated or old fashioned. It seems as though black rad-icalism in the twenty-first century continues to represent a riddle, or series of riddles, which remain the hallowed hallmark(s) of the "wretched of the earth," and this even though "conventional" critical theorists consistently downplay and attempt to diminish the salience of race, racism, racial violence, and, of course, white su-premacy. Black radicalism has been all but banished in contemporary critical the-ory, as it was with classical critical theory, blithely relegated to the status of a ruse put forward by the unruly (dare I say, "buckwild!") blacks of bygone eras—that is, those "Pan-African insurgents," "Negritude nuisances," "Civil Rights radicals," and, of course, "Black Power pests" of the past.

However, for those of us with unquenchable commitments to continuing the fight for freedom, for those of us deeply disturbed by what is going on in our global warming and war-torn world, and for those of us who desperately search for solu-tions to our most pressing social and political problems, black radicals' anti-impe-rialist ideas and actions, black radicals' increasing commitments to gender justice and women's liberation, black radicals' revolutionary humanist political vision and theories of social change are far from antiquated and have historically and continue currently to offer a much needed *Africana* alternative to, and through, the mazes of ever-increasing Eurocentrism, postmodernism, postcolonialism, postfeminism, and post-Marxism, among other contemporary conceptual distractions and disruptions. Along with other black radical figures, like Marcus Garvey, Claudia Jones, Ella Baker, Malcolm X, Fannie Lou Hamer, Bayard Rustin, and Audre Lorde, the examples of W. E. B. Du Bois, C. L. R. James, Aime Cesaire, Leopold Senghor, Frantz Fanon, and Amilcar Cabral can serve as models of, and provide the means through which we begin critically rethinking the possibilities of resistance to, and the transgressive transformation of the new global imperialism(s) of our age. Their collective thought and texts clearly cut across several disciplines and, therefore, closes the chasm between

Africana Studies and critical theory, constantly demanding that intellectuals not simply think deep thoughts, develop new theories, and theoretically support radical politics, but *be* and constantly *become* political activists, social organizers, and cultural workers—that is, folk the Italian critical theorist Antonio Gramsci referred to as "organic intellectuals." In this sense, then, the series of studies gathered in *Africana Critical Theory* contribute not only to African Studies, African American Studies, Caribbean Studies, Cultural Studies, Postcolonial Studies, Postnational Studies, and Women's Studies, but also to contemporary critical theoretical discourse across an amazingly wide-range of "traditional" disciplines, and radical political activism outside of (and, in many instances, absolutely *against*) Europe's insidious ivory towers and the apartheid-like absurdities of the American academy.

## CRITICAL THEORETICAL AND RADICAL POLITICAL THINGS AIN'T WHAT THEY USED TO BE

Besides building on the research of my previous books, *Africana Critical Theory: Reconstructing the Black Radical Tradition, from W. E. B. Du Bois and C. L. R. James to Frantz Fanon and Amilcar Cabral* is loosely based on my doctoral dissertation and, consequently, identifies and analyzes continental and diasporan African contributions to classical and contemporary critical theory. The present volume is earnestly intended to be a climatic critical theoretical clincher that cogently demonstrates how Du Bois's rarely discussed dialectical thought, transdisciplinarity, intellectual history-making radical political activism, and world-historical multiple liberation movement leadership helped to inaugurate a distinct Africana tradition of critical theory. With chapters on, of course, W. E. B. Du Bois (African American), C. L. R. James (Caribbean), Negritude: Aime Cesaire (Caribbean) and Leopold Senghor (African), Frantz Fanon (Caribbean), and Amilcar Cabral (African), *Africana Critical Theory* endeavors to accessibly offer contemporary critical theorists an intellectual archaeology of the Africana tradition of critical theory and a much-needed dialectical deconstruction and reconstruction of black radical politics. These six seminal figures are certainly not Africana critical theory's only intellectual-activist ancestors and, as I alluded above, there is an almost innumerable wealth and wide-range of unexplored Africana "organic intellectuals," political activists and cultural workers whose thought and texts desperately deserve to be identified and analyzed for their contribution to the Africana tradition of critical theory in specific, as well as the wider world of radical politics and critical social theory in general.

The subsequent series of studies, in addition, will analyze and explain the many tensions and ambiguities, contradictions and conundrums in the Africana tradition of critical theory by demonstrating how these six seminal figures' thought and texts are deeply connected to, and, as is usually the case, in critical dialogue with specific historical happenings, cultural conditions, and political practices both within and without the African world. This dialectical approach will enable us to see, first, how Frankfurt School and the more Marxian brands of critical theory have long overlooked racism, sexism, and colonialism, thus, in most instances, making their versions of critical theory the very "one-dimensional" thought that the Frankfurt

School critical theorist, Herbert Marcuse (1964), woefully warned against. Second, a dialectical approach will allow us to observe how Africana Studies and black radicalism relates to the deconstruction and reconstruction of critical theory. Over the last quarter of a century there have been consistent calls within critical theoretical discourse for a "return to Marx" in order to reconstruct critical theory and make it more viable in light of the vicissitudes of contemporary capitalism. However, what many of these otherwise sophisticated critical social theorists fail to perceive is that it was and remains their over-dependency on Marx and Marxism that has made so much of their work theoretically myopic and intellectually insular.

Like a dog chasing its own tail, many white Marxists and critical theorists have locked their discourses into a vicious cycle, a hermeneutic circle, going round and round, covering a lot of the same theoretical terrain and identifying similar economic issues as the infinite cause of contemporary social suffering without opening their conceptual universes to the world of ideas and the radical thought-traditions of those of "other races and other colors," as Marcuse (1964) aptly put it in *One-Dimensional Man* (p. 256). Many of these same Marxists and critical theorists bemoan the sorry state of contemporary critical social theory, but are either too intellectually timid, too intellectually elitist or, dare I say, too racially exclusivist to move beyond merely mentioning the fact that critical theory should be *equally* anti-racist, anti-sexist, and anti-colonialist. Mentioning racism, sexism, and/or colonialism in passing, at the end of an article, or at the back of a book, and always in subordination to "the evils of capitalism," does not do the, literally, billions of human beings who suffer at the hands of these overlapping, interlocking, and intersecting systems of exploitation, oppression, and violence a favor. In fact, if the truth be told, it is the exact kind of curt *cosmetic multiculturalism* and tired *textual tokenism* that profoundly perturbs non-European/non-white radical and revolutionary intellectual-activists and makes them constantly question the sincerity of white "critical" social theorists.

If, indeed, critical theory is theory critical of domination and discrimination, and a social theory that simultaneously offers accessible and ethical alternatives to the key social and political problems of the present age, then, any theory claiming to be a "critical theory of contemporary society" must thoroughly theorize not only capitalism, but also racism, sexism, and colonialism, and how each of the aforementioned overlaps, interconnects, and intersects to deform and destroy life and the ongoing prospects of liberation and democratic socialist transformation. Africana critical theory, thus, emerges from the succeeding series of studies as a transdisciplinary, critical social scientific, philosophically fascinating, and mixed and multimethod tradition of radicalism whose theoretical advances and actual socio-political revolutions indisputably contributes to contemporary efforts to reconceptualize and reconstruct radical politics and critical theory. Critical theory cannot and will not be able to revise itself unless and until it seriously considers the contributions of non-European/non-white social theorists and intellectual-activists. This generation of critical theorists, then, has a unique and time-sensitive task before it and, simply said, it is as follows: we must put into principled practice *immediately* what critical theory has so long advanced theoretically and rhetorically. In terms of the Africana tradition of critical theory that critical theoretical admonition, perhaps, has been best captured by Frantz Fanon (1967), in *Black Skin, White Mask*, when he wrote:

> I, the man of color, want only this:
> That the tool never possess the man. That enslavement of man by man cease forever. That is, of one by another. That it be possible for me to discover and to love man, wherever he may be . . .
> It is through the effort to recapture the self and to scrutinize the self, it is through the lasting tension of their freedom that men will be able to create the ideal conditions of existence for a human world.
> Superiority? Inferiority?
> Why not the quite simple attempt to touch the other, to feel the other, to explain the other to myself?
> Was my freedom not given to me then in order to build the world of the *You*? (pp. 231–232; emphasis in original)

## IN A SENTIMENTAL MOOD: SAYING ASANTE SANA TO MY FRIENDS AND FAMILY, TO MY COLLEAGUES AND COMRADES

*Africana Critical Theory* is not simply an intellectual exercise about the long-overlooked Africana tradition of critical theory, but it also stands as a testament to what the many people who have contributed to my personal, professional, and radical political development have taught me. W. E. B. Du Bois, C. L. R. James, Aime Cesaire, Leopold Senghor, Frantz Fanon, and Amilcar Cabral, as I will repeat throughout the text, represent radical political intellectual-activist ancestors who provide me with several paradigms and points of departure to explore Africana Studies' contributions to the deconstruction and reconstruction of critical theory. Though their thought provides the primary points of departure, the theories and praxes of many, many others have influenced and informed my conceptions of radical politics and critical social theory. Each chapter of this book bears the imprint of the diverse—though often disconnected—intellectual and political arenas and agendas I draw from and endeavor to establish critical dialogue with. As a consequence, the list of intellectuals, activists, archivists, institutions, and organizations to which I am indebted is, indeed, enormous. Such being the case, I hope I may be forgiven for deciding that the most appropriate way in which to acknowledge my sincere appreciation is simply to list them below without the protracted praise each has so solemnly earned. My deepest gratitude and most heartfelt *asante sana* (a thousand thanks) is offered, first and foremost, to my family: my mother, Marilyn Giles; my grandmothers, Lizzie Mae Davis (deceased) and Elva Rita Warren; my great aunt, Arcressia Charlene Connor; my older brother and his wife, Robert Smith II and Karen Smith; my younger brother and his wife, Dwight Clewis and Terica Clewis; my nieces and nephews, Journey Clewis, Dominique Clewis, Robert Smith III, Ryan Smith, Kalyn Smith, Remington Smith; my father, Robert Smith I; my grandfather, Joseph Warren (deceased); and, my innumerable aunts, uncles, and cousins throughout the Americas, the Caribbean, and Africa.

An undertaking as ambitious as *Africana Critical Theory* would have been impossible without the assistance of colleagues and comrades, both far and wide. I express my earnest appreciation to the following fine folk, who each in their own special way contributed to the composition and completion of this book: Lucius Outlaw; Rhonda Tankerson; De Reef Jamison; Denise Lovett; Adam Clark; Elzie Billops; Sigmund Washington; Patrick DeWalt; Nelson Keith; Stacey Smith; Lamya Al-Kharusi; Toroitich Chereno; Anthony Lemelle; Katherine Bankole; Onye Ozuzu; Troy Barnes; April Sweeney; Nicole Barcliff; Zachary Epps; Ursula Lindqvist; La'Neice Littleton; Marissa Manriquez; Sara Bloom; Tiya Trent; Lewis Gordon; Paget Henry; Joy James; Alan Sica; Alison Jaggar; Vincent Harding; Kimberly Marshall; Cali Harris; Otis L. Scott; George Junne; Andrew Smallwood; Mpozi Tolbert (deceased); and, Vincent Woodard (deceased).

I cannot adequately convey the depth of my gratitude to the National Council for Black Studies (NCBS) for providing me with the critical feedback and fora to deepen and develop my relationship with the Africana tradition of critical theory. I have been presenting my research on Africana critical theory at NCBS's annual conferences for more than a decade. Along with saying *nashukuru sana* (special thanks) to NCBS in general, I would be remiss not to single out several members whose key contributions and intellectual encouragement have made the present volume possible. I express my earnest appreciation to the following NCBS colleagues and comrades: Molefi Asante; Maulana Karenga; James Turner; Delores Aldridge; James Stewart; Ronald Stephens; James Conyers; Charles Jones; Sundiata Cha-Jua; Perry Hall; Shirley Weber; Barbara Wheeler; Alfred Young; Bill Little (deceased); Munasha Furusa; Akinyele Umoja; Fred Hord; Terry Kershaw; Jeffrey Ogbar; Scot Brown; Alan Colon; Abdul Nanji; Christel Temple; Patricia Reid-Merritt; Kevin Cokley; Salim Faraji; Cecil Gray; Ricky Jones; and, Mark Christian.

The faculty, staff, and students in the Department of Ethnic Studies and the Center for Studies of Ethnicity and Race in America (CSERA) at the University of Colorado at Boulder deserve special thanks for their patience and critical support. *Nashukuru sana* to our steadfast staff, especially Sandra Lane and Susan Armstrong, for always being there and lending a brother a helping hand. I am also deeply indebted to my colleagues and comrades who selflessly serve on the fine faculty in the Department of Ethnic Studies, each of them have patiently listened to me rant and rave about the Africana tradition of critical theory over the last couple of years. I say *nashukuru sana*, therefore, to William King, Albert Ramirez, Arturo Aldama, Elisa Facio, Emma Perez, Daryl Maeda, Ken Orona, Deward Walker, Seema Sohi, William Takamatsu, Stewart Lawler, Linda Hogan, Patricia Kaurouma, Vivian Delgado, and Jose Lugo. William King, a former president of NCBS, and his lovely wife Carla welcomed me to Boulder with open arms, and we have shared many memorable meals filled with love-laced words, lots of laughter and heated discussions and critical debates about everything from the state of Africana Studies to the aesthetic evolution of jazz and "soul music" (as opposed to "rhythm and blues"). Bill has been a model mentor, and I humbly hope that the best of my teaching and research reflect my profound respect for him and what he has shared with me over the last couple of years. Also, I say *asante sana* (a thousand thanks) to the incredibly insightful students who took my seminars on W. E. B. Du Bois, C. L. R. James, Frantz Fanon, Critical Race Theory, and Africana Philosophy at the University of Colorado at Boulder. This book has greatly benefited from the critical questions and eloquent answers they offered me (and the Africana tradition of critical theory).

Several libraries, research centers, special collections, and archives hosted and helped me transform this book from an inchoate idea into its fully realized form. I am indelibly indebted to the directors, research fellows, and staffs of: the W. E. B. Du Bois Memorial Center for Pan-African Culture, Accra, Ghana; Africana Rare Books Room, Balme Library, University of Ghana, Legon; Institute of African Studies, Nnamdi Azikiwe Library, University of Nigeria, Nsukka; West African Research Center (WARC), Dakar, Senegal; Institut Fondamental d'Afrique Noire (IFAN), Cheikh Anta Diop University, Dakar, Senegal; C. L. R. James Collection, West Indiana and Special Collections, Main Library, University of the West Indies at St. Augustine, Trinidad and Tobago; The West Indies Collection and University Collection, Main Library, University of the West Indies at Mona, Jamaica; George Padmore Institute, London; Center of African Studies, School of Oriental and African Studies, University of London; Department of the Languages and Cultures of Africa, School of Oriental and African Studies, University of London; Center for Ethnic Minority Studies, School of Oriental and African Studies, University of London; American Studies Research Center, King's College London, University of London; Eccles Center for American Studies, British Library, London; African Studies Center, University of Oxford; Rothermere American Institute, University of Oxford; School of American and Canadian Studies, University of Nottingham; Center for American Studies, University of Leicester; Center of African Studies, University of Cambridge; Ferguson Center for African and Asian Studies, Open University; Center for African Studies, University of Leeds; Center of West African Studies (CWAS), University of Birmingham; Center of African Studies, University of Edinburgh; W. E. B. Du Bois Papers, Department of Special Collections and University Archives, W. E. B. Du Bois Library, University of Massachusetts at Amherst; W. E. B. Du Bois Institute for African and African American Research, Harvard University; Arthur A. Houghton, Jr., Library, Harvard University; Center for African American Studies, Wesleyan University; Schomburg Center for Research in Black Culture, New York Public Library; Nicholas Murray Butler Library, Columbia University; John Henrik Clarke Africana Library, Africana Studies and Research Center, Cornell University; African American Collection, Hillman Library, University of Pittsburgh; Africana Research Center, Pennsylvania State University; Charles L. Blockson African American Collection, Temple University; Center for African American History and Culture, Temple University; Center for Africana Studies, University of Pennsylvania; Moorland-Spingarn Research Center, Howard University; African American Studies Research and Resource Center, George Mason University; John Hope Franklin Collection for African and African American Documentation, Rare Book, Manuscript, and Special Collections Library, Duke University; Carter G. Woodson Center for African American and African Studies, University of Virginia; Robert W. Woodruff Library, Atlanta University Center Archives; Manuscript Sources for African American History, Special Collections, Emory University; Fisk University Library, Fisk University; Amistad Research Center, Tulane University; Center for African and African American Studies, University of Texas at Austin; Center for African American Studies, University of Houston; St. Clair Drake Center for African and African American Studies, Roosevelt University; Center for African American and African Studies, University of Michigan; African Studies Center, Michigan State University; Neal-Marshall African American

Cultural Center, Indiana University; African and African American Collection, University Library, University of California, Berkeley; Ralph J. Bunche Center for African American Studies, University of California, Los Angeles; Center for Black Studies, University of California, Santa Barbara; Blair-Caldwell African American Research Library, Denver Public Library; and, Center for African American Policy, University of Denver.

My astute editor, Michael Sisskin, and the Lexington Books editorial board deserve very special thanks (*nashukuru sana*) for seeing the potential in this book project and prodding me along during the many months it took me to revise the manuscript and prepare it for production. I would like to formally thank Michael, Julie Kirsch, and Jessica Bradfield for the care and promptness with which they have handled my book projects, and for their patience with my extremely erratic (if not a bit eccentric) research and writing regimen, which in this instance took me to more than three dozen university and public libraries, archives, and research centers in Africa, the Caribbean, Europe, and the United States. I am not by any means the easiest person to get in touch with when I am working, but throughout the entire research and writing process they have calmly fielded my questions and coolly encouraged me to complete my book.

It would be extremely irresponsible of me not acknowledge the enormous debt I owe to Edward Kennedy Ellington, whose music has served as a constant source of inspiration for me during the research and writing of, not only *Africana Critical Theory*, but, if truth be told, both of my previous books. To openly admit that my affinity for the music of Duke Ellington is comparable to my intellectual love affair with Du Bois is to finally put into print something that most of friends and family have known for the better part of my life. Ellington (with Sun Ra coming in an uncomfortably close second!) is unequivocally my favorite composer, and it would not be stretching the truth to say that I have, literally, listened to hundreds and hundreds of his compositions during the research and writing of this book—Ellington composed more than 5,000 compositions, and one of my life's goals is to listen to his corpus; yes, meaning, each and every one of his works. As it was with Du Bois, the road to success (actually fame and fortune), did not come easily for Ellington. Few folk wanted to hear his early "rags," and even fewer folk had open ears for his innovative, music history-making contributions to jazz, which he initially called "Jungle Music," then "Mood Music." Ellington meticulously labored long and hard on his compositions, but I would be remiss not too mention that though he is generally regarded as the greatest "American"—as well as African American—composer of the twentieth century, few have fully grasped the genius of his piano playing, and Ellington himself was often extremely self-effacing when it came to his playing, most often modestly pointing to the innovative improvisations of his extraordinarily talented orchestra members (see Ellington, 1973; M. Tucker, 1993).

It was my grandmother who first exposed me to Ellington's music, and then, upon learning of my musical love affair with the maestro, it was my mother who bought me his albums and took me to the library to borrow books on him and his music (i.e., "Ellingtonia"). Like Du Bois, Ellington has traveled with me from adolescence to adulthood—that is, from boyhood to manhood. Where Du Bois provides me with intellectual and political guidance and direction, Ellington offers a unique Africana aesthetic that is part musical and, very importantly, part spiritual and cultural. He, too, then, has influenced my research method(s) and writing style(s), and it is in reference to his lifework, which is much more than mere "music" to me, that the title and subtitles of this preface smacks of and is smitten with.

This book is lovingly dedicated to my nieces and nephews and, as with all of my work, it is also dedicated to my mother, grandmothers, and great aunt—and they individually and collectively know the many millions of reasons why. I cannot properly put into words what my nieces and nephews mean to me. They are my inspiration, and constant sources of joy. I sincerely hope and pray that my lifework will be like a bright light shining in this dark world where they, too, will have to eke out an existence and, even more, a "good" life. I do not pretend to know what they have suffered, nor what they more than likely will suffer, but this I do know: Life is not now, and has never been predetermined (not even for black folk in an anti-black racist and white supremacist world). Like Harriet Tubman and Frederick Douglass, like Anna Julia Cooper and W. E. B. Du Bois, like Fannie Lou Hamer and Malcolm X who came long before them, my nieces and nephews need to know that they do not have to suffer in silence, they can and must knuckle and brawl to transform themselves and the world they live in. I write all of this especially to Robert Dean Smith III, my most beloved "Tré," who has suffered for so long with leukemia and epilepsy, among other ailments, and who through all of his ordeals has remained resilient and resolute. This book is most especially for him, in sickness and in health, on "bad" days and on "good" days.

I am also at a loss for words to express my love to and my most profound reverence for my mother, grandmothers, and great aunt. They reared and raised me, loved me and listened to me, berated and believed in me when so many others seemed not the least bit concerned whether I, literally, lived or died. Though my brothers and I grew up in a most acute abject poverty, it was my mother, grandmothers, and great aunt who constantly reminded us that our poverty did not automatically deny our human dignity. They double-dared us to dream but, even more, they encouraged us to humbly and diligently work toward turning our dreams into our realities. Though they could have discouraged me from pursuing higher education, since no one in our immediate family has ever attended a college or university, they instead encouraged and supported me. Why or how, remains unbeknownst to me. I suppose this is love in its purest and most unadulterated form. So, once again, to them, I say simply, *nakupenda sana*—I love, admire, and adore you more any words can express.

If, then, my gentle readers, any inspiration or insights are gathered from my journey through the jungles of radical politics and critical social theory, I pray you will attribute them to the aforementioned. However, if (and when) you find foibles and intellectual idiosyncrasies, I humbly hope you will neither associate them with any of the forenamed nor, most especially, W. E. B. Du Bois, C. L. R. James, Aime Cesaire, Leopold Senghor, Frantz Fanon, or Amilcar Cabral. I, and I alone, am responsible for what herein is written. *Nkosi Sikelel' iAfrika . . . .*[1]

—Reiland Rabaka
The Maghreb (al-Maġrib al-Arabī)

## NOTES

1. Translation: "God bless Africa" in Xhosa. Azania or South Africa's national anthem, *Nkosi Sikelel' iAfrika*, was composed in 1897 by Enoch Mankayi Sontonga, a Xhosa teacher and choirmaster at a Methodist mission school in Johannesburg. Since it was first sung in 1899 at the ordination of Reverend Boweni, a minister in the Methodist tradition, it has been adopted as the anthem of the African National Congress and the national anthem of both Tanzania and Zambia. Additionally, it was sung in Zimbabwe and Namibia during their respective struggles against racial colonialism. Most of Sontonga's songs were heart-wrenching odes, somewhere between the spirituals and the blues, often grappling with the human suffering and social misery of black life under apartheid. Sontonga, a reportedly deeply religious man, is said to have repeatedly recited this prayer and taught it to his many pupils. The African National Congress continues to close its meetings with this song, and it has been reported that, upon his release from being unjustly imprisoned for 27 years on Robben Island, Madiba Nelson Rolihlahla Mandela was so moved by the solemn singing of it that once elected the president of South Africa he declared Sontonga's grave a national monument and erected a memorial in his honor. Therefore, in my earnest effort to show my sincere solidarity with my known and unknown kith and kin throughout continental and diasporan Africa, I know of no better way to conclude this preface and begin my beloved book: *Nkosi Sikelel' iAfrika*.

# 1

# (Re)Introducing the Africana Tradition of Critical Theory: Posing Problems and Searching for Solutions

Critical theory envisions philosophy not so much as an abstract or general engagement with questions of human existence; rather, it envisions a productive relationship between philosophy and other disciplines—for example, sociology, cultural studies, feminist theory, African American studies—and the use of this knowledge in projects to radically transform society. Critical theory, as formulated and founded by the Frankfurt School—which included Horkheimer and Marcuse—has as its goal the transformation of society, not simply the transformation of ideas, but social transformation and thus the reduction and elimination of human misery. It was on the basis of this insistence on the social implementation of critical ideas that I was able to envision a relationship between philosophy and black liberation.

—Angela Y. Davis, *African American Philosophers: 17 Conversations*, p. 22

The framework of critical social theory, joined with praxis aimed at revolutionary or evolutionary sociohistorical development, provides a context of understanding within which we people of African descent (and others) can assess our situations and achieve enhanced clarity regarding which concrete historical possibilities are in our best interest. To the extent that we do so within this context of understanding, conditioned by a commitment to generalized progressive human development, then it is clear that our interest in our own well-being cannot be limited to narrow self-interest.

—Lucius T. Outlaw Jr., *Critical Social Theory in the Interests of Black Folk*, p. 27

[C]ritical social theory encompasses bodies of knowledge and sets of institutional practices that actively grapple with the central questions facing groups of people differently placed in specific political, social, and historical contexts characterized by injustice. What makes critical social theory "critical" is its commitment to justice, for ones own group and/or for other groups.

—Patricia Hill Collins, *Fighting Words: Black Women and the Search for Social Justice*, p. xiv

1

Black Studies/African American Studies/Africana Studies was born with the express purpose of *decolonizing the minds of people, especially black people*. Although much knowledge can be produced by writing histories and social scientific studies, no amount of information could get very far in the absence of minds unable to see or understand it. Important as empirical work has been and continues to be, without interpretation, even at the level of the methods used for organizing the research and gathering data, such work would be meaningless. The power of interpretation is such, however, that it, too, is embedded in a special type of interpretation or hermeneutic without which it, as well, would be meaningless. And that interpretation we call theory.

—Lewis R. Gordon and Jane Anna Gordon, *Not Only the Master's Tools:*
*African American Studies in Theory and Practice*, p. x

[I]t is a common habit to study the thought of black thinkers as primarily derivative. . . . What this means is that thinkers like C. L. R. James, Frantz Fanon, and W. E. B. Du Bois are never credited with intellectual independence and originality. Their ideas exist only *in relationship to* and *because* of the already accepted systems of thought. Consequently, there is a great chain of thought constructed around hierarchical order wherein Africana thinkers are located on the margins. In this chain, radical Africana thinkers piggyback on Marx or Sartre, their intellectual validation passing through the ideas of the accepted "giants." . . . The study of radical black intellectuals requires us to excavate the ideas of black radicals, to probe and discover the questions they raise in their political discourses and practices.

—Anthony Bogues, *Black Heretics, Black Prophets:*
*Radical Political Intellectuals*, pp. 2, 9

## TO BEGIN, AGAIN: REVISITING AND
## REVISING THE BLACK RADICAL TRADITION

As we quickly move from the dawn to the first decade of the twenty-first century, W. E. B. Du Bois's provocative prophecies and Frantz Fanon's critical candor continue to haunt their intellectual and political heirs and opponents. The thought and texts of these two towering figures have been recurrently deified and demonized, exalted and ignored, defended and disproved to such an extent that it almost invariably makes contemporary discussions of their offerings to the social sciences and the humanities—as well as the *transdisciplinary discipline* of Africana Studies in specific—suspect. In other words, critically engaging Du Bois and Fanon, and the thought-tradition(s) their work extended and expanded, and continues extending and expanding, is not for folk who are intellectually or politically faint of heart. The series of studies that constitute *Africana Critical Theory: Reconstructing the Black Radical Tradition, from W. E. B. Du Bois and C. L. R. James to Frantz Fanon and Amilcar Cabral* are not simply about Du Bois and Fanon, nor the other quartet of comrades who fill its pages. Much more, this book is about remembering a tradition (or, rather, *traditions*) of radicalism, and about how remembering that tradition (or, again, those *traditions*) in the twenty-first century; in the midst of the reemergence of anti-black racism, (neo)colonialism, and a new unprecedented stage of global capitalist imperialism; in light of the advances of critical race theory, philosophy of race, history of race, sociology of race, psychology of race, anthropology of race, geography of race and, most especially, Africana Studies' anti-racism and critique of Eurocentrism and white supremacy, provides us with an ideal opportunity to not only *reflect* on our inherited tradition(s) of radicalism but—and this cuts to the core of the matter—it offers us a rare occasion to *deconstruct* and *reconstruct* classical and *create* and *recreate* new, contemporary thought- and practice- tradition(s) of radicalism. In subsequent chapters in this volume I shall critically engage Du Bois and Fanon, therefore, here there is no need to summarily define or defend their theories and praxes. However, here I would like to briefly highlight how their thought and practices, among others, helps contemporary intellectual-activists *revisit* and *revise* the black radical tradition.[1]

Why return to, and critically deconstruct and reconstruct, the black radical tradition? Because we are witnessing and living through one of the most pervasive and profound crisis in the history of human culture and civilization, and, more specifically, in the histories, cultures, and struggles of continental and diasporan Africans—Du Bois's most beloved but still bitterly embattled "black folk," and Fanon's famous but somehow either ill-remembered or completely forgotten "wretched of the earth." The current crisis is both old and new, known and unknown, visible and invisible, and seemingly has the ability to elude even the keenest and most critical observers, who at their best have identified the key contemporary issues as follows: racism, sexism, capitalism, colonialism, heterosexism, Eurocentrism, religious intolerance, war, nuclear annihilation, ecological devastation, and animal extinction. This book is about the solutions that continental and diasporan Africans, and the black radical tradition in particular, historically has, and currently continues to offer to these pressing problems.

Invoking the black radical tradition in an epoch of war and religious rivalry, at a time when our global warming and war-torn world seems closer than ever before to that final fiery moment, may shock and awe many of my more conservative and (neo)liberal readers. However, I believe that it is important to humbly, albeit strongly stress that this often-despised, routinely overlooked, and frequently unengaged tradition of radicalism has, and continues to provide viable solutions to many of the problems confronting the contemporary world. Further, it is my belief that the enigmatic issues of the contemporary world are illuminated by black radicals in unique ways in which they have not been and are not now by Marxists, feminists, pragmatists, existentialists, phenomenologists, hermeneuticists, deconstructionists, poststructuralists, postmodernists, postcolonialists, critical pedagogues, liberation theologians, and (neo)liberals, among others.

The black radical tradition is much more than a deconstructive response to white supremacy, European modernity, the African holocaust, racial enslavement, racial colonialism and racist capitalism, and the theories and praxes produced by its practitioners should not be ghettoized and quarantined to "black folk" and/or "the black experience." In *Prophesy Deliverance!* the acclaimed African American philosopher Cornel West (1982) has persuasively argued that Africans were central to, if not the unacknowledged motors inside of, the monstrous machines of, European modernity and its aftermaths (see also West, 1993c, 1993d, 1999; Yancy, 2001). Therefore, to truly comprehend the issues arising out of European modernity and, even more, the pastiche and pitfalls of postmodernity, a critical engagement of, not simply "the black experience," but Africana history, culture, and thought, and specifically the black radical tradition, is probably prudent if not outright necessary.

European modernity globalized, among other things, white supremacy, and the black radical tradition has consistently countered it, often providing glowing and irrefutable examples of its inhumanity, among other contradictions. In this sense, then, the black radical tradition offers more than five hundred years of theory and praxis that could potentially aid contemporary continental and diasporan Africans, as well as other people of color and white "race traitors," in their efforts to rupture their relationships with, not simply white supremacy but, considering the historical (and *herstorical*) discourses and ongoing developments in womanism, black feminism, black liberation theology, revolutionary black nationalism, black Marxism, African socialism, and revolutionary decolonization, among others, the ways in which white supremacy overlaps, interlocks, and intersects with sexism, capitalism, and colonialism. What is often overlooked, and what I intend to critically accent, is the historical fact that there is an undeniable and inextricable relationship between European modernity and the African holocaust, racial enslavement, racial colonialism, and the rise and racist nature of capitalism. Moving far beyond, and actually going against, conventional (read: Eurocentric and white supremacist) conceptions of European modernity, from the critical points of view of non-Europeans this insidious epoch had the exact opposite effects as it did for Europe and Europeans.

Where we are told that European modernity bequeathed "radical" political breakthroughs with regard to the American Revolution of 1776 and the French Revolution of 1789, during this same period both the Americans and the French, among other European nations, participated in holocausts against, and the enslavement and colonization of, people of color, particularly Native Americans and Africans. Where it is said that European modernity ushered in new notions of empire, what is most often not said is that they erected their empires on the carnage and ruins of the nation-states, nay, even more, on the cultures and civilizations, on the sciences and technologies of various peoples of color. Where we are told time and time again that European modernity contributed the modern philosophical foundation for the arts and the sciences, no mention is made of the many millions of ways in which non-Europeans have not simply influenced and inspired European artists and scientists, but in many instances provided them with points of departure, the basic architecture, if you will, and the very tools through which they have built their modern haunted houses and postmodern plantations (see Adams, Clemens, and Orloff, 2005; Appadurai, 1996; Bartolovich and Lazarus, 2002; Bauman, 1987, 1989, 1991, 1992a, 1997, 2000, 2004a; Docherty, 1999; Fischer, 2004; Giddens, 1991; Goody, 2004; Held, Hubert, Thompson and Hall, 1996; Himmelfarb, 2004; Kosik, 1995; D. Scott, 2004; Tester, 1992; K. Wilson, 2004; Winks and Neuberger, 2005).

European modernity, and its postmodern interpretation, has always been and remains one long self-congratulatory and narcissistic narrative, which has at its heart a centuries-spanning celebration of Europe's Europeanization, Europe's "civilization" and Christianization, Europe's white-washing of the entire "dark," "unenlightened," non-European world. Deeply embedded in the discourse of, and the discourse on, European modernity is a latent *Eurocentric intellectual insularity* and *Eurocentric epistemic exclusiveness* that has been universalized and normalized as a result of Europe's international imperialism. This means, then, that almost *all* modern and postmodern intellectual activity, whether by whites or non-whites, unless it is critically conscious of white supremacy, adheres in one way or another to Eurocentric paradigms of intellectualism, "scholarly" research, radicalism and, even, "revolution" (M. Christian 2002, 2006). Consequently, this conundrum, this riddle of modern and postmodern radicalism, has profoundly influenced and impacted the history of classical and contemporary thought in general, and the study of modern Africana intellectual history in particular. Therefore, even though Africana Studies, among other (re)emerging disciplines, has made many strong strides in developing *deconstructive* devices for the critique of Eurocentrism in the arts, sciences, and society at large, it has been woefully weak in self-reflexively putting forward *reconstructive* tools and theories that move beyond the critique of Eurocentrism and emphasize the importance of revisiting and revising, as well as extending and expanding traditions of black radicalism and, equally important, traditions of revolutionary humanism. This is the major motif and main concern of the present volume, my little labor of love, if you will.

Much more than neo-black radicalism, *Africana critical theory* is a twenty-first century outgrowth of efforts aimed at accenting the dialects of deconstruction and reconstruction, and the dialectics of domination and liberation in classical and contemporary, continental and diasporan African life-worlds and lived-experiences. Its major preoccupation has been and remains synthesizing classical and contemporary black radical theory with black revolutionary praxis. Consequently, Africana Studies provides Africana critical theory with its philosophical foundation(s) and primary point(s) of departure, as it, Africana Studies, decidedly moves beyond monodisciplinary approaches to Africana phenomena. More than any other intellectual arena, Africana Studies has consistently offered the black radical tradition its highest commendations and its most meticulous criticisms. It is, also, the academic discipline that most inspired Africana critical theory's unique method—"unique" especially when compared to other forms of critical theory that emerge from traditional disciplines—because Africana Studies is a *transdisciplinary discipline*—that is, *a discipline that transgresses, transverses, and transcends the academic boundaries and intellectual borders, the color-lines and racial chasms, and the jingoism and gender injustice of traditional single phenomenon-focused disciplines, owing to the fact that at its best it poses problems and seeks solutions on behalf of Africana (and other struggling) people employing the theoretic innovations of both the social sciences and humanities, as well as the political breakthroughs of grassroots radical and revolutionary social movements.*[2]

By critically examining the theories and praxes of half a dozen carefully chosen major Africana intellectual-activists, this book (re)introduces, chronicles, and analyzes several of the significant features of Africana critical theory. Here I am primarily, and almost exclusively, concerned with the Africana intellectual-activists' theoretical and political legacies—that is, with the ways in which they constructed, deconstructed, and reconstructed theory and the aims, objectives, and concrete outcomes of their theoretical applications and discursive practices. Beginning with W. E. B. Du Bois's radical, and later revolutionary, theory and praxis, and then time-traveling and globe-trotting from C. L. R. James to Negritude to Frantz Fanon and, finally, concluding with Amilcar Cabral, this study chronicles and critiques, revisits and revises the black radical tradition with an eye toward the ways in which classical black radicalism informs, or *should* inform, not only contemporary black radicalism but contemporary efforts to create a new *anti-racist, anti-sexist, anti-capitalist, anti-colonialist, and sexual orientation-sensitive critical theory of contemporary society*, what I call *Africana critical theory*.[3]

"But," the critics of Africana critical theory have been quick to query, "isn't 'critical theory' Eurocentric?" I usually respond speaking almost in a whisper so that they will know that I am sincere when I say gently but emphatically, "no." Then I go on, "Frankfurt School critical theory may be Eurocentric, but critical theory, in a general sense, is not Eurocentric. If we take that argument, the assertion that 'critical theory' is Eurocentric, to its logical conclusion, then, ultimately, we are saying that critical thinking, that deep theorizing, that philosophizing is Eurocentric. And, what is worst, we are saying this without really taking into critical consideration that most forms of philosophy or theorizing are interrelated and have roots in ancient or classical thought traditions and, most, if not all, Africana Studies scholars and students know that ancient African thought traditions, take Kemet or Egypt as an initial example, provided the very foundations upon which philosophy was built" (see Asante, 2000; C.A. Diop, 1974, 1987, 1991; Frye, 1988; Gordon, 2008; Lott and Pittman, 2003; Karenga, 2004; Obenga, 1990, 1993, 2004; Ogunmodede, 2004; Onyewuenyi, 1993; Sumner, 1985; Wiredu, 2004).

Part of the problem, I surmise, has to do with the fact that frequently the only form of critical theory that most people (including Africana Studies scholars and students) have been exposed to is Frankfurt School critical theory. However, truth be told, there are many forms, many traditions, of critical theory.[4] What the critics of Africana critical theory fail to understand is that the body of literature that constitutes the Frankfurt School of critical theory is but one European groups' efforts to identify what they understand to be the most pressing problems of their age and put forward viable solutions to those problems.[5] In a nutshell, this is what critical theory, in a general sense, entails; this is its basic method. That so many sophisticated theorists, in Africana Studies in specific, cannot seem to comprehend that *posing problems and searching for solutions* to those problems, not only preceded the Frankfurt School but, especially in the Africana tradition of critical theory, raised questions and offered answers above and beyond the intellectual, ethical, and political universe(s) of the Eurocentric tradition of critical theory, is truly astonishing and, it seems to me, symptomatic of their intense internalization of what Du Bois dubbed "double-consciousness," and what I have identified as *intellectual historical amnesia* and *the diabolical dialectic of white intellectual superiority and black intellectual inferiority*.

In point of fact, W. E. B. Du Bois, who provides Africana critical theory with its primary point of departure, graduated from Harvard University with a Ph.D. in history in 1895, the very same year that the oldest member of the Frankfurt School of critical theory, Max Horkheimer, was born. Prior to graduating with a Ph.D. from Harvard, Du Bois, as is well-known, earned a bachelor's degree from Fisk University, where he studied German, Greek, Latin, classical literature, philosophy, ethics, chemistry, and physics; received a second bachelor's degree, *cum laude*, in philosophy, and a master's degree in history, both from Harvard; and, completed his doctoral studies, studying history, economics, politics, and political economy, at Friedrich Wilhelm University, now the University of Berlin, in Germany. Therefore, he, literally, was *developing* and *doing* authentic interdisciplinary critical social theory either before the Frankfurt School critical theorists were born or, at the least, when they were toddlers. One need look no further, for instance, than his early, critical politico-sociological works, which helped to inaugurate American sociology and, especially, sociology of race, and his early interdisciplinary "social" and "community" studies of black life and culture with which he, of course, initiated Africana Studies: *The Suppression of the African Slave Trade to the United States of America, 1638–1870,* "The Conservation of Races," "Careers Open to College-Bred Negroes," *The Philadelphia Negro: A Social Study, The Atlanta University Publications* under his editorship, *The Souls of Black Folk,* "The Talented Tenth," and his early "social" and "community" studies posthumously published in *W. E. B. Du Bois on Sociology and the Black Community* (1978) and *The Social Theory of W. E. B. Du Bois* (2004), among others.

Some of my critics have said, "Well, why are you calling your work 'critical theory,' then, if it is not Eurocentric? Why not call it something else?" Again, I calmly, almost quietly, respond saying, "Another element of critical theory that intellectually attracted me to it was its almost inherent emphasis on linking theory with praxis. Now, as I understand Africana histories, cultures, and struggles, we black folk have been connecting our words and deeds, our ideas and actions for quite some time. So, since this is, perhaps one of the most popular, intellectual and political terms designating *praxis-promoting theory* or *theory with practical intent,* then, I decided to employ it—as one of my mentors, Lucius Outlaw (2005), is found of saying—'in the interests of black folk'."

I have also pointed out to many of my critics that I am fairly fluent in Swahili and could have easily provided Africana critical theory with a Swahili name (*unafahamu?*), but my intention is to make my work accessible to as wide an audience as possible (across the "lines" of race, gender, class, sexual orientation, and religious affiliation), not simply to black academics and Africana Studies scholars nationally, but to the black masses, other people of color, and, even, white anti-racists and white "race traitors" internationally. On several occasions I have pointed out the fallacy of attempting to dismiss Africana critical theory solely on the basis of nomenclature by observing that many of its critics continue to work in "disciplines," in "the academy," and "critique" and produce "theory." Even if we were to critically engage just one of these European language based terms, say, "theory," it, too, is not free from Eurocentric baggage. For example, the etymology of the word "theory" is derived from the Greek word *theoria,* which means, "to view." There are correlations between *theoria* and another Greek word, *theos* or *theus* or *Zeus,* each of which means "God," and each of which goes far to demonstrate that for the Greeks the theorist is supposed "to view" the world as God would (Denyer, 1991; Gerson, 1990; A. A. Long, 1999; Nightingale, 2004; Sedley, 2003; Vlastos, 1995). And, consequently, in seeing the world the way God would, the theorist is suppose to search for and see "the truth," and reveal "the truth" about the world. I seriously doubt that Africana Studies scholars will suddenly stop calling their conceptual generations "theory" because it is derived from a Greek word and emerges from Greek history, Greek culture, and Greek mythology. Therefore, we must all keep in mind that the great bulk of our modern discourse has taken and is taking place in European colonial languages and in a white supremacist world, and that what we have to do for the foreseeable future is *Africanize* anything that can be used in our efforts to continue and further develop *the dialectical process of revolutionary decolonization and revolutionary re-Africanization*. This means, then, that Africana critical theory is incomprehensible without a thorough and critical knowledge of Africana intellectual history, the history of Africana philosophy, and the controversial history of *anti-Eurocentric Africana appropriation and Africanization* of European, among other cultures and civilizations', languages, thoughts, and practices.

Therefore, those who quickly and uncritically claim that Africana critical theory is Eurocentric because they hold the historically and intellectually uninformed belief that "all critical theory is Eurocentric," not only misunderstand and misrepresent critical theory in a general sense, but they also put their internalized Eurocentrism, intellectual historical amnesia, ungroundedness in Africana intellectual history, and, perhaps even, their *anti-Africana conceptual generation*, on display. The critics of Africana critical theory seriously error when they argue, often without undertaking a thorough investigation of Africana critical theory, that it is nothing other than Frankfurt School critical theory in blackface, or black Marcusean or black Habermasian critical social theory. As has been witnessed above (especially in Angela Davis's epigraph) and as will be witnessed below (in the subsequent sections), although several Africana critical social theorists (myself included) have been influenced by the Frankfurt School tradition of critical theory, it would be foolhardy and fallacious to assume that such influence functions as a prerequisite or, even more, as a "cause" as opposed to a unique paradigmatic opportunity that is actually more indicative of the Eurocentric colonization of intellectual history and the world of ideas. What is more, and as will be discussed in detail below, if any thought tradition(s) or classical theorists serve as progenitors and prerequisites for Africana critical theory, undoubtedly that honor should be bestowed on W. E. B. Du Bois and Frantz Fanon, because they above and beyond all others have prefigured and provided the primary paradigms and preeminent points of departure for the discourse and development of an Africana critical theory of contemporary society.

To take this a step further, even in its *anti-Eurocentric Africana appropriation and Africanization* of certain models and methods of the Frankfurt School or other European traditions of critical theory, Africana critical theory utilizes the revolutionary rationale and the revolutionary intellectual and political resources of its own tradition of critical theory as a *critical theoretical criteria*. In particular, and as will be discussed in detail in chapter 6 of this study, it is the words and wisdom of the Cape Verdean and Guinea-Bissaun revolutionary, Amilcar Cabral (1979), which has indelibly influenced Africana critical theory's emphasis on appropriation and Africanization, and especially when he wisely warned: "A people who free themselves from foreign domination will not be culturally free unless, without underestimating the importance of positive contributions from the oppressor's culture and other cultures, they return to the upwards paths of their own culture" (p. 143). To "return" to the "upwards paths of [our] own culture" would mean, at least in part, side-stepping racial and cultural essentialists' claims against, and narrow-minded nationalists' knee-jerk reactions to, everything European or non-African, and it would also mean making a critical and, even more, a dialectical distinction between the abominations and undeniable negatives of white supremacy and Eurocentrism, on the one hand, and the positives of European and other cultures' authentic contributions to progressive human culture and civilization, on the other hand (see the more detailed discussion of Cabral's contributions to Africana critical theory in chapter 6).

Again, the Africana tradition of critical theory precedes the Eurocentric tradition of critical theory, and it takes classical Africana intellectual-activists, such as W. E. B. Du Bois and C. L. R. James as points of departure, not the Frankfurt School critical theorists. However, and I should emphasize this, Africana critical theory is not afraid to intellectually interrogate, critically dialogue with, and/or astutely appropriate theoretic breakthroughs contributed by the Frankfurt School and other traditions of critical theory if it can *Africanize* them and put them to critical use in our efforts to continue and further develop *the dialectical process of revolutionary decolonization and revolutionary re-Africanization.* It is, therefore, extremely intellectually insincere of the critics of Africana critical theory to harp on a handful of Eurocentric influences without critically grappling with and attempting to grasp *how* or *the ways in which* it seeks to *Africanize* and utilize aspects of Eurocentric theory and methods *against* the Europeanization process and, even further, I reiterate, in our efforts to continue and further develop *the dialectical process of revolutionary decolonization and revolutionary re-Africanization.* It is, also, extremely intellectually disingenuous on the part of the critics of Africana critical theory to hoot and holler about the inclusion of some carefully and critically selected insights from a couple of the critical theorists of the Frankfurt School without critically comprehending that *all* of the primary points of departure of Africana critical theory have been and continue to be drawn from classical and contemporary, continental and diasporan African intellectual-activists, lifeworlds, and lived-experiences. In other words, to contend that European critical theorists were the initiators of critical theory, to place them as the "cause" and Africana critical theory and Africana critical theorists as the "effect" is, quite simply, to place the proverbial cart before the horse. It is to intellectually erase or, at the least, to render intellectually invisible, continental and diasporan Africans as *intellectual and political agents and inventors.* It is, as the Anthony Bogues (2003) observed in the final epigraph above, "to study the thought of black thinkers as primarily derivative" and this, of course, only continues Europeanization and Eurocentric intellectual colonization, because Africana thinkers, then, "are never credited with intellectual independence and originality" (p. 2; see also Bogues, 1998, 2002, 2004, 2005, 2008).

Part of my task in the remainder of this introduction entails further elaborating on the distinct conception of critical theory that will be employed in the chapters to follow. This conception of critical theory, Africana critical theory, is grounded in and grows out of Africana Studies, and specifically the discourses of Africana philosophy, Africana social and political theory, and Africana intellectual history. Contrary to the plethora of polemics, simplifications, mystifications, and misinterpretations of the black radical tradition, it indeed does make several significant contributions to the discourses of Africana Studies and contemporary critical theory. In an effort to emphasize these contributions, I shall discuss the relationship between black radical theory and black revolutionary praxis, critical social theory in general, and, ultimately, my conception of Africana critical theory.

By analyzing and criticizing black radical thought, and the politico-economic and socio-cultural situations to which it responds, its theories and praxes can be accessed and assessed for their contribution to: (1) contemporary Africana Studies and critical social theory; (2) grassroots and mass movements calling for radical/revolutionary social transformation, from the Harlem Renaissance, Negritude, Civil Rights and Black Power movements, to the brewing anti-war and peace movements at the dawn of the twenty-first century; and (3) future moral and multicultural social thought and practices. In what follows I shall, first, discuss some of the distinct differences between Africana critical theory, critical race theory, critical class theory, Eurocentric or white Marxism, black Marxism, and black radicalism. Second, I shall examine the relationship between black radical theory and black revolutionary praxis, all the while exploring the contours of the Africana tradition of critical theory. Third, I shall critically engage the nature and nuances of philosophy, radical politics, and social theory in Africana Studies in an effort to further demonstrate Africana critical theory's distinct continental and diasporan African primary sources of knowledge and primary sites of struggle. And, finally, I conclude this introduction by emphasizing the book's recurring theme of the radical reconstruction of contemporary critical social theory and outlining the distinct theoretical thrusts of each of the subsequent chapters.

## THE CRISIS OF CONTEMPORARY CRITICAL SOCIAL THEORY: TRANSGRESSING THE WHITE MARXIST TRADITION OF CRITICAL THEORY, TRANSCENDING THE BLACK MARXIST TRADITION OF RADICALISM

For over a decade critical social theorists have been issuing calls for "a more multicultural, race and gender focused, and broad[er]-based" critical theory (Kellner, 1995, p. 20). Unfortunately, however, few of their fellow critical theorists have taken their summons seriously. One of the glaring ironies and intellectual injustices of contemporary critical theory is that even with the academic popularity of feminism, postcolonialism, and, more recently, critical race theory, the white and male dominated discourse(s) of critical theory have yet to develop meaningful and in depth dialogues with these discursive communities. In the introduction to their groundbreaking volume, *New Critical Theory*, William Wilkerson and Jeffrey Paris (2001) admit: "The challenge to critical theorists to rethink their presuppositions according to the realities of non-European cultures and technologies remains the most underthematized aspect of critical theories new and old" (p.8).

Part of the current crisis of critical theory has to do with its often-uncritical reliance on classical Marxist concepts and categories without sufficiently revising and synthesizing them with new, especially non-Marxian and non-European, theoretical and political developments. Classical Marxism privileged class and the proletariat as the agents of revolutionary social transformation, while unwittingly neglecting the overlapping, interlocking, and intersecting nature of racism and sexism in capitalist and colonial societies. In "The Obsolescence of Marxism?," one of the leading European American critical theorists, Douglas Kellner (1995), argues that it is "widely accepted that classical Marxism exaggerates the primacy of class and downplays the salience of gender and race. Clearly, oppression takes place in many more spheres than just the economic and the workplace, so a radical politics of the future should take account of gender and race as well as class" (p. 20). Notice that Kellner is not calling for a complete rejection of Marxism and class theory but coupling it, revising and synthesizing it with cutting-edge race and gender theory. Many black radicals and multicultural Marxists, I believe, would partially agree with Kellner when he writes further:

> [W]e need to build on viable political and theoretical perspectives and resources of the past, and I would argue that Marxism continues to provide vital resources for radical theory and politics today. . . . In sum, I believe that we need new theoretical and political syntheses, drawing on the best of classical Enlightenment theory, Marxian theory, feminism, and other progressive theoretical and political currents of the present. Key aspects for such new syntheses, however, are found in the Marxian tradition, and those who prematurely abandon it are turning away from a tradition that has been valuable since Marx's day and will continue to be so in the foreseeable future. Consequently, Marxism is not yet obsolete. Rather, the Marxian theory continues to provide resources and stimulus for critical theory and radical politics in the present age. (pp. 25–26)[6]

Kellner and Africana critical theory, however, part company when and where he gives a detailed discussion of the relevance of European derived and developed theories or, rather, Eurocentric theories—Enlightenment theory, Marxism, and feminism—and only alludes to the work of non-European theorists or, as he put it, "*other* progressive theoretical and political currents" for renewing radical politics and critical theory in the present (my emphasis). To his credit, Kellner states, "radical politics today should be more multicultural, race and gender focused, and broad-based than the original Marxian theory" (p. 20). But, he does not identify or critically engage the "other progressive theoretical and political currents" the way, nor to the depth and detail to which he does a plethora of white male radical thinkers whose thought, he believes, contributes indelibly to the reconstruction of critical social theory.

Kellner is not alone in arguing for the continued importance of Marxism for contemporary radical politics and the reconstruction of critical social theory. In "Toward a New Critical Theory," another leading European American critical theorist, James Marsh (2001), audaciously asserts, "a critical theory without Marx" is a "critical theory that is insufficiently critical" (p. 57). He further contends:

> I think we need a much fuller appropriation and use of Marx than is going on in either postmodernism or Habermasian critical theory. If capitalism is deeply pathological and unjust, as I think it is and as I have argued in all of my works, then we need the resources of what still remains the deepest and most comprehensive critique of capitalist political economy, that which occurs in the late Marx in the pages of the *Grundrisse*, *Capital*, and *Theories of Surplus Value*, a total of seven volumes that are more relevant than ever. For these reasons, I draw on Marx's theory of exploited labor in the workplace, his theory of tyranny, in which the economy and money impinge on noneconomic aspects of the lifeworld in a way that is absurd, his theory of a marginalized industrial reserve army, his theory of value and surplus value, and his account of substantive socialism. Capitalist pathology is not just colonization of lifeworld by system, although that is certainly an important part of such pathology, but includes exploitation, tyranny, domination, and marginalization as well. (p. 57)

As with Kellner's claims, Marsh is on point when he asserts the comprehensive character of Marx's critique of capitalism. Similar to Kellner, he warns contemporary critical theorists about the intellectual insularity and epistemic exclusiveness of their discourse and even goes so far to say that "both modern and postmodern critical theory runs the risk of being idealistic in a bad sense, that is, insufficiently attentive to the task of interpreting, criticizing, and overcoming late capitalism in its racist, sexist, classist, and heterosexist aspects. We, modernists and postmodernists alike, need to get down to the job of social transformation" (p. 53). Now, after taking all this in, one of the first critical thoughts that passes through the mind of an anti-sexist critical social theorist of color is: How will radical politics and critical theory become "more multicultural, and race and gender focused," as Kellner contends, if it does not turn to the thought and texts of the most progressive and, even further, *critical* race and gender theorists; some of whom happen to be radical theorists and revolutionary intellectual-activists of color, particularly folk of African origin or descent, and some of whom, of course, are women, and women of color in specific?

According to the Caribbean radical political theorist, Anthony Bogues (2003), who wrote in *Black Heretics, Black Prophets: Radical Political Intellectuals*, "in radical historical studies, when one excavates a different archive, alternative categories are opened up" (p. 86). To be sure, black radical theorists, such as Du Bois, C. L. R. James, Frantz Fanon, Amilcar Cabral and Angela Davis, "deployed Marxism, but in [their] hands the categories used to describe historical processes were wrought into something else" (p. 81). That "something else" which Marxian categories were shaped and molded into by these theorists was based on their critical understanding of continental and diasporan African history, culture, and struggle.

Africana history, culture, and struggle are the deeply disregarded "different archives" that black radicals work with and operate from. These archives are not only in many senses distinctly divergent from the archives of white Marxists, but embedded in them are recurring racial motifs that shade and color black radical politics and social theory. White Marxists' efforts to diminish and downplay racial domination and discrimination have made black radicals' marriage to Marxism a turbulent and very unhappy one. For example, in *From Class to Race: Essays in White Marxism and Black Radicalism*, the Caribbean philosopher Charles W. Mills (2003a) maintains:

> Throughout the twentieth century, many people of color were attracted to Marxism because of its far-ranging historical perspective, its theoretical centering of oppression, and its promise of liberation. But many of these recruits would later become disillusioned, both with Marxist theory and the practice of actual (white) Marxist parties. The historical vision turned out to be Eurocentric; the specificities of their racial oppression were often not recognized but were dissolved into supposedly all encompassing class categories; and the liberation envisaged did not include as a necessary goal the dismantling of white supremacy in all its aspects. Cedric Robinson's pioneering *Black Marxism* (2000), first published in 1983, recounts the long-troubled history of left-wing black diasporic intellectuals (W. E. B. Du Bois, C. L. R. James, George Padmore, Richard Wright, Aimé Césaire) with "white Marxism," and it argues for the existence of a distinct "black radical political tradition" whose historic foci and concerns cannot be simply assimilated to mainstream white Marxist theory. So even if the origin of white supremacy is most plausibly explained within a historical materialist framework that locates it in imperialist European expansionism—as the product, ultimately, of class forces and bourgeois class interests—race as an international global structure then achieves an intersubjective reality whose dialectic cannot simply be reduced to a class dynamic. (p. xvi)

In other words, black radicals' issues with white Marxism often stem from the fact that they understand racism to be both economic *and* experiential. Racial oppression has more than merely an economic exploitative or class dimension that can coolly and calmly be conjectured by well-meaning white Marxist social scientists (see Goldberg, 1990, 1993, 1997, 2001; L. Harris, 1999b; Marable, 1995, 1996, 1997; Mullen, 2002; Outlaw, 1996a, 2005; C.J. Robinson, 2000, 2001). As I discussed in detail in *W. E. B. Du Bois and the Problems of the Twenty-First Century*, racism is malleable and motive, and white Marxists' insensitive attempts to reduce it to an outgrowth or offshoot of class struggle, or something internal to class conflict, robs the economically exploited *and* racially oppressed of an opportunity to critically theorize their lived-reality and a major determinant of their historical, cultural, social and political identities (Rabaka, 2007a).

Many black radicals, especially black Marxists, are at pains to point out that their criticisms "should not be taken in the spirit of a complete repudiation of Marxism," since, they maintain, "a *modified* historical materialism might be able to carry out an adequate conceptualization of the significance of race" (C.W. Mills, 2003a, pp. xvi–xvii, emphasis in original). But, the longstanding problem has been and remains white Marxists' inconsideration and unwillingness to critically grasp and grapple with the political economy of race and racism, in both capitalist and colonial societies, in their extension and expansion of Marxian concepts and categories. Black Marxists have historically exhibited an epistemic openness, one quite characteristic of the Africana tradition of critical theory, to critical class theory in a way brazenly counter to white Marxists' almost universal unreceptiveness to, intellectual disinterestedness in, and gnarly neglect of, critical race theory.[7]

Critical race theory, which could be defined as *anti-racist praxis-promoting theory critical of the ways in which white supremacy impacts institutions and individuals*, has its origins in the works of several civil rights lawyers in the early 1980s. Often associated with the Critical Legal Studies (CLS) movement, which demonstrated in dizzying ways that law is neither neutral nor apolitical, critical race theory began by challenging the racial neutrality of the law (Crenshaw, Gotanda, Peller, and Thomas, 1995; Delgado, 1995; Delgado and Stefancic, 2001; Essed and Goldberg, 2001; Goldberg, Musheno, and Bower, 2001; Valdes, Culp, and Harris, 2002). Legal scholars of color, in complete agreement with the argument that law is non-neutral, criticized the mostly white male leaders of the CLS movement for failing to recognize and critically theorize the crucial role and continued relevance of *race* in social and political interactions and institutions. Their work was quickly recognized as *critical race theory*, and they themselves as *critical race theorists*. In recent years, the term critical race theory has become what the Palestinian intellectual-activist Edward Said (1999, 2000) referred to as a "traveling theory," moving in and out of intellectual and political discursive communities far from its theoretical and intellectual origins, and with each move taking on new or multiple meanings and losing some of its original intent and logic.

In this sense, then, I argue that critical race theory should not be thought of as an uncritical coupling of anti-racism with Marxism/critical class theory, or limited to the work of the last twenty-five years explicitly identified under the rubric of "critical race theory." Its intellectual history and political journey, like that of the Africana tradition of critical theory, has been much more complicated than previously noted, especially when read against the backdrop of Africana intellectual history, black radical theory, and black revolutionary praxis. Within the Africana world of ideas and Africana intellectual history there has been and remains radical anti-racist thought on racial domination and discrimination, and specifically white supremacy, that prefigures and provides a black radical point of departure for contemporary critical race theory, and, if truth be told, critical white studies (Rabaka, 2006c, 2006d, 2007a, 2007b, 2008a). Here I am hinting at what could be called *classical critical race theory*, which is not now and has never been an outgrowth of white Marxism or the Frankfurt School tradition of critical theory and, in fact, was underway long before the birth of Karl Marx.

Well ahead of Marxism and the Frankfurt School, as W. E. B. Du Bois's *Black Reconstruction* and C. L. R. James's *The Black Jacobins* eloquently illustrate, enslaved Africans developed critical anti-racist thought traditions in their efforts to topple white supremacy and cut capitalism and colonialism off at their knees (Du Bois, 1995b; C. L. R. James, 1963). Enslaved African intellectual-activists sought solutions to social and political problems as passionately and radically as—indeed, even more passionately and radically than—the white working-class, who, as the Caribbean historian and leader Eric Williams (1966) observed in *Capitalism and Slavery*, profited from, were complicit in, and racially privileged as a result of the very white supremacist and enslaving system dominating and discriminating against blacks and other non-whites. Usually critical theory is linked to modernity and the European Enlightenment, and "modernity" is only thought of from a Eurocentric point of view—that is, in the aftermath of European imperial expansion around the globe what it means to be "modern" translates into how well Europeans and non-Europeans emulate European *imperial* thought, culture, politics, etc. But, if one were to critically call into question Eurocentric and imperial conceptions of what it means to be "modern," then, the very "alternative categories" that Bogues discussed above, "are opened up," and contemporary critical theorists are able to observe, perhaps for the first time: first, that it was on the fringes of Europe's imperial free-for-all, in the imperial outposts in the colored world where racism and colonialism were naturalized, where modernity was conceived, and in some senses aborted, and, second, that many of modernity's most perplexing problems were initially put forward and keenly considered by non-European, racialized and colonized, indigenous and enslaved intellectual-activists. Charles W. Mills (2003a) writes poignantly of this paradox and oft ignored predicament, and his penetrating words are worth quoting at length:

> All the issues we now think of as defining critical theory's concerns were brought home to the racially subordinated, the colonized and enslaved, in the most intimate and brutal way: the human alienation, the instrumentalization and deformation of reason in the service of power, the critique of abstract individualism, the paradox of reconciling proclamations of humanism with mass murder, the need to harness normative theory to the practical task of human liberation. So if Marx's proletariat too often had to have proletarian consciousness "imputed" (in Georg Lukács infamous phrase) to them, and if the relation between Marxism and the actual working-class outlook was often more a matter of faith and hopeful counterfactuals than actuality (what the workers *would* think if only . . . ), then oppositional ideas on race have shaped the consciousness of the racially subordinated for centuries. If white workers have been alienated from their

product, then people of color, especially black slaves, have been alienated from their personhood; if Enlightenment reason has been complicit with bourgeois projects, then it has been even more thoroughly corrupted by its accommodation to white supremacy; if liberal individualism has not always taken white workers fully into account, then it has often excluded nonwhites altogether; if it was a post-World War II challenge to explain how the "civilized" Germany of Goethe and Beethoven could have carried out the Jewish and Romani Holocausts, then it is a far older challenge to explain how "civilized" Europe as a whole could have carried out the savage genocide of indigenous populations and the barbaric enslavement of millions; and finally, if Marx's proletarians have been called upon to see and lose their chains (and have often seemed quite well-adjusted to them), then people of color (Native American populations, enslaved and later Jim Crowed Africans in the New World, the colonized) have historically had little difficulty in recognizing their oppression—after all, the chains were often literal! —and in seeking to throw it off. So if the ideal of fusing intellectual history with political practice has been the long-term goal of critical class theory, it has been far more frequently realized in the nascent critical race theory of the racially subordinated, whose oppression has been more blatant and unmediated and for whom the urgency of their situation has necessitated a direct connection between the normative and practical emancipation. (p. xviii)

Critical theories are not simply a synthesis of radical politics and social theory, but also a combination of cultural criticism and historical theory. Each version of critical theory, whether critical race theory or critical class theory, seeks to radically reinterpret and revise history in light of, for example, race and racism for critical race theorists, or capitalism and class struggle for critical class theorists. In order to thoroughly comprehend a given phenomenon, critical theorists believe that one must contextualize it within its historical context, testing and teasing-out tensions between the phenomenon and the cultural, social, political, economic, scientific, aesthetic and religious, among other, institutions and struggles of its epoch.

Mills makes the point that though white Marxists/critical class theorists have repeatedly revisited the connection(s) between theory and praxis, more often than not the "revolutions" their works spawned have been theoretical and one-dimensional (obsessively focused on the critique of capitalism) as opposed to practical and multidimensional (simultaneously critiquing capitalism *and* racism *and* colonialism). Black radicals/critical race theorists, he observes, have frequently been more successful at linking radical (anti-racist and anti-capitalist) theory to liberation struggles and social movements because their "oppression has been more blatant and unmediated," and because "their situation has necessitated a direct connection between the normative and practical emancipation." The "situation" that Mills is referring to is simultaneously historical, social, political, and economic, not to mention deeply raced and gendered. So, though critical race theorists and critical class theorists both have macro-sociohistorical concerns, in the end it all comes down to, not necessarily the way they shift and bend the critical theoretical method for their particular purposes, but *what* they shift and bend the critical theoretical method to address. For most white Marxists race and racism are nonentities, but for many black Marxists capitalism is utterly incomprehensible without connecting it to the rise of race, racism, racial violence, white supremacy, and racial colonialism. Hence, black radicals' constant creations of timelines and topographies of the political economy of race and racism in capitalist and colonial contexts, and emphasis on revising and advancing alternatives to Eurocentric historiography and Marxist historical materialism in light of white supremacist and European imperial concepts and ruling race narratives that render race and racism historically invisible, obsolete, or nonexistent.

Where white Marxists/critical class theorists have a longstanding history of neglecting, not only the political economy of race and racism but the distinct radical thought traditions, life-worlds and lived-experiences of continental and diasporan Africans in capitalist and colonial contexts, primarily utilizing the black radical tradition, Africana critical theory endeavors to accent the overlapping, interlocking, and intersecting character of capitalism, colonialism, racism, and sexism, among other forms of domination, oppression, and exploitation. This means, then, that Africana critical theory transgresses and transcends the white Marxist tradition of critical theory in light of its epistemic openness and emphasis on continuously critically and dialectically deepening and developing the basic concepts and categories of its socio-theoretical framework and synthesizing disparate discourses into its own original *anti-racist, anti-sexist, anti-capitalist, anti-colonial and sexual orientation-sensitive critical theory of contemporary society*. Let us, then, take a deeper, perhaps, more dialectical look at the contour(s) and character of this new conception of critical social theory that utilizes Africana intellectual history, and the black radical tradition in particular, as its primary point of departure.

## THE CONTOUR(S) AND CHARACTER OF AFRICANA CRITICAL THEORY: RECONNECTING BLACK RADICAL THEORY WITH BLACK REVOLUTIONARY PRAXIS

At its core, Africana critical theory advances and applies two major dialectical presuppositions: *the dialectics of deconstruction and reconstruction* and *the dialectics of domination and liberation*, and its major preoccupation is synthesizing classical and contemporary, national and international black radical theory with black revolutionary praxis. It will be recalled that Africana critical theory's dialectics of deconstruction and reconstruction were discussed above and, consequently, need not be reiterated in great detail here. Therefore, it is to the dialectics of domination and liberation that our current discussion will be devoted. In addition, then, to being a critical theory of deconstruction and reconstruction, Africana critical theory is *theory critical of domination and discrimination in classical and contemporary, continental and diasporan African life-worlds and lived-experiences*. It is a style of critical theorizing, inextricably linked to progressive political practice(s), that highlights and accents black radicals' and black revolutionaries' answers to the key questions posed by the major forms and forces of domination and discrimination that have historically and continue currently to shape and mold our modern/postmodern and/or neocolonial/postcolonial world.

Africana critical theory involves not only the critique of domination and discrimination, but also a deep commitment to human liberation and radical/revolutionary social transformation. Similar to other traditions of critical social theory, Africana critical theory is concerned with thoroughly analyzing contemporary society "in light of its used and unused or abused capabilities for improving the human [and deteriorating environmental] condition" (Marcuse, 1964, p. xlii; see also

Rabaka, 2006a; Wilkerson and Paris, 2001). What distinguishes and helps to define Africana critical theory is its emphasis on the often-overlooked continental and diasporan African contributions to critical theory. It draws from critical thought and philosophical traditions rooted in the realities of continental and diasporan African history, culture, and struggle. Which, in other words, is to say that Africana critical theory inherently employs a methodological orientation that highlights and accents black radicalism and Africana philosophies, as Leonard Harris (1983) said, "born of struggle."[8] And, if it need be said at this point, the black liberation struggle is simultaneously national and international, transgender and transgenerational and, therefore, requires multidimensional and multiperspectival theory in which to interpret and explain the various diverse phenomena, philosophical motifs and social and political movements characteristic of—to use Fanon's famous phrase—*l'expérience vécue du Noir* ("the lived-experience of the black"), that is, the reality of constantly and simultaneously wrestling and wrangling with racism, sexism, capitalism, and colonialism, among other forms of domination, oppression and exploitation (Fanon, 2001; see also Gordon, Sharpley-Whiting, and White, 1996; Sharpley-Whiting, 1997; Weate, 2001).

Why, one may ask, focus on black radicals and black revolutionaries' theories of social change? An initial answer to this question takes us directly to Du Bois's (1986a) dictum, in "The Conservation of Races," that people of African origin and descent "have a contribution to make to civilization and humanity" that their historic experiences of holocaust, enslavement, colonization, and segregation have long throttled and thwarted (p. 825). He maintained that, "[t]he methods which we evolved for opposing slavery and fighting prejudice are not to be forgotten, but learned for our own and others' instruction" (Du Bois, 1973, p. 144). Hence, Du Bois solemnly suggested that black liberation struggle(s)—i.e., the combined continental and diasporan African fight(s) for freedom—may have much to contribute to critical theory, and his comments here also hit at the heart of one of the core concepts of critical theory, the *critique of domination and discrimination* (see Agger, 1992a; Malpas and Wake, 2006; O'Neill, 1976; Shumaker, 1964; Snedeker, 2004; Rasmussen and Swindal, 2004; Rush, 2004; Schroyer, 1975; Wexler, 1991).

From a methodological point of view, critical theory seeks to simultaneously: (1) comprehend the established society; (2) criticize its contradictions and conflicts; and (3) create egalitarian (most often radical/revolutionary democratic socialist) alternatives (Arato, 1993; Barrow, 1993; B. Cannon, 2001; Cohen, 1987; Morrow, 1994; Outlaw, 2005). The ultimate emphasis on the creation and offering of alternatives brings to the fore another core concept of critical theory, its *theory of liberation and radical/revolutionary democratic social(ist) transformation* (Marcuse, 1968, 1969a; Marsh, 1995, 1999; Ray, 1993).[9] The paradigms and points of departure for critical theorists vary depending on the theorists' race, gender, intellectual interests, and political persuasions. For instance, many European critical theorists turn to Hegel, Marx, Weber, Freud, and/or the Frankfurt School (Adorno, Benjamin, Fromm, Habermas, Horkheimer, and Marcuse), among others, because they understand these thinkers' thoughts and texts to speak in special ways to European modern and/or "postmodern" life-worlds and lived-experiences (see Held, 1980; Jay, 1984, 1985a, 1985b, 1996; Kellner, 1989; Wiggerhaus, 1995; Wolin, 1992, 1994, 1995, 2006).

My work, Africana critical theory, utilizes the thought and texts of Africana intellectual-activist ancestors as critical theoretical paradigms and points of departure because so much of their thought is not simply *problem-posing* but *solution-providing*
where the specific life-struggles of persons of African descent (or "black people") are
concerned—human life-struggles, it should be said with no hyperbole and high-
sounding words, which European critical theorists (who are usually Eurocentric and
often unwittingly white supremacist) have woefully neglected in their classical and
contemporary critical theoretical discourse; a discourse that ironically has consistently congratulated itself on the universality of its interests, all the while, for the
most part, side-stepping the centrality of racism and colonialism within its own discursive communities and out in the wider world. Moreover, my conception of critical theory is critically preoccupied with classical Africana thought traditions, not
only because of the long unlearned lessons they have to teach contemporary critical
theorists about the dialectics of being simultaneously radically humanist and
morally committed agents of a specific continent, nation, or cultural groups' liberation and social(ist) transformation, but also because the ideas and ideals of continental and diasporan African intellectual-activists of the past indisputably prefigure
and provide a foundation for contemporary Africana Studies, and Africana philosophy in specific. In fact, in many ways, Africana critical theory, besides being
grounded in and growing of out the discourse of Africana Studies, can be said to be
an offshoot of Africana philosophy, which according to the acclaimed African American philosopher, Lucius Outlaw (1997a), is:

> a "gathering" notion under which to situate the articulations (writings, speeches, etc.),
> and traditions of the same, of Africans and peoples of African descent collectively, as
> well as the sub-discipline or field-forming, tradition-defining, tradition-organizing re-
> constructive efforts which are (to be) regarded as philosophy. However, "Africana phi-
> losophy" is to include, as well, the work of those persons who are neither African nor of
> African descent but who recognize the legitimacy and importance of the issues and en-
> deavors that constitute the disciplinary activities of African or [African Caribbean or]
> African American philosophy and contribute to the efforts—persons whose work justi-
> fies their being called "Africanists." Use of the qualifier "Africana" is consistent with the
> practice of naming intellectual traditions and practices in terms of the national, geo-
> graphic, cultural, racial, and/or ethnic descriptor or identity of the persons who initiated
> and were/are the primary practitioners—and/or are the subjects and objects—of the
> practices and traditions in question (e.g., "American," "British," "French," "German," or
> "continental" philosophy). (p. 64)

Africana critical theory is distinguished from Africana philosophy by the fact that
critical theory cannot be situated within the world of conventional academic disciplines and divisions of labor. It transverses and transgresses boundaries between traditional disciplines and accents the interconnections and intersections of philosophy, history, politics, economics, the arts, psychology, and sociology, among other
disciplines. Critical theory is contrasted with mainstream, monodisciplinary social
theory through its multidisciplinary methodology and its efforts to develop a comprehensive dialectical theory of domination and liberation specific to the special
needs of contemporary society (see Agger, 2006; J.C. Alexander, 2001; Blackburn,
1972; Bronner, 2002; Habermas, 1984, 1987a, 1988, 1989b; Rush, 2004). Africana

philosophy has a very different agenda, one that seems to me more meta-philosophical than philosophical at this point, because it entails theorizing-on-tradition
and tradition-reconstruction more than tradition extension and expansion through
the production of normative theory and critical pedagogical praxis aimed at application (i.e., immediate radical/revolutionary self and social transformation).[10]

The primary purpose of critical theory is to relate radical thought to revolutionary
practice, which is to say that its focus—philosophical, social and political—is always
and ever the search for ethical alternatives and viable moral solutions to the most
pressing problems of our present age. Critical theory is not about, or rather *should
not* be about allegiance to intellectual ancestors and/or ancient schools of thought,
but about using *all* (without regard to race, gender, class, sexual orientation, and/or
religious affiliation) accumulated radical thought and revolutionary practices in the
interest of human liberation and social(ist) transformation. With this in mind, Cornel West's (1982) contentions concerning "Afro-American critical thought" offer an
outline for the type of theorizing that Africana critical theory endeavors:

> The object of inquiry for Afro-American critical thought is the past and present, the do-
> ings and the sufferings of African people in the United States. Rather than a new scien-
> tific discipline or field of study, it is a genre of writing, a textuality, a mode of discourse
> that interprets, describes, and evaluates Afro-American life in order comprehensively to
> understand and effectively to transform it. It is not concerned with "foundations" or tran-
> scendental "grounds" but with how to build its language in such a way that the configu-
> ration of sentences and the constellation of paragraphs themselves create a textuality and
> distinctive discourse which are a material force for Afro-American freedom. (p. 15)

Though Africana critical theory encompasses and is concerned with much more
than the life-worlds and lived-experiences of "African people in the United States,"
West's comments here are helpful, as they give us a glimpse at the kind of connections critical theorists make in terms of their ideas having an impact and significant
influence on society. Africana critical theory is not thought-for-thought's sake (as it
often seems is the case with so much contemporary philosophy—Africana philosophy notwithstanding), but thought-for-life-and-liberation's sake. It is not only a
style of writing which focuses on radicalism and revolution, but a new way of *thinking* and *doing* revolution that is based and constantly being built on the radicalisms
and revolutions of the past, and the black radical and black revolutionary past in
particular.

From West's frame of reference, "Afro-American philosophy expresses the particular American variation of European modernity that Afro-Americans helped shape in
this country and must contend with in the future. While it might be possible to articulate a competing Afro-American philosophy based principally on African norms
and notions, it is likely that the result would be theoretically thin" (p. 24). Contrary
to West's comments, Africana critical theory represents and registers as that "possible articulat[ion] of a competing [Africana] philosophy based principally on African
norms and notions," and though he thinks that the results will be "theoretically
thin," Africana critical theory—following Fanon (1965, 1967, 1968, 1969)—understands this risk to be part of the price the wretched of the earth must be willing to
pay for their (intellectual, political, psychological, and physical) freedom. Intellectually audacious, especially considering the widespread Eurocentrism and white

supremacism of contemporary conceptual generation, Africana critical theory does not acquiesce or give priority and special privilege to European history, culture and thought. It turns to the long overlooked thought and texts of women and men of African descent who have developed and contributed radical thought and revolutionary practices that could possibly aid us in our endeavors to continuously create an *anti-racist, anti-sexist, anti-capitalist, anti-colonial and sexual orientation-sensitive critical theory of contemporary society.*

Above and beyond all of the aforementioned, Africana critical theory is about offering alternatives to *what is* (domination and discrimination), by projecting possibilities of *what ought to be* and/or *what could be* (human liberation and radical/revolutionary social transformation). To reiterate, it is not afraid, to put it as plainly as possible, to critically engage and dialogue deeply with European and/or other cultural groups' thought traditions. In fact, it often finds critical cross-cultural dialogue necessary considering the historical conundrums and current shared conditions and shared crises of the modern or postmodern, transnational, and almost completely multicultural world (see Goldberg, 1994; Goldberg and Solomos, 2002; McLaren, 1997). Africana critical theory, quite simply, does not privilege or give priority to European and/or other cultural groups' thought traditions since its philosophical foci and primary purpose revolves around the search for solutions to the most pressing social and political problems in continental and diasporan African life-worlds and lived-experiences in the present age.

## EPISTEMIC STRENGTHS AND THEORETIC WEAKNESSES: ON THE PROSPECTS AND PROBLEMATICS OF EPISTEMIC OPENNESS AND INTELLECTUAL EXCLUSIVENESS IN AFRICANA THOUGHT TRADITIONS

Africana critical theory navigates many theoretic spaces that extend well beyond the established intellectual boundaries of Africana Studies. At this point, it is clearly characterized by an *epistemic openness* to theories and methodologies usually understood to be incompatible with one another. Besides providing it with a simultaneously creative and critical tension, Africana critical theory's *antithetical conceptual contraction* (i.e., its utilization of concepts perceived to be contradictory to, and in conflict and competing with one another) also gives it its theoretic rebelliousness and untamable academic quality. Which is to say that Africana critical theory exists or is able to exist well beyond the boundaries of the academy and academic disciplines because the bulk of its theoretic base, its primary points of departure, are radical and revolutionary Africana political practices and social movements. The word "theory," then, in the appellation "Africana critical theory" is being defined and, perhaps, radically refined, for specific *transdisciplinary* discursive purposes and practices. This is extremely important to point out because there has been a long intellectual history of chaos concerning the nature and tasks of "theory" in Africana Studies.

To an Africana critical theorist, it seems highly questionable, if not simply downright silly at this juncture in the history of Africana thought, to seek a theoretical Holy Grail that will serve as a panacea to our search for the secrets to being, culture, politics, society or, even more, liberation. Taking our cue from W. E. B. Du Bois and

C. L. R. James, it may be better to conceive of theory as an "instrument" or, as Frantz Fanon and Amilcar Cabral would have it, a "weapon" used to attack certain targets of domination and discrimination. Theories are, among many other things, optics, ways of seeing; they are perspectives that illuminate specific phenomena. However, as with any perspective, position or standpoint, each theory has its blind spots and lens limitations, what we call in the contemporary discourse of Africana philosophy, *theoretical myopia.*

Recent theoretical debates in Africana Studies have made us painfully aware of the fact that theories are discipline-specific constructs and products, created in particular intellectual contexts, for particular intellectual purposes (see Aldridge and James, 2007; Aldridge and Young, 2000; Anderson and Stewart, 2007; Asante and Karenga, 2006; Bobo and Michel, 2000; Bobo, Hudley and Michel, 2004; Conyers, 2005; P.A. Hall, 1999; Gordon and Gordon, 2006a, 2006b; Marable, 2000, 2005). Contemporary Africana thought has also enabled us see that theories are always grounded in and grow out of specific social discourses, political practices, and national and international institutions. In *The Hermeneutics of African Philosophy*, the Eritrean philosopher, Tsenay Serequeberhan (1994), correctly contends that "political 'neutrality' in philosophy, as in most other things, is at best a 'harmless' naïveté, and at worst a pernicious subterfuge for hidden agendas" (p. 4). Each discipline has an academic agenda. Therefore, the theories and methodologies of a discipline promote the development of that particular discipline. Theories emerging from traditional disciplines that claim to provide an eternal philosophical foundation or universal and neutral knowledge transcendent of historical horizons, cultural conditions and social struggles, or a metatheory (i.e., a theory about theorizing) that purports absolute truth that transcends the interests of specific theorists and their theories, have been and are being vigorously rejected by Africana Studies scholars and students (see Asante, 1990, 1998, 2003a, 2007a; Azevedo, 2005; Ba Nikongo, 1997; Bonilla-Silva and Zuberi, 2008; Conyers, 2003; Gordon, 2006a; Norment, 2007a, 2007b; Zuberi, 2001). Theory, then, as Serequeberhan (1994) says of philosophy, is a "critical and explorative engagement of one's own cultural specificity and lived historicalness. It is a critically aware explorative appropriation of our cultural, political, and historical existence" (p. 23).[11]

Theoretic discourse does not simply fall from the sky like wind-blown rain, leaving no traces of the direction from which it came and its initial point of departure. On the contrary, it registers as, and often radically represents, critical concerns interior to epistemologies and experiences arising out of a specific cultural condition and historical horizon within which it is located and discursively situated. In other words, similar to a finely crafted woodcarving or hand-woven garment, theories retain the intellectual and cultural markings of their makers, and though they can and do "travel" and "cross borders," they are optimal in their original settings and when applied to the original phenomena that inspired their creation (Said, 1999, 2000; Giroux, 1992).

A more modest conception of theory sees it, then, as an instrument (or, as Michel Foucault would have it, a "tool") to help us illuminate and navigate specific social spaces, pointing to present and potential problems, interpreting and criticizing them, and ultimately offering ethical and egalitarian alternatives to them (e.g., see Foucault, 1977a, 1977b, 1984, 1988, 1997, 1998, 2000). At their best, theories not only illuminate social realities, but they help individuals make sense of their life-worlds and lived-experiences. To do this effectively, theories usually utilize metaphor, allegory, images, symbols, discursive concepts, counter arguments, conversational language, rhetorical devices, and narratives. Modern metatheory often accents the interesting fact that theories have literary components and qualities: they narrate or tell stories, employ rhetoric and semiotics and, similar to literature, often offer accessible interpretations of classical and contemporary life. However, theories also have cognitive and kinship components that allow them to connect with other theories' concepts and common critical features, as when a variety of disparate theories of Africana Studies discourse raise questions concerning race and racism, or questions of identity and liberation.

There are many different types of theory, from literary theory to linguistic theory, cultural theory to aesthetic theory, and political theory to postmodern theory. Africana critical theory is a critical conceptual framework that seeks an ongoing synthesis of the most emancipatory elements of a wide-range of *social theory* in the interests of continental and diasporan Africans, among other struggling people. This means that Africana critical theory often identifies and isolates the social implications of various theories, some of which were not created to have any concrete connections with the social world (and certainly not the African world), but currently do as a consequence of the ways they have been appropriated, (re)articulated and, in terms of Africana critical theory, *decolonized* and *Africanized*.

Here, it is extremely important to recall the history of theory. Theories are instruments and, therefore, can be put to use in a multiplicity of manners. Historically, theories have always traveled outside of their original contexts, but two points of importance should be made here. The first point has to do with something the Palestinian literary theorist and political activist Edward Said (1999, 2000) said long ago, that is, that theories lose some of their original power when taken out of their original intellectual and cultural contexts, because the sociopolitical situation is different, the suffering and/or struggling people are different, and the aims and objectives of their movements are different. The second point is reflexive and has to do with the modern moment in the history of theory: Never before have so many theories traveled so many mental miles away from their intellectual milieux. This speaks to the new and novel theoretical times that we are passing through. Part of what we have to do, then, is identify those theories ("instruments" and/or "weapons," if you prefer) that will aid us most in our struggles against racism, sexism, capitalism, and colonialism, among other epochal imperial issues.

The turn toward and emphasis on social theory suggests several of Africana critical theory's key concerns, such as the development of a synthetic sociopolitical discourse that earnestly and accessibly addresses issues arising from: everyday black life and experiences in white supremacist societies; women's daily lives in male supremacist (or, if you prefer, patriarchal) societies; and, the commonalities of and the distinct differences between black life in colonial and capitalist countries, among other issues. Social theoretical discourse is important because it provides individuals and groups with topographies of their social terrains. This discourse, especially when it is "critical," also often offers concepts and categories that aid individuals and groups in critically engaging and radically altering their social worlds (see Agger, 2006; J.C. Alexander, 2001; Birt, 2002; Blackburn, 1972; Calhoun, 1995; Dant,

2003; P.H. Collins, 1998; R. Collins, 2000; Elliott, 2003; Rhoads, 1991; Sica, 1998; B.S. Turner, 1996).

Social theories, in a general sense, are simultaneously heuristic and discursive devices for exploring and explaining the social world. They accent social conditions and can often provoke social action and political praxis. Social theories endeavor to provide a panoramic picture that enables individuals to conceptualize and contextualize their life-worlds and lived-experiences within the wider field of sociopolitical relations and institutions. Additionally, social theories can aid individuals in their efforts to understand and alter particular sociopolitical events and artifacts by analyzing their receptions, relations, and ongoing effects.

In addition to socio-theoretical discourse, Africana critical theory draws directly from the discourse of *dialectics* because it seeks to understand and, if necessary, alter society as a whole, not simply some isolated or culturally confined series of phenomena. The emphasis on dialectics also sends a signal to those social theorists and others who are easily intellectually intimidated by efforts to grasp and grapple with the whole of human history, culture and our current crises, that Africana critical theory is not in any sense a traditional social theory but, unapologetically, *a social activist and political praxis-promoting theory* that seriously seeks the radical/revolutionary redistribution of social wealth and political power. The dialectical dimension of Africana critical theory enables it to make connections between seemingly isolated and unrelated parts of society, demonstrating how, for instance, neutral social terrain, such as the education industries, the entertainment industries, the prison industrial complex, the political electoral process, or the realm of religion are sites and sources of ruling race, gender, and/or class privilege and power.[12]

Dialectics, the art of demonstrating the interconnectedness of parts to each other and to the overarching system or framework as a whole, distinguishes Africana critical theory from other theories in Africana Studies because it simultaneously searches for progressive and retrogressive aspects of Africana, Eurocentric, and other cultural groups' thought traditions. This means, then, that Africana critical theory offers an external and internal critique, which is also to say that it is unrepentantly *a self-reflexive social theory*: a social theory that relentlessly reexamines and refines its own philosophical foundations, methods, positions, and presuppositions. Africana critical theory's dialectical dimension also distinguishes it from other traditions and versions of critical theory because the connections it makes between social parts and the social whole are those that directly and profoundly affect Africana life-worlds and lived-experiences. No other tradition or version of critical theory has historically or currently claims to highlight and accent *sites of domination* and *sources of liberation* in the interests of continental and diasporan Africans, as well as humanity as a whole.

## STRUGGLE ALWAYS: WEAPONS OF THEORY, THOUGHT TRADITIONS OF PRAXIS, AND AFRICANA CRITICAL THEORY'S AVERSION TO EPISTEMIC EXCLUSIVENESS AND INTELLECTUAL INSULARITY

In "The Weapon of Theory," the Cape Verdean and Guinea-Bissaun freedom fighter, Amilcar Cabral (1979), asserted: "every practice gives birth to a theory. If it is true that a revolution can fail, even though it be nurtured on perfectly conceived theories, no one has yet successfully practiced revolution without a revolutionary theory" (p. 123). Africana critical theory is a "revolutionary theory" and a beacon symbolizing the birth of a theoretical revolution in Africana Studies and critical social theory. Its basic aims and objectives speak to its radical character and critical qualities. It is unique in that it is theory preoccupied with promoting social activism and political practice geared toward radical/revolutionary social transformation and the development of an ethical and egalitarian anti-imperial society by pointing to: what needs to be transformed; what strategies and tactics might be most useful in the transformative efforts; and, which agents and agencies could potentially carry out the radical/revolutionary social transformation.

Following Cabral (1972, 1973, 1979), Africana critical theory conceives of theory as a "weapon," and the history of Africana thought, and the black radical thought tradition in particular, as its essential arsenal. As with any arsenal, a weapon is chosen or left behind based on the specifics of the mission, such as the target, terrain and time-sensitivity. The same may be said concerning "the weapon of theory." Different theories can be used for different purposes in disparate situations. The usefulness or uselessness of a particular theory depends on the task(s) at hand and whether the theory in question is deemed appropriate for the task(s). Theory can be extremely useful, but it is indeed a great and grave mistake to believe that there is a grand narrative, super-theory or theoretical god that will provide the interpretive or explanatory keys to the political and intellectual kingdom (or queendom). Instead of arguing for a new super-theory, as so many theories emerging from European modernity and postmodernity seem to, Africana critical theory advocates an ongoing synthesis of the most moral and radical political elements of classical and contemporary, continental and diasporan African thought-traditions with other cultural groups' progressive (i.e., radical/revolutionary) thought and political practices in the interest of critically engaging and ethically altering local *and* global, national *and* international, African *and* human problems in the present age.

Contemporary society requires a continuous and increasingly high level of socio-political mapping because of the intensity of recent politico-ideological maneuvers–what the Italian critical theorist, Antonio Gramsci (2000, pp. 222–245), identified as "wars of position" and "wars of maneuver"—and the urgency of present socio-economic transformations.[13] History has unfolded to this in-between epoch of immense and provocative change, and many theories of contemporary society outline and attempt to explain an aspect of this change, and, as a result, are relevant with regard to certain social phenomena. But, no single theory captures the complete *constantly-changing* socio-political picture, though there are plethoras that religiously profess to, and promise to provide their adherents and converts with theoretical salvation in the sin-sick world of theory. It should be stated outright: *All theories have blind spots and lens limitations,* and *all theories (theoretically) make critical conceptual contributions.* Consequently, Africana critical theory advocates combining classical and contemporary theory from diverse academic disciplines and intellectual-activist traditions; though Africana thought traditions, and the black radical tradition in specific, it must be made clear, is always and ever Africana critical theory's primary point of departure. My conception of critical social theory keeps in mind that the mappings of each theory potentially provide specific new and novel insights but, it must be admitted, these insights alone are not enough to affect the type of radical/revolutionary social change required. It is with this understanding that Africana critical theory eschews epistemic exclusiveness and intellectual insularity, and instead emphasizes epistemic openness and, on principle, practices *antithetical conceptual contraction* by generously drawing from the diverse discursive formations and theoretic practices of a wide-range of classical and contemporary, continental and diasporan African thought traditions, such as: African, African American, African Caribbean, Afro-Asian, Afro-European, Afro-Latino, Afro-Native American, and Africana philosophy and theory; Negritude; revolutionary Pan-Africanism; prophetic pragmatism; womanism; black feminism; black postmodernism; black existentialism; black radicalism; black Marxism; revolutionary black nationalism; black liberation theology; critical race theory; philosophy of race; sociology of race, psychology of race; anthropology of race; history of race; and, geography of race, among others.

Africana critical theory relentlessly examines its own aims, objectives, positions, and methods, constantly putting them in question in an effort to radically refine and revise them. It is, thus, epistemically open, flexible and non-dogmatic, constantly exhibiting the ability to critically engage opposing theories and appropriate and incorporate progressive strains and reject retrogressive strains from them. It is here that Africana critical theory exhibits its theoretic sophistication and epistemic strength and stamina. Along with the various Africana theoretical perspectives that Africana critical theory employs as its primary points of departure, it also often critically engages many of the other major theoretical discourses of the modern moment, such as: Marxism; feminism; pragmatism; historicism; existentialism; phenomenology; hermeneutics; semiotics; Frankfurt School critical theory; critical pedagogy; poststructuralism; postmodernism; and, postcolonialism, among others.

Africana critical theory engages other, non-Africana discursive formations and theoretic practices because it is aware of the long history of appropriation and re-articulation in Africana thought traditions. This takes us right back to the critical debates raging all around about black people employing white theory to explore and explain black experiences (Asante and Karenga, 2006; Conyers, 2003, 2005; Gordon and Gordon, 2006a, 2006b; Rojas, 2007; Rooks, 2006). Instead of simply side-stepping this important intellectual history, Africana critical theory conscientiously confronts it in an effort to understand and, if need be, alter it in an attempt to actualize black liberation on terms interior to contemporary Africana life-worlds and lived-experiences. This brings to mind the Caribbean philosopher, Lewis Gordon's (1997a), contention that,

> [T]heory, any theory, gains its sustenance from that which it offers *for* and *through* the lived-reality of those who are expected to formulate it. Africana philosophy's history of Christian, Marxist, Feminist, Pragmatist, Analytical, and Phenomenological thought has therefore been a matter of what specific dimensions each had to offer the existential realities of theorizing blackness. For Marxism, for instance, it was not so much its notion of "science" over all other forms of socialist theory, nor its promise of a world to win, that may have struck a resonating chord in the hearts of black Marxists. It was, instead, Marx and Engels' famous encomium of the proletarians' having nothing to lose but their chains. Such a call has obvious affinity for a people who have been so strongly identified with chattel slavery. (p. 4, emphasis in original)

It is important to understand and critically engage *why* continental and diasporan Africans have historically and continue currently to embrace Eurocentric theory. Saying simply that blacks who did or who do embrace some aspects of white theory are intellectually insane or have an intellectual inferiority complex logically leads us to yet another discourse on black pathology; all the while we will be, however inadvertently, side-stepping the confrontation and critique of white supremacy as a history-making and culture-shaping global imperialism (Bonilla-Silva, 2001, 2003; Bonilla-Silva and Doane, 2003; Bonilla-Silva and Zuberi, 2008; C.W. Mills, 1999, 2001, 2003b). Persons of African origin and descent have been preoccupied in the modern moment with struggles against various forms and forces of domination, oppression, and exploitation. They, therefore, have been and remain attracted to theories that they understand to promise or provide tools to combat their domination, oppression, and/or exploitation. Though blacks in white supremacist societies are often rendered anonymous and/or are virtually invisible, they do not have a "collective mind" and have reached no consensus concerning which theories make the best weapons to combat their domination, oppression, and/or exploitation.[14] This means, then, that the way is epistemically open, and that those blacks who embrace or appropriate an aspect of white theory are not theoretically "lost" but, perhaps, simply employing the theoretical tools they understand to be most applicable and most readily available to them in their neocolonial contexts and their particular emancipatory efforts.

Fanon spoke to this issue in a special way in *Black Skin, White Masks*, where he declared "the discoveries of Freud are of no use to us here" in the hyper-racialized and hyper-colonized life-worlds and lived-experiences of black folk, and in *The Wretched of the Earth*, where he asserted "Marxist analysis should always be slightly stretched every time we have to do with the colonial problem. Everything up to and including the very nature of pre-capitalist society, so well explained by Marx, must here be thought out again" (1967, p. 104, 1968, p. 40). Fanon (1967) did not find anything of use in Freud for the particular kind of critical theoretical work he was doing in *Black Skin, White Masks*, and he even went so far to say that "there is a dialectical substitution when one goes from the psychology of the white man to that of the black" (p. 151). However, he was able to employ some aspects of Marxism for the kind of critical theoretical work he was doing in *The Wretched of the Earth*, but—and this is the main point—he critically engaged Marxism from his own critical subjective and radical political position as a hyper-racialized and hyper-colonized black man in a white supremacist capitalist and colonial world. In other words, his Africanity, or non-Europeanness, was never left in abeyance or abandoned for the sake of Eurocentric theoretical synthesis. Approaching Marxism from this Africana critical theoretical angle, essentially employing it as a tool and not as a tenet, Fanon was able to extend and expand the critical theoretical and radical political range and reach of Marxism; more than merely Africanizing it, but seminally building on and moving beyond it to critically engage phenomena, life-worlds, and lived-experiences that Marx and his Eurocentric heirs have shamefully shoved to the intellectual outposts of their quite quarantined racial and colonial (and patriarchal) world of ideas.

It is quite possible, even with the advent and academization of Africana Studies from the mid-1960s to the present, that many contemporary intellectuals and activists of African descent are unaware of Africana intellectual history, and especially

Africana critical thought traditions, which is very different than saying that they are unattracted to or find little or nothing of use in Africana critical thought traditions. Contemporary Africana theorists must take as one of their primary tasks making classical and contemporary black radical and Africana critical thought traditions more accessible and attractive, particularly to blacks but also to non-African anti-imperial others. There simply is no substitute for the kinds of easily-intelligible and epistemically open critical theoretical genealogies and contemporary conceptual generations that Africana Studies scholars must produce and propound to the Africana intelligentsia, the masses of black folk, well-meaning anti-racist whites, and multicultural, multiracial, and transethnic others if, not simply Africana Studies, but the souls of humble and hard-working black folk, are to survive and continue to contribute to human culture and civilization.

Africana critical theory engages a wide and diverse range of theory emerging from the insurgent intellectuals of the academy and the activist-intellectuals of radical and revolutionary socio-political movements. It understands each theory to offer enigmatic and illuminating insights because the more theory a theorist has at her or his disposal, the more issues and objects they can address, the more tasks they can perform, and the more theoretical targets they can terminate. As stated above, theories are optics or perspectives, and it is with this understanding that Africana critical theory contends that bringing a multiplicity of perspectives to bear on a phenomenon promises a greater grasp and a more thorough engagement and understanding of that phenomenon. For instance, many theories of race and racism arising from the discourse of Africana Studies have historically exhibited a serious weakness where sexism, and particularly patriarchy, is concerned. This situation was (to a certain extent) remedied and these theories were strengthened when Africana Women's Studies scholars diagnosed these one-dimensional and uni-gendered theories of race and racism, and coupled them with their own unique anti-racist interpretations of women's domination and discrimination and gender relations (see Butler and Walter, 1991; Guy-Sheftall, 1995; Hull, Scott and Smith, 1982; James and Sharpley-Whiting, 2000; Nnaemeka, 1998). Indeed this is an ongoing effort, and clearly there is no consensus in Africana Studies as to the importance of critically engaging gender domination and discrimination in continental and diasporan African life-worlds and lived-experiences. But, whether we have consensus or not, which we probably never will, the key concern to keep in mind is that though it may not be theoretically fashionable to engage certain phenomena it does not necessarily mean that it is not theoretically and/or practically important to engage that phenomena. As theorists part of our task is to bring unseen or often overlooked issues to the fore. In order to do this we may have to develop new concepts and new categories so that others might be able to coherently comprehend these enigmatic issues.

In calling for bringing many theories to bear on a phenomenon, Africana critical theory is not eluding the fact that in many instances a single theory may be the best source of insight. For example, Pan-Africanism offers a paradigm for analyzing the history of Africana anti-colonialism and decolonization; where black Marxism accents the interconnections of racism and capitalism in black life; while black feminism often speaks to the intersection(s) of racism and sexism in black women's life-worlds. Africana critical theory chooses to deploy a theory based on its overarching aims and objectives, which are constantly informed by the ongoing quest for human freedom and black liberation. It is not interested in an eclectic combination of theories—that is, *theoretical eclecticism*—simply for the sake of theoretical synthesis and contributing to the world of ideas, but its earnest interest lies in radical and revolutionary social(ist) transformation in the interest of Africana and other oppressed people.

## LOOKING BACKWARD TO THE BLACK RADICAL TRADITION, LOOKING FORWARD TO THE AFRICANA TRADITION OF CRITICAL THEORY: EPISTEMIC TOPOGRAPHIES AND CHAPTER SUMMARIES

The following chapter will focus on the polymathic and pioneering thought and texts of W. E. B. Du Bois and, specifically, his four quintessential contributions to Africana critical theory; contributions, it should be said at the outset, which continue to either elude or intimidate contemporary Africana, among other, intellectual-activists. Though he made many critical theoretical breakthroughs and, as we will see, covered and crisscrossed a great deal of uncharted and oft time treacherous intellectual terrain, many of Du Bois's major positions arise and recur as he addressed issues involving race, gender, and the dual dimensions of capitalist and colonial exploitation and oppression in Africana life-worlds and lived-experiences. In an effort to accent and highlight what I have identified as Du Bois's seminal and most significant donations to the discourse and development of the Africana tradition of critical theory, I undertake extended analyses of his concepts of race, anti-racism and critical race theory; his critique of sexism, and particularly patriarchy; his anti-colonialism, discourse on decolonization, and (proto) postcolonial theory; and, lastly, his concept of a race-centered and racism-conscious critique of capitalism and Marxism.

Critically challenging the traditional interpretations of the Trinidadian radical, C. L. R. James, in chapter 3 I shall argue that James, similar to Du Bois and the other intellectual-activist ancestors of the Africana tradition of critical theory explored in this study, was, first, more a critic of Marxism than a Marxist in any orthodox, or dogmatic, or Eurocentric sense. Second, I situate James in the black radical and Africana critical thought traditions. This is extremely important because it has become commonplace in studies on James to analyze his philosophy and social and political theory, almost exclusively, in light of white Marxist and other Eurocentric schools of thought, as if he had little or no relationship with the black radical tradition. Finally, I articulate what I consider to be James's most substantial contributions to the discourse and development of a critical theory of contemporary society with an emphasis on the most crucial issues confronting modern Africa and its diaspora.

Chapter 4 begins with an engagement of the multiple meanings of Negritude, exploring the supposedly divergent and "clearly distinguished" versions of the theory as advanced by Aime Césaire, Leopold Senghor, and Jean Paul Sartre. Then, an exploration of Negritude's connections to the radicalism of the Harlem Renaissance will be undertaken. Similar to Negritude, the Harlem Renaissance, it will be argued, provided both continental and diasporan Africans with fora where the most pressing social and political problems confounding and confronting their respective countries and communities could be critically and collectively engaged. In this way, much of Negritude, as theory and/or movement, is incomprehensible without exploring its critical connections to the radicalism of the Harlem Renaissance, among other black radical traditions and movements. And, finally, the chapter concludes with an analysis of Negritude's significance for Africana Studies, and most especially with an accent on the concept's contributions to the discourse and development of the Africana tradition of critical theory.

In chapter 5, I confront conventional interpretations of Fanon that either seek to turn him and his work into psychoanalytic theory, postcolonial theory, or a derivative of some other form of Eurocentric philosophy or theory by reinterpreting his ideas and actions from the vantage point of the black radical tradition. Employing Africana critical theory as my basic interpretive framework, I carefully and critically sift through Fanon's work, all the while focusing on its often-overlooked radical and revolutionary socio-theoretical dimensions. From this angle, Fanon is viewed as a critical social theorist of extraordinary depth and insight, especially with regard to issues involving Europe's supposed white superiority and Africa's alleged black inferiority; racism, sexism, colonialism and neocolonialism; revolutionary self-determination and revolutionary decolonization; the nature of revolutionary nationalism and its interconnections with revolutionary humanism; colonial violence and anticolonial violence; national consciousness, national culture and national liberation; the psychology of both the colonizer and the colonized; and, the prospects and problematics of a truly "postcolonial" African state.

In chapter 6, I explore and explicate Amilcar Cabral's extremely important, albeit often-overlooked, contributions to Africana Studies and critical social theory; contributions, I argue, which conceptualize and earnestly attempt to think through the borderlines and boundaries between, and the dialectics at play in, various stages of "underdevelopment" and "development," tradition and modernity, and nationalism and humanism in racial colonial and racist capitalist societies. The chapter will commence with a critical engagement of Cabral's concept(s) of colonialism and emphasis on the importance of ideology and concrete philosophy. Then, it engages the unique ways in which he synthesized radical theory with revolutionary praxis (or, rather, revolutionary nationalism with guerilla warfare). Next, analysis is given to his thesis of "return to the source" and the importance and inextricability of national history and national culture in his distinctive conceptions of national liberation and *the dialectical process of revolutionary decolonization and revolutionary re-Africanization*. Finally, the chapter concludes with a brief assessment and interpretation of some of the deficiencies of Cabral's contributions to the new critical theory of the twenty-first century.

The concluding chapter engages Africana critical theory as an unfinished project of human liberation and radical/revolutionary social transformation. It points to some of the pitfalls and problematics of previous interpretations and criticisms of black radicalism and strongly stresses the necessity of future studies to examine black radicalism as theory as opposed to ideology. I also make note of many of the remaining tasks for redeveloping critical theory of contemporary society and argue that henceforth it must be much more multiracial, multicultural, transethnic, transgender, transgenerational, sexual orientation-sensitive, and have a broader base than classical black radicalism and conventional (i.e., white or Eurocentric) critical theory.

Contemporary critical theory, and Africana critical theory in particular, I contend, must initiate the arduous and intricate task of simultaneously and dialectically re-developing and revising its classical philosophical foundation(s), move beyond its now inadequate and/or obsolete positions, and constantly synthesize itself with the most critical and cutting-edge social and political theory available. A redefined and revised black radical tradition and, even more, the Africana tradition of critical theory, I end the book asserting, offers an almost ideal source of and site for the radical reconstruction of, not simply Africana Studies and critical theory but, more importantly, contemporary culture and society. Let us now begin our journey by taking a critical look at Du Bois's key contributions to the Africana tradition of critical theory.

## NOTES

1. In terms of "black radicalism" and the "black radical tradition," I should observe at the outset that though it has been consistently discussed and heatedly debated over the years, few scholars have endeavored extended studies in this area. Often a paragraph or, at most, a journal article or book chapter surfaces every now and then, but book-length studies of this tradition have been and remain extremely rare. Consequently, I have relied on a wide-range of sources to deconstruct and reconstruct the black radical tradition. Most helpful in this regard were: Alkebulan (2007), Bogues (1983, 2003), Bush (1999), Cha-Jua (2001), O.C. Cox (1948, 1959, 1962, 1964, 1976, 1987), Cruse (1965, 1967, 1969, 2002) Foley (2003), Foner (1976, 1977), Foner and Allen (1987), Foner and Lewis (1989), Foner and Shapiro (1991), Geggus (2002), Haines (1988), C. L. R. James (1963, 1994, 1995, 1996a, 1999), J.A. James (1996a, 1997, 1999), W. James (1998), C. Johnson (2007), Joseph (2006a, 2006b), R.D.G. Kelley (1990, 1994, 1997a, 2002), Kornweibel (1998, 2002), Lazerow and Williams (2006), Lemelle and Kelley (1994), Marable (1983, 1985a, 1986, 1987, 1996, 2000, 2002, 2005, 2006), Meeks (1993, 1996, 2000), Meeks and Lindahl (2001), C.W. Mills (2003a), Moten (2003), Mullen (1999, 2002, 2004), Mullen and Ho (2008), Mullen and Linkon (1996), (Mullen and Smethurst (2003), Naison (1983), Ogbar (2004), Parascandola (2005), Payne and Green (2003), Pulido (2006), C.J. Robinson (1997, 2000, 2001), Schor (1977), Singh (2004), Springer (1999, 2005), Theoharis and Woodard (2003, 2005), J. Tyner (2006), West (1988b, 1993a, 1999), Wilmore (1998), and J. Woods (2004).

2. The literature on Africana Studies, which in its most comprehensive sense includes African, African American, Afro-American, Afro-Asian, Afro-European, Afro-Latino, Afro-Native American, Caribbean, Pan-African, Black British and, of course, Black Studies, is diverse and extensive. The most noteworthy overviews and critical analyses are: Aldridge (1988), Aldridge and James (2007), Aldridge and Young (2000), Alkalimat (1986, 1990), Allen (1974), Anderson (1990), Anderson and Stewart (2007), Asante (1990, 1998, 2003a, 2007a), Asante and Abarry (1996), Asante and Karenga (2006), Azevedo (2005), R. Bailey (1970), Baker, Diawara, and Lindeborg (1996), Ba Nikongo (1997), Barrett and Carey (2003), Bates, Mudimbe and O'Barr (1993), Blassingame (1973), Bobo and Michel (2000), Bobo, Hudley and Michel (2004), Butler (1981, 2000, 2001), Cha-Jua (2000), Conyers (2003, 2005), Cortada (1974), Croutchett (1971), P.T.K. Daniels (1980, 1981), Davies, Gadsby, Peterson and Williams (2003), Fierce (1991), Ford (1973), Fossett and Tucker (1997), Frye (1978), Geggus (2002), Gordon and Gordon (2006a, 2006b), P.A. Hall (1999), Hare (1972, 1998), Harris, Hine, and McKay (1990), Hayes (2000), Hudson-Weems (2004, 2007), Johnson and Henderson (2005), Johnson and Lyne (2002), Karenga (1988, 2001, 2002), R.D.G. Kelley (1997b), Kershaw (1989, 1992, 2003), Kilson (1973, 2000a), Kopano and Williams (2004),

Marable (2000, 2005), Marable and Mullings (2000), Mazrui (1967, 1974, 1978, 1980, 1986, 1993, 2002a, 2002c, 2004), Mazrui, Okpewho and Davies (1999), Mercer (1994), Mullen and Ho (2008), Norment (2007a, 2007b), Prashad (2000, 2001), Robinson, Foster and Ogilvie (1969), Rojas (2007), Rooks (2006), J.B. Stewart (1979, 1981, 1992, 1996b, 2004), Turner and McGann (1980), J. Turner (1984), Walton (1969), and Whitten and Torres (1998).

3. I advance this book, then, as a continuation of the Africana Critical Theory (ACT) intellectual archaeology project, which was initiated with my doctoral dissertation, "Africana Critical Theory: From W. E. B. Du Bois and C. L. R. James's Discourse on Domination and Liberation to Frantz Fanon and Amilcar Cabral's Dialectics of Decolonization" (2001). The present volume, however, represents much more than an uncomplicated revision of my dissertation on account of the fact that it endeavors to build on and go beyond my previous books, *Du Bois and the Problems of the Twenty-First Century* and *Du Bois's Dialectics*—that is, works in which I deepened and developed my conception of critical theory and identified Du Bois as the primary and preeminent point of departure and paradigmatic figure for the Africana tradition of critical theory. Where *Du Bois and the Problems of the Twenty-First Century* innovatively examined Du Bois's contributions to classical critical theory, *Du Bois's Dialectics* audaciously upped the ante by asserting that Du Bois did not only contribute to classical critical theory but also offers much to the resuscitation and reconstruction of contemporary critical theory, what has been referred to as "new critical theory," which seeks to bring critical class theory (mostly Marxism) into discursive dialogue with critical race theory, feminist theory, queer theory, postmodern theory, and postcolonial theory, among others (see Cornell, 2008; N. Fraser, 1989, 1997; Malpas and Wake, 2006; Mendieta, 2007; C.W. Mills, 2003a; Wilkerson and Paris, 2001). *Africana Critical Theory*, as an ongoing intellectual archaeology project, of course, revisits Du Bois's contributions to the deconstruction and reconstruction of critical theory but also, taking a bold turn toward often overlooked and unengaged Africana intellectual-activist ancestors and history, chronicles a heretofore hidden history and tradition of critical theory: from W. E. B. Du Bois to C. L. R. James, Negritude to Frantz Fanon, and Frantz Fanon to Amilcar Cabral. It need be noted at the outset, and in agreement with the British political theorist, David Held (1980), "[c]ritical theory, it should be emphasized, does *not* form a unity; it does not mean the same thing to all its adherents" (p. 14, emphasis in original). For instance, Steven Best and Douglas Kellner (1991) employ the term "critical theory" in a general sense in their critique of postmodern theory, stating: "We are using 'critical theory' here in the general sense of critical social and cultural theory and not in the specific sense that refers to the critical theory of society developed by the Frankfurt School" (p. 33). Further, Raymond Morrow (1994) has forwarded that the term *critical theory* "has its origins in the work of a group of German scholars [of Jewish descent] (collectively referred to as the *Frankfurt School*) in the 1920's who used the term initially (*Kritische Theorie* in German) to designate a specific approach to interpreting Marxist theory. But the term has taken on new meanings in the interim and can be neither exclusively identified with the Marxist tradition from which it has become increasingly distinct nor reserved exclusively to the Frankfurt School, given extensive new variations outside the original German context" (p. 6). Finally, in his study of Marx, Foucault, and Habermas's philosophies of history and contributions to critical theory, Steven Best (1995) uses the term *critical theory* "in the most general sense, designating simply a critical social theory, that is, a social theory critical of present forms of domination, injustice, coercion, and inequality" (p. xvii). He, therefore, does not "limit the term to refer to only the Frankfurt School" (p. xvii). This means, then, that the term "critical theory" and the methods, presuppositions and positions it has come to be associated with in the humanities and social sciences: (1) connotes and continues to exhibit an *epistemic openness* and style of radical cultural criticism that highlights and accents the historical alternatives and emancipatory possibilities of a specific age and/or sociocultural condition; (2) is not the

exclusive domain of Marxists, neo-Marxists, post-Marxists, feminists, post-feminists, post-structuralists, postmodernists, and/or Habermasians; and, (3) can be radically reinterpreted and redefined to identify and encompass *classical and contemporary, continental and diasporan African liberation theory and revolutionary praxis.* For a few of the more noteworthy histories of the Frankfurt School and their philosophical project and various sociopolitical programs, see Bernstein (1995), Bottomore (1984, 2002), Bubner (1988), Dews (1987), Freundlieb, Hudson and Rundell (2004), Friedman (1980), Geuss (1981), Held (1980), Ingram (1990), Jay (1996), Kellner (1989), Kohlenbach and Geuss (2005), T. McCarthy (1991), McCarthy and Hoy (1994), Morrow (1994), Nealon and Irr (2002), O'Neill (1976), Pensky (2005), Rasmussen (1996), Rasmussen and Swindal (2004), Stirk (2000), J.B. Thompson (1990), Wiggerhaus (1995), and Wolin (1992, 1994, 1995, 2006). And, for further discussion of the Africana tradition of critical theory, see Rabaka (2002, 2003a, 2003b, 2003c, 2003d, 2003e, 2004, 2005a, 2006a, 2006b, 2006c, 2006d, 2007a, 2007b, 2008a, 2008b, 2008c).

4. Several works, which fall under the rubric of what is currently being called "new critical theory," are already taking up the challenge of making critical theory speak to more than merely European, European American, patriarchal, and heterosexual crises, cultures, and sociopolitical problems. These works lucidly demonstrate that there are many forms and many traditions of critical theory. For further discussion, see Agger (1992b, 1993), Arisaka (2001), P.H. Collins (1998, 2000, 2004), Essed and Goldberg (2002), N. Fraser (1989), Hames-Garcia (2001), L. Harris (1999b), Huntington (2001), Jafri (2004), Mendieta (2007), Outlaw (2005), Pulitano (2003), Rabaka (2007a, 2008a), L.C. Simpson (2003), Willet (2001), and Wilkerson and Paris (2001).

5. For further discussion of critical theory, or critical social theory, "in a general sense" and/or beyond the Frankfurt School's conception of critical theory, see Agger (1992b, 2006), J.C. Alexander (2001), Best (1995), Blackburn (1972), Crossley (2005), Dant (2003), Elliott (2003), N. Fraser (1989, 1997), How (2003), Lichtmann (1993), Outlaw (2005), Pensky (2005), Peters, Olssen and Lankshear (2003), Peters, Lankshear and Olssen (2003), Rabaka (2006a), Ray (1993), Rhoads (1991), Sica (1998), and J.B. Thompson (1990).

6. Since its inception Marxism has been in crisis, but this does not negate the fact that it has historically and continues currently to provide one of, if not *the* most penetrating and provocative critiques of capitalism. In response to constant criticisms that Marxism had been falsified, Herbert Marcuse (1978b) may have put it best when he asserted in a 1978 BBC interview:

> [I] do not believe that the theory [Marxism], as such, has been falsified. What has happened is that some of the concepts of Marxian theory, as I said before, have had to be re-examined; but this is not something from outside brought into Marxist theory, it is something which Marxist theory itself, as an historical and dialectical theory, demands. It would be relatively easy for me to enumerate, or give you a catalogue of, those decisive concepts of Marx which have been corroborated by the development of capitalism; the concentration of economic power, the fusion of economic and political power, the increasing intervention of the state into the economy, the decline in the rate of profit, the need for engaging in a neo-imperialist policy in order to create markets and opportunity of enlarged accumulation of capital, and so on. This is a formidable catalogue—and it speaks a lot for Marxian theory. . . . Marxian theory would be falsified when the conflict between our ever-increasing social wealth and its destructive use were to be solved within the framework of Capitalism; when the poisoning of the life environment were to be eliminated; when capital could expand in a peaceful way; when the gap between rich and poor were being continuously reduced; when technical progress were to be made to serve the growth of human freedom—and all this, I repeat, within the framework of Capitalism. (pp. 72–73; see also Marcuse, 1967)

Many black radicals, especially black Marxists, concede with their white Marxists counterparts that capitalism does not enhance but inhibits human life and liberation. However, in contradistinction to white Marxists, black Marxists also emphasize the political economy of race and racism and, often employing a reconstructed race-conscious and racism-critical historical materialist framework, point to the interconnections and parallel historical evolution of racism and capitalism. As early as his 1907 essays, "Socialist of the Path" and "The Negro and Socialism," for instance, W. E. B. Du Bois (1985c) detected and detailed deficiencies in the Marxist tradition which included, among other things, a silence on and/or an inattention to: race, racism, and anti-racist struggle; colonialism and anti-colonial struggle; and the ways in which *both* capitalism and colonialism exacerbate not simply the economic exploitation of non-Europeans, but continues (both physical and psychological) colonization beyond the realm of political economy. Du Bois, therefore, laboring long and critically with Marxian theory and methodology, deconstructed it and developed his own original radical democratic socialist theory that: simultaneously built on his pioneering work as a (classical) critical race theorist and anti-colonialist; called for the radical transformation of U.S. society and the power relations of the world; was deeply concerned about and committed to world peace and demanded disarmament; and, advocated the liberation of all colonized, politically oppressed, and economically exploited persons (see Horne, 1986; Marable, 1986; Mullen, 2002; Rabaka, 2007a, 2008a; C.J. Robinson, 2000).

7. For further discussion of black radicals and black Marxists' ragged relationship with white Marxism and white Marxist party politics and movements, see Baraka (1966, 1970, 1971, 1972, 1984, 1994, 1995, 1997, 2000), Bogues (1983, 2003), O.C. Cox (1959, 1987), Cruse (1967, 2002), A.Y. Davis (1998a), Duffield (1988), Foner and Allen (1987), Grigsby (1987), Haywood (1934, 1948, 1978), Hennessey (1992), P. Henry (2000), Holcomb (2007), C. L. R. James (1992, 1994, 1996a), W. James (1998), Kelley (1990, 1994, 2002), Kornweibel (1998), Marable (1983, 1985a, 1987, 1996), Mullen (2002); Naison (1983), Outlaw (1983a, 1983b, 1987), Serequeberhan (1990), Sivanandan (1990), C.J. Robinson (2000), Watts (2001), West (1988b, 1993a, 1999) and K. Woodard (1999, 2000).

8. Along with Africana Studies and more general critical social scientific research methods, Africana critical theory has also been deeply influenced by the monumental meta-methodological studies of Bonilla-Silva and Zuberi (2008), Gunaratnam (2003), Sandoval (2000), and L.T. Smith (1999), which each seek to decolonize research methods and emphasize their importance in developing critical theories of white supremacist patriarchal capitalist and colonial societies. The influence of these works on Africana critical theory's methodological orientation cannot be overstated.

9. In his introduction to *One-Dimensional Man*, the Frankfurt School critical theorist Herbert Marcuse (1964) argues that, "[s]ocial theory is concerned with the historical alternatives which haunt the established society as subversive tendencies and forces" (pp. xliii–xliv). Part of the task of a critical theory of contemporary society, then, lies in its ability to critique society "in light of its used and unused or abused capabilities for improving the human condition" (p. xlii). When I write of "ethical," "historical," and/or "radical" alternatives here, I am advocating new modes of human existence and interaction predicated on practices rooted in the realities of our past, present, and hoped for future. I am following in the footsteps of one of the great impresarios of the Black Arts movement, Larry Neal (1989), who taught us that one of the most urgent tasks of radical artists and intellectual-activists is to offer "visions of a liberated future." In offering *ethical alternatives* to the established order, critical theorists highlight and accent right and wrong thought and action, perhaps the single most important issue in the field of moral philosophy (Frey and Wellman, 2003; Lafollette, 1999, 2003; Singer, 1993; Sterba, 1998). The critique of racism, sexism and colonialism register, or rather *should* register right alongside the critique of capitalism in critical theorists' conceptual universe(s), because part of the established order's ideology and, in particular, part of its political and economic agenda, involves domination and discrimination based on race, gender, and capitalist and/or colonial class/caste. Anti-racist, anti-sexist, and anti-colonial thought, practices, and social movements help to provide *historical alternatives* that Marx and Marxists'

criticisms of capitalism, to date, have not been able to adequately translate into reality (Aronson, 1995; Best, 1995; Callari, Cullenberg and Biewener, 1995; Gottlieb, 1992; Magnus and Cullenberg, 1995; Nelson and Grossberg, 1988). In fact, many former and neo- Marxists openly acknowledge that "classical" Marxism privileged class and gave special priority to economic issues that enabled it to easily overlook and/or omit the multiple issues arising from the socio-historical realities of racism, sexism, and colonialism in modern history, culture, politics, and society (Agger, 1992a, 1998; Cohen, 1987; A.Y. Davis, 1981, 1989, 1998a; Di Stephano, 1991, 2008; Dussel, 1985, 1995, 1996; Ingram, 1990; Kellner, 1989, 1995; Kuhn and Wolpe, 1978; Marsh, 1995, 1999, 2001; Matustik, 1998; C.W. Mills, 1987, 1997, 1998, 2003a; Nelson and Grossberg, 1988; Sargent, 1981; Vogel, 1983, 1995; Weinbaum, 1978; West, 1988b, 1993a). What I am calling for here, though, is not a neglect of class and the role that political economy plays in contemporary culture and society, but rather the placing of critical class theory in dialogue and on equal theoretical terms with critical race theory, women's liberation theory, and postcolonial theory, among other theory, in order to develop a broader-based, polyvocal radical political theory of contemporary society. The sites and sources of oppression and exploitation in contemporary culture and society are multiple and do not emerge from the economy and the crises of capitalism alone. New critical theory must take into consideration the long neglected or often overlooked new and novel forces and forms of domination and discrimination. Africana critical theory is an effort aimed at chronicling classical and contemporary, continental and diasporan African radicals and revolutionaries' contributions to a critical theory of contemporary society. For further discussion, see Rabaka (2007a, 2008a).

10. Part of Africana philosophy's current meta-philosophical character has to due with both its critical and uncritical appropriation of several Western European philosophical concepts and categories. As more philosophers of African origin and descent receive training in and/or dialogue with Africana Studies theory and methodology, the basic notions and nature of Africana philosophy will undoubtedly change. Needless to say, Africana philosophy has an intellectual arena and engages issues that are often distinctly different from the phenomena that preoccupy and have long plagued Western European and European American philosophy. I am not criticizing the meta-philosophical motivations in the discourse of contemporary Africana philosophy as much as I am pleading with workers in the field to develop a "division of labor"—à la Du Bois's classic caveat(s) to continental and diasporan Africans in the face of white supremacy (see Du Bois, 1973, 2002). A move should be made away from "philosophizing on Africana philosophy" (i.e., meta-philosophy), and more Africana philosophical attention should be directed toward the cultural crises and social and political problems of the present age. In order to do this, Africana philosophers will have to turn to the advances of Africana Studies scholars working in history, cultural criticism, economics, politics, and social theory, among other areas. For a more detailed discussion of the nature and tasks of Africana philosophy, see Lucius Outlaw's groundbreaking, "Africana Philosophy" and "African, African American, Africana Philosophy" (Outlaw, 1996a, 1997a). Also of immense importance and extremely influential with regard to my interpretation (and criticisms) of Africana philosophy have been: Abanuka (2003, 2004), Appiah (1992, 2003, 2005, 2006, 2008), Asouzu (2004), Azenabor (1998), Babbitt and Campbell (1999), R.H. Bell (2002), L.M. Brown (2004), Chukwu (2002), Coetzee and Roux (1998), Dawson (1994, 2001), English and Kalumba (1996), Ekei (2001), Etuk (1989), Eze (1997a, 1997b), Gordon (1997a, 1997b, 1998, 2000, 2003, 2006a, 2006b, 2008), Gbadegesin (1991), Gyekye (1988, 1995, 1996, 1997), Hallen (2002, 2006), Hallen and Sodipo (1981, 1986), Hamminga (2005), L. Harris (1983), P. Henry (2000), Hord and Lee (1995), Hountondji (1996), Imbo (1998, 2002), Karp and Bird (1980), Karp and Masolo (2000), Kebede (1999, 2004), Kiros (1992, 1994, 2001, 2005), Kwame (1995), Locke (1983, 1989, 1992), Lott (2002), Lott and Pittman (2003), Mkabela (1997), Masolo (1994), May (2007), Mburu (2003), Mezu (1965), C.W.

Mills (1998), Montmarquet and Hardy (2000), Moses (2004), Mosley (1995a), Mudimbe (1988, 1994), Ndubuisi (2005), Nwigwe (2004), Nzegwu (2006), Ogunmodede (2001, 2004), Okere (1971, 1991, 2005), Okrah (2003), C.B. Okolo (1985, 1987, 1990a, 1990b, 1993a, 1993b, 1993c, 1994a, 1994b, 1996), Oladipo (1992, 1996, 1998a, 1998b, 2002, 2006), Olaniyan (1995), Onyewuenyi (1993), Oruka (1990a, 1990b), Owomoyela (1996), Peters (1982), Pinn (2001), Pittman (1997), Praeg (2000), Ramose (1999), Ruch (1984), Scott and Franklin (2006), Scriven (2007), Serequeberhan (1991, 1994, 1997, 2000, 2007), Shelby (2005), Sodipo (2004), Sogolo (1993), Sumner (1962, 1970, 1974, 1985, 1986, 1999), Sumner and Wolde (2002), P.C. Taylor (2004), Tedla (1995), Unah (1995, 1996, 1999, 2002), Waters and Conaway (2007), D. Wells (1993), Wintz (1996a), Wiredu (1980, 1995, 1996, 2004), R.A. Wright (1984), and Yancy (1998, 2004, 2005, 2007, 2008).

11. Here, and throughout the remainder of this section of the introduction, I draw heavily from the discourse of Africana hermeneutics, or Africana philosophy of interpretation, in an effort to emphasize the importance of culturally grounded inquiry and interpretation in Africana critical theory. As Okonda Okolo (1991) observed in his classic essay, "Tradition and Destiny: Horizons of an African Philosophical Hermeneutics," Africana hermeneutics, as with almost all hermeneutical endeavors, centers on the ideas of tradition and destiny and how successive generations interpret, explain and embrace their historical, cultural and intellectual heritage. In his own words:

> For our part, we want to test the resources but also the limits of our hermeneutical models and practices, by examining the two notions that encompass our interpretative efforts in an unconquerable circle—the notions of Tradition and Destiny. These notions simultaneously define the object, the subject, the horizons, and the limits of interpretation. To interpret is always to close the circle of the subject and the object. We cannot, however, make this circle our own if we do not lay it out beyond the thought of the subject and the object, toward a thinking of our horizons and the limits of our interpretation defined by the reality of our traditions and the ideality of our destiny. (p. 202)

Okolo, among other Africana hermeneuticists, highlights the abstruse issues that arise in interpretative theory and praxis in our present social world and world of ideas. Historical and cultural experiences determine and, often subtly, define what we interpret and the way we interpret. If, for instance, Africana thought-traditions are not known to, and not shared with, theorists and philosophers of African descent and other interested scholars, then they will assume there is no history of theory or philosophy in the African world (see L. Harris, 1983; Eze, 1997a; Gordon and Gordon 2006a, 2006b; Lott and Pittman, 2003; Wiredu, 2004). These would-be Africana theorists will draw from another cultural group's schools of thought, because human existence, as the Africana philosophers of existence have pointed out, is nothing other than our constant confrontation with ontological issues and questions. What is more, the nature of theory, especially in the current postcolonial/postmodern period, is that it incessantly builds on other theories. In other words, a competent theorist must not only be familiar with the history and evolutionary character of theory, but the intellectual origins of theories—that is, with *who*, *where*, and *why* specific theories were created to describe and explain a particular subject and/or object. For further discussion of Africana hermeneutics, see Okere (1971, 1991), Outlaw (1974, 1983a, 1983c), and Serequeberhan (1991, 2000, 2007).

12. Most notably, my interpretation of dialectics has been influenced by C. L. R. James's *Notebooks on Dialectics: Hegel, Marx, Lenin* (1980), Robert I. Allen's *Dialectics of Black Power* (1968), Raya Dunayevskaya's *Women's Liberation and the Dialectics of Revolution: Reaching for the Future* (1996), Anouar Abdel-Malek's *Social Dialectics* (1981), and John H. McClendon's *C. L. R. James's Notes on Dialectics: Left-Hegelianism or Marxist-Leninism?* (2005). Similar to critical social theory, it should be emphasized that dialectics is not the exclusive theoretical domain or intellectual terrain of Marxists or Marxist-Leninists, but a specific kind of critical thinking, open to all, that constantly compares, contrasts, and counters *what is* with *what*

*could be* or *what ought to be.* In this sense, each human culture and civilization has its own unique version of dialectical thinking, and it is from this discourse that Africana critical theory deepens and develops its dialectical dimension (see Rabaka, 2008a). For further discussion of dialectics, in a general sense, see Albritton (1999), Albritton and Simoulidis (2003), Anived (2003), Bongmba (2006), D. Cooper (1968), DeGrood (1978), Erickson (1990), Fatton (1986), Kosik (1976), McClennen (2004), Moscovici (2002), Nuckolls (1996), T.J. Reiss (2002), Rescher (1977, 2006), J.D. Saldivar (1991), R. Saldivar (1990), T.M. Shaw (1985), Shusterman (2002), Solomon (1976), Widmer (1988), and Vogeler and de Souza (1980).

13. Here and throughout this section in addition to Amilcar Cabral's critical theory, I am generously drawing from Antonio Gramsci's conceptual contributions: "ideological hegemony," "organic intellectual," "historical bloc," "war of position," "war of maneuver," and "ensemble of ideas and social relations," and so on. His work has deeply influenced my conception of critical theory as a form of ideological and cultural critique, as well as a radical political praxis-promoting social theory. In particular, Gramsci's assertion that class domination is exercised as much through popular and unconscious consensus (or the internalization of imperialism) as through physical coercion (or the threat of it) by the state apparatus—especially in advanced capitalist societies where politics, education, religion, law, medicine, media, and popular culture, among other areas, are covetously controlled by the ruling class—his work innovatively emphasizes the ideological and counter-hegemonic dimension that radical politics and critical social theory today must deepen and further develop. However, in terms of Africana critical theory of contemporary society and the life-worlds of people of African origin and descent, and people of color in general, class domination and capitalism represent one of many overlapping, interlocking, and intersecting systems of domination and discrimination that must be ideologically and physically combated and discontinued. Therefore, Gramsci's work provides several insights, but must be synthesized with other theory, especially critical race theory, anti-racist feminist theory, womanist theory, postcolonial theory, critical pedagogy, and liberation theology, among others, if it is to aid in the (re)construction of a new, more multicultural, radical anti-racist, gender justice-seeking, and sexuality sensitive critical theory of contemporary society. For further discussion, see Gramsci (1967, 1971, 1975, 1977, 1978, 1985, 1992, 1994a, 1994b, 1995a, 1995b, 1996, 2000).

14. My interpretation of black invisibility and anonymity has, of course, been deeply influenced by Ralph Ellison's *Invisible Man* (1980) and Toni Morrison's *Playing in the Dark: Whiteness and the Literary Imagination* (1990), but has been enhanced most by Lewis Gordon's *Bad Faith and Anti-Black Racism* (1995a), "Existential Dynamics of Theorizing Black Invisibility" (1997a, pp. 69–79), "Context: Ruminations on Violence and Anonymity" (1997b, pp. 13–24), and "Existential Borders of Anonymity and Superfluous Invisibility" (2000a, pp. 153–163). On the black collective mind and African communal thought theses, see Robin Horton's *Modes of Thought: Essays on Thinking in Western and Non-Western Societies* (1973) and his controversial sequel *Patterns of Thought in Africa and the West: Essays on Magic, Religion, and Science* (1993), as well as Paulin Hountondji's *African Philosophy: Myth and Reality* (1996). And, for solid criticisms of these theses, see Kwasi Wiredu's *Philosophy and an African Culture* (1980) and Kwame Gyekye's *An Essay on African Philosophical Thought* (1995).

# 2

## W. E. B. Du Bois: The Soul of a Pan-African Marxist Male-Feminist

Du Bois detected early, along with and presumably independently of his German contemporaries associated with the Frankfurt Institute, the fundamental homology uniting Fascism, Bolshevism, and the New Deal; he expressed a need to adjust the orthodox critique of capitalism to account for the rise of a "new class of technical engineers and managers" and other internal systemic changes in the twentieth century, and he demonstrated a sense of the significance of the mass-culture apparatus, planned obsolescence and intensified marketing in the contemporary social management synthesis.

—Adolph L. Reed Jr., *W. E. B. Du Bois and American Political Thought: Fabianism and the Color-Line*, pp. 217–218

With a politics remarkably progressive for his time (and ours), Du Bois confronted race, class, and gender oppression while maintaining conceptual and political linkages between the struggles to end racism, sexism, and war. . . . In his analysis integrating the various components of African American liberation and world peace, gender and later economic analyses were indispensable.

—Joy A. James, *Transcending the Talented Tenth*, pp. 36–37

He [Du Bois] virtually, before anyone else and more than anyone else, demolished the lies about Negroes in their most important and creative periods of history. The truths he revealed are not yet the property of all Americans but they have been recorded and arm us for our contemporary battles. . . . Dr. Du Bois was not only an intellectual giant exploring the frontiers of knowledge, he was in the first place a teacher. He would have wanted his life to teach us something about our tasks of emancipation.

—Martin Luther King Jr., "Honoring Dr. Du Bois," pp. 20, 24

## INTRODUCTION: W. E. B. DU BOIS
## AND THE SOUL OF CRITICAL SOCIAL THEORY

The African holocaust and anti-colonial struggle; Pan-Africanism and the peace movement; Marxism and male-feminism; the African American struggle for human and civil rights; intellectual adoration of and admiration for Frederick Douglass and Alexander Crummell; disputations with Booker T. Washington and Marcus Garvey—an enigmatic and eclectic combination of critical ideas and interests unfolds across the landscape of William Edward Burghardt Du Bois's life and work. For many he represents one of the most critical and contradictory race theorists of the twentieth century. Another host argues that he is "the father of Pan-Africanism" and a pioneering architect of anti-colonial theory and praxis. For others, such as Cedric Robinson (2000) in *Black Marxism*, Du Bois was one of the most sophisticated Marxist theorists in American radical history, though "his work had origins independent of the impulses of Western liberal and radical thought" (p. 186). Still others, such as Joy James, Beverly Guy-Sheftall, Cheryl Townsend Gilkes, and Nellie McKay contend that Du Bois's name, along with those of Charles Lenox Remond and Frederick Douglass, belongs on that very short list of men who openly advocated gender equality and spoke out against female domination and discrimination. His work, in many senses similar to that of C. L. R. James and Frantz Fanon, and due no doubt to its highly porous nature, has been critically analyzed and appropriated by scores of academics and political activists who harbor harrowingly different intellectual and ideological agendas.

Though his thought took several crucial philosophical and political twists and turns in his eighty-year publishing career (from 1883 to 1963), it is Du Bois's concepts of race and anti-racism, Pan-Africanism and anti-colonialism, critique of capitalism and critical Marxism and, most recently, his anti-sexism and male-feminism that have come under the greatest scholarly scrutiny and can be said to have ushered in the contemporary Du Bois renaissance.[1] But, I should bellow from the beginning, rarely if ever have these central themes in Du Bois's oeuvre been juxtaposed and examined for their import to *critical theory*. To be sure, Du Bois's thought has traveled an almost unfathomable tract of intellectual terrain, receiving commentary and criticism from philosophers, historians, political scientists, economists, literary theorists, feminists, womanists, Pan-Africanists, and Marxists, to name only a few intellectual and political communities. However, on no occasion (my previous work withstanding) has his thought and texts been critically engaged for their contribution to critical theory of contemporary society.

This chapter will analyze W. E. B. Du Bois's thought for its contribution to contemporary critical theory in particular, and Africana radical politics and revolutionary social movements more generally. Consequently, it is not my intention to offer a definitive or even exhaustive treatment of his biography or life-work, which would seem rather redundant coming so quickly on the heels of David Levering Lewis's Pulitzer Prize-winning volumes (see D.L. Lewis, 1993, 2000). I am concerned here primarily, and almost exclusively, with Du Bois's theoretical and political legacy— that is, with the ways he constructed, deconstructed, and reconstructed theory and the aims, objectives, and outcomes of his theoretical applications and discursive practices. He consistently appropriated, revised and rejected disparate concepts, always integrating what he perceived to be the most radical (and later *revolutionary*) thought into his critical socio-theoretical discourse. His work, in several senses, lends itself to critical social theory because it provides an alternative model and methodology to chart and affect progressive social change.[2]

The following sections will focus on Du Bois's four key contributions to critical theory, and specifically critical theory in the interest of continental and diasporan Africans—what I have referred to elsewhere as *Africana critical theory* (Rabaka, 2006a, 2007a, 2008a). Though he made many theoretical breakthroughs and, as we will see, covered and crisscrossed a great deal of uncharted and oft time treacherous intellectual terrain, many of Du Bois's major positions arise and recur as he addressed issues involving race, gender, and the dual dimensions of capitalist and colonialist exploitation and oppression in Africana life-worlds and lived-experiences. In an effort to focus exclusively, but not superficially, on what I have identified as Du Bois's seminal and most significant donations to the discourse and development of critical social theory, I undertake extended analyses of his concepts of race, anti-racism and critical race theory; his critique of sexism, and particularly patriarchy; his anti-colonialism and critical postcolonial theory; and, his concept of a race-centered and racism-conscious critique of capitalism *and* Marxism. We begin with his philosophy of race, anti-racism, and contributions to critical race theory.

## THE SOULS OF BLACK AND WHITE FOLK: W. E. B. DU BOIS'S PHILOSOPHY OF RACE, ANTI-RACISM, AND CRITICAL RACE THEORY

Du Bois's corpus contains an astounding body of literature on, and knowledge of, race and racism. His philosophy of race figures prominently, and has consistently been featured in both classical and contemporary racial discourse. Moreover, race critics have chronicled his concepts of race from a multiplicity of disciplinary and theoretic perspectives, often arguing against and, at other times, agreeing with his critical writings on race and racism, which have been documented to have dominated racial discourse for the first half of the twentieth century (Bay, 1998; Bobo, 2000; Bruce, 1995; Chaffee, 1956; Holt, 1990, 1998; Meade, 1987; Mostern, 1996; Rampersad, 1996b; C.M. Taylor, 1981).

The history of Du Bois's philosophy of race and anti-racist theory is not an easy tale to tell, but one that must be told. Why? One may ask. Why do we need another (re)interpretation of Du Bois's concept(s) of race and critique(s) of racism? Why should we revisit the discourse of race and racism anyway? Isn't race, and therefore racism, a thing of the past or, at the least, a superstitious social construction that science tells us has never existed or certainly no longer exists? Didn't Anthony Appiah's analytic philosophical assault debunk Du Bois's philosophy of race once and for all, exposing its pseudo-scientific and narrow nationalistic underpinnings? And, after all the smoke has cleared and all the dust settled, isn't Du Bois just another over-engaged "race man" posthumously positioned as a radical theorist?[3]

Throughout this section I will address these questions (and probably problematize and raise many others) by arguing that Du Bois's writings on race are relevant and contribute to contemporary racial discourse for four fundamental reasons. First, his philosophy of race is often interpreted as an "ideology of race"—that is, an inert, inflexible, fixed and fast, singular notion of what race is, and which groups constitute constituent races. This is not only a gross misinterpretation of Du Bois's constantly evolving philosophy of race, but an example of the type of intellectual disingenuousness and invisibility that plagues Africana intellectuals of every political persuasion and social station.

Critically engaging Du Bois's philosophy of race offers objective interpreters and critics of race and racism an opportunity to analyze a theoretically rich and thoroughgoing series of ruminations on race and racism by a pioneer *critical* race theorist who almost infinitely harbored a hardnosed skepticism toward the supposed scientific and/or biological bases of race. This skepticism, coupled with his own homegrown pragmatism, often led Du Bois to contradictory conclusions regarding race (Glaude, 2007; West, 1989). However, he repetitiously reminded his readers that he was not searching for a sound, scientific concept of race as much as he was on a quest to either locate or create a vehicle for Africana (as well as other non-whites') cultural development, political empowerment, and social survival.

The meaning of race has always moved, as the very idea of race has consistently traveled far and wide since its inception. Du Bois has the distinction of being one of the first persons of African descent to scientifically research and write on race (Durr, 2001; B.S. Edwards, 2001; Juguo, 2001; D.L. Lewis, 1993, 2000; Lott, 1999, 2001). His Africanity, or blackness, is important insofar as Africans, or blacks, have historically and continue currently to be considered one of the most thoroughly racialized groups—though under theorized from their own historical horizons, cultural conditions, social situations and political positions—in the history of race and racism (Gordon, 1995a, 2006b; Marable, 1983, 1993, 2002; C.W. Mills, 1997, 1998, 1999, 2001, 2003b). From an increasingly Africana history-, culture-, and philosophy-informed critical perspective, Du Bois studied the history of race with an intense interest in its origins and originators, and the purpose(s) of its origination. This alone should distinguish his writings on race as more than mere intellectual artifacts, but there is more, as a matter of fact, much more.

His concepts of race harbor an inherent and radical humanism (which is to say a humanism that extends well beyond his beloved black folk) that is often complex and seemingly contradictory, but which nonetheless is part and parcel of his overarching philosophy of race. In specific, Du Bois developed what I will crudely call, a "gift theory" which, in short, elaborated that each race has specific and special "gifts" to contribute to national and international culture and civilization. In works such as *The Souls of Black Folk*, "The People of Peoples and Their Gifts to Men," and *Darkwater*, and most especially in later works like *The Gift of Black Folk*, "The Black Man Brings His Gifts," *Black Reconstruction of Democracy in America*, *Black Folk, Then and Now*, *Dusk of Dawn: An Essay Toward an Autobiography of a Race Concept* and *The World and Africa*, Du Bois put forward concepts of race that were not biologically based, but predicated on political, social, historical, and cultural "common" characteristics and experiences shared by continental and diasporan Africans. In Du Bois's gift theory, these characteristics represent Africana peoples' "gifts" or race-specific, black existential contributions to the forward flow of human history.

Second, and falling fast on the heels of the first point, it is important for us to revisit Du Bois's concept(s) of race because what we now know of his race theory is almost utterly predicated on and relegated to his early writings. For instance, most contemporary critics of Du Bois's theory of race begin and often end with his 1897 address to the American Negro Academy, "The Conservation of Races." Some critics go as far as his early career classics, "The Study of the American Negro Problem," *The Philadelphia Negro*, and, of course, *The Souls of Black Folk*. Further than these texts, however, contemporary race critics do not dare venture, which to my mind seems absurd considering the fact that Du Bois continued to publish for another 60 years. Scant attention has been given to Du Bois's writings on race and racism after *The Souls of Black Folk*, and, when on rare occasions they are engaged, more is made of his infamously alleged and highly controversial collapsing of race into class in his 1935 classic, *Black Reconstruction of Democracy in America*. Maybe those who argue that Du Bois (1982c) collapsed race into class and that he uncritically accepted communism have never read his 1936 essay, "Social Planning for the Negro, Past and Present," where he roars against the supposed racelessness and political panacea thesis of the white socialists and communists: "There is no automatic power in socialism to override and suppress race prejudice. . . . One of the worst things that Negroes could do today would be to join the American Communist Party or any of its many branches" (p. 38). Du Bois, then, as I will demonstrate in a subsequent section, was a much more astute interpreter of Marxian philosophy and class theory than many contemporary race theorists may be aware of. Without a thorough understanding of why, and the ways in which he critically engaged, as opposed to openly embraced Marxism, many critics of his concepts of race are doomed to do Du Bois a disservice by misinterpreting his motivations for emphasizing certain aspects of race and racism at specific socio-historic and politico-economic intervals. It may not be too much of an overstatement to say that Du Bois developed a discourse on race in order to critique racism and provide a philosophical foundation for antiracist struggle. This is the second reason his work has import for contemporary race and racism discourse: because it may offer methods and models for us to further our critiques of race and to combat racism.

The third reason Du Bois's writings on race are important for contemporary race and racism discourse is because of the recent emergence of critical white studies and the emphasis on whiteness, white racelessness or white racial neutrality and universality, and white supremacy. In several pioneering publications in historical sociology and political economy he deftly and defiantly hit at the heart of whiteness, chronicling its rise alongside the concept of race, noting that to be white is to be raceless, to be powerful or, at the least, to have access to power or people in positions of power. In the logic of the white world, race is something that soils the social status of sub-humans, it politically pollutes their thinking, thus rendering them powerless, irrational, and in need of clear conceptions concerning themselves and the world. Since whites are the only group that is not plagued by race, they then have been burdened by God with the task of leading the lost, raced "natives," "barbarians," "savages," and sub-humans to the higher level or "heaven" of humanity. Du Bois resented whites' racial mythmaking, and directed a significant portion of his writings on race and racism to critiquing whiteness and white supremacy. His writings, such as "Race Friction Between Black and White," "The Souls of White Folk," "Of The Culture of White Folk," "White Co-Workers," "The Superior Race," "The White Worker," "The White Proletariat in Alabama, Georgia, and Florida," "The White World" and "The White Folk Have a Right to Be Ashamed," represent and register as early and sustained efforts that critique whiteness and white supremacy. Du Bois's work in this area, then, can be said to prefigure and provide a paradigm and point of departure for the contemporary discourse and debates of critical white studies (Rabaka, 2006d, 2007b).

Finally, Du Bois's writings on race are relevant with regard to contemporary race and racism criticism as they contribute significantly to the discourse of critical race theory. No longer considered the exclusive domain of legal studies scholars and radical civil rights lawyers and law professors, critical race theory has blossomed and currently encompasses and includes a wide range of theory and theorists from diverse academic disciplines. In a nutshell the core concerns of critical race theory include: race and racism's centrality to European imperial expansion and modernity; racism's interconnection with sexism and capitalism; white supremacy; white normativity and neutrality; state-sanctioned (or, "legal") racial domination and discrimination; and, liberative race-consciousness amongst non-whites or, rather "people of color" (Bulmer and Solomos, 1999a, 1999b, 2004; Crenshaw, Gotanda, Peller and Thomas, 1995; Delgado, 1995; Delgado and Stefancic 2001; Dixson and Rosseau, 2006; Essed and Goldberg, 2001; Goldberg, Musheno, and Bower, 2001; Goldberg and Solomos, 2002; Matsuda, 1993; Parker, Deyhle and Villenas, 1999; Solomos and Back, 2000; Solomos and Muji, 2005; Valdes, Culp and Harris, 2002; Wing, 1997, 2000). Du Bois's philosophy of race in many senses foreshadows contemporary critical race theory and, therefore, contributes several paradigms and points of departure. However, as with so many other aspects of his dialectical thought, Du Bois's writings on race and racism have been relegated to the realm, at best, of sociology (especially sociology of race), which downplays and diminishes their transdisciplinarity and significance for the deconstruction and reconstruction of radical politics and contemporary critical social theory. Therefore, his writings on race have been virtually overlooked and/or rendered intellectually invisible by critical race theorists (Rabaka, 2006c).

As Joy James (1997) and Cheryl Townsend Gilkes (1996) argue, and as I will discuss in greater detail in an ensuing section of this chapter, Du Bois was critically conscious of some of the ways in which *race is gendered* and *gender is raced.* Emerging in the fifteenth century, and coinciding with European imperial expansion around the globe, racial domination threw fuel on the wildfire of gender discrimination. As an astute student of gender relations, Du Bois accented the interconnections and intersections of racism and sexism, specifically white supremacy and patriarchy. This means, then, that at the least some of his anti-racist social theorizing may serve as a model for critical race theory in the sense that it seeks a similar goal: To make visible the long invisible interconnections between racial and gender domination and discrimination, not only in law but in medicine, politics, education and religion, among other aspects and areas of contemporary society. What is intellectually amazing and seminally significant is that Du Bois developed *a gender-sensitive* and *sexism-critical conception of race and racism* almost a hundred years prior to the current critical race theory and critical race feminist movements, which is to say that Du Bois's work for all theoretical and practical purposes could (and, I think, should) be considered *classical critical race theory.*[4]

Du Bois was also an early exponent of the race/class thesis that contended that though class struggle had been a part of human history for several centuries, the

modern concept of race and the sociopolitical practice of racism, coupled with capitalism and colonialism exacerbated class conflicts (amongst both colonizers and
the colonized). Though often unacknowledged, similar to C. L. R. James (1977a,
1980a, 1980c, 1984, 1992, 1994, 1996a, 1999) and Oliver C. Cox (1948, 1959,
1962, 1964, 1976, 1987, 2000), Du Bois was a pioneer in terms of analyzing the political economy of race and racism, which is to say that he often argued against
studying race independent of class. Race and class, as we have seen with race and
gender in Du Bois's *gender-centered* and *sexism-critical conception of race and racism*,
are inextricable and incessantly intersecting and reconfiguring, constantly forming,
reforming and deforming, creating a racist dimension in modern class theory and
struggle, and a classist or economically exploitive dimension in anti-racist politics
and struggle.

Race and racism were European modernity's weapons of choice. A (sub)person,
from the modern white world's frame of reference, was economically exploited
based on biology or ethnicity. That is, the degree(s) to which one was dominated
and/or discriminated against was predicated on European-invented racial classifica-
tions and ethno-cultural categorizations (L.D. Baker, 1998; Black, 2004; Bonilla-
Silva, 2001, 2003; Bonilla-Silva and Doane, 2003; Goldberg, 1993, 1994, 2001;
Gossett, 1953, 1997; Graves, 2001, 2004; Gregory and Sanjek, 1994; Hannaford,
1996; Smedley, 2007). Du Bois's writings on the political economy of race and
racism provide another paradigm for contemporary critical race theory to build on
and bolster its calls for racial, economic, and gender justice.

A large part of the racially ruled's anti-racist theory and praxis has been preoccupied with colonialism and the prospects of decolonization—issues which remarkably have yet to resonate or register as central concerns in the discourse of contemporary critical race theory. This is extremely curious considering the fact that many
of the earliest expressions of radicalism amongst the racially oppressed were aimed
at critiquing various forms and forces of *colonial racism* and/or *racial colonialism*. Du
Bois was one of the major doyens of this discourse and, by most accounts, is considered to have made his most lasting contributions as a pioneer Pan-Africanist and
radical anti-colonialist. As a consequence, the ensuing section will analyze Du Bois's
critical theory of the colonial world for its contribution to the discourse and development of a critical theory of contemporary society that is as critical of (neo)colo-
nialism as it is of the predatory and nefarious nature of capitalism.

## THE SOULS OF COLONIZED COLORED FOLK: W. E. B.
## DU BOIS'S CRITICAL THEORY OF THE (NEO)COLONIAL
## WORLD AND CONTRIBUTIONS TO DECOLONIZATION

W. E. B. Du Bois offers contemporary colonial and postcolonial theorists a critical
conception of colonialism and neocolonialism in several ways. First, by analyzing
colonialism's fundamental features (which will be outlined below), and, second, by
focusing his readers' attention on the world-historic fluctuations and mutations of
colonialism, Du Bois highlights—as Tejumola Olaniyan (2000) recently noted—the
varied nature of colonialism, not simply in topographical terms, but also insofar as
the particularities of the colonized peoples' pre-existing or "pre-colonial" cultures

are concerned. This is an extremely important point to make because many post-colonial theorists have a tendency to gloss over the specificities and the different degrees to which various peoples were historically and currently continue to be colonized—not to mention colonized *and* racialized (see Barrington, 2006; Chambers and Curti, 1996; Chatterjee, 1993; Feathersome, 2005; Goldberg, 2000; Goldberg and Quayson, 1999; Joseph and Wilson, 2006; Krishnaswamy and Hawley, 2008; Loomba, 2005; J. McLeod, 2007; Moore-Gilbert, 1997; Parry, 2004; Poddar and Johnson, 2005; Puri, 2004; Schwarz and Ray, 2000; Syrotinski, 2007; Venn, 2006). Finally, by linking colonialism with capitalism, and by refusing to isolate economic exploitation from racial domination and gender discrimination, Du Bois's conception of colonialism prefigures and provides a paradigm for and a critique of contemporary critical theoretical and postcolonial discourse.

By "deliberately using the word 'colonial' in a much broader sense than is usually given it," and by asserting that "there are manifestly groups of people, countries and nations, which while not colonies in the strict sense of the word, yet so approach the colonial system as to merit the designation *semicolonial*," Du Bois (1985a) not only anticipates, but contributes the concept of "semi-colonialism" to postcolonial discourse (pp. 229, 236; my emphasis). It is this concept of "semi-" or "quasi-" colonialism that distinguishes Du Bois's conception of colonialism from Cesaire (1972), Fanon (1965, 1967, 1968, 1969), Nkrumah (1964, 1965, 1970b, 1973a), Cabral (1972, 1973, 1979), and a whole host of classical anti-colonial and de-colonial theorists. Moreover, it is this same theory of "semi-colonialism" that enables me to assert that, on the one hand, Africana Studies scholars, and Du Bois scholars in specific, may find much of interest in postcolonial theory. We need mince no words in laying bare the fact that both Africana and postcolonial theorists are involved in similar (and, I would aver often identical) projects of radical critique. For Africana theorists, to speak generally, great and grave issues emanate from the socio-historical realities of not simply anti-African racism and racial colonialism, but sexism and capitalism as well. For postcolonial theorists, again generally speaking, criticisms have been leveled against each of the aforementioned and, in specific, the ways in which past and present forms of colonialism exacerbate and perpetuate racism, sexism and capitalism. Indeed, a burgeoning philosophical framework that brings diverse discourse on colonialism, anti-colonialism, and the coming *post*-colonial world into dialogue is on the rise.

On the other hand, it should be stated outright, Du Bois—an intellectual-activist who consistently critiqued colonialism throughout his eighty-year publishing career—has been relegated to the periphery of postcolonial discourse. As a result, as I argue throughout this section, postcolonial theorists in many senses undermine and do themselves a disastrous disservice because they ignore and/or erase a wealth of critical concepts and categories, such as "semi-colonialism," that could very well aid them in their efforts to theorize and bring into being a truly *post*-colonial world.

In arguing that there are partially colonized peoples and countries, Du Bois offers postcolonial theorists a concept that helps to highlight the continuation of colonialism in our modern moment. If "[a] colony, strictly speaking, is a country which belongs to another country, forms part of the mother country's industrial organization, and exercises such powers of government, and such civic and cultural freedom, as the dominant country allows," then there exists today, even *after* independence, in Africa, in the Americas and the Caribbean, in Asia and in Australia, colonies—albeit "quasi-" or "semi-" colonies, but colonies nonetheless (Du Bois, 1985a, p. 229). Du Bois's concept of colonialism is predicated on what he understands to be universal or common characteristics, "certain characteristics of colonial peoples, which are so common and obvious that we seldom discuss them and often actually forget them." These characteristics, which remain part and parcel of the life-worlds and lived-experiences of the wretched of the earth, essentially entail the following: (1) physical and/or psychological violence, racio-biological domination and discrimination; (2) economic exploitation; (3) poverty; (4) illiteracy; (5) lawlessness, stealing and crime; (6) starvation; (7) death; (8) disaster; (9) disease; (10) disenfranchisement; (11) the denial of "cultural equality;" and, (12) the denial of participation in political processes (pp. 229–236).[5]

Moving beyond the "narrower definition" and "the strict sense of the word" colony—and, I would like to suggest, "colonialism"—Du Bois's conceptualization of colonialism challenges postcolonial theorists to be cognizant of the fact that the prefix "post" in "postcolonialism," on the one hand, may very well signify a rupture with that which preceded it. But, on the other hand, the "post" in postcolonialism can also be said to signify a dependence on, a continuity with, and a filial connection to, that which follows it. Which, of course, has led some critics to argue that what is currently being called "postcolonial" is actually an intensification of the colonial.[6]

The noted Nigerian philosopher, Emmanuel Eze (1997b), has argued that "post" should be employed as a prefix insofar as colonialism is concerned, "only as far as the lived actuality of the peoples and the lands formerly occupied by European imperial powers can suggest, or confirm, in some meaningful ways, the sense of that word, the 'post' of the (post)colonial" (p. 341). Ashcroft and associates assert that there is "a continuity of preoccupations throughout the historical process initiated by European imperial aggression," so much so that "all the culture affected by the imperial process from the moment of colonization to the present day" must, to paraphrase Fanon, be called into question (Ashcroft, Griffiths and Tiffin, 1989, p. 2; Fanon, 1968, p. 37). And, the Ghanaian philosopher Anthony Appiah (1992) avers, "[t]o theorize certain central features of contemporary culture as *post* anything, is, of course, inevitably to invoke a narrative, and from the Enlightenment on, in Europe and in European-derived [and dominated] cultures, that 'after' has also meant 'above and beyond'" (pp. 140–141; emphasis in original).[7] Now, the critical questions confronting us are: Have we really reached the *post-* (as in, *after*) colonial period? How can we be in the period *after* colonialism when most of the fundamental features of colonialism continue to plague "three-quarters of the people living in the world today"? Is it possible that we have gotten "above and beyond" colonialism when it is understood that even with "political independence" the impact and influence of European imperial powers continue to "displace" pre-colonial philosophical, spiritual and axiological systems and traditions? (Ashcroft, Griffiths and Tiffin, 1989, pp. 1, 8–10).[8]

Here it will be helpful to compare Du Bois's concept of colonialism with that of other leading Pan-African and radical anti-colonial theorists. According to Amilcar

Cabral (1979) there have historically been two major forms of imperialist domination that have affected Africana people:

1. Direct domination: by means of a political power made up of agents foreign
   to the dominated people (armed forces, police, administrative agents and settlers)—which is conventionally called *classical colonialism* or *colonialism*.
2. Indirect domination: by means of a political power made up mainly or completely of native [African] agents—which is conventionally called *neocolonialism*. (p. 128)

Cabral's concept and categories of colonialism, especially when compared with
Du Bois's, accents and enables us to conceive of colonialism not so much as an historical and cultural coordinate of the past, but as one of the present. For Cabral
(1979), colonialism (whether direct or indirect) has the same basic objective and effect: the "denial of the historical process of the dominated people, by means of violent usurpation of the freedom of the process of development of the national productive forces" (pp. 129–130).[9] Furthermore, those forces that are most productive
to a people struggling for national liberation are the ones that help them create
thought and practices that not only confront and contradict the established imperial order, but also bring into being the "new humanity" and "new society" that Du
Bois, Fanon, Che Guevara, and Herbert Marcuse wrote and spoke so passionately
about.[10] Coupling Du Bois's conception of colonialism with Cabral's, we see, then,
that it is possible for "classical colonialism," as "direct domination," to come to an
end without neocolonialism—and the "indirect domination" it entails—being ex-
hausted and extinguished.

In fact, Kwame Nkrumah (1965) contended that most African nations were
"nominally independent"—that is, independent only in name, not in fact—because
even after "independence" their economic systems and, therefore, their social and
political policies were directed by, and dictated from, non-African or foreign forces
(p. ix). More credence is given to this line of thinking when it is understood that
neocolonialism, like the form(s) of classical colonialism that preceded it, is predicated upon the paralysis and retardation of the historical process(es) or "historicity"
of Africana and other colonized peoples. "The reality of colonialism," suggests the
Eritrean philosopher Tsenay Serequeberhan (1994), is "the violent superimposition
of European historicity on African historicity" (p. 111). In other words, classical
colonialism and neocolonialism, and all the dogma and domination they necessi-
tate, represent and register as "the negation of the cultural difference and specificity
that constitutes the historicity and thus humanity of the non-European world" (p.
58). These conclusions bring us to a discussion of the period between colonialism
and postcolonialism.

Postcolonial theory, literature, culture and the like, denotes the intellectual productions of formerly colonized peoples *after* colonization. Considering the fact that
"[h]istorical epochs do not rise and fall in neat patterns or at precise chronological
moments," and considering the fact that the culture of the colonizing country continues to effect the culture of the colonized even *after* "independence," much of the
discourse of postcolonialism is extremely misleading (Best and Kellner, 1997, p. 31;
Loomba, 1998, pp. 10–12). Based on Du Bois's conceptualization of colonialism, it

seems safe to say that we are not in a *post*colonial period, but in a transitional stage/state between a now-aging colonial era and an emerging postcolonial era that remains to be adequately conceptualized, charted, and mapped. Transition from one era to the next, we are told, is always "protracted, contradictory, and usually painful" (Best and Kellner, 1997, p. 31). But, the task for contemporary critical theorists is not to jump on the (extremely "premature") postcolonial bandwagon (Loomba, 1998, p. 7). On the contrary, our task is to attempt to explore this transitional moment, to grasp the connections between "classical colonialism" and "neocolonialism," and to project present and future postcolonial possibilities. Hence, one of the most important tasks of a critical anti-colonial theory of contemporary society is to capture and critique both the continuities and discontinuities of the colonial and neocolonial in order to make sense of our currently quite colonized life- and language-worlds.

Although it is prudent to be skeptical and critical of certain segments of postcolonial discourse, and especially the extreme forms of this discourse which attempt to render the assumptions and assertions of anti-colonialists and decolonialists of the past obsolete. It must be admitted that significant changes have taken, and are taking place, and that many of the classical anti-colonial and decolonial theories and practices no longer adequately describe or explain contemporary (neo)colonialism. Whereas the "classical colonial" period, as Cabral (1979) pointed out, was distinguished by "direct domination," since the gaining of "independence" African and other colonized people, neocolonized people, if you will, have experienced "indirect domination," which unrepentantly remains, I should add, a form of domination nonetheless (p. 128).

Africana critical thought at its best has consistently been anti-colonial, and this is especially evident when we turn to the treasure trove of theoretical and practical insights of the Pan-African tradition.[11] Keeping a keen and critical eye on Du Bois's concept of "semi-colonialism," it must be born in mind that colonial status has consistently been extended and expanded to encompass and include the lived-experiences and life-worlds of the Africans of the diaspora.[12] Further, following Du Bois's line of thinking, and as asserted above, the nature, processes, and effects of colonization have changed, and colonialism in its new forms—just as Du Bois pointed out with the "classical," direct domination forms of colonialism—is not something that can be confined simply to "people of color" in "third world" and/or "underdeveloped" countries. If we dare attempt to fully grasp and grapple with this expanded Du Boisian definition of colonialism, then, one of the most daunting questions besetting and bombarding contemporary Africana and other radical anti-colonial theorists is: If the injustices and other inequities of racial colonial rule have not, in fact, been eradicated, and if colonialism continues, albeit in another indirect and/or covert form, how, then, can we combat colonialism in the modern moment? It is here, I think, that we can come to appreciate several aspects of classical anti-colonial *and* contemporary postcolonial discourse.

Loomba (1998) stated, "the grand narrative of decolonization has, for the moment, been adequately told and widely accepted. Smaller narratives are now needed, with attention paid to local topography, so that maps can become fuller" (p. 252). Many postcolonial theorists are involved in projects of constructing regional or national narratives and, similar to some postmodernists, are excited by the "multiplicity of histories" that challenge political and cultural "monocentricism," and especially Eurocentrism and other linear conceptions of history.[13] Postcolonial discourse has also often provided (neo)colonized, anti-colonial and decolonial theorists with a much-needed network and discursive arena in which to compare, contrast, and create coalitions based on common historical experiences and endurances.

However, I would be the first to say that contemporary anti-colonial theorists should be suspicious of extreme or "strong" postcolonialism, and especially those versions which assert that the "post" in "postcolonialism" literally means "after," as in "after-colonialism." For some postcolonial theorists, the extremists, colonialism is a thing of the past and we have already entered into the postcolonial period. Without understanding the reconfiguring nature of colonialism, some postcolonial theorists have conflated changes in the character of colonialism with the "death," demise, and/or destruction of colonialism—this is, again, precisely why I assert that Du Bois's concepts of colonialism and semi-colonialism are so important for contemporary anti-colonial, decolonial, and postcolonial theory and praxis.

Loomba (1998) claims, "colonialism was challenged from a variety of perspectives by people who were not all oppressed in the same way or to the same extent" (p. 8). This statement helps to highlight the heterogeneous nature of both classical colonialism and neocolonialism. Colonialism took, and is taking place in the lives and on the lands of various peoples who have had comparably different historical experiences. This means, then, that it is important not to gloss over the precolonial, colonial, and possible postcolonial life- and language-worlds of historically and currently colonized people. In our attempts to engage "the colonial problem" and put forward postcolonial solutions, we should keep in mind that, "[o]pposition to colonial rule was spearheaded by forms of national struggle which cannot offer a blueprint for dealing with inequities of the contemporary world order" (p. 14). Why? Because the "contemporary world" is not the world of classical colonialism, and as Arif Dirlik (1994, 1997, 2007) and Crystal Bartolovich (2000) have pointed out, the connections and power relations between neocolonialism and global (multi-national and corporate) capitalism have intensified and are often obscured by the poststructuralist and/or postmodernist conceptually incarcerating jargon of postcolonial theorists.

Du Bois serves as a critic and critique of postcolonialism insofar as his discourse demystifies and destabilizes several of the main tenets of postcolonialism. Where it is argued that postcolonialism represents a specific species of thought that theorizes the world "after" colonialism, Du Bois puts forward the principle features of colonialism, which in turn helps to highlight the fact that although we are not enduring "classical colonialism," we are, as Cabral and Nkrumah asserted, experiencing "neocolonialism." Du Bois can also be seen as a critic and critique of postcolonialism when it is understood that he refused to reduce colonialism to direct domination or strictly economic exploitation.

For Du Bois (1985a) capitalism and colonialism, as they emanate from European "mother countries" and metropolises, represent "two of the most destructive [forces] in human history" and are "today threatening further human death and disaster" (p. 233). We, then, as critical and radical anti-colonial theorists, have a solemn duty to develop theory and praxis that counters and combats not only capitalism and colonialism, but also any and all forms of imperialism. We must consistently build bridges between classical and contemporary anti-colonial thought and practices. Additionally, as Du Bois's discourse accents, there is a real need to critically engage Pan-African and Africana anti-colonial thought-traditions, as these traditions may offer much of interest and much that can be instructive in our current struggle(s) against the ever-present colonialism in most of our lives. Du Bois (1971b) reminds us once again that the anti-colonial struggle has consistently had as its aim "intellectual understanding and cooperation" among all colonized peoples "in order to bring about at the earliest possible time . . . industrial and spiritual emancipation" (p. 208). Finally, we must not be fooled into believing that either colonialism or capitalism, or racial domination and discrimination are things of the past so long as they determine, define, and deform our present. We must consistently fight for freedom, keeping Cabral's (1972) caveat in mind:

> [L]et us go forward, weapons in hand . . . let us prepare ourselves . . . each day, and be vigilant, so as not to allow a new form of colonialism to be established in our countries, so as not to allow in our countries any form of imperialism, so as not to allow neocolonialism, already a cancerous growth in certain parts of Africa and of the world, to reach our own countries. (p. 85)

Du Bois's engagement of colonialism soon gave way to a more serious critique of capitalism. As a system of oppression, colonialism has historically been primarily predicated on robbing people of color of their resources, land and labor—in a word (or, in a couple of words), colonialism loots their very lives and livelihood. Capitalism, on the other hand, has never conceded to the conventions of the color-line. It economically exploits and underdevelops poor whites as well as blacks and other people of color. However, when and where capitalism connects with colonialism, which is almost everywhere considering the historical fact that the rise of capitalism coincides with European imperial expansion around the globe, it exploits people of color in ways in which it does not white workers, because workers of color under a white supremacist capitalist system not only lose their labor, but their sense of self and their kinship with their history and culture.

For Du Bois, colonialism and capitalism are two very different oppressive systems that, especially considering their racial (or racist) character, intersect in the lives of people of color, and twice (or thrice) threaten their humanity and ability to contribute to human culture and civilization. The racial political economic aspects of colonialism and capitalism have historically made them inextricable; where one was found, the other was always there somewhere, in someway as well. This being the case, Du Bois developed what was conceivably the first critical *race* theory of capitalism. However, he observed at the outset of this venture that one of the major differences involved in the critique of colonialism and the critique of capitalism was the fact that capitalism's economic exploitation extended well-beyond the world of color and workers of color.

White workers had long leveled serious criticisms of capitalism, and undeniably during the late nineteenth and early twentieth centuries their best work in this vein was embodied in Marxism. Yet, Du Bois pointed out, white Marxists overlooked the racist character of capitalism and diminished and downplayed the political economy of race and racism in their discourse when Pan-African Marxists consistently brought these issues to the fore. It was with this in mind that Du Bois developed not only a critical race theory of capitalism, but a critical race theory of the Eurocentrism and white supremacism of Marxism as well. His relationship with Marxian theory (and dogma) was long, varied and intricate, and often obfuscated by both black and white Marxists wishing to claim him for their respective "radical" camps. In the next section I discuss Du Bois's critiques of capitalism and Marxism, as well as his development of a conception of critical multicultural and transethnic democratic socialism that sought an alternative egalitarian society free from the machinations of racism, capitalism and colonialism.

## THE SOULS OF BLACK AND WHITE MARXISTS: W. E. B. DU BOIS'S CRITICAL RACE THEORY OF CAPITALISM AND MARXISM

As intimated in the previous section, Du Bois's critique of colonialism is inextricable from his critique of capitalism. In some senses it could be averred that as he developed his simultaneously socio-historic and politico-economic analyses, beginning with race and racism and quickly connecting them to colonialism and decolonization, Du Bois eventually added capitalism to his anti-imperialist agenda as a major target of oppression and exploitation to be eliminated. On the one hand, one of many things that distinguish his criticisms of capitalism from colonialism involves the fact that from his optic capitalism and colonialism are two very different—albeit intimately interrelated—violent, oppressive, and exploitive systems that must be approached in a manner that speaks to their specificities. On the other hand, another contributing defining and distinguishing marker of Du Bois's critique of capitalism is linked to the fact that some whites, that is, some members of the ruling race, also understood capitalism to be a violent, oppressive, and exploitive system and had developed critical theory and praxis traditions that could be loosely drawn from and put to use in the Africana fight for freedom and justice. Though, as Du Bois observed early, most white critics of capitalism focused almost exclusively on capitalism's economic exploitative aspects without so much as mentioning how it intersected with and exacerbated racial violence (physical and psychological violence) and racial oppression. This led Du Bois at the outset of his critique of capitalism to simultaneously critique capitalism *and* the white critics (and their critiques) of capitalism.

The white critics of capitalism were critical of it for very different reasons than those of their colored "comrades." And, Du Bois was one of the first radical theorists of color, and, perhaps, without a doubt, the first Africana theorist to register this difference. As several interpreters of Du Bois have observed, he had a critical and dialectical relationship with the white critics of capitalism, especially Marxist socialist and communist thought and practice. According to Adolph Reed (1997), in *W. E. B. Du Bois and American Political Thought*, "everyone agrees that Du Bois died a socialist, but few agree on when he became one or on what kind of socialist he was" (p. 83).

In *W. E. B. Du Bois: Negro Leader in a Time of Crisis*, the brutally polemical Francis Broderick (1959) explains that Du Bois's thought may be difficult to periodize in the manner that many intellectual historians are accustomed to on account of the fact that "[h]is ideas changed constantly, but the major changes came gradually, with a considerable overlap" (p. 124). This is an important point, especially considering the present examination of Du Bois's contributions to the deconstruction and reconstruction of radical politics and critical social theory, because it speaks to the systematic, multidimensional, and transdisciplinary quality and character of his thought. Broderick's (1959) comments in this regard deserve further quotation:

> Writing month after month on current events, he [Du Bois] did not, of course, abruptly end one period of intellectual change and begin another. He might drop a hint, then wait twenty years before picking it up for further development. His praise of self-sufficient, segregated Negro communities came at the flood tide of the Niagara Movement. He was making advances to socialism in 1907, although in early 1908 he affirmed his attachment to the principles of the Republican party. Africa had an almost mystical fascination for him even on his twenty-fifth birthday, but thirty years elapsed before the fascination produced a program of action. Even as the hope for alliance with workers and colored men dominated his thought in the 1930s, a minor theme, self-sufficiency for the Negro community, was rising in a crescendo which by the early 1930s would make it dominant. Conversely, as new ideas came to prominence after the World War, the old ones did not disappear: the essence of his lecture "Race Relations in the United States," for the American Academy of Political and Social Science in 1928 could have been written twenty-five years before. His ideas changed constantly, but the major changes came gradually, with considerable overlap. (pp. 123–124; see also Du Bois, 1982b, pp. 303–308)

Du Bois's "socialism," to use this term loosely, may have never been as scientific, dogmatic, and/or orthodox Marxist as many intellectual historians have claimed, or would like to claim. As he matured, both personally and professionally, his thought took on a chameleonic character, crisscrossing back and forth between the chasms of race and class. His thought often exhibited internal tensions, sometimes appearing unrepentantly race-centered, intensely Pan-African and bluntly black nationalist, and at other times seeming overly concerned with class, labor, and economic (in)justice issues. In addition, the complexity and multidimensionality of his thought gave it a contradictory and often confusing character, which, as we will soon see in the subsequent section, was exacerbated by the fact that sexism (particularly patriarchy and/or male supremacy) was also a major item on his anti-imperial agenda right alongside racism, colonialism, and capitalism. Du Bois's criticisms of capitalism, then, are distinguished from those of the white critics of capitalism, especially the Marxists, because his criticisms harbored an acute sensitivity to, and critical employment of subjugated knowledge regarding the ways in which capitalist oppression overlaps, intersects and interconnects with racial and sexual domination and discrimination.[14]

Du Bois, indeed, was a "socialist," and he openly admitted as much. But, as many black and white Marxist theorists have pointed out, what it meant to be a "Marxist" or "socialist" prior to the Russian Revolution of 1917 was very different than claiming to be one after this historic event (Kolakowski, 1978b, 1978c; Service, 1999, 2007; Wade, 1969, 1984, 2001, 2005). Prior to the Russian Revolution, socialism generally entailed a belief in non-violent social revolution or, rather, social reform, trade and industrial unionism, public ownership of utilities and properties, munic-ipal improvement, corporate regulation, and a wide-range of other economic and public policies and programs. After the Russian Revolution, socialism became the bane of many social circles in capitalist countries because it was purported to be the transitional state between capitalism and communism, as claimed by Karl Marx and his disciples in their theorizations. The Russian Revolution was not the prim and proper, prudent non-violent textbook revolution that so many French, English, and white American socialists had hoped for and long dreamed about (Buhle, 1991; Carr, 1966; Fitzpatrick, 2001). In fact, according to Roger Gottlieb (1992), in *Marx-ism 1844–1990*, though the Russian communists took state power in the spirit of the ideas of Marx and Engels, their interpretation and practice of communism "had vir-tually nothing in common with Marx's vision of socialism" (p. 77; see also Fromm, 1941, 1947, 1955, 1960b, 1961a, 1961b, 1965; Marcuse, 1958). None of this, of course, stopped the Russian communists' actions and interpretations from staining Marxism and socialism in the American social imagination, as the hysteria of the House Committee on Un-American Activities under the auspices of Senator Joseph McCarthy clearly illustrated (Doherty, 2003; Fried, 1997; T. Morgan, 2003; Schrecker, 1998, 2002; Theoharis, 2002). In the final analysis, similar to the term *race* (and the terms of racism) at the turn of and throughout the twentieth-century, *socialism* had/has a mercurial and malleable meaning, or set of meanings.[15]

Du Bois critically engaged various versions of socialism (or, more generally, Marxism) for many of the same reasons that the Trinidadian triumvirate of C. L. R. James, Oliver C. Cox, and Eric Williams did: because it offered an array of criticisms of capitalism that cut to its core and made visible its obstinately invisible imperial machinations. However, it must be borne in mind that each of the aforementioned continuously criticized Marxism for its neglect of the racial and racist aspects of capitalist culture and political economy. They were never Marxist in any orthodox or doctrinaire sense because, as Du Bois and James's radical thought regularly re-minds us, blacks and other non-whites were often seen as threats to white workers, white trade unions, and white labor movements' strides toward economic justice. White supremacy shaped and shaded the white critics of capitalism's theorizations and politics, especially in the socialist and communist parties. This had the effect of placing Du Bois and the other black critics of capitalism outside of the orthodox Marxist orbit. In a sense, this forced them to develop their own race-centered and racism-conscious critiques of capitalism; something the white Marxists had never even dared dream of doing. It also led the black radicals to a critical and, at times, volatile relationship with the white critics of capitalism, Marxism, and Marxist party politics.[16]

Just as he had pioneered as a philosopher of race, sociologist of race, Pan-African-ist and anti-colonial theorist, Du Bois recusantly reinterpreted and critically engaged Marxism from perspectives that previously had not been considered by either Marx-ist or non-Marxist theorists. That is to say that when he critically questioned Marx-ian theory from an Africana historical, cultural, social, and political frame of refer-ence, and/or from the position of colored and colonized people generally, he identified several of its theoretic inadequacies. It is the identification of these inad-equacies and his development of a distinct critical race theory of capitalism that makes Du Bois stand out among Africana radical theorists.

Whether they agreed or disagreed with him, few could escape Du Bois's enormous and almost unfathomable influence on black radicalism during his day. For instance, take into consideration, perhaps, the most noted of the Trinidadian triumvirate, C. L. R. James, who is by many accounts one of the greatest intellectuals the Caribbean has produced, and the subject of the succeeding chapter. In *C. L. R. James and Revolutionary Marxism*, Scott McLemee (1994) argues that though James was highly critical of Du Bois, Du Bois did, in fact, "deeply influence him" (p. 225). In an often-overlooked 1965 tribute to the then recently deceased Du Bois, James (1977a) revealingly wrote:

> There is no need to subscribe to all that Dr. Du Bois has said and done. . . . Only the future can tell to what degree the historical audacities of Du Bois are viable. . . . Dr. Du Bois has always been put forward as one of the great black men and one of the great leaders of the black people. But, I have said that he is one of the great intellectuals—American intellectuals—of the twentieth century, and today and in years to come his work will continue to expand in importance while the work of others declines. (pp. 202, 211)

Du Bois's thought appealed to James and others of his ilk because it was culturally grounded, critical, and dialectical. In his approach to Marxism, Du Bois consistently demonstrated his ability to distinguish between its progressive and retrogressive elements. One of the many areas that Du Bois—among many other Africana radical theorists—found Marxism wanting was in its neglect to theorize the lifeworlds and lived-experiences of the racially oppressed (blacks as well as other non-whites).

As early as his 1907 essay, "The Negro and Socialism," Du Bois detected and detailed deficiencies in the Marxist tradition which included, among other things, a silence on and/or an inattention to: race, racism, and anti-racist struggle; colonialism and anti-colonial struggle; and, the ways in which *both* capitalism and colonialism exacerbate not simply the economic exploitation of non-European peoples, but continues (both physical and psychological) colonization beyond the realm of political economy. Du Bois, therefore, laboring long and critically with Marxian theory and methodology, deconstructed it and developed his own original radical (and later *revolutionary*) democratic socialist theory that: simultaneously built on his pioneering work as a race theorist and anti-colonialist; called for the radical transformation of U.S. society and the power relations of the world; was deeply concerned about and committed to world peace and demanded disarmament; and, advocated the liberation of all colonized, politically oppressed, and economically exploited persons.

Du Bois was well aware of the fact that anyone in the citadel of super-capitalism, the United States, who openly embraced socialism or Marxism in any of its manifestations would quickly become a social and political pariah. But, against a barrage of black bourgeois and white conservative criticism he sought democratic socialism and a methodical and meticulous understanding of Marxism. As discussed in greater detail below, Du Bois did not believe that the Russian communists had a monopoly on Marxism any more than he believed that the Marxists put a patent on the critique of capitalism. Marxism was merely one of many tools in Du Bois's ever-evolving critical socio-theoretical framework, and just as the meaning of socialism and Marxism changed as a result of revolutionary praxis and re-theorization, so too did Du Bois's relationship with and critical appreciation and/or race-conscious rejection of certain aspects of Marxism change.

In his classic study, *The Golden Age of Black Nationalism, 1850–1925*, Wilson Moses (1978) correctly contends, "Du Bois was an anticapitalist long before he was a socialist" (p. 138). In 1903, the year he published his watershed work, *The Souls of Black Folk*, Du Bois wanted nothing whatsoever to do with what he called "a cheap and dangerous socialism" (cited in Moses, 1978, p. 138). There has long been a tendency in Du Bois studies, and especially among those working on his racial and radical thought, to either exclusively engage his work prior to and including *The Souls of Black Folk*, or to disavow his early articulations and emphasize the radicalism of his later years. But, this is intellectually disingenuous and, it would seem to me, a great disservice to Du Bois, who spoke and wrote endlessly of our ethical obligation to constantly search for both scientific and social truth. In addition, this elision creates an arbitrary and artificial dichotomy in Du Bois's *oeuvre* that robs contemporary radicals of a paradigm and an opportunity to chart the political growth and development of a classical radical theorist and critic.

Traditionally when Du Bois's radical thought and relationship to socialism has been engaged three themes predominate the discourse. First, Du Bois is argued to have rashly turned to radicalism, embracing a brand of socialism based on the articulations of white critics of capitalism (this includes Marxists, anti-Marxists, and non-Marxists). Second, the Russian Revolution is reported to have convinced him once and for all of the sanctity of socialism and Marxism. And, third,—and the most common claim—his magisterial black Marxian text, *Black Reconstruction of Democracy in America*, is asserted to represent the completion of his conversion to Marxism. However, Du Bois's texts tell a different tale, and it is to these neglected narratives that I now intend to turn. I will briefly treat each of the three themes before discussing his distinct and constantly developing conception of democratic socialism.

With regard to the first theme, Moses (1978) maintains, "Du Bois is remembered as one of the great socialists of the twentieth century and it is easy to forget the conservatism of his intellectual origins" (p. 138). However, we should mince no words and make no mistakes about it, though Du Bois ultimately arrived at socialism, he only "became a socialist by gradual stages" (p. 138). His embrace of socialism did not entail the type of religious "leap of faith" or rituals of religious conversion that have historically been associated with some theorists' turn to Marxism. The careful and critical Du Bois came to socialism only after years of studying its theories and observing its practices, and, even after he came to it, it is difficult to say with any accuracy what type of socialism he initially embraced.[17]

Though much has been made of Du Bois's 1907 essays, "Socialist of the Path" and "The Negro and Socialism," which, of course, reveal his turn to "radical thought" and socialism, few have commented on the fact that even after his supposed "socialist turn," Du Bois continued to carry out one of the most thorough criticisms of Marxian theory in radical intellectual history. Many Du Bois scholars have observed his historic 1907 turn to socialism, but they do not provide an intellectual archaeology of the crucial *why* and *how* he decided to embrace socialism as a political theory and praxis. Further, most Du Bois scholars pass over roughly thirty years of his critical writings on socialism and Marxism to quickly get to the tried and true example of his employment of Marxian methodology and major contribution to what is currently called "black Marxism" (C. J. Robinson, 2000, 2001). I am, of course, referring to Du Bois's 1935 classic *Black Reconstruction of Democracy in America*.[18]

Du Bois was a consistent critic of Marxism, and not an uncritical and impetuous demagogue and disciple of the white critics of capitalism and their theories. In 1911 he officially joined the Socialist Party. Ironically, in that same year he delivered an address in New York entitled, "Socialism Is Too Narrow for Negroes," before an audience of one thousand socialists. In his speech he told his "comrades":

> You come to us, and with all the faith that your idea, the idea of Socialism inspires you, and you tell the Negro race to join the Socialist movement, which aims at the abolition of all ills and inequalities. You will find, however, that the Negro race will look upon you, upon the Socialists, with the same suspicion that it looks upon all white men. It will regard you as enemies just as it has been taught to regard all white men. (Du Bois, 1982b, p. 40)

Why will Du Bois's beloved black folk look at the socialists "with the same suspicion that [they] look upon all white men," we are all asking? Because, Du Bois decidedly continued:

> the Socialist movement really does not offer such a remedy for the race problem as Socialists generally think. The Socialist movement, like a great many reform movements in religion, in humanitarian and social relations of men, in the labor movement, have been movements which have concerned themselves with the European civilization, with the white races. So long as the Socialist movement can put a ban upon any race because of its color, whether that color be yellow or black, the Negro will not feel at home in it. (p. 40)

In so many words, Du Bois was calling his socialist comrades white supremacists and Eurocentrists because their brand of socialism was racially exclusive, focusing narrowly on "the European civilization" and "the white races," as he put it above. Surely this type of intra-party criticism (again, Du Bois was a member of the party at this point) was unprecedented in socialist circles at the time. But, because most Du Bois scholars rush to *Black Reconstruction*, they miss many of his seminal criticisms of (Eurocentric) socialism that led him to develop the distinct methodology of their most beloved book. Now, one may also be wondering: well, why did Du Bois join the Socialist Party if he knew it was racist? He quickly and coolly answered: the Socialists were "the only party which openly recognizes Negro manhood." According to Manning Marable (1986), in *W. E. B. Du Bois: Black Radical Democrat*, Du Bois's motivations for joining the Socialist Party also grew out of his associations with several of the white socialists who helped him found the National Association for the Advancement of Colored People (NAACP) and his "overriding commitment to racial and economic justice" (p. 90). Soon, says Marable, "Socialism was integrated into his larger struggle against racial inequality" (p. 90).[19]

Du Bois's tenure in the Socialist Party was very brief, only lasting one year, from 1911 to 1912. As he revealed in *Darkwater*, he simply could not stomach the fact that his so-called socialist "comrades," and a political organization that he was a member of, "openly excluded Negroes and Asiatics" (Du Bois, 1996a, p. 552). Du Bois's prompt departure from the party was precipitated by what he perceived to be its timidity toward concrete criticisms of, as opposed to radical rhetoric against, racial discrimination and racist exclusions within its own ranks. Soon after joining the party he began a campaign to recruit and elect African American officers. But, the white socialists would not budge. Marable (1986) correctly contends that though Du Bois "may have resigned from the Socialist Party, . . . he remained a Socialist" (p. 90).

The second recurring theme that dominates the discourse on Du Bois's radical thought involves his impression and interpretation of the Russian Revolution and its impact on his outlook. Clearly the Soviet experiment with communism had a deep and profound impact on Du Bois. But, again, his interest in the Russian Revolution has often been interpreted as an unequivocal and unflinching acceptance of everything that revolution entailed. However, and in the fashion of his foray into socialism, and Marxism in general, Du Bois continued to critically question Russian communism. In fact, he exhibited such an uncharacteristic reticence regarding the Russian Revolution and its immediate aftermath that he was harshly criticized by the Jamaican poet laureate and black radical, Claude McKay.[20]

From McKay's optic, Du Bois had written critically of the Russian Revolution and was therefore a traitor to the working classes and black masses because, as McKay fumed, "the Negro in politics and social life is ostracized only technically by the distinction of color; in reality the Negro is discriminated against because he is the lowest type of worker" (McKay quoted in Du Bois, 1995a, p. 531). Now, it is Du Bois's rejoinder to McKay that sheds light on his position on the Russian Revolution and possibly lays to rest incredulous claims regarding his early, extremely critical interpretation of it. Du Bois's blazing response to McKay was entitled, "The Negro and Radical Thought." In the essay he takes "Mr. McKay" to task for privileging class over race (something several critics of Du Bois would argue that he did in his later work) and making the erroneous assumption that he "sneered" at the Russian Revolution. Du Bois (1995a) declared:

> [W]e have one chief cause—the emancipation of the Negro, and to this all else must be subordinated—not because other questions are not important but because to our mind the most important social question today is recognition of the darker races.
>
>   Turning now to that marvelous set of phenomena known as the Russian Revolution, Mr. McKay is wrong in thinking that we have ever intentionally sneered at it. On the contrary, time may prove, as he believes, that the Russian Revolution is the greatest event of the nineteenth and twentieth centuries, and its leaders the most unselfish prophets. At the same time *The Crisis* does not know this to be true. Russia is incredibly vast, and the happenings there in the last five years have been intricate to a degree that must make any student pause. We sit, therefore, with waiting hands and listening ears, seeing some splendid results from Russia . . . and hearing other things which frighten us. (p. 532)

At first issue is Du Bois's unapologetic display of black nationalism. In his words, "we have one chief cause . . . the emancipation of the Negro." In addition, and this should be underscored, it must be borne in mind that he made this statement well-nigh fifteen years after his supposed "socialist turn" in 1907. Again, I refute the claim that he was a Marxist-socialist in any orthodox or doctrinaire sense. In fact, what we see here is Du Bois being highly critical of a radical of African descent—the fact that he was a "Negro poet of distinction" notwithstanding—who had accepted the orthodox Marxist obsession with economics and overemphasis on class struggle (p. 531). And finally, Du Bois's comments on the Russian Revolution reveal that five years after "that marvelous set of phenomena" he was still not convinced or committed to the Russian version of communism. However, and in characteristic fashion, he did remind his radical "Negro" readers that "the immediate work for the American Negro lies in America and not in Russia" (pp. 532–533). He also counseled black radicals to continue to question socialism and communism, all the while he was extending and expanding his critique or, rather, his critical race theory of Marxism. Du Bois rhetorically questioned and answered:

> What is today the right program of socialism? The editor of *The Crisis* considers himself a Socialist but he does not believe that German State Socialism or the dictatorship of the proletariat are perfect panaceas. He believes with most thinking men that the present method of creating, controlling and distributing wealth is desperately wrong; that there must come and is coming a social control of wealth; but he does not know just what form that control is going to take, and he is not prepared to dogmatize with Marx or Lenin. Further than that, and more fundamental to the duty and outlook of *The Crisis*, is this question: How far can the colored people of the world, and particularly the Negroes of the United States, trust the working classes?
>
> Many honest thinking Negroes assume, and Mr. McKay seems to be one of these, that we have only to embrace the working class program to have the working class embrace ours; that we have only to join Trade Unionism and Socialism or even Communism, as they are today expounded, to have Union Labor and Socialists and Communists believe and act on the equality of mankind and the abolition of the color line. *The Crisis* wishes that this were true, but it is forced to the conclusion that it is not. (p. 533)

Fifteen years after his supposed socialist turn, and five years after the Russian Revolution, Du Bois considered himself a socialist but was "not prepared to dogmatize with Marx or Lenin." This may seem curious to many contemporary readers but, again, Du Bois did not think that the Marxists had a monopoly on socialism. In 1921 he continued to carry out his critique of Marxism, calling into question its usefulness to the racially oppressed, and particularly people of African origin and descent.

It was racial discrimination and racist exclusionism, not only by white capitalists but also by white workers that distinguished the plight of the black worker. Black workers were *black* before they were ever even considered *workers*, which in many white supremacist capitalists, unionists, labor organizers, and workers' minds precluded blacks from ever being workers in either a Marxian or non-Marxian sense. This is to say that black workers were never thought of in the raceless terms in which white workers were thought of when white Marxists, economists, labor scholars, political scientists and sociologists, among many others, theorized "the working class" (R.D.G. Kelley, 1994, 1997a). Black workers were always and ever *raced first*, to shamelessly appropriate Marcus Garvey's famous phrase for my own critical theoretical purposes. The bottom line, and the main point Du Bois wanted to make in the passage above was that white workers undeniably suffer severely within a capitalist system. But, he emphatically emphasized, being a white worker within a white supremacist capitalist system is not nearly as tragic and traumatic as being black *and* a worker in a white supremacist capitalist system (Marable, 1983, 1993, 1995, 1996, 1997, 2002).

Fifteen years after "The Negro and Radical Thought," Du Bois produced what many critics have long hailed as his definitive statement on the differences between the white worker and the black worker, his 1935 masterpiece *Black Reconstruction of Democracy in America*. This, of course, brings us to the third and final theme that dominates the discourse on Du Bois's radicalism and distinct democratic socialism. With the publication of *Black Reconstruction*, a book C. L. R. James (1977a, p. 211) said "is and is likely to continue to be one of the finest history books ever written," Du Bois is purported to have finally shown his hand and crossed over completely to Marxism. Critics have taken great pleasure in pointing out this or that Marxian element or influence in his later radical writings, especially in *Black Reconstruction*. But, the truth of the matter is: one-dimensional, narrow-minded, and Eurocentric interpretations of Du Bois do his (Africana intellectual history-making) legacy a great disservice and robs contemporary critical theorists of an opportunity to explore the richness and wide-range and reach of his dialectical thought.

Indeed, *Black Reconstruction* is one of many watershed works in Du Bois's corpus, and my critical remarks here should not be confused with criticisms of the book (which, incidentally, will not be directly engaged in this instance), but more criticisms of the book's reception. *Black Reconstruction*'s reception—and we could say, contemporary reception of classical reception of this text—is important here in terms of developing Africana critical theory because if this important work in black radicalism is interpreted as a work wholly within the Marxian tradition, then, Du Bois quickly and logically (from a mainstream Marxist and Eurocentrist frame of reference, which are virtual one and the same) becomes a disciple or, worst, an ideologue in a tradition in which he actually innovated, created, and contributed new critical concepts and categories of analysis and praxis. My efforts here are primarily geared toward exposing the fact that even after he wrote *Black Reconstruction*, Du Bois did not uncritically accept Marxism, but continued to draw from those aspects of the theory which he understood to offer the greatest contribution to his "one chief cause—the emancipation of the Negro." Moreover, let us bear in mind that for Du Bois "all else must be subordinated" to the "one chief cause," "not because other questions are not important but because to our mind the most important social question today is recognition of the darker races."

I utterly agree with the two-time Pulitzer Prize-winning Du Bois biographer, David Levering Lewis in *W. E. B. Du Bois: The Fight for Equality and the American Century, 1919–1963*, when he noted: "The book [*Black Reconstruction*] represented one of those genuine paradigm shifts periodically experienced in a field of knowledge, one that sunders regnant interpretations into the before-and-after of its sudden, disorienting emergence. Had he ventured to paraphrase Marx, who both inspires and deforms the book, Du Bois might well have observed that he had set reconstruction historiography upright after finding it standing on its head" (D.L. Lewis, 2000, p. 367). *Black Reconstruction* represents and registers as a "genuine paradigm shift" because it recasts both Reconstruction historiography and Marxian historical materialism from "the black point of view," a cool-penned Lewis quipped regarding the methodological orientation of Du Bois's Reconstruction research from his 1910 bombshell "Reconstruction and Its Benefits" through to *Black Reconstruction* (p. 351).

Du Bois maintained a critical relationship with Marxism from the time of his supposed socialist turn in 1907 and up to and even after the publication of *Black Reconstruction* in 1935. In 1936, ironically a year after *Black Reconstruction* had a ripple effect on Reconstruction historiography and supposedly made him the black Marxist *par excellence*, Du Bois continued to carry out his criticism of socialism and communism in an obscure and often overlooked *Journal of Negro Education* essay entitled, "Social Planning for the Negro: Past and Present." The essay is essentially a history of African American's social and political thought and movements, from enslavement to his epoch, then 1936. After accenting the rebellions of Denmark Vesey and Nat Turner; noting Harriet Tubman and the Underground Railroad; highlighting Paul Cuffe's emigration plan; praising John Brown and Frederick Douglass for their revolutionary abolitionism; and, writing almost objectively of Booker T. Washington and his accommodationist program, the essay gives way to its concluding section, which Du Bois dubbed "The Present Dilemma."

Emphasis should be placed on the last section of Du Bois's essay because it represents one of the first times he discussed African Americans and their then current conditions after the publication of *Black Reconstruction*. *Black Reconstruction* was a critical look at African Americans' past from "the black point of view" (à la Lewis), where "Social Planning for the Negro: Past and Present," as the title suggests, was an examination of African Americans' classical and contemporary conditions from "the black point of view." In addition, the final section of Du Bois's essay is a clarion example of his continued critical relationship with Marxism after the publication of *Black Reconstruction*.

Du Bois (1982c) begins the section, "The Present Dilemma," by putting forward his long held contention that "the problem of race discrimination always cuts across and hinders the settlement of other problems" (p. 36). The problem he is hinting at here has to do with both race and class, actually racial oppression and economic exploitation in the forms of racism and capitalism. Faced with the reality of the economic depression in the U.S. at that time, Du Bois argued that African Americans had three options available to them: "(1) toward invoking the protection of restored capitalism, (2) a movement toward alliance with organized labor, and (3) a movement toward socialism" (p. 36). With regard to the first and second options, Du Bois succinctly stated:

> There is only one haven of refuge for the American Negro. He must recognize that his attempt to enter the ranks of capital as an exploiter came too late, if it were ever a worthy ideal for a group of workers. He is now forever excluded by the extraordinary monopoly which white capital and credit have upon the machines and materials of the world. Moreover, that solution after all was possible only for the few. The great mass of Negroes belong to the laboring class. (pp. 37–38)

African Americans simply could not join with the capitalists and bourgeois bureaucrats because they had no capital, and even if and when they did produce or procure capital, racism still reared its ugly head (and horns!). Besides, Du Bois questioned, is it a "worthy ideal," economically exploiting others? And, considering African Americans' historical experiences at the hands (and under the boots!) of white supremacist capitalists: aren't blacks almost inherently anti-capitalist or, rather, *shouldn't* (based on their historical experiences and endurances) blacks be almost inherently anti-capitalist? Keep in mind, Du Bois declared, "The great mass of Negroes belong to the laboring class" and historically have been ever since Africans first came to the Americas in shackles and chains at the dawn of the sixteenth century. The first option was, therefore, quickly dispelled.

As far as the second option of African Americans joining the unions, racism again proved a decisive factor. The unionists, as Du Bois discussed in "The American Federation of Labor and the Negro," were white supremacists who saw blacks as job-stealers and would not allow them to join the unions. There went the second option, dismissed with Du Bois's characteristic quick-wit and uncomplicated brevity. This left, then, the third and final option, socialism. Du Bois (1982c) demurrly mused:

> Suppose, now, that the Negro turns to the promise of socialism whither I have long looked for salvation. I was once a member of the celebrated Local No. 1 in New York. I am convinced of the essential truth of the Marxian philosophy and believe that eventually land, machines and materials must belong to the state; that private profit must be abolished; that the system of exploiting labor must disappear; that people who work must have essentially equal income; and that in their hands the political rulership of the state must eventually rest.
>
> Notwithstanding the fact that I believe this is the truth and that this truth is being gradually exemplified by the Russian experiment, I must nevertheless ask myself seriously; how far can American Negroes forward this eventual end? What part can they expect to have in a socialistic state and what can they do now to bring about this realization? And my answer to this has long been clear. There is no automatic power in socialism to override and suppress race prejudice. This has been proven in America, it was true in Germany before Hitler and the analogy of the Jews in Russia is for our case entirely false and misleading. One of the worst things that Negroes could do today would be to join the American Communist Party or any of its many branches. The Communists of America have become dogmatic exponents of the inspired word of Karl Marx as they read it. They believe, apparently in immediate, violent and bloody revolution, and they are willing to try any and all means of raising hell anywhere and under any circumstances. This is a silly program even for white men. For American colored men, it is suicide. In the first place, its logical basis is by no means sound. The great and fundamental change in the organization of industry which Karl Marx with his splendid mind and untiring sacrifice visualized must, to be sure, be brought about by revolution, but whether in all times and places and under all circumstances that revolution is going to involve war and bloodshed, is a question which every sincere follower of Marx has a right to doubt. (p. 38)

Du Bois began on a sincere and somber note, revealing his belief in "the promise of socialism" and "the essential truth of the Marxian philosophy." Next, he outlines socialism and solemnly sings some of its praises, laying bare its emphasis on utilizing natural, technological, and human resources in the best interest of the most needy among the masses, the laboring classes, and future generations. Socialism had a certain longstanding appeal for Du Bois (1986c) not simply because he believed that it was "the end to economic reform" (pp. 49–53). But, it also appealed to him because it was a system of social organization that resembled ancient African communalism, where "crops are divided, not necessarily according to the amount of work that the man does or the efficiency of it, but according to the needs of the members of the tribe" (Du Bois, 1971c, p. 165). This last point is one that often goes overlooked by students of Du Bois's radical writings, even those working in Africana Studies, but it is extremely important nevertheless.[21]

Now, back to the previous passage, we come to the crux of Du Bois's criticisms of Marxist socialism and communism: "There is no automatic power in socialism [or communism] to override and suppress race prejudice." Du Bois had read those well-worn famous first few pages of the *Communist Manifesto*, where Karl Marx and Friedrich Engels wrote with great glee of the global triumph of the white bourgeoisie over the colonized colored world's cultural and historical formations. In an almost knee-jerk reaction, which has since become an unspoken rite of passage among black radicals, Du Bois critically queried: what happens when socialists or communists are white supremacists and Eurocentrists? This is a question that Karl Marx and many of his communist comrades never considered, because very frequently they suffered from white supremacism and Eurocentrism, and looked on European imperial expansion as a "necessary evil" that "opened up fresh ground for the rising bourgeoisie" that would ultimately forge "weapons that bring death to itself" (Marx and Engels, 1978, pp. 474, 478; see also Marx, 1972; C.W. Mills, 2003a; Rabaka, 2008a; C.J. Robinson, 2000, 2001; Serequeberhan, 1990, 1994). Du Bois pleaded with African Americans and other "colored men" not to join the Communist or Socialist Party, as he had done, but to organize among themselves, study socialism and communism from their own independent frames of reference, and develop race-centered and racism-conscious critiques of capitalism, as well as Marxism.[22]

It was not simply the racism and Eurocentrism of the white socialists and communists that Du Bois took issue with. He also felt that their emphasis on "immediate, violent and bloody revolution" was not feasible for African Americans who at the time constituted less than 10 percent of the U.S. population. White communists and socialists could advocate "immediate, violent and bloody revolution" to the white working class because they were the majority of the U.S. population and, thus, stood a greater chance of destabilizing the imperial economic order. However, for black folk to take this position, from Du Bois's optic, was not only untenable but quite simply "suicide." In an extremely unorthodox and heretic manner, Du Bois (1982c) was searching for an alternative to violent social revolution, but he never ruled out self-defensive violence as a last resort, stating: "We abhor violence and bloodshed; we will join no movement that advocates a program of violence, except as the last defense against aggression" (p. 39).[23]

Du Bois was acutely aware of blacks' social status and political position in the white supremacist world. By this time, circa 1936, he had undertaken several studies of lynching and mob violence and, as a result, was painfully cognizant of the fact that white supremacists had no regard whatsoever for black life.[24] His criticisms of Marxism here were groundbreaking in the sense that he exposed the nexus between white conservatives, white liberals, and white radicals: their whiteness and (conscious and/or unconscious) adherence to white supremacy. Du Bois may have been duped when he joined the Socialist Party in 1911, but now he knew that the white socialists and communists could be just as white supremacist as the white capitalists. The white communists and socialists had volumes of radical rhetoric regarding the "brotherhood of mankind" and the equality and inherent rights of all workers, when in all actuality they meant *white* workers and even more, as we will see in the next section, they meant white *male* workers.

Each time Du Bois criticized the white socialists or communists it forced him to dig deeper and develop his own independent version of democratic socialism, one distinctly race-centered and racism-conscious. It was premature to spend too much time theorizing communism since, along orthodox Marxist lines, Du Bois believed that socialism must proceed communism. As he asserted in "The Negro and Social-ism," "the salvation" of persons of color, and people of African descent in particu-lar, "lies in socialism" (Du Bois, 2000a, p. 418). However, he was extremely adamant in stating that continental and diasporan Africans should not graft Euro-centric (Marxist-Leninist) and/or Asiocentric (Maoist) communism or socialism onto Africana life-worlds, but that they should "study socialism, its rise in Europe and Asia, and its peculiar suitability for the emancipation of Africa" and its diaspora (p. 416). Du Bois maintained that the "question of the method by which the so-cialist state can be achieved must be worked out by experiment and reason and not by dogma. Whether or not methods which were right and clear in Russia and China fit our circumstances is for our intelligence to decide" (p. 418).

In its broadest sense, "socialism," according to Du Bois in "Socialism and the American Negro," means "the ownership of capital by the state; the regulation of all industry in the interests of citizens and not for private profit of the few; and the building of a welfare state where all men work according to ability and share income according to need" (1985a, p. 295). However, he is quick to point out that "[t]he complete socialism called communism has been reached by no nation," and he in-cluded the politico-economic experiments of the Soviet Union (Russia) and China in his analysis (p. 295). In attempting to understand Du Bois's connections and contributions to the deconstruction and reconstruction of radical politics and criti-cal social theory, it is important to point out—as Cedric Robinson (2000) has in *Black Marxism*—that, "Du Bois was one of the first American theorists to sympa-thetically confront Marxist thought in critical and independent terms" (p. 207). Be-cause of the brevity of his tenure in the Socialist Party, which he felt betrayed African Americans on account of its internal racial hierarchy (which replicated U.S. society and the European imperial impulse) and the socialists' non-existent (or, at the least, half-hearted) external critique and confrontation of racism, and considering his longstanding distrust of the Communist Party, the Party which drove him to un-flinchingly state: "American Negroes do not propose to be the shock troops of the Communist Revolution, driven out in front to death, cruelty and humiliation in or-der to win victories for whites workers"—it is not hard to understand *how* or *why* I, following Robinson, read Du Bois as more of a critic of Marxism than a Marxist in any dogmatic, orthodox, or Eurocentric sense (Du Bois, 1995a, p. 591; C.J. Robin-son, 2000, p. 228).

Du Bois is easily understood to be a contributor to the deconstruction and re-construction of radical politics and critical social theory when and where the cri-tique of *both* capitalism and Marxism are acknowledged as basic characteristics of radical politics and critical social theory (Agger, 1992a, 1992b, 2006; Kellner, 1989, 1990b, 1990c, 1993, 1995; Wilkerson and Paris, 2001). And, when his critiques of capitalism and Marxism are coupled with his pioneering work as an anti-racist and anti-colonial theorist, Du Bois immediately emerges as an innovator in the critical theory tradition, Africana or otherwise. An innovator who broadened critical theory's base by using Africana liberation thought and revolutionary practices as his foundation and grounding point of departure.

It was not simply capitalism and class struggle that impeded socialism from Du Bois's increasingly radical point of view, but equally racial domination and discrimination weighed in. Where he began his adventure in socialism toying with its most conservative, reformist, and gradualist strains, historical happenings on the world scene and the acute and increasing economic exploitation of blacks in white supremacist capitalist societies led him to couple his critical race and anti-colonial theory with critical class theory. As a consequence, Du Bois developed some of the first race/class theory and criticisms of Marxism from an Africana frame of reference. However, race and class were not the only issues Du Bois believed were deterring a democratic socialist society. There was also the problem of gender domination and discrimination, something the prophet of problems wrote extensively about, but an issue that Du Bois scholars and critics have buried beneath a barrage of criticism regarding his race manhood, black radicalness, and/or lack of skills as a littérateur. The concluding section of this chapter, then, will be devoted to the often-overlooked anti-sexist dimension(s) of Du Bois's dialectical thought and critical socio-theoretical discourse.

## THE SOULS OF BLACK FEMALE FOLK: W. E. B. DU BOIS'S ANTI-SEXIST CRITICAL THEORY OF CONTEMPORARY SOCIETY

Du Bois's contributions to critical theory, and Africana critical theory in specific, are perhaps ultimately most distinguished by his passionate pro-women politics or, what Michael Awkward (2000) dubs, Du Bois's "male-feminism," which amazingly integrates each of the aforementioned areas of critical inquiry—(anti)racism, (anti)colonialism, and (anti)capitalism—into a full-fledged critical socio-theoretical framework. Du Bois claimed in his classic essay, "The Study of Negro Problems" (1898), that the omission of persons of African descent from the realm of social scientific study, and their relegation and reduction to paradigms *par excellence* of pathology when they are studied, robs all "true lovers of humanity" who "hold higher the pure ideals of science" of the rigorous and robust practice of a truly human science (p. 23). In this same vein, he also argued that there could be no authentic human science unless and until the contradictions and conundrums of women's *sociality*—that is, women's socio-political lived-experiences and lived-endurances, their social life-realities in this "man-ruled world," and their relations among themselves and to men—were critically reflected in social scientific and other humanistic studies of the social world (Du Bois, 1995a, p. 297).[25]

Though many read him as an archetypal "race man," according to Joy James (1997) in *Transcending the Talented Tenth*, Du Bois actually practiced "a politics remarkably progressive for his time and ours" (p. 36).[26] James notes, "Du Bois confronted race, class, and gender oppression while maintaining conceptual and political linkages between the struggles to end racism, sexism, and war" (pp. 36-37). His socio-theoretical framework was dynamic and constantly integrated diverse components of African American liberation theory; Pan-Africanism and anti-colonial theory; women's liberation theory; peace and international political theory; and Marxist and non-Marxist class theory, among others.

In "The Souls of Black Women Folk in the Writings of W. E. B. Du Bois," the greatly esteemed African American feminist and literary theorist Nellie McKay (1990) contends: "At a time when black male writers concentrated their efforts on the social, economic, and educational advancement of black men as the 'leaders' of the race, Du Bois is something of an anomaly in his recognition that black women were equal partners in the struggle to claim the human dignity all black people were seeking" (p. 236). Moreover, in *Daughters of Sorrow: Attitudes Toward Black Women, 1880–1920*, the lionized African American literary and feminist theorist Beverly Guy-Sheftall (1990) maintains that Du Bois was not only one of "the most passionate defenders of black women," but also one of the "most outspoken [male-] feminists" in African American history and, more generally, American history (p. 13). In fact, in Guy-Sheftall's opinion, Du Bois "devote[d] his life's work to the emancipation of blacks *and* women" (p. 161, emphasis in original).[27]

In *W. E. B. Du Bois: Black Radical Democrat*, celebrated African American historian, political scientist, and social theorist Manning Marable (1986) echoes Guy-Sheftall's observations, declaring, "[l]ike Douglass, Du Bois was probably the most advanced male leader of his era on the question of gender inequality" and woman suffrage, though he was deeply "troubled by the racism within the white women's movement" (p. 85). Particularly perplexing for Du Bois was the white women's movement's inattention to and perpetuation of racism. For instance, Du Bois was bothered by the racial politics of the National American Woman Suffrage Association, whose president, Carrie Chapman Catt, asserted that democratic rights had been granted to African American men "with possibly ill-advised haste," producing "[p]erilous conditions" in U.S. society as it introduced "into the body politic vast numbers of irresponsible citizens." Belle Kearney, the Mississippi suffragist leader, practiced an even more overtly anti-black racist politics by advocating that white women's enfranchisement would guarantee, among other things, an "immediate and [more] durable white supremacy" (cited in Marable, 1986, p. 85; see also Blee, 1991, 2002; Caraway, 1991; Ferber, 2004; Newman, 1999; Roth, 2003; Twine and Blee, 2001; Ware, 1992). Du Bois (1995a), in characteristic fashion, shot back: "Every argument for Negro suffrage is an argument for woman's suffrage; every argument for woman's suffrage is an argument for Negro suffrage; both are great movements in democracy" (p. 298).

In terms of developing Africana critical theory of contemporary society, what I am most interested in here is how Du Bois maintained, as James put it above, "conceptual and political linkages" between various anti-racist, anti-sexist, anti-colonial, and anti-capitalist thought-traditions and socio-political movements. Unlike most of the critics in the Frankfurt School tradition of critical theory, Du Bois did not downplay gender domination and discrimination (N. Fraser, 1991; Heberle, 2006; Meehan, 1995). On the contrary, he placed the critique of sexism and racism right alongside the critique of capitalism, class analysis, and class conflict theory. In tune with the thinking of many Marxist feminists and socialist feminists, Du Bois was critical of both capitalism and patriarchy (Gillman and Weinbaum, 2007; A.E. Weinbaum, 2001; see also M.J. Buhle, 1981; Eisenstein, 1979; Holmstrom, 2002; Sargent, 1981; B. Weinbaum, 1978). He understood women, in general, to have great potential as agents of social transformation because of their simultaneous ex-perience of capitalist exploitation and sexist oppression. However, similar to con-temporary Africana anti-sexist social theorists, both black feminists and womanists, Du Bois understood women of African origin and descent, in particular, to have even greater potential as agents of radical social change on account of their simul-taneous experience of racism, sexism and economic exploitation, whether under capitalism or colonialism (Guy-Sheftall, 1995; hooks, 1981, 1984, 1995; Hudson-Weems, 1995, 1997, 2004; James and Sharpley-Whiting, 2000; Nnaemeka, 1998). Du Bois's socio-theoretical framework, therefore, has immense import for the dis-cussion at hand so far as it provides Africana critical theory with a paradigm and point of departure for developing a multi-perspectival social theory that is simulta-neously critical of racism, sexism, capitalism, and colonialism.

Du Bois developed theory that was simultaneously critical of racism, colonialism, capitalism, and traditional Marxism. In the remainder of this chapter I will bring this thought into dialogue with his contributions to women's decolonization and women's liberation. Similar to the iconic African American intellectual-activist an-cestor Frederick Douglass (1992), Du Bois demanded that women's human and civil rights be respected and protected. But, beyond Douglass, DuBois thoroughly theorized and "strategized woman suffrage and female equality," argues Gary Lemons (2001) and Nellie McKay (1985, 1990), "from a standpoint grounded in the lived experiences," literature and critical thought of black women (Lemons, 2001, p. 74). Bringing his critique of capitalism and careful study of modern polit-ical economy to bear on "this man-ruled world" and its absurd "sex conditions," Du Bois—again, faithfully following Frederick Douglass—advocated that women have "equal pay for equal work," stating: "We cannot abolish the new economic freedom of women. We cannot imprison women again in a home or require them all on pain of death to be nurses and housekeepers" (Du Bois, 1995a, pp. 289, 297, 309; see also Douglass, 1992, pp. 63–65).[28]

Many Du Bois scholars have pointed out that Du Bois prophesied that "the prob-lem of the twentieth century" would be "the problem of the color line" (see Ander-son and Zuberi, 2000; Andrews, 1985; Bell, Grosholz and Stewart, 1996; Clarke, Jackson, Kaiser and O'Dell, 1970; Fontenot, 2001; Fontenot and Keller, 2007). How-ever, what many of these scholars have often failed to mention is the fact that Du Bois made this statement in 1900 (in "To the Nations of the World"), and that he augmented and revised this thesis *several times* within the remaining sixty-three years of his life (see Du Bois, 1995a, pp. 639–641; see also Rabaka, 2007a). In fact, by the time he published *Darkwater* in 1920, Du Bois (1995a) stressed not only the "sex conditions," "sex equality" and "sex freedom" of women, but he also asserted that "women are passing through, not only a moral, but an economic revolution" (pp. 308, 311). Further, forty-three years before his death, Du Bois—seemingly unbe-knownst to the great majority of past and present Du Bois scholars and critics—stated: "The uplift of women is, next to the problem of the color line and the peace movement, our greatest modern cause" (p. 309; see also Gillman and Weinbaum, 2007).[29]

Du Bois developed a "critical sociology," according to the noted black feminist so-ciologist Cheryl Townsend Gilkes (1996), which "emphasized that gender, race, and class intersected in the lives of black women to foster an important critical perspective or standpoint" (pp. 117, 112; see also Lucal, 1996). "Standpoint" is a term currently employed in black feminist discourse, and feminist discourse in general, to denote, as another noted black feminist sociologist, Patricia Hill Collins (1996), points out, the fact that:

> First, Black women's political and economic status provides them with a distinctive set of experiences that offers a different view of material reality than that available to other groups. The unpaid and paid work that Black women perform, the types of communities in which they live, and the kinds of relationships they have with others suggest that African American women, as a group, experience a different world than those who are not Black and female. Second, these experiences stimulate a distinctive Black feminist consciousness concerning that material reality. In brief, a subordinate group not only experiences a different reality than a group that rules, but a subordinate group may interpret that reality differently than a dominant group. (p. 223)[30]

Du Bois believed that women, and women of African descent in particular, were (within white and male supremacist societies) a "subordinate group" who by dint of hard labor and harsh living conditions had developed a distinct gender, racial and class consciousness.[31] With "[a]ll the virtues of her sex . . . utterly ignored," "the primal black All-Mother of men," "the African mother" endured, on Du Bois's (1995a) account, "[t]he crushing weight of slavery" only to be re-subjugated in a world that claimed to "worship both virgins and mothers," but "in the end despises motherhood and despoils virgins" (pp. 304, 300, 301, 300). African American women, in the period after *de jure* "American slavery," were flung into a world where they were dominated and discriminated against simultaneously on account of their race and gender. Their subordination, then, was inherent—though implicit on many accounts—in the evolving social ontology and social ecology of white and male supremacist U.S. society.[32] The chronic experience and effects of the interlocking, intersecting and overlapping nature of race, gender, class and, as of late, sexuality have led many Africana women's liberation theorists to posit that women of African descent experience a reality that is distinctly different from the lived-experiences and life-struggles of those persons who are not black *and* female. Theories of "double," "triple," and "multiple" jeopardy abound but, curiously, rarely if ever has Du Bois's contributions to women's decolonization and women's liberation figured prominently in this discourse.[33]

Du Bois spent the great bulk of his life and intellectual energy wrestling with different forms of domination and discrimination, and though he often missed the mark in his personal life (I am tempted to say, in his personal "affairs") with women, specifically his wife and daughter, there remains much that can (and *should*) be salvaged from his anti-sexist social thought. To leave Du Bois to the traditional "race man" line is, to my logic, to throw the baby out with the bath water. The more radical and critical thing to do is to search for and salvage what we can from Du Bois's life-work that will aid us in our endeavors to develop an Africana critical theory of contemporary society, which includes a definite and distinctive anti-sexist dimension alongside its anti-racism, anti-colonialism, and anti-capitalism. This, then, is an effort to build on and go beyond Du Bois; it is aimed at bringing his anti-sexist social thought into dialogue with past and present Africana women's liberation theorists.

As with any thought-system or philosophical method there are things that are positive and others that are negative in Du Bois's discourse, which, of course, brings us to the question of dialectics (Rabaka, 2008a). A dialectical approach to Du Bois enables us to simultaneously acknowledge the sexism he practiced at specific intervals in his private life, while focusing on his production and promotion of anti-sexist positions and policies in his public life. This approach, also, opens objective interpreters of Du Bois to the fact that he—as is common with many men struggling against their sexist socialization and the madness of male supremacy—may very well have concomitantly and contradictorily had instances of sexist thought and behavior in both his public and private life-worlds.

However, were we to highlight Du Bois's sexism without accenting his anti-sexism (or, vice versa) we would be producing and practicing the very type of one-dimensional interpretation and thought that critical theory purports to be combating and offering ethical and radical alternatives. Because he has long been cast in the "race man" cloak, it is difficult for many Du Bois scholars and critics to look at his life and work from multidimensional theoretical optics. What I wish to accent here, above all else, are those aspects of Du Bois's life-work that contribute to the development of Africana critical theory, which means that I am primarily concerned with those aspects of his discourse that critique domination and provide the promise of liberation. The Du Bois that I am interested in, then, indeed did sometimes harbor subtle sexist sentiments but, by the same token, the Du Bois that I am engaging here also did not shy away from the forms of domination and discrimination that women, and particularly women of African descent, experienced as a result of white *and* male supremacy. Surely his essays such as, "The Work of Negro Women in Society," "The Black Mother," "Hail Columbia!," "Woman Suffrage," "The Damnation of Women," and "Sex and Racism," to name only a few, are sincere testimonies and solemn testaments that affirm his heartfelt assertion in the last paragraph of "The Damnation of Women": "I honor the women of my race" (Du Bois, 1995a, p. 311).[34]

Divulging the fact that "women of African descent have struggled with the multiple realities of gender, racial, and economic or caste oppression," Joy James, similar to Cheryl Townsend Gilkes, contends that Africana women have "created . . . space for a more viable democracy" (James and Sharpley-Whiting, 2000, p. 1; see also Gilkes, 1996, pp. 114, 116–117). Democracy, one of the most prevalent and pervasive themes in Du Bois's discourse, has not and will never exist so long as any human group, no matter how small or so-called "minority," is excluded from the civic decision making-processes of their respective national communities and the international community. Du Bois included women when he spoke of "peasants," "laborers," and "socially damned" persons who must always be considered if the United States, or any nation for that matter, is to achieve anything remotely close to democracy. For instance, in *Darkwater*, in the chapter ironically entitled "Of the Ruling of Men," Du Bois (1969a) asserted:

Today we are gradually coming to realize that government by temporary coalition of small and diverse groups may easily become the most efficient method of expressing the will of man and of setting the human soul free. . . . [N]o nation, race, or sex, has a monopoly on ability or ideas . . . no human group is so small as to deserve to be ignored as a part, and as an integral and respected part, of the mass of men . . . above all, no group of twelve million black folk, even though they are at the physical mercy of a hundred million white majority, can be deprived of a voice in government and of the right to self-development without a blow at the very foundations of all democracy and all human uplift. . . . [N]o modern nation can shut the gates of opportunity in the face of its women, its peasants, its laborers, or its socially damned. How astounded the future world-citizen will be to know that as late as 1918 great and civilized nations were making desperate endeavor to confine the development of ability and individuality to one sex,—that is, to one-half of the nation; and he will probably learn that a similar effort to confine humanity to one race lasted a hundred years longer. (pp. 153–154)

Du Bois directed his intellectual attention to the plight of black women, and they were so far as he was concerned, "an integral and respected part" of his beloved "black folk." In fact, the woman of African descent, "the primal black All-Mother of men," could not and would not be held in check, neither by white nor male supremacy. Why? Because she was leading both a "moral" and an "economic" revolution (Du Bois, 1995a, pp. 300, 308). Gilkes (1996) contends that "for Du Bois, black women represent a unique force for progressive change in the United States" because of the degree(s) to which they experience and endure various forms of racial and gender oppression and economic exploitation (p. 113).

Where most of the male social theorists of his age placed a greater emphasis on class theory, class formation, class consciousness and the impact of political economy on culture and society, Du Bois engaged the intersections of class, race, *and* gender utilizing Africana lived-experiences and liberation thought and practices as a model for his theories of social change and concept of an ever-expanding, all-inclusive transethnic, transgender, and transgenerational democracy. Gilkes goes on to say, "Du Bois's vision pointed to a society that could confront, respect, and embrace the gifts of all" (p. 133). His was a critical sociological imagination and prophetic radical democratic vision that neither limited itself to the issues of the white male bourgeoisie nor the white male proletariat, as was the dominant sociological trend of his day, but Du Bois decidedly and solemnly sought to develop "a broad theory of history that concerned itself with" an even broader and bolder conception and "development of democracy and of American culture" (p. 114). Going against the socio-theoretical grain of his times, as Gilkes observes, Du Bois staunchly opposed the "subordination of the problems of gender and race in the development of sociological theory" (p. 117). Hence, here again, Du Bois's critical socio-theoretical framework is distinguished from that of classical European, white American, and Frankfurt School social theorists', who by most accounts relegated race and gender—and, more specifically, *racism* and *sexism*—not merely to the margins, but to intellectual and actual oblivion (see J.C. Alexander, 2001; Alexander, Boudon and Cherkaoui, 1997; Boudon, Cherkaoui and Alexander, 1997; Calhoun, 2002; Ferrarotti, 2003; Giddens, 1971; Hughes, Sharrock and Martin, 2003; Ray, 1999; Roche de Coppens, 1976; K.H. Tucker, 2002; B.S. Turner, 1999). When race and gender did/do register in classical and contemporary Eurocentric "critical" and social theory they are usually seen as social negatives that somehow fell from the sky, as though Europeans (or whites) were not the architects of modern (and postmodern) conceptions and social constructions of race and racism, and as though men were not the masterminds behind, and continue to be the major perpetuators and perpetrators of gender domination and discrimination against women and other gen-der justice-seeking men who embrace and endorse what bell hooks calls, "alterna-tive masculinities" (hooks, 1991; see also Bennett, 2006; Bulmer and Solomos, 1999a, 1999b, 2004; Essed and Goldberg, 2001; Essed, Goldberg and Kobayashi, 2005; Goldberg, 1990; 1993; Goldberg and Solomos, 2002; L. Harris, 1999b; Jain, 2005; P. Miller, 1998; Schloesser, 2002; Solomos, 1988, 1995, 1996; Solomos and Back, 2000; Solomos and Murji, 2005; Solomos and Jenkins, 1987; Walby, 1990).

It was precisely "the problems of gender and race" which Karl Marx, Emile Durkheim and Max Weber—the "three names [that] rank above all others," accord-ing to the esteemed British sociologist Anthony Giddens (1971)—downplayed in their "development of sociological theory" (p. vii; see also Bologh, 1990; Bonilla-Silva, 2001, 2003; Bonilla-Silva and Doane, 2003; Bonilla-Silva and Zuberi, 2008; Di Stephano, 1991, 2008; Lehmann, 1994; McKee, 1993). Du Bois's socio-theoreti-cal framework is distinguished by the fact that it sought solutions to the problems of racism, sexism, and colonialism, while keeping a keen and critical eye on the ways that capitalism defines, deforms and destroys an ever-expanding, all-inclusive transethnic, transgender, and transgenerational democracy. On the prevalence of "the problem of class" in early modern social theory, Gilkes (1996) observes:

> Although issues of class, race, and gender ought to be addressed, most early social the-ory only focused on class and not on gender or race. In spite of its prominence in Amer-ican society, the problem of race relations was not accorded the same theoretical im-portance as were issues centered on class, change, and social structure. Critical theories that assumed the primacy of human action and enterprise in the process of social change often dismissed the issues of race and gender as subordinate to or derived from the problem of class. The result . . . has been a neglect of gender and of racial-ethnic op-pressions. (p. 113)

Because of the sociohistorical fact of their suffering, what black feminist sociolo-gist Deborah King (1995) calls the "multiple jeopardy" of being black, female, poor, and perpetually hyper-sexualized—which, in other words, is to say that black women to varying degrees simultaneously experience and endure racism, sexism, and the ravaging effects of economic exploitation, whether under capitalism or colo-nialism, among other existential issues—Du Bois understood women of African de-scent to be the almost ideal agents of radical social change. In Africana women and their lived-experiences, in their lived-actualities and life-struggles, Du Bois found radical subjects for social change and the spreading of authentic democratic thought and practice. Though rarely referred to, Du Bois's "perspectives on African American women," asserts Gilkes (1996), "anticipated and influenced concepts and ideas we currently use to examine the intersection of gender, race, and class with reference to African American women" (p. 132). She continues, "his work is the earliest self-con-sciously sociological interpretation of the role of African American women as agents of social change" and, therefore, offers modern radical theorists and activists a multi-perspective model on which to build an anti-racist, anti-sexist, anti-colonial and anti-capitalist critical theory of contemporary society (p. 134).

Gilkes reminds us that African American women were an integral part of all three of the "great revolutions" Du Bois prophesied in *Darkwater* which must take place if America (and the wider world) was to truly achieve democracy: the revolution against racism or the color-line; the revolution against sexism, and specifically the subordination of women; and the revolution against economic exploitation, which included both capitalism and colonialism. Here we see most clearly how Du Bois went about confronting and contesting the major and most daunting existential issues of his epoch (and ours): racism, sexism, capitalism, and colonialism. Of the "great revolutions," first, there was the revolt of the masses of colored peoples against colonialism and the color-line. This, of course, translated itself in Du Bois's discourse into his anti-colonial and anti-racist writings in *The Moon, Horizon*, the *Crisis, Phylon*, and *The National Guardian*, amongst other publications, public intellectualism, and radical political activism. Women of African descent were cast in a "messianic" or "prophetic" role in the revolution against racial domination and discrimination, because Du Bois believed their sufferings "provided them with a legitimate voice of challenge" (Gilkes, 1996, p. 120). Who knew then, and who would know now, perhaps more so than any other class of citizens, the deficiencies of U.S. democracy than those persons experiencing and enduring both white *and* male supremacy, as well as capitalist-colonialist economic exploitation? Prefiguring Patricia Hill Collins's notion of "subjugated knowledge," Du Bois attempted to accent and highlight the "hidden" and/or "suppressed" knowledge produced by black women as they confronted, combated, and often contradicted both white and male supremacy (see P.H. Collins, 1990, pp. 3–40, 201–238, 1998, pp. 95–123, 2000, pp. 51–90).

The second "great revolution" that Africana women were to participate in, according to Du Bois (1995a), was the revolution of womanhood. He contended that it was the "new revolutionary ideals" of women, and especially black women, "which must in time have vast influence on the thought and action of this land [i.e., the United States of America]" (p. 311). Here he is clearly drawing from the social theory of several Africana women's liberation theorists of his era: Anna Julia Cooper, Ida B. Wells, Josephine St. Pierre Ruffin, Frances Ellen Watkins Harper, and Maria Stewart, among them. Ever the serious student of African American sociopolitical thought and culture in its totality, Du Bois was keenly conscious of African American women's liberation thought-traditions: from the anti-sexist abolitionism of Maria Stewart, Sojurner Truth and Frances Harper, to the black women's club and civil rights activism of Anna Julia Cooper, Ida B. Wells, Mary Church Terrell, and Mary McLeod Bethune.

Frances Harper in particular was distinguished and deserved recognition, according to Du Bois (1911), on account of her incessant efforts "to forward literature among colored people" (p. 20). Harper, Du Bois epiphatically intoned, was "a worthy member of that dynasty, beginning with the dark Phyllis [Wheatley] in 1773 and coming on down to Dunbar, Chesnutt and Braithwaite of our day" (p. 21). It is highly plausible that Harper's women's liberation theory, and especially her classic 1893 essay, "Woman's Political Future," had an impact on the development of Du Bois's women's rights consciousness when we consider the fact that Harper was a major force in both the black women's club movement and the then burgeoning black literary tradition (see Harper, 1988, 1990, 1994, 2007).[35] It is hard to overlook the similarities in Harper and Du Bois's women's liberation theory, both of which highlight and hinge upon women's character and their distinct moral mission, nationally and internationally. Take the following passage from Harper's (1995) essay, "Woman's Political Future," as an initial example:

Today there are red-handed men in our republic, who walk unwhipped of justice, who richly deserve to exchange the ballot of the freeman for the wristlets of the felon; brutal and cowardly men, who torture, burn, and lynch their fellow-men, men whose defenselessness should be their best defense and their weakness an ensign of protection. More than the changing of institutions we need the development of a national conscience, and the upbuilding of national character. Men may boast of the aristocracy of blood, may glory in the aristocracy of talent, and be proud of the aristocracy of wealth, but there is one aristocracy which must ever outrank them all, and that is the aristocracy of character; and it is the women of a country who help to mold its character, and to influence if not determine its destiny; and in the political future of our nation woman will not have done what she could if she does not endeavor to have our republic stand foremost among the nations of the earth, wearing sobriety as a crown and righteousness as a garment and a girdle. In coming into her political estate woman will find a mass of illiteracy to be dispelled. If knowledge is power, ignorance is also power. The power that educates wickedness may manipulate and dash against the pillars of any state when they are undermined and honeycombed by injustice. (p. 41)

Harper's words help to drive home the point that women, and women of African descent in particular, were believed by many—again, Du Bois among them—to be destined to make great contributions to the deconstruction and radical reconstruction of (American) democracy. Similar to Maria Stewart—who in 1832 queried, "How long shall the fair daughters of Africa be compelled to bury their minds and talents beneath a load of iron pots and kettles?" (M.W. Stewart, 1987, p. 38)— Harper held-fast to the notion that though women were relegated to the home and housework, there would come a time, in a not too distant future, when the ruling race/gender/class would have to come to terms with women's growing sociopolitical power. That power, unlike men's power, would not rest on the "might-makes-right" theses of the Western European social contract tradition (e.g., Jean-Jacques Rousseau, *Discourse on the Origins and Foundations of Inequality*; Thomas Hobbes, *Leviathan*; John Locke, *Two Treatise of Government*; and Immanuel Kant, *The Metaphysics of Morals*), but would revolve around women's contributions to "the development of a national conscience, and the upbuilding of national character."[36] Harper (1995) continues in this vein:

Political life in our country has plowed in muddy channels, and needs the infusion of clearer and cleaner waters. I am not sure that women are naturally so much better than men that they will clear the stream by the virtue of their womanhood; it is not through sex but through character that the best influence of women upon the life of the nation must be exerted.
. . . O women of America! into your hands God has pressed one of the sublimest opportunities that ever came into the hands of the women of any race or people. It is yours to create a healthy public sentiment; to demand justice, simple justice, as the right of every race; to brand with everlasting infamy the lawless and brutal cowardice that lynches, burns, and tortures your own countrymen. (p. 42)

Also a dominant theme in Du Bois's women's decolonization discourse, as we shall soon see, "character" was the cornerstone of Harper's conception of womanhood and it laid at the heart of her women's liberation theory as well. Women would "mold" the country's character, help to "determine its destiny," and "create a healthy public sentiment," not by mimicking the ruling race/gender/class—who so-ciohistorically have been simultaneously racist, sexist and classist—but, by "de-mand[ing] justice, simple justice, as the right of every race."

In *A Voice from the South: By A Black Woman of the South*, published in 1892, the noted Africana women's liberation theorist, Anna Julia Cooper (1998), echoes Harper's contentions of black women's social, political and cultural contributions through their special character by asserting that: "The colored woman of today oc-cupies, one may say, a unique position in this country" (p. 112). She continues, "[i]n a period of itself transitional and unsettled, her status seems one of the least ascertainable and definitive of all the forces which make for our civilization." Where white men in mobs, as Harper alluded to above, had historically "lynch[ed], burn[ed], and torture[d]" their black fellow "countrymen," and where white women and black men had long been vying with one another—in light of the white and male supremacy of the U.S. government—for the right to vote, Cooper maintained that each of the aforementioned ("all of the forces which make for our civilization") could learn many lessons from black women's lived-experiences and liberation thought and practices. Why, we feel compelled to query? Because the black woman "is confronted by both a woman question and a race problem, and is as yet an un-known or a unacknowledged factor in both" (pp. 112–113).[37]

Harper charged women in general with the task of "demand[ing] justice, simple justice, as the right of every race." Cooper, however, took this claim a step further and focused in no uncertain terms on "the BLACK WOMAN," her plight and so-ciopolitical position (p. 63). For Cooper, what distinguished the black (or "col-ored") woman's standpoint from that of white men, white women, and even that of black men, was the sociohistorical fact that she "is confronted by both a woman question and a race problem." In critically engaging racism and sexism, the black woman, the "unknown" and "unacknowledged factor in both," had developed a "unique position," a "peculiar coigne of vantage," which enabled her to "weigh and judge and advise" (p. 114). So, where Harper charged women in general with the task of "demand[ing] justice, simple justice, as the right of every race," Cooper, we could say, charged black women with the task of *demanding justice, simple justice, as the right of every race and both sexes*. On the unique vocation of black women, Cooper wrote:

> What a responsibility then to have the sole management of the primal lights and shad-ows! Such is the colored woman's office. She must stamp weal or woe on the coming history of this people. May she see her opportunity and vindicate her high prerogative. (p. 117)

The majority of black women had long been "thoughtful spectators," standing "aloof from the heated scramble . . . above the turmoil and din of corruption and selfishness." This helped to foster their "unique position," their "peculiar coigne of vantage," which enabled them to critically look at and carefully listen for "the teach-ings of eternal truth and righteousness" rising out of the furious fight for the soul, not simply of America, but the soul of humanity. Cooper continues:

> One needs occasionally to stand aside from the hum and rush of human interests and passions to hear the voices of God. And it not unfrequently [sic] happens that the All-

loving gives a great push to certain souls to thrust them out, as it were, from the distracting current for awhile to promote their discipline and growth, or to enrich them by communion and reflection. And similarly it may be woman's privilege from her peculiar coigne of vantage as a quiet observer, to whisper just the needed suggestion or the almost forgotten truth. The colored woman, then, should not be ignored because her bark is resting in the silent waters of the sheltered cove. She is watching the movements of the contestants none the less and is all the better qualified, perhaps, to weigh and judge and advise because not herself in the excitement of the race. Her voice, too, has always been heard in clear, unfaltering tones, ringing the changes on those deeper interests which make for permanent good. She is always sound and orthodox on questions affecting the well-being of her race. (p. 114)

For Cooper, it was not simply black women's character, but also their "unique [sociohistorical] position" that fostered their moral mission and enabled them to speak their special moral message. This is a point that was not lost on Du Bois, who put his own special spin on this thesis in his classic essay, "The Damnation of Women." Du Bois, as the lionized literary theorist Eric Sundquist (1993) observed, "appears to have absorbed a good deal from others without leaving the fullest accounts of his tutelage" (p. 552). Surely this was the case when it came to Africana women's liberation theory, and Cooper's contributions in specific. For instance, both Joy James (1997) and Charles Lemert (1998) have noted that Cooper and Du Bois met at and participated in the 1900 Pan-African Congress in London and "over the years, had corresponded . . . over several notable race matters" (Lemert, 1998, p. 12; see also A.J. Cooper, 1998, p. 336).

Cooper's woman-centered sociopolitical concepts increasingly crept their way into Du Bois's discourse as he continued to develop his critical theory of contemporary society. In his most sustained offering to Africana women's liberation theory, "The Damnation of Women," Du Bois quoted Cooper's famous "when and where I enter" sentence, but unforgivably failed to mention Cooper by name or to cite the source of the sentence. Du Bois (1995a) wrote:

As one of our women writes: "Only the black women can say 'when and where I enter, in the quiet, undisputed dignity of my womanhood, without violence and without suing or special patronage, then and there the whole Negro race enters with me'." (pp. 304–305)

The unnamed woman writer, and the unacknowledged source of the sentence, in a sense, "allows Cooper to disappear as her words appear," Joy James (1997) convincingly argues (pp. 42–46). This, in turn, renders Cooper anonymous and robs Du Bois's readers of an opportunity not simply to engage Cooper's woman-centered cultural criticism, but also to compare Cooper and Du Bois's women's rights work and social theories, respectively. Cooper's anonymity enables Du Bois and his Africana women's liberation theory to appear as an androgynous or "transgender representative for the entire vilified and oppressed race," James jabs (p. 45). This, to put it plainly, is not only problematic, but helps to demonstrate an instance were Du Bois was intellectually dishonest and, in a way, embraced his "race man" intellectual reputation. He should have given Cooper credit for her ideas and acknowledged her work as his point of departure for this section of his essay. Instead, he did the intellectually (and ethically) inexcusable: He rendered Cooper anonymous and placed himself in the traditional "race man" position of omniscient intellectual-leader and "protector and provider" of black women, those dark damsels in distress, if you will. Indeed, Du Bois did, as Sundquist asserted above, gather "a good deal from others without leaving the fullest accounts of his tutelage." This scenario may actually be even more pronounced when his women's rights work is further critically approached and thoroughly analyzed.

Recall earlier I observed that Du Bois stated, "women of Negro descent . . . are passing through, not only a moral, but an economic revolution." Here Du Bois is, perhaps, following Frances Harper and, surely, Anna Julia Cooper with his emphasis on black women's special moral message and ethical obligation to black liberation. For Du Bois, as it was for Harper and Cooper, it was character that rested at the heart of the moral revolution that women of African descent were bringing into being. Character was one of the many great contributions Africana women were counted on to make to the development and dissemination of democracy in the modern moment. In *Darkwater*, which was written almost a quarter of a century after Harper delivered "Woman's Political Future" and Cooper published *A Voice from the South*, Du Bois (1995a) commented on the character of black women, austerely stating:

> So some few women are born free, and some amid insult and scarlet letters achieve freedom; but our women in black had freedom thrust contemptuously upon them. With that freedom they are buying an untrammeled independence and dear as is the price they pay for it, it will in the end be worth every taunt and groan. Today the dreams of the mothers are coming true. We still have our poverty and degradation, our lewdness and our cruel toil; but we have, too, a vast group of women of Negro blood who for strength of character, cleanness of soul, and unselfish devotion of purpose, is today easily the peer of any group of women in the civilized world. (p. 311)

Here Du Bois defies white and male supremacist notions of womanhood, and constructs what could be termed a part Pan-African, part black nationalist-feminist/womanist version of womanhood. He encouraged "our women in black" to struggle for liberation in both the public and privates spheres (pp. 309–311). Moreover, Du Bois—in the fashion of Cooper's woman-centered sociocultural criticism—thought it important to point out that women of African descent were attempting to grasp and grapple with distinctly different social and political issues than their white counterparts, though both groups of women were discriminated against on account of their gender. Race, racism, and anti-racist struggle made and continues to make distinct differences in the lived-experiences, life-worlds, and liberation theory and praxis of women of African descent, and this is especially true when coupled with their simultaneous struggles for gender justice and an end to economic exploitation. To put it another way, gender *and* racial domination and discrimination, and the theory and praxis developed to combat these oppressions, have and continue to serve as central determining factors in Africana women's lived-experiences and life-worlds, and it is this stubborn socio-historical fact, combined with the contradictions of capitalism and/or colonialism, that have routinely put many Africana women's liberation theorists at loggerheads with the inexcusable racial lethargy and lacunae of ruling race/class feminists and feminism(s) (see, e.g., Alcoff, 1998; Allan, 1995; Bambara, 1970; Caraway, 1991; B. Christian, 1985, 1989, 1994; P.H. Collins,

1993, 1995, 1998, 2000; A.Y. Davis, 1981, 1989, 1998a; Dill, 1979, 1983; Dove, 1998a; Floyd-Thomas, 2006a, 2006b; Guy-Sheftall, 1995; Harley and Terborg-Penn, 1978; hooks, 1981, 1984, 1989, 1990, 1991; Houston and Idriss, 2002; Hudson-Weems, 1997, 1998a, 1998b, 2004; Hull, Scott and Smith, 1982; James and Sharpley-Whiting, 2000; Lorde, 1984, 1988, 1996, 2004; Marsh-Lockett, 1997; Nnaemeka, 1998; L. Phillips, 2006; B. Smith, 1983, 1998; V. Smith, 1998; Steady, 1981; Terborg-Penn, Harley and Rushing, 1987; and Thiam, 1978).

Du Bois seems to have possessed the ability to synthesize disparate discourses into his own somewhat sophisticated critical social theory. For instance, it is interesting to point out that though he initially drew from elite black women's work that cast bourgeoisie black women in leadership roles, work such as that of Anna Julia Cooper and some of the members of the black women's club movement, he continued to deepen and develop his concept(s) of class(ism) and the political economy of race(ism) and sex(ism) (Blair, 1980; Cash, 1986, 2001; Dickson, 1982; Hendricks, 1998; E.B. Higginbotham, 1993; Knupfer, 1996; K.O. T. Miller, 2001; Perkins, 1981, 1997; S.J. Shaw, 1991; Terborg-Penn, 1998; Waters and Conaway, 2007; C.H. Wesley, 1984; D.G. White, 1999). Ultimately, Du Bois developed a critical sociotheoretical framework that transcended and transgressed, if you will, the gender (male) and class (bourgeoisie) elitism of his younger years. Critically comparing Cooper and Du Bois's social theory, Joy James (1997) helps to corroborate my contentions:

> Cooper's gender politics revolved around poor black women's struggles and elite black women's agency. But Du Bois's evolving class politics allowed him to, theoretically, attribute greater agency to *poor* black women workers and laborers. Du Bois's later writings surpass Cooper's 1892 work in democratizing agency. Cooper repudiates masculine elites, or privileged black male intellectuals. However, her repudiations do not extend to feminine elites, or privileged black female intellectuals. Cooper countered the dominance of male elites with that of female elites and remained somewhat oblivious of the limitations of her caste and class-based ideology. Cooper's 1892 book [*A Voice from the South*] failed to argue that the intellectual and leadership abilities of black women laborers equaled those of black women college graduates, whereas Du Bois's later revisions of the Talented Tenth included nonelite black women and men. In this respect, we see that Du Bois's maturing politics were less hampered by the cultural conservatism of bourgeois notions of respectability for (black) women. (p. 45, emphasis in original; see also May, 2007; Rabaka, 2008a)

It is not my intention here to (re)interpret and (re)inscribe Du Bois as some sort of super anti-sexist social theorist, which he, if the truth be told, and simply said, was not. I am well aware of the ways that an anti-sexist male perspective in a male supremacist society is not as suspect as an anti-sexist female perspective—though I would concede that an anti-sexist male perspective *is* suspect to a certain degree, and that gender progressive males are marginalized and ostracized in such a social world, though they have never been marginalized and ostracized to the extent to which (anti-sexist) women have historically been in the said social world. However, and in all intellectual honesty, an anti-sexist male (with the most minute amount of academic credentials and/or institutional affiliation) can quickly become, in the minds of the ruling race/gender/class and their media machines in a male supremacist social world, an authoritative anti-sexist "voice of reason." This, of course, is similar in many senses to the ways that white "race traitors" and white anti-racists are exalted as the definitive voices of anti-racist reason and radical anti-racist political practice in white supremacist society. Du Bois's discourse destabilizes and resists efforts to position him purely (and, disingenuously I believe) as "race man," or "male-feminist"/"male-womanist," or "Marxist," or "Pan-Africanist," or "black nationalist," or even "integrationist," because—as I stated above—he continuously deepened and developed the basic concepts and categories of his socio-theoretical framework and synthesized disparate discourses into his own original critical theory of contemporary society.

To read "The Conservation of Races," *The Souls of Black Folk*, *Darkwater* and *Dusk of Dawn* is to read not merely studies in race, but also studies in class and caste. To read *Black Reconstruction*, *Color and Democracy* and *The World and Africa* is not simply to read studies in race, caste and class, but also studies in Pan-Africanism and anti-colonialism. And, finally, when "The Damnation of Women," "The Work of Negro Women in Society," "The Black Mother," "Suffering Suffragettes," "Hail Columbia!," "The Burden of Black Women" and "Sex and Racism" are read, what one is reading are not just studies in race and class theory, but also critical analyses of gender domination and discrimination, and especially as these overlapping, interlocking and intersecting systems of violence, oppression, and exploitation effect the life-worlds and lived-experiences of black women. It is the multidimensionality of Du Bois's discourse that makes it difficult for opportunistic interpreters to appropriate and (re)articulate his thought and texts in a monodimensional manner. Moreover, it is this same multidimensionality in Du Bois's discourse that provides paradigmatic examples of some of the ways male anti-sexist social theorists can simultaneously avoid being appropriated as "the" authoritative and most rational voices of gender justice, and connect critiques of sexism with those of racism and classism.

If male anti-sexist social theorists openly and honestly dialogue with, document and disseminate the community and campus work of female anti-sexist social theorists, then, it will be very hard for male supremacist media machines to project the gender progressive male voice as the definitive voice of gender justice. Critically engaging women's liberation theory and practice by actively participating in the said theory and practice, male anti-sexist social theorists can and should expand the range and use(s) of women's liberation theory and other anti-sexist social theory to include the work of both women *and* men who sought and are actively seeking gender justice. Male anti-sexist social theorists must simultaneously (re)claim and (re)construct male anti-sexist, gender justice, and women's liberation theory and praxis traditions, and share the knowledge they discover and create with gender justice-seeking women and men. In fact, one of the special tasks of anti-sexist men is to encourage our brother-friends to critically examine ways that they embrace patriarchy and perpetuate and exacerbate sexism and female domination and discrimination. Male anti-sexist social theorists and activists are long overdue in articulating to sexist men the violent psychological and physical consequences of male supremacist thought and behavior, and how, as quiet as it is kept, this thought and behavior not only robs women of their human and civil rights, but also often causes serious life-threatening conflicts and contradictions among men.

What I am calling for here is for anti-sexist men to unflinchingly encourage sexist men to self-consciously confront and correct their sexist socialization and sexist thought and behavior. Anti-sexist men must embrace the revolutionary responsibility of providing new paradigms for modern masculinity. We must show the world, and especially women, our sister-friends, that patriarchal, phallocentric, militaristic and misogynistic masculinity are not definitive practices or modes of masculinity but deformations and destructions of masculinity. Masculinity, henceforth and forevermore, must be predicated on moral practice. What it means to be a "man" must begin to be bound up with males' embrace of the ethical obligation to end female domination and discrimination and their promotion of women's decolonization, women's liberation, and radical anti-sexist social reorganization.

Africana male anti-sexist social theorists and activists must be bold enough and brave enough to take our cue from our anti-sexist forefathers, men (dare I say, "father figures") like Charles Lenox Remond, Frederick Douglass, and W. E. B. Du Bois, among others, who—as I have earnestly endeavored to illustrate above—possessed problematic but nonetheless progressive stances on gender justice and, specifically, Africana women's decolonization and liberation. However, and even more than turning to the anti-sexist thought and practice traditions of our forefathers, anti-sexist men of African descent must humbly learn the many lessons our freedom fighting foremothers' legacies of liberation thought and practice have to teach. This impulse to learn radical life-saving and life-enhancing lessons from our foremothers must also extend to the thought, texts and practices of anti-sexist Africana women in our present age. A common characteristic of both black feminist and womanist discourse is the notion that theory and practice must simultaneously speak to the special needs of women of African descent *and* the emancipatory aspirations of African people (which includes black men) nationally and internationally. This means, then, that (most) modern black feminists and womanists do not adhere to the constraints of European and European American constructions of gender and/or sex roles. The only "role" we, women and men of African descent, have is that of resilient black revolutionaries: radical anti-racist, anti-sexist, anti-colonialist, and anti-capitalist rebels and renegades.

C. L. R. James was certainly a radical, though his work is probably weakest when and where we come to the problems of patriarchy and sexist sentiment among black men, especially black male radicals. He was a pioneering Pan-African Marxist who innovatively deepened and developed many of the themes found in Du Bois's discourse—again, Du Bois's contributions to women's decolonization and liberation theory withstanding. James is correctly considered one of the major "most-underrated" and "most-sophisticated" Marxist social theorists of the twentieth century, but curiously his work has had, at best, a lukewarm and generally lethargic reception, ironically, especially amongst Africana Studies scholars and students. Part of the problem has to do with the sprawling nature of his *oeuvre*, and the maverick manner in which he researched, wrote, raised critical consciousness, and participated in radical politics. The following chapter critically engages James's contributions to the Africana tradition of critical theory by examining his unique synthesis of Pan-Africanism and Marxism during his initial intellectual history-making decade-long sojourn in the United States, from 1938 to 1948. It was during this period that James made his most lasting early contributions to, not simply Pan-Africanism and Marxism, but also to the African American struggle for human and civil rights, as well as black radical politics in the United States. Let us now, therefore, leave the discourse on W. E. B. Du Bois and begin what promises to be a beguiling journey into the radical politics and polymathy of C. L. R. James.

## NOTES

1.  With regard to what I am referring to as "the contemporary Du Bois renaissance," I have in mind not only the plethora of recent reprints by Du Bois, but also David Levering Lewis's Pulitzer Prize-winning volumes and the spate of works in Du Boisia that preceded those texts and closed the twentieth and opened the twenty-first centuries. See, for example, Andrews (1985), Bloom (2001), Blum (2007), Byerman (1994), Durr (2001), Horne (1986), B.L. Johnson (2008), Juguo (2001), D.L. Lewis (1993, 2000), Marable (1986), Reed (1997), Wolters (2001) and Zamir (1995, 2008). A number of noteworthy doctoral dissertations were produced during this period as well, see Alridge (1997), Braley (1994), Chandler (1997), W.A. Drake (1985), Drummer (1995), Edelin (1981), B.S. Edwards (2001), Gabbidon (1996), Greco (1984), Higbee (1995a), Hwang (1988), Makang (1993), Meade (1987), P.L. Moore (1998), H.J. Morrison (2000), T.R. Neal (1984), Nwankwo (1989), Okoro (1982), Quainoo (1993), N. Warren (1984), J.M. Wortham (1997), W.D. Wright (1985) and Yuan (1998). There were also several conferences on and commemorations and centennial celebrations of his books and classic essays which rekindled intellectual and politic interest in Du Bois, see Anderson and Zuberi (2000), Bell, Grosholz and Stewart (1996), Crouch and Benjamin (2002), Fontenot (2001), and Katz and Sugrue (1998). Moreover, many of Du Bois's speeches and his audio autobiography have been recently reissued on compact disc, see Du Bois (1960a, 1960b, 2000c). Finally, curiosity concerning Du Bois's long buried radical legacy has been revived by two documentaries produced in the last decade of the twentieth century, see Baulding (1992) and Massiah (1995). The Massiah documentary is far superior to the Baulding production and is considered the definitive work in this genre, but Baulding paints a more nuanced picture of Du Bois's early years, family life and initial intellectual formation. Taken along with the aforementioned studies, dissertations, conference proceedings and compact discs, these documentaries (which both aired on PBS multiple times) have brought Du Bois back to intellectual life and introduced him to yet another youthful generation of social justice seekers.

2.  For a more detailed discussion of Du Bois's life and work, see first and foremost his own adventures in autobiography: "The Celebration of My Twenty-fifth Birthday," *The Souls of Black Folk*, "Credo," "I Am Resolved," *Darkwater: Voices from Within the Veil*, "So the Girl Marries," "On Being Ashamed of Oneself: An Essay on Race Pride," *A Pageant in Seven Decades, 1868-1938*, *Dusk of Dawn: An Essay Toward an Autobiography of a Race Concept*, "My Evolving Program for Negro Freedom," "My Golden Wedding," "I Bury My Wife," "I Take My Stand," *In Battle for Peace: The Story of My 83rd Birthday*, "A Vista of Ninety Fruitful Years," "My Last Message to the World," "To an American Born Last Christmas Day," "Advice to a Great-Grandson," "A Negro Student at Harvard at the End of the Nineteenth Century," *W. E. B. Du Bois: A Recorded Autobiography*, and *The Autobiography of W. E. B. Du Bois: A Soliloquy on Viewing My Life from the Last Decade of Its First Century* (see Du Bois, 1938, 1952, 1960a, 1968a, 1968b, 1969a, 1969b, 1970d, 1985a, 1997a). One should also consult his posthumously published, *Against Racism: Unpublished Essays, Papers, Addresses, 1887–1961*, and the three-volume collection of his correspondence, *The Correspondence of W. E. B. Du Bois, 1877–1963* (Du Bois, 1985a, 1997b, 1997c, 1995a, 1997d). Also, helpful in this regard are several secondary sources which often reveal more about various trends and traditions in Africana social and political theory and praxis as they do Du Bois's intellectual development and biography, see, for example, Broderick (1955, 1958a, 1958b, 1959, 1974), Cain (1990a), Chandler (1997), Clarke, Jackson, Kraiser, and O'Dell (1970), W.A. Davis (1974), DeMarco (1974), S.C. Drake

(1986/87), W.A. Drake (1985), Drummer (1995), Durr (2001), Franklin (1995), Golden and Milikan (1966), Guzman (1961), Higbee (1995b), Katznelson (1999), Lester (1971), D.L. Lewis (1993, 2000, 2008), R.W. Logan (1971), Marable (1985a, 1986, 1996, 1998), J.B. Moore (1981), Moses (1975, 1978b, 1993a, 1996, 1998), Rampersad (1990), Reed (1985, 1997), Rudwick (1956, 1960, 1968, 1982a), Stuckey (1987), Sundquist (1993, 1996), Tuttle (1957, 1973), J. Tyner (1997), Walden (1966, 1977), R. Williams (2001), Wolters (2001), F. Woodard (1976), and Zamir (1995, 2008).

3. With regard to Anthony Appiah's (1992) assault on Du Bois's philosophy of race, his "The Uncompleted Argument: Du Bois and the Illusion of Race," originally published in *Critical Inquiry* in 1985, was revised, re-titled, and reprinted as "Illusions of Race," in his *In My Father's House: Africa in the Philosophy of Culture* (pp. 28–46). In "Race, Culture, Identity: Misunderstood Connections," Appiah (1996) amends some his argument(s) against Du Bois's so-called "socio-historical" conception of race, and claims that Du Bois was up to much more than he, Appiah, had initially realized. For hard-hitting critiques of Appiah's criticisms of Du Bois's concepts of race and critiques of racism, see Patrick Goodin's "Du Bois and Appiah: The Politics of Race and Racial Identity" (2002), Paul C. Taylor's "Appiah's Uncompleted Argument: W. E. B. Du Bois and the Reality of Race" (2000), and Lucius Outlaw's legendary and heatedly debated "defense" of Du Bois, "'Conserve' Races?: In Defense of W. E. B. Du Bois" (1996b). Further, for a vociferous yet not vicious critique of Du Bois, Appiah and Outlaw's discourse and debates on Du Bois, race, culture and identity, see Robert Gooding-Williams's "Outlaw, Appiah, and Du Bois's 'The Conservation of Races'"(1996). Concerning the claim that Du Bois may very well be "just another over-engaged 'race man' posthumously positioned as a radical theorist," see the concluding section of the present chapter where I discuss the disingenuousness and difficulties of reading a multidimensional theorist such as Du Bois from a one-dimensional frame of reference.

4. For more on the provocative discourse of critical race feminism, please see Wing (1997, 2000).

5. For further discussion of Du Bois's concept(s) of colonialism's "common characteristics," see Du Bois (1930a, 1930b, 1945, 1958, 1961a, 1965, 1968b, 1970a).

6. In light of the fact that many, if not most, of the formerly colonized countries remain under some mutated and/or (post)modern form of colonialism, Amilcar Cabral's assertions concerning *classical colonialism* as "direct domination," and *neocolonialism* as "indirect domination" help to highlight and accent a bitter and brutal truth: We—meaning formerly and currently colonized people—are not in a *post*colonial period, which is to say that we are not in a period *after* colonialism when and where we understand colonialism as Cabral (1979) did: as interlocking and intersecting systems of racial and gender domination and discrimination and economic exploitation (p. 128). In fact, at this point it seems safe to say that we are actually in a transitional stage/state between a now-aging colonial era and an emerging postcolonial era that remains to be adequately conceptualized, charted, and mapped. This point will be discussed in greater detail in the subsequent paragraphs. For other examples of works which question and confront the "post" in "postcolonial," see Appiah (1992), McClintock (1992, 1995), McClintock, Mufti, and Shobat (1997), During (1987), Mishra and Hodge (1991), Lazarus (2004), Loomba (1998), Olaniyan (1992, 2000), Parry (1987, 2004), Rattansi (1997), Sadar (1998), San Juan (1998), and Shohat (1993, 1998). Cabral's conception of colonialism will be discussed further very briefly below and, then, more fully in chapter 6 of the present volume.

7. Tejumola Olaniyan also addresses this issue in "Narrativizing Postcoloniality" (1992).

8. For a fuller discussion and other corroborating claims, see Prakash (1995) and Rajan and Mohanran (1995).

9. As with Fanon in *The Wretched of the Earth* (see chapter 1: "Concerning Violence"), Cabral's concept of violence extends well-beyond the realm of physical violation and encompasses those psychological factors and forces that inhibit human wholeness, critical

self-consciousness, and free and full development. Which, in other words, is to say that the ethical and justificatory hub and hinge of Cabral's concept of violence is a struggling peoples' right to *self-definition, self-determination,* and *self-defense.* For further discussion, see Bienen (1977), Blackey (1974), Chabal (1981a, 1983), Chilcote (1968, 1991), McCollester (1973), McCulloch (1983b), Taiwo (1999a, 1999b), and Serequeberhan (1994), as well as chapter 6 of the present volume.

10. See, for instance, Du Bois (1945, 1968b, 1999), Fanon (1967, 1968), Guevara (1968), and Marcuse (1969a, 1972a). On national liberation, see Fanon, "The Pitfalls of National Consciousness" and "On National Culture," both in *The Wretched of the Earth* (1968); Fanon, "Decolonization and Independence" and "Unity and Effective Solidarity are the Conditions for African Liberation," both in *Toward the African Revolution* (1969); Nkrumah, *Towards Colonial Freedom* (1962), *Consciencism: Philosophy and Ideology for Decolonization* (1964), *Neo-Colonialism: The Last Stage of Imperialism* (1965), *Africa Must Unite* (1970a), *Class Struggle in Africa* (1970b), *Revolutionary Path* (1973a), and *The Struggle Continues* (1973b); Cabral, "National Liberation and Peace: Cornerstones of Non-Alignment," "The National Movements of the Portuguese Colonies," and "The Development of the Struggle," all in *Revolution in Guinea* (1972); Cabral, "National Liberation and Culture" and "Identity and Dignity in the Context of National Liberation Struggle," both in *Return to the Source* (1973); Cabral, "Presuppositions and Objectives of National Liberation in Relation to Social Structure," in *Unity and Struggle* (1979); and Chabal, "National Liberation in Portuguese Guinea, 1956-1974" (1981b).

11. For critical discussions of Pan-African theory and praxis, see Axelsen (1984), English and Kalumba (1996), Esedebe (1994), Geiss (1974), Langley (1973, 1979), Serequeberhan (1994), V. B. Thompson (1969), and Walters (1993). And, for discussions of Pan-Africanism that details Du Bois's position as doyen of this discourse, see Contee (1969a, 1969b, 1971, 1972), Efrat (1967), Gbadegesin (1996), Gershoni (1995), Martin and Yeakey (1982), R. B. Moore (1970), Rabaka (2005a), Recht (1971), Reed (1975, 1997), Rogers (1955), and Romero (1976).

12. For further discussion, see Du Bois (1945, 1958, 1965), Ashcroft, Griffiths, and Tiffin (1989, p. 2), Loomba (1998, p. 12), Cook and Henderson (1969), Drachler (1975), J. E. Harris (1993), Lemelle and Kelley (1994), V. B. Thompson (1987), Von Eschen (1997), and Walters (1993).

13. For a discussion, see Alva (1995) and Ashcroft, Griffiths and Tiffin (1989, pp. 11-12). On postmodern conceptions of history and the history of ideas, see Appleby, Covington, Hoyt, Latham, and Snieder (1996). And, for strong critiques of Eurocentrism and other linear conceptions of human history, see Abu-Lughod (1991), Chatterjee (1993), Blaut (1993), Gran (1996), M. Keita (2000), Shohat and Stam (1994), and Wallerstein (1974, 1979, 1980a, 1980b, 1981, 1983, 1984, 1989, 1991a, 2004, 2006).

14. My interpretation of (white) Marxism here and throughout this chapter has been primarily drawn from several "Hegelian" or "Western" Marxist works, as well as a few of the more philosophy-focused texts in Marxist studies, see P. Anderson (1976), N. S. Arnold (1990), Aronson (1995), P. Buhle (1991), Callari, Cullenberg and Biewener (1995), Castoriadis (1991, 1997), Gottlieb (1989, 1992), Gouldner (1980), Hindess (1993), Howard (1972, 1988), Howard and Klare (1972), Jacoby (1981), Jameson (1971, 1975, 1979a, 1979b, 1990), Jay (1984, 1985a), Kellner (1989, 1995), Kelly (1982), Kolakowski (1978a, 1978b, 1978c), Leonhard (1971), Lichtheim (1965, 1966), Marcuse (1960, 1967, 1970b), Nelson and Grossberg (1988), and Therborn (1996).

15. For a discussion socialism's fluidity and malleability throughout the twentieth century, and especially at the century's end, see Aronson (1995), Boggs (1982, 1995), Callari, Cullenberg and Biewener (1995), Castoriadis (1988a, 1998b, 1993), Cole (1953, 1955, 1957, 1959, 1960), Ferguson (1998), Laclau and Mouffe (1985, 1987), Magnus and Cullenberg (1995), Marcuse (1965a, 1965b), Nelson and Grossberg (1988), and Self (1993).

16. For further discussion of black Marxism and black Marxists' relationship with the white critics of capitalism and white Marxism, see Bogues (1983), O.C. Cox (1959, 1987), Cruse (1967, 2002), A.Y. Davis (1998a), C. L. R. James (1992, 1994, 1996a), Kelley (1990, 1994, 2002), Marable (1985a, 1987, 1996), C.W. Mills (2003a), Mullen (2002), Outlaw (1983a, 1983b, 1987), Serequeberhan (1990), Rabaka (2007a, 2008a), C.J. Robinson (2000), and West (1988b, 1993a, 1999). And, for analyses of the Trinidadian triumvirate, among other African Caribbean intellectuals' communion with Marxism, see Bogues (2003), Boodhoo (1986, 2001), Cateau and Carrington (2000), Deosaran (1981), Hennessey (1992), P. Henry (2000), W. James (1998), W.A. Lewis (1994), McAuley (2004), Palmer (2006), and Solow and Engerman (1987).

17. My claims here, and much of my interpretation of Du Bois's socialism and relationship to Marxism has been critically culled from two excellent, though ultimately flawed, unpublished doctoral dissertations, among several other sources cited in the text. See, William Wright's "The Socialist Analysis of W. E. B. Du Bois" (1985) and Ji Yuan's "W. E. B. Du Bois and His Socialist Thought" (1998). Because these works are extended studies that focus exclusively on Du Bois's democratic socialist thought they offer students of Du Bois's democratic socialism some of the best criticisms available of his ever-increasing radicalism, and a long overdue look at the myriad meanings of Marxism, socialism, and communism in twentieth century black radical discourse. My analysis here has also benefited from my colleague Joseph DeMarco's contributions to Du Bois studies, "The Rationale and Foundation of Du Bois's Theory of Economic Cooperation" (1974) and, of course, his classic *The Social Thought of W. E. B. Du Bois* (1983).

18. With regard to the "roughly thirty years" of Du Bois's critical writings on socialism, Marxism, and radical thought (including his labor studies) that many Du Bois scholars have had a tendency to pass over in order to get to *Black Reconstruction*, see, for instance: "Socialist of the Path," "The Negro and Socialism," "The Economic Aspects of Race Prejudice," "The Economics of Negro Emancipation in the United States," "Socialism Is Too Narrow For Negroes," "A Field for Socialists," "Socialism and the Negro Problem," "The Problem of Problems," "Brothers, Come North," "Of Work and Wealth," "Of the Ruling of Men," "The Social Equality of Blacks and Whites," "Socialism and the Negro," "The Negro and Radical Thought," "Class Struggle," "Communists Boring into Negro Labor," "Russia, 1926," "The Denial of Economic Justice to Negroes," "The American Federation of Labor and the Negro," "The Negro and Communism," "Communists and the Color Line," "Socialism in England," "Karl Marx and the Negro," "Marxism and the Negro Problem," "The U.S. Will Come to Communism," "Where Do We Go From Here?: An Essay on the Negroes' Economic Plight," "The Present Economic Problem of the American Negro," and "A Negro Nation Within the Nation." My interpretation and reconstruction of Du Bois's concept of democratic socialism, and critique of capitalism and Marxism, as well as my general argument here, derives in part from careful and critical investigation of these extremely important articles and essays (see Du Bois 1965, 1970c, 1970d, 1971a, 1971b 1985a, 1986a, 1995a, 1996a).

19. Similar to Moses (1978, p. 138), who contends that Du Bois "became a socialist by gradual stages," Marable (1986) argues:

> Du Bois's introduction to Marxism and socialism was extremely fragmentary. At Harvard, Marx's work was briefly discussed, "but only incidentally and as one whose doubtful theories had long since been refuted," Du Bois wrote later. "Socialism as dream of philanthropy or as will-o-wisp of hotheads was dismissed as unimportant." At [the University of] Berlin, Karl Marx was mentioned, only to point out how thoroughly his theses had been disproven; of his theory itself almost nothing was said." Only at Atlanta University did Du Bois begin to acquaint himself with writings by socialists and radical liberals. . . . In the second issue of the *Horizon*, in February 1908, Du Bois stated that he considered himself a "Socialist-of-the-Path." Du Bois had certain misgivings about the Socialist party, but still believed that "the socialist trend" represented the "one great hope of the

Negro American." As the Socialist party acquired a mass following, Du Bois monitored its progress as an ally to the democratic struggles of blacks. In February 1908, Du Bois advised readers of the *Horizon* that "the only party today which treats Negroes as men, North and South, are the Socialists." (p. 89)

From the foregoing it seems clear that even Du Bois's early relationship with Marxism was critical, complex, and extremely complicated. Similar to the thought of many black radicals, Du Bois's radical ruminations cannot easily and one-dimensionally be characterized as Marxist, or "black Marxist" because, as we will soon see, his thought routinely re-theorized Marxist class theory by combining it with a critical race component, and by emphasizing racial strife within the working class. At times in Du Bois's later discourse race simply was not as central as many black nationalist and other race-centered theorists would like. But, it would be difficult for these theorists to argue that race occupies a secondary or tertiary position in his critical socio-theoretical framework. Race and racism were consistent foci of his discourse, but as his thinking evolved, and he identified capitalism and sexism as oppressive systems that overlap, intersect and interlock with racism, each system was often simultaneously engaged. It is the simultaneity (and, I should add, the transdisciplinary nature) of Du Bois's engagement of these overlapping, interlocking and intersecting oppressive systems that misleads many Du Bois scholars and critics into arguing that in his later years he privileged class over race. This issue does not arise as much where Du Bois's discourse on colonialism is concerned because of the overt racially oppressive character of colonialism (hence, *racial colonialism*) in continental and diasporan African modernity.

20. For further discussion of McKay, his poetic imagination, literary prowess, and radical politics, see W.F. Cooper (1982, 1987), Gayle (1972), Giles (1976), Gosciak (2006), Holcomb (2007), W. James (2000, 2003), C. McKay (1953, 1968, 1970, 1973, 1998, 2004), A.L. McLeod (1992), Ramesh (2006), and Tillery (1992).

21. In *Black Folk: Then and Now* and *The World and Africa*, Du Bois made a few cursory remarks concerning "cooperative movements in Africa" and "West African collectivism" that emphasized communist and socialist sentiments in ancient and pre-colonial Africa (i.e., before Karl Marx was born and Europe made colonial contact). He believed that contemporary communist and socialist societies could learn many valuable lessons from classical African social organization, politics, and economics because in ancient Africa, to speak very generally, each of these systems was interrelated and stressed collectivism over individualism. The contention that Africa's past possibly offers us useful paradigms to improve our *Africana* present has been echoed recently by the Ghanaian philosopher, Kwasi Wiredu (1991), who asserted, "the philosophical thought of a traditional (i.e., preliterate and nonindustrialized) society may hold some lessons of moral significance for a more industrialized society" (p. 98). However, Du Bois was not completely nostalgic about ancient Africa and proved to be a harsh critic where ruling classes privileged their personal or familial wants and whims over the vital needs of the masses. For further discussion, see Du Bois (1939, pp. 296–299, 1965, pp. 160–161). Widely considered "the father of Pan-Africanism," Du Bois's accent on ancient African communist and socialist sentiment was extremely influential on several of the mid-twentieth century pioneer Pan-Africanists; particularly Kwame Nkrumah, who, along with Sekou Toure and Julius Nyerere, went the furthest (theoretically and practically) in terms of developing a distinctly African version of socialism that purported to be loosely based on classical African social organization and political systems. An astute statesman and theoretician, Nyerere went so far to dub his "definition of socialism in Tanzanian terms," *Ujamaa*, which essentially means "familyhood," to emphasize Africans' filial connections to each other and all humanity. On Nkrumah, Nyerere, and Toure's Pan-African socialism, see Nkrumah (1964, 1965, 1970a, 1970b, 1973a, 1973b), Nyerere (1966, 1968, 1969,1970, 1973, 1974, 1977, 1978), and Toure (1959, 1972, 1973, 1974, 1975, 1976, 1977, 1978, 1979, 1980).

22. For a discussion, see Du Bois's post-*Black Reconstruction* radical writings: "Lifting from the Bottom," "A Social Program for Black and White Americans," "A Program of Organization for Realizing Democracy in the United States by Securing to Americans of Negro Descent the Full Rights of Citizens," "My Evolving Program for Negro Freedom," "The Negro and Imperialism," "Behold the Land," "Socialism," "A Petition to the Human Rights Commission of the Social and Economic Council of the United Nations; and to the General Assembly of the United Nations; and to Several Delegations of the Member States of the United Nations," "There Must Come a Vast Social Change in the United States," "Address at the American Labor Party Election," "Negroes and the Crisis of Capitalism in the United States," "Colonialism and the Russian Revolution," "Ethiopia: State Socialism Under An Emperor," "The Stalin Era," "Socialism and Democracy," "Negroes and Socialism," "A Future for Pan-Africa: Freedom, Peace, Socialism," "The Future of All Africa Lies In Socialism," "The Negro and Socialism," "The Dream of Socialism," "The Vast Miracle of China Today," "Socialism and the American Negro," *Socialism Today*, "Whither Now and Why," and "Application for Membership in the Communist Party of the United States of America" (see Du Bois, 1965, 1970c, 1970d, 1971a, 1971b 1985a, 1986a, 1995a, 1996a). One of the best studies of Du Bois's later years, particularly the period after the second European world war (i.e., "World War II"), was researched and written by the acclaimed African American radical historian Gerald Horne, *Black and Red: W. E. B. Du Bois and the Afro-American Response to the Cold War, 1944–1963* (1986), which I have relied on heavily here to develop my argument.

23. One of Du Bois's best statements on black self-defense against white supremacist violence is his classic September 1919 *Crisis* essay, "Let Us Reason Together." In the essay he exploded in moral outrage in the aftermath of a heated six-month period of violent racial conflict, which James Weldon Johnson famously referred to as the "Red Summer of 1919." During this nadir in U.S. race relations more than twenty-five cities and small towns erupted in white supremacist and anti-black racist violence. Black blood flowed in the streets, not simply in Southern cities, but also in Chicago and Washington D.C., the nations' capital! Where Claude McKay captured the wrathful and resilient mood of the masses of black folk in his protest poem, "If We Must Die," similarly Du Bois (1971b) decidedly summoned blacks to defend themselves in "Let Us Reason Together," thundering:

> Brothers, we are on the Great Deep. We have cast off on the vast voyage which will lead to Freedom or Death. For three centuries we have suffered and cowered. No race ever gave Passive Resistance and Submission to Evil longer, more piteous trial. Today we raise the terrible weapon of Self-Defense. When the murderer comes, he shall no longer strike us in the back. When the armed lynchers gather, we too must gather armed. When the mob moves, we propose to meet it with bricks and clubs and guns. But we must tread here with solemn caution. We must never let justifiable self-defense against individuals become blind and lawless offense against all white folk. We must not seek reform by violence. We must not seek vengeance. "Vengeance is Mine," saith the Lord; or to put it otherwise, only Infinite Justice and Knowledge can assign blame in this poor world, and we ourselves are sinful men, struggling desperately with our homes, our wives and children against the lawless stint or hesitation; but we must carefully and scrupulously avoid on our own part bitter and unjustifiable aggression against anybody. (pp. 14–15)

Here, Du Bois not only foreshadows and lays a foundation for many of the central themes of the Civil Rights and Black Power movements, but he also displays an ability to articulate black anger and outrage in a rational and morally mature manner. Both Martin Luther King, Jr., and Malcolm X would later echo aspects of the argument Du Bois laid out above, each taking elements of the ideas in their own distinct direction. The main point that I want to place emphasis on here has to do with Du Bois's advocacy of black self-defense and the fact that more like Malcolm X (especially in his later years), and unlike King or Bayard Rustin, Du Bois was not unerringly wedded to any specific social strategy or political tactic (e.g., passive resistance, civil disobediance, and/or non-violence). He was consistently open to using what he understood to be the best plans of defense and social survival thought and practices available to blacks in white supremacist capitalist society. An additional issue that distinguishes Du Bois's critical social theorizing stems from his constant coupling of diverse and disparate (Africana *and*, much to the chagrin of many black nationalists, European) radical thought-traditions: from Pan-Africanism to Pragmatism, Marxism to Feminism, and Black Nationalism to German Romanticism (see Anderson and Zuberi, 2000; Aptheker, 1989; Beck, 1996; Bell, Grosholz and Stewart, 1996; Berman, 1997; Boxill, 1996; Broderick, 1958b, 1959, 1974; Cain, 1993; Clarke, Jackson, Kaiser, O'Dell, 1970; W.A. Drake, 1985; Gilroy, 1993a; J.A. James, 1997; Meier, 1959, 1963; Moses, 1975, 1978, 1998; Rabaka, 2007a, 2008a; Rampersad, 1990; Reed, 1997; Rudwick, 1960, 1968, 1982; Sundquist, 1993; West, 1989, 1996; Zamir, 1994, 1995, 2008).

24. Du Bois's most noteworthy studies of lynching and mob violence are: "Race Friction Between Black and White," "A Litany of Atlanta," "Agitation," "Does Race Antagonism Serve Any Good Purpose?," "Lynching," "The Lynching Industry," "Houston," "The Massacre of East St. Louis," "Rape," "Let Us Reason Together," "Jim Crow," "The Technique of Race Prejudice," "The Tragedy of Jim Crow," "A University Course in Lynching," "Lynchings," "Mob Tactics," "Lynchings," "Violence," and "Prospects of a World Without Race Conflict" (see, Du Bois, 1970c, 1971b, 1983a, 1983b, 1986a). On the U.S. legacy of lynching and anti-black racist violence and, more generally, Du Bois's place in this discourse, see Charles A. Frye's *Values in Conflict: Blacks and the American Ambivalence Toward Violence* (1980) and Herbert Shapiro's watershed work *White Violence and Black Response: From Reconstruction to Montgomery* (1988).

25. For a discussion of Du Bois's philosophy of social science and social scientific methodology, see Du Bois (1978, 1996b, 2004), Anderson and Zuberi (2000), Bulmer (1991), Burbridge (1999), Dennis (1975), Edelin (1981), B.S. Edwards (2001), Everage (1979), K.K. Gaines (1996), Gilkes (1996), Gordon (2000b, 2000c), D.S. Green (1973), A.L. Johnson (1949), A.J. Jones (1976), Juguo (2001), Katz and Sugrue (1998), Larue (1971), McDaniel (1998), T.R. Neal (1984), Outlaw (2000), Reed (1997), Rudwick (1969, 1974), C.M. Taylor (1981), E. Wright (2001) and Zamir (1995, 2008).

26. On Du Bois and his "race man" reputation, see Carby (1998).

27. Some may find Guy-Sheftall's (re)construction of Du Bois as a male-"feminist" troubling. However, as Hazel Carby (1998) contends, it should be held in mind that Du Bois means "many things to many people" (p. 14). He is one of the many male and female "rediscovered ancestors" whose thought and texts are currently being engaged by contemporary theorists "in response to the needs of various agendas," academic and otherwise (p. 14). Where Guy-Sheftall (1990) and McKay (1990) read Du Bois as a male-"feminist," Joy James (1996b, 1997) proffered a "pro-feminist" Du Bois. More recently, Gary Lemons (2001) argued that Du Bois's pro-women's rights and women's suffrage work can actually be read as both "black feminist" *and* "womanist." It is not the intention of this section to argue whether Du Bois was a "womanist" or a "feminist"—two terms, it should be pointed out, that were not *en vogue* in Africana intellectual arenas until well-after his death. The primary purpose here is to discover what implications Du Bois's pro-women's rights and women's suffrage work has for the development of an anti-racist, anti-sexist, anti-capitalist, and anti-colonial critical theory of contemporary society, what I am currently calling Africana critical theory. Therefore, this section, as well as this study in general, will draw from the women's decolonization and women's liberation theory of a wide-range of women *and* men of African descent who self-describe and self-define themselves as: "womanists," "Africana womanists," "black feminists," and "African feminists," among other nomenclature (see A.Y. Davis, 1998a; hooks, 1991, 1984, 2000b; Hudson-Weems, 1998b, 1998c, 2001a, 2004; Hull, Scott, and Smith, 1982; Lorde, 1984, 1996, 2004).

28. For treatments of male-feminism, and black male-feminism or black male-womanism in particular, see Adams and Sayran (2002), Adu-Poku (2001), Awkward (1995, 2000), Brod

(1987), Brod and Kaufman (1994), Buchbinder (1994), Byrd and Guy-Sheftall (2001), Carbado (1999), H. Christian (1994), Dench (1996), Digby (1998), Douglass (1992, 1996, 1999), Gardiner (2002), D.D. Gilmore (1990), Goldrick-Jones (2002), Jardine and Smith (1987), Kiberd (1985), Kimmel (1995, 2004a, 2004b), Kimmel and Mosmiller (1992), Lemons (1997, 2001), May, Strikwerda, and Hopkins (1996), P. Murphy (2004), D. Porter (1992), Schacht and Ewing (1998), Seidler (1991), Spender (1981), Sterba (2000), Stoltenberg (1993), and Whitehead and Barrett (2001). And, concerning Du Bois's assertion that women receive "equal pay for equal work," it is interesting to note that this claim lies at the heart of modern Marxist feminist discourse, and especially the "comparable worth" theorists' work. See, for example, Amott and Matthaei (1999), M. Barrett (1980), Bose, Feldberg, and Sokoloff (1987), Fox (1980), Gunderson (1994), Guettel (1974), Kuhn and Wolpe (1978), Malos (1980), and Mullaney (1983).

29. Nellie McKay, Gary Lemons, and Hazel Carby each bemoan the fact that there is a strong tendency in Du Bois studies to read him primarily as a "race man" and downplay the "feminist" and/or "womanist" dimensions of his discourse. In her essay, "The Souls of Black Women Folk in the Writings of W. E. B. Du Bois," McKay (1990) claims that Du Bois was one of very few black men who wrote "feminist autobiography": "More than any other black man in our history, his three autobiographies [*Darkwater, Dusk of Dawn,* and *The Autobiography of W. E. B. Du Bois*] demonstrate that black women have been central to the development of his intellectual thought" (pp. 229, 231). McKay argues that one of the reasons that so many Du Bois scholars and critics read him as a "race man" is because they often overlook his "more creative, less sociological works, where most of his thoughts on women and his own fundamental spirituality are expressed" (p. 230). "Few people, even those who have spent years reading and studying Du Bois," quips McKay, "know that he wrote five novels and published a volume of poetry" (p. 231). In "'When and Where [We] Enter': In Search of a Feminist Forefather—Reclaiming the Womanist Legacy of W. E. B. Du Bois," Lemons (2001) laments: Du Bois's "womanist activism remains to be fully claimed by contemporary Black men, as he continues to be viewed primarily as a 'race man'" (p. 72). What perplexes Lemons is the fact that the critics who elide and erase Du Bois's donations to women's decolonization and women's liberation do not simply do Du Bois a great disservice, but rob contemporary men, and men of African descent in particular, of an Africana male *anti-sexist* role model. According to Lemons, "not only" was Du Bois's "conception of anti-racist resistance feminist-inspired, his worldview was profoundly influenced by Black women" (p. 73). Finally, in the first chapter of her book, *Race Men,* "The Souls of Black Men," Hazel Carby (1998) offers contemporary academics and political activists a deconstruction of Du Bois as "race man" that acknowledges that he "advocated equality for women and consistently supported feminist causes" (p. 12). Carby, who asserts that it is not her intention to claim that Du Bois was "a sexist male individual," is not, however, as concerned with Du Bois's "male-feminist" thought—though she gives it a thorough critical treatment—as with many black male intellectuals' erasure and omission of that thought from their discourse on Du Bois and their obsessive concerns with "the reproduction of Race Men" (pp. 12, 25). She further states: "If, as intellectuals and as activists, we are committed, like Du Bois, to struggles for liberation and democratic egalitarianism, then surely it is not contradictory also to struggle to be critically aware of the ways in which *ideologies of gender* have undermined our egalitarian visions in the past and continue to do so in the present" (p. 12, my emphasis). Carby's caveat, like the cautions of McKay and Lemons, essentially asks that we be cognizant of not only the "ideologies of gender" in the present, but also the "ideologies of gender" of the past, and how this specific species of ideology may have and/or, more than likely, influenced the ways our intellectual-activist ancestors theorized about this or that issue. In other words, we must make ourselves, as well as others, critically conscious of sexist sentiment and patriarchal pretensions in both classical and contemporary Africana liberation thought and practice traditions. My work here, then, registers as an effort to simultaneously deepen and develop the anti-sexist aspects

of Africana critical theory, and an attempt to move beyond one-dimensional interpretations of Du Bois which downplay the multidimensionality and transdisciplinarity of his thought and texts. It is, once again, important here to note that because of the richness and wide range and reach of Du Bois's thought, within Du Bois studies there are various research areas and agendas—for example, history, philosophy, social theory, politics, economics, aesthetics, religion, education, and so forth. Depending on one's intellectual orientation and academic training and discipline, his thought and texts may serve a multiplicity of purposes and may be approached from a wide array of dialectical and discursive directions. Needless to say, my interpretations of Du Bois have been deeply influenced by my training in and trek through Africana studies, and specifically Africana philosophy, social theory, and radical politics.

30. Collins's contentions here are right in line with the arguments of many of the major feminist standpoint theorists: Sandra Harding's *The Feminist Standpoint Theory Reader* (2004), Nancy Harstock's *The Feminist Standpoint Revisited and Other Essays* (1998), and Sara Ruddick's "Maternal Thinking as a Feminist Standpoint" (1999) immediately come to mind. However, what distinguishes Collins's standpoint theory from those of Harstock and Ruddick is her emphasis on race and the realities of racism in the life-worlds and life-struggles of women of color, and women of African descent in particular. For further discussion, see P.H. Collins (1993, 1998, 2000, 2005, 2006).

31. For Africana womanist, black feminist, and/or feminist discussions of the intersection and interconnections of race, gender, and class, see Awkward (2000), Bambara (1970), Bobo (2001), Busby (1992), B. Christian (1985, 1989, 1994), P.H. Collins (1993, 1998, 2000), A.Y. Davis (1981, 1989, 1998a), Dill (1979, 1983), Dove (1998a, 1998b), Guy-Sheftall (1990, 1995), hooks (1981, 1984, 1989, 1990, 1991, 1995, 2000a), Hudson-Weems (1995, 1997, 1998a, 1998b, 2000, 2004), Hull, Scott, and Smith (1982), James and Busia (1993), J.A. James (1996a, 1996b, 1997, 1999), James and Sharpley-Whiting (2000), Lorde (1984, 1988, 1996, 2004), Marsh-Lockett (1997), Nnaemeka (1998), B. Smith (1983, 1998), Terborg-Penn, Harley, and Rushing (1987), Zack (1997, 2000), and Zack, Shrage, and Sartwell (1998). Black feminist/womanist historians have also engaged the overlapping nature of race, gender, and class in the lives of women of African descent. A few of the most noteworthy major studies are: Giddings (1984), Hine (1990, 1994a, 1994b), Hine, King, and Reed (1995), Hine and Thompson (1998), J. Jones (1985), Noble (1978), and D.G. White (1999).

32. For a discussion, consult Angela Davis's essay, "Reflections on the Black Woman's Role in the Community of Slaves" (1995), which remains one of the best introductions to African American women's existential universe during enslavement. In "Sexism and the Black Female Slave Experience," and in *Ain't I A Woman* generally, bell hooks (1981) provides a provocative and penetrating analysis of sexual stereotypes and racial myth-making that was and continues to be created in white and male supremacist efforts to socio-politically control and "steer" black women away from the sites and sources of power, and also the people in/with power away from black women's lived-experiences and life-worlds (pp. 15–49). Patricia Hill Collins (2000), also, comments on sexual stereotypes and racial myth-making, and particularly with regard to "the politics of the maternal," in "Mammies, Matriarchs, and Other Controlling Images" (pp. 69-96). She, too, is critical of white and male supremacist efforts to socio-politically control and "steer" black women and has put forward a blistering critique in, "The More Things Change, the More They Stay the Same: African American Women and the New Politics of Containment" (P.H. Collins, 1998, pp. 11–43). In a similar spirit, Hammond (1997) and Towns (1974) offer a couple of the best critical genealogies of the mythification of black women's sexuality. And finally, Joy James (1999), in "Depoliticizing Representations: Sexual-Racial Stereotypes," critiques some of the ways black women's radicalism (during and after enslavement) has been downplayed because of the over-sexualization, "mammification," and "bitchification" of black women in modern mass media and the entertainment industry (pp. 123–150).

33. For a discussion of sexuality and/or sexual orientation's import to the overlapping, interlocking and intersecting nature of race, gender and class, see P.H. Collins (1993, 1998, 2000, 2005), A.Y. Davis (1981, 1989), Guy-Sheftall (1995), hooks (1990, 1991, 1994b), Hull, Scott and Smith (1982), J.A. James (1996a, 1999), James and Sharpley-Whiting (2000), Lorde (1984, 1988, 1996, 2004), B. Smith (1983, 1998), V. Smith (1998), Zack (1997), and Zack, Shrage and Sartwell (1998). With regard to the "jeopardy" theses, see Frances Beale's "Double Jeopardy: To Be Black and Female" (1995) and Deborah King's "Multiple Jeopardy, Multiple Consciousness: The Context of Black Feminist Ideology" (1995).

34. Each of the aforementioned essays can be found in Du Bois (1995a), with the exception of "The Work of Negro Women in Society," which was originally published in the *Spelman Messenger* in February 1902, see Du Bois (1982a).

35. For biographical, political, and philosophical explorations of Harper's life and legacy, see Boyd (1994), Carby (1987), Collier-Thomas (1997), Foster (1993), Giddings (1984), Graham (1973, 1986), Greer (1952), Hine and Thompson (1998), and D.G. White (1999). The claim that it is "highly plausible" that Harper influenced, however indirectly, the development of Du Bois's women's liberation theory is based on Jesse Michael Lang's "Anticipations of the Booker T. Washington-W. E. B. Du Bois Dialectic in the Writings of Frances E.W. Harper, Ida B. Wells, and Anna Julia Cooper" (1992).

36. Gatens (1991), Grimshaw (1986), G. Lloyd (1984), Nagl-Docekal (1998), Okin (1992), Pateman (1988, 1989), and Tuana (1992) provide a few of the more salutary and sustained feminist critiques of the Western social contract tradition, while Boxill (1992), Lawson (1992), Lott (1998), McGary and Lawson (1992), McGary (1999), C.W. Mills (1997, 1998), Outlaw (1983a, 1983b, 1987, 1991, 1995, 1996a), and West (1982, 1988a, 1989, 1993a) offer some of the more noteworthy Africana (male) critiques of both contractarianism and Western social and political philosophy in general.

37. For critical engagements of Cooper's intellectual biography, women's liberation theory, and philosophy of education, see E. Alexander (1995), Baker-Fletcher (1991, 1994), L.C. Gabel (1982), L. Hutchinson (1981, 1993), K.A. Johnson (2000), and May (2007). Further, for a fuller discussion of what Harper and I are referring to when we write of the "white men in mobs . . . 'lynch[ing], burn[ing], and tortur[ing]' their black fellow 'countrymen'" (I take her to include black women, their fellow *countrywomen*, here), see: Angela Y. Davis (1998a), "Violence Against Women and the Ongoing Challenge to Racism," among her many other writings on "racialized punishment" and the criminalization of people of color, collected in *The Angela Y. Davis Reader*; Joy James (1996a, 1997), "Erasing the Spectacle of Racialized State Violence," in *Resisting State Violence*, and "On Racial Violence and Democracy," in *Transcending the Talented Tenth*; Manning Marable's (1983) classic, "The Meaning of Racist Violence in Late Capitalism," in *How Capitalism Underdeveloped Black America*; and, by far the best study on this subject to date, Herbert Shapiro's (1988) *White Violence and Black Response: From Reconstruction to Montgomery*. Du Bois, of course, wrote a great deal concerning white violence, both physical and psychological, and the need for both black self-defensive violence and nonviolence. See, for example: *John Brown*, "The Souls of White Folk," "Cowardice," "The Massacre of East St. Louis," "Let Us Reason Together," *Darkwater*, "A University Course in Lynching," "Mob Tactics," *Black Reconstruction*, *Black Folk Then and Now*, *Color and Democracy: Colonies and Peace*, *African in Battle Against Colonialism, Racism, and Imperialism*, and *Against Racism* (see Du Bois, 1939, 1945, 1960, 1962, 1970c, 1971a, 1972a, 1972b, 1983, 1985a).

# 3

## C. L. R. James: Pan-African Marxism Beyond All Boundaries

James's research also constituted a preliminary approach to international black history, hardly even a concept at that point [in the 1930s]. In the same years that James pursued his researches, veteran black political-intellectual leader W. E. B. Du Bois, foremost sponsor of Pan-African gatherings, had begun consolidating the studies leading to his book *Black Reconstruction*. The relative youngster (and political neophyte) James, and the distinguished Du Bois evolved simultaneously toward Marxism, on history's account. They could solve the intellectual problems before them in no other manner.

—Paul Buhle, *C. L. R. James: The Artist as Revolutionary*, pp. 41–42

The lacuna in Western political thought regarding the importance of the black struggle and its impact on the nature of politics again puts black political thinkers outside the Western intellectual tradition and its radical legacies. Consequently, the conceptions of Western Marxism are white and European, and literature on Marxism after Marx does not mention black thinkers or the nature of the racial question. Yet it is the works of C. L. R. James and W. E. B. Du Bois which raise some of the fundamental issues of Western society about the nature and limitations of equality, freedom and democracy, because the nature of the black radical tradition in all its heterogeneity is both a critique of and a fundamental enquiry into these classical notions. The universality of the Enlightenment stopped short on race. The black radical tradition offers a larger dimension to these issues.

—Anthony Bogues, *Caliban's Freedom:*
*The Early Political Thought of C. L. R. James*, p. 168

Over half a century ago, a group of radical black intellectuals, most notably W. E. B. Du Bois, George Padmore, Eric Williams, and C. L. R. James, came to the conclusion that African people in the Western hemisphere have been at the fulcrum of the most important social and political transformations in the modern world. . . . James was rare among fellow Marxists for his recognition of the revolutionary

potential of black nationalism. . . . James was convinced of the necessity of black
nationalism as an essential element of the black freedom struggle.

—R.D.G. Kelley, "The World the Diaspora Made:
C. L. R. James and the Politics of History," pp. 104, 115–116

## INTRODUCTION: C. L. R. JAMES AND
## REVOLUTIONARY PAN-AFRICAN MARXISM

Cricket and calypso, Toussaint L'Ouverture and the Haitian Revolution, the history
of Pan-African revolt, Marxist-Leninism and world revolution, the African American
struggle for human and civil rights, William Shakespeare, W. E. B. Du Bois, Herman
Melville, and Richard Wright—an enigmatic and eclectic combination of ideas and
interests unfolds across the landscape of Cyril Lionel Robert James's life and work.
He has been, of no doubt due to the highly porous nature of his writings, read and
re-read from a multiplicity of academic and non-academic angles (P. Buhle, 1986a;
Cha-Jua, 1998; Cudjoe and Cain, 1995; Farred, 1996; Henry and Buhle, 1992). Initially in James studies it was mostly Marxists (of various persuasions) whom mined
James's mind for the precious dialectical diamonds interned there. In time, and due
undoubtedly to the fact that James began to teach in university and other academic
settings, his thought and texts procured praise and criticism far exceeding any other
purported "black Marxist" or "Marxist of African descent," Du Bois's dialectics, of
course, withstanding (Bogues, 2003; P. Henry, 2000; C.J. Robinson, 2000; West,
1991).

James was born in 1901 on the Caribbean island of Trinidad, which was a British
colony at the time. Early in life he developed an anti-authoritarian approach and,
though his family was firmly middle-class, he harbored an intense interest in working-class culture and politics. Refusing to be a "good" colonized intellectual, though
he was exceptionally gifted and intellectually advanced, much to his parents' chagrin the young James opted to pursue a career as a writer and political radical. He
migrated to England in 1932 to bring his literary ambitions to fruition, but once
there he became intensely involved in Marxist, anticolonial, and Pan-African politics. He quickly became one of the leading lights of the international Marxist movement in Europe, publishing a history of Marxist-Leninism and the Russian Revolution in 1936, *World Revolution, 1917–1936* (C. L. R. James, 1993c). James also had a
lifelong love affair with cricket and became a leading cricket correspondent for the
*Manchester Guardian* (Renton, 2007; Worcester, 1985). During this period he published a novel and wrote several plays (one of which starred the acclaimed African
American actor and orator Paul Robeson) as well.

From England James migrated to America, then back to England, then to the
Caribbean, then again back to England, and along the way he developed his own
unique Pan-African Marxist perspective in a number of jaw-dropping and genre-ex-
ploding works: *The Black Jacobins, A History of Pan-African Revolt, Notes on Dialectics,
State Capitalism and World Revolution, American Civilization, Mariners, Renegades, and
Castaways, Modern Politics, Beyond a Boundary,* and *Nkrumah and the Ghana Revolution,* among others (see C. L. R. James 1960, 1963, 1969, 1977b, 1980b, 1985,
1993a, 1993b, 1995; see also P. Buhle, 1988; McClendon, 2005; Worcester, 1995).

Throughout much of his life his work was marginalized and overlooked by both Pan-Africanists and Marxists, though in his own eyes he humbly saw himself as a faithful disciple of both traditions. Similar to Du Bois, what James did not realize, at least not until much later in his life, was how uncommon and intimidating combining Pan-Africanism and Marxism was for both Pan-Africanists and Marxists *and* both capitalist and colonialist governments. He was, in a word, a political pariah because his social and political vision encompassed and integrated aspects of both African and European radical thought traditions; intellectual and popular culture; and, academic and folk philosophy. During the last quarter of his life the intellectual eclipse ended (although his radical politics remained suspect) and he received praise and honor in certain circles.

In the 1970s, *Radical America* devoted an entire issue to James's life and work, an unprecedented occurrence in that publication's history. The 1980s witnessed not only a special issue of *Urgent Tasks* dedicated exclusively to James studies, but also the publication of four volumes of his selected writings: *Cricket, At the Rendezvous of Victory, The Future in the Present,* and *Spheres of Existence.* In 1988, a year before James's death, acclaimed European American Marxist, Paul Buhle (1988), published the first full-length James biography, *C. L. R. James: The Artist as Revolutionary.* By the 1990s several collections of James's writings and scholarly criticisms of his work appeared in print, and at the turn of the twenty-first century and well into its first decade James studies has only continued to deepen and develop, with scores of scholars identifying or taking issue with this or that aspect of James's innovative and intellectual history-making *oeuvre.*

Of particular interest with regard to the present study is the wide range and reach of Jamesian theory; that is to say, the *beyond interdisciplinary* and, more accurately, *transdisciplinary* import of James's ideas and interests and their relevance for contemporary radical politics and the reconstruction of critical social theory. For example, Grace Lee Boggs (1993, 1995), Anthony Bogues (1997, 2003), Paul Idahosa (1995), Walton Look Lai (1992), Neil Lazarus (1992), Scott McLemee (1994, 1996), James Millette (1995), Glen Richards (1995), Rick Roderick (1995), Andrew Ross (1996), Brett St. Louis (2007), and Kent Worcester (1984, 1985, 1991, 1992a, 1992b, 1995, 1996) have each undertaken critical studies of Jamesian political theory. Paul Buhle (1986b, 1988), Cornelius Castoriadis (1995), Martin Glaberman (1995, 1999), Stuart Hall (1992), Paul Le Blanc (1994), Farrukh Dhondy (2001), John McClendon (2005), Cedric Robinson (1995, 2000), and Frank Rosengarten (2008) have each examined James as a Marxist cultural critic and aesthete; hence, the current contentions of James as a doyen in cultural studies discourse (Gair, 2006; Larsen, 1996; Lazarus, 1992; Levi, 1991). Sylvia Wynter (1986, 1992), Aldon Nielsen (1995, 1997), Frank Birbalsingh (1984), Helen Pyne-Timothy (1995), Kara Rabbitt (1995), and Nicole King (2001) have read James as a literary artist and theorist, while Paget Henry (1992a, 1992b, 1997, 2000) and Lewis Gordon (1997a, 1997b, 2000) have long viewed James as a social and political philosopher. Further, the radical historian, Robin D.G. Kelley (1996), has critically engaged James as an historian and notes that James "radically revised African and diasporic history by placing it firmly in the history of the West and by focusing on the masses" (p. 104).

Though he has been read from the aforementioned angles, C. L. R. James has on no occasion to this writer's knowledge been approached and appropriated as a critical theorist. Similar to Du Bois, James sought to construct a systematic and comprehensive social theory in the interest of solving the key social, political and cultural problems of his day. Hence, and in line with the other theorists excavated and appropriated for the Africana critical theory intellectual archaeology project, James offers contemporary critical theorists radical (re)interpretations of various forms of imperialism. In remarking on his strengths as a revolutionary thinker, Paul Le Blanc (1994) perceptively points to James's

> great intellectual breadth, which is evidenced in the quality of his Marxism, reflecting a serious concern with philosophy, history, economics, culture, and practical political work. There is also his capacity to see things that aren't quite "there" yet, but that are in the process of coming into being. Related to this are his capacity to identify fruitful connections between seemingly disparate phenomena and his consequent ability to take what is "peripheral" and show that it is, in fact, central to an adequate understanding of politics and society. (p. 26)

Corroborating Robin Kelley's aforementioned assertion that James "radically revised African and diasporic history by placing it firmly in the history of the West and by focusing on the masses," Le Blanc helps to highlight the fact that James, in viewing the Africana experience as integral to any understanding of Western culture and civilization, adhered to an inchoate Africana critical theoretical and black radical political approach to "seemingly disparate phenomena." By placing that which is purported to be "peripheral" at the "center" of his analyses, James's radicalism dovetails with Du Bois's more Marxist-oriented work. Both theorists exposed the Eurocentrism of Marxism and offer anti-racist critical theorists, and critical race theorists in particular, creative paradigms with which to construct a new critical theory of contemporary society that intensely explores the political economy of race and racism and the Eurocentric pitfalls of the original Marxian paradigm, which after all, from Marx through to Marcuse, has consistently prided itself on being a "world-historical" and "global" theory of revolution (Aronson, 1995; D'Amato, 2006; Gottlieb, 1992; Jay, 1984; Kellner, 1989; Kolakowski, 1978a, 1978b, 1978c). However, this is not to say that Du Bois and James did not internalize some of the Eurocentrism of Marxism even as they were at pains to point it out. It is often these kinds of creative tensions that place Africana and other non-European/non-white critical theorists on distinctly different theoretical terrain(s), making much of their social and political theory heresy in orthodox Marxist *and* Pan-Africanist circles. When compared with Du Bois's Marxist writings, James may have developed a more nuanced relationship with, and understanding of Marxism, but at the same time his work frequently displays some of the same Eurocentric pitfalls that Marxism so often does.

On the one hand, it must be conceded that James *can* and *should*, at specific instances in his *oeuvre*, be read as a Marxist, and particularly as a Marxist innovator for his critically acclaimed contributions of several "Marxist" concepts and categories (P. Buhle, 1986b; Gelderen, 1994; Hamilton, 1992; P. Henry, 1992b; Le Blanc, 1994; McClendon, 2005; McLemee, 1994, 1996). On the other hand, it should be emphasized that there are a multiplicity of deficiencies that arise when employing Marxist methods to engage James, because he was not merely a Marxist, but *also* a revolutionary Pan-Africanist.[1] For example, and with regard to James's innovations in the Marxist tradition, Bogues (1997), Kelley (1996), and C.J. Robinson (2000) have each observed that James, alongside Du Bois, should be considered one of the preeminent pioneers in Marxian theory because of his emphasis on the ways in which race is exacerbated and interlocks and intersects with class in capitalist societies. Also, Bogues (1997) and McLemee (1994) have both noted that James, "having recognized the limitations of the Trotskyist movement . . . attempted the massive project of reconstructing Marxism for the immediate post-World War II period" (Bogues, 1997, p. 1). In undertaking such an endeavor, James's aim is reported to have been "similar in some respects to that of the Italian Marxist thinker Antonio Gramsci" (p. 1). Like Gramsci, James's social theory and political discourse extended a tradition in Marxism that focused on *culture* and *critical consciousness*. However, unlike Gramsci, Marx or Lenin, James's subtext and subjects were not Europe and Europeans, but Africa and Africans, continental and diasporan, as well as other non-whites. James revealed and remarked upon his Africana historical materialism when he wrote in the "Preface" of the 1980 edition of *The Black Jacobins*: "The book was written not with the Caribbean but with Africa in mind" (p. vi).

Upon his arrival in the United States in October 1938, C. L. R. James observed: "In America the situation is different" (quoted in Bogues, 1997, p. 86). By this he wished to convey to his comrades that they were faced with a new situation, one that neither Marx nor Lenin, or any of the other members of the Marxist pantheon, had dared approach. A new situation, a new interlocking form of domination and discrimination demanded new critical liberation theory, theory that not only critiqued capitalism, but also colonialism, racism, sexism, and, perhaps most importantly for the young James, Marxism.

It is the James who—after his arrival in America and experience of American apartheid—never wearied of noting the deficiencies of Marxist thought, and especially with regard to persons of African descent, that Africana critical theory draws from and seeks to illuminate; that James (1994) who exclaimed, "[t]he classics of Marxism are European in origin and content" (p. 223); that James (1996a) who thundered with utterly unchecked passion, "[t]he Negro people . . . on the basis of their own experiences, approach the conclusions of Marxism" (p. 140); that James (1996a) who stated without an ounce of hyperbole, "[t]hey [persons of African descent] may not formulate their beliefs in Marxist terms, but their experience drives them to reject this shibboleth of bourgeois democracy" (p. 140). It is that same James that Africana critical theory comprehends to offer alternatives to Eurocentric radical politics and critical social theory.

In contrast to conventional interpretations of C. L. R. James, I shall argue in this chapter that James, similar to Du Bois, Cesaire, Senghor, Fanon, and Cabral, was first, more a critic of Marxism than a Marxist in any orthodox or dogmatic sense.[2] Second, I situate James in continental and diasporan African intellectual and political traditions. This is extremely important because it has become commonplace in James studies to analyze James's philosophy and social and political theory in light of Western European schools of thought (e.g., P. Buhle, 1986c, 1988, 1994; Castoriadis, 1995; Gelderen, 1994; Glaberman, 1966, 1995, 1999; Le Blanc, 1994; McClendon, 2005; Roderick, 1995; L. Turner, 1995). However, to acknowledge that he was influenced and inspired by Western European thought without acknowledging all the Africana intellectual and political influences on him, in my mind, is to do James (and James studies) a great and grave disservice. Employing the Africana critical theoretical framework, I read James, not as an appendage of, or "black bastard" within Western European/white "radical" thought traditions, but as a Pan-African Marxist revolutionary theorist whose contentious and frequently contradictory corpus provides contemporary critical theorists with much more than previously noted. Finally, I articulate what I consider to be James's most substantial contributions to the discourse and development of a critical theory of contemporary society with an emphasis on the most crucial issues plaguing "postcolonial" and "postmodern" Africa and its diaspora.

## TRANSFORMATION THROUGH REVOLUTION: C. L. R. JAMES, PAN-AFRICAN MARXISM, AND AFRICANA INTELLECTUAL HISTORY

In order to interpret James, one must not only be in full command of past and present Marxist discourse (and eminently attentive to the divergent discourses of multiracial and multicultural Marxists), but also, and as I shall argue *especially*, classical and contemporary Pan-African discourse. Moreover, it would seem to me an utter impossibility to understand the plausibility of my assertions of James as a *critic of Marxism* as opposed to a mere *Marxist critic* unless one had a thorough knowledge of Africana intellectual history. In this section I intend, in brief, to explicate and illustrate James in relation to Africana radical thought and traditions, and particularly Pan-Africanism.[3]

Early in his intellectual life James exhibited the kind of critical Pan-African approach to continental and diasporan history and culture that would come to characterize most of his corpus (Blackburn, 1995; Dupuy, 1995; Hamilton, 1992; Lai, 1992; Lazarus, 1992; Moitt, 1995; Pyne-Timothy, 1995; Rabbitt, 1995; Richards, 1995; Singham, 1970). Several James scholars have noted that he studied Marxism and joined and participated in Marxist party politics during his residence in Europe between 1932 and 1938 (Bogues, 1997; P. Buhle, 1988; R.A. Hill, 1986; Worcester, 1984). However, what most of these scholars fail to effectively highlight and accent in their studies is the fact that James composed not one, but two classic texts in Pan-Africanist thought, both in 1938, just before he set sail for America. *The Black Jacobins* and *A History of Pan-African Revolt* stand today as testaments to James's early commitment to Pan-African revolt, and monuments to his legacy as a revolutionary Pan-Africanist *par excellence*.

Although there is no nice and neat definition of Pan-Africanism, for discursive purposes I would like to offer a sort of working definition for the sake of clarity and accessibility. According to several Pan-African scholars (Du Bois, 1958; Esedebe, 1994; Langley, 1979; Legum, 1962; Ofuatey-Kudjoe, 1986; V.B. Thompson, 1969; Walters, 1993), the principal aims and objectives of twentieth-century Pan-Africanism revolved around several combinations of the following component ideas:

1. Africa as the homeland of both continental and diasporan Africans.
2. Unity with all persons of African origin and descent.
3. Belief in a distinct *African personality*.
4. Firm belief in the rehabilitation of past and present Africa (which includes struggles to rescue and rehabilitate Africa).

5. Pride in African history and culture.
6. Africa for Africans in church and state (i.e., in both the sacred and secular spheres of existence).
7. Faith in and hope for a united and glorious future for Africa and its diaspora.

Based upon the above and with some simplification, we can say that Pan-Africanism is *a social, political, and cultural theory and praxis which regards continental and diasporan Africa and Africans as a collective unit and force for national and international transformation in the best interest of persons of African origin and descent.* Though James may not have ever adhered to all of these ideas, he did at several intervals in his intellectual adventure subscribe to and seek to wed many of them with his homegrown and simultaneously cosmopolitan critical Marxism.

James's early predilection for Pan-Africanism can be ascertained by his consistent raising of anticolonial issues whilst a member of the British Marxist movement (Bogues, 1997; Worcester, 1984). For instance, the Italian invasion of Ethiopia in 1935 in particular made James aware of the fact that not only were the Marxists Eurocentric, because they did not see the invasion of Ethiopia as a crucial rallying point for Africans and other oppressed ("Third World") people worldwide, but also because many of them refused to condemn the Soviet Union when it was discovered that Stalin was selling arms to Italy. This betrayal, perhaps more than any other in his long coquetry with Marxism, made James well-aware of the fact that Marxism, as a school of purported "radical" thought, was deficient and had neither fully nor adequately dealt with the questions of race, racism (especially white supremacist anti-black racism), and colonialism (especially racial colonialism). Remarking on James's insider-outsider relationship with respect to white Marxism's anti-black racism, Bogues (1997) writes:

> Black colonial intellectuals are a distinct social group in the "mother country." Equipped with the intellectual tools learnt from the colonial power, and although having absorbed the language, norms and values of the colonial power, they remain outsiders. A key factor here is race. It would have been unusual for James not to have been aware of this, and indeed his first sustained piece of political writing was anti-colonial and his first practical political activity in England was as a popular anti-colonial speaker where he would have had to confront the question of race. The problem of synthesizing different political currents would arise as he moved to embrace Marxism. But as a West Indian intellectual, James was particularly well suited to this task. (p. 38)

This brings us to the question of what Marxism may have meant to James. As Bogues relates, "his [James's] Marxist commitment meant fighting imperialism internationally" (p. 39). James's corpus is shot-through with indicting comments on, criticisms of, and corrections for Marxism's utter inadequacy in grasping and grappling with the various forms of imperialism that effect and influence the contemporary world, especially the non-European/non-white world. However, if Marxism "meant fighting imperialism internationally" for James, and it meant not criticizing its own perpetuation of imperialism (i.e., Marxist party's anti-black racist policies and paternalistic attitude toward non-whites in general and the Soviet's selling arms to fascist Italy, amongst other acts of imperialism), then James quickly disqualified himself as a Marxist. It is precisely this conundrum that Bogues has in mind when he contends above, "[t]he problem of synthesizing different political currents would arise as he [James] moved to embrace Marxism." Bogues perceptively poses the tension in James's *oeuvre* with regard to Marxism and Pan-Africanism as a "problem," which sheds light on why I characterized James's corpus as "contentious" and "contradictory" above.

James, however, may be read as contradicting not so much himself as Marxism, and particularly the types of Marxism adhered to by many of the major Western European and European American political theorists and activists. For instance, James's (1995) pioneering studies on Pan-African revolutionary history were undertaken to smash racist myths and reveal that "the Negro was no docile animal. He revolted continuously" (p. 57). Long before Fanon wrote *The Wretched of the Earth* in 1961, James (1994) understood that "change will take place, by violence and by reason combined" (p. 85). James was also perceptive when he wrote: "Long before Karl Marx wrote 'Workers of the world, Unite!,' the revolution was international" (p. 81). In highlighting Pan-African revolutionary history, James, according to Robin Kelley (1995), "excoriated imperialism and placed Black laborers at the center of world events when the leading historians of his day believed Africans were savages, colonialism was a civilizing mission, and slavery was a somewhat benevolent institution" (p. 2). It is his placing of Africa and Africans "at the center of world events" that makes James, in my mind, an ideal intellectual-activist ancestor for those of us interested in developing theories critical of the multifarious forms and forces of imperialism confronting contemporary continental and diasporan African culture(s) and civilization(s).

When and where James chronicles the radical and revolutionary thought and practices of continental and diasporan Africans in their quest for freedom; when and where he "see[s] things that aren't quite 'there' yet, but that are in the process of coming into being" (Le Blanc, 1994, p. 26); when and where he "take[s] what is 'peripheral' and show[s] that it is, in fact, central to an adequate understanding of politics and society" (p. 26); and, finally, when and where he places persons of African descent "at the center of world events" is precisely *when* and *where* he steps onto the terrain and enters into the insurgent intellectual orbit of the Africana tradition of critical theory (Kelley, 1995, p. 2). *The Black Jacobins* provides an excellent example of James's relationship with the Africana tradition of critical theory and is considered by many to be a highpoint in both Pan-African and Marxist discourse, because it is a narrative about the energies and capacities of persons, once enslaved, who transformed themselves and their society through revolution. This is a point that should be emphasized, because it is this issue, with all of its existential and ontological baggage, that I shall argue is the *leitmotif*, or the major recurring theme in the Jamesian journey; a journey which incessantly emphasized *transformation through revolution*.

C. L. R. James was attracted to Pan-Africanism and Marxism because each in their own way offered *transformation through revolution*. By "transformation" I wish to imply here not merely *social transformation*, but equally *self-transformation*, a type of change that alters both the public and private spheres of existence. When he discovered that Marxism had not and could not provide emancipatory answers to the race and colonial questions, James developed a theory of revolution that accented Africana agency and the creative capacities of other oppressed peoples independent of many of the major tenets and variables of Marxism (Bogues, 1997, pp. 153–169; also see McLemee, 1994, 1996; Worcester, 1995, 1996). It is in this light that I intend to engage *The Black Jacobins*.

*The Black Jacobins* stands in James's *oeuvre* as a major work of literature, an unparalleled piece of radical historiography, and an inaugural text integral to any understanding of James as a *critical Marxist* and *critic of Marxism*. At one level, the book can be read as the story of the Haitian revolutionary Toussaint L'Ouverture. The narrative, in distinctly Jamesian fashion, details not merely L'Ouverture's acumen as a leader, but also the fact that "[t]he slave trade and slavery were the economic basis of the French Revolution" and that it was the French Revolution, with Africa and Africans at its heart, that inspired and influenced the Haitian Revolution (C. L. R. James, 1963, p. 47). As James (1994) saw it, the Haitian Revolution "had a profound effect on the struggle for the cessation of the slave trade," and it was this historical event, this act of Africana agency, that he utilized as his point of departure (p. 81).

At the level of social and political theory four distinct issues emerge from *The Black Jacobins*: first, the nature of diasporan African (and particularly Caribbean) societies; second, the role of African enslavement and colonization in the development of the modern capitalist world; third, the relationship between a dominant personality (a leader) and society (the masses); and, fourth, a theory of social change. James exploded Marxian concepts and categories by emphasizing the role of the enslaved (the racially oppressed *and* economically exploited) in the process of revolutionary social transformation. For example, James challenged Leninistic notions of *vanguardism*: a vanguard party leading the oppressed on the path through revolution to liberation.[4] For James (1963), it was not L'Ouverture who made the revolution, but the "revolution had made him" (p. 249). In fact, James relates, "it is impossible to say where the social forces end and the impress of personality begins" (p. 240). However, James did not like all that history had to tell of L'Ouverture's leadership style and revolutionary politics. He candidly contended: "Criticism is not enough. What should Toussaint have done? A hundred and fifty years of history and the scientific study of revolution begun by Marx and Engels, and amplified by Lenin and Trotsky, justify us in pointing to an alternative course" (p. 282).

Not only is *The Black Jacobins* a critique of Marxism-Leninism, it is also a critique of Pan-Africanism and, more particularly, Pan-African leaders. Certainly there have been those who have quickly quipped that James practiced paternalism by utilizing Marxist-Leninism to critique Pan-Africanism (and black nationalism), but that read is theoretically thin because it negates the fact that James, first, as Bogues (1997) correctly argued above, saw Marxism more as a means to "fight imperialism internationally" (p. 39). And, second, it negates the fact that James understood the Marxist tradition to be, among other things, "[a] hundred and fifty years of history and scientific study of revolution." This, of course, leads us to an exploration of Lenin's place in the Jamesian journey. For James, Lenin more than any other Marxist had taken Marxism, as a revolutionary theory, and applied it; that is to say that Lenin, in James's mind, had moved Marxism from the level of a *revolutionary theory* to that of a *revolutionary praxis*. However, James was no naïve Marxist in blackface. One of the things that he admired most about Lenin and the Russian revolution was that Lenin, as leader of the Bolsheviks, had augmented Marxism and made it speak to the specific conditions of the Russian people and their epochal and enigmatic issues (see C. L. R. James, 1992, pp. 327–346; see also McClendon, 2005).

In employing Marxist-Leninism to critique Pan-Africanism James did not do so because he was an erstwhile Europhile, but because he understood Marxism to be a *method* (in the social scientific sense) that offered possibilities of *transformation through revolution*. Marxism was not any more "radical" or "revolutionary" than Pan-Africanism in James's intellectual universe. However, Marxism was much better documented and developed than Pan-Africanism, then and now, and as a philosopher, historian, political scientist and social theorist of revolution, James attempted to provide examples and alternatives of and for radical change utilizing what he perceived to be the *lingua franca* of modern revolution. This is something, or so it seems, that has escaped both James's Pan-African and Marxist critics. James himself said that Marxism represented "[a] hundred and fifty years of history and scientific study of revolution." But, it must be borne in mind that this quote is ironically culled from a book on the first successful African diasporan revolution, which predates not merely Marxism, but the birth of Karl Marx.[5] In fact, from the Africana critical theoretical perspective, both *The Black Jacobins* and *A History of Pan-African Revolt* can in many senses be read as direct and unequivocal critiques of Marxists' purported monopoly on revolutionary theory and praxis.

So, in a sense Kelley (1996) is correct when he asserts above that James "radically revised African and diasporic history by placing it firmly in the history of the West and by focusing on the masses" (p. 104). However, Kelley, as radical historian himself, does not go far enough in explicating just *how*, *why*, and *the ways in which* James "radically revised" revolutionary history and theory in the Marxist tradition. As I read him, James, and especially through *The Black Jacobins* and *A History of Pan-African Revolt*, offered alternatives to the stalemate situation Stalinism had produced in the Marxist world. But, the inverse is also true. Just as James felt the Pan-African tradition had much to offer the Marxists, so, too, did he believe the Marxist tradition had much to offer the Pan-Africanists (as well as the black nationalist, if truth be told [see C. L. R. James, 1996a]). Here we have stumbled upon yet another dialectic in the Jamesian journey. Contracting Lenin as a critique of L'Ouverture, James (1963) revealingly wrote:

> It was in method, and not in principle, that Toussaint failed. The race question is subsidiary to the class question in politics, and to think of imperialism in terms of race is disastrous. But to neglect the racial factor as merely incidental is an error only less grave than to make it fundamental. . . . But whereas Lenin kept the party and masses thoroughly aware of every step, and explained carefully the exact position of the bourgeois servants of the Workers' State, Toussaint explained nothing, and allowed the masses to think that their old enemies were being favored at their expense. In allowing himself to be looked upon as taking the side of the whites against the blacks, Toussaint committed the unpardonable crime in the eyes of a community where the whites stood for so much evil. That they should get back their property was bad enough. That they should be privileged was intolerable. And to shoot Moïse, the black, for the sake of the whites was more than an error, it was a crime. It was almost as if Lenin had had Trotsky shot for taking the side of the proletariat against the bourgeoisie. (pp. 283–284)

James simultaneously and dialectically critiqued the Marxists and Pan-Africanists by first emphasizing "the racial factor," the very factor which he felt the Marxists had never adequately dealt. In "good" Marxist fashion he subordinated race to class, but even in doing this he still challenged the Marxian method by stating, "to neglect the racial factor as merely incidental is an error only less grave than to make it fundamental." This statement in and of itself was heresy in the orthodox Marxist camp. So, even though he was still caught in the quagmires of Marxist economic determinism, James (1996a) understood that though persons of African descent "may not formulate their beliefs in Marxist terms . . . their experience drives them to reject [the] shibboleth[s] of bourgeois democracy" (p. 140). In critiquing L'Ouverture's perceived acquiescence to the whites whom we are told, "stood for so much evil," James uses Lenin as an example not so much because he was European or, rather, Russian to be more precise, or a Marxist even, but because Lenin represented an archetypal "good" leader for James. What made Lenin an ideal leader in James's thinking was the fact that he, Lenin, sought to create strong connections between the vanguard party, the proletariat, and the peasants, and he contributed a global perspective that comprehended capitalism to be a world system of imperialism rather than a series of isolated capitalist nations.

For James, both L'Ouverture and Lenin were "good" leaders, however this was not enough. History, time and circumstance demanded much more of leaders. It demanded that leaders cease to be leaders; meaning that in the ideal Jamesian society people collectively lead themselves (Rosengarten, 2008). In *Notes on Dialectics*, James (1980) thundered: "Now if the party is the knowing of the proletariat, then the coming of age of the proletariat means the abolition of the party. That is our new universal" (p. 175; see also McClendon, 2005). In stating this, James was not only going against both Lenin and Trotsky's notions of "the vanguard party," but he was also offering a caveat to the emerging African independence movement and its leaders.

In response to the Italian invasion of Ethiopia, C. L. R. James, George Padmore, Amy Ashwood Garvey, Ras Makonnen, and Jomo Kenyatta formed the International African Service Bureau (IASB) in 1936; an historical fact often overlooked by the more Marxist-oriented James scholars. According to Bogues (1997), "[t]he IASB was a non-party organization which represented the democratic demands of Africans. It was 'an organization which supported democratic rights and liberties and self-determination'" (p. 40). The IASB's organizational paper was the *International African Opinion* in which they "agitated and published anti-colonial material, all of which served as one of the bases for the modern black anti-colonial movement" (p. 40). Here, Bogues places my thesis in bold relief: James was never merely a Marxist, but from the beginning acknowledged an affinity with Pan-African radical politics. Further, not only did James have an affinity to Pan-Africanism, he also, according to Bogues, was a progenitor in this discourse by emphasizing the political economy and inextricability of racism, colonialism *and* capitalism.

From his first sustained piece of political writing and his first practical political activity in England, James stressed the need for Marxists to rethink revolution in terms of racism, colonialism and capitalism. In "Revolution and the Negro" he wrote: "What we as Marxist have to see is the tremendous role played by Negroes in the transformation of Western civilization from feudalism to capitalism. It is only from this vantage-ground that we shall be able to appreciate (and prepare for) the still greater role they must of necessity play in the transformation from capitalism to socialism" (C. L. R. James, 1994, p. 77). Again, accenting Africans as critical actors and radical agents in the unfolding high drama of human history, James assigns them a central position in the major movements of the modern world, but James does not do so simply because he is a person of African descent, or because he wishes other Africans to "feel good" about themselves, their history and their culture. Quite the contrary, James documented the radical ideas and revolutionary deeds of continental and diasporan Africans, because he, as it was with Du Bois, believed that the Pan-African tradition of radicalism could provide alternatives and answers to the most pressing existential issues of his epoch.

James, the consummate intellectual and political cosmopolitan, has an extremely contradictory place in Africana intellectual history, but he, indeed, *does* have a place in this history. From the foregoing it may be concluded that James is neither a pure Pan-Africanist nor a Marxist in any orthodox sense, but more a *Pan-African Marxist* whose life and intellectual legacy offers theorists and activists in both the Pan-African and Marxist schools of thought a rich reservoir for radical theory and revolutionary praxis. Let us now, then, take a long-overdue look at James's Pan-African criticisms of Marxism.

## C. L. R. JAMES'S REVOLUTIONARY ANSWER TO THE RACE PROBLEM: EXPLORING AND EXPLODING WHITE MARXIST CONCEPTS AND CATEGORIES, EXTENDING AND EXPANDING THE PAN-AFRICAN MARXIST TRADITION

In "Preliminary Notes on the Negro Question," published in 1939, C. L. R. James (1996a) stated, "[t]he [Communist and Socialist] party members and sympathizers must be educated to the significance of the Negro question" (p. 4). Without understanding the role persons of African descent had played and must of necessity continue to play in the production and construction of radical theory and the application and implementation of revolutionary praxis, James argued that no significant global (and certainly not "critical") social theory could be developed.[6] Critical theories of societies with Africana populations that did not take into consideration the myriad ways in which Africana intellectuals and activists contributed to the radical transformation of those societies were deemed deficient from James's point of view. After the publication of *The Black Jacobins* James's Marxism grew increasingly critical of Eurocentric Marxists' neglect of the political economy of race and racism in capitalist and colonial societies. "The proletariat . . . must lead the struggles of *all oppressed* and *all those who are persecuted* by capitalism," quipped James (p. 139, my emphasis). The moment white Marxists attempted to develop theories of world revolution without including black and other racially oppressed people is precisely the moment, in Jamesian Marxism, that white Marxism practiced a form of subtle white supremacism or, at the very least, liberal racism. That Marxism could be a form of liberal racism, or an extremely racist paternalism, in James's thinking, can be easily ascertained from the essays compiled in *C. L. R. James on the "Negro Question"* (1996a). In his "Preliminary Notes" he maintained:

1. The Negro represents potentially the most revolutionary section of the population.
2. He is ready to respond to militant leadership.

3. He will respond to political situations abroad which concern him.
4. He is today more militant than ever. (p. 4)

For James (1994) there were no two ways about it: Marxists needed to thoroughly comprehend "the tremendous role played by Negroes in the transformation of Western civilization from feudalism to capitalism. It is only from this vantage-ground that [they would] be able to appreciate (and prepare for) the still greater role [Negroes] must of necessity play in the transformation from capitalism to socialism" (p. 77). His first point above, as was his wont on numerous occasions, was to accent and emphasize, first and foremost, blacks as agents of historical and social change. James argued this point over and over again, whether in *The Black Jacobins* and *A History of Pan-African Revolt*, or in *American Civilization* or *Beyond A Boundary*. He essentially reiterated, deepened and radically developed this theme throughout his corpus: "The Negro represents *potentially* the most revolutionary section of the population" (my emphasis).

Now, the question we must ask ourselves is: Why would one of the most astute and sophisticated Marxists of the modern era place such emphasis on the revolutionary potential of Africana people—a people historians have consistently referred to as "docile" and "servile"? This query may quickly be answered by James (1996a) in the following manner: "[T]he *Negro question*, as an integral part of the American revolution, can no longer be neglected. *The Negro helped materially to win the Civil War* and he can make the difference between success and failure in any given revolutionary situation," because "[e]conomic exploitation and the crudest forms of racial discrimination make . . . radicalization inevitable" (pp. 3, 4, emphasis in original). Though I disagree with the Marxist "principle of inevitability" (C. L. R. James, 1992, p. 159), because I understand it to rob human beings of freedom of choice and agency, and it often falls hard on the heels of fatalism, I do agree with James when and where he observes and emphasizes Africana folk as historical actors and revolutionary agents. What we need to understand is, first, why James felt it was necessary to consistently accent and acknowledge Africana people as historical actors and revolutionary agents. And, second, how his placing emphasis on Africana people as *soldiers of social change* critiqued and collapsed Marxist concepts and categories, as well as simultaneously and dialectically extended and expanded Marxist discourse. In this section I intend to briefly touch on these most important matters.

James employed the second point above, that Africana people are "ready to respond to militant leadership," as an opportunity to critique Marxist paternalism towards persons of African origin and descent. He stated explicitly:

This question of the Negro organization is one that deserves the closest study. As far as I can see, no white leader or organization is going to build a mass organization among the Negroes, either in Africa or in America . . .

The party will base itself in the everyday needs of the Negro. *It must aim at being a mass organization or it will be useless and mischievous . . .*

The white proletariat will have to demonstrate concretely its value to the Negro not once, but many times, before it wins the Negro's confidence. (1996a, pp. 7, 9, emphasis in original)

Even the most minor interpretation of James's comments above must concede that he is, on the one hand, exposing the official Marxist parties, both the Communist and Socialist parties, as essentially white working-class parties that in most instances cater to, of course, the white working-classes. Which is, of course, why he maintains, "[a]s far I can see, no *white* leader or organization is going to build a mass organization among the Negroes, either in Africa or in America" (my emphasis). Thus, the communist and socialist parties, being essentially white workers' parties, have historically relegated Africana and other racially oppressed people, and their anti-racist and anti-colonial sociopolitical demands and desires, to marginal or peripheral positions in their "Marxist" revolutionary theories and praxes. On the other hand, James's (1971b) comments also shed light on the fact that he firmly believed that:

> Black people have the right to struggle against oppression. *They don't have to be stimulated by the communist party; they needn't be socialist; they needn't be subject to any of these doctrines, but to struggle against oppression is their absolute right; it is their duty.* (p. 8, my emphasis)

James reveals his primary interest in radical political discourse and critical social theory, whether Marxist or Pan-Africanist, and that is *revolution*. This is the trope that McLemee (1994) forcefully argues "connects James's British years with his American sojourn" (p. 218). To James it mattered little whether one was a communist or a socialist, a black nationalist or a Pan-Africanist, or any combination of the aforementioned. What mattered most was that one was "struggl[ing] against oppression," that "the party" and "the proletariat" were struggling in the best interest of "all oppressed and all those who are persecuted by capitalism." When he realized, whilst on his "American sojourn," that the communist and socialist parties were excluding African Americans—a group he regarded as "potentially the most revolutionary section of the [U.S.] population" (see James, 1996a, pp. 4, 63–89)—just as he had noted the deficiencies of Pan-Africanism, James critiqued and offered correctives to American Marxism.[7]

Where in 1939 he wrong-headedly stated, "the Negro, fortunately for Socialism, does not want self-determination," by 1948 James would confidently quip: "The Negro people . . . on the basis of their own experiences, approach the conclusions of Marxism. . . . They may not formulate their belief[s] in Marxist terms, but their experience drives them to reject the shibboleth of bourgeois democracy" (pp. 8, 140). The James of the 1939 "Preliminary Notes on the Negro Question" was a very different intellectual-activist from the one who composed the hard-hitting, Marxist mind-blowing 1948 essay, "The Revolutionary Answer to the Negro Problem in the United States."

In the "Preliminary Notes" James stated, "self-determination for the American Negroes is (1) economically reactionary and (2) politically false because no Negroes (except C.P. [Communist Party] stooges) want it" (p. 8). As misguided a Marxist as ever existed, James seemed to initially lack confidence in the self-activity and self-organization of African Americans, though he ironically advocated "the organization of a Negro movement" (p. 8). He looked upon the NAACP, the National Urban League, the Garvey Movement, and Father Divine with disdain, going so far as to call Divine "merely a super-preacher and demagogue combined" (pp. 7, 13, 15). James's abhorrence for autonomous African American social and political activity was in keeping with the mainstream Marxist view of Africana and other racially oppressed groups' social and political struggles as merely episodic in value to "the" struggle—

that is, the struggle of "the proletariat" (the white, mostly male, working-class) against capitalism.

Though he had labored in both the Pan-African liberation and British Marxist movements in England from 1932 onward, by the time he had arrived in America in the fall of 1938 James was, in many senses, still snared in the Marxist method, often privileging it over (as opposed to synthesizing it with) the Pan-African radical political paradigm. In his "Preliminary Notes on the Negro Question," he contended, "[o]ur great weapon at the present is Marxism by which we illuminate every grave social and political problem of the day. The party's first task, therefore, is to do what no organization, white or Negro, can do completely unless it is based on the principles of Marxism, study the Negro question in relation to the national and international situation" (p. 12). At this point, 1939, James was still very wedded to the idea that Marxism was superior to all other methods of sociopolitical analysis because it was purported to be a science.[8] However, he soon realized that the African American struggle for liberation had "a vitality and a validity of its own" (p. 139). That is to say that James, by 1948, understood the African American struggle for human and civil rights, independent of Marxism, to be an "absolute right," one that "needn't be subject to any [Marxist] doctrines" (C. L. R. James, 1971b, p. 8).

Almost a decade of social theorizing and political praxis in the U.S. would pass before James would come to the conclusions of his infamous "The Revolutionary Answer to the Negro Problem in the Unites States." In the interim he vacillated between advocating (a) an independent "Negro movement," in which he asserted that "[t]he Party's attitude towards such a movement should . . . be one of frank, sincere, and unwavering support" and (b) a cell of communist/socialist "Negroes" within their respective ideological parties charged with the task of "assist[ing] the [Negro] movement in every way and, while pointing out the political differences and showing that revolutionary socialism is the ultimate road, work[ing] side by side to influence this movement by criticism and activity" (p. 9). The foregoing reveals that James did not come to his "revolutionary" and/or "independent" Marxism over night (see, Le Blanc, 1994, pp. 1-40; Bogues, 1997, pp. 153-169). Quite the contrary, James remained caught in the quandary of conventional Marxist interpretations of the African American experience from 1938 to 1948, and much of this time he oscillated between advocating autonomous African American social and political activity, with the support of the Marxists, and a type of Marxist paternalism that was then very much in vogue in Marxist and other white Leftist circles.

According to the James (1996a) of the "Preliminary Notes on the Negro Question," Marxism could "illuminate every grave social and political problem of the day," and "do what no organization, white or Negro, can do completely unless it is based on the principles of Marxism, study the Negro question in relation to the national and international situation" (p. 12). Perhaps James here is having a moment of historical amnesia, because the Pan-African movement, and especially under W. E. B. Du Bois's auspices, had been up and running since 1900, a fact James certainly should have been conscious of, and especially considering the fact that he, James, co-founded the International African Service Bureau with prominent Pan-African personalities, such as Amy Ashwood Garvey, George Padmore, and Jomo Kenyatta, in the wake of the Italian invasion of Ethiopia in 1935 (Bogues, 1997, p. 40; Worcester, 1996, pp. 32–33). Pan-Africanism "stud[ied] the Negro question in relation to the national and international situation," but it did not do so "based on the principles of Marxism," which we are to presume is why James made no mention of it. However, by omitting Pan-Africansim as an alternative "revolutionary path" (Nkrumah, 1973a) to not only capitalism but also colonialism, James misses an ideal opportunity to link the African American struggle, a national struggle, with the Pan-African liberation movement, an international struggle. At this point in his thinking James was so incarcerated in Marxist ideology that he believed (a) that "revolutionary socialism [was] the ultimate road;" and, (b) that Marxism could "illuminate every grave social and political problem of the day."

Certainly socialism has proven to be compatible with Pan-Africansim—as the work of Du Bois, Cesaire, Senghor, Nkrumah, Toure, Nyerere, Fanon, and Cabral attests—but, by not engaging Pan-Africanism, and to a certain extent erasing it from his discourse when addressing the communist and socialist parties of the USA, James foregoes an excellent opportunity to explicate, first, the inextricable nature of capitalism from colonialism, and vice versa. And, second, by temporarily abandoning his Pan-African politics, James falls prey to the very Marxist paternalism that he would soon critique so mercilessly in "The Revolutionary Answer." In advocating that a cadre of communist/socialist "Negroes" assist and influence African Americans in their struggle for human and civil rights, "pointing out the political differences and showing that revolutionary socialism is the ultimate road," James exhibits his own unique brand of Marxist Eurocentrism. Without critically engaging, first and foremost, the historical and contemporary solutions African Americans had put forward with regard to "the Negro problem in the United States," and, second, the ways in which Marxism may have on many occasions marred Africana agency, James treats the African American struggle as a subordinate struggle to "the" struggle, i.e., "the" struggle of "the proletarian" (the white, mostly male, working-class) against capitalism. James (1996a) stated: "Negro persecution will fall only with the fall of capitalism" (p. 136). But, African Americans were not then, and are not now, white workers in black-face, and just as white workers have needs and desires that are particular to their life-histories and lived-experiences, so, too, do African American and other economically exploited non-white workers possess needs and desires that are particular to their life-histories and lived-experiences. What is more, at this point in his intellectual-activist journey James seems to lack a critical comprehension of the simple fact that often when white Marxists speak of "revolution" or "revolutionary socialism," their theories of revolution rarely include a radical anti-racist rejection of white supremacy; their "revolution" is unerringly against capitalism, not what Cedric Robinson, in *Black Marxism*, has eloquently illustrated is "racial capitalism" (the racist character of capitalism); and, their "revolution" is not against what Charles Mills, in his groundbreaking essay "White Supremacy," has recently referred to as "a multidimensional system of domination, encompassing not merely the 'formally' political that is limited to the juridico-political realm of the official governing bodies and laws, but . . . extending to white domination in economic, cultural, cognitive-moral, somatic, and in a sense even 'metaphysical' spheres" (C.J. Robinson, 2000, p. 3; C.W. Mills, 2003b, p. 274).

James traveled an immense amount of terrain—social, political, philosophical, and physical—in the ten years that passed between his 1938 arrival and experience of American apartheid in New Orleans (see McLemee, 1996, pp. xxi–xxii) and the

1948 publication of "The Revolutionary Answer to the Negro Problem in the United States." After a decade of activity and writing on the African American struggle for human and civil rights, "The Revolutionary Answer" represented the climatic culmination of James critical theorizing on "the Negro question." On the American terrain C. L. R. James the black British Marxist and Pan-African radical blossomed into C. L. R. James the political leader, social theorist, philosopher, cultural critic, and radical historian. Amongst watershed works, such as "Negro Liberation Through Revolutionary Socialism," "Revolution and the Negro," "Imperialism in Africa," "The Destiny of the Negro: An Historical Overview," "The Historical Development of the Negroes in American Society," and "Dialectical Materialism and the Fate of Humanity," James's "Revolutionary Answer" stands out. After a brief introduction where he acknowledged that Richard Wright's *Native Son* had helped to popularize the "Negro question," James (1996a), going against Marxism, Leninism, Trotskyism, and Stalinism stated:

> We can compare what we have to say that is new by comparing it to previous positions on the Negro question in the socialist movement. The proletariat, as we know, must lead the struggle of all the oppressed and all those who are persecuted by capitalism. But this has been interpreted in the past—and by some very good socialist too—in the following sense: the independent struggles of the Negro people have not got much more than an episodic value and, as a matter of fact, can constitute a great danger not only to the Negroes themselves, but to the organized labor movement. The real leadership of the Negro struggle must rest in the hands of organized labor and of the Marxist party. Without that the Negro struggle is not only weak, but is likely to cause difficulties for the Negroes and dangers to organized labor. This, as I say, is the position held by many socialists in the past. Some great socialists in the United States have been associated with this attitude. We, on the other hand, say something entirely different. (p. 139)

As far back as his 1939 "Preliminary Notes on the Negro Question" James asserted that, "[t]he constant domination of whites, whether by the bourgeoisie or in workers' movements, more and more irks the Negro" (p. 9). He knew from harsh, bitter experience that in such situations African American issues and black social and political concerns were placed on the periphery, always subordinate to the white (mostly male) working-class struggle(s) against capitalism. But, African Americans did not, and do not now suffer the consequences of capitalism alone. In other words, it was not and is not on account of economic exploitation, in and of itself, that African Americans have been, and to a certain extent remain, one of the most dominated, denuded, degraded, and disenfranchised groups in the history of the United States of America.

In ten years time, during his first decade in the USA, James had come to experience and know first hand that racial discrimination often proved to be more penetrating and pernicious in the life-worlds of African Americans than economic exploitation. However, James, in good Marxist fashion, understood economic exploitation to be an integral and interfacing aspect of African American's particular and peculiar oppression. And, it is precisely on these grounds that he challenged Marxist paternalism toward African Americans. Again utilizing his distinct dialectics, James inferred that the communist and socialist parties of the USA had much to offer African Americans in their struggle for freedom. But, by the same token, James also averred that African American struggles for human and civil rights, African Americans' fight for recognition as human beings and as U.S. citizens, could teach communists and socialists, in the U.S. and abroad, much about the overlapping, interlocking and intersecting nature of capitalism *and* racism *and* colonialism in the modern world.

To be sure, James indicted himself in his criticisms of the "previous positions on the Negro question in the socialist movement." However, he knew this was no time to be politically timid, too many people were suffering, and too many supposed "radicals" and "revolutionaries" were talking about, but not doing anything practical with regard to this suffering. Where he himself had once harbored the very Marxist paternalistic positions he now criticized, "The Revolutionary Answer" not only symbolizes James as critic of Marxism, but also James as critic of James. He knew good and well, as I am certain many of his comrades did too, that he had advocated that leadership of the African American struggle be placed in the hands of the Eurocentric American Marxist parties. But, "The Revolutionary Answer" revealed a new even more radical James; a James just as critical of Marxism as he was of capitalism, racism, and colonialism. The new James thundered:

> We say, number one, that the Negro struggle, the independent Negro struggle, has a vitality and a validity of its own; that it has deep historic roots in the past of America and in present struggles; it has an organic political perspective, along which it is traveling, to one degree or another, and everything shows that at the present time it is traveling with great speed and vigor. (p. 139)

Long gone is the James who once looked upon autonomous African American social and political activity, that is, social and political activity unguided by white Marxists and labor leaders, with disdain. This new James claimed that the African American struggle for freedom had a "vitality and validity of its own." It was not necessary for an African American freedom fighter to be communist or socialist, or any other brand of Marxist. What mattered most to James at this point was that those who struggled, produced radical political theory, and plotted revolution worked in the best interest of "all the oppressed and all those who are persecuted by capitalism."

Delivering an incredible and unheard of "insider-outsider" critique of the American Marxist movement, James employed his simultaneous identities and political positions as Caribbean immigrant in exile, intellectual-activist of African descent, radical Pan-Africanist, and critical Marxist to forge yet another political position: *dialectical critic of Marxism*. In "The Revolutionary Answer" James is unequivocal, African American and other racially oppressed people have never and should not now begin to bow to the Eurocentric Marxist ideology of revolution, that ideology which vaingloriously speaks of revolution "for all the oppressed and all those persecuted by capitalism," and yet has thoroughly maintained a racist and sexist hierarchy and "chauvinism" which excludes and erases the radicalism of persons non-white and non-male from its political discourse (pp. 9, 11).

As Pan-African critic of Marxism, James asserted that African Americans have made and will continue to make significant contributions to the progressive transformation of American society, thus highlighting the recurring theme in his corpus, *transformation through revolution*. However, at this point James no longer advocates that African Americans rely on Marxism and/or Marxists for their political direction and political education. James, the dialectical critic of Marxism, as opposed to James the critical Marxist, now promulgates and promotes African Americans working in concert and coalition with the communists and socialists, but maintaining a critical distance and independence so as not to allow their, African Americans', distinct social and political demands and desires for justice (racial, gender, economic, and social justice) to be co-opted and confused with those of the white working-classes. James was explicit:

> We say, number two, that this independent Negro movement is able to intervene with terrific force upon the general social and political life of the nation, despite the fact that it is waged under the banner of democratic rights, and is not led necessarily either by the organized labor movement or the Marxist party. We say, number three, and this is the most important, that it is able to exercise a powerful influence upon the revolutionary proletariat, that it has got a great contribution to make to the development of the proletariat in the United States, and that it is in itself a constituent part of the struggle for socialism. In this way we challenge directly any attempt to subordinate or to push to the rear the social and political significance of the independent Negro struggle for democratic rights. That is our position. (p. 139)

It was "the independent Negro movement" that James now understood to be the most viable social and political position and platform from which to advocate and agitate for African American human and civil rights. Too often when working with communists and socialists African American issues and concerns were "subordinate[d] or . . . push[ed] to the rear." From his new radical political perspective James understood (a) that independent of Marxism, African Americans (as a social and political force) had a long history and had produced a heritage of resistance, radicalism and revolution that could—if engaged critically and appreciatively, which is to say, *dialectically*—contribute to contemporary anti-capitalist and anti-racist social transformation; and, (b) that Marxism, as with any and all other purported "radical" and/or "revolutionary" social and political theory, was in need of constant critique and correction, that is, continuous deconstruction and reconstruction.

In emphasizing the influence African Americans have had, and the role(s) they have played, in every major "American revolution" (he lists the American Revolution of 1776, the Civil War, and both [European] World Wars [i.e., "World War I" and "World War II"), the James of "The Revolutionary Answer" comes full circle and connects with the James of the 1939 "Revolution and the Negro" when he wrote: "What we as Marxist have to see is the tremendous role played by Negroes in the transformation of Western civilization from feudalism to capitalism. It is only from this vantage-ground that we shall be able to appreciate (and prepare for) the still greater role they must of necessity play in the transition from capitalism to socialism" (1994, p. 77). This statement may be read, and has been read here, as the trope that binds James's disparate words and deeds of this period, 1938 to 1948, together.

## C. L. R. JAMES AND (AFRICANA)
## CRITICAL THEORY OF CONTEMPORARY SOCIETY

James's ideas and actions represent and register as a rupture, a schism in Marxism. He demonstrated, in word and deed, not merely that Marxism was deficient with regard to enhancing the quality of continental and diasporan African life-worlds and lived-experiences. But, going much further, James illustrates some of the ways in which Marxism mars human existence and experience as it purports at almost every instance to be a "rational" attempt to reconstruct it.[9] In disentangling him from some of the almost inherent Eurocentrism of Marxist discourse, I have sought to illuminate those aspects of the Jamesian journey which provide contemporary critical theorists with an alternative "revolutionary path" (Nkrumah, 1973a) and paradigm that, on the one hand, is critical of what continental and diasporan Africans have done, and are doing, to liberate themselves; and, on the other hand, is critical of Western European and European American "radical"/"revolutionary" social and political theory and movements, Marxist or otherwise, which do not seriously consider the political economy of race and racism in white supremacist capitalist and colonial societies.

Similar in many senses to the contributions of Du Bois, James's work as a radical historian, political theorist, and social activist helped to concretize the connections between the revolutionary traditions of the Africana Atlantic world—i.e., Africa, the Americas, the Caribbean, and Europe. During his "American years" in the 1940s, James developed a critical theory grounded in Marxism and Pan-Africanism (and black nationalism) that linked the enslavement and colonization of persons of African origin and descent with the rise of racism, colonialism, and capitalism. Before the watershed works of Eric Williams (*Capitalism and Slavery*) and Walter Rodney (*How Europe Underdeveloped Africa*), both of whom were students of James, he asserted that "the greatest progressive revolution that mankind had so far experienced," the transition from feudalism to capitalism, had simultaneously symbolized the period of the greatest death and destruction in the histories, cultures and civilizations of Africa, the Americas, and the Caribbean (Rodney, 1972; E.E. Williams, 1966; see also O.C. Cox, 1948, 1959, 1962, 1964, 1976, 1987, 2000). The conundrums of capitalism, and all of the conflicts and contradictions in spawned, constantly rearranged not only the economies and cultural architecture of Africa, the Americas, the Caribbean, and Europe, but rendered racism and colonialism (and sexism) universal and socially, politically, legally, and religiously acceptable if one could, or wickedly wanted to capitalize or profit by perpetuating it. With the fall of feudalism, capitalism and a new racial colonialism rose in its wake, and the modern world witnessed the intense racialization of the human species. On James's account, white Marxists had done a fairly good job of critiquing and offering alternatives to capitalism, but much of their analysis sorely lacked an anti-racist and anti-colonial dimension that seriously considered the racist character of capitalism, what Cedric Robinson referred to as "racial capitalism." Therefore, James's work as a radical historian, political theorist, and social activist was preoccupied with recollecting the politics and social relevance of the history (and the dialectic) of domination and liberation, so that contemporary radical politics and social movements could (re)emerge with greater revolutionary fervor and perspicuity.

It is James's conscious contradictions of, and contributions to Marxism that distinguish his work and offers an alternative paradigm for critical theorists seeking to move beyond Marxism's Eurocentrism. Traditionally critical theory has taken as its primary preoccupation the vicissitudes of capitalism, and particularly as it impacts and affects Europe and North America. Moreover, critical theory has historically employed Marxism as its weapon of choice in its war against capitalist exploitation. But, if Marxism has long-overlooked racism and the racist character of capitalism, then the Marxist tradition of critical theory more than likely will have/has many of the same limitations that mainstream Marxism does when it comes to engaging the myriad inextricable connections between capitalism, colonialism, and racism. James's Pan-African Marxism not only critiques and offers correctives to classical Marxism, but it contributes a much-needed anti-racist and anti-colonial dimension to the discourse and development of a "new critical theory," that is, a critical theory of "really existing" or "actually existing" contemporary society (Aronson, 1995; Benner, 1995; Nove, 1986; Wilkerson and Paris, 2001).

Read against the backdrop of Africana intellectual history, James, to be sure, in many instances exhibits an extreme Eurocentrism. However, and as I have argued above, James traveled an immense amount of terrain—social, political, philosophical, and physical—in the ten years that passed between his 1938 arrival and experience of American apartheid and the 1948 publication of "The Revolutionary Answer to the Negro Problem in the United States." Over and against attempts to label James a mere "Marxist," it has been my intention to illustrate that though he may have embraced certain elements of Marxist thought throughout his intellectual journey, he was by no means a Marxist in any orthodox sense. As argued above, James's affinity to Pan-African liberation struggles and movements, past and present, often left him at loggerheads with mainstream Marxist party politics and movements. He was in this sense an outsider amongst the outsiders, an exile even among the exiles. James's thought and texts reveal their relevance to the Africana critical theory intellectual archaeology project in so far as it is understood that (1) he was not simply a critical Marxist but more an anti-racist and anti-colonialist critic of Marxism; (2) it was his Pan-African inclinations that complicated, conflicted with, and often contradicted his purported Marxism; and, (3) he alerts us to the fact that even the most "radical"/"revolutionary" thought-traditions stand in need of constant critique and correction, that is, continuous deconstruction and reconstruction.

In many respects C. L. R. James and W. E. B. Du Bois represent the pillars and pinnacle of early Pan-African Marxism and classical Africana contributions to critical theory. Their intellectual and political legacies directly and indirectly influenced countless social theorists and political activists, one group being the African and Caribbean theorists of Negritude, particularly Aime Cesaire and Leopold Senghor, whose poems, plays, and radical politics synthesized Pan-Africanism, Marxism, and Surrealism, among other theories. The Negritude theorists exerted an enormous influence on the future of Pan-African Marxism and anti-colonial struggles, and their writings and radical politics represent an often-overlooked and greatly misunderstood contribution to contemporary critical theory. The following chapter, therefore, will explore Negritude's connections and contributions to the discourse and development of critical theory of contemporary society.

## NOTES

1. For a discussion of the deficiencies of Marxism, and specifically with regard to racial and gender domination and discrimination, see Bogues (1983, 2003), O.C. Cox (1959, 1987), Cruse (1967, 2002), A.Y. Davis (1989, 1998a, 1998b), Hennessey (1992), W. James (1998), Kelley (1990, 1994, 2002), Marable (1983, 1996), C.W. Mills (2003a), C.J. Robinson (2000), and C. West (1988a, 1988b).

2. On orthodox Marxism, see Gottlieb (1992) and Kolakowski (1978a); and for hard-hitting contemporary critiques of the Marxist tradition, see Aronson (1995) and Howard (1972, 1988). It should be noted that in these works "Marxism" is the exclusive domain of Europeans, not a single Marxist of color is critically engaged. We witness, again, Eurocentrism rearing its ugly head, even in contemporary neo-Marxist and post-Marxist discourse.

3. On Pan-Africanism, see Cook and Henderson (1969), Drachler (1963), Du Bois (1958), Kohn and Sokolsky (1965), Langley (1973, 1979), Legum (1962), Lemelle and Kelley (1994), Ofuatey-Kudjoe (1986), Schwartz and Sangeeta (2000), Rothberg and Mazrui (1970), Schall (1975), V.B. Thompson (1969, 1987), and Walters (1993).

4. On Lenin, Leninism, and vanguardism, see Robert Tucker's introduction to Lenin (1975), and Henry Christman's introduction to Lenin (1987). And, for Lenin's classic statements on vanguardism, see Lenin (1975 [esp., pp. 1–153], 1960c, 1960d, 1965c, 1987).

5. Karl Marx was born on May 5th, 1818. On Marx's life and thought, see McLellan (1970, 1971, 1973, 1979, 1983a, 1983b, 2006).

6. On critical theory as an "intrinsically global and historical" theory that attempts to provide "the 'big picture' that portrays the fundamental outlines of socio-economic development and the ways in which the vicissitudes of capitalism structure social life and can in turn be replaced by a socialist society," see Kellner (1989, p. 48).

7. For a discussion of the specificities and particularities of "American Marxism," see Buhle (1987), Diggins (1992), and Buhle, Buhle, and Georgakas (1992).

8. On Marxism as a science, see Gottlieb (1992, pp. 59–76) and Aronowitz (1988).

9. Habermas (1979, 1984, 1986b, 1986c, 1987a, 1989a, 1989b, 1998b, 2000) provide excellent overviews, examples, and critiques of Marxism as a "rational" reconstruction project. Also of interest on this issue are, Aronson (1995), Gottlieb (1992), and Jay (1984).

# 4

## Aimé Césaire and Léopold Senghor: Revolutionary Negritude and Radical New Negroes

Negritude is what one race brings to the common rendezvous where all will strive for the new world of the poet's vision.

—C. L. R. James, cited in Julio Finn, *Voices of Negritude*, p. xi

The revolutionary black is a negation because he wishes to be in complete nudity: in order to build his Truth, he must first destroy the Truth of others. . . . Negritude, to use Heidegger's language, is the black's *Being-in-the-world*.

—Jean Paul Sartre, "Black Orpheus," pp. 124, 129

It is the white man who creates the Negro. But it is the Negro who creates Negritude.

—Frantz Fanon, *Black Skin, White Masks*, p. 47

[A]ll the poets of 'Negritude' confess that they owe the sweep of their arguments and the force of their self-awareness to the rediscovery of African philosophy.

—Janheinz Jahn, *Muntu: African Culture and the Western World*, p. 118

### "BLACK-BEING-IN-THE-WORLD": SARTREAN NEGRITUDE, BLACK MILITANT MARXIST-SURREALISTS, ANTI-RACIST RACISM, AND CRITICAL SOCIAL THEORY

With the "Great Depression" of the 1930s in the U.S. came the decline and eventual end of the Harlem Renaissance. However, as Ako (1982), Bamikunle (1982), and Fabre (1993), among others, have eruditiously observed, it was not the end of the Africana "renaissance" in arts and letters but, perhaps, a new beginning. As the economic and cultural scene changed because of the fluctuations of the U.S. capitalist economy, continental and diasporan Africans began to congregate in Paris and develop a critical concept that, as the Nigerian literary theorist Abiola Irele (1986) has asserted, remains one of "the most comprehensive and coherent efforts of reflection upon the African situation" (p. 393). Irele is, of course, referring to Negritude.[1]

Negritude holds a prominent place in Africana intellectual history because it was able to synthesize a wide-range of black and white radical perspectives, as well as leave a controversial legacy for future anti-racist, anti-colonialist, and anti-capitalist radicalism. The theorists of Negritude were *guerilla intellectuals* in the sense that they used everything and anything they could get their hands on in their struggle(s) against racism, colonialism, and capitalism: from W. E. B. Du Bois and C. L. R. James's Pan-African Marxism, to the radicalism of the Harlem Renaissance; from Jean-Paul Sartre's existentialism, to André Breton's surrealism. Negritude is unique in that it was one of the first modern black aesthetic movements whose central credo was the spiritual and cultural redemption of continental and diasporan Africans. In the aftermath of the African holocaust, enslavement, colonization, and segregation, Negritude redefined and radically politicized the black aesthetic, making it more modern by bringing black art into dialogue with Pan-Africanism, black nationalism, and African socialism, as well as, and equally important, Marxism, existentialism, and surrealism.

As a theory and movement of continental and diasporan African cultural continuum, Negritude was expressed most eloquently by Aimé Césaire and Léopold Sedar Senghor in their prose, poetry, and radical politics.[2] However, as noted by James Clifford (1988), "the Negritude of Léopold Senghor and that of Césaire are clearly distinguished" (p. 177). Clifford observes that from those first faithful days of the concept's conception (circa 1931) there was a "Césairean Negritude" and a "Senghorian Negritude."

An extremely important, though often-overlooked, third stream of Negritude was also controversially conceptualized by the acclaimed French philosopher Jean-Paul Sartre, who undoubtedly introduced and helped to popularize the theory amongst white Marxists, leftists, and academics (Bennetta, 2007). "Sartrean Negritude," if you will, has had a life both dependent on and independent of Césairean and Senghorian Negritude, partly because of Sartre's popularity within white Marxist and leftist circles, especially from the mid-1950s until his death in 1980, and also because Sartre's articulation of Negritude was intentionally geared toward explaining Negritude to whites and emphasized its alleged temporality and transient nature. Thus, Sartre was and remains Negritude's preeminent proponent and interlocutor of European descent. To his credit, he and his philosophy are distinguished from a host of well-meaning and would-be anti-racist philosophers of European descent in the sense that he entered into critical dialogue with Césaire and Senghor, and later Fanon, on not only "the class question," but also "the colonial question" and "the race question" (Sartre, 1948, 1965, 1995, 1997). Consequently, Sartre's work provides a missing link and extremely important point of departure in any effort geared toward understanding and thoroughly assessing the significance of Negritude for the development of an anti-racist, anti-capitalist, and anti-colonial critical theory of contemporary society.

This chapter, therefore, will begin by engaging the multiple meanings of Negritude, exploring the (supposed) divergent and "clearly distinguished" versions of the theory as put forward by Césaire, Senghor, and Sartre. Then, an exploration of Negritude's connections to the radicalism of the Harlem Renaissance will be undertaken.

Similar to Negritude, the Harlem Renaissance provided both continental and diasporan Africans with fora where the most pressing social and political problems confounding and confronting their respective countries and communities could be critically and collectively engaged. In this way, much of Negritude, as theory and/or movement, is incomprehensible without exploring its critical connections to the radicalism of the Harlem Renaissance, among other black radical movements. And, finally, the chapter concludes with an analysis of Negritude's significance for Africana Studies, especially with an emphasis on the concept's contributions to the discourse and development of Africana critical theory of contemporary society.

Ironically, according to the Kenyan philosopher Dismas Masolo (1994), Jean-Paul Sartre contributed the "first systematic definition" of Negritude in his 1948 essay "Orphée Noir," or "Black Orpheus" (p. 29).[3] Since Sartre's articulation of the theory will be engaged below only insofar as it relates to Senghor and/or Césaire's Negritude and the Africana tradition of critical theory, and considering the conceptual importance of "Sartrean Negritude," a brief explication (and interrogation) may prove beneficial at the outset. As distinct from both Césairean and Senghorian Negritude, Sartrean Negritude understands the black's "affective attitude towards the world"— that is, his or her "Negritude"—to be a necessary "negativity," an "anti-racist racism [that] is the only way by which to abolish racial differences" (Sartre, 2001, pp. 129, 118). Neither Césaire nor Senghor advocated, as Sartre (1948, p. xlii) did, "a society without race[s]" as the end result of Negritude, but because (both Africana and European) scholars in the francophone and anglophone academic worlds have given greater attention and critical acclaim to Sartre's writings on Negritude, he has, in a sense, become the go-to-guy for knowledge on Negritude and, by default, "the" philosopher of Negritude. However, Irene Gendzier (1973) has stated that Sartre was, indeed, "sympathetic of Negritude," but may have been "uncertain as to precisely what the movement was about" (pp. 37–38). Sartre's supposed uncertainty, the resultant conceptual ambiguity, and his refusal to revise and/or revisit his articulation of Negritude, as Césaire and Senghor did, has—to many contemporary workers in black radical thought—rendered his "Negritude," at best, lethargic (see Gordon, 1995b, pp. 30–35; Masolo, 1994, pp. 30–37; Sekyi-Otu, 1996, pp. 16–17).

Sartre makes a distinction between Césaire's "subjective" Negritude and Senghor's "objective" Negritude. Senghorian Negritude seeks to rescue and reclaim ancient African civilizations, customs, myths, values, and so on, where Césairean Negritude endeavors to "return to the source" (à la Amilcar Cabral) only insofar as the past pertains to, or can be shown to have a meaningful impact on, eradicating racial oppression and colonial exploitation in the present (and the longed-for liberated future). Despite making this distinction, Sartre, much to the dismay of Negritudists of both persuasions, argued that Césairean and Senghorian Negritude ultimately yield the same result, which contradicts his assertion that Césaire's subjective Negritude is "revolutionary" because it "asserts [its] solidarity with the oppressed of every color" and "pursues the liberation of all" (Sartre, 2001, pp. 136–137). Sartre did not challenge Senghor's "black soul" Negritude as much as he assimilated it, and translated it into what he termed "the Being-in-the-world of the black." Ironically, even after embracing certain aspects of Senghor's backward-looking or, rather, nostalgic Negritude, Sartre goes on to claim that the only "road" that can lead to the "abolition of differences of race" is a "subjective" one—one remarkably similar to the "road" traveled by the synoptic Césaire, and very soon—as will be subsequently seen—Fanon and Cabral, among others. The journey down the subjective "road" is very brief; it is only a "moment of separation or negativity," as Sartre is quick to racially essentialize blacks and whites, putting forward an almost ontological division or, as Du Bois might have said, a "color-line" between Africans and Europeans (p. 118). From Sartre's point of view, what is objective for the black is not necessarily the lived-experience and lived-endurance of racism and colonialism, but—and here he is foolishly following Senghor—black "soul," black "nature," and "the Essence of blackness" (p. 119). In "Black Orpheus," then, Sartre exhibits a tendency to associate blacks with peasants, agriculture, sex, "erotic mysticism," "phallic erection" and the earth, and, in a sense, he puts forward a Negritude of black naturalness that unwittingly places his existential phenomenological Eurocentrism, Marxist/white leftist racism, and, let it be said, liberal white supremacist humanism into bold relief (see Champigny, 1972; Sartre, 1973, 2007). Sartre (2001) proudly proclaimed:

> Techniques have contaminated the white peasant, but the black peasant remains the great male of the earth, the sperm of the world. His existence is the great vegetal patience; his work is the repetition from year to year of the sacred coitus. Creating and nourished because he creates. To till, to plant, to eat, is to make love with nature . . . it is in this that they join the dances and the phallic rites of the black Africans. (p. 131)

It would be difficult to deny Sartre's digestion of and preoccupation with Senghor's Negritude of black naturalness, replete with racist and sexist references (Bartok, 2003; Bennetta, 2007; Gordon, 1995a, 1995c, 2002; Haddour, 2005; Howell, 1992; Mann, 2004; Marcano, 2003; Masolo, 1998; J.S. Murphy, 1999, 2002). Sartrean Negritude refashions colonial anthropology and unwittingly contributes to ethnophilosophy with its emphasis on "the dances and the phallic rites of the black Africans," African primitiveness, and ancient African rituals and customs, as well as its preoccupation with the sexual potency of primordial or "primitive" African men, "the great male[s] of the earth, the sperm of the world," as he put it. For Sartre, Negritude celebrates black creation, black sexuality, black spirituality, black bodies, black firm phalluses, black workers, and black consciousness; "it is based upon a black soul," he asserted drawing from Senghor, and "on a certain quality common to the thoughts and to the behavior of blacks." Observe the abstractness and ambiguity in Sartre's discourse on Negritude. Part of the problem has to do with the pronouncements of the objective Negritudists and, most especially, their nostalgic claims of a single black essence, despite countless historical and cultural records and artifacts that point to black folks' very varied, multicultural, transethnic and transgenerational *lived-experiences* and *lived-endurances* of holocaust, enslavement, colonization, segregation, and assimilation, not only in the diaspora but, truth be told, on the African continent as well.

In contrast to Senghor's objective Negritude, Sartre identifies Césaire's subjective Negritude, a Negritude that moves beyond a mere chronicling of the "great" African past; a Negritude with one foot on the continental past and the other on the diasporan present; and, finally, a Negritude that pulls no punches and exhibits an extreme "passion for liberty," said Sartre. Césaire's Negritude, we are told, is *revolutionary Negritude* because it is focused on black "being" and "becoming" in the present and future, not ancient rituals, "the mysterious bubbling of black blood," or African polyrhythms (Sartre, 2001, p. 138). It is not a Negritude of universality, but one of specificity and, as Sartre observed, it is based on a "sense of revolt and love of liberty." He continues: "What Césaire destroys is not *all* culture but rather white culture; what he brings to light is not desire for *everything* but rather the revolutionary aspirations of the oppressed black; what he touches in his very depths is not the spirit but a certain specific, concrete form of humanity" (p. 127, all emphasis in original). Césaire snatches surrealism, "that European poetic movement," away from the Europeans who created it and, to use Sartre's term, "de-Frenchifize[s]" it, and *Africanizes* it to speak to the special needs of the (continental *and* diasporan) African world (pp. 128, 123). Césaire's poetry, then, signals the de(con)struction of surrealism and the reconstruction of Negritude, or "Africanity," as Senghor would soon suggest.

Even after his intense analysis of Senghorian and Césairean Negritude, which is to say, though he devoted the bulk of his essay to a critical treatment of objective and subjective Negritude, or the divergent "degrees of Negritude," Sartre took an odd turn and ended the piece emphasizing "the temporality of black existence," unequivocally announcing that "Negritude is for destroying itself," it is "the root of its own destruction" (pp. 133, 136–173; see also Fanon, 1967, p. 133). This is the "more serious" matter that "the prophets of Negritude" bring to the fore, a matter of intellectual, political, and racial life and death. The following passage from Sartre's "Black Orpheus," which was made famous by Frantz Fanon in *Black Skin, White Masks*, perhaps captures the conundrum best and, consequently, should be quoted at length:

> But there is something more important: The black, as we have said, creates an anti-racist racism for himself. In no sense does he wish to rule the world: He seeks the abolition of all ethnic privileges, wherever they come from; he asserts his solidarity with the oppressed of all colors. At once the subjective, existential, ethnic idea of *Negritude* "passes," as Hegel puts it, into the objective, positive, exact idea of the *proletariat*. "For Césaire," Senghor says, "the white man is the symbol of capital as the Negro is the labor. . . . Beyond the black-skinned men of his race it is the battle of the world proletariat that is his song." That is easy to say, but less easy to think out. And undoubtedly it is no coincidence that the most ardent poets of Negritude are at the same time militant Marxists. But that does not prevent the idea of race from mingling with that of class: The first is concrete and particular, the second is universal and abstract; the one stems from what Jasper calls understanding and the other from intellection; the first is the result of a psychobiological syncretism and the second is a methodical construction based on experience. In fact, Negritude appears as the minor term of a dialectical progression: The theoretical and practical assertion of the supremacy of the white man is the thesis; the position of Negritude as an antithetical value is the moment of negativity. But this negative moment is insufficient by itself, and the blacks who employ it know this very well; they know that it is intended to prepare the synthesis or realization of the human in a society without races. Thus Negritude is the root of its own destruction, it is a transition and not a conclusion, a means and not an ultimate end. (Sartre, 2001, p. 137, all emphasis in original; see also Fanon, 1967, pp. 132–133)

For Sartre, Negritude was merely a "negative moment," which was ultimately "insufficient by itself." What Negritude lacked, from the Sartrean point of view, was precisely what blacks lacked: an openness to assimilation, which actually meant an openness to Europeanization parading under the guise of modernization, and a more in-depth understanding of Hegel and, especially, Marx, who, perhaps *not* unbeknownst to Sartre, were both—sometimes subtle and sometimes not so subtle—white supremacists or, at the least, extreme Eurocentrists. As with so many white Marxists or white leftists before him, Sartre understood racism and colonialism to be important factors impacting the modern world, but—and here's the real rub—racism and colonialism were particular to blacks' "being-in-the-world" and the life-worlds and lived-experiences of other colored and colonized people, whereas capitalism and class struggle represented the ultimate "universal Revolution," a struggle that would not only liberate colored and colonized folk, but also "the proletariat," by which Sartre means "white workers" (p. 128).

It must be honestly admitted that Sartre did not exaggerate when he wrote, "undoubtedly it is no coincidence that the most ardent poets of Negritude are at the same time militant Marxists." However, what Sartre's analysis circumvents is the crucial fact that non-white radicals are usually initially attracted to Marxism because of its wide-ranging historical and political perspective; its critical theoretical preoccupation with exploitation, alienation, oppression, and domination; and, its emphasis on social transformation and the promise of liberation. But, as soon as non-white radicals realize that when white Marxists speak of "exploitation" or "oppression" rarely is racism critically considered, and colonialism almost always takes a secondary position to the evils of capitalism, they immediately find Marxism to be a false doctrine, its historical vision horribly Eurocentric and surreptitiously white supremacist, and its supposedly all-encompassing conceptual categories to be so narrowly focused on class and obsessed with capitalist corruption, that Marxism, for all radical political purposes in the interest of anti-racism, anti-colonialism *and* anti-capitalism, often inhibits much more than it inspires revolutionary anti-imperialist movements (B. Camara, 2008).

Sartre quickly collapses Negritude (and, in some senses, Pan-Africanism and black nationalism) into Marxism before he has a good understanding of what Negritude is, why it was created, and what it was created to do. As soon as black radicalism out-distances white radicalism, which, of course, has long been embodied in Marxism, Sartre counsels blacks to take a hard turn toward revolutionary humanism and transcend their newly discovered radical blackness or racial particularity. By Sartre's own admission, the revolutionary Negritudists had surely put the white Surrealists to shame, making a mockery of the "emptiness," the "verbal impotence," and the "silent densities" of their, the white Surrealists' poetry (p. 122). But, even in winning, blacks still lose. Sartre was dead serious when he wrote of "the *moment* of separation or negativity" that Negritude represents. A "moment" is a very brief period of time, and that is precisely how long Sartre envisioned blacks' dire need to speak their special truths to each other, whites, and the wider world about their collective experiences and collective endurances in a white supremacist world. In so many words, Sartre was saying that blacks were justified in their deep desire to separate from and/or critique white supremacy and European global imperialism, but just as soon as he admits this *he* (as opposed to the really and truly "wretched of the earth") sets a time limit on how long blacks should journey down the road of racial justice.

Negritude, indeed, is an "anti-racist racism" from the Sartrean perspective, but "this anti-racist racism is the only road that will lead to the abolition of racial differences" (p. 118). Even as they embrace race in a revolutionary anti-racist manner, in the interest of a revolutionary anti-racist movement, the racially ruled are simultaneously told by the progeny of the inventors of race, the modern racial rulers, to transcend race, to erase race, to deal it the final deathblow. From Sartre's point of view, then, Negritude is temporary and, like a child throwing a temper tantrum, it should be tolerated for the time being, but it cannot and will not last long. In his own existential phenomenological paternalistic words,

> Negritude is not a state, it is a simple surpassing of itself, it is love. It is when Negritude renounces itself that it finds itself; it is when it accepts losing that it has won: the colored man—and he alone—can be asked to renounce the pride of his color. He is the one who is walking on this ridge between past particularism—which he has just climbed—and future universalism, which will be the twilight of his Negritude; he is the one who looks to the end of particularism in order to find the dawn of the universal. Undoubtedly, the white worker also becomes conscious of his class in order to deny it, since he wants the advent of a classless society: but once again, the definition of class is objective; it sums up only the conditions of the white worker's alienation; whereas it is in the bottom of his heart that the black finds race, and he must tear out his heart. (p. 138)

In Negritude, continental and diasporan Africans are simultaneously issued a long-overdue special invitation to rescue, reclaim and, perhaps, modernize African culture and, also, almost immediately admonished to transcend their newfound (or newly created) culture for the greater good, not of humanity, as Sartre would slyly have us believe, but for white workers. Note that blacks "find" race, not in the white supremacist world they are mercilessly and maliciously flung into, but "in the bottom of [their] heart[s]" and they, therefore, "must tear out [their] heart[s]." Why? Because the most pressing social and political problems are capitalism and class struggle; the very problems that white Marxists have long been perplexingly preoccupied with. Sartre tells us that white workers want a "classless society," however he does not extend his analysis to black and other colored and colonized workers who want not only a "classless society," but an anti-racist, dare I say, post-white supremacist society (and world) as well. If, indeed, race is in blacks' hearts, as Sartre suggests, then how did it get there? What is the relationship between racism and capitalism? Racism and colonialism? And, furthermore, colonialism and capitalism? Is it a coincidence that the rise of race and racism parallels the historical and cultural development of capitalism? Who invented racial categories? When, where and why were racial categories invented and disparaging racial distinctions made? Césairean and Senghorian Negritude offers answers—dissimilar answers, but answers nonetheless—to these questions. Sartrean Negritude side-steps answering these crucial questions and makes a mad-dash to desultorily dissolve Negritude into Marxism.

Sartre, however, is correct to suggest that Negritude contains the seeds of revolutionary humanism—one need only turn to Fanon's four volumes to see the fruits of Negritude's revolutionary humanism pushed to their pinnacle—but, Sartre is wrong, retrogressively wrong to euphemize the importance of Pan-Africanism and black nationalism for black radical politics and black revolutionary social movements. He is on point when and where he states that the "black revolutionary . . .

asserts his solidarity with the oppressed of every color," and "because he has suffered from capitalistic exploitation more than all others, he [the black revolutionary] has acquired a sense of revolt and a love of liberty more than all others. And because he is *the most oppressed*, he necessarily pursues the liberation of all, when he works for his own deliverance" (pp. 126, 136–137, emphasis in original). However, Sartre fails to see *how* and *why* the black liberation struggle, of which Negritude is an important though often overlooked part, fuels the fires of black revolutionary humanism (Gerard, 1962, 1964).

If black revolutionaries are "pursu[ing] the liberation of all," even as they embrace their blackness, then the problem is not with blackness, but more perhaps with the way that blackness is (mis)represented and devalued in a white supremacist world. Sartre, perhaps, should be admonishing whites, especially white Marxists, to renounce their race (or, sense of racelessness or racial neutrality or racial universality), since historically when whites embrace their race it has usually translated into racism, white supremacy in particular, and the physical and cultural decimation and/or colonization of non-whites. Sartre is in very "bad faith"—to borrow one of his favorite existential phenomenological phrases—when he suggests that black revolutionaries transcend race in their efforts to abolish racism without so much as mentioning that whites, especially white workers and white Marxists, would do well (finally they would do right moral and ethically) in doing the same. We seem to have stumbled upon a Sartrean double standard here; a racial riddle, or a racial colonial conundrum, if you will.

The "abolition of racial differences" is not or, rather, should not be quarantined to blacks, black revolutionaries, and/or black revolutionary movements, but should be incorporated into all anti-imperialist movements, especially white Marxist and white leftist movements. It is quite cowardly, if not subtly anti-black racist, of Sartre and other white Marxists to nobly volunteer to fight in the war against capitalism and entreat and enlist black revolutionaries in class struggle (often as the "shook troops," as Du Bois declared in "The Negro and Communism"), and then abandon blacks in their parlous struggle against racism, and white supremacy in particular (Du Bois 1995a, p. 591). Insult is added to the injury when many white Marxists and white leftists refuse to acknowledge the ways that they themselves are complicit in and contribute to white supremacy by downplaying and neglecting the ways in which racism, colonialism *and* capitalism are incessant overlapping, interlocking and intersecting systems of oppression that thrice threaten black life-worlds and lived-experiences.

It seems utterly absurd that an extremely perceptive philosopher and radical social theorist such as Jean-Paul Sartre would double-deal the Negritude theorists, and blacks in general, at the very moment that they turned to him for camaraderie. However, in Sartre's defense it could be pointed out that he did earnestly admit in the middle of "Black Orpheus": "It must first be stated that a white man could hardly speak about it [Negritude] suitably, since he had no inner experience of it and since European languages lack words to describe it" (Sartre, 2001, p. 129; see also Sartre, 1995). If, indeed, "a white man could hardly speak about it suitably," then, why did he suggest over and over again throughout "Black Orpheus" that Negritude was fleeting, momentary, and/or temporary? On what grounds did he make these audacious assertions and, we must honestly ask, why? What is more, why was Sartre so eager to suggest that the Negritude theorists, and black revolutionaries in general, transcend their blackness, their "past particularism" for a "future universalism" without at the same time issuing a similar caveat to white Marxists and other white leftists, if not whites in general? Sartre knows good and well that the black revolutionary "wishes in no way to dominate the world: he desires the abolition of ethnic privileges, wherever they come from." So, it seems extremely curious that he would prematurely eulogize Negritude and eloquently write its epitaph (p. 137). Perhaps there is a deep double meaning, dare I say a deep *Sartrean double-consciousness*, when he writes near the end of "Black Orpheus": "One more step and Negritude will disappear completely" (p. 138).

One of Negritude's heirs and harshest critics, Frantz Fanon, as we shall observe in the following chapter, found the theory wanting, and particularly the Senghorian and Sartrean articulations. According to Fanon (1967), "[h]elp had been sought from a friend [Sartre] of the colored peoples, and that friend had found no better response than to point out the relativity of what they were doing" (p. 133). Sartre, fumed Fanon, "robbed" the theorists and practitioners of Negritude of their "last chance" (p. 133). As he deconstructed "the old Negritude," Fanon developed a neo-Negritude that simultaneously confronted and contested what he believed to be Senghor's search for a "Negritude of the sources" and Sartre's dialectical negation of Negritude.[4]

Although he was increasingly critical of Césairean Negritude, Fanon found within Césaire's poetry and radical political writings, especially *Discourse on Colonialism*, a working concept of anti-colonialism and a theory of decolonization. For this reason, Fanon sardonically stated in *Black Skin, White Masks*: "I come back once more to Césaire," and then, "[o]nce again I come back to Césaire; I wish that more black intellectuals would turn to him for their inspiration" (pp. 90, 187). In his critique of Sartre's "Black Orpheus," Fanon (1967, pp. 91, 124, 131, 198) employs Césaire's *Discourse on Colonialism*, *Notebook of a Return to the Native Land*, *The Miraculous Weapons*, and his introduction to Victor Schoelcher's *Esclavage et Colonisation*, commenting ultimately that it was Césaire and his Negritude that "had prepared us" (p. 195) to combat "cultural imposition" (p. 193) and inspired Negroes pursuing their "Negrohood" (p. 197). Césaire can be said to be Fanon's philosophical father and, as will be discussed in the ensuing chapter, the black radical theorist's work that Fanon most consistently and critically builds on and goes beyond when he constructs his critical theory of the colonial world, specifically in texts such as *Black Skin, White Masks* and *The Wretched of the Earth*. We turn now, then, to one of the seminal sources of Fanon's radicalism: Aimé Césaire's revolutionary Negritude.

## AIMÉ CÉSAIRE, REVOLUTIONARY NEGRITUDE, AND THE CRITICAL (RE)TURN TO RADICAL TRADITIONAL AFRICAN PHILOSOPHY: ENGAGING FANON'S PHILOSOPHICAL FATHER

Negritude has lived through all kinds of adventures. . . . I would like to say that everyone has his [or her] own Negritude. . . . There has been too much theorizing about Negritude.

—Aime Césaire, *Discourse on Colonialism*, p. 75

Aimé Césaire is reported to have coined the term "Negritude" in 1939, using it first in his long prose-poem *Notebook of a Return to the Native Land* (*Cahier d'un Retour au*

*Pays Natal*).⁵ Jean-Paul Sartre, André Breton, and a host of others have argued that Césaire's *Notebook* is the quintessential revolutionary Negritude poem, and that his call to Caribbean people to rediscover their African roots was simultaneously seminal, radical, evocative, and abstruse. Fanon (1969) famously asserted in "West Indians and Africans," from *Toward the African Revolution*:

> Until 1939 the West Indian lived, thought, dreamed (we have shown this in *Black Skin, White Masks*), composed poems, wrote novels exactly as a white man would have done. We understand now why it was not possible for him, as for the African poets, to sing the black night, "The black woman with pink heels." Before Césaire, West Indian literature was a literature of Europeans. The West Indian identified himself with the white man, adopted a white man's attitude, "was a white man." (p. 26)

Césaire's poem "created a scandal," Fanon gleefully recalled, because Césaire was an educated black, and educated blacks simply did not want to be black: they wanted to be white, and absurdly thought of themselves and their work as white and/or contributions to European culture and "civilization"—I am, of course, using the word "civilization" in an extremely sardonic sense, especially considering the conundrum of a supposed "civilization" that colonizes and decimates non-European cultures and civilizations. In fact, as Fanon observed in several of his studies, black intellectuals have long lived in a make-believe world of their own: rejected by the white world, and relentlessly rejecting the black world (à la Du Bois's concept of double-consciousness). Césaire sought to "return" to and reconnect, not only with Caribbean history and culture, but with what he understood to be the roots of Caribbean history and culture: pre-colonial and anti-colonial indigenous, continental and diasporan African history and culture. Fanon gives us a sense of how unusual and unique Césaire's critical rediscovery project was in Martinique, and the Caribbean in general, at the same time, displaying his, Fanon's, own intense awe and the irony of Césaire's breakthrough and brilliance:

> For the first time a *lycée* teacher—a man, therefore, who was apparently worthy of respect—was seen to announce quite simply to West Indian society "that it is fine and good to be a Negro." To be sure, this created a scandal. It was said at the time that he was a little mad and his colleagues went out of their way to give details as to his supposed ailments. What indeed could be more grotesque than an educated man, a man with a diploma, having in consequence understood a good many things, among others that "it was unfortunate to be a Negro," proclaiming that his skin was beautiful and that the "big black hole" was a source of truth. Neither the mulattoes nor the Negroes understood this delirium. The mulattoes because they had escaped from the night, the Negroes because they aspired to get away from it. Two centuries of white truth proved this man wrong. He must be mad, for it was unthinkable that he could be right. (pp. 21–22)

Fanon is careful and critical to note Césaire's deconstruction of "white truth," which takes us right back to Sartre's assertion in "Black Orpheus" that, "The revolutionary black is a negation because he wishes to be in complete nudity: in order to build his Truth, he must first destroy the Truth of others." Through Negritude, Césaire seeks to deracinate continental and diasporan Africans' internalization of anti-black racism and Eurocentrism. He knows all to well that blacks have been told time and time again that they are, and have always been uncivilized, unintelligent, primitive and promiscuous, and with his work he strives to counter colonialism and racism by rediscovering and, if need be, creating new anti-imperialist African values. Césaire's deconstruction of "white truth" and Sartre's contention that, "The revolutionary black is a negation because he wishes to be in complete nudity," also illustrates Césairean Negritude's intense emphasis on decolonization and re-Africanization (Touré, 1959). When Sartre writes of "nudity," he is acknowledging that part of the Negritude project involves deracination, or stripping or suspending (perhaps in a existential phenomenological sense) blacks of their current conception(s) of themselves and their life-worlds, which has more often than not been diabolically bequeathed to them by the white supremacist world.

With *Notebook of a Return to the Native Land*, Césaire introduced several concepts, and two in particular, which would later turn out to be central to the discourse on black identity and Africana philosophy, and determinant of a new direction in the francophone and pan-African production and representation of knowledge about Africa and its diaspora. The two core concepts were, first, of course, "Negritude," and secondly, Césaire's special use(s) of the word "return." I will first treat Césairean Negritude, and then explore his Negritudian notion of "return."

## CÉSAIRE'S RADICALISM AND REVOLUTIONARY NEGRITUDE

Negritude, according to Césaire, is at once "a violent affirmation" of "Negrohood"— or "Africanity," as Senghor would later phrase it—as well as "a struggle against alienation;" "an awareness of the [need for] solidarity among blacks;" "a resistance to the politics of assimilation;" "a decolonization of consciousness;" "a reaction of enraged youth;" "a concrete rather than abstract coming to consciousness;" and, a "search for . . . identity" (Césaire, 1972, pp. 72-76; see also Senghor, 1995a, p. 123, 1996, p. 49). Negritude, therefore, from Césaire's point of view, is wide-ranging and grounded in black radical politics and a distinct pan-African perspective; a purposeful perspective aimed not only at "returning" to and reclaiming Africa but, perhaps more importantly, consciously creating an authentic African or black self. In order to convey both the usable parts of Africa's past and blacks' present intense "search for . . . identity," Césaire (1972) created a new language to more adequately express the new Africana logic, "an Antillean French, a black French," as he contended (p. 67). In his efforts to create a new language, he demonstrates Negritude's connections to surrealism, and also Negritude's commitments to revolution, decolonization, and re-Africanization. As Lilyan Kesteloot (1991) has observed in *Black Writers in French: A Literary History of Negritude*, for Césaire surrealism "was synonymous with revolution; if [he] preferred the former, it was not only because of political censorship, but because [he] wanted to show that it referred not merely to social reform but to a more radical change aimed at the very depths of individual awareness" (p. 263). With Negritude, Césaire deconstructed the French language and attempted to decolonize "French Africa" and "French Africans." He was adamant about creating a new language to communicate his new logic, *Negritude*, stating: "I want to emphasize very strongly that—while using as a point of departure the elements that French literature gave me—at the same time I have always strived to create a new language, one capable of communicating the African heritage" (Césaire, 1972, p. 67).[6]

Césairean Negritude, as is made clear by the aforementioned, is rooted in "the African heritage," that is, the historicity of African people, and similar to Senghorian Negritude and Du Boisian discourse, understands that people of African descent, like all other human groups, have—as Du Bois said—a "great message . . . for humanity" (Du Bois 1986a, p. 820). Césaire (1972) stated: "[T]here were things to tell the world. We [the theorists of Negritude] were not dazzled by European civilization. We bore the imprint of European civilization but we thought that Africa could make a contribution to Europe" (pp. 76–77).

In *Discourse on Colonialism*, Césaire relates that "European civilization" had "two major problems to which its existence [had] given rise: the problem of the proletariat and the colonial problem" (p. 9). Negritude, then, as postulated by Césaire, had the onus of engaging capitalism *and* colonialism. It was there, located in the locus of the dialectic of European civilization and African colonization that Césairean Negritude—much like the critical theories of Du Bois and James—confronted and contested the "howling savagery" and "barbarity," as Césaire put it, of "the negation of civilization" (pp. 15, 18).

Césaire understands European civilization to rest on the colonization of non-Europeans, their lives, labor and lands. His Negritude, like Du Bois and James's discourse, was a revolutionary humanist enterprise that was sympathetic to the sufferings of "non-European peoples," especially "Indians . . . Hindus . . . South Sea islanders . . . [and] Africans" (pp. 14, 58). Moreover, Césairean Negritude viewed European civilization as a "decadent" and "dying civilization" that had "undermined civilizations, destroyed countries, ruined nationalities, [and] extirpated 'the root of diversity'" (pp. 9, 59). To combat and counter the global destructiveness of European "civilization," Césaire suggested that persons of African descent, working in concert with other colonized, exploited, and alienated human beings, rebel and revolt against the savagery, barbarity, and brutality of European conquerors, colonizers, and capitalists (p. 13). He thundered:

> [C]apitalist society, at its present stage, is incapable of establishing a concept of the rights of all men, just as it has proved incapable of establishing a system of individual ethics. . . . Which comes down to saying that the salvation of Europe is not a matter of revolution in methods. It is a matter of the Revolution—the one which, until such time as there is a classless society, will substitute for the narrow tyranny of a dehumanized bourgeoisie the preponderance of the only class that still has a universal mission, because it suffers in its flesh from all the wrongs of history, from all the universal wrongs: the proletariat. (pp. 15, 61)

Césaire's Negritude is "revolutionary," not because it critically engages and appropriates certain aspects of Marxism, surrealism, and existentialism, but by virtue of the fact that it understands that: "Marx is all right, but we [the enslaved, colonized, exploited, and alienated] need to complete Marx" (p. 70).[7] Just what does Césaire mean, "we need to complete Marx?" Part of what he is suggesting is that it is important for the economically exploited and racially oppressed to come to the discomforting realization (especially for many non-white Marxists, and black Marxists in particular) that "the" revolution that Karl Marx had in mind was a war to be waged not on behalf of a "universal" proletariat, but on behalf of the proletariat of his, Marx's, time and mind: white, working-class men (Di Stephano, 1991, 2008;

Ferguson, 1998). Moreover, Marx, unlike Friedrich Engels in *The Origin of the Family, Private Property, and the State,* rarely wrote a flattering word concerning women. So, women as gender oppressed and exploited workers were not a part of his anti-capitalist theorizations either.[8] Furthermore, it is a known fact that both Marx and Engels believed that the enslavement of people of African descent and the colonization of the colored world was a "necessary evil."[9] For example, in his article "The British Rule in India," Marx related to his readers:

> England, it is true, in causing a social revolution in Hindustan [India], was actuated only by the vilest interests, and was stupid in her manner of enforcing them. But that is not the question. The question is: Can [white, working-class male] mankind fulfill its destiny without a fundamental revolution in the social state of Asia? If not, whatever may have been the crimes of England, she was the unconscious tool of history in bringing about that revolution. Then, whatever bitterness the spectacle of the crumbling of an ancient world may have for our personal feelings, we have the right, in point of history, to exclaim with Goethe:
>> Should this torture then torment us
>> Since it brings us greater pleasure?
>> Were not through the rule of Timur
>> Souls devoured without measure?
> (Marx and Engels, 1972, p. 41)

Engels, echoing Marx's pro-colonialism in an essay entitled, "Defense of Progressive Imperialism in Algeria," stated with a stark confidence that would have surely made Fanon's blood boil:

> Upon the whole it is, in our opinion, very fortunate that the Arabian chief [Abd-el-Kader] has been taken. The struggle of the Bedouins was a hopeless one, and though the manner in which brutal soldiers, like Bugeaud, have carried on the war is highly blamable, the conquest of Algeria is an important and fortunate fact for the progress of [European] civilization. . . . [T]he conquest of Algeria has already forced the Beys of Tunis and Tripoli, and even the Emperor of Morocco, to enter upon the road of [European] civilization. . . . All these nations of free barbarians look very proud, noble, and glorious at a distance, but only come near them and you will find that they, as well as the more civilized nations, are ruled by the lust of gain, and only employ ruder and more cruel means. And after all, the modern [European] bourgeois, with civilization, industry, order, and at least relative enlightenment following him, is preferable to the feudal lord or to the marauding robber, with the barbarian state of society to which they belong. (Marx and Engels, 1989, pp. 450–451)

What should be taken note of and emphasized here—and this extends well-beyond colonial India and Algeria to the rest of the colored/colonized (non-European/non-white) world—is the disconcerting fact that neither Marx nor Engels compassionately considered the "howling savagery" and hypocrisy, the "barbarity" and "brutality" that European colonial rule wreaked upon the wretched of the earth. Moreover, the writings of both Marx and Engels attest to the fact that European imperial expansion—that is, the violent colonial conquest of the non-European/non-white world—has been, and continues to be carried out precisely as Fanon (1968) said it must be if the oppressive and exploitative divide between the colonized and the colonizer, the racially ruled and the racial rulers, is to remain: "by dint of a great array of bayonets and cannons" (p. 36). Césairean Negritude, similar to Fanonian philosophy as we shall see in the succeeding chapter, understands that the "globalization of European civilization presupposes and is grounded on the systematic destruction of non-European civilizations" (Serequeberhan, 1994, p. 61). When and where Marx exonerates British or European rule in India, or any other non-European continent or country, and when and where Engels advocates "progressive imperialism" in Algeria—as if imperialism in any form could be "progressive"—is precisely when and where Du Bois, James, Césaire, Fanon and Cabral, among many other black radicals, move away from Marx's and Marxist Eurocentrism and/or white supremacism (see C.J. Robinson, 2000; Serequeberhan, 1990).

In contradistinction to the "revolutionary" rhetoric of the white Marxists (communists and socialists alike), who have historically produced empty page after page of promises to colored and colonized people, Césairean Negritude, a "Negritude [of and] in action," knows "that the emancipation of the Negro consist[s] of more than just political freedom." Césairean Negritude, it should be reiterated, is among other things an intense "search for . . . identity," an ever-evolving exploration of Africanity and freedom ("more than just political freedom"), which is fundamental to the formation of any human(e) identity (Césaire, 1972, pp. 75, 70, 76).[10] In other words, Africans will never know who they have been, who they are, or who they are (capable of) becoming unless they have the freedoms (plural) to explore and examine their inherited historicity and the very human right to determine their own destiny.

"Colonialism petrifies the subjugated culture," writes Eritrean philosopher Tsenay Serequeberhan (1994, p. 101). Under colonialism neither the colonized nor the colonizer knows himself or herself. The colonized live lives of "double-consciousness," as Du Bois put it, or "third-person consciousness," as Fanon would have it, and the sad reality of their situation forces "the urge for freedom" upon them (Du Bois, 1997a, pp. 38–39; Fanon, 1967, p. 110; Jahn, 1968, p. 241). Grappling with "the urge for freedom" places the colonized squarely in existential and ontological opposition to the colonizer, leaving both sides with dialectical and extremely perplexing onuses: on the one hand, the struggle to maintain racial and colonial domination and discrimination, and, on the other hand, the fight for freedoms—that is, emancipation in every sphere of human existence (Bernasconi, 2002; G. Wilder, 2003b, 2004, 2005). Césaire (1972) said, "it is the colonized man who wants to move forward, and the colonizer who holds things back" (p. 25). The colonizer "who holds things back," moreover, asphyxiates and/or retards the colonized person's "being-in-the-world," their very perception and experience of the world in which they inhabit and have inherited. It is precisely at this moment that the colonized human being is reduced to a mere object or thing in the colonizer's mind, and in the colonial world in general. Note Césaire's colonial equation: "colonization = thingification" (p. 21). He observes, however, that both the colonized and the colonizer suffer the consequences of colonialism:

[C]olonization, I repeat, dehumanizes even the most civilized man; that colonial activity, colonial enterprise, colonial conquest, which is based on contempt for the native and justified by that contempt, inevitably tends to change him who undertakes it; that the colonizer, who in order to ease his conscience gets into the habit of seeing the other man as *an animal*, accustoms himself to treating him like an animal, and tends objectively to transform *himself* into an animal. It is this result, this boomerang effect of colonization, that I wanted to point out. (pp.19–20, emphasis in original)

Césaire turned to the horrifying history of Hitler's Nazi Germany to ground his "boomerang effect of colonization" thesis. He intentionally chose an example that he knew was fresh in the European imagination, and one that would shock and awe his white readers. Similar to *Notebook of a Return to the Native Land*, *Discourse on Colonialism* was written and structured in a way to express an intense sense of struggle—both internal and external struggle—and, perhaps more importantly, the development of Negritude; the development, in other words, of a new black consciousness, a necessarily "negative" or critical consciousness in an anti-black racist and white supremacist world. *Discourse on Colonialism*, then, paints a picture in prose, as opposed to the surrealistic poetry of *Notebook of a Return to the Native Land*, which reveals the double-consciousness and life-threatening dialectic of blacks' intense and incessant struggle to transgress and transcend the color-lines and morally corrupting chasms of racism and colonialism.

Much more than surrealism in blackface, Césairean Negritude represents *fighting words*; words used as weapons, weapons which bring revolution and cultural renewal. Césaire's work, his words and ideas were aggressively argued in French with the express intent of countering French racism and French colonialism. In "Black Orpheus" Sartre (2001) observed that because "the oppressor is present in the very language that they [the theorists of Negritude] speak, they will speak this language in order to destroy it." He also pointed out that the surrealists did not have the same agenda: "The contemporary European poet tries to dehumanize words in order to give them back to nature; the black herald is going to *de-Frenchifize* them; he will crush them, break their usual associations, he will violently couple them" (pp. 122–123, emphasis in original). Césaire's violent, *self-defensive* and *anti-colonial counter-violent*, coupling of words as weapons was also symbolic of the ubiquitous violence of black lived-experiences and life-struggles in an anti-black racist and white supremacist world.

*Notebook of a Return to the Native Land* opens with a poetic portrait of Martinique's capital, Fort-de-France. The Caribbean capital city is contrasted with France's metropolises, and specifically Paris. Fort-de-France is described as flat, lacking life, and filled with colonial zombies but it, nevertheless, is constantly on the brink of violence. However, not the violence of liberation but the violence of survival, the violence of lives lived under a brutal, spirit-breaking, assimilation-advocating colonialism: the "black-on-black violence" of the internal colony within the colony, the ghetto, and its vicious, breath-takingly brutal, and deeply dehumanizing violence. For Césaire, his work must not simply speak to this violence, but combat it, and in this sense his poetry, as he pointed out, is "a cursed poetry . . . because it was knowledge and no longer entertainment" (quoted in Kesteloot, 1991, p. 261). His work was also "cursed," he believed, because "it lifted the ban on all things black" (p. 261). Once more, surrealism made no efforts to do any of this, and this is precisely where Césairean Negritude, and Negritude in general, distinguishes itself from surrealism (and, I am wont to aver, phenomenology, existentialism, pragmatism, Marxism, communism, socialism, etc.).

Césairean Negritude surpasses surrealism in its efforts to simultaneously combat capitalism, colonialism, *and* racism. It also puts the premium on revolutionary humanism by extending its discourse well beyond African life-worlds and lived-experiences. In the following passage, Césaire connects the holocausts of countless racialized and colonized peoples with the Jewish holocaust and questions Europe's supposed moral conscience, and emphasizes racism's irrationality. Therefore, when Césaire writes above of the "boomerang effect of colonization," he is saying, very similar to Malcolm X, that "the chickens always come home to roost," and that it is not only non-whites/non-Europeans who suffer the violence of white supremacy and European imperialism: *imperialism does not offer allegiance to anyone*. Césairean Negritude, again going back to Sartre (2001), reframes the Jewish holocaust by creating "what Bataille calls the holocaust of words" (p. 122; see also Sartre, 1965). In clear, sardonic prose Césaire (1972) explained:

> [B]efore they were its victims, they were its accomplices; that they tolerated that Nazism before it was inflicted on them, that they absolved it, shut their eyes to it, legitimized it, because, until then, it had been applied only to non-European peoples; that they have cultivated that Nazism, that they are responsible for it, and that before engulfing the whole of Western, Christian civilization in its reddened waters, it oozes, seeps, and trickles from every crack.
>
> Yes, it would be worthwhile to study clinically, in detail, the steps taken by Hitler and Hitlerism and to reveal to the very distinguished, very humanistic, very Christian bourgeois of the twentieth century that without his being aware of it, he has a Hitler inside him, that Hitler *inhabits* him, that Hitler is his *demon*, that if he rails against him, he is being inconsistent and that, at bottom, what he cannot forgive Hitler for is not *crime* in itself, *the crime against man*, it is not *the humiliation of man as such*, it is the crime against the white man, the humiliation of the white man, and the fact that he applied to Europe colonialist procedures which until then had been reserved exclusively for the Arabs of Algeria, the coolies of India, and the blacks of Africa. (p. 14, all emphasis in original)

The violence of colonial conquest, according to Césaire, dehumanizes both the colonized and the colonizer. As the colonizer ruthlessly dominates the colonized person's life-world and language-world, the colonized experiences not merely dehumanization, but *deracination*, which means "[l]iterally, to pluck or tear up by the roots; to eradicate or exterminate" (Ashcroft, Griffiths, and Tiffin, 1998, p. 68). For Césaire (1972), the deracination of Africans must be countered and/or combated by "a violent affirmation" of their Africanity, which includes not only their distinct identity but also their unique historicity; hence, their Negritude, their distinctly African attitude toward the world (p. 74). What is more, Negritude, being nothing other than "a concrete rather than abstract coming into [African] consciousness," knows that "it is equally necessary to decolonize our minds, our inner life, at the same time that we decolonize society" (pp. 76, 78). Decolonization, as Fanon eloquently observed in *Toward the African Revolution* and *The Wretched of the Earth*, demands a *critical return* to the precolonial history and culture of the colonized nation, a radical rediscovery of the precolonial history and culture of the colonized people. In his own words:

> The settler makes history and is conscious of making it. And because he constantly refers to the history of his mother country, he clearly indicates that he himself is the extension

of that mother country. Thus the history which he writes is not the history of the country which he plunders but the history of his own nation in regard to all that she skims off, all that she violates and starves. The immobility to which the native is condemned can only be called into question if the native decides to put an end to the history of colonization—the history of pillage—and bring into existence the history of the nation—the history of decolonization. (Fanon, 1968, p. 51)

In order for the colonized to "put an end to the history of colonization" and "bring into existence the history of the nation," they must make a critical distinction between their history and culture and that of the colonizer. Moreover, they must move beyond their current colonized culture and critically return to and deeply ground themselves in their own precolonial history, culture, and struggle(s). But—and this is where we dance with the dialectic—as they "return" to their precolonial past they must not romanticize and find Utopia on every page of their hidden history. Their engagement of their precolonial past must be critical, expressly seeking to salvage those things from the past which provide paradigms for liberation in the present and future. Long before Fanon, Césaire argued for a critical return to Africa's precolonial past, a past he understood to offer many contributions to the ongoing Africana (and worldwide) liberation and decolonization struggle.

## CÉSAIRE'S CRITICAL (RE)TURN TO RADICAL TRADITIONAL AFRICAN PHILOSOPHY

In *Black Skin, White Masks* Fanon (1967) asserted: "Without a Negro past, without a Negro future it is impossible for me to live my Negrohood" (p. 138). The future, for Fanon, is predicated on how one understands her or his past, and that is why he contends that if "the Negro" is robbed of critical knowledge of her or his past, then, a "Negro future" becomes questionable, and with it the very idea of "the Negro" and her or his "Negrohood" or Negritude. The Ghanaian political theorist, Ato Sekyi-Otu (1996), contends that in Fanonian philosophy the "ideal of the postcolonial future was in its essential details called forth by a particular memory of the colonial past" (p. 205). For Fanon, then, the very process of decolonization is "called forth" by the revolutionary reclamation and remembrance of the violence of the "colonial past."

However, there was a "past" long before colonialism, observed Césaire (1972), a precolonial past of "beautiful and important black civilizations," and it is this part of the "past" that is "worthy of respect" and which should be radically reclaimed and rehabilitated because it "contains certain elements of great value" (p. 76). Sekyi-Otu (1996) suggests that for Fanon "political education" meant nothing other than "*the practice of teaching the people a remembrance of their sovereignty*" (p. 211, emphasis in original). When precisely were "the people" sovereign? Yes! You've guessed it: In precolonial Africa, before the European interruption of and intervention into African life-worlds and lived-experiences. But, is this so? Were "the people" really sovereign then? One thing is for certain, "the people" will never know unless they critically encounter and dialectically engage their inherited historicity, that which has been bequeathed to them by their ancestors.

The past is inextricable from the present and the future in Césairean Negritude. It is, or would be, impossible to "decolonize our minds, our inner life, at the same time that we decolonize society" if we did not (or "legally" could not) posses critical knowledge of our "Negro past." In order to procure appropriate and applicable knowledge of our historicity and Africanity—that is, the lived-experiences of our ancestors and their, if truth be told, multicultural and transethnic identities—it is necessary, Césaire maintained, for us to *return* to (or, as I would prefer, *rediscover*) the lives and cultures of our ancestors to learn the lessons of Africa's tragedies and triumphs. In *African Philosophy in Search of Identity*, the Kenyan philosopher Dismas Masolo (1994) importantly mused:

> Closely related to the concept of Negritude, the idea of "return" gives the dignity, the personhood or humanity, of black people its historicity; it turns it into consciousness or awareness, into a state (of mind) which is subject to manipulations of history, of power relations. It is this idea of "return" which opens the way to the definition of Negritude as a historical commitment, as a movement. In the poem [*Notebook of a Return to the Native Land*], then, the word "return" has two meanings, one real, depicting Césaire's historical repatriation to a geographical or perceptual space, Martinique; the other metaphorical, depicting a "return" to or a regaining of a conceptual space in which culture is both field and process—first of alienation and domination, but now, most importantly, of rebellion and self-refinding [sic]. Today, this "return" is a deconstructivist term which symbolizes many aspects of the struggle of the peoples of African origin to control their own identity. . . . For many black people, slavery and [the] slave trade had provided the context for the need for a social and racial solidarity among themselves. Solidarity was their strength and a weapon with which to counter Westernism's arrogant and aggressive Eurocentric culture. Césaire's "return to the native land" was therefore a symbolic call to all black peoples to rally together around the idea of common origin and in a struggle to defend that unifying commonality. To Césaire, Negritude meant exactly this—a uniting idea of common origin for all black peoples. It became their rallying point, their identity tag, and part of the language of resistance to the stereotype of the African "savage." (pp. 1–2)

In grappling with Césaire's Negritudian notion of "return," it is important to understand that he, in no way, advocated a "return" to a "glorious," antiquated African past. To read Césaire in this way would be to severely misread him. What Césaire advocated was an earnest engagement and acknowledgement of black humanity and historicity, and the authentic Africanity that accompanies them. African identity, that is, our "Africanity," does not exist outside of the discourse and horizon of history, and African history in particular (Serequeberhan, 1991, 1998, 2003). That is to say that we must constantly consider the fact that European imperialism—whether it expresses itself as racial, gender or cultural oppression, or economic exploitation—has been, and remains a perpetual part of Africans' (and other non-Europeans/non-whites') lived-experiences since the fifteenth century (Blaut, 1993; Eze, 1997b, 1997c; J.E. Harris, 1993; Pieterse, 1992; Rodney, 1972).

The "return," for Césaire, was not so much to an African past as it was to a set of African values, an African axiology, if you will (Arnold, 1981; Hale, 1974; Jahn, 1958; Maldonado-Torres, 2006; Scharfman, 1987). Moreover, what Césaire (1972), very similar to Du Bois, appreciated most about "the African past" was its "communal societies," its "societies that were . . . *anti-capitalist*," its "democratic societies," its "cooperative societies, [and] fraternal societies" (p. 23, emphasis in original). In comparing the African societies of the precolonial past with the neocolonial, as opposed to "postcolonial," African societies of his present, then 1955, Césaire stated that "despite their faults" the societies of Africa's precolonial past contained and could convey "values that could still make an important contribution to the world" (pp. 23, 76).

Here Césaire, similar to Herbert Marcuse in *Counterrevolution and Revolt*, promotes a "return," not to some imagined perfect past, but to the real, concrete historical experiences and desires of actual ancestors. Marcuse (1972a) asserted that the *anamnesis*, the recollecting or remembrance of past events, "is not remembrance of a Golden Past (which never existed), of childhood innocence, primitive man, et cetera" (p. 70). On the contrary, what must be remembered by "man," contended Marcuse (1966) in *Eros and Civilization*, are those promises and potentialities "which had once been fulfilled in his dim past. . . . The past remains present; it is the very life of the spirit; what has been decides on what is. Freedom implies reconciliation—redemption of the past." A critical demystifying engagement of "the past" must not only concern itself with what "had once been fulfilled" or accomplished or achieved in the past, but should also bear sober witness to the sufferings of the past. Marcuse mused: "[E]ven the ultimate advent of freedom cannot redeem those who died in pain. It is the remembrance of them, and the accumulated guilt of mankind against its victims, that darken the prospect of a civilization without repression" (pp. 18, 106, 216).

In *An Essay on Liberation*, Marcuse (1970a) continues this theme and maintained that the "return" to the past is not an attempt at "regression to a previous stage of civilization, but return to an imaginary *temps perdu* in the real life of mankind" (p. 90). The "real life of mankind," as most of Marcuse's work attests to, is a life lived in many instances in pain and suffering due to domination: human over human domination, and human over nature domination (see also Marcuse, 1964, 1965c, 1968, 1973, 1997a, 2001, 2004). This domination, maintained Marcuse (1978) in *The Aesthetic Dimension*, must be remembered because losing track of, or "forgetting past suffering and past joy" produces a historical amnesia that prevents the critical engagement and "conquest of suffering," and the possibilities of and for "the permanence of joy" (p. 73).

Césaire's notion of "return" is rooted in the "real life" (i.e., lived-experiences and lived-endurances) of people of African origin and descent and it, like Marcuse's theory of remembrance, understands that revolutionary motivation may well stem more from moral outrage over the indignities suffered by ancestors than hope for the comfort of our children and our children's children. This may, indeed, explain why African diasporan historical figures and events, such as Toussaint L'Ouverture, Henri Christope and the Haitian Revolution, became recurring themes in Césaire's work. One need look no further than his book-length essay *Toussaint L'Ouverture: La Revolution Francaise et le Probleme Colonial* and his play *La Tragedie du roi Christophe*. "Haiti," Césaire (1972) contended, "is the country where Negro people stood up for the first time, affirming their determination to shape a new world, a free world" (p. 75). It was this spirit of affirmation and determination that made the Negritude movement, and Césairean Negritude in particular, according to Eshleman and Smith (1983), "set as its initial goal a renewed awareness of being black, the acceptance of one's destiny, history, and culture, *as well as a sense of responsibility toward the past*" (p. 6, emphasis added). What does it mean to have "a sense of responsibility toward the past?" It meant for Césaire, perhaps, precisely what it meant for Marx (1964), that "[t]he tradition of all the dead generations weighs like a nightmare on the brain of the living." Or, perhaps, having "a sense of responsibility toward the past" may have meant for Césaire something similar to what it did for Walter Benjamin (1969), who revealingly wrote:

> There is a secret agreement between past generations and the present one. Our coming was expected on earth. Like every generation that preceded us, we have been endowed with *weak* Messianic power, a power to which the past has a claim . . . nothing that has ever happened should be regarded as lost for history. (p. 254, emphasis in original; see also Benjamin, 1996, 1999b, 2002, 2003, 2007, 2008)

Césaire desires to "return" to the past no more than Marx, Marcuse, and Benjamin exhibit a predilection to digress from their epochs to a "Golden Past," which as Marcuse reminded us above, "never existed." It is not a "return" to a "Golden Past" which Césaire seeks, but a "return" to, or remembrance or rediscovering of Africa's historicity. Hence, Césaire suggests that the cultural workers in black radical politics and black revolutionary social movements recollect the "truths" (of their ancestors and elders' thought) that have been scattered throughout the globe as a result of the European interruption of and intervention into African life-worlds and lived-experiences. Certainly, then, Césaire knows, as European American pragmatist Richard Rorty (1979) does, that "we cannot get along without our heroes. . . . We need to tell ourselves detailed stories of the mighty dead in order to make our hopes of surpassing them concrete" (p. 12; see also Rorty 1982, 1998, 1999, 2007).

Thus, Césaire's "return" to Africa is more spiritual and cultural than physical, and it requires a critical (dare I say, *dialectical*) exploration of the past, which for many continental and, especially, diasporan Africans means salvaging what we can in the aftermath of the horrors of the African holocaust, enslavement, colonization, segregation, and Eurocentric assimilation. Césairean Negritude engages the absurdity of the African holocaust and enslavement, and at one point in his *Notebook* he solemnly memorializes African ancestors lost, like Toussaint L'Ouverture, to "white death" (Césaire, 1983, p. 47). The thought of so many blacks dying meaningless and misery-filled deaths at the hands of merciless white enslavers, colonists, and capitalists compels Césaire to claim "madness": "the madness that remembers/ the madness that howls/ the madness that sees/ the madness that is unleashed/and you know the rest" (p. 49). If whites claim "Reason," then blacks claim "madness": "Because we hate you and your reason, we claim kinship with dementia praecox with the flaming madness of persistent cannibalism" (p. 49). Here, as Eshelmen and Smith (1983) have observed,

> Cannibalism carries to its fullest degree the idea of participation; it symbolically eradicates the distinction between the I and the Other, between human and nonhuman, between what is (anthropologically) edible and what is not and, finally, between the subject and the object. It goes insolently against the grain of Western insistence on discrete

entities and categories. . . . Ultimately, in a political frame of reference, cannibalism may summarize the devouring of the colonized country by the colonizing power—or, vice versa, the latent desire of the oppressed to do away with the oppressor, the wishful dreaming of the weak projecting themselves as warriors and predators. (p. 13)

Within the world of Césairean Negritude, cannibalism can be both an embrace and rejection of the stereotypical (mis)representation of human-eating Africans, un-civilizable subhumans, and "savages" at play in their carnival of carnage. What may be more important in terms of Césaire's Negritude is *which* humans his imaginary cannibals are eating, and *why*. Césaire's embrace of the stereotype of human-eating Africans, black cannibals, if you will, may seem absurd, but only if his claim of mad-ness is overlooked. Black madness is deeply connected to blood memory. In his *Notebook* he announced: "So much blood in my memory! . . . My memory is encir-cled with blood. My memory has a belt of corpses!" (Césaire, 1983, p. 59). As with madness, memory and remembering are very perplexing and painful for blacks, but it is only by overcoming *the madness of white supremacy* and *the irrationality of anti-black racism*, and by returning to, remembering and reconstructing Africa, that blacks or, more appropriately, *Africans* can truly be free (Brundage, 2005; Ndongo, 2007; Pitcaithley, 2003). Remembering Africa means challenging both *whites' demonization* and *blacks' romanticization* of Africa, and it also means bearing in mind that not all whites' demonize Africa, just as surely as not all blacks romanticize Africa. However, I would be one of the first to point out that in a white-supremacist society it is quite common for almost everyone living within that society to see Africa or, what is worse "black Africa," just as Joseph Conrad (2006) did, as "the heart of darkness," or Henry Stanley (1899) did, as "the dark continent" (see also, Conrad, 1984, 2007; Hibbert, 1984; M. McCarthy, 1983). Césairean Negritude, therefore, opens up criti-cal questions; questions concerning *which* Africa, or *whose* representation of Africa contemporary continental and diasporan Africans should "return" to in order to dis-cover a usable past and ensure a present and a promising (truly *postcolonial*) future.

Similar to Cesairian Negritude, Senghorian Negritude advocated a critical return to the precolonial African past but, unlike Césaire, Senghor's work consistently ex-hibited an intense preoccupation with and openness to contemporary European colonial, particularly French, philosophy and culture. Where Cesairian Negritude can best be characterized by its emphasis on Africana self-determination, Africana history, Africana culture, and the struggle(s) of the black proletariat, Senghorian Negritude is best captured with the words assimilation, synthesis, symbiosis, (African) socialism, and elitism. However, it is important to point out that, similar to Césaire, Senghor's thought is highly complex and often draws from and con-tributes to both African and European radical philosophical and political thought-traditions. Senghor sought to utilize and synthesize what he took to be the best of African and European culture and create, following the French philosophical an-thropologist, Pierre Teilhard de Chardin, a "Civilization of the Universal." The sub-sequent section, therefore, explores Senghorian Negritude with an eye toward its contributions to contemporary radical politics and the reconstruction of critical so-cial theory.

# A SATREAN AFRICAN PHILOSOPHER?: LÉOPOLD SENGHOR, NEGRITUDE, AFRICANITY, AND THE POLITICS OF (ANTI-)COLONIAL ASSIMILATION

Negritude is the whole complex of civilized values—cultural, economic, social and political—which characterize the black peoples, or more precisely, the black-African world. All these values are essentially informed by intuitive reason. Because this sentient reason, the reason which comes to grips, expresses itself emotionally, through that self-surrender, that coalescence of subject and object; through myths, by which I mean the archetypal images of the Collective Soul; above all, through primordial rhythms, synchronized with those of the cosmos. In other words, the sense of communion, the gift of myth-making, the gift of rhythm, such are the essential elements of Negritude, which you will find indelibly stamped on all the works and activities of the black man.

—Leopold Senghor, "Negritude and African Socialism," p. 440

[O]ur Negritude should be the effective instrument of liberation.

—Leopold Senghor, *The Foundations of "Africanité" or "Negritude" and "Arabite,"* p. 51

Senghorian Negritude is at once a rebellious (albeit, not by any means *revolutionary*) affirmation of Africanity in the face of the politics of assimilation and, similar to Césairean Negritude, a search for and an attempt to overcome "the loss of identity suffered by Africans due to a history of slavery, colonialism, and racism" (Shutte, 1998, p. 429). For Senghor, Negritude is "the awareness, defense, and development of African cultural values," but it also "welcomes the complementary values of Europe and the white man" (Senghor, 1996, p. 49, 1998, p. 441). It has been argued that Senghor's extreme openness to "the complementary values of Europe and the white man" represents one of the major distinguishing features between his and Césaire's Negritude. Nigel Gibson (2003) has even gone so far to say that, "[a]lthough Senghor emphasized African sources of his philosophy, it would be possible to identify European sources for every one of his ideas," ironically, "including Catholicism, which he merged into Negritude" (p. 69).

As with Césairean Negritude, Senghorian Negritude pivots on an axiological foundation that does not seek to "return to the Negritude of the past, the Negritude of the sources," but to affirm contemporary (neo)colonial Africanity (Senghor, 1971, p. 51). The sources of Senghor's Negritude, however subtly on first sight, are different from Césaire's, and different enough to constitute two distinct versions of Negritude, which may very well share a common language, a common interest in the reclamation and recreation of African culture, and a common social vision, but which nevertheless developed and employed divergent strategies and tactics in pursuit of differing goals. In his classic, *African Philosophy: Myth and Reality*, the Beninese philosopher Paulin Hountondji (1996) characterized Senghor's Negritude as a kind of "culturalism," which overemphasizes "the cultural aspect of foreign domination" while downplaying and diminishing the significance of politics and economics—that is, the political economy of colonialism, capitalism, and racism, and how each oppressive system incessantly overlaps, intersects, and interlocks in African life-worlds and lived-experiences (p. 160). Speaking directly about the distinct differences between Césairean and Senghorian Negritude, Hountondji asserted,

> whereas for Césaire the exaltation of black cultures functions merely as a supporting argument in favor of political liberation, in Senghor it works as an alibi for evading the political problem of national liberation. Hypertrophy of cultural nationalism generally serves to compensate for the hypertrophy of political nationalism. This is probably why Césaire spoke so soberly about culture and never mentioned it without explicitly subordinating it to the more fundamental problems of political liberation. This also explains why, in works like *Liberté I*, Senghor, as a good Catholic and disciple of Teilhard de Chardin, emphasizes rather artificial cultural problems, elaborating lengthy definitions of the unique black mode of being and of being-in-the-world, and systematically evades the problem of the struggle against imperialism. (pp. 159–160; see also Senghor, 1964b)

In side-stepping the political by collapsing it into the cultural, Senghorian Negritude connects with and in some senses becomes an imperial agent for colonial policy, colonial anthropology, and colonial ethnology. It, perhaps, unwittingly distorts the primacy of political and economic problems in the colonial world and serves as a colonial decoy, redirecting Africans' attention from the political economy of their neocolonial conditions, to endless comparisons with European, and particularly French culture. What is worst is that these comparisons and cultural problems are themselves grossly simplified—à la Placide Tempels's *Bantu Philosophy*, Alexis Kagame's *Philosophie Bantou-Rwandaise de L'Etre*, Marcel Griaule's *Conversations with Ogotemmeli*, and John Mbiti's *African Religions and Philosophy*—so as to reduce African culture to folklore, mysticism and, almost exclusively, black popular culture, or "Afro-Pop," if you will; the most manifest exterior and gaudy aspects of contemporary continental and diasporan African cultures. The interiority of culture, its inner-life and internal contradictions, the dialectics and dynamism of culture and, more importantly, critical questions concerning the ways in which colonialism and racism impact culture are all abandoned, along with cultural history, cultural developments and, of course, cultural revolutions. Senghorian Negritude, thus, solidifies African culture, painting a sad and synchronic picture, a dull and purposely "primitive" picture of African culture that is then contrasted with European culture, which, if truth be told, is also rendered one-dimensionally and schematized for the purposes of pseudo-scientific, philosophically phony, and politically pointless comparisons.

It would be very difficult to deny the seminal importance of Senghorian Negritude and its conceptual contributions, especially to contemporary Africana philosophy. But, it would be equally difficult, if not impossible, to overlook that fact that Senghor's theory of Negritude, with its extreme openness to "the complementary values of Europe and the white man," has consistently glossed over the specificities of African cultures in an effort to present a "unified conception of the black race" and a Pan-African folk philosophy, not necessarily to blacks, but more often than not (à la Sartrean Negritude) to whites. This is an unrealistic and utterly absurd portrait Senghor is attempting to paint, especially considering the horrific and deeply divergent nature of the African holocaust, enslavement, colonization, segregation, and assimilation, but it is a fictitious and surrealistic portrait which nonetheless won him many French (and some pseudo-Pan-African) patrons. In this sense, then, Senghorian Negritude has often been interpreted as running interference for European imperialists by downplaying the differences and specificities of African cultures and embracing white supremacist and Eurocentric misconceptions about continental and diasporan Africans. Hountondji (1996) captured this sentiment best when he contended:

> It is not often realized in the English-speaking world that Senghor's theory of Negritude has stirred up a controversy in francophone Africa which is, if anything, even more intense than the generally hostile reception it has met with from English-speaking African intellectuals. While Senghor's francophone critics accept the historical necessity for the rehabilitation of the black man and the revaluation of African culture, they have advanced strong theoretical objections to his formulation of Negritude as a unified conception of the black race. Negritude is presented in these objections as not only too static to account for the diversified forms of concrete life in African societies but also, because of its "biologism," as a form of acquiescence in the ideological presuppositions of European racism. Senghor's theory has been felt to be too thoroughly implicated in the system of imperialist ideas to be considered an effective challenge to its practical applications. The question of African identity required, from this point of view, a different approach which could not play into the hands of imperialism, which offered no form of compromise with its theory or practice. (p. 21)

Clearly Senghor's work is complicated and full of contradictions, but there are several contemporary Senghorian philosophers who defend his positions, often while simultaneously acknowledging the contradictory character of his Negritude and contrasting it with that of Césaire and sometimes Sartre. His work has also influenced the interpretation of African literature, culture, and politics, usually providing philosophical fodder for revolutionary and anti-assimilationist Pan-Africanists, black nationalists, and black Marxists. Janice Spleth (1985) has importantly identified three periods that can be used to chronicle and critique Senghor's evolving theory of Negritude (pp. 21–27; see also Spleth, 1993). The first period covers the 1930s and 1940s when Senghor and other black intellectuals in Paris acknowledged a tension between African and European epistemologies, especially with regard to racism, colonialism, and humanism. Negritude quickly became a radical Pan-African intellectual path that enabled continental and diasporan Africans to search for and (re)create a modern, anti-colonial and anti-capitalist identity that challenged and destabilized the myriad racist myths and stereotypes that French, and other European imperialists held with regard to Africa and Africans. Senghor's emphasis on a reclaimed, if not reconstructed, anti-colonial and anti-capitalist African humanity, personality, and identity is what he came to call, as will be discussed in detail below, "Africanity."

During the second period, which began with his service in the French army of World War II and ended with Senegal's independence in 1960, Senghor advocated for African autonomy, particularly in Senegal, and a kind of quasi-cultural nationalism that synthesized Pan-Africanism, black nationalism, surrealism, and existentialism. At this time he characterized his quasi-cultural nationalist Negritude, following Sartre in "Black Orpheus," as an "anti-racial racialism" aimed at European colonialism and racism. And in the third period, since Senegal's independence, Senghor has employed Negritude as a tool for what he understood to be "progressive" national and cultural development. It was during this period, the post-independence period, that Senghor began to emphasize—much to the dismay of many revolutionary Pan-Africanists and black nationalists—that Negritude was not simply "the awareness, defense, and development of African cultural values," but it also "welcomes the complementary values of Europe and the white man." In particular, Senghor endeavored to illustrate the value of intuitive, emotional reasoning, which he saw as *African epistemology*, and its connections to discursive, predictive reasoning, which he understood to be *European epistemology*. Moreover, he attempted to illustrate the value of discursive (European) reasoning as he thought it should be developed in relation to intuitive (African) reasoning, which brings us to a critical discussion of his concept of "Africanity."

Similar to his definition of Negritude, Senghor (1971) defined Africanity as the "values common to all Africans and permanent at the same time" (p. 7). These "values," he quickly contended, "are essentially *cultural*," which gives credence to Hountondji's above characterization of Senghorian Negritude as a kind of "culturalism" that is preoccupied with and privileges "the cultural aspects of foreign domination" and "emphasizes rather artificial cultural problems, elaborating lengthy definitions of the unique black mode of being or being-in-the-world," while glaringly glossing over the political and economic aspects of racial colonialism (Senghor, 1971, p. 8, emphasis in original; Hountondji, 1996, p. 160). Senghor's concept of Africanity, then, serves as a complement to his version of Negritude, and each is as esoteric as the other and often intended, or so it seems, for a non-African audience: Negritude explains black-being-in-the-world to whites, and Africanity, initially, explains black-being-in-the-world to Arabs. On this last point, the connection between Africanity and its intended Arabian audience, in *The Foundations of Africanité or Négritude and Arabité*, Senghor (1971) arcanely asserted: "I have often defined *Africanité* as the complementary symbiosis of the values of *Arabism* and the values of *Négritude*. Today I prefer to call the former *Arabité*" (p. 8, all emphasis in original).

In introducing his concept of Africanity Senghor quickly discovered that whites did not like the term Negritude and, in his incessant efforts to appeal to whites, in the early 1960s he began using Negritude and Africanity, in most instances, synonymously depending on his intended audience. Africanity was no longer simply the "complementary symbiosis of the values of *Arabism* and the values of *Négritude*," but now the complete "contributions from us, the peoples of sub-Saharan Africa . . . to the building of the Civilization of the Universal" (Senghor, 1996, p. 49). Senghor's concept of Africanity contains at its core an axiological proposition that in many senses boils down to the question of how best to "integrate Negro-African values" into Africa's fight for freedom. Here, then, his concept of Africanity exhibits its (quasi)anti-colonialism and (quasi)Pan-Africanism, but we will soon see why they are characterized as "quasi." "There is no question," Senghor (1959) said, "of reviving the past, of living in a Negro-African museum; the question is to inspire this world, here and now, with the values of our past" (p. 291). But, really now, what are these values? As he observed in "The Spirit of Civilization or the Laws of African Culture," a seminal text presented at the First Congress of Negro-African Writers and Artists in Paris in 1956, these values, "the values of our past," are the very values that characterize and capture the humanity of the human in African life-worlds and lived-experiences (see Senghor, 1956).

The African has an intense ontological affinity with nature that is apparently absent from European humanity. According to Senghor, "the Negro is the man of Nature." He further explained: "By tradition he [the African] lives off the soil and with the soil, in and by the Cosmos." He is "sensual, a being with open senses, with no intermediary between subject and object, himself at once subject and object." Because, for the African, this special kinship with and immediacy to nature is "first of all, sounds, scents, rhythms, forms and colors; I would say that he is touch, before being eye like the white European. He feels more than he sees; he feels himself" (Senghor, 1956, p. 52). For Senghor, this is the black's-being-in-the-world—an acquiescing, ultra-accommodating immediacy, in tune and in rhythm with nature and the cosmos. It is this servility, this docility to nature that is super-significant for Senghor, and he privileges it above all else in his characterization and articulation of the essence of the African, the authentic ontology of the African or, as Sartre has said, "black-being-in-the-world." Senghor suggests that these formerly negative images and assertions about the primitivity of "black nature" are now somehow, as if with the waving of a magic wand, inverted, positive pejoratives pointing to idealized Africans' pristine primitivisms. This, in a nutshell, then, is Senghor's much-touted and often-mangled concept of Africanity.

From the Senghorian point of view, whether looking through the lens of Negritude or Africanity, there is fundamentally a qualitative ontological difference between European and African rationality and epistemology. "The Negro," declared Senghor in his defense, is "not devoid of reason, as I am supposed to have said. But his reason is not discursive: it is synthetic. It is not antagonistic: it is sympathetic. It is another form of knowledge." Furthermore, "Negro reason does not impoverish things, it does not mould them into rigid patterns by eliminating the roots and the sap: it flows in the arteries of things, it weds all their contours to dwell in the living heart of the real." As if sensing the abstraction and absurdity of the preceding remarks, Senghor sought to clarify, stating: "White reason is analytic through utilization: Negro reason is intuitive through participation" (p. 52). Continuing to contrast African and European rationality, Senghor puts forward full-fledged definitions and descriptions of black and white reason, asserting that European reason is undoubtedly discursive and utilitarian and seeks to capture, control, and convert: The "European is empiric," where "the African is mystic" (p. 59). The European, he went on to explain,

> takes pleasure in recognizing the world through the reproduction of the object . . . the African from knowing it vitally through image and rhythm. With the European the chords of the senses lead to the heart and the head, with the African Negro to the heart and the belly. (p. 58)

Ironically, asserted Senghor, the African

> does not realize that he thinks: he feels that he feels, he feels his existence, he feels himself; and because he feels the Other, he is drawn towards the other, into the rhythm of the Other, to be reborn in knowledge of the world. Thus the act of knowledge is an "agreement of conciliation" with the world, the simultaneous consciousness and creation of the world in its indivisible unity. (p. 64)

Here it is important to emphasize that, for Senghor, the above (racist) definitions and descriptions of the African are not simply historical and, ipso facto, contingent characteristics pertaining to a particular history and culture at a particular point in time. Quite the contrary, similar to the white supremacists and Eurocentrists who put forward their imperial interpretation of history as though it were the definitive and divine, indeed, the universal and undisputed "truth" of history, Senghor in a similar—though highly reactionary—fashion, which illustrates his intense internalization of Eurocentric and colonial conceptions of Africa and Africans, put forward the above definitions and descriptions concerning the distinct differences between African and European rationality and epistemology. It is imperative here to emphasize that Senghor does not understand himself to be casually articulating an interpretation, or a culture- or region-specific aspect of the African approach to knowledge; instead, he conceives of himself as a conduit through which the definitive "truth" about Africa and Africans, as a whole, is finally being revealed. What excites Senghor even more is that some higher power has honored and ordained him, brought him to a higher consciousness, and bestowed the burden of the revelation on him, which he jubilantly—and eloquently, I might add—articulates.

Sounding more like a prophet than a poet, Senghor said: "Nature has arranged things well in willing that each people, each race, each continent, should cultivate with special affection certain of the virtues of man; that is precisely where originality lies" (p. 64). But, this assertion begs the question: from what metaphysical or supernatural vantage point does Senghor cite and derive the "truth" that he articulates? In other words, what are the sources of his Africanity? The former is a question that has remained unanswered for more than half a century, and one that I will audaciously venture to say cannot be answered because Senghor's concept of Africanity, similar to his notion of Negritude, is conceptually incarcerated within the prison house of the Otherness of the Other as projected and presented by Europe's Eurocentric metaphysical and supernatural, indeed, divine and delusional, self-(mis)conception. It is from within the confines of his cell inside the prison house of this centuries-spanning Eurocentric racial-colonial presentation and projection that Senghor conceived Africanity. Senghorian Africanity, then, as Sartre sadly said of Negritude, was born only to die, because it cannot and does not exist outside of the Manichaean world and the imperial machinations of Europe.

From Senghor's epistemically suspect point of view, Africa is to enrich human culture and civilization through its intuitive reason, and Europe through the development of its discursive reason, and, ultimately, humanity will achieve Teilhard de Chardin's "Civilization of the Universal." Here, then, lies the "originality" that Senghor mentioned above, and also here, in plain view, is his conception of the "true" or authentic—ontologically speaking—complementarity of African and European rationality and epistemology. Africanity's axiology, therefore, was purposely produced, from within the prison house of a white supremacist and European imperial world, as a politically impotent, insult-embracing, racism-accepting, and colonialism-condoning search for African (sub)humanity, identity and personality. So, is it any wonder that Africanity's values often mirror the very values that European colonizers and white enslavers projected onto Africa and Africans: intuitive reason, emotional, sensational, sensuousness, instinctual, feeling, rhythm, creative, imaginative, natural, agricultural, primitive, athletic, animalistic, hyper-sexual, spiritual, exotic, and erotic, etc.

Without critically engaging the negative portraits and mischaracterizations of Africans put forward by the plethora of Eurocentric missionaries, philosophers, anthropologists, and ethnologists to which his work constantly refers, Senghor falls prey to the "culturalism" that Hountondji charged him with above. The Eurocentric mischaracterizations of Africa and Africans that Senghor develops his ideas out of constantly destabilizes the discursive foundation of his work and gives it its characteristic, if not infamous, contradictory character. His Africanity and Negritude naturalizes negative views of, and abominable projections of primitivity onto, Africans and turns these "views" into timeless "truths."

Drawing from the pseudo-scientific and amorphous philosophical anthropology of Teilhard de Chardin, the racist and morally reprehensible ethnography of Count de Gobineau, the flimsy and flippant existential-phenomenological remarks on race and racism of Jean-Paul Sartre, and the inchoate colonial ontological conjectures of Father Placide Tempels, among others, Senghor is overjoyed to invent an "authentic" African essence. Critical readers are quick to query: how does he "invent" an "authentic" African essence? Quite simply, he inverts Eurocentric diabolical descriptions and explanations of Africa and Africans, re-inscribes them, and then re-presents them as positive, "authentic" African evidence of an ontological difference in and for black-being-in-the-world. Senghor cannot comprehend that these descriptions are invariably situated within the contours of the Eurocentric prison house, which constantly conceptually incarcerates and (re)colonizes non-European cultures and civilizations because European culture and civilization is always and ever put forward as the model and measure of "true" human culture and civilization. By unwittingly utilizing Europe as the model and measure of humanity, Senghor (re)inferiorizes Africa and Africans, making them Europe's ideal Others, and leaving Europe exactly where the Eurocentric missionaries, philosophers, anthropologists, and ethnologists he continually quotes would like it to be left, *at the center* of all human history, culture, and civilization.

Senghor asserted, "I felt divided before my rebirth, torn as I was between my Christian conscience and my Serer blood. . . . Now, I am no longer ashamed of my diversity; I find joy and reassurance in embracing in one catholic gesture all these complementary worlds" (Senghor quoted in Ba, 1973, p. 49). It would seem that Senghor offers us an answer to Du Bois's classic question of "double consciousness" but, as observed above, Senghorian Negritude often concedes and, what is worst, embraces many of the anti-black racist myths and stereotypes about Africans without adequately challenging, or radically refuting them. What is more, Senghorian Negritude has a tendency to acquiesce to colonial assimilation, even as it purports to defend "African cultural values." Therefore, Senghorian "double consciousness," if you will, often exhibits a hyperconsciousness of French and other Eurocentric views and values, and especially in terms of interpreting and articulating African history and culture, and it rarely reverses this practice and employs African views and values as a rubric for interpreting French and other European history and culture. This is not a "double consciousness," at least not in the Du Boisian sense, as much as it is a *single consciousness*, or a *colonized consciousness*, a *false consciousness* that is predicated on and privileges Eurocentric views and values and does not challenge or destabilize Europe's long-held anti-black racist and colonial conceptions of Africa and Africans.

Senghor's early writings on Negritude were greatly influenced by Sartre's "Black Orpheus," and as a result bear the stamp of what Fanon (1967) would later term "Sartre's . . . Hegelian . . . negative . . . [destruction] of black zeal" (pp. 133–35).[11] Recall for Sartre, Negritude is a "negative moment" that "is not sufficient in itself." Sartre saw "the black's-being-in-the-world"—that is, blacks' struggle to be African in a European imperial world—as merely another moment in a Hegelian-Marxist dialectical progression towards "a society without races."[12] However, what he failed to realize was that he, like Marx and Engels before him, reduced persons of African origin (and other colored and colonized people) to anonymous *racial* entities, or "human things," as Fanon (1968) put it (p. 205). Sartre spoke as if Africans and other non-Europeans did not exist outside of this "insufficient" "negative moment," or solely for the sake of "the goal of all vulgar dialectics: synthesis" (Sekyi-Otu, 1996, p. 201). Moreover, Sartre—again, as with his philosophical fathers, Marx and Engels—is quick to forget that it was Europeans, and white philosophers and white racist pseudo-scientists in particular, who contributed to the development of, and, in many senses, perpetuated the concept of race throughout the globe (Essed and Goldberg, 2002; Eze, 1997c; Ward and Lott, 2002; Zack, 1996).

When Senghor digests, for lack of a better term, Sartre's dependency theory of Negritude and places it within the wider discourse of African philosophy, he, in a sense, does precisely what he claims "the Negro" or "the African" does when she or he encounters an object or "the Other": "He dies to himself to be reborn in the Other. He does not assimilate it, but himself. He does not take the Other's life, but strengthens his own with its life" (Senghor, 1995a, p. 120). Senghor does not say what will happen to the African if "the Other" is "negative," or unjust, unethical, immoral or irreligious. What he and Sartre fail to question is the reason why Africans, or any other colored and colonized group, would want to synthesize their respective cultures and civilizations with those of Europeans, whose thought and behavior have historically been horribly xenophobic and jingoistic and, even more, downright brutal and genocidal, towards non-European cultures and civilizations (Blaut, 1993; Rodney, 1967, 1972, 1981, 1990; Schwarz and Ray, 2000).

Perhaps Senghor and Sartre allude to the fact that non-Europeans, their lives, labor, lands, languages and cultures, have been and remain dominated and decimated by European imperialism and that, at this juncture in human history, they have but two choices, those of adhering to white supremacist racialization and dehumanization, or certain and soon deracination. Surely Senghorian and Sartrean Negritude reek of biological determinism and racial essentialism. Human beings of whatever hue are not unalterably predestined to do or not do anything, and non-Europeans, and African people in particular, must be bold enough to challenge their past and change their present colonial and neocolonial conditions.

Early Senghorian Negritude, being grounded on and in Sartre's "negative" conception of Negritude, is an alienated Negritude, a Negritude that finds itself often at odds with Césairean Negritude, which claimed that "[o]ur struggle was a struggle against alienation" (Césaire, 1972, p. 73). Where Césaire understands Negritude to be "a concrete rather than abstract coming into [African] consciousness," Senghor (1996) sees Negritude, via Sartre, as a transient, temporal state on the way to "synthesis"

(p. 50). Senghor's Negritude may be characterized as "cultural mulattoism" because, similar to the literature on and/or about "mulattoes," there appears to be a constant, tragic threat of being forced to decide whether one is a participant of and contributor to African (Senegalese) or European (French) culture and civilization.[13] Senghor, similar to Du Bois (1986a, p. 820) in "The Conservation of Races," seems to be asking himself the black existential question: "What, after all, am I? Am I an American [Frenchmen] or am I a Negro [African]? Can I be both? Or is it my duty to cease to be a Negro [African] as soon as possible and be an American [Frenchmen]?"

Senghor (1996) suggests assimilation as the solution to the problem, but notes at the outset that many may misunderstand or misinterpret what he means by "assimilation": "There is a danger that the word assimilation may lead to confusion and ambiguity. . . . To assimilate is not to identify, to make identical . . . we must go beyond the false alternative of association or assimilation and say association *and* assimilation" (p. 51, emphasis in original). He does not stop there, taking his assimilation theory one step further, and as if adding insult to injury, Senghor, first applauds "the colonial policies of Great Britain and France," and then explains how he intends, in so many words, to continue the French colonization of Senegal. Observe Senghor's (1998) hat-in-hand and utterly unbelievable celebration of the European colonization of Africa:

> [T]he colonial policies of Great Britain and France have proved successful complements to each other, and black Africa has benefited. The policies of the former tended to reinforce the traditional native civilization. As for France's policy, although we have often reviled it in the past, it too ended with a credit balance, through forcing us actively to assimilate European civilization. This fertilized our sense of Negritude. Today, our Negritude no longer expresses itself as opposition to European values, but as a complement to them. Henceforth, its militants will be concerned, as I have often said, not to be assimilated, but to assimilate. They will use European values to arouse the slumbering values of Negritude, which they will bring as their contribution to the Civilization of the Universal. (p. 441)

First, observe Senghor's openness to colonial assimilation and, second, his own admission that Africans have been (and are being) robbed of their basic human rights when and where he writes of the French "forcing us actively to assimilate European civilization." With all of his discourse on Negritude as a humanism it is a wonder that Senghor did not take a principled stand against French colonialism, pointing to its denial of the basic humanity and right to self-determination of African people, its racial oppression, and its economic exploitation. Instead, Senghor celebrated French colonialism and European imperialism, absurdly asserting, "although we have often reviled it in the past, it too ended with a credit balance." What is worst is when Senghor explained his "first Four-Year Plan," which he initiated as the President of Senegal soon after its independence in 1960:

> [W]e had to eliminate the flaws of colonial rule while preserving its positive contributions, such as the economic and the technical infrastructure and the teaching of the French language; *in spite of everything, the balance sheet of colonization is positive rather than negative* . . . these positive contributions had to be rooted in Negritude by a series of comparisons between existing systems. (p. 445, emphasis added)

Senghorian Negritude amazingly understands the colonization of Africa to be "positive rather than negative," and even encourages the continued teaching of "the French language"—not Wolof, one of the most widespread Senegalese languages, but French—even after Senegal's so-called "independence." The "comparisons between existing systems" which he alludes to, then, are clearly comparisons between Eurocentric imperial systems. Even after independence, France and French language, history, and culture remained Senghor's point of departure. He unwittingly overlooked literally hundreds of indigenous African social systems, institutions and arrangements; he boldly paraded his preoccupation with France; and, throughout his Presidency (1960–1980), he openly sought to assimilate and *recolonize* (as opposed to decolonize) Senegal. Moreover, Senghor astoundingly admitted that "the backwardness of black Africa . . . has been caused less by colonization than by the slave trade, which in three centuries carried off some two hundred million victims, *blacks hosts* (p. 442, emphasis in original). But, he then concluded in the customary contradictory nature of his Negritude: "Capitalism, then, thanks to the accumulation of financial resources and its development of the means of production, was a factor of progress for Europe and also for Africa" (p. 442).

After giving a brief discussion of the "cultural borrowing[s]" between civilizations, Senghor asserts that: "the civilization of the future must be . . . the outcome of a sym-bio-sis [sic]" (p. 51). Symbiosis, "the intimate living together of two kinds of organisms, especially if such an association is of mutual advantage," is not exactly what one is wont to term the history of power relations between Africa and Europe. In order for there to be true "assimilation," "synthesis," and/or "symbiosis," Africa and Europe would both have to bring to the treasure houses of human culture and civilization their "great message[s]," as Du Bois (1986) said, "for humanity" (p. 820). Africa, along with the rest of the non-European/non-white world, has had its mouth gagged, hands tied, and feet bound since the fifteenth century. Europe and Europe alone speaks, and the remainder of humanity, all colored and colonized eighty-five to ninety percent, is literally forced—by the threat of nuclear annihilation—to hear and heed. As Fanon (1967) poignantly and painfully put it: "The white man wants the world; he wants it for himself alone. He finds himself predestined master of this world. He enslaves it" (p. 128).

## SENGHORIAN SOCIALISM: NEOCOLONIALISM, NEGRITUDE, AFRICANITY, AND THE ADVENTURES OF AFRICAN SOCIALISM

The foregoing provides a theoretical portrait, a conceptual snapshot, if you will, of Senghor's early Sartrean existential phenomenology-influenced articulation of Negritude. But, as the Pan-African independence boom gained momentum, he revised his Negritude and began to stress the importance of African views and values, African identity and, perhaps most importantly, an "African mode of socialism."[14] A decade after Sartre had pronounced Negritude a mere reaction to, and antithetical "negation" of white supremacy, born only to die, Senghor (1996) stated, "the struggle for Negritude must not be *negation* but *affirmation*" (p. 49, emphasis in original). Affirming both the humanity and distinct identity—that is, the authentic

*Africanity*—of Africans, Senghor posits that Africa, too, has its part to play in the great drama of human history.[15] He asks the question: "Is there any people, any nation, which does not consider itself superior, and the holder of a unique message?" (Senghor, 1998, p. 439). As with Du Bois's contention that each human group has a "great message for humanity," Senghor's revised Negritude maintained that Africa has a "unique message" for the world, but that the world must be bold enough to hear and heed the special message.

The message that Africa can and must contribute to the world is, according to Senghor, contained in traditional African thought, that is, the historical views and values of African people.[16] In this sense, then, Senghor (1998) asserted, the Negritudists "were justified in fostering the values of Negritude, and arousing the energy slumbering within us." In fact, he continued, "it must be in order to pour them into the mainstream of cultural miscegenation (biological process taking place spontaneously). They must flow towards the meeting point of all humanity; they must be our contribution to the Civilization of the Universal" (p. 440). Where Senghor had previously asserted that the African "does not assimilate, he is assimilated," employing his reconstructed concept of Negritude, he now claimed that the African is concerned "not to be assimilated, but to assimilate" (1996, p. 47, 1998, p. 441). Breaking away from Sartrean "negative" Negritude, Senghor swings in the direction of Césaire and suggests a reengagement and reconstruction of traditional African views and values. However, Senghor, similar to Césaire, advocates a "return"—to use Césaire's term—not to the precolonial African past, but to radical "traditional" African views and values, because he feels there is much that could be appropriated and applied to the neocolonial African present. Senghor (1996) said:

> The problem which we, Africans in 1959, are set with is how to integrate African values into the world of 1959. It is not a case of reviving the past so as to live on in an African museum. It is a case of animating this world, here and now, with the values that come from our past. This after all is what the American Negroes have begun to do. (p. 51)

One of the definitive "values" from the African past that Senghor, Sekou Toure, Kwame Nkrumah, Julius Nyerere and Amilcar Cabral, among others, strongly felt should be integrated into and animate Africa's present was "African socialism." "The African mode of socialism," asserted Senghor (1998), "is not that of Europe. It is neither atheistic communism nor, quite, the democratic socialism of the Second International of the Labor Party" (p. 442). On the contrary, he continued:

> The specific objective of African socialism, after the Second World War, was to fight against foreign capitalism and its slave economy; to do away, not with the inequality resulting from the domination of one class by another, but with the inequality resulting from the domination of the European conquest, from the domination of one people by another, of one race by another. (p. 444)

For Senghor, and many of the other African socialists, Western Marxism and/or Eurocentric socialism was simply "too narrow" to fully engage the existential and ontological issues of neocolonial Africa. He declared: "For, Marx's world-view, although that of a genius, remained too narrow; it was neither sufficiently *retrospective*, nor sufficiently *prospective*" to speak to the specials needs of Africa and Africans (p.

445, emphasis in original). Where Césaire (1972, p. 70) said, "Marx is all right, but we need to complete Marx," and Fanon (1968, p. 40) fumed, "Marxist analysis should always be slightly stretched every time we have to do with the colonial problem. Everything up to and including the very nature of pre-capitalist society, so well explained by Marx, must here be thought out again." Senghor (1998) sternly stated:

> Marx nowhere deals with this form of inequality [racial colonialism], this domination, and the struggle for freedom which they were to provoke. That was one of his omissions, which we had to repair by starting from our own situation, extrapolating, nevertheless, from his analyses and his theory, pressing them home to the very last of their logical implications and of their practical implications. For the celebrated solidarity of the world proletariat has remained purely theoretical, even among Marx's disciples. In hard fact, as we must have the clear sight—and the courage—to admit, the rise in the standard of living of the European worker has been effected, through a colonial slave economy, to the detriment of the masses of Asia and Africa. Hence the difficulties of decolonization. . . . [W]e can form a new world-vision which takes in the whole of matter and life: a *Weltanschauung* deeper and more complete than Marx's, and therefore more human. (pp. 444–445)

Long before Marxism and the Frankfurt School tradition of critical theory, as Du Bois's *Black Reconstruction*, James's *The Black Jacobins*, and Césaire's *Discourse on Colonialism* eloquently illustrate, enslaved, racialized and colonized Africans developed critical theories of race and racism in their efforts to topple white supremacy and cut capitalism and colonialism off at their knees (Du Bois, 1995b; James, 1963; Césaire, 1972). They sought solutions to social and political problems as passionately and radically as—again I say, even more passionately and more radically than—the white working-class, who—as Eric Williams acutely observed in *Capitalism and Slavery* (1966), as Walter Rodney perceptively and persuasively waxed in *How Europe Underdeveloped Africa* (1972), and as Manning Marable eloquently illustrated in *How Capitalism Underdeveloped Black America* (1983)—profited from and were complicit in the very white supremacist, enslaving, and colonizing system(s) oppressing and exploiting blacks, among other non-whites. Usually critical theory is comprehended as a critique of and an heir to modernity and the Enlightenment, and "modernity" is only thought of from a Eurocentric point of view—that is, in the aftermath of European imperial expansion around the globe what it means to be "modern" translates into how well Europeans and non-Europeans emulate European *imperial* thought, culture, politics, etc. But, if one were to critically call into question Eurocentric and imperial conceptions of what it means to be "modern," then, alternative categories—anti-racist, anti-colonial, and anti-capitalist categories—are opened up, and contemporary critical theorists are able to observe, perhaps for the first time: first, that it was on the fringes of Europe's imperial free-for-all, in the imperial outposts in the colored world where racism and colonialism were naturalized, where modernity was initially conceived, and in some senses aborted; second, that many of modernity's most perplexing problems were initially put forward and keenly considered by non-European, racialized, and colonized intellectual-activists; and, lastly, that Negritude is, however problematic and contradictory, a continuation and seminal part of the black radical tradition that should no longer be left in the lurch because of its perceived associations with or allegiance to Eurocentric existentialism, surrealism, and socialism. As the above analysis of Negritude illustrates, there simply is no substitute, no easy-out for critical theorists, and Africana critical theorists in particular, who should sift through Negritude's divergent discourse(s), including Sartrean Negritude, and salvage anything that might be useful in our ongoing efforts to not simply deconstruct and reconstruct radical politics and critical social theory but, even more importantly, contemporary culture, society, and humanity.

Senghor's newly revised Negritude of the 1960's understood that it was not colonialism alone that the colonized must wage war against, but capitalism as well. Once "independent" many of the formerly colonized countries continued to depend on European powers for their national wellbeing, Senghor's Senegal notwithstanding. To break the monopoly European powers had on Africa and Africans Senghor (1998) suggested an "African mode of socialism" that went well beyond Marx and "old scientific socialism . . . by plugging the holes in it, and by opening up its blind alleys" (p. 446). However, and here is where Senghorian Negritude's characteristic contradictory nature surfaces once again, even as he advocated for an African socialism, Senghor continued to encourage Pan-Africanists to "borrow from the socialist experiments" of Europe and white Marxists (p. 443). This, in and of itself, its not problematic, but it does in the long-run prove problematic when and where Senghor does not clearly articulate that African interests, and the interests of other colored and colonized peoples should be critically held in mind in the event that transethnic anti-imperialists and multicultural Marxists "borrow from the socialist experiments" of Europe and white Marxists.

Ironically, unlike Césaire, Senghor suggested "returning" to and/or "cultural borrowing," not from the burgeoning tradition of Pan-African socialism and black Marxism, which was initiated by Du Bois, James, and several of the radicals of the Harlem Renaissance, but from European socialists and white Marxists during one of the most intense periods of revolutionary Pan-African political and intellectual activity in modern history.[17] One need look no further, for example, than Du Bois's *Black Reconstruction, Color and Democracy*, and *The World and Africa*; James's *The Black Jacobins* and *A History of Pan-African Revolt*; Kwame Nkrumah's *Towards Colonial Freedom, Africa Must Unite, Consciencism: Philosophy and Ideology for Decolonization*, and *Neo-Colonialism: The Last Stage of Imperialism*; Sékou Touré's *Africa in Motion, Africa and the Revolution, Africa and Imperialism*, and *Towards Full Re-Africanization*; Julius Nyerere's *Ujamaa: Essays on Socialism, Freedom and Unity, Freedom and Socialism*, and *Freedom and Development*; and, finally, Amilcar Cabral's *Revolution in Guinea, Return to the Source*, and *Unity and Struggle*. Overlooking all of this, Senghor urges black Marxists and Pan-African socialists, in essence, to continue their colonial relationship with Europe, stating: "It is a question, once again, of modernizing our values by borrowing from European socialism, its science and technical skills, above all, its spirit of progress" (p. 443).

In *On African Socialism* Senghor (1964a) critically engages white/Western Marxism and endeavors, not to illustrate its inadequacies in terms of confronting racial oppression and racial colonial domination, but ways in which it informs an "African mode of socialism" predicated on the projected African primitivisms of Eurocentrism and white supremacism. Senghorian socialism, similar to his versions of Negritude and Africanity, is conceptually incarcerated in the horror-filled holding-cell that Europe's invented Africa has long been held in. Again, similar to his versions of Negritude and Africanity, Senghorian socialism does display a penchant for quasi-Pan-African radical politics (not to mention black radical rhetoric), but its would-be radical politics are constantly diluted and destabilized by his incessant advocacy of a synthesis and "symbiosis" of European and African rationality, which, because both descriptions and interpretations of black and white reason are one-dimensional and figments of his fantastic imagination, he unwittingly ultimately advocates for the subordination of (his highly-imaginary and super-surrealistic) "Africa" to (his unbelievably over-inflated and over-exaggerated) "Europe" on the same pseudo-scientific, philosophically phony, and politically pointless Eurocentric metaphysical grounds that rendered his versions of Negritude and Africanity fatally-flawed. So, given the foregoing, it might make sense to ask a serious question, such as: Is Senghorian socialism, when all is said and done, a *socialism of subordination*; a *socialism of servility*; a Eurocentric "African mode of socialism," which is not an "African mode of socialism" at all, but a gentler and more generous form of neo-colonialism in blackface? Is it surreptitiously—it seriously saddens me to ask—*an anti-African* and *anti-socialist* socialism?

Sadly, even after independence, even after advocating an "African mode of socialism," Senghor was unable to break free from the French colonial cathedral where he had so solemnly and faithfully worshiped for so long. France, and Europe in general, from Senghor's surrealist, artificial Pan-African point of view, simultaneously represented Africa's death (crucifixion?) and neocolonial new life or afterlife (resurrection?), and African socialism—again, from Senghor's Eurocentric surrealist, faux Pan-African point of view—was simply another symbol of Africa's inferiority or, as he put it above, "the backwardness of black Africa." In other words, even in their fight for freedom, Senghor counseled the colonized to turn to the twisted teachings of their colonizers, thus intellectually re-enslaving, theoretically recolonizing and, eventually, psychologically and physically redelivering the racially ruled to the egregious and epoch-encompassing violence of their racial rulers. Senghorian Negritude, though it clearly quantitatively surpasses Césairean Negritude in its critical engagement of European socialism and white Marxism, not to mention Sartrean existential phenomenology and Teilhard de Chardin's philosophical anthropology, it is nonetheless qualitatively inferior to Césairean Negritude on account of its ultimate acquiescence to Eurocentric conceptions of Africa, Africans, blackness, and socialism. Yet and still, taken together both Senghorian and Césairean Negritude contribute to the Africana tradition of critical theory, and it is to their contributions that we will now turn.

## NEGRITUDE'S CONNECTIONS AND CONTRIBUTIONS TO AFRICANA CRITICAL THEORY

Negritude, as an aesthetic attitude, a lyrical literary movement, and a social and political philosophy, connects and contributes to the discourse of Africana critical theory in several ways. First, Negritude's nexus to the African anti-colonial struggle, and the theory and praxis of Pan-Africanism in particular, can hardly be denied (Berrian and Long, 1967; Finn, 1988; Irele, 1965a, 1965b; E.A. Jones, 1971; Wanja, 1974). Senghor wrote of "the Negro-African personality" and "our Collective Soul," where

Césaire said, "I have always recognized that what was happening to my brothers in Algeria and the United States had its repercussions in me" (Senghor, 1998, p. 439, 1996, p. 50; Césaire, 1972, p. 77). Secondly, Negritude possesses a cultural kinship with the Harlem Renaissance, the first modern black aesthetic movement and axiological explosion (Ako, 1982; Bamikunle, 1982; Fabre, 1993; Irele, 2004; Shuttlesworth-Davidson, 1980). The breakthroughs of the Renaissance fanned and fueled the wildfires that would eventually spread around the colored and colonial world. The radicals of the Renaissance contributed an existential engagement of the African self-image and identity, which in the hands of Senghor and Césaire would translate and transform itself into the Negritudian notion of "Africanity" (Carroll, 2005; S.K. Lewis, 2006; Wylie, 1985). With regard to the Harlem Renaissance, it must be remembered, as Nathan Huggins (1995) asserted, "[i]dentity was central" (p. 9). Meaning, identity was an integral part of, and an organizing principal for, African American aesthetic attitudes. Huggins continued, "Afro-American identity was then, as it is now, a major preoccupation with black artists and writers" (p. 11).

Thirdly, Césaire and Senghor's emphasis on the need to "return" to, or better yet the *re-discovering*, appropriating and applying, extending and expanding of indigenous African thought and practices in an effort to reconstruct an African identity—i.e., Africanity—certainly links with and sheds light on the fact that Negritude, as quiet as it is kept, laid the foundation for what has been dubbed, by some positively and others pejoratively, "ethnophilosophy" (Bell, 2002; L.M. Brown, 2004; Gordon, 2008; Horton, 1973, 1993; Hountondji, 1996; Imbo, 1998, 2002; Karp and Bird, 1980; Karp and Masolo, 2000; Wiredu, 1980, 1995, 1996, 2004). Fourthly, from within the vortex of Africana philosophy Negritude registers, however "un-systematically," one of the earliest critiques and rejections of the grafting of Western European philosophical concepts and categories onto persons of African origin and descent and Africana cultures (Masolo, 1994, p. 29). For example, Césaire's excellent engagement of Placide Tempels' *Bantu Philosophy*, and Senghor's seminal and signal critique of Marx and white Marxist socialism (Césaire 1972, pp. 33–39; Senghor 1998, pp. 438–448). And, finally, Negritude reminds the workers of Africana critical theory once again that no matter what other human groups understand "philosophy" to be, in the African world—a world currently experiencing the ongoing effects of violent colonial conquest—we need functional philosophy or, as the Italian philosopher Antonio Gramsci (1971) would have it, a "philosophy of praxis": philosophy that is at once intellectual and political, academic *and* activist. Let us, then, take a deeper, more dialectical look at the connections or contributions of Negritude (and Africanity) to the Africana tradition of critical theory.

## NEGRITUDE AND THE PARADOXICAL PREDICAMENT OF EARLY TWENTIETH CENTURY PAN-AFRICANISM

Janheinz Jahn (1968) maintained that, "the semantic, rhythmical and thematic achievements of Negritude have a fruitful connection with each other as characteristics of a specific philosophy and attitude to the world, the conception of an African style and the unity of an African culture" (p. 249). Negritude, being at once "a specific philosophy and attitude to [or toward] the world" binds disparate aspects of transethnic African cultures together by the very fact that it asserts that there is such a thing as an "African reality," or "African metaphysics."[18] Jahn stated, "The aim of the subject matter [of Negritude] is to capture the African reality," and this "reality," in both its continental and diasporan forms, is a "reality" that has been shaped and molded by the violence unleashed by European imperialism (p. 249; see also Blaut, 1993; Chinweizu, 1975; Rodney, 1972; Serequeberhan, 1994). In considering the nexus of Negritude to Pan-Africanism one must concede that Negritude, being ultimately concerned with "Africanity," sought to forge an African identity out of the raw materials of both continental *and* diasporan life-worlds and lived-experiences (N.R. Shapiro, 1970; Wanja, 1974; Wylie, 1985). We would do well to emphasize this point. Pan-Africanism, a precursor of Negritude and the Negritudian notion of Africanity, is—as Du Bois (1958, 1960c, 1963, 1965) asserted at several intervals throughout his dialectical development of the theory of Pan-Africanism—concerned not merely with improving the lived-experiences of the Africans on the continent, but with the whole of the colored and colonized world. In "Pan-Africa and New Radical Philosophy," Du Bois (1971b) declared:

> We have considered all these matters [European imperialism and the colonial problem] in relation to the American Negro but our underlying thought has been continually that they can and must be seen not against any narrow, provincial or even national background, but in relation to the great problem of the colored races of the world and particularly those of African descent. . . . [I]f this young, black American is going to survive and live a life, he must calmly face the fact that however much he is an American there are interests which draw him nearer to the darker people outside of America than to his white fellow citizens. And those interests are the same matters of color caste, of discrimination, of exploitation for the sake of profit, of public insult and oppression, against which the colored peoples of Mexico, South America, the West Indies and all Africa, and every country in Asia, complain and have long been complaining. It is, therefore, simply a matter of ordinary common sense that these people draw together in spiritual sympathy and intellectual co-operation [sic], to see what can be done for the freedom of the human spirit which happens to be incased in dark skin. (pp. 206–207)

Negritude, as reported by Césaire (1972) in *Discourse on Colonialism*, is among many other things "a coming to consciousness among Negroes," and "an affirmation of our solidarity" (p. 70). As with Pan-Africanism, Negritude serves as a counter to the reifying nature of the Europeanization of the non-European world through colonial conquest; Césaire's colonial equation should be recalled here: "colonization = thingification" (p. 21). Further, Negritude surely speaks to the "spiritual sympathy and intellectual co-operation" that Du Bois above claims must exist if anything is to be done in the direction of "the freedom of the human spirit which happens to be incased in dark skin." Freedom, a signal theme in black radical thought traditions, is the trope that binds Negritude and Pan-Africanism (Ackah, 1999; Adi, 2003; Axelsen, 1984; Cook and Henderson, 1969; Eze, 1997a; Kohn and Sokolsky, 1965; Langley, 1973, 1979; Legum, 1962; Lemelle and Kelley, 1994; Ofuatey-Kudjoe, 1986; Otite, 1978; Rothberg and Mazrui, 1970; Schall, 1975; V.B. Thompson, 1969, 1987, 2000). As Du Bois observed, it is precisely black collective interests in "matters of color caste, of discrimination, of exploitation for the sake of profit, of public insult and oppression" that places persons of African origin and

descent "nearer to the darker people" than persons who immorally inherit unprecedented power, privilege and prestige as a result of European imperialism and
white world supremacy.

## NEGRITUDE'S NEXUS TO THE
## RADICALISM OF THE HARLEM RENAISSANCE

With regard to the Harlem Renaissance, Nathan Huggins (1995) has reported that
the "New Negro" predecessors of the Renaissance called for "Afro-American identity
with Africa and for some form of Pan-African Unity. Whether in the studied language of W. E. B. Du Bois or in the more flamboyant rhetoric of Marcus Garvey, they
were announcing a striking new independence for black Americans" (p. 9; see also
Carroll, 2005; Favor, 1999; Wintz, 1996a). Huggins correctly observed a sense of
"new independence" amongst the "New Negroes," but he surreptitiously attempts
to characterize the New Negro movement and the "striking new independence" as
an exclusively African American affair. It was not merely "black Americans" that
made up the cadre of radical New Negroes, but also Caribbean cultural icons, such
as Marcus Garvey, Amy Jacques Garvey, Claude McKay, Hubert Harrison, Claudia
Jones, Cyril Briggs, Richard B. Moore, and W.A. Domingo, who filled their ranks
(C.B. Davies, 2007; W. James, 1998; Parascandola, 2005; Naison, 1983; U.Y. Taylor,
2002; J.M. Turner, 2005). The radical New Negroes, in calling for "some form of
Pan-African Unity," knew full well the interlocking and interconnecting ways in
which the image of "the black"—in the language of Fanon (1967) in *Black Skin,
White Masks*—was inextricable to the working white supremacist notion that *all* persons of African origin and descent were subhumans, subpersons, or just down-right
"savages" (pp. 117, 119-120, see also C.W. Mills, 1997; Pieterse, 1992). This is an
important point to accent, because without acknowledging the Caribbean impact
and influence on the New Negro movement and the Harlem Renaissance we will
not be able to grapple with and/or fully grasp the significance of these movements
for Negritude and subsequent black radical thought traditions. In fact, it was Huggins (1995) himself who unwittingly relayed that "Blacks were coming to the city
[New York] not only from the South but also from the French and British West Indies and Africa" (p. 6). This means, then, that the Harlem Renaissance cannot and
should not be characterized as an exclusively African American affair, but more
properly as an early twentieth-century *Africana* affair.

The radical New Negroes of the Harlem Renaissance took the "primitivism" and
"exoticism" associated with the "Old Negro" and Africa and began to forge a "new
self-concept" that understood African ancestry to be a positive as opposed to a negative: "Africans and Afro-Americans found positive value in the very stereotypes that
had formerly marked them as limited" (pp. 7-8). Further, in *African Philosophy in
Search of Identity*, Dismas Masolo (1994) related that many members of the Renaissance—he lists "Claude McKay, Langston Hughes, Jean Toomer, Countee Cullen,
and Sterling Brown"—"saw Africa, with its rawness and anchorage to bare natural
forces, as an essential antithesis to the domineering industrial civilization of the
white world" (p. 13). It was this axiological inversion "along the color-line" that
made the writings of the radicals of the Harlem Renaissance so enduring and intriguing to the architects of the Negritude movement.

Masolo contends that the primary aim of the Harlem Renaissance was "to rehabilitate the image of the black man wherever he was; it was the expression of the
black personality" (p. 10). He goes on to explain that the Renaissance, as a literary
movement, was a seminal and central "predecessor of the more widely known cog-
nate, Negritude." In fact, according to Masolo, in order "[t]o characterize Negritude
as a legitimate origin of philosophical discussion in Africa, we must . . . trace its origins and roots to [the] writings on race by African Americans in the United States,
especially in the 1920's" (pp. 10–11). More to the point, "[t]he Harlem Renaissance," mused Masolo, "gave Negritude both its form and its content" (p. 10). Masolo, in explicating that the Renaissance was concerned to "rehabilitate the image of
the black man wherever he was," speaks not only to the fact that the radicalism of
the Harlem Renaissance was informed by Pan-Africanism (in both its Du Boisian
and Garveyite forms), but also to the fact that it was in Harlem, as Huggins (1995)
related, where there was a "cross-fertilization of black intelligence and culture as in
no other place in the world" (p. 6). The Harlem Renaissance, therefore, served as a
signal paradigm for subsequent Africana philosophical and radical political activity,
and Negritude in particular symbolizes the hard won harvest of Africana conceptual
generations and discursive formations in the period immediately following the
Harlem Renaissance.[19]

In highlighting the roots of Negritude's radicalism, Lilyan Kesteloot (1991) asserted that it was the militants of the Harlem movement who "were the first to
broach the subject . . . [of] the existence of a racial problem," and that prior to them
"the only right of the black man that was recognized was the right to amuse whites"
(pp. 57, 60). One of, if not *the* major contribution of the radicals of the Renaissance
was their insistent engagement and appreciation of Africa—though their engagement and appreciation of Africa, it should be earnestly observed, was often caught
within the confines of the prison house of Eurocentric projected African "primitivisms," à la Senghorian Negritude and, to a certain extent, Senghorian Africanity.
According to Kesteloot, "[t]he acknowledgement of Africa was one of the pervasive
characteristics of the Harlem Renaissance" (p. 71). The acknowledgement and appreciation of Africa led the radicals of the Renaissance to critique and collapse many
of the cultural values of Europe and engage and extract African values that they felt
had gone unjustly unrecognized for far too long, not simply by whites and Europe,
but also by persons of African descent, continental and diasporan. Kesteloot contended:

> However, mixed in with the folklore, the black writers [of the Harlem Renaissance]
> sowed ideas in their books which some ten years later became the leaven of the Negri-
> tude movement. They resolutely turned their backs on the preceding generation which
> had been "characterized by intellectual acceptance of white American values and, in lit-
> erature, by sentimental lyricism over the misfortunes of an oppressed and exiled race,"
> in order to commit themselves to a "vigorous though not boastful affirmation of their
> original values." (pp. 60–61)

Kesteloot carefully concluded:

> . . . [T]he [African] American literature already contained seeds of the main themes of
> Negritude. Hence, one can assert that the real fathers of the Negro cultural renaissance
> in France were neither the writers of the West Indian tradition, nor the surrealist poets,

nor the French novelists of the era between the two wars, but black writers of the United States. They made a very deep impression on French Negro writers by claiming to represent an entire race, launching a cry with which all blacks identified—the first cry of rebellion. (p. 57)

Corroborating Kesteloot's claims, Jahn (1968) stressed that "[b]ecause they [the theorists of Negritude] claimed to feel and represent their own dynamic 'being-in-the-world,' these writers looked on all Afro-American writers before them as their forerunners and discovered Negritude in the earlier writers' works" (p. 253). However, Jahn is quick to offer a caveat: "Whatever the Negritude writers may owe to their predecessors, they brought it into the great complex of their own conception. Even when borrowing or taking over, they often excelled those earlier writers in inspiration and poetic power. Their self-confidence was firmly based on real achievement" (pp. 260–261). Both Kesteloot and Jahn contend that the theorists of Negritude were drawn to the writers of the Harlem Renaissance because the Harlem writers professed to "represent an entire race," and because it was these writers' words and wisdom concerning "the question of color" in a white supremacist world that contained the kernel from which Negritude, as theory and praxis, originated (Kesteloot, 1991, p. 57).

Jahn acknowledged that the theorists of Negritude "borrow[ed]" from the writers of the Renaissance, which speaks to the notion of continuity in black radical thought traditions. However, he, as with Huggins, was too quick to label all of the radicals of the Harlem Renaissance as "Afro-Americans." Jahn's insipid read of the Renaissance as an exclusively "Afro-American" affair notwithstanding, he touched on an issue that importantly cuts to the very core of our discussion. Jahn observed that no matter what the theorists of Negritude may have borrowed or taken over from the writers of the Harlem Renaissance, they "brought it into the great complex of their own conception." By this I take Jahn to mean that the theorists of Negritude did as they admonished others to do, they appropriated and applied liberating visions, views, and values from the precolonial African past to their then colonial and neocolonial present. This, of course, is why Jahn felt compelled to highlight the fact that the theorists of Negritude's "self-confidence was based firmly on real achievement." The "real achievement" that Jahn alluded to is, of course, the "real"—meaning "concrete" as opposed to "abstract"—*political* achievements of Negritude as it moved from the theoretical level to the practical (application) level. More to the point, the "real achievement" of Negritude translated itself into Césaire and Senghor's political breakthroughs with regard to their respective "native" lands. For example, Césaire was elected mayor of, and went on represent Martinique in the French National Assembly, and Senghor was elected and served as president of Senegal for two decades (1960–1980).

That the radical political poets of Negritude understood their school of thought to be an extension and expansion of the cultural revolution initiated by the radicals of the Harlem Renaissance can hardly be questioned. Janet Vaillant, in *Black, French, and African: A Life of Léopold Sedar Senghor*, related that Senghor was first exposed to the writings of the Harlem Renaissance by Louis Achille, Jr., a former professor at Howard University, who entertained several of the leading African American intellectuals of the era in his Parisian apartment, and Paulette Nardal, whose apartment served as the gathering house for African, African American, and Caribbean students in Paris (Sharpley-Whiting, 2002). Vaillant (1990) revealingly wrote:

> It is here that Senghor first began to learn about the writers of the Harlem Renaissance and the New Negro movement in the United States. In time, he began to meet the black Americans, who were always welcome in the Achilles' bilingual household. He discovered with surprise that there was a whole world, even if a small one, that was as preoccupied as he was by the question of color. (pp. 91–92)

Corroborating Vaillant's claims, Kesteloot (1991) related "Senghor, Césaire, and Damas, the founders of what came to be known as the Negritude movement, acknowledge that, between 1930 and 1940, African and West Indian students living in Paris were in close contact with American Negro writers Claude McKay, Jean Toomer, Langston Hughes, and Countee Cullen," and that they read these writers' work and were personally acquainted with them (p. 56). As the theorists of Negritude read the writings of the radicals of the Harlem Renaissance they began to appropriate the aesthetic insights and axiological inversions of the Harlem school, and it is here that the strongest line(s) of continuity between these two schools may be ascertained. Huggins (1995) observed that for the radicals of the Harlem Renaissance "[i]dentity was central" and that "Blackness, clearly, was not only a color, it was a state of mind" (p. 9). In like fashion, following the Harlem radicals' lead, Césaire (1972) fastidiously stated:

> I have always thought that the black man was searching for his identity. And it has seemed to me that if what we want is to establish this identity, then we must have a concrete consciousness of what we are—that is, of the first fact of our lives; that we are black; that we were black and have a history, a history that contains certain cultural elements of great value; and that Negroes were not, as you [René Depestre] put it, born yesterday, because there have been beautiful and important black civilizations. At the time we began to write people could write a history of world civilization without devoting a single chapter to Africa, as if Africa had made no contributions to the world. Therefore, we affirmed that we were Negroes and that we were proud of it, and that we thought that Africa was not some sort of blank page in the history of humanity; in sum, we asserted that our Negro heritage was worthy of respect, and that this heritage was not relegated to the past, that its values were values that could still make an important contribution to the world. (p. 76)

## NEGRITUDE AND THE CRITICAL (RE)TURN TO TRADITIONAL/PRECOLONIAL AFRICAN THOUGHT

This search for identity, exacerbated by European imperialism, led the theorists of Negritude—as it had the members of the Harlem Reniassance—to confront and contest the supposed "universal" applicability of Western European, or, rather Eurocentric values insofar as the colored and colonized world was concerned. Césaire was extremely explicit, "our Negro heritage [is] worthy of respect." The "heritage" of which Césaire speaks symbolizes the cultural inheritance of persons of African descent, and must not be "relegated to the past," but engaged and examined for its relevance to the contemporary "African reality" (Serequeberhan, 2000). Césaire further stated that the values of the African past are "values that could still make an important contribution to the world." Here Césaire's critical faith in African ancestral traditions places him squarely on terrain (re)covered by the African American philosopher Alain Locke (1968) in his essay, "The Legacy of the Ancestral Arts," where he thundered, "the Negro is not a cultural foundling without his own inheritance" (p. 256).[20] Locke asserted that contemporary persons of African origin would do well to extend and expand the traditions of their forebears, and he went on to retort, "[n]o great art will impose alien canons upon its subject matter" (p. 264). On the extension and expansion of the legacy left by the ancestors, Locke remarked:

> [W]hat the Negro artist of today has most to gain from the arts of the forefathers is perhaps not cultural inspiration or technical innovations, but the lesson of a classical background, the lesson of discipline, of style, of technical control pushed to the limits of technical mastery. A more highly stylized art does not exist than the African. If after absorbing the new content of American life and experience, and after assimilating new patterns of art, the original artistic endowment can be sufficiently augmented to express itself with equal power in more complex patterns and substance, then the Negro may well become what some have predicted, the artist of American life. (pp. 257–258)[21]

For Locke, as with Césaire and Senghor, it was never a question of "returning" to an antiquated African past merely for the sake of highlighting and accenting the "great" achievements of Africa, but, on the contrary, he counseled his contemporaries to *discover* the lessons of "a classical background," "discipline," "style," and technique. It was only after continental and diasporan African aesthetes had thoroughly engaged and examined the artistic legacy of their forebears that Locke suggested they should "augment" the "original artistic endowment." The theorists of Negritude, who studied with Locke personally, heeded the African American philosopher's words and became the preeminent heirs of the radicalism bequeathed by the Harlem Renaissance to the discourses of Africana philosophy, black radical politics, and critical social theory (Masolo, 1994, p. 25).[22]

Senghor (1998) said, "we unsheathed our native knives and stormed the values of Europe" (p. 439). However, he also asserted "our Negritude no longer expresses itself as opposition to European values, but as a *complement* to them" (1996, p. 50, emphasis in original). Africans, as well as Europeans, according to Senghor, are to remain "open" to the views and values of "Others," and appropriate and apply the things which they understand to be applicable to their life-worlds: "We Negro-Africans and you Europeans thus have a common interest in fostering our specifically native values, whilst remaining open to the values of the Others" (Senghor, 1998, p. 440). Western European views and values are not negative in and of themselves—and this is the point that both the Harlem Renaissance and Negritude thought-traditions highlight and accent—but, when and where Eurocentric axiology and aesthetics are foisted or superimposed onto the colored and colonized world is precisely the place where a cultural mishap has taken place. In fact, Senghor perceptively pointed out that the colored and colonized world has not historically chosen European views and values because they felt that these were the best, or healthiest, or most humane views and values. But, because they have had no choice: "For if European civilization were to be imposed [as it historically has been], unmodified, on all peoples and continents, it could only be by *force*" (Senghor, 1998, p. 441, emphasis added). European views and values have been and continue to be "forced" onto non-Europeans, their cultures and continents, and it must be remembered here, as both Fanon (1960b, 1968, 1969) and Foucault (1978, 1997, 2000) have asserted, "force" always entails some form of violence, whether physical or psychological.

Senghor suggested "cultural borrowing" as a solution to the "colonial problem." "[C]ultural borrowing" would "enable . . . us to adapt ourselves to the new situation" or, at the least, "make a better adaptation to the situation" (Senghor, 1996, p. 51). However, Senghor surreptitiously side-steps the fact that "the new situation" remains a "situation" where past and present European imperialism ubiquitously bequeaths an unprecedented amount of power, privilege, and prestige to Europeans/whites. His concept of "cultural borrowing" fails to take the historicity of the colored and colonized world into critical consideration (Serequeberhan, 1991a, 1991b, 2000). For, if the "power relations"—to use Foucault's phrase—of the "new situation" are identical to those of the "old situation," then what, pray tell, makes it a "new situation"? This is not to say that Senghor's concept of "cultural borrowing" does not and should not resonate deeply within the world of Africana philosophy and critical theory, but that his concept is ahistorical and does not adequately grapple with and/or engage the world (European and non-European) as it actually exists. "Cultural borrowing" lacks historical depth and for that reason needs to be rooted in the realities of the non-European world, before and beyond European imperialism.

At the heart of the theory of Negritude, Senghor (1996) observed, is "the awareness, defense, and development of African cultural values" (p. 49). In advocating a "return" to and/or the rediscovering of "African cultural values" in an effort to ascertain their applicability to the modern moment, the theorists of Negritude helped to spawn the contemporary discourse on "traditional" African and "ethnophilosophy."[23] Whether we understand "ethnophilosophy," as Paulin Hountondji (1996) does, to be "the imaginary search for an immutable, collective philosophy, common to all Africans" (p. 38). Or, if we interpret "ethnophilosophy" as Kwasi Wiredu does, as "the philosophy implicit in the life, thought, and talk of the traditional African," this aspect of African thought-traditions must consistently be critically and dialectically engaged because, as Césaire said, the African past contains "values that could still make an important contribution to the world" (Wiredu, 1991, p. 88; Césaire, 1972, p. 76).

The theorists of Negritude, in suggesting that Africans excavate their past for appropriate and applicable views and values with regard to their present, laid the foundation for the discourse of and on "ethno-" or "traditional" African philosophy. However, unfortunately Placide Tempels, via his work *Bantu Philosophy*, is often considered by the workers in African philosophy as the founder or "father" of this discourse (Imbo, 1998, pp. 8–11; Masolo, 1994, pp. 46–67). Tempels did mine the worldview of the Bantus, but he did so with the wicked intention of opening up the "ethno-mind," laying the "primitive thought" of these "primitive people" to bear, before a European colonial readership (Van Niekerk, 1998, p. 74). Further, it should be importantly pointed out that Tempels' volume was not published until 1945, a whole decade after the theorists of Negritude had initiated their poetic, political, and philosophical movement that rested on a recurring theoretical theme of "return."[24] This motif of "return"—the engagement of the views and values of the past in order to appropriate and apply the insights to the present—has trickled down to our modern moment and has contributed to the discourse of Africana philosophy a fertile conceptual ground that promises to yield an abundant harvest. Although many Western European-trained philosophers of African descent have criticized the workers in "ethno-" or "traditional" African philosophy, Wiredu reminds us that "when we speak of the philosophy of a people we are talking of a tradition," and the "study of both traditional African philosophy and various systems of modern philosophy is likely to be existentially beneficial," because, as Kwame Gyekye put it, "we cannot create (or re-create) African philosophy . . . out of the European heritage: If we could, it would not . . . be *African* philosophy" (Wiredu, 1991, p. 94; Gyekye, 1995, p. 9, emphasis added).

If, indeed, "when we speak of the philosophy of a people we are talking of a tradition," Africana philosophy, then, as with other cultural group's philosophical traditions, must out of necessity be based, almost inherently, on the historicity, the lived-experiences, the life-worlds and life-struggles of both continental and diasporan Africans. Philosophy invariably emerges out of and should engage a cultural context and a (particular) historical coordinate or problematic, and even the most "universal" of philosophical thought is and may be "located" within the locus of a particular people's life-worlds and language-worlds. Take, for example, Western European philosophical thought, Gyekye (1995) asserted, "Western philosophy was itself brewed in a cultural soup whose ingredients were the mentalities, experiences, and the folk thought and folkways of Western peoples" (p. 34). This means, then, that "[i]n attempting to establish an African [or Africana] philosophical tradition one should rather start one's investigation from the beliefs, thought, and linguistic categories of African peoples" (p. 35). The theorists of Negritude, taking their cue from the radicals of the Harlem Renaissance, advocated that persons of African descent "return" to, or rather *rediscover*, the teachings and texts, logic(s) and lessons of their ancestors in order to provide interpretations, clarifications, and solutions to the conceptual puzzles that confront Africans, as well as others, in the present. Both Wiredu and Gyekye assign a similar role to the contemporary workers in/of African philosophy. In "On Defining African Philosophy," Wiredu (1991) charged:

> [T]his is the time when there is the maximum need to study African traditional philosophy. Because of the historical accident of colonialism, the main part of the philosophical training of contemporary African scholars has come to derive from foreign sources. Why should the African uncritically assimilate the conceptual schemes embedded in foreign languages and cultures? Philosophical truth can indeed be disentangled from cultural contingencies. But for this purpose nothing is more useful than the ability to compare different languages and cultures in relation to their philosophical prepossessions. Insofar as a study of traditional philosophy may enable one to do just this, it can be philosophically beneficial to the African as well as the non-African. . . . [T]he philosophical thought of a traditional (i.e., preliterate and non-industrialized) society may hold some lessons of moral significance for a more industrialized society. (p. 98)

And, in a similar vein, Gyekye (1995) conscientiously contended:

[M]odern African philosophers must base themselves in the cultural life and experiences of the community. While reflecting modern circumstances, such philosophical activity may commit itself to refining aspects of traditional thought in the light of modern knowledge and experience. The cultural or social basis (or relevance) of the philosophical enterprise seems to indicate that if a philosophy produced by a modern African has no basis in the culture and experience of African peoples, then it cannot appropriately claim to be an *African* philosophy, even though it was created by an African philosopher. I suggest therefore that *the starting points, the organizing concepts and categories of modern African philosophy be extracted from the cultural, linguistic, and historical background of African peoples*, if that philosophy is to have relevance and meaning for the people, if it is to enrich their lives. (pp. 33, 42, all emphasis in original)

Taking the above comments into critical consideration, this means then that workers in Africana philosophy need more than a mere perfunctory knowledge of the historicity of African peoples ("precolonial," "colonial," "neocolonial" and/or "postcolonial"), their thought-traditions, belief-systems, and socio-political struggles. More to the point, Africana philosophy draws from and takes as its point of departure "traditional African philosophy," and seeks to graft the insights gleaned from the critical engagement of the said discourse onto "the contemporary African situation" (Gyekye, 1995, pp. 11, 40). This "situation" is, "because of the historical accident of colonialism," one which currently extends well beyond the geographical circumference of the African continent. Continental Africans do not and should not be allowed to have a monopoly on African identity, or rather "Africanity," as the theorists of Negritude put it. In this regard, Nigerian Nobel laureate Wole Soyinka (1990), in his essay "The African World and the Ethno-Cultural Debate," sardonically queried: "How can we as intelligent human beings submit to the self-imprisonment of a 'saline consciousness' which insists that, contrary to all historic evidence, Africa stops wherever salt water licks its shores? Or that, conversely, all that is bound by salt water on the African continent is necessarily African?" (p. 19). We would do well to cautiously consider Soyinka's queries. Soyinka knows, as should the workers of Africana philosophy, that "Africa"—whether "invention" or "idea," as Mudimbe (1988, 1994) would have it—is more than a mere material/physical spatial reality, but a conglomeration of multicultural, transethnic, and transgenerational thought-traditions, belief-systems, life-worlds, and language-worlds that are drawn from and contributed to by persons of African descent (and, if truth be told, "Africanists"—i.e., non-African scholars and cultural workers) wherever they exist.

In stating that "Africa" and "the contemporary African situation" does not pertain exclusively to the physical land mass, nor the persons who reside on what is currently called "the African continent," but extends to persons of African descent the world over, I wish to allude to the fact that both Wiredu and Soyinka acknowledge the historical reality of the diabolical dispersion and colonial conquest of African peoples in the contemporary context. "[B]ecause of the historical accident of colonialism," "Africa" and what it means to be "African" have been altered indefinitely (albeit, not irreparably, since culture is an ever-evolving *shared human product* and *shared human project*). This means, then, that cultural workers of African descent (and Africanists) must, from within the vortex of this insoluble situation, "return" to or *rediscover* and wring meaning from not merely an aspect of "the contemporary African situation," that is, the *continental* African situation, but the whole of the *contemporary* African situation, which includes the African diaspora just as much as it does the African continent. In short, any discussion of the contemporary African situation, as opposed to, say, the "Nigerian," or "Ethiopian," or "Kenyan," or "Zimbabwean" situation, must by default include the Africans of the diaspora, or else what one is really referring to is the "continental" African situation. Of course, we desperately need studies that focus on particular continental and diasporan African cultural groups, but these studies should be appropriately titled so as not to mislead the students and scholars of Africana Studies, and Africana philosophy and critical theory in specific, considering the present discussion.

## NEGRITUDE'S DECONSTRUCTIVE AND RECONSTRUCTIVE CHALLENGES TO AFRICANA, EUROPEAN, AND EUROPEAN AMERICAN PHILOSOPHY

In "African 'Philosophy'?: Deconstructive and Reconstructive Challenges," Lucius Outlaw (1996a) stated that Negritude is "one of the most deconstructive forms of African philosophizing," because it registers "a major challenge to the notion and ideal of what it means for *Africans* to be human" (pp. 66–67, emphasis in original). If we follow Mudimbe (1988), then we, to a certain extent, understand "Africa" to be an invention and/or creation not wholly of our (i.e., Africans') own construction. Therefore, what it means to be "African"—again, "to a certain extent"—must be confronted, contested, and critically and dialectically engaged with an understanding of the history of the African experience, past and present, continental and diasporan. The theoreticians of Negritude, in advocating that persons of African descent "return" to, or *rediscover* African views and values, sought to reclaim and rehabilitate African thought-systems and identities, and by doing so they challenged the very— as Ato Sekyi-Otu (1996) put it—"imperial and pure universals" that Western European culture and civilization prides itself on (p. 104). In Negritude, Outlaw (1996a) acutely observed,

> [W]e have the reclamation of the place of Africans on the stage of human history, but now cast in roles defined by Africans who have structured those roles out of what *they* take to be the meanings of African histories and existences, both of which are seen as decidedly different (or ought to be) from the histories and existences of peoples of Europe. But the complex of strategies that we now refer to as Negritude involved much more than the rehabilitation of Africa. In addition to the construction of a philosophical anthropology carved out of African ebony, there was also an effort to displace from its dominating position the paradigm of rationalist epistemology championed by proponents of Philosophy by arguing in favor of an epistemology that had its basis in African racial/bio-cultural life-worlds. . . . In addition, for Senghor and other Negritude writers, African historical-cultural life-worlds are shaped by values and aesthetics particular to African peoples. Part of the Negritude agenda was to identify the elements and practices constituting these life-worlds and to reclaim and rehabilitate them from the twisted amnesia resulting from European colonialism and enslavement. Thus, in addition to arguments in behalf of an African epistemology, Negritude bequeathed African-centered aesthetics, axiology, and socio-political philosophies. (p. 67, emphasis in original)

This challenges conventional conceptions, Africana and otherwise, of Negritude, and it also enables us to reframe the discourse on Negritude's contributions to radical politics and the Africana tradition of critical theory. What places Outlaw's analysis of Negritude on a different plane is the simple fact that he moves beyond the conventional one-dimensional critique of Negritude, which usually argues that it has little or nothing to offer to contemporary Africana Studies, and Africana philosophy in particular, and critically interrogates it with an eye toward the ways in which, when viewed from an "African-centered" perspective, it contributes important paradigms and points of departure. In other words, Outlaw's analysis of Negritude is distinguished in that it is *dialectical*; carefully distinguishing between its progressive Africana elements and its retrogressive Eurocentric elements, and vice versa. This should be stressed, as all too often Africana theoretical traditions and Africana theorists are engaged in extremely rigid and unrealistic ways, which usually focus more on the ways in which they are either similar or dissimilar to Eurocentric theories and theorists, without asking what I believe to be the more important questions, such as: What distinct contributions does the Africana tradition of critical theory make to critical theory in a general—i.e., white *and* non-white, world-historical–sense? What are the major theoretic motifs and methods, and who are the major theorists of the Africana tradition of critical theory? What were the ancient and precolonial African conceptions of wisdom, philosophy, and theory that might be most useful for contemporary critical theorists, Africana and otherwise, deeply preoccupied with the deconstruction and reconstruction of radical politics and critical social theory? What lessons can contemporary societies learn from classical and traditional African social and political theories, movements, and systems?

If, indeed, one of the main motifs of Negritude involves a critical "return" to precolonial, traditional, and/or authentic African views and values, then, part of its contribution to the Africana tradition of critical theory revolves around its emphasis on a sense of history and a deeper, more critical relationship with African culture(s) and struggle(s). This is often obscured by many Africana philosophers preoccupation with and over-focus on the misguided and mealy-minded nature of Senghorian Negritude, without a clear delineation of the ways in which Senghor and his, however nebulous, Negritude, when taken along with Cesairean (and Sartrean) Negritude, in the final analysis registers in the world of black radical politics as one of the great challenges to European imperialism, to white world supremacy, and to the Eurocentric idea and invention of Africa and Africans. Speaking directly to this issue, Outlaw importantly asserted:

> Like all discursive ventures, Negritude was not a homogeneous unity, nor is there consensus regarding the meaning of the term. And there continue[s] to be powerful (and sometimes persuasive) criticisms of Senghorian Negritude. Nonetheless, the Negritude arguments, fundamentally, involved a profound displacement of the African invented by Europeans. It is this African challenge and displacement, through radical critique and counter-construction, that have been deconstructive in particularly powerful and influential ways: involving direct attacks on the assumed embodiment of the paragon of humanity in whites of Europe, an attack that forces this embodiment back upon itself, forces it to confront its own historicity, its own wretched history of atrocities, and the stench of the decay announcing the impending death of the hegemonic ideal of the Greco-European Rational Man. (p. 67)

Negritude deconstructs "the hegemonic ideal of the Greco-European Rational Man" precisely at the moment that it "reclaims and rehabilitates" the "values and aesthetics" that are purportedly, according to Outlaw, "particular to African peoples." In no uncertain terms Negritude advanced the notion that African people can and should "reclaim and rehabilitate"—i.e. "return" to, or as I would prefer "rediscover"—"African-centered aesthetics, axiology, and socio-political philosophies." In challenging "the African invented by Europeans," Negritude contributes to the discourses of Africana philosophy and Africana critical theory a type of philosophical praxis that is concurrently a "radical critique" of Eurocentric concepts of "Man" and a "counter-construction" of the African that is "cast in roles defined by Africans who have structured those roles out of what *they* take to be the meanings of African histories and existences." Put another way, Negritude provides philosophers and critical theorists of African descent, as well as Africanists, with an emulative model that is rooted in and grows out of the lives and lessons, thoughts and texts of both continental and diasporan Africans, and it demonstrates that Africana philosophy and Africana critical theory must out of historical necessity dialectically "deconstruct" Eurocentric concepts and categories simultaneously as it "reconstructs" "African epistemology," and "African-centered aesthetics, axiology, and socio-political philosophies."[25]

Negritude, by steering Africana Studies scholars and, more particularly, specialists in Africana philosophy and Africana critical theory, in the direction of an engagement with "traditional" African philosophy, in a sense promotes the contextualization and historicization of Africana philosophical and political thought. This is precisely what forced Senghor to "deconstruct" his early Sartre-influenced conception of Negritude and "reconstruct" it into the more "African identity"—i.e., "Africanity"—affirming conception that he is now famous (if not infamous) for in Africana philosophical circles (Imbo, 1998; English, 1996; English and Kalumba, 1996; Hord and Lee, 1995; Irele, 1965a, 1965b, 1970, 1971, 1977; Masolo, 1994; Shutte, 1998; Towa, 1971). Senghor realized, one could say, that in order to "reconstruct" the African, he would, in a certain sense, have to "deconstruct" the European and, further, that the African—in opposition to the Hegelian philosophy of history— does not exist outside of the bounds of human history. Sartre robbed the oppressed of their agency. Senghor sought, however subtly and servilely, to reclaim it. Moreover, it should be recalled that Sartre maintained that Negritude was a reactionary "moment," "the minor term" of a "dialectical progression," but Senghor (1996) said, "the struggle for *Negritude* must not be *negation* but *affirmation*" (p. 49; emphasis in original). In affirming Africanity, Senghor snatched the attempted abortment of African agency away from Sartre, resuscitated it, and initiated the contemporary critique by Africana philosophers of Western European philosophical and cultural categories and conceptions being grafted onto Africana life-worlds and lived-experiences.[26]

When Senghor (1996) stated, "our Negritude no longer expresses itself as opposition to European values, but as a *complement* to them," he, in a way, confuted Sartre's assertion that Negritude, being an "antithetical value," is a "negative moment" that is "insufficient by itself" (p. 50). Negritude, being "the awareness by a particular social group or people of its own situation in the world," insofar as Senghor was concerned, was not "insufficient by itself" by the very fact that it was historically housed diametrically adjacent to "the supremacy of the white man," as Sartre put it (p. 49). On the contrary, "the supremacy of the white man" may perhaps be "insufficient by itself," because it inherently depends on an "Other," someone outside of itself and its life-world and language-worlds, which it seeks to denude, degrade, and dominate—and, if that "Other" is not a non-white, though they usually are, this hegemony has historically translated itself into sexism, patriarchy, or the gender oppression of women of European descent (Bell and Blumenfeld, 1995; Gould, 1973, 1984; Gould and Wartofsky, 1976; Jackson, 1993; Jaggar and Young, 1998; Kauffman, 1993; G. Lloyd, 1984; Pateman, 1988, 1989; Tong, 1989; Tuana, 1995; Tuana and Tong, 1995).[27] One need not meditate long on Sartre's cryptic comments announcing the death of Negritude in order to detect a Hegelian line of thinking that leads directly to Hegel's infamous "master/slave" dialectic. However, Fanon (1967) debunked this Sartrean, one-dimensional interpretation and projection of the Hegelian dialectic onto the "White master"/"Black slave" situation long ago, stating:

> There is not an open conflict between white and black.
> One day the White Master, *without conflict*, recognized the Negro slave.
> But the former slave wants to *make himself recognized*.
> At the foundation of [the] Hegelian dialectic there is an absolute reciprocity which must be emphasized. It is in the degree to which I go beyond my own immediate being that I apprehend the existence of the other as a natural and more than natural reality. If I close the circuit, if I prevent the accomplishment of movement in two directions, I keep the other within himself. Ultimately, I deprive him even of this being-for-itself. . . . In its immediacy, consciousness of self is simple being-for-itself. In order to win the certainty of oneself, the incorporation of the concept of recognition is essential. Similarly, the other is waiting for recognition by us, in order to burgeon into the universal consciousness of self. Each consciousness of self is in quest of absoluteness. It wants to be recognized as a primal value without reference to life, as a transformation of subjective certainty (*Gewissheit*) into objective truth (*Wahrheit*). . . . Self-consciousness accepts the risk of its life, and consequently it threatens the other in his physical being. . . . Thus human reality in-itself-for-itself can be achieved only through conflict and through the risk that conflict implies. This risk means that I go beyond life toward a supreme good that is the transformation of subjective certainty of my own worth into a universally valid objective truth. (pp. 217–218, all emphasis in original)

Following Fanon, both "the supremacy of the white man" and Negritude are inadequate because of the "absolute reciprocity" that must exist if either is to be a "universally valid objective truth." In order to be "universally valid" both positions of the dialectic must not only "recognize" and "reciprocate" the other's "primal value," or human worth, but both must "go beyond life toward a supreme good." Senghor swung in this direction when he stated, "our Negritude no longer expresses itself as opposition to European values, but as a *complement* to them." But, it must be reiterated that Senghor's concept of the African is in large part culled from Eurocentric and white supremacist projections of primitivism onto Africa and Africans. Negritude nevertheless, unlike "the supremacy of the white man," does not seek to deprive any human being or cultural group of its "being-for-itself," of its humanity, and Sartre is well aware that "the supremacy of the white man" is a defiling and deforming, inhuman digressive discursive formation and praxis that rests on faulty logic and pseudo-science. As Sartre (1968) self-reflexively and eloquently observed in his preface to Fanon's *The Wretched of the Earth*:

> We [Europeans] were men at his [the racialized and colonized's] expense, he makes himself man at ours: a different man; of higher quality. . . . With us, to be a man is to be an accomplice of colonialism, since all of us without exception have profited by colonial exploitation. . . . [F]or with us there is nothing more consistent than a racist humanism since the European has only been able to become a man through creating slaves and monsters. (pp. 24–26; see also Sartre, 1995)

In opposition to "the supremacy of the white man" Senghor (1998) put forward his borrowed (from Teilhard de Chardin) concept of "the Civilization of the Universal," which maintained that "if European civilization were to be imposed, unmodified [as it historically has been], on all peoples and continents, it could only be by force" and, therefore, "it would not be *humanistic*, for it would cut itself off from the complementary values of the greater part of humanity" (p. 441). Realizing, as Sartre did, the "racist humanism" of European culture and civilization, Senghor, perhaps taking his cue from Fanon, went "beyond life [or his own immediate situation] toward a supreme good" that recognized and reciprocated "primal values," or the human worth of other peoples and their cultures and civilizations. Senghor, conceiving of Negritude as a "complement" to European values, side-steps Sartre's Hegelian dialectical progression which, of course, ends (*telos*) in synthesis, and offers up a seminal theoretical theme from Africana philosophical discourse, *complementarity*. Negritude, for Senghor, was no longer an "antithetical value," or an "anti-racist racism" as it was for Sartre, but an affirmation of African humanity that was perpetually open to revision and redefinition. Disentangling his theory of Negritude from Sartre's, Senghor solemnly said:

> [O]ur revised Negritude is humanistic, I repeat, it welcomes the complementary values of Europe and the white man, and indeed, of all other races and continents. But it welcomes them in order to fertilize and reinvigorate its own values, which it then offers for the construction of a civilization which shall embrace all mankind. The *neo-Humanism* of the twentieth century stands at the point where the paths of all nations, races, and continents cross, where the four winds of the spirit blow. (p. 441)[28]

Countering the "racist humanism" of Europe, Senghor's revised "humanistic" Negritude breaks free from Sartre's Hegelian dialectical progression and Manichean thinking, and openly acknowledges that "the" world, as it actually exists, is not merely a series of binary oppositions between blacks and whites, or Africans and Europeans, but a world full of "other races [and cultures] and continents." Senghor's new Negritude welcomed the values of the rest of the racialized and colonized world "in order to fertilize and reinvigorate its own values," hence the concept of "cultural borrowing," and it is interested ultimately in "the construction of a civilization which shall embrace all mankind." Negritude, like Du Bois and James's Pan-African Marxism and, as we shall soon see, Fanon's discourse on decolonization, was ultimately concerned with the greater good, the "supreme good" of humanity—that is, it was profoundly, nay radically, humanistic. In this sense, then, it contributes and helps to highlight another important theme of the discourse of Africana critical theory: its revolutionary humanism, its deep and abiding concern not merely for "the contemporary African situation," but for the "supreme good," to use Fanon's phrase, of suffering humanity as a whole.

Where the theorists of Negritude synthesized Pan-Africanism, black nationalism, Marxism, existentialism and surrealism into their own extremely original artistic, intellectual and political project, Frantz Fanon—as I have hinted at throughout this chapter—wielded a new form of Negritude, a neo-Negritude, if you will, against the new forms of racism, sexism, capitalism, and colonialism. His thought and texts challenge the very foundations of Africana (as well as European and European American) philosophy, and makes several seminal contributions to Africana critical theory in the sense that his offerings acutely accent the constantly changing character of imperialism, especially as it expresses itself as racism and colonialism, or what has been termed *racial colonialism*. For Fanon, colonized and racialized people, especially black folk, needed to do much more than "return" to the traditions of their ancestors, as it would seem that Senghor and—to a certain extent—Cesaire would have it. From Fanon's perspective, more than a mere cultural revolution was needed as well. What Fanon proposed was a complete revolution, one that encompassed not only cultural reclamation, but also self and social transformation. He argued that it was not simply continents and cultures that had been colonized, but many of the very concepts that racialized and colonized people were using in their efforts to attain their freedom. As a consequence, he developed one of the most important discourses on decolonization in recent memory. Therefore, the next chapter will be devoted to a critical exploration of Fanon's discourse on decolonization and its contributions to the Africana tradition of critical theory.

## NOTES

1. For further discussion of connections between the Harlem Renaissance, the development of Negritude, and Paris, see the aforementioned, Ako (1982), Bamikunle (1982), Fabre (1993), as well as, more recent research by Archer-Straw (2000), Cazenave (2005), Irele (2004), and Jules-Rosette (1998).

2. On Negritude's implications for radical politics, see Berrian and Long (1967), Chikwendu (1977), Cismaru (1974), Climo (1976), English (1996), Fabre (1975), Feuser (1966), Finn (1988), Flather (1966), Gbadegesin (1991b), Hale (1974), Irele (1965a, 1965b, 1968, 1970, 1971, 1986), Jeanpierre (1961), E.A. Jones (1971), Kennedy (1968, 1988), Kennedy and Trout (1966) Kesteloot (1990, 1991), Knight (1974), Lagneau (1961), Lindfors (1970, 1980), R. Long (1969), Luvai (1974), Markovitz (1967, 1969), Mohome (1968), Senghor (1998), Shelton (1964), Simon (1963), L.V. Thomas (1965), Towa (1969a, 1969b, 1971), Trout and Kennedy (1968), Wake (1963), and Wanja (1974).

3. For a discussion of the various critiques of "Sartrean Negritude," see Masolo (1994, pp. 30–37), "The Critics of 'Orphée Noir'."

4. On the notion of "negation" in Negritude, see Knipp (1974).

5. For full-scale treatments Césaire's literary career, see Arnold (1981), G. Davies (1997), Scharfman (1987), and Frutkin (1973). Hale (1974) and Pallister (1991) provide excellent analyses of both Césaire's literary and political writings, while M.W. Bailey (1992) and Irele (1968) focus specifically on Césaire's political plays. Cismaru (1974), B.H. Edwards (2005), Jahn (1958), Kennedy (1968, 1988), Kesteloot (1995), Nesbitt (2000), Tomich (1979), and Towa (1969a, 1969b) are a few of the more noteworthy and seminal articles/essays in Césaire studies.

6. In order to fully understand Negritude it is important to critically engage France and French citizens' ambivalent relationship with French colonialism (nay, French imperialism) in Africa and the Caribbean. There are all sorts of tall-tales and mythmaking concerning French colonialism—with the most common claim being that the French form of colonialism, when contrasted with that of other European colonial empires, was somehow more benevolent and not as violent—this, to be perfectly honest and historically accurate, is quite simply not true. Most certainly, it is extremely important to revisit Fanon's *The Wretched of the Earth* and Gillo Pontecorvo's *The Battle of Algiers*, but it is equally important to turn to the scores of scholarly texts produced since these watershed works first exploded the myth of French colonial benevolence. For further, more critical and historical discussions of "French Africa," "French Africans," "Francophone Africa," and French colonialism in Africa and the Caribbean, see Genova (2004), Laroussi and Miller (2003), S.K. Lewis (2006), Manning (1998), C.L. Miller (1985, 1990, 1998), D.R.D. Thomas (2002), and G. Wilder (2003a, 2003c, 2005).

7. On Césaire's Negritude as a "revolutionary Negritude," see Serequeberhan (1996, p. 245), Towa (1969), and G. Wilder (2004). For a discussion of Negritude in relation to Surrealism, Marxism, and Existentialism, see Eshelman and Smith (1983, pp. 3–8, 14–18), Finn (1988, pp. 40–57), Kesteloot (1991, pp. 19–46, 102–119, 253–279), Knight (1974), and Sellen (1967).

8. See Engels (1972). For a critique of Engels's "feminism," see Lane (1976).

9. See Marx and Engels (1972). For a critique of Marx's pro-colonial stance, see Said (1978, pp. 153–157) and Serequeberhan (1990).

10. For a discussion of Negritude's implications for African identity, and especially in relation to the onslaught of European imperialism, see A. Diop (1962), Drachler (1963), and Wylie (1985).

11. On Senghor and Senghorian Negritude, see Beier (1959), Berrian and Long (1967), Chikwendu (1977), Climo (1976), Finn (1988), Hyman (1971), E.A. Jones (1971), Kesteloot (1990), Lagneau (1961), Markovitz (1969), L.V. Thomas (1965), and Towa (1971). On "Sartrean Negritude," see Jahn (1968) and Kesteloot (1991, pp. 105–115).

12. On "Hegelian Marxism," which on several authors' accounts is synonymous with "Western Marxism," see Gottlieb (1992), Jameson (1971), and Jay (1984).

13. My thinking concerning "mulattos" and "cultural mulattoism" has been deeply influenced by Zack (1993, 1995, 1998).

14. Senghor produced half a dozen major works in the area of "African socialism," and it is these texts that inform my analysis and critique of Senghorian socialism throughout this section; please see, Senghor (1959, 1961, 1962, 1964a, 1964b, 1970).

15. Senghor's extended treatment of "Africanity" may be found in Senghor (1971). For critiques of "Africanity," as concieved by Senghor, see Jack (1996), Melady (1971), Serequeberhan (1998), Simon (1963), Spleth (1993), and Towa (1971).

16. For a critical discussion of Senghor's interpretation and articulation of "traditional African thought," see Augustine Shutte, "African and European Philosophizings: Senghor's 'Civilization of the Universal'" (1998).

17. With regard to what I am referring to as "the radicalism of the Harlem Renaissance," please see, Bassett (1992), Favor (1999), G. Hutchinson (1995, 2007), E.E. Johnson (1997), Kramer and Russ (1997), D.L. Lewis (1989), T. Martin (1991), Naison (1983), Tarver and Barnes (2006), B.M. Tyler (1992), R.E. Washington (2001), Watson (1995), and Wintz (1996b).

18. On Negritude's assertion of an "African reality," see Gonzales-Cruz (1979), Irele (1977), and Shelton (1964). For a discussion of "African metaphysics," see Teffo and Roux (1998, pp. 134–149), which engages and delineates metaphysical concepts and categories that are appropriate and applicable to African life-worlds and lived-experiences.

19. Masolo is not alone in asserting the Harlem Renaissance's influence on Negritude, see Fabre (1975, 1993), Feuser (1976), Gerard (1964, 1970, 1971, 1981, 1986, 1990, 1992), Irele (2004), Jahn (1961, 1968), Jeanpierre (1961), Kennedy and Trout (1966), Kesteloot (1991), Kesteloot and Kennedy (1974) and Mohome (1968), among the other works cited in the text.

20. Locke is an extremely important figure in the history of Africana philosophy, and more specifically African American philosophy, not simply for the fact that he was the first African American to be awarded a Ph.D. in philosophy from Harvard University in 1917, but because he made several seminal contributions to areas as diverse as aesthetics, value theory, philosophy of race, philosophy of culture, philosophy of education, and social and political philosophy. On Locke's life and philosophy, see L. Harris (1989, 1999a), Linnemann (1982), Locke (1983, 1989, 1992), and J. Washington (1986, 1994).

21. For critical discussions of Locke's philosophy of art and concept of African aesthetics as they relate to his notions of axiological inheritance and African ancestral legacy, see Barnes (1982) and Helbling (1999).

22. There are several essays in the anthologies of L. Harris (1999a) and Linnemann (1982) which treat Locke's theory of art (aesthetics) and value theory (axiology), see Cureau (1982), G. Hall (1982), Harvey (1982), Mason (1982), Duran and Stewart (1999) J.M. Green (1999), and Scholz (1999).

23. Appiah (1992), Biakolo (1998), Hountondji (1996), Imbo (1998), Kaphagawani (1998), Masolo (1994), Oruka (1990a, 1990b), Van Nierkerk (1998), and Van Staden (1998) provide historical and critical discussions of ethnophilosophy.

24. On the thematic and conceptual thrust(s) of Negritude, see Bastide (1961), Beier (1959), Berrian and Long (1967), Blair (1961a, 1961b), Cismaru (1974), E.A. Jones (1971), Lagneau (1961), Long (1969), Melone (1963), and L.V. Thomas (1965).

25. For further discussion of "African epistemology," see Kaphagawani (1998) and Sogolo (1998b).

26. Negritude, and more specifically, Senghorian Negritude, then, can be said to prefigure the Horton-Wiredu debate in which Robin Horton (1993) compares, "African traditional thought" to Western Science, and Kwasi Wiredu (1980) counter argues that the comparison Horton makes is problematic because it presupposes that "African traditional thought" is "non-scientific," or either the product of a "pre-scientific stage of development." Masolo (1994) offers an excellent—albeit critical—commentary on the Horton-Wiredu/Western science vs. African thought debate.

27. To date, one of the best works on Negritude and feminism is, of course, T. Denean Sharpley-Whiting's *Negritude Women* (2002). However, my analysis here has also been informed by Omofolabo Ajayi's "Negritude, Feminism, and the Quest for Identity" (1997).

28. For critical discussions of Negritude's contributions and connections to radical (or, rather, revolutionary) anti-racist humanism, see Fabre and Eburne (2005), Gerard (1962), Moulard-Leonard (2005), and G. Wilder (2005).

# 5

# Frantz Fanon: Revolutionizing the Wretched of the Earth, Radicalizing the Discourse on Decolonization

I am not merely here-and-now, sealed into thingness. I am for somewhere else and for something else. I demand that notice be taken of my negating activity insofar as I pursue something other than life; insofar as I do battle for the creation of a human world—that is, of a world of reciprocal recognitions. He who is reluctant to recognize me opposes me. In a savage struggle I am willing to accept convulsions of death, invincible dissolution, but also the possibility of the impossible.

—Frantz Fanon, *Black Skin, White Masks*, p. 218

Fanon hides nothing: in order to fight against us the former colony must fight against itself: or, rather, the two struggles form part of a whole.

—Jean-Paul Sartre, "Preface to *The Wretched of the Earth*," p. 11

Everything, on Fanon's account of the social and symbolic conditions of postcolonial existence, requires to be reread and rewritten. Everything is an invitation to "invention."

—Ato Sekyi-Otu, *Fanon's Dialectic of Experience*, p. 40

Fanon is not simply a man of action, he is also a critic of reactive action.

—Nigel C. Gibson, *Fanon: The Postcolonial Imagination*, p. 41

Severed from its body, Fanon's thought can signify everything and nothing at the same time.

—E. San Juan, Jr., 1999, p. 126

I do not come with timeless truths.

—Frantz Fanon, *Black Skin, White Masks*, p. 7

## THE FACTS OF FANON'S REVOLUTIONARY BLACKNESS

Frantz Fanon was born in the folds of French colonialism on July 20, 1925 on the Caribbean island of Martinique. Unlike Du Bois, but very similar to his Caribbean comrades James and Césaire, his family was firmly "upper middle-class" and, in the "typically complicated Martiniquan manner," hyper-preoccupied with all the questions concerning race, color, and class (Gendzier, 1973, p. 10; see also Macey, 2004). Fanon's father, Félix Casimir Fanon, was of mixed Indian and Martiniquan origin, while his mother, Elénore Médélice Fanon, was of Alsatian extraction, herself "the illegitimate daughter of parents of mixed blood" and heritages (Gendzier, 1973, p. 10). Frantz Fanon's first name, of course, reflected his mother's Alsatian ancestry. He was the fourth, youngest, and middle son of his parent's eight children, and—in keeping with the unique color complex(es) of the Caribbean, it is extremely important to observe—he was the darkest member of his family. The "fact of [his] blackness," as he himself put it in *Black Skin, White Masks*, was never allowed to be forgotten, neither among his family and friends, nor, most especially, among the Martiniquan public at large.

At age eighteen Fanon enlisted in the Free French unit, then believing that "his own freedom, that of Martinique and that of France were inextricably bound together" (Macey, 2000, p. 91). Between 1944 and 1946 he served in Algeria, where he also came into contact with Senegalese soldiers. This, to say the least, was an eye-opening and life-altering experience for him, and it was there in Africa that he began to develop a critical consciousness of colonialism and its physical and psychological effects on the colonized. After he was wounded and discharged from the French Army he opted to study psychiatry because of its synthesis of medicine, psychology and philosophy, he believed, would enable him to pursue his increasing interests in the psychological effects of racism and colonialism on *both* the colonizer and the colonized. He studied first in Paris and then in Lyon, from 1947 to 1951. Following the successful completion of his qualifying exams, Fanon began to practice initially in Saint Ylie, France, then in Pontorson, Normandy, and finally in Blida-Joinville, Algeria, where he was appointed *Chef de service* in 1953. In 1952 he was wed to a Frenchwoman of Corsican-gypsy descent, Marie-Josephe Dublé (known to all as Josie), whom he met in 1949 when she was eighteen years old and still a classics student at her lycée.

It was in Algeria as the *Chef de service* at the Psychiatric Hospital of Blida-Joinville that Fanon acquired significant clinical experience and engaged in seminal psychiatric experiments through his work with 165 European women and 220 Algerian men. During these decisive years Fanon honed his ideas on the social, political and cultural causes and effects of many mental illnesses. He resigned from the psychiatric hospital in 1956 to join the Front de Libération Nationale (the FLN), the revolutionary anti-colonial movement that successfully waged armed struggle for an independent (and Islamic) Algeria free from French colonialism. Fanon was not content with the supposed neutrality his status as a medical doctor offered him. In his letter of resignation he unequivocally intoned, "There comes a time when silence becomes dishonesty" (Fanon, 1969, p. 54). He was determined to use his military and medical training in the interest of Algeria's liberation and all of Africa's decolonization (see P. Adams, 1970; Bulhan, 1980b, 1985; Hopton, 1995; Macey, 1999; Razanajao, Postel and Allen, 1996; Ucelli, 2001; Youssef and Fadl, 1996).

Fanon began his formal association with the FLN as early as 1954 when he "counseled" (in the psychiatric sense) several Algerian freedom fighters suffering from "mental problems" as a result of the war. David Macey (2000), a leading Fanon biographer, maintains that Fanon's "growing commitment to the nationalist movement took the classic pattern of an initial contact, the rendering of minor 'favors' and the establishment of both trust and deeper involvement" (p. 265). Before long Fanon was fully integrated into the FLN, working as a medic, freedom fighter, revolutionary writer, and Algerian ambassador. He addressed the All-African Peoples Congress held in Accra, Ghana, from December 8 to 12, 1958, as a member of the Algerian delegation. There he rendezvoused with acclaimed Pan-African revolutionaries, such as Patrice Lumumba, Tom M'Boya, Roberto Holden, and, of course, the then President of Ghana, Kwame Nkrumah.

It was at this crucial Pan-African congress that Fanon forcefully argued that the Algerian struggle for freedom was, indeed, integral to the overarching Pan-African movement, and introduced what would later become his controversial views on violence and decolonization. Although the congress of over two hundred delegates, representing twenty-five countries, as a rule emphasized non-violence and negotiation, especially Lumumba, M'Boya, and Nkrumah, Fanon shocked and awed his audience with passionate pleas, exhorting the delegates to "never rule out recourse to violence" (p. 368). For Fanon, racism and colonialism at their core are nothing other than outright, naked violence, both physical and psychological violence. Therefore, "[f]reedom fighters and nationalist leaders had to adopt *all* forms of struggle and could not rely on peaceful negotiations alone" (p. 368, emphasis in original).

Out of his insistence that "[f]reedom fighters and nationalist leaders had to adopt *all* forms of struggle and could not rely on peaceful negotiations alone" the African Legion project was born. Often-overlooked in the commentary—critical and otherwise—on Fanon, Macey contends that "the idea of an 'African Legion' came to mean a great deal to Fanon" (p. 369). As much is evident when we turn to the concluding section of Fanon's (1969) essay entitled, "Accra: Africa Affirms Its Unity and Defines Its Strategy," where he wrote:

> In the settlement of colonies of the type of Kenya, Algeria, and South Africa there is unanimity: only armed struggle will bring about the defeat of the occupying nation. And the African Legion, the principle of which was adopted in Accra, is the concrete response of the African peoples to the will to colonial domination of the Europeans. In deciding to create a corps of volunteers in all the territories the African peoples mean clearly to manifest their solidarity with one another, thus expressing the realization that national liberation is linked to the liberation of the continent. (pp. 156–157)

Shortly after his tendentious success at the Accra conference, Fanon was appointed the Gouvernement Provisoire de la République Algérienne's (the GPRA's) ambassador to Ghana in 1959, and went on to represent the GPRA at several international conferences, including, the Conference for Peace and Security, Accra, Ghana, April 7–10, 1960; the Afro-Asian Conference, Conarky, Guinea, April 12–15, 1960; and, the Third Conference of Independent African States, Addis Abba, Ethiopia, June 17–19, 1960. Though it has often been downplayed by Fanon's Eurocentric critics, from the foregoing it is easily ascertained that he was, indeed, a Pan-Africanist. However, I should quickly quip, his Pan-Africanism was often at loggerheads with many of the more nationalist-oriented leaders of his time. It should also be pointed out that though he was not religious in any sense of the word, he was willing to devote his life to a liberation struggle that had as its end goal an Islamic state. Clearly, then, Fanon was a complex and complicated person, committed, perhaps above all else, to racially colonized peoples' right to self-definition, self-determination and decolonization. In neglecting Fanon's nuanced engagement of Pan-Africanism, African socialism, and Algerian nationalism, many of his critics have created or, rather, insidiously invented an ahistorical, fantastic, often inexcusably Eurocentric, and extremely violent Fanon.

Fanon's four books—*Black Skin, White Masks, A Dying Colonialism, The Wretched of the Earth*, and *Toward the African Revolution*—reveal a dialectical thinker and critical theorist of extraordinary depth and insight, especially with regard to issues involving Europe's supposed white superiority and Africa's alleged black inferiority; racism, sexism, colonialism and neocolonialism; revolutionary self-determination and revolutionary decolonization; the nature of revolutionary nationalism and its interconnections with revolutionary humanism; colonial violence and anticolonial violence; national consciousness, national culture and national liberation; the psychology of both the colonizer and the colonized; and, the prospects and problematics of a truly "postcolonial" African state. The man who came to be called, "the apostle of violence," "the prophet of a violent Third World revolution," "the prisoner of hate," and "the preacher of the gospel of the wretched of the earth," died of leukemia on December 6, 1961 at the unforgivably young age of thirty-six (E. Hansen, 1977, p. 52; Macey, 2000, p. 2). Macey (2000), perhaps, captured the ever-evolving posthumous life of Frantz Fanon best when he wrote at the dawn of the twenty-first century, "[o]ver forty years after his death, Fanon remains a surprisingly enigmatic and elusive figure. Whether he should be regarded as 'Martiniquan,' 'Algerian,' 'French,' or simply 'Black' is not a question that can be decided easily. It is also a long-standing question" (p. 7).[1]

Undoubtedly, Fanon has profoundly influenced twentieth and, already, twenty-first century thinking about racism and colonialism, and whether his readers understand him to have been Caribbean, African, or French—or some synthesis of each of the foresaid—it is extremely important to emphasize that he desired, above all else, to be regarded quite simply as *human*, as a brother in the house of hard-working, humble humanity. However, as the Ethiopian philosopher, Teodros Kiros (2004), readily reminds us, "[w]e are the children of geography and history, born to a given race, a given region, at a particular time, in a particular place" (p. 217). Fanon, no matter how radically humanist, was not during his lifetime, and certainly is not now, immune to these inescapable facts—the facts, as he himself said, of his blackness. "An accomplished writer," Kiros contends, "Frantz Fanon is regarded by many as one of the greatest revolutionary thinkers of the twentieth century" (p. 217). He holds a special place in the hearts and minds of black radicals, revolutionary nationalists, and Pan-Africanists because, Kiros continues: "He was a Pan-Africanist who did not divide Africa into north and south, and he made it his mission always to remind the Algerians of their Africanity, and other Africans of the Africanity of the north of the continent. His activities and writings were always guided by a Pan-African lodestar" (p. 216).

Fanon (1968), then, was not simply against the colonization of African people and the African continent, but he was also against the colonization of African thought, what he termed in *The Wretched of the Earth*, the "racialization of thought" (p. 212). In this chapter I examine what I understand to be Fanon's major contributions to Africana critical theory, most of which were included in the litany above where I detailed the wide-range of issues his four books address. However, I should emphasize at the outset, because his work has been engaged and appropriated by scholars and activists of disparate disciplinary and political perspectives, Fanon's discourse on decolonization will be employed as the primary point of departure and *leitmotif* in an effort to make his contributions to Africana critical theory accessible to as broad an audience, academic and otherwise, as possible. His discourse on decolonization, though, will be almost utterly incomprehensible without first (re)turning to the anticolonialism of Aimé Césaire and intricately exploring what Fanon borrowed from, and how he built on and went beyond, Césaire's revolutionary Negritude and discourse on decolonization.

## FANON, CÉSAIRE, AND (DIS)CONTINUITY IN THE DISCOURSE ON DECOLONIZATION

I come back once more to Césaire . . .
I feel that I can still hear Césaire . . .
Once again I come back to Césaire; I wish that many black intellectuals would turn to him for their inspiration.

—Frantz Fanon, *Black Skin, White Masks*, pp. 90, 187

Fanon's pronouncements are underwritten by the spectre of Negritude.

—Ato Sekyi-Otu, *Fanon's Dialectic of Experience*, p. 44

Preceding Fanon, one of the early decolonizers and, perhaps, his greatest (single) Africana influence, particularly with regard to the concept of decolonization, was the Martiniquan poet and theorist of Negritude and radical politician, Aime Cesaire.[2] Cesaire's influence on Fanon is, quite simply, immeasurable and, seemingly, ubiquitous throughout his corpus. Fanon's earliest post-war political activities can be linked to Cesaire and, as the highly regarded Ghanaian political scientist Emmanuel Hansen (1977) has noted in his groundbreaking study, *Frantz Fanon: Social and Political Thought*, though "[t]here is no evidence that Fanon was at this time [1946] sympathetic to the Communist cause. He was more interested in the cultural nationalism of Cesaire. His participation in the campaign activities of Aime Cesaire was very instructive" (p. 27). Further exploring Fanon's intellectual and political relationship with Césaire, the French intellectual historian, David Caute (1970), contends, "Fanon took his . . . lead from Césaire" (p. 15). Caute continues: "Fanon's first debt was to Aimé Césaire, and particularly to his masterpieces *Cahier d'un retour au pays natal* [*Return to My Native Land*] and *Discours sur le colonialisme* [*Discourse on Colonialism*]. In Fanon's view, Césaire had virtually single-handed fostered the spirit of black pride in the people of the Antilles" (pp. 17–18).

Fanon, as anyone who has ever perused the pages of *Black Skin, White Masks* shall surely tell you, was extremely enamored by Césaire. So much so, that he bemoaned the fact that more intellectuals of African descent did not "turn to him [Césaire] for their inspiration" (Fanon, 1967, p. 187). Césaire, in many senses, provided Fanon with an anomalous anticolonial political education that would, by the time of the writing of *The Wretched of the Earth*, translate itself into a full-blown praxis-promoting theory of decolonization. Besides and, to a certain extent, beyond literally providing Fanon with political education—no matter how flawed upon critical reflection[3]—Césaire contributed the concept of black consciousness (or, "black pride," as Caute would have it) to Fanon's critical theory of the colonial world. This "spirit of black pride" that Césaire is reported to have fostered in Antilleans has been commented upon by several of Fanon's biographers as having a life-altering effect on him and his thinking.[4] As mentioned above, Fanon's crucial years between his discharge from the French army and his higher education in France were both intellectually and politically pivotal, and Cesaire's centrality during this period of his development cannot be overstated.

Fanon did not merely engage the thoughts and texts of Césaire. By no means, he, Fanon, ever the radical willing unerringly to act on his ideas and couple his passion with politics, participated—at the behest of his elder brother, Joby—in Césaire's 1946 campaign, under the auspices of the French Communist Party, for the Prime Ministership of Martinique (see J. Fanon, 2004). In *Fanon: The Revolutionary as Prophet*, Peter Geismar (1971), one of Fanon's first critical biographers, revealingly wrote:

> Frantz and Joby Fanon based their hopes for a better society on Aimé Césaire, [then] running as the Communist Party's parliamentary candidate from Martinique in the first election of the Fourth Republic . . . Césaire had been at the head of a group of intellectual refugees from the Antilles who put out their own review in Paris, *Legitime Defense*, with articles dissecting all aspects of Caribbean colonial society. Earlier than Fanon, he despaired of these islands where the blacks treated each other as "dirty niggers." Martinique, he said, was the bastard of Europe and Africa, dripping with self-hatred. Yet he returned—to seek a political solution to the cultural desolation. The Communists, Césaire felt, could begin to renovate Martinique's economic infrastructure; a more healthy society might develop. . . . That Frantz Fanon worked for Césaire's election in 1946 indicates not that the former was a confirmed Marxist at this early time [Fanon was but 21], or a revolutionary, but only that Fanon felt that things were not quite as perfect as they might be within the French Republic, or in Martinique. Still, this first political endeavor was instructive; he began to think about the mechanics of social change. . . . The 1946 excursion, which had originally been planned so that they could listen to the fine oratory of Césaire, and aid him when possible, led to quite different patterns of thought. (pp. 40-41)[5]

Geismar relates that Ceasire—and this should be emphasized—sought "a political solution" to the Antillean problem of "cultural desolation."[6] Césaire was not merely a "theorist," or some sort of armchair revolutionary promoting Negritude and a new black consciousness. Much more, he was one of its greatest practitioners. Negritude, as discussed in the preceding chapter, and as too few academics and activists have acknowledged, was not simply a theory of "return," or cultural recuperation, or "nativism," as some have consistently charged (Anise, 1974; Bastide, 1961;

Beier, 1959; Berrian and Long, 1967; Blair, 1966; E.A. Jones, 1971; Melone, 1963). Quite the contrary, Negritude, in the heads, hearts, and hands of Aimé Césaire, Leopold Sedar Senghor and Leon Damas, was a *theory* that encompassed and engaged "trans-African" aesthetics, politics, economics, history, psychology, culture, philosophy, and society (Berrian and Long, 1967; Cismaru, 1974; Finn, 1988; Gonzales-Cruz, 1979; E.A. Jones, 1971; Kennedy, 1990; Kesteloot, 1991; Lagneau, 1961; C.L. Miller, 1990; N.R. Shapiro, 1970; Simon, 1963; Tomich, 1979; Wauthier, 1967). Negritude was a theory that promoted *praxis* toward the end of transforming the aforementioned aspects of African life-worlds in the best interest of persons of African descent in their specific colonial, neocolonial, and/or postcolonial settings, circumstances, or situations (Irele, 1970, 1977). Negritude, and it perhaps would be hard to overstate it, was the very foundation upon which Frantz Fanon developed his discourse on decolonization (Caute, 1970, pp. 17–28; Gendzier, 1973, pp. 36–44; Macey, 2000, pp. 127–132, 177–186). However, even at this early age, Fanon was not an uncritical disciple of Cesairean Negritude.

It was Joby, Fanon's elder brother, who awakened him to the weaknesses of Cesaire's campaign by emphasizing the problems and serious pitfalls of social and political mobilization on a colonial island such as Martinique. According to Joby, the major flaw of Cesaire's campaign was that "he never succeeded in reaching the peasants and the countryside" (E. Hansen, 1977, p. 27). Cesaire's cultural nationalism smacked of the very vanguardism and top-down tactics of continental African colonial aristocrats and bourgeois bureaucrats that Fanon would take to task several years later in *The Wretched of the Earth*. What is important here to observe is that it was Joby, not Frantz, who insisted on the peasantry's involvement in Martiniquan politics. He accented the irony of a militant black Marxist such as Cesaire overlooking, perhaps, the most downtrodden on the island, the peasantry and rural folk, all the while espousing communism, worker's rights, and radical economic reform. By the time he wrote *The Wretched of the Earth*, Fanon's concept of decolonization included, not only the colonized proletariat, but also the colonized lumpenproletariat, the "landless peasant," and the "mass of the country people" (Fanon, 1968, pp. 44, 80, 111). Here, we can see that even from his first exposure to Cesairean Negritude Fanon developed a dialectical rapport and critical relationship with it, and that he also, very early in his political life, began a practice of appropriating aspects of others' arguments, synthesizing them with contrasting concepts, and then pushing them to their extreme, at times dialectically redeveloping them in ways their inventors may have never fully fathomed. As with his brother's critique of Cesaire's 1946 campaign, it can be said that Fanon appropriated much from Cesaire, and especially his seminal text, *Discourse on Colonialism*. Let us now, therefore, turn to *Discourse on Colonialism*, where it may be said the real roots of Fanon's dialectic of decolonization and liberation lie.

When Fanon (1968) wrote, in *The Wretched of the Earth*, "decolonization is always a violent phenomenon" (p. 35), he knew—as he had illustrated as far back as his essays in *El Moudjahid* and *A Dying Colonialism*—that Césaire (1972), in *Discourse on Colonialism*, had passionately and polemically argued that:

> no one colonizes innocently, that no one colonizes with impunity either; that a nation which colonizes, that a civilization which justifies colonization—and therefore force—is already a sick civilization, a civilization that is morally diseased, that irresistibly,

progressing from one consequence to another, one repudiation to another, calls for its Hitler, I mean its punishment. (pp. 17–18)

The "force" which Césaire writes of above is none other than outright, naked violence. The "colonizers" literally "force," through violent and other means, the "natives" to relinquish their lives, lands, and labor. This is a tale told many times over all throughout Africa, the Americas, Asia, and Australia. However, as often as the tale has been told, few theorists involved in the discourse on decolonization have explored the legitimacy and validity of *retribution*—that is, "punishment for evil done or reward for good done"—with the depth and piercing precision of Aimé Césaire (Irele, 1968; Tomich, 1979; Towa, 1969a, 1969b). In stating that "a civilization which justifies colonization . . . is already a sick civilization, a civilization that is morally diseased," and then invoking retributive justice through "punishment," Césaire cuts-to-the-chase, if you will. He wishes to make it known, to the colonized and otherwise, that the colonial world—an immoral world, an unethical world, an irreligious world—yearns for, and demands: "Violence! The violence of the weak . . . the violence of revolutionary action" (Césaire, 1972, pp. 28, 34). The "revolutionary action" that Césaire claims the "colonial situation" calls for, is definitely what he, Fanon, and, as we shall soon observe, the Kenyan revolutionary writer, Ngugi wa Thiongo, term: *decolonization*.

For those who would argue that Césaire is a naïve "nativist," one who simply espouses a radical rhetoric of "return" or "cultural recuperation," it would be prudent to consider his concept of cultural exchange. He believes that cultural "contacts" between divergent "civilizations" is "a good thing," but despises and detests, and rightly so, "humanity," having been, or being, "reduced to a monologue" (pp. 11, 57). Césaire said:

> I admit that it is a good thing to place different civilizations in contact with each other; that it is an excellent thing to blend different worlds; that whatever its own particular genius may be, a civilization that withdraws into itself atrophies; that for civilizations, exchange is oxygen; that the great good fortune of Europe is to have been a crossroads, and that because it was the locus of all ideas, the receptacle of all philosophies, the meeting place of all sentiments, it was the best center for the redistribution of energy.
>
> But then I ask the following question: has colonization really *placed civilizations in contact*? Or, if you prefer, of all the ways of *establishing contact*, was it the best?
>
> I answer *no*.
>
> . . . between *colonization* and *civilization* there is an infinite distance; that out of all the colonial expeditions that have been undertaken, out of all the colonial statutes that have been drawn up, out of all the memoranda that have been dispatched by all the ministries, there could not come a single human value. (pp. 11–12, emphasis in original)

Césaire supports cultural exchange and the placing of civilizations in contact with one another. What he does not agree with, however, is the domination of one human, social, political, and/or cultural group over that of any or all others. Hence, here his comments point to a distinct anticolonial conception of *self-determination*. Domination, whether colonialist or capitalist (or both), demands "revolutionary action," and this "action," as stated above, has been designated, defined, and described as—the process(es) and program(s) of—decolonization.

Fanon's conception of decolonization, what Hansen (1977, p. 27) has termed "revolutionary decolonization," is inscrutable without linking it to Cesaire's *Discourse on Colonialism*. Cesaire's emphasis on not simply decolonization, but self-determination and African consciousness were appropriated by Fanon and, as was his custom, synthesized with contrasting anticolonial concepts (including Sartre's critiques of capitalism and colonialism), and then belabored to their extreme (see Sartre, 1948, 1963, 1976, 1995). Just as he had done with Joby's critique of Cesaire's 1946 campaign, which would also impact his thinking in *The Wretched of the Earth*, Fanon took Cesaire's discourse on colonialism and Africanized (or, rather, Algeriaized) it and, even more, he dialectically deepened and further developed its revolutionary dimensions.

As stated above, Fanon (1968) asserted that "decolonization is always a violent phenomenon" (p. 35) This is so because "the agents of [the colonial] government speak the language of pure force" (p. 38). It is this "force," this—according to the Eritrean philosopher, Tsenay Serequeberhan (1994)—virtual "primordial violence" that spawns the "reactive," or, as I would prefer, *counteractive* violence *contra*, not simply the colonizers, but the internalization of colonialism and racism on the part of the racially colonized and the entire white supremacist colonialist-capitalist world (p. 73).

The "colonizer," Fanon (1968) insisted, "is the bringer of violence into the home and into the mind of the native" (p. 38). However, this is not to say that Africa (or any part of the "colored," non-white world) was non-violent prior to European colonial conquest(s). By no means should this falsehood be allowed to pass unchecked (see Bodunrin, 1984, pp. 7–8; and also Mazrui, 1967, 1978, 1980, 1986, 2002b, 2004). What Fanon meant here is that "the colonizer" brought the violence that *white supremacist* or *racial* colonialism is to African and other racially colonized peoples' life-worlds and lived-experiences, thus drawing them, the colonized, into Europe's global imperial orbit, which presently includes peoples and continents constitutive of 75 percent of the earth's population and surface (Blaut, 1993; Said, 1979, 1993). With the "colonizers" came violence of such immensity and intensity, such global enormity, that the preexisting violence—dare I say, the "precolonial" violence—on hindsight appears to be no more than mere local or, at most, national skirmishes; scant squabbles that historically have been documented to have been commonplace, and to have plagued human beings in almost every epoch of human history, culture, and civilization.

Colonialism is, quite simply, "violence in its natural state," and, this epoch-breaking and epoch-making violence, asserted Fanon (1968), "will only yield when confronted with greater violence" (p. 61). The colonized, under these circumstances knows, and especially after enduring centuries of exploitation and alienation at the hands of colonialists and the colonial system, that she or he has no other recourse: Decolonization or (continued) dehumanization. It is at, and in, this momentous moment, the moment the colonized commits to, and takes up the banner of decolonization, that Fanon contended:

> He of whom *they* have never stopped saying that the only language he understands is that of force, decides to give utterance by force. In fact, as always, the settler has shown him the way he should take if he is to become free. The argument the native chooses has

been furnished by the settler, and by an ironic turning of the tables it is the native who now affirms that the colonialist understands nothing but force. The colonial regime owes its legitimacy to force and at no time tries to hide this aspect of things. (p. 84, emphasis in original)

What is important to emphasize here is that the "argument the native chooses has been furnished," at least in part, "by the settler"; by the settler's colonial actions, by their "force," by their colonial violence and, it also needs to be accentuated, by the European liberals' and the white left's anticolonial inaction. That the white left, both of Europe and America, has long practiced a policy of benign and often naked neglect where racial colonies and the racially colonized are concerned, to put it plainly, is nothing new. In fact, if truth be told, white liberals and the white left's policy of benign and naked neglect is perfectly "normal" in the abnormal and absurd white supremacist colonialist-capitalist world. However, the fact that the racially colonized have appropriated aspects of the white left's (mainly Marxist) arguments might come as a surprise, and especially to those who remain unaware of the long tradition of black radicalism, which, in all political and intellectual honesty, can be said to reach back as far as the Abolitionist and Pan-Africanist movements, and stretch across several centuries to our modern movements for racial, gender, and economic justice.[7] Which aspects of the colonized's anticolonial argument(s) have been furnished by the settler, or the settler's metropolitan Marxist siblings? Do the colonized uncritically digest the colonizers' arguments? Can anything of anticolonial value be found in the radical/revolutionary tradition of the colonizers' cousins and kinfolk back in the colonialist-capitalist metropole? This last question begs to be asked and answered, especially considering Audre Lorde's (1984) haunting harangue, "The Master's Tools Will Never Dismantle the Master's House" (pp. 110–113).

Prior to engaging Fanon's contributions to the discourse on decolonization, and in order to critically comprehend his pioneering conception of revolutionary decolonization, we would do well to attend to each of the queries above, particularly the latter. In so doing, it may be most helpful to bear in mind Trinidadian historian Tony Martin's contention that there is an explicit indication of Fanon's "affinity to Marx," which is "evident even without a close look at his philosophy." Martin (1999) continues, "the fact [is], for example, that two of his three books bore titles directly suggestive of a conscious identification with Marx: *Les Damnes de la Terre*, which is taken from the first line of the "Internationale" and *L'An Cinq de la Revolution Algerienne* which bears an obvious similarity to Marx's *The Eighteenth Brumaire of Louis Bonaparte*" (p. 85). Fanon's revolutionary decolonization was informed by, not only Pan-Africanism and various strands of African nationalism, but also by his critical and ever-evolving relationship with Marxism. This critical dialogue with Fanon would yield very little if his much-mangled dialectical rapport and critical relationship with Marxism were left in the lurch.

## FANONIAN MARXISM AND/OR MARXIST FANONISM: FANON'S CRITIQUE, APPRECIATION, APPROPRIATION, AND MODIFICATION OF MARXISM IN THE INTEREST OF REVOLUTIONARY DECOLONIZATION

> Marxist analysis should always be slightly stretched every time we have to do with the colonial problem. Everything up to and including the very nature of pre-capitalist society, so well explained by Marx, must here be thought out again.
>
> —Frantz Fanon, *The Wretched of the Earth*, p. 40

> Fanon can be considered a Marxist. This is not to say that he adhered rigidly to every word that has come down to us from Marx's pen. He didn't. But he was Marxist in the sense that Lenin or Castro or Mao are Marxist. That is, he accepted Marx's basic analysis of society as given and proceeded from there to elaborate on that analysis and modify it where necessary to suit his own historical and geographical context.
>
> —Tony Martin, "Rescuing Fanon from the Critics," p. 87

> Fanon can be considered a Marxist-humanist, in the sense that he is not championing a static notion of human nature, but a human "potential" which can be "created by revolutionary beginnings," and where social relationships give meaning to life.
>
> —Nigel C. Gibson, "Introduction to *Rethinking Fanon*," p. 117

Decolonization is the logical consequence of colonization (Kang, 2004; Kawash, 1999; Lazarus, 1999). Therefore, those who would label decolonizers and their discourse, "nativists" and "nativism," should read very slowly, and very carefully, the following line from Fanon: "The argument the native chooses has been furnished by the settler. . . ." That "the native" "chooses" violence as a means toward the end of "total liberation" should surprise no one, and least of all colonialists, capitalists, and those associated with the ruling race, ruling gender, and ruling class(es) of the modern (neo)imperial "world-system" (Fanon, 1968, p. 310). Karl Marx and Friedrich Engels had written on, and of, the imminent revolution for many years by the time Du Bois, James, Césaire, Senghor, and Fanon developed, in the twentieth century, their discourse(s) on decolonization. Marx and Engels (1978) stated quite cryptically in *The Communist Manifesto*:

> All previous historical movements were movements of minorities, or in the interest of minorities. The proletarian movement is the self-conscious, independent movement of the immense majority, in the interest of the immense majority. The proletariat, the lowest stratum of our present society, cannot stir, cannot raise itself up, without the whole superincumbent strata of official [bourgeoisie] society being exploded into the air. (p. 482)

Decolonization is essentially this paragraph magnified ten times over, and then dropped into the context of our (post)modern moment of undercover colonialism, or, as Kwame Nkrumah (1965) and Samir Amin (1973) would have it, "neocolonialsim." Were one to substitute "racialized/colonized" for "proletarian" and "proletariat" above, then, perhaps, Fanon's assertion might make more sense. The argument(s) chosen and augmented, adopted and adapted by the racially colonized *were* and *are*, to a certain extent, supplied by the "radical" and "revolutionary" traditions of racist, colonialist, and capitalist Europe and the United States (Assimeng, 1990; I. Cox, 1966; Isbister, 2001; Lopes, 1988). One need look no further than C. L. R. James's magisterial *The Black Jacobins* to comprehend that the "first" successful revolution by people of African descent in the modern era was deeply influenced by the French Revolution of 1789. However, Fanon (1968) forwards that "Marxist analysis," or any other "radical" or "revolutionary" tradition, that does not arise out of the particular and peculiar, concrete historicity of the racially colonized, should be deconstructed and reconstructed so as to encompass and suit the needs, as well as address the current neocolonial crises, of their specific time and circumstances (p. 40).

In "Rescuing Fanon from the Critics," Tony Martin (1999), perhaps more so than any other Fanonist, has asserted that although "Fanon's writings reveal the influence of several people—Hegel, Marx, Sartre, and Césaire, to name but a few," most critics and commentators have generally "evaluated his philosophy around the concept of Marxism" (p. 85).[8] However, Fanon, similar to only a hand-full of Marxist theorists, understood well what Marx, writing in *The Eighteenth Brumaire of Louis Bonaparte*, meant when he wrote: "The social revolution . . . cannot draw its poetry from the past, but only from the future" (Marx and Engels, 1978, p. 597; also quoted in Fanon, 1967, p. 223; see also T. Martin, 1999, p. 86). For although "[t]he argument the native chooses has been furnished by the settler," it must constantly be kept in mind that Fanon (1968) himself said: "Marxist analysis should always be slightly stretched every time we have to do with the colonial problem. Everything up to and including the very nature of pre-capitalist society, so well explained by Marx, must here be thought out again" (p. 40). Fanon set for himself the task of enhancing ("slightly stretch[ing]") "Marxist analysis." He asserted that "everything" "so well explained by Marx" needed to be, out of historical, cultural, and geographical necessity, "thought out again."

What does it mean to "stretch," to extend and expand "Marxists analysis" in our search for solutions to "the colonial problem," especially racial colonialism? What does it mean to rethink social transformation in light of the anti-imperial onuses that both colonialism *and* capitalism present, and specifically—in contradistinction to comrade Karl Marx's corpus—to non-Europeans/non-whites? Fanon, perhaps, would have replied that there are no social or political panaceas for the plethora of problems which presently plague humanity. Even if "[t]he argument the native chooses has been furnished by the settler," "the native" does not and should not conceptually incarcerate, or intellectually emaciate herself or himself in "the colonial vocabulary" (p. 43). Fanon discerned that "Marxist analysis" was part and parcel of capitalism, *not* colonialism.[9]

Indeed, Marx and the *critical* (as opposed to "vulgar," "orthodox," and/or "mechanical") Marxists provide one of, if not "the," most comprehensive and sophisticated critiques of capitalism. However, they have consistently neglected to factor capitalism's interconnections with racism and colonialism into their analyses. That is why Fanon's emphasis on a more elastic interpretation and application of Marxism, particularly outside of the conventional capitalist context, is so seminal. He challenged the anticolonial intellectual-activist to not only be anticolonial, but also anticapitalist and antiracist. It was Lewis Gordon (1997b), one of the leading and more critical Fanon scholars, who asserted that Fanon's thought might best be characterized as "conjunctive analysis" which critically engaged racism *and* colonialism *and* capitalism (pp. 35–36). The Fanonian intellectual-activist, then, is much more than a mere Marxist disciple. The Fanonian intellectual-activist is more than a mere critical race theorist and anticolonialist. The Fanonian intellectual-activist is not, under any circumstances, a mere academic, ivory tower overseer, or armchair revolutionary. The Fanonian intellectual-activist is a critical theorist and revolutionary humanist, and also a constant critic of internalized colonialism, racism, and capitalism on the part of the colonized (Osei-Nyame, 2002; Pithouse, 2003). This is the dual mandate that Fanon ascribed to the revolutionary intellectual-activist. Noted Fanon scholar, Nigel Gibson (1999b), eloquently addressed this issue when he wrote: "Rather than applying an *a priori*, a crucial task for the Fanonian intellectual was to confront the intellectual's internalization of colonial ideology that had become mentally debilitating. The native intellectual, therefore, does not simply uncover subjugated knowledges but has to challenge the underdeveloped and Manichean ways of thinking produced by colonial rule" (p. 114).

Colonialism inherently gives colonized intellectuals an intellectual inferiority complex. In order to initiate the process of decolonization, the anticolonial (on-the-path-to-becoming-a-truly-*postcolonial*) intellectual must radically rupture their relationship with their (neo)colonial (mis)education and practice critical conceptual generation, putting forward dialectical theory and praxis particular to, and in the best interest of, their specific historical struggle(s) against colonialism, capitalism, and racism, among other (post)modern sociopolitical ills. In a word, colonized intellectuals must "decolonize their minds," as Ngugi (1986) put it, and become revolutionary intellectual-activists. Again, Gibson (1999b) offers insights:

> The revolutionary intellectual who explicitly attempts to develop the often conflictual relationship between mental and manual labor, therefore, is grounded in two interpenetrated though different types of knowledge: the explication of subjugated knowledges and knowledges born of resistance, in their myriad (and not simply practical) forms; and what Fanon meant by working out new concepts, namely, the history of the idea of freedom. These knowledges are connected: revolutionary thought is also a conceptualization of the historical memory of struggle. (p. 120)

In "challeng[ing] the underdeveloped and Manichean ways of thinking produced by colonial rule" the Fanonian intellectual-activist must also bear in mind something that the Cape Verdean and Guinea-Bissaun revolutionary, Amilcar Cabral (1979)—as will be discussed in greater detail in the subsequent chapter—contended: "A people who free themselves from foreign domination will not be free culturally unless, without underestimating the importance of positive contributions from the oppressor's culture and other cultures, they return to the upwards paths of their own culture" (p. 143). The Fanonian intellectual-activist, similar to the

Cabralian intellectual-activist, has a deeply dialectical and critical relationship with Marxism, one that simultaneously critiques most Marxists' inattention to racism and colonialism, but greatly appreciates their thoroughgoing critique of capitalism and its infamous constantly changing character. From the point of view of Fanon's critical theoretical framework, Marxism can be effectively used toward anticolonial ends and, more importantly, in the process of decolonization. However, here we would do well to keep in mind his admonition that, "Marxist analysis should always be slightly stretched every time we have to do with the colonial problem" (see Ayalew, 1975; W. Hansen, 1997; D. Lloyd, 2003; Moreira, 1989; C.J. Robinson, 1993; Serequeberhan, 1988).

In *The Class Struggle in France*, Marx wrote: "A new revolution is possible only in consequence of a new crisis. It is, however, just as certain as this crisis" (Marx and Engels, 1978 p. 593, emphasis omitted). For Fanon, it could be said that racial colonialism presented humanity with "a new crisis" and, therefore, "[a] new revolution," a whole new conception of revolution was required, one that took into consideration not merely the ravaging effects of capitalism, but also those of colonialism and racism. It was incumbent on "the wretched of the earth," without turning a blind-eye to the predatory and vampiric nature of capitalism, to acutely analyze and assess their own racial and colonial oppression, exploitation, and alienation. The revolutionary intellectual-activists who think and act in the best interest of, and in concert with "the wretched of the earth," must do precisely what Fanon (1968) admonished them to do at the close of *The Wretched of the Earth*; they must "waste no time in sterile litanies and nauseating mimicry" of Eurocentric and capitalist political economy-obsessed Marxists (p. 312).

Fanon forcefully challenged the wretched of the earth's revolutionary intellectual-activists to intellectually, politically, and culturally "[l]eave . . . Europe" (p. 311). He critically continued: "Let us decide not to imitate Europe; let us combine our muscles and our brains in a new direction. Let us try to create the whole man, whom Europe has been incapable of bringing to triumphant birth" (p. 313). Fanon was well aware that we, like any people involved in a life or death struggle for human liberation, "need a model," that "we want blueprints and examples." He earnestly admitted that "[f]or many among us the European model is the most inspiring" (p. 312). This is so because (neo)colonial (mis)education exclusively and purposely exposes colonized intellectuals to Eurocentric models, social movements, political thought, philosophy, culture, and so on. Colonized intellectuals, therefore, are just that, *colonized*, and the only way they can decolonize their minds is by plunging themselves into the depths of those elements of their indigenous thought, culture, and traditions—precolonial, colonial, and neocolonial—which could potentially aid them in their efforts to develop revolutionary theory and praxis. They must, however, do this without losing sight of those "positive contributions from the oppressor's culture and other cultures," as Cabral asserted, which could, if employed in the revolutionary interest of the wretched of the earth, provide them not only with critical theories of, but critical praxes in, the racial colonial and racist capitalist world.

According to Fanon, the "nauseating mimicry" and "imitation" of "the European model" on the part of racially colonized intellectuals, and the racialized/colonized in general, has led to "mortifying setbacks," which of his four books *Black Skin, White Masks* and *The Wretched of the Earth* most explicitly engage these issues. It was both shameful and horrifying to Fanon that as more African countries gained "independence," what Nkrumah (1965) in his conception of neocolonialism called "nominal independence," and as more Africans in the diaspora secured greater access to education and basic civil rights, they not only continued to turn to Europe, but willingly and increasingly deepened and developed their racial colonial relationship with European "mother countries." Fanon (1968) fumed:

> European achievements, European techniques, and the European style ought no longer to tempt us and to throw us off our balance. When I search for Man in the technique and the style of Europe, I see only a succession of negations of man, and an avalanche of murders. The human condition, plans for mankind, and collaboration between men in those tasks which increase the sum total of humanity are new problems, which demand true inventions. (pp. 312–313)

Fanon dared the racially colonized to leave Europe and think critically about "the new problems, which demand true inventions." The "European game has finally ended," he said, "we must find something different" (p. 312). The "new problems, which demand true inventions" are precisely those problems which the racial and colonial proletariat have long been struggling against: racism and colonialism, and the intersections and interconnections between and betwixt capitalism *and* colonialism *and* racism. Above, when Fanon asserted that "we," the wretched of the earth's revolutionary intellectual-activists, must "combine our muscles and our brains in a new direction," the "new direction" that he had in mind was one that simultaneously built on and went well-beyond Marxist analyses of the vicissitudes and vampiric nature of capitalism. For Fanon, as for Africana critical theorists, Marxism is but one of many theoretical tools or weapons to be deployed in the struggle against (neo)imperialism, which includes the new and constantly changing forms of, not only capitalism, but colonialism and racism as well. Europe should not be the measure and model for what it means to be "human," or "civilized," or "cultured," or "modern." In fact, Fanon announced, when the racially colonized intellectual embraces critical consciousness, which is to say, when the racially colonized intellectual shifts from being "colonized" and begins the arduous and protracted process(es) of becoming the wretched of the earth's revolutionary intellectual-activist, anything is possible. Why? Because revolution, real revolution as opposed to theoretical or rhetorical revolution, is nothing other than the concrete creation of historical possibilities, the innovative opening up of alternatives. What may have appeared impossible before the embrace of their revolutionary responsibilities, now seems quite possible to the formerly colonized—but, currently on the road to becoming a real *revolutionary*—intellectual. Fanon was unequivocally critical of, and critically optimistic about, the wretched of the earth's revolutionary intellectual-activists: "We today can do everything, so long as we do not imitate Europe, so long as we are not obsessed by the desire to catch up with Europe" (p. 312).

Really now, a Fanonian query begs, what has Europe contributed to human culture and civilization that the racialized and colonized, intellectual-activists or otherwise, should want to spend their entire lives in "nauseating mimicry," uncritically imitating? It will be recalled that I asserted above, *the only way anticolonial intellectual-activists can decolonize their minds is by plunging themselves into the depths of those elements of their indigenous thought, culture, and traditions—precolonial, colonial, and neocolonial—which could potentially aid them in their efforts to develop revolutionary theory and praxis.* It is with this in mind that I return to the important work of the noted Ghanaian philosopher, Kwasi Wiredu (1991), who makes two important points with regard to the discussion at hand. The first point is that "it seems to be a fact about human beings generally that technical progress is apt to outstrip moral insight" (p. 98). In this sense, he continues, "the philosophical thought of a traditional (i.e., preliterate and nonindustrialized) society may hold some lessons of moral significance for a more industrialized society" (p. 98). These comments connect with Fanon's when we recollect his assertion that we must move "in a new direction," and turn our attention to the "new problems, which demand true inventions." The "new direction" that Fanon has in mind here is not a Senghorian Negritude nostalgic embrace of all things "primitive" in precolonial Africa, but an Africana critical theoretical archaeology of those aspects of Africa's past—precolonial, colonial, neocolonial—that could potentially be utilized in our present struggle(s) for human liberation and a higher level of human life.

Wiredu's work is insightful in that it helps to highlight, not simply some of the distinct differences between Africana and European thought, but that Africana thought, as with European thought, has aspects that are simultaneously particular and universal, and that European theorists, among others, could gather a great deal from Africana thought. This brings us to the second point that Wiredu's work helps to highlight. In his own words:

> An obvious fact about the thought of a traditional society is that it is communalistic in orientation. By contrast, the more industrialized a society is, the more individualistic it seems to become. Now it is quite plain that some of the most unlovable aspects of life in the so-called advanced countries are connected with individualism. It is reasonable to expect that a critical examination of individualism in the context of a study of a communally oriented philosophy might yield some useful insights for people engaged in the quest for industrialization as well as for those who are far advanced in that process. Of course, both communalism and individualism may have their strengths and weaknesses. But, an objective appraisal of them is likely to be hampered if studied exclusively from the point of view of any one of these modes of life. (pp. 98–99)

Contemporary continental and diasporan Africans live in both advanced industrial and nonindustrial societies, colonial and capitalist societies, literate and semi-literate societies and, therefore, the revolutionary intellectual-activists who have been charged by Fanon with the task of searching for solutions to the wretched of the earth's "new problems, which demand true inventions," must take all of this into consideration and also heed Wiredu's words when he observed that "both communalism and individualism may have their strengths and weaknesses." The wretched of the earth's revolutionary intellectual-activists must undertake "an objective appraisal" of both communalism and individualism, all the while bearing in mind that their assessment "is likely to be hampered if studied exclusively from the point of view of any one of these modes of life." Wiredu's work enables the wretched of the earth's revolutionary intellectual-activists to call into question Eurocentric conceptions of "progress" and "modernization" and demonstrates that because of, what he terms, "the historical accident of colonialism" Africa is underdeveloped in many, though not by any means all, areas (p. 98; see also Rodney, 1972,

1990). However, by the same token, his work accents the often-overlooked fact that though Europe may be technically and scientifically overdeveloped when compared to Africa, in many other areas, especially ethics and morality, Africa (among other "underdeveloped" continents) is clearly more advanced. Wiredu's ideas on this subject have been recently echoed by Gibson (1999b), who wrote, "it is now the European who must catch up with the African" (p. 119).

Instead of mindlessly mimicking Eurocentric Marxists, which if truth be told most Marxists have been and remain unrepentantly Eurocentric, the revolutionary intellectual-activists who think and act in the best interest of, and in concert with, the wretched of the earth should systematically and critically study their own history and culture—precolonial, colonial, and neocolonial—with an eye toward anything and everything that could be employed in the present anti-imperial struggle. Wiredu's words must be held in mind, and Fanonian intellectual-activists should unceasingly encourage racially colonized, as well as other intellectuals to rethink the contributions that non-European and/or so-called "underdeveloped" cultures could make, not merely to Marxism and other radical political theories, but to modern (i.e., twenty-first century) human culture and civilization in general (see Amin, 1976, 1989, 1990a, 1998a, 2003; Kosukhin, 1985). Fanon (1968) declared, "[t]oday we are present at the stasis of Europe," and Eurocentric, capitalist economy-obsessed Marxism is an outgrowth of European thought and culture, which similar to Europe in general has reached an impasse (p. 314). Fanon refused to bite his tongue, even in the midst of his (French, African, and other) Marxist comrades. Long before the postmodernists (and post-Marxists), Fanon noted Marxism's "obscene narcissism" and pointed to the contradictions at its conceptual core (Callari, Cullenberg, and Biewener, 1995; Magnus and Cullenberg, 1995; Nelson and Grossberg, 1988). I quote the pertinent passage at length:

> A permanent dialogue with oneself and an increasingly obscene narcissism never ceased to prepare the way for a half delirious state, where intellectual work became suffering and the reality was not at all that of a living man, working and creating himself, but rather words, different combinations of words, and the tensions springing from the meanings contained in words. Yet some Europeans were found to urge the European workers to shatter this narcissism and to break with this unreality. But in general, the workers of Europe have not replied to these calls; for the workers believe, too, that they are part of the prodigious adventure of the European spirit. (Fanon, 1968, p. 313)

Fanon's critique of Marxism and the metropolitan proletariat did not stop here. As if defending his embrace and espousal of certain elements of Cesairean Negritude, Pan-Africanism, African nationalism, African socialism, and the African Legion project, Fanon dealt Eurocentric Marxists and white leftist-liberals a theoretical death-blow:

> All the elements of a solution to the great problems of humanity have, at different times, existed in European thought. But the action of European men has not carried out the mission which fell to them, and which consisted of bringing their whole weight violently to bear upon these elements, of modifying their arrangement and their nature, of changing them and finally of bringing the problem of mankind to an infinitely higher plane. (p. 314)

In his unceasing efforts to bring "the problem of mankind to an infinitely higher plane," Fanon challenged white supremacist colonialists and Eurocentric Marxists. This represents a significant contribution to the discourse on decolonization insofar as we understand that Fanon took issue with both racial colonialism *and* Eurocentric radicalism. His work went even further to reveal that racially colonized intellectuals, racially colonized politicians, and the national bourgeoisie were willing to side with white supremacist colonialists if it meant that they could trade places or, at the least, share the spoils with the white colonialists and recolonize the nominally independent nation in their own nefarious neocolonial interests. However, Fanon acutely asserted: "Under the colonial system, a middle class which accumulates capital is an impossible phenomenon. Now, precisely, it would seem that the historical vocation of an authentic national middle class in an underdeveloped country is to repudiate its own nature in so far as it is bourgeois, that is to say in so far as it is the tool of capitalism, and to make itself the willing slave of that revolutionary capital which is the people" (p. 150).

As for those colonized intellectuals coming into a critical consciousness of (neo)colonialism, Fanon cautions them about their embrace of, and conceptual incarceration in, Eurocentric radicalism, Marxist or otherwise. Africa's specific historicity, Africa's particular experience of racial colonialism, and Europe's incessant imperial efforts to *de-Africanize* Africa must be borne in mind and integrally incorporated into any theory that seeks to contribute to the liberation of Africa and its diaspora. Marxism does not now, and has never, claimed to speak to the special needs of Africa and Africans. This point should be emphasized, so that if (or, should I say, *when*) (neo)colonized African intellectuals begin to develop an anticolonial critical consciousness and initiate their sincere search for solutions to the problems of Africa and its diaspora they will realize that though Marxism, among many other schools of European thought, may have much to offer black radicalism and Africana revolutionary praxis, European schools of thought, European history and culture, European religion, and European conceptions of science and civilization cannot and should never be used as the paradigms and theoretical points of departure for decolonization, re-Africanization, and blueprints for an authentic *postcolonial* Africa and its diaspora.

The basic parameters of Marxism are actually too narrow to categorize and conceptually capture Fanon's critical theory, which to reiterate includes critiques of racism *and* colonialism *and* capitalism *and*, if truth be told, sexism (Bergner, 1995; Gibson, 1999a; Gordon, Sharpley-Whiting and White, 1996; Read, 1996; Sharpley-Whiting, 1997). Similar to Du Bois, James, Cesaire, Senghor, and Cabral, Fanon extends and expands and, at times, explodes Marxism. He synthesizes it with the wider and too-often uncharted Africana world of ideas and black radical tradition. To uncritically categorize Fanon's dialectical thought as "Marxism" (or even "black Marxism," for that matter) and leave it there, is similar to attempting to force his feet into a pair of too-tight shoes simply because Marxists and others caught in the quagmires of Eurocentric critical theory think the shoes will look good on his feet. This, in all intellectual honesty, is utterly unfair to Fanon and, what adds insult to injury, is that when his work is carefully and critically read, when it is critically engaged and the historical and cultural contexts, as well as the social and political milieus in which he composed the texts are taken into critical consideration, then his work, literally his words, defy the lazy labeling and simpleminded synopses of Marxists and others conceptually incarcerated in Eurocentric critical theory. This is, precisely, why Melesse Ayalew (1975), Emmanuel Hansen (1977), Lewis Gordon (1995b), L. Adele Jinadu (1986), Ato Sekyi-Otu (1996), Tsenay Serequeberhan (1994), and Renate Zahar (1974), among others, consider Fanon more an "innovator" within the Marxist tradition and a too-often unrecognized rightful member of the Marxian pantheon than a disciple of Marxism—that is, I should importantly add, if he is to be considered as a "Marxist" at all. In 1970, less than a decade after Fanon's untimely death, Marcus Garvey scholar Tony Martin (1999) mused:

> Fanon can be considered a Marxist. This is not to say that he adhered rigidly to every word that has come down to us from Marx's pen. He didn't. But he was Marxist in the sense that Lenin or Castro or Mao are Marxist. That is, he accepted Marx's basic analysis of society as given and proceeded from there to elaborate on that analysis and modify it where necessary to suit his own historical and geographical context. (p. 87)

It is the latter part of Martin's last sentence that resonates the deepest with the discussion at hand: Fanon "accepted Marx's basic analysis of society as given and proceeded from there to elaborate on that analysis and modify it where necessary to suit his own historical and geographical context." Clearly Martin and I are not in agreement when he asserts that Fanon "accepted Marx's basic analysis of society as given," because I do not understand how he could make such a claim when, as I am sure he knows all too well, neither Karl Marx nor his myriad disciples engaged the colonial world, or the racial world to the discursive depth and critical detail to which they have the capitalist world (see Marx and Engels, 1972). How could Fanon have "accepted Marx's basic analysis of society as given" when he consistently emphasized that racial oppression and colonial exploitation, that racism and colonialism, if you will, are equally as oppressive, exploitative, and alienating as the evils of capitalism?

To be fair to Martin, whom I greatly intellectually admire, it could be that because Fanon often emphasized the political economy of race, racism, and colonialism in a white supremacist colonialist–capitalist world, he is open to being interpreted as a Marxist, especially since the search for and critique of the political economy of "things" in a capitalist society is one of the most common characteristics of Marxism. In fact, Martin maintained: "Like the good Marxist that he is, Fanon sees the economic base of most things. This includes racism and colonialism" (p. 88). It is true that Fanon pointed to "the economic base of most things," but what distinguishes his work from that of most Marxists are the very varied "things," the colonial and racial "things" that captured his critical attention and to which he sought to apply Marxism. Fanon, indeed, employed the Marxian method, but he also observed its limitations and deficiencies when we come to the colonial and racial world. Is he automatically a "Marxist" simply because he utilized certain elements of the Marxian method? If so, then, he may also be labeled a Pan-Africanist, African nationalist, African socialist, Negritudist, existentialist, and phenomenologist, among others. Is he really a "Marxist" when his corpus—yes, every single work—in one way or another collapses Marxian critiques of capitalism by pointing to the ways in which capitalism is interconnected with and inextricable from colonialism and racism? Fanon may have "accepted Marx's basic analysis of [*capitalist*] society as given," but he, on principle, found Marxism inexcusably inadequate and loathsomely silent when it came to colonial society, or racist society or, heaven help us, a simultaneously white supremacist colonialist-capitalist society.

I am not denying or taking issue in any way with the intellectual and political fact that "Fanon can be considered a Marxist," as Martin put it above. I am only emphasizing that he was much more than a Marxist, and that Martin himself hints at as much when he wrote in the latter part of the sentence under scrutiny that Fanon "elaborate[d]" or built on Marx's analysis and "modif[ied] it where necessary to suit his own historical and geographical context." It is precisely when and where he "modified"—or "stretched," as he himself said—Marxism that Fanon made his most enduring contributions to both the discourse on decolonization *and* Marxism, bringing them into critical dialogue in a way they had not been before and—Amilcar Cabral's critical theory withstanding—have not been since. In as much as socialism existed long before Karl Marx, and considering Wiredu's, among others', characterization of precolonial and traditional African societies as "communal," it could very well be that Fanon, similar to Sekou Toure, Kwame Nkrumah, Julius Nyerere, Amilcar Cabral and, to a certain extent, Leopold Senghor, was searching for a socialism suitable for Africa and its modern needs. In order for socialism, or any political economic system, to really address the authentic human needs of Africa and Africans, it would have to be grounded in, and grow out of Africa's particular history and culture, Africa's multicultural and transenthic conceptions of social organization, politics, ethics, and so on.[10] Fanon (1968) firmly challenged the wretched of the earth's revolutionary intellectual-activists to develop their own history-, culture-, and struggle-specific radical political theory to guide their revolutionary praxis:

> The Third World ought not to be content to define itself in the terms of values which have preceded it. On the contrary, the underdeveloped countries ought to do their utmost to find their own particular values and methods and a style which shall be peculiar to them. The concrete problem we find ourselves up against is not that of a choice, cost what it may, between socialism and capitalism as they have been defined by men of other continents and of other ages. . . . Capitalist exploitation and cartels and monopoly are the enemies of underdeveloped countries . . . the choice of a socialist regime, a regime which is completely orientated toward the people as a whole and based on the principle that man is the most precious of all possessions, will allow us to go forward more quickly and more harmoniously, and thus make impossible that caricature of society where all economic and political power is held in the hands of a few who regard the nation as a whole with scorn and contempt. (p. 99)

Fanon was pro-socialist, but he was against Eurocentric conceptions of socialism being imposed or superimposed on Africa and Africans either by European or, it must be underscored, by African Marxists (Assimeng, 1990; Keller and Rothchild, 1987; Ottaway, 1986; see also the *Journal of African Marxists*). He understood "Marxist analysis" to be part of "the colonial vocabulary" and, therefore, it needed to be called into question along with everything else in "the colonial situation" (Fanon, 1968, pp. 40, 43, 37). He was, to put it mildly, *suspicious* of the thought and texts that emanated from Europe, since it was this same Europe that perpetually spoke of "the welfare of Man" yet "murder men everywhere they find them" (pp. 311–312). He was, indeed, *suspicious* of Marx and his disciples' chosen agents of social revolution, the metropolitan proletariat, particularly the white workers of Europe and America, who were purportedly destined to deal capitalism its deathblow. Fanon, in fact, had little or no faith in white workers rising up in revolution against capitalism because, as he observed above, "the [white] workers believe, too, that they are part of the prodigious adventure of the European spirit." White workers, as well as white Marxists and the white bourgeoisie, simply did not, dare I say *do not*, understand a crucial historical and cultural fact: "Europe is literally the creation of the Third World. The wealth which smothers her is that which was stolen from the underdeveloped peoples" (p. 102). And, if the Marxists should fix their faces to claim that they are well aware of all of this, then, the question remains: Why have they consistently neglected to factor colonialism and racism into their theories of socialist (or communist) revolution? This query, of course, leads to other critical questions, questions I—along with, it seems to me, Du Bois, James, Cabral, Nkrumah, Toure, Nyerere, Malcolm X, Angela Davis, Samir Amin, Amiri Baraka, Cedric Robinson, bell hooks, Cornel West, Manning Marable, Joy James and Robin Kelley, among many others—have longed to ask and, to be perfectly honest, have been asking: If colonialism and racism are finally factored into Marxian critical theories of contemporary society, then, will the end goal of their (or, should I say, *our*) socialist (or communist) revolution remain an anticapitalist classless society? Wouldn't a new revolutionary agenda be needed, one that includes a *telos* of an antiracist, anticolonialist, *and* anticapitalist classless society? What about the distinct forms of domination and discrimination that women experience, especially in patriarchal capitalist societies? What of women of color in white supremacist patriarchal colonialist capitalist societies? What about homosexuals in heterosexist white supremacist patriarchal colonialist capitalist societies? I am almost certain that my readers register the point that Fanon and I are making here. The critical questions are, literally, infinite when asked from the epistemically open Africana critical theoretical framework.

Fanon was not fooled by the radical rhetoric of the Eurocentric Marxists. He stated, almost emphatically, that "[t]ruth"—meaning, that which is positive and progressive, and in the best interesting of colonized people—is precisely that which "hurries on the break-up of the colonialist regime" (p. 50). It was only through the radical, nay revolutionary, transformation of self and society that "the break-up of the colonialist regime" was to be brought into being. However, and this is where and why Fanon, the African socialists, and the so-called black Marxists remain at odds with the orthodox and capitalist economy-obsessed Eurocentric Marxists, "the colonialist regime" is inseparable from *the capitalist regime*, and both the colonialist and capitalist regimes are utterly inextricable from *the racist regime*. To reiterate, Fanon, the African socialists, and the so-called black Marxists do not deny the pervasive and predatory nature of capitalism but, and here's the real rub, they cannot in good conscience (or, in "good faith," as Sartre might have said) repudiate the ravaging and retarding effects of racism; they cannot downplay and diminish the tragic historic fact that colonialism and neocolonialism have negatively impacted Africa and its diaspora as much as, nay, in certain instances, *even more than*, capitalism; and, finally, they cannot overlook the myriad ways in which racism, colonialism, and capitalism constantly intersect and interconnect in the life-worlds and lived-experiences of the wretched of the earth (Bogues, 2003; Kelley, 2002; Marable, 1983,

1987, 1996; C.W. Mills, 2003a; Mullen, 2002; C.J. Robinson, 2000, 2001; San Juan, 1988, 1992, 2002, 2003).

Marx asserted, as Fanon soon would, that in forging the revolution the oppressed change themselves, because the revolution requires and brings into being radical transformations of such massive proportions, that nothing existing in the "new" society remains as it was prior to the revolution. That is to say that the revolution that Marx envisioned, and the process(es) of decolonization that Fanon (1968) conceived, were to be "total" and "complete," and for Fanon, in contradistinction to Marx, "[w]ithout any period of transition" (p. 35).[11] As the society is altered, so are the individuals that collectively constitute that society. In *The German Ideology*, Marx (1983) contended:

> Both for the production on a mass scale of the Communist consciousness, and for the success of the cause itself, the alteration of men on a mass scale is necessary, an alteration which can only take place in a practical movement, in a revolution; this revolution is necessary, therefore, not only because the ruling class cannot be overthrown in any other way, but also because the class overthrowing it can only in a revolution succeed in ridding itself of all the muck of ages and become fitted to found society anew. (p.187)

Revolution, according to Marx, was "necessary," not merely for the forging and fostering of a "new" society, but for the development of "new" selves. Marx, again similar to Fanon, felt that "the ruling class cannot be overthrown any other way." Oppressed people, to put it bluntly, have very few options; they either come to the conclusion that they are, or have been, forced to fight, or they succumb and sink back, deeper and deeper, into their present state(s) of dehumanization and neocolonization. Revolutionary decolonization was Fanon's solution to "the colonial problem." However, we are to be reminded here that he began his first book by stating: "I do not come with timeless truths" (Fanon, 1967, p. 7). This means, quite simply, that Fanon foresaw the need for future generations of *critical* theorists to revise and retheorize the concept of decolonization in light of the existential issues of their specific life-worlds and lived-experiences. It was, indeed, Fanon (1968) who wrote without rancor or self-righteousness: "Each generation must out of relative obscurity discover its mission, fulfill it, or betray it" (p. 206). It seems safe to say that decolonization remains on our revolutionary agenda as we come to the close of the first decade of the twenty-first century, and we, as Fanon exhorted, are obliged, "out of relative obscurity," to "discover [our] mission, fulfill it, or betray it." It is in the unequivocal interest of aiding the wretched of the earth of the twenty-first century in their (or, rather, *our*) efforts to "discover [our] mission" (or mission*s*) that I now critically engage and expound on Fanon's discourse on revolutionary decolonization.

## "TRUE" VS. "FALSE" DECOLONIZATION: FANON AND THE DISCOURSE ON REVOLUTIONARY DECOLONIZATION

> [F]or proof of what is acknowledged to be happening it is no longer necessary to consult the classical Marxist writers.
>
> —Kwame Nkrumah, *Neo-Colonialism: The Last Stage of Imperialism*, p. xvii

Where Marx's main focus was on "communist revolution," Fanon's was on "decolonization." Decolonization, fundamentally, is a form of revolution waged by, and
in the best interests of, racially colonized peoples, "the wretched of the earth." It is
a process of simultaneous revolutionary transformation of self and society that seeks
to eschew the direct, as well as indirect, imposition of imperial—Eurocentric or otherwise—cultural, racist, colonialist, and capitalist values and models. Decolonization is "a process" insofar as it understands that "independence" is not gained at the
moment the colonized country is "given" its "liberty," and "allowed" to raise its national flag and sing its national anthem. On the contrary, according to Fanon, political independence is merely the beginning, and it, political independence, in no
way indicates and/or insures that the colonized have been freed from colonial values, for these values—which include aesthetic, spiritual, social, political, cultural,
intellectual, and psychological mores and models—have historically persisted and
plagued the purportedly "post-"colonial people and society long after political independence. Grappling with this historical fact, Fanon (1968) wrote:

> During the colonial period the people are called upon to fight against oppression; after
> national liberation, they are called upon to fight against poverty, illiteracy, and under-
> development. The struggle, they say, goes on. The people realize that life is an unending
> contest. (pp. 93–94)

Indeed, "life *is* an unending contest," especially life lived in the racial colonialist-
capitalist world, thus, Fanon's concept of decolonization seeks to call into question
not simply racial colonialism, but also racial (or, rather, *racist*) capitalism. His concept is open-ended, radically dialectical, and self-reflexively critical, and the new nation and the "new men," nay the "new humanity," who are to bring this new nation
into being, can be achieved through a wide-range of revolutionary strategies and tactics, provided—and here I return to Fanon's faithful caveat—the postcolonial nation
and postcolonial humanity "do not imitate Europe, so long as [they] are not obsessed by the desire to catch up with Europe" (pp. 36, 312). If the nation-state that
arises from the ashes of racial colonialism becomes dominated by the racially colonized middle class, Fanon's "greedy" and ever-groveling "national bourgeoisie,"
then, not only will the cancer that is neocolonialism have been brought into existence, but racial capitalism, racist-capitalist social relations, racist-capitalist political
economy, racist-capitalist culture, etcetera, will tighten the already too-tight, in-
creasingly-asphyxiating noose it has long had around the wretched of the earth's
necks. This we may call, following the noted literary and cultural theorist, Neil
Lazarus (1999), the "neo-colonial option" (p. 163). This "option," which when critically engaged from the point of view of the wretched of the earth is revealed *not* to
be an "option" at all, enables the racially colonized to be more completely capital-
ized! It enables the super-exploited to be further exploited in new and unimagin-
able ways; to be perpetually dehumanized and disenfranchised; and, to be eternally
confined to the prison house that imperial Europe and America has constructed
with the express purpose of quarantining the racialized-colonized.

The "neo-colonial option" encourages the racially colonized to choose between
the lesser of two evils: racial colonialism or racist capitalism. However, capitalism,
white supremacist or otherwise, is utterly inextricable from racial colonialism.

Lazarus sheds light on this issue when he writes that the "neo-colonial option" is essentially "a capitalist world system made up—'after colonialism'—of nominally independent nation-states, bound together by the logic of combined and uneven development, the historical dialectic of core and periphery, development and underdevelopment" (p. 163; see also Lazarus, 1990, 2000, 2004). If the colonized middle class, Fanon's "national bourgeoisie," comes to power in the "postcolonial" nation-state, then, only cosmetic changes to racial colonialism will have been made—or, as Fanon (1968) put it, "there's nothing but a fancy-dress parade and the blare of the trumpets. There's nothing save a minimum of readaptation, a few reforms at the top, a flag waving: and down there at the bottom an undivided mass, still living in the middle ages, endlessly marking time" (p. 147).

The truth of the matter is that "[i]n its narcissism, the national middle class is easily convinced that it can advantageously replace the middle class of the mother country" (p. 149). National independence, in this sense, offers the racially colonized middle class opportunities to create new relationships with both the colonizers and the colonized. In terms of the colonized, we have already seen that the racially colonized middle class wishes to exploit them more efficiently in the interest of the European and American bourgeoisies and their imperial interests. With regard to "the middle class of the mother country," the racially colonized bourgeoisie "discovers its historic mission: that of intermediary" (p. 152). To the racially colonized bourgeoisie, "nationalization quite simply means the transfer into native hands of those unfair advantages which are a legacy of the colonial period" (p. 152). Below I quote at length a stunning passage in which Fanon drives the point home that the racially colonized middle class, because it will not "consider as its bounden duty to betray the calling fate has marked out for it," becomes for all intents and purposes neocolonialism's midwife and European and American imperialisms' smokescreen (p. 150).

> Seen through its eyes, its mission has nothing to do with transforming the nation; it consists, prosaically, of being the transmission line between the nation and a capitalism, rampant though camouflaged, which today puts on the mask of neocolonialism. The national bourgeoisie will be quite content with the role of the Western bourgeoisie's business agent, and it will play its part without any complexes in a most dignified manner. But this same lucrative role, this cheap-Jack's function, this meanness of outlook and this absence of all ambition symbolize the incapability of the national middle class to fulfill its historic role of bourgeoisie. Here, the dynamic, pioneer aspect, the characteristics of the inventor and of the discoverer of new worlds which are found in all national bourgeoisies are lamentably absent. In the colonial countries, the spirit of indulgence is dominant at the core of the bourgeoisie; and this is because the national bourgeoisie identifies itself with the Western bourgeoisie, from whom it has learnt its lessons. It follows the Western bourgeoisie along its path of negation and decadence without ever having emulated it in its first stages of exploration and invention, stages which are an acquisition of that Western bourgeoisie whatever the circumstances. In its beginnings, the national bourgeoisie of the colonial countries identifies itself with the decadence of the bourgeoisie of the West. (pp. 152–153)

From the foregoing the need for the dialectical dimension of decolonization appears crystal-clear: decolonization is inherently critical of bourgeois values and culture, whether European *or* African, Eurocentric *or* Africana; it self-reflexively brings dialectical thought to bear on the liberation strategies and tactics, that is, on the liberation theories and praxes undertaken in the revolution against imperialism to achieve an authentically postcolonial world; and, equally important, it applies this same self-reflexive critique to the proponents and opponents, agents and adversaries of revolutionary social, political, and cultural transformation (Duara, 2003; Egbuna, 1986; Osei-Nyame, 1999).

Fanon critically comprehended that European capitalists and colonized African elites were willing to work together, even "after colonialism," to continue colonialism, to initiate a new covert form of colonialism, a kinder, gentler form of colonialism. This is why Fanon ceaselessly searched for a version of democratic socialism suitable to the particular historical and cultural needs of Africa and its diaspora, because it could never be enough to simply *decolonize* Africa and its diaspora, or any former colony: colonialism must be deracinated, literally, ripped out at the roots. Lazarus (1999), again, offers insights: "for Fanon the *national* project also has the capacity to become the vehicle—the means of articulation—of a *social*(ist) demand which extends beyond decolonization in the merely technical sense, and which calls for a fundamental transformation rather than a mere restructuring of the prevailing social order" (p. 163, emphasis in original).

This means, then, in the same process in which the wretched of the earth's intellectual-activists deracinate colonialism from their lives and homelands, they must also offer history- and culture-specific *anticolonial options*. Alternative egalitarian and revolutionary social organizations, political systems, cultural forms, and human relations have to be recreated or, in many instances, *created*; indigenous traditions must be rescued and returned to, in a Cesairean sense, and new ones must be initiated; and, special emphasis should be placed here, decolonization, de-Europeanization, and *revolutionary re-Africanization* ought to be ongoing—yet, I return to Cabral's caveat, ongoing "without underestimating the importance of positive contributions from the oppressor's culture and other cultures," which the wretched of the earth could (and, I honestly believe, *should*) appropriate and adapt as "they return to the upwards paths of their own culture." Behold the dialectics of what Fanon referred to as "true decolonization"! In his own words:

> Nowadays a theoretical problem of prime importance is being set, on the historical plane as well as on the level of political tactics, by the liberation of the colonies: when can one affirm that the situation is ripe for a movement of national liberation? In what form should it first be manifested? Because the various means whereby decolonization has been carried out have appeared in many different aspects, reason hesitates and refuses to say which is a true decolonization, and which is a false. We shall see that for a man who is in the thick of the fight it is an urgent matter to decide on the means and the tactics to employ: that is to say, how to conduct and organize the movement. If this coherence is not present there is only a blind will toward freedom, with the terribly reactionary risks which it entails. (Fanon, 1968, pp. 58–59)

Clearly, decolonization is a complicated phenomenon, one in which Africa's perplexing class politics and, in specific, the peculiar politics of Africa's colonized classes, plays itself out, though not without the eager, ever-watchful eyes and wicked intentions of various colonialist-capitalist bourgeoisies, European or otherwise

(Amin, 1980; Amin and Cohen, 1977; S. Katz, 1980; Magubane and Ntalaia, 1983; Staniland, 1968). The wretched of the earth's revolutionary intellectual-activists, therefore, not only have to decolonize the world the colonizers made—and, "the colonizer's model of the world," as James Blaut (1993) perceptively put it—but also, the world the begrudging racially colonized bourgeoisie deeply wishes and desperately wants to make. False decolonization is, quite simply, the "fancy-dress parade and the blare of the trumpets" that Fanon made mention of above. Absolutely nothing accept the color of the colonizers' skins will be changed. "There's nothing," fumed Fanon, "save a minimum of readaptation, a few reforms at the top, a flag waving: and down there at the bottom an undivided mass, still living in the middle ages, endlessly marking time." Fanon's concept of revolutionary decolonization, therefore, makes a distinction between the class politics and class projects of the racially colonized bourgeoisie and the wretched of the earth. From this critical Fanonian frame of reference, it can be ascertained that decolonization is not neutral and, consequently, not always automatically in the best interest of the wretched of the earth. There are different directions that decolonization can take, just as there are different, extremely devious directions that colonialism (*and* capitalism *and* racism *and* sexism) can take, and the racially colonized bourgeoisie seeks to initiate and establish a neocolonial nation-state by means of a *bourgeois decolonization*—that is, decolonization in the interest of the racially colonized bourgeoisie who, to strike the iron while it is hot, want nothing other than to further underdevelop "their" countries in the imperial interests of the upper and middle classes of the "mother country" and, especially, foreign capitalist corporations. Not to be fooled by African colonial elites false decolonization, which is nothing other than another name for Eurocentric imperial *recolonization*, Fanon (1968) disparages the racially colonized bourgeoisie's concept of decolonization, its false decolonization, by emphasizing the interconnection of their interests with those of the upper and middle classes of the "mother country."

> The national bourgeoisie will be greatly helped on its way toward decadence by the Western bourgeoisie, who come to it as tourists avid for the exotic, for big game hunting, and for casinos. The national bourgeoisie organizes centers of rest and relaxation and pleasure resorts to meet the wishes of the Western bourgeoisie. Such activity is given the name tourism, and for the occasion will be built up as a national industry . . . all these are the stigma of this depravation of the national middle class. Because it is bereft of ideas, because it lives to itself and cuts itself off from the people, undermined by its hereditary incapacity to think in terms of all the problems of the nation as seen from the point of view of the whole of that nation, the national middle class will have nothing better to do than to take on the role of manager for Western enterprise, and it will in practice set up its country as the brothel of Europe. (pp. 153–154)

The dialectics of decolonization is simultaneously aimed at the concreteness of the colonial past and the possibilities of the postcolonial future and, for all its openness it remains, like all dialectics, preoccupied with both internal and external contradictions, which, as we have witnessed above, means that it is as critical of the pseudo-bourgeoisie in neocolonial Africa as it is of the super-bourgeoisies in Europe and America. The dialectics of decolonization, thus, is grounded in, and grows out of, the crossroads where the concreteness of the colonial past and the possibilities of the postcolonial future converge, the place where world-historical facts meet racial colonial fictions, the place where the wretched of the earth, through their revolutionary decolonization, begin the process(es) of freeing themselves from the claws and confines of colonialism. I observed above that decolonization critically engages the proponents and opponents, as well as the agents and adversaries of revolutionary social, political, and cultural transformation, this is necessary because of the constraints of colonial history: the fact, namely, that the historical narratives of colonizing countries—dare I say colonizing continents—by default dehumanizes the colonized; the colonial (mis)education system, which the colonized find very difficult to get around if they desire to be "successful" and survive in the colonial world, brainwashes them and their children into believing that Europe and Europeans—nay, as Du Bois (1995a) declared, "white folk"—are quite literally "supermen" and "world-mastering demi-gods" (p. 456; see also Rabaka 2006d, 2007b). Is it any wonder, then, that racial colonialism and racist capitalism implants a deep and pervasive sense of inferiority into the consciousnesses of the colonized, who get caught in the tangled web of undeniable intraracial antagonisms and curious transethnic kinships, bitter battles and concealed complicity? Is it any wonder that these same racially colonized social agents, who seem to live their lives on the brink of the most excruciating schizophrenia (how could it be otherwise?), are (true to their double-conscious racial colonial condition) simultaneously capable of the narrowest nationalism and most heartfelt humanism, unrepentant religious intolerance and openness to agnosticism, ethnic chauvinism and deep commitment to critical multiculturalism, and, searing selfishness and draw-dropping selflessness (Hanley, 1976; JanMohamed, 1984, 1985, 1988; Lazarus, 2000; Maldonado-Torres, 2005b; T.O. Moore, 2005; Ngugi, 1972, 1983).

It is important for the wretched of the earth's revolutionary intellectual-activists to redefine revolutionary decolonization for their specific struggle, always keeping in mind that colonialism and capitalism, as with racism and sexism, are always and ever changing, which is to say, that each of the aforementioned are extremely malleable and motive, constantly shifting from one epoch or milieu to the next. Fanon's distinction between true and false decolonization provides an important paradigm and critical theoretical point of departure, one that enables the wretched of the earth to gauge whether true decolonization has taken, or is actually taking place. With this in mind, we are compelled to briefly—albeit *critically*—examine Fanon's concept of revolutionary decolonization.

For Fanon (1968) decolonization is "a program," "a historical process," and a "period" which follows neither laws, nor logic that can be comprehended by either "the colonizer" or "the colonized" *a priori*, that is, prior to its emergence (pp. 36, 43, 36). It overturns every "thing," nothing survives unaltered (pp. 36–37). Decolonization is "quite simply the replacing of a certain 'species' of men by another 'species' of men" (p. 35). It is part of a "historical process" that can and will end only when the entire "colonial world," that is, the "whole social structure," is "changed from the bottom up" (pp. 36, 37, 35). However, decolonization goes a lot further, and cuts considerably deeper into the social setting. It, in a word, "influences" not merely the social setting but also those individuals who undertake it or, rather, experience it.

Fanon tells us that just as decolonization changes the "whole social structure," it also alters and "influences individuals," it "modifies them fundamentally": "the 'thing' which has been colonized becomes man during the same process by which it frees itself" (pp. 36–37). For, decolonization, at minimum, "is the veritable creation of new men," who speak a "new language" to express their "new humanity" (p. 36). But, it should be underscored, the "new men" that Fanon envisioned were not merely racially colonized males. Quite the contrary, he included "the colonizers" or "the settlers," as well as the females of both of these "two forces ["the colonized" and "the colonizers"], opposed to each other by their very nature" (p. 36).[12] Fanon wrote: "The need for this change [decolonization] exists in its crude state, impetuous and compelling, in the consciousness and in the lives of the men *and* women who are colonized. But the possibility of this change is equally experienced in the form of a terrifying future in the consciousness of another 'species' of men and women: the colonizers" (pp. 35–36, my emphasis).[13]

In an anarchic moment, in many respects reminiscent of the Russian revolutionary, Mikhail Bakunin, Fanon sternly stated: "Decolonization, which sets out to change the order of the world, is, obviously, a program of complete disorder" (p. 36). It is by and through this "period" of "complete disorder" that Fanon claims racially colonized peoples finally have the opportunity to question "the colonizers," "the colonial world," and, perhaps most importantly, themselves: "In decolonization, there is therefore the need of a complete calling in question of the colonial situation" (p. 37). This "complete calling in question of the colonial situation" opens the colonized and the colonizing peoples to the potential and possibilities that they—by and for themselves—have of (re)creating and (re)constructing selves and societies predicated on "[t]otal liberation" (pp. 43, 310).

"Total liberation" entails freedom, and the freedom which Fanon envisioned had a double dimension: it is at once political and individual. With regard to the former, Fanon has in mind the freedom of the nation-state and/or governmental apparatus. Concerning the later, he envisions an *existential freedom*, which refers to an individual's consciousness of their freedom and free choice. The Fanonian concept of freedom bitterly understands that "[t]he starving peasant, outside the class system, is the first among the exploited to discover that only violence pays" and that she or he has "nothing to lose and everything to gain," and for this reason, in the past where "they [the 'peasants'] were completely irresponsible; today they mean to understand everything and make all decisions" (pp. 61, 94). The freedom Fanon envisaged is one where the "peasants" and politicians are one and the same because all citizens know and understand that "[n]obody, neither leader nor rank-and-filer, can hold back the truth" (p. 199). And, "the truth," according to Fanon, "is that which hurries on the break-up of the colonialist regime" (p. 50). He went far to put his faith in "the people" in full view when he wrote, "[e]verything can be explained to the people, on the single condition that you really want them to understand" (p. 189). However, here Fanon is quick to offer a caveat: "You will not be able to do all this [i.e., decolonize and attain and maintain revolutionary freedom] unless you give the people some political education" (p. 180).

Freedom in the public and political sphere requires the absence of external control over the State (Gramsci, 1971, 1977, 1978; Kipfer, 2004). It is in this sense that Fanon (1968), especially in "The Pitfalls of National Consciousness," criticizes anti-democratic, single party, tsarist, militarist, fascist, dictatorial, and puppet politics in post-independence "underdeveloped" countries (pp. 148–205).[14] Through the lens and lessons of history and betrayal, and perhaps following Fanon, Kwame Nkrumah (1965) would later write about and term this phenomenon in so-called "Third World" politics: "neo-colonialism." Colonialism remained just that, "colonialism," merely mutating into "its final and perhaps most dangerous stage" (Nkrumah, 1965, p. ix). It, colonialism, quite simply, went by another name, and Du Bois, Fanon, Nkrumah, Cabral, and a whole host of anticolonial Africana (among other) thinkers have expressed and offered bits and pieces of the truth and reality of this matter. Nkrumah comprehended that "[n]eo-colonialism is by no means exclusively an African question" (p. xvii). Quite the contrary, Nkrumah, a life-long disciple of Du Bois and Pan-African comrade of Fanon's, contended:

> Long before it was practiced on any large scale in Africa it was an established system in other parts of the world. Nowhere has it proved successful, either in raising living standards or in ultimately benefiting the countries which have indulged in it. Marx predicted that the growing gap between the wealth of the possessing classes and the workers it employs would ultimately produce a conflict fatal to capitalism in each individual capitalist State. This conflict between the rich and the poor has now transferred on to the international scene, but for proof of what is acknowledged to be happening it is no longer necessary to consult the classical Marxist writers. (p. xvii)

"[I]t is no longer necessary to consult the classical Marxist writers," because the "classical Marxist writers," in all their prescience and ranting and raving of revolution and social transformation, never fully figured, nor felt they needed to critically figure into their analyses, the "classical" or contemporary situations and circumstances of the racialized and colonized world. That is precisely why, following Renate Zahar (1974), Lewis Gordon (1995b) correctly observes that "although Fanon was more in line with Marxist-Leninism," his contribution(s) to Marxist, and particularly "Western Marxist," discourse and theory "was more as an innovator, not a disciple" (p. 93). It was not long after Nkrumah (1973b) wrote, "for proof of what is acknowledged to be happening it is no longer necessary to consult the classical Marxist writers," that he, ousted from his presidency in Ghana in 1966, turned to and drew from Fanon, and, in no uncertain terms, stated sternly: "There is no middle road between capitalism and socialism" (p. 74; see also Nkrumah, 1970b, 1973a, 1973c, 1990). For Nkrumah, as for Fanon, decolonization, and all that it entails, is a necessary *means* if "the wretched of the earth" (in Fanon's phraseology) or "the oppressed and exploited of the earth" (in Nkrumah's terminology) are to reach the *end* of both colonial and neocolonial exploitation, alienation, and oppression, and usher in the ugly-beauty of "total liberation" (Fanon, 1968, p. 310; Nkrumah, 1973b, p. 74). Gordon, following Zahar (1974), asserts that Fanon was no mere card-carrying, party-preaching Marxist-Leninist, but "more . . . an innovator" within the worlds of Marxist and liberation theory. One of Fanon's major innovations and contributions to the discourses of Marxism, liberation theory, and Africana critical theory was his articulation of revolutionary decolonization.

Although many of the major Fanon scholars and critics hardly discuss his concept of *revolutionary* decolonization, and make little or no distinction between true and false decolonization, it has been and remains one of Fanon's most pervasive, profound, and provocative contributions to psychoanalytic, social, political, postcolonial and postmodern theory. With regard to Marxism, Fanon's articulation of revolutionary decolonization enabled him to do precisely what he advocated others engaging and enduring "the colonial problem" do, stretch it, "slightly." The classic line, it will be recalled, reads: "Marxist analysis should always be slightly stretched every time we have to do with the colonial problem" (Fanon, 1968, p. 40). Fanon, specifically in "Concerning Violence," literally augments and updates Marxist theory, and appropriates those aspects and elements from it which he believed would enable him to "call into question the colonial situation," that is, begin "the historical process" of revolutionary decolonization (pp. 36–37). By "stretching" "Marxist analysis," Fanon placed a new praxis-promoting critical theory, radical politics, and revolutionary decolonization, not merely on Marxists', but Pan-Africanists, African socialists, African nationalists, black nationalists, existentialists, phenomenologists, and radical humanists' discursive and political agendas.

## FANON'S FURY: COLONIAL VIOLENCE, ANTI-COLONIAL VIOLENCE, AND THE DISCOURSE ON REVOLUTIONARY DECOLONIZATION

Fanon first broached the subject of the inferiority complex that colonialism instills in the racially colonized in *Black Skin, White Masks*. Racial colonialism and the racially colonized person's inferiority complex was something that he more or less psychologized in his early work, pointing to the profundity of the racial colonial problem and the racially colonized's double-conscious racial colonial condition as a result (P. Adams, 1970; Bulhan, 1980a, 1985; Cooppan, 1996; T.O. Moore, 2005; Razanajao, Postel and Allen, 1996; Ysern-Borras, 1985). With *The Wretched of the Earth*, written a decade after *Black Skin, White Masks*, Fanon believed that he had found an extremely important part of the solution to the racial colonial problem and the racially colonized's inferiority complex: self-defensive anticolonial violence. Though it has long rubbed many of Fanon's readers the wrong way, few can deny how intriguing his views on anticolonial violence are; in a sense, they provide a leitmotif for critically comprehending *A Dying Colonialism*, *The Wretched of the Earth*, and most of essays in *Toward the African Revolution*, which is to say, the bulk of his body of work.

Few have understood, or engaged critically, Fanon's concept of revolutionary decolonization, its advocacy of self-defensive anticolonial violence or otherwise. When he is read, as mentioned above, he is often read as "a philosopher of violence," but, similar to Malcolm X, Frantz Fanon cannot and should not be allowed to be reduced to a few misquoted statements concerning counter or self-defensive anticolonial violence (Rabaka, 2002, 2008b). In point of fact, colonialism is a code word for a complex kind of violence that plays itself out in the heads and hearts, in the lives and homelands of both the colonized and the colonizer. However, the colonized and the colonizer approach violence in two completely different, yet deeply interconnected, ways. On the one hand, the colonizer introduces the colonized to *colonial violence*, and this is a point that should be strongly stressed. Even so, we must be clear here to highlight the historical fact that violence existed long before the colonizer came. What makes the colonizer's violence different from the preexisting precolonial violence is that the colonizer's violence is *colonial violence*: violence for the sake of colonialism, and, more specifically, racial colonialism. The colonized, on the other hand, engages in anticolonial violence in reaction to the colonizer's colonial violence, to counter the colonizer's colonial violence.

The colonized comes to realize that colonialism has its own code of ethics, or *etiquette of anti-ethics*, if you will. The colonizer cannot and does not under any circumstance acknowledge the humanity or right to self-determination of the colonized, because to do so would completely undermine the bad faith and false legitimacy of colonialism, which has been established on the imperial assumption that the colonized, left to their precolonial political systems and social organizations, are utterly incapable of governing themselves. What is more, insofar as the colonized does not forfeit their rightful claim to self-determination and resist the imposition of racial colonial rule, the colonial nation-state, that is, the colonial government, the exportation of European imperial social and political models and Eurocentric modes of existence cannot be guaranteed to take root (Memmi, 1967, 1969, 1984, 2000). In order to plant the seeds of European imperial social and political models and Eurocentric modes of existence, the colonizer employs various forms of violence, overt and covert kinds of violence, to quarantine the colonized to the colonial world. Fanon contended that no matter how benevolent the colonizer might appear, the reality of the racial colonial matter is that she or he will not recognize the human rights of the racially colonized, or, in the event that some semblances of the humanity of the racially colonized are acknowledged, the colonizer will not permit it unless the acknowledgement simultaneously perpetuates the continued devaluation and humiliation of the humanity of the racially colonized. In other words, racial colonialism is willing to make certain concessions or exceptions to its racist rules, but these concessions with the racially colonized, usually with the racially colonized bourgeoisie, are few and far between.

It is primarily because of colonialism's violent denial of the racially colonized's humanity and history that Fanon argued that the wretched of the earth *must* rescue and reclaim their humanity and history from the dark, dank dungeon that the colonizer has confined it to, and completely topple the racial colonial world. The racially colonized, therefore, must be mentally and physically prepared to *violate* the "dividing line[s]"—social, political, cultural, metaphysical, physical, epistemological, and ethical—imposed by the colonizer if they are to "return to the upwards paths of their own culture," as Cabral contended, and in like fashion, as Fanon importantly asserted, *rehumanize* the colonizer and return them to their lost humanity as well (Cabral, 1979, p. 143; Fanon, 1968, p. 38; see also Bernasconi, 1996). In *The Hermeneutics of African Philosophy*, Tsenay Serequeberhan (1994) importantly emphasized:

> the fundamental concern of the colonized is to retake the initiative of history: to again become historical Being. It is to *negate the negation* of its lived historicalness and overcome the violence of merely being an object in the historicity of European existence that the colonized fights. Thus, it is the inter-implicative dialectic of this primordial violence, and the counter-violence it evokes, that we need to concretely grasp. (p. 57, emphasis in original)

Heeding the words of Serequeberhan, and employing his caveat as my point of departure, what I seek to do here is to "concretely grasp" the role and relevance of violence in the process(es) of decolonization. It must be underscored at the outset that the first sentence of Fanon's last book, *The Wretched of the Earth*, reads: "National liberation, national consciousness, the restoration of nationhood to the people, commonwealth: whatever may be the headings used or the new formulas introduced, *decolonization is always a violent phenomenon*" (p. 35, emphasis added). From Fanon's perspective, that the racially colonized turn to anticolonial and self-defensive violence should shock no one, least of all the colonizer and reprehensibly racializing and colonizing nation-states. Colonialism, the whole colonial system, the entire colonial world, is nothing other than violence. Violence is not simply physical; there are also psychological dimensions to violence. What is more, colonial violence is extremely predatory and pervasive and seeks to racialize and colonize as many aspects of the colonized's life-worlds and lived-experiences, as many elements of their history and culture as it inhumanly and possibly can: from politics to economics, education to religion, psychology to social organization, aesthetics to ethics, and on and on.

Recall, Fanon (1968) contended that it is the colonizer who "is the bringer of violence into the home and into the mind of the native" (p. 38). All that we know as "Europe" and "European" has been, and remains, established on "the negation" of the lives, lands, languages, cultures, histories, and, therefore, humanity of the non-European world (see Blaut, 1993; Chinweizu, 1978; Mudimbe, 1988, 1994; Said, 1979, 1993). The colonized, "back . . . to the wall, . . . knife . . . at [their] throat[s]," realizes that there exists but one way out of the wicked world "the settlers" have made, and that is "gun in hand," "ready for violence at all times" (Fanon, 1968, pp. 58, 37). Fanon went further: "The native who decides to put the program [of decolonization] into practice, and to become its moving force, is ready for violence at all times. From birth it is clear to him that this narrow world, strewn with prohibitions, can only be called in question by absolute violence" (p. 37).

Under the auspices of the program of decolonization, a struggle, one of "absolute violence," a "murderous and decisive struggle between the two protagonists [the colonized and the colonizers]" thus ensues (p. 37). No "thing" remains as it was prior to this "struggle," which, of course, is why the violence of this struggle is characterized as "absolute." Absolute—meaning "total," "complete," "unconditional" and "infinite"—the violence of this "murderous and decisive struggle" alters all that was, and opens the oppressed, and, by default, the oppressors, to the possibility and potential of that which *should have been*, and that which they—meaning, both the colonized and the colonizers—begin to critically understand *ought to be*. The colonized, again, "back . . . to the wall, . . . knife . . . at [their] throat[s]," knows that they have no other recourse but to fight for their liberty, and on behalf, and in the interest of their long denied humanity. The colonized knows that the world in which she or he has, literally, been *flung* into, a "narrow world, strewn with prohibitions," is a world predicated on the primordial violence of colonialism. Colonialism is, quite simply, "violence in its natural state" (p. 61). It was violence, "absolute violence," which marked the beginning of colonial conquest, and it shall be nothing other than violence, "absolute violence," which will symbolize and signify the end of colonial conquest. The form that the colonized's anticolonial violence takes is not in any way predetermined by the colonial violence of the colonizer. Colonial violence, ironically, opens the colonized to new versions of violence, violence heretofore unimagined in the precolonial world (Gines, 2003; Gueddi, 1991; Kebede, 2001; Makuru, 2005; Seshadri-Crooks, 2002).

On the initial encounter between the colonized and the colonizers, Fanon (1968) wrote: "Their first encounter was marked by violence and their existence together—that is to say the exploitation of the native by the settler—was carried on by dint of a great array of bayonets and cannons" (p. 36). The colonized's history, culture, social and political systems, language, religion, art, and "customs of dress," are supplanted, literally *deracinated*—that is, plucked or torn up or out by the roots; eradicated or exterminated—so as to make colonialism, "violence in its natural state," complete, total, or "absolute," as Fanon would have it. Commenting on the "break up," that is, the decolonization of the colonial world, Fanon commented:

> The violence which has ruled over the ordering of the colonial world, which has ceaselessly drummed the rhythm for the destruction of native social forms and broken up without reserve the systems of reference of the economy, the customs of dress and external life, that same violence will be claimed and taken over by the native at the moment when, deciding to embody history in his own person, he surges into forbidden quarters. To wreck the colonial world is henceforward a mental picture of action which is very clear, very easy to understand and which may be assumed by each one of the individuals which constitute the colonized people. (pp. 40–41)

Fanon, unlike many Marxist theorists, did not ascribe fixed and fast roles to specific social and political economic classes: decolonization, he declared, "may be assumed by each one of the individuals which constitute the colonized people." Where Marx thought certain social and political economic classes, take, for example, the "lumpenproletariat," were a "dangerous class" and "social scum" whose "conditions of life prepare it for the part of a bribed tool of reactionary intrigue" (Marx and Engels, 1978, p. 482). Fanon (1968), on the other hand, argued that "the lumpenproletariat, that horde of starving men, uprooted from their tribe and from their clan, constitutes one of the most spontaneous and most radically revolutionary forces of a colonized people" (p. 129; see also C.P. Peterson, 2007; Sekyi-Otu, 1996; Wallerstein, 1979). This is because the colonized lumpenproletariat constitute a class who constantly have to do without the most basic human needs, and whose members are systematically denied entrée into the most minuscule so-called "benevolences" and "benefits" of colonialism and Eurocentric imperial modernity. Their lives, their very existence serve as a constant reminder that the racially colonized bourgeoisie is nothing other than a bunch of buck-dancing and bootlicking neocolonial carpetbaggers whose pseudo-lavish Eurocentric lifestyles accentuate the gross political and economic injustices of the established racial colonial order (Farber, 1981; Memmi, 2006; Sabbagh, 1982; Staniland, 1968; G.A. Thomas, 1999).

The colonized lumpenproletariat's lives also painfully point to the fact that their relationships with their precolonial history and culture have been brutally ruptured, which is one of the reasons Fanon wrote that they have been "uprooted from their tribe and from their clan." The "tribe" and the "clan" symbolize the colonized lumpenproletariat's precolonial history and culture, their precolonial political systems and social organizations and, though Marx may have thought of them as a bunch of mindless mercenaries, Fanon believed that they could potentially represent "one of the most spontaneous and most radically revolutionary forces of a colonized people." Why? Because the colonized lumpenproletariat, long locked out of the colonial world that both the European bourgeoisie and the colonized African bourgeoisie greedily share, constitute the group farthest away from the crumbs that fall from (neo)colonialism's imperial table. Their relationship with European modernity, which is to say their relationship with the evolution of Europe's anti-black racist capitalism and colonialism, has been and remains a violent one.

For Fanon (1968), violence "ruled over" in the colonial world, it alone was "absolute." It was the most pervasive characteristic of colonialism, and no one and no "thing" went unscathed. In fact, the "government" that the "governing race" and "classes" erected can be, and has been, described as a "reign of violence" (pp. 40, 88). Because violence was the "absolute," "ordering" and organizing principle of the racial colonial world, Fanon felt that only "greater violence" could and would bring "disorder" long enough to forge a new (antiracist, anticolonialist, and anticapitalist) world: "colonialism is not a thinking machine, nor a body with reasoning faculties. It is violence in its natural state, and it will only yield when confronted with greater violence" (p. 61). Therefore, the anticolonial violence of the racially colonized is nothing other than the long overdue answer to the conundrum that the primordial violence of racial colonial conquest has, and continues to present to the wretched of the earth, who are, I should reiterate, the masses of the earth. The colonized, through anticolonial violence, intend to "wreck" or "break up" the established order of the racial colonial world (pp. 40–41). Once again Serequeberhan (1994) offers important insights:

> The first act of freedom that the colonized engages in is the attempt to *violently* disrupt the "normality" which European colonial society presupposes. The tranquil existence of the colonizer is grounded on the chaotic, abnormal, and subhuman existence of the colonized. The "new societies" that replicate Europe in the non-European world are built on "vacated space" which hitherto was the uncontested *terra firma* of different and differing peoples and histories.
>
> The dawn and normalcy of colonial society—i.e., the birth and establishment of the modern European world, as Karl Marx approvingly points out in the first few pages of the *Communist Manifesto*—is grounded on the negation of the cultural difference and specificity that constitutes the historicity and thus humanity of the non-European world. European modernity establishes itself globally by violently negating indigenous cultures. This violence in replication, furthermore, accentuates the regressive and despotic/aristocratic aspects internal to the histories of the colonizing European societies. (p. 58, emphasis in original)

The imposition of European "normality" onto non-European lives and lands signals and symbolizes the very terms, the very grounds upon which the "murderous and decisive struggle" between the oppressed and their oppressors is fought. As Fanon (1968) contended: "The cause is the consequence; you are rich because you are white, you are white because you are rich" (p. 40). To take this line of thinking a step further, it could be said that one is human because one is white, and that one is white insofar as one is human. By negating the history of the racially colonized, the colonizers also negate the identity, and therefore the humanity of the conquered peoples. Serequeberhan (1994) maintains that "[t]he colonized is a member of a defeated history" (p. 69). By this, I take him to mean two things. First, that the racially colonized is a member of a group that has suffered a historical defeat. And, second, that the racially colonized's history, "the process of his communal becoming," has been violently suspended or "interrupted" and, from the colonial point of view, definitively (p. 69).

In "defeating" or conquering the racially colonized, the colonizer also "defeated" and conquered the historicity—that is, the lived and concrete actuality, the life-worlds and life-struggles—of the racially colonized. The racially colonized no longer comes into being, or becomes a *human being* on her or his own, she or he only registers on the record of "History" when and where the colonizers allow her or him to do so; which, to be perfectly honest, is rarely, if ever. Further, when and where the racially colonized does rear her or his head in "History," she or he is painted as a "subhuman" "savage," "a sort of quintessence of evil" (Fanon, 1968, p. 41; see also, Jordan, 1968; Pieterse, 1992). This in turn creates a "situation," a "world" where there exists two "'species' of men [and women]": those who are white, European, and human and, as a consequence, have human rights which are to be respected and protected; and, those who are racialized, colonized, non-European, non-white and, therefore, *not* human, and have no human rights which are to be respected and protected in a white supremacist colonialist capitalist world.[15]

In this world, and in this situation, it is not hard to discern why Fanon would write: "On the logical plane, the Manicheism of the settler produces a Manicheism of the native" (p. 93). That is to say that "the native," imbued with the horror and hell of racial colonialism, sets out to decolonize, literally de-center and destroy, the racial colonial world. The racially colonized has no choice. As I have said, the oppressed have few options. Barred by the colonizers—and sometimes their own self-negation and self-hatred—from the annuals of history, the racially colonized seek nothing less than to reclaim her or his place on the stage of the miraculous drama of human existence and experience. Hence, Serequeberhan (1994) said: "Conflict and violence are not a choice, they are an existential need negatively arising out of the colonial situation which serves as a prelude to the rehumanization of the colonized" (p. 73). Serequeberhan acknowledges that violence is only a "prelude"—that is, it is literally a preface, an introduction, an opening—through which the racially colonized might step back on to the stage of human history, and (re)construct human being(s) and a humane world where each person critically understands her or his identity and dignity and, therefore, humanity, to rest on the respect and recognition of other persons' identity and dignity and, therefore, humanity.[16] This line of logic is, perhaps, most pronounced when and where we observe Fanon's critiques of the ways in which colonialism overlaps, interlocks, and intersects with, not only racism and capitalism, but also sexism, and particularly patriarchy. In other words, race is not only colonized and inextricable from colonialism in the realm of racial colonialism, but it is also gendered and hyper-sexualized or, rather, eroticized and exotified in racist colonialist capitalist contexts, which are always and ever, however sometimes subtly, racist colonialist capitalist *sexist* situations.

## UNVEILING FRANTZ FANON, UNVEILING MALE FEMINISM, UNVEILING MALE WOMANISM: FANON'S CONTRIBUTIONS TO WOMEN'S DECOLONIZATION AND WOMEN'S LIBERATION

Fanon has a contradictory, controversial, and regularly contested relationship with feminism, womanism, and women's studies. As the growing body of criticism on "Fanon's feminism" demonstrates, it would be extremely difficult to deny his contributions—again, however contradictory, controversial and contested—to women's quest to decolonize their distinct life-worlds and lived-experiences in the male supremacist world in which they find themselves (Sharpley-Whiting, 1997). Fanon's commitment to women's liberation was deeply connected to, and, even more, inextricable from his commitments to decolonization, democratic socialism and human liberation, and, as with each of the aforementioned, his theory of women's liberation has progressive and retrogressive aspects. There is a knee-jerk tendency among theorists, both male and female, who engage Fanon's contributions to feminism, womanism, and women's liberation to argue either that Fanon was gender progressive or that Fanon was gender regressive. I openly acknowledge, in all intellectual honesty, that Fanon was *both*: in his texts he seems to be schizophrenically, at times, a staunch advocate for women's rights and women's liberation, and, at other times, completely oblivious of his "Freudian slips" and blind-spots with regard to gender justice and the ways in which his work, his own words speak to, not the *decolonization* of women's life-worlds and lived-experiences, but the *recolonization* of women's life-worlds and lived-experiences (Chow, 1999; Fuss, 1995; McClintock, 1995).

Much has been made of Fanon's brutal, but powerfully persuasive, critique of Martiniquan writer Mayotte Capecia in *Black Skin, White Masks*. Many feminist theorists find his critique of Capecia so merciless and his words so acerbic that his work seems to be rarely read beyond his first book, and this, insofar as I am concerned, is the main part of the problem. In speaking on this issue in "Who Is that Masked Woman? Or, the Role of Gender in Fanon's *Black Skin, White Masks*," feminist theorist Gwen Bergner (1995), perhaps, put it best when she wrote: "Typically, contemporary readers dismiss Fanon's condemnation as so obviously sexist that it does not merit analysis" (p. 83). What these otherwise, I can only assume, "sophisticated" readers fail to see is that they not only do Fanon a disservice, but they do themselves a great and grave disservice by re-inscribing Fanon's supposed sexism and theoretically freeze-framing him as an "anti-feminist" in a way that they do not (and probably would not dare to dream of) when it comes to the oftentimes unrepentantly sexist *and* racist thought of Kant, Hegel, Marx, Nietzsche, or Heidegger (Bernasconi, 2001, 2003; Carver, 1998; Di Stephano, 2008; Holland and Huntingdon, 2001; P.J. Mills, 1996; Oliver and Pearsall, 1998; Schott, 1997; Scott and Franklin, 2006; Ward and Lott, 2002). I am not in any way suggesting that Fanon, or any other black male thinker, be given a "pass" when and where we come to women's liberation, as much as I am pleading with feminists and other women's liberationists to do away with their longstanding double-standard when and where we come to non-white men's contributions to women's decolonization and women's liberation.

I raise the issue of feminist misinterpretations of Fanon, not to defend or apologize for Fanon's *textual masculinism*, which I find morally repugnant and ethically reprehensible, but to humbly make a critical distinction between masculinism and sexism, as well as gender progressivism and anti-feminism. Fanon, for the most part was, indeed, a masculinist, but I believe the feminists go too far in making blanket condemnations and charging him and his corpus with "symbolic matricide" and anti-feminism. This kind of one-dimensional interpretation of an extremely multi-dimensional figure such as Fanon does not simply diminish or neglect what some have called "Fanon's feminism," but it actually negates, erases or, at the very least, renders invisible his innovative and concrete contributions to women's decolonization and women's liberation. In *Transcending the Talented Tenth*, the African American feminist philosopher Joy James (1997) importantly asserts that masculinism is different from misogynism and anti-feminism:

> Since masculinism does not explicitly advocate male superiority or rigid gender social roles, it is not identical to patriarchal ideology. Masculinism can share patriarchy's presupposition of the male as normative without its anti-female politics and rhetoric. Men who support feminist politics, as pro-feminists, may advocate the equality or even superiority of women. . . . However, even without patriarchal intent, certain works replicate conventional gender roles. (p. 36)

The fault lies, therefore, not so much with the feminists, but more so with the masculinists, these men who are theoretically not patriarchs and anti-feminists, but who do not critically comprehend that their masculinist worldview, though not identical to the patriarchal and misogynistic worldviews, nonetheless diminishes their gender progressivism, rendering their well-meaning thought and actions on behalf of women's decolonization and women's liberation, at best, paternalistic and schizophrenic and, at worst, ultimately, a deeply disguised, clandestine contribution to women's re-colonization and women's continued domination. This, again, speaks to the necessity of bringing the dialectic to bear on male feminism and male womanism, and strongly stressing the need for anti-sexist men to consciously and consistently practice sincere self-criticism and self-correction. Anti-sexist men must do more than theoretically commit themselves to women's decolonization and women's liberation but, even more, they must develop dialectical rapports and critical theoretical relationships with the ideologies of women's decolonization and women's liberation and embrace and practice feminism or womanism, hence, epistemically and politically incorporating women's liberation theory into their worldview(s). Without developing dialectical rapports and critical theoretical relationships with women's liberation theory and praxis well-meaning anti-sexist men's worldview(s), and, therefore, their thoughts and actions, remain nothing other than a well-meaning masculinism, which in no uncertain terms perpetuates and exacerbates patriarchy and the continued colonization of women's life-worlds and lived-experiences. Joy James' words and wisdom, once again, find their way into the fray:

> Like some types of anti-racism, certain forms of feminism and pro-feminism are disingenuous. Consider that anti-racist stances guided by a Eurocentrism that presents European (American) culture as normative inadvertently reproduce white dominance; this re-inscription of white privilege occurs despite the avowed racial egalitarianism. Likewise, despite their gender progressivism, anti-sexists or pro-feminists whose politics unfolds within a meta-paradigm that establishes the male as normative reinforce male dominance. (p. 35)

By making a critical distinction between masculinism and misogynism we are able to simultaneously and dialectically acknowledge that Fanon was for the most part a masculinist with pro-feminist fragments scattered throughout his corpus, and that it is extremely intellectually disingenuous to interpret (or, rather, misinterpret) him and his oeuvre as misogynist or anti-feminist. In taking a dialectical and critical theoretical approach to Fanon we are given license to unflinchingly conduct an

intellectual archaeology of his contributions to women's decolonization and
women's liberation, with the critical understanding that many first-rate feminist theorists may have fallen into their own form of *feminist bad faith* by, whether consciously or unconsciously, denying Fanon's contributions to women's decolonization and women's liberation. In *Feminism Is for Everybody*, the foremost
contemporary black feminist bell hooks (2000) writes about an anti-male faction
within the feminist movement who resent "the presence of anti-sexist men because
their presence serve[s] to counter any insistence that all men are oppressors, or that
all men hate women" (p. 68). Revolutionary feminists, such as hooks, challenge reactionary anti-male feminists who project nice, "neat categories of oppressor/op-
pressed" onto men and women in their efforts to portray "all men as the enemy in
order to represent all women as victims" (p. 68). Revolutionary feminists counter by
arguing that "from the onset of the movement there was a small group of men who
recognized that feminist movement was as valid a movement for social justice as any
and all other radical movements in our nation's history that men had supported.
These men became our comrades in our struggle and our allies" (p. 68).

Instead of approaching Fanon as a simple sexist, I will critically engage the pro-
feminist fragments scattered throughout his texts. Following in the intellectual and
political footsteps of revolutionary feminists, such as bell hooks and Joy James, who
advocate a critical openness to male feminists and male womanists, below I explore
"Fanon's feminism" as a paradigmatic point of departure for the critique of both
masculinism and misogynism, as well as anti-male feminists' gender bias against
male feminists, male womanists and their contributions to women's decolonization
and women's liberation. My major preoccupation here is premised on T. Denean
Sharpley-Whiting's (1997) assertion in her watershed work, *Frantz Fanon: Conflicts
and Feminisms*, where she astutely stated:

> Fanon is . . . neither silent on the question of gender, which exists as part of feminists'
> conflicts, nor sexually indifferent. I would argue that his use of masculinist paradigms
> of oppression and alienation in *Black Skin, White Masks* (or elsewhere) does not impor-
> tantly posit male superiority. Masculinism is categorically different from anti-feminism
> and misogyny. . . . [A] thorough reading of Fanon's writings on women, liberation, and
> resistance in *A Dying Colonialism, Toward the African Revolution, The Wretched of the Earth,*
> and *Black Skin, White Masks* provides an important frame of reference for a liberatory
> feminist theory and praxis for women existing under various guises of colonial and neo-
> colonial oppression and sexist domination within their own countries and communi-
> ties. (pp. 9–11)

Fanon, then, does make a distinct contribution to women's decolonization and
women's liberation, and the issue I wish to humbly highlight here is whether or not
we, female *and* male women's liberationists of the twenty-first century, are willing
and able to epistemically open ourselves to his—however fragmented and foible-
filled—contributions, even though they are often couched in masculinist (and
sometimes seemingly sexist) language and, also, in spite of the fact that Fanon's pro-
feminism and gender progressivism, in many instances, may be (and most likely *is*)
very different from our own. What lessons can we learn from Fanon's contributions
to women's decolonization and women's liberation? How can his work help men
(and may be even some women) "unlearn sexism" and learn to embrace and prac-

tice anti-sexism, whether through feminism or womanism, or both, as with Africana critical theory? What does it say about the state of the women's liberation movement if sincere anti-sexist and gender progressive men feel that from many feminists' points of view they are "damned if they do, and damned if they don't," and upon admission of their disdain for, and disavowal of their sexist socialization and patriarchal pretensions they are quickly quarantined to a purgatory for former patriarchs by the very feminists and womanists they were sincerely seeking camaraderie with?

Again, hooks (1984) put the premium on revolutionary feminist principles in *Feminist Theory* when she sternly stated, "men should assume responsibility for actively struggling to end sexist oppression" (p. 67). Some feminists and womanists have argued that Fanon, in his own unique way, was grappling with gender domination and discrimination and, even more specifically, women's decolonization and women's liberation. He is not to be applauded for devoting a book chapter or two to women's life-worlds and lived-experiences, because—in all intellectual and political honesty, and hoping not to sound too harsh—anything that men do to "end sexist oppression" is simply what any real revolutionary is morally responsible for, and ethically obligated to do to bring a real (as opposed to a masculinist) revolution into being. I am not asking, therefore, for a special place or any special favors for male feminists and male womanists in the women's liberation movement, as much as I am humbly pleading with women's liberationists to critically engage the precarious and perplexing position of many pro-feminist and pro-womanist men who feel that they have been quarantined to the "damned if you do, and damned if you don't" purgatory for former patriarchs by feminists and womanists, and routinely ridiculed and rendered socially and politically impotent in the male supremacist world by anti-feminist and anti-womanist men. This means, then, that many, if not most, male feminists and male womanists exist, literally, in a "no-man's land," where they receive the cold shoulder from feminists and womanists, and are shamelessly shunned by male anti-feminists and anti-womanists and the sexist men who rule the male supremacist world. Speaking directly to this issue with her characteristic special insight and astuteness, hooks observes: "Men who have dared to be honest about sexism and sexist oppression, who have chosen to assume responsibility for opposing and resisting it, often find themselves isolated. Their politics are disdained by anti-feminist men and women, and are often ignored by women active in feminist movement" (p. 67).

It would be a great intellectual injustice for feminists and womanists, female and male, to leave Fanon's contributions to women's decolonization and women's liberation in the lurch. I reiterate that he probably was not a "feminist" or a "womanist" by past or present standards but, from my understanding, with regard to revolutionary feminism, this is all beside the point. The point is to take what we can from Fanon's critical intellectual and radical political legacy that will aid us in our quest to deepen and further develop revolutionary feminism, "end sexist oppression," and bring a post-patriarchal world in being. What, pray-tell, you perhaps have been incessantly asking, are Fanon's contributions to women's decolonization and women's liberation?

In many feminist circles, *Black Skin, White Masks* has long been held up as proof positive of Fanon's "misogyny." First, leading the charge is a literary criticism,

Fanon's normative use of masculinist language, such as "man," "men," "mankind," "the black man," "the man of color," and "colored brothers," combined with cold and calculated masculinist constructions and projections of gender and sexuality, culminated into an unforgivable erasure of women's, especially black women's, agency and subjectivity (Bergner, 1995; Chow, 1999; McClintock, 1995). The second mark of Fanon's "misogyny" is said to be his masculinist-reductionist approach to women, psychosexuality, and sexual violence in the text and, consequently, it is argued that he rudely reduced and rendered women, and white women in particular, neurotics and, ultimately, argued that their sexuality, their preferred sexual experiences and deep-seated sexual desires, are basically, and often unalterably, masochistic (Doane, 1991; Fuss, 1995). Finally, and by far the most common and condemning example of Fanon's "misogyny" is his merciless critique of Mayotte Capecia, which for many feminists demonstrates once and for all that Fanon was simply another sexist man parading his patriarchy and sometimes subtle sexism at the expense of black women, unwittingly illustrating his deep-seated desire to colonize (or, rather, re-colonize) and control black women's life-worlds and lived-experiences, and their bodies, sexuality, and dreams in particular (Sharpley-Whiting, 1996, 1999).

At the outset of *Black Skin, White Masks* Fanon shared with his readers, in all intellectual honesty, that his work was simultaneously a clinical study and a psycho-existential-experimental narrative. It, therefore, was the beginning of his critical exploration and proactive process of "disalienation" and decolonization. He was still in the process of developing his "weapons of theory," critical theoretical arsenal, and critical language, and, sad to say, many extremely important issues that he raises, not simply in *Black Skin, White Masks* but throughout his oeuvre, went and remain either undeveloped or underdeveloped at the time of his untimely death. Clearly, his inchoate ideas on women's decolonization and women's liberation were either undeveloped or underdeveloped, but, yet and still, these pro-feminist fragments, if pieced together properly and fused with more fully developed revolutionary feminist and womanist theory may nevertheless provide an important paradigm, point of departure, and anti-sexist alternative to phallocentric, patriarchal, misogynistic, and militaristic masculinity distinctly different from those historically and currently available to male feminists and male womanists, as well as radical and revolutionary feminists and womanist theorists and activists.

Here I feel obliged to ask: Is Fanon at fault for his use of masculinist language anymore than those female theorists who, writing during the same era, not only use male normative language, but put their intense internalization of male supremacy on display by either rendering sexism and patriarchy nonexistent or invisible in their thought and texts, or openly (and often vehemently) criticizing feminism and womanism and carefully composing unambiguously anti-feminist and anti-womanist theories and texts? Many feminists give these female theorists a "pass," one which seems to smack of gender bias, or anti-male feminism, or *feminist sexism*, especially when and where Fanon's text demonstrate that he did, indeed, grapple with and seek to critically grasp gender oppression, women's exploitation, and sexual violence against women. He may not have engaged these issues from an orthodox feminist standpoint, or employing the freshest and flyest feminist theory, but that is all beside the point that I am making here, and that is that if and when Fanon's corpus is re-read and re-interpreted from revolutionary feminist and womanist perspectives it is discovered to make several seminal and significant contributions to women's decolonization and women's liberation, not to mention male feminism and male womanism. I, in all earnestness, am not convinced that Fanon's use of masculinist language translates into misogyny. Nor am I adequately persuaded that his use of masculinist language immediately and automatically disqualifies his undeniable contributions to women's decolonization and women's liberation.

Were more of Fanon's feminist critics to epistemically open themselves to his—however unorthodox and imperfect—contributions to women's decolonization and women's liberation, then, they might be able to salvage something from his work by critically re-reading and re-interpreting his texts from dialectical and revolutionary feminist perspectives that would enable them to simultaneously critique *and* appreciate both his gender-exclusive (masculinist) and gender-inclusive (revolutionary humanist) donations to women's decolonization and women's liberation. It is, in truth, extremely important to point out that Fanon used masculinist language, which I concede. However, it is wholly another issue to deduce from his use of masculinist language that he was either silent on gender issues, and women's life-worlds and lived-experiences in particular, or, even worse, that he was somehow a sexist.

Fanon, indeed, did theorize gender and women's life-worlds and lived-experiences in *Black Skin, White Masks* in the chapters, "The Woman of Color and the White Man" and "The Man of Color and the White Woman." Although, it must be solemnly said, many feminists do not agree with, or have serious issues with his analysis of women's life-worlds and lived-experiences. Even so, there is a big difference between arguing that Fanon was silent on women's life-worlds and lived-experiences, and disagreeing with his actually existing analysis on feminist or womanist principles—and, it should be observed, that just because one group of feminists disagree with Fanon's analysis of women does not mean that all feminists or womanists have to, or will disagree with his analysis. This speaks to the myriad ways in which feminists and womanists interpret and re-interprets thought and texts. T. Denean Sharpley-Whiting (1997) asserts that there is no single, unified form of *feminism*, not *one* form of feminism, but several *forms* of *feminisms*, just as Fanon (1967) correctly contended that, "Negro experience is not a whole, for there is not merely *one* Negro, there are *Negroes*" (p. 136, all emphasis in original). Here we can also see the distinct differences between revolutionary feminism and more liberal and conservative forms of feminism: the revolutionary feminists, the feminists with real revolutionary principles, are willing and able to draw from both female *and* male radical and revolutionary sources and incorporate them into their vision of a liberated future, which includes anti-sexist men in the process of creating a *post-patriarchal masculinity* predicated on revolutionary humanist (which always and ever includes revolutionary feminist) principles; where the liberal and conservative feminists limit their conceptions of the women's liberation movement to "women only" and surreptitiously continue to re-inscribe patriarchal gender relations by consciously and/or unconsciously embracing and perpetuating the very antagonistic sexist sex roles, women-as-victims stereotypes, femme fatale fantasies, damsels in distress daydreams, and male supremacist myths that they purport to be feminist freedom fighting against. In *Feminist Theory*, bell hooks (1984), critically captured this conundrum best when she wrote:

> Individuals committed to feminist revolution must address ways that men can unlearn sexism. Women were never encouraged in contemporary feminist movement to point out to men their responsibility. Some feminist rhetoric "put down" women who related to men at all. Most women's liberationists were saying "women have nurtured, helped, and supported others for too long—now we must fend for ourselves." Having helped and supported men for centuries by acting in complicity with sexism, women were suddenly encouraged to withdraw their support when it came to the issue of "liberation." The insistence on a concentrated focus on individualism, on the primacy of self, deemed "liberatory" by women's liberationists, was not a visionary, radical concept of freedom. It did provide individual solutions for women, however. It was the same idea of independence perpetuated by the imperial patriarchal state which equates independence with narcissism and lack of concern with triumph over others. In this way, women active in feminist movement were simply inverting the dominant ideology of the culture— they were not attacking it. They were not presenting practical alternatives to the status quo. In fact, even the statement "men are the enemy" was basically an inversion of the male supremacist doctrine that "women are the enemy"—the old Adam and Eve version of reality. (p. 76)

When the chapters "The Woman of Color and the White Man" and "The Man of Color and the White Woman" in *Black Skin, White Masks* are carefully and critically read from revolutionary feminist and womanist perspectives, which means from epistemically open optics that eschew both weak-minded masculinists *and* backward-thinking bourgeois feminists' theoretical nepotism and intellectual insularity, then, it is revealed that Fanon does not always and in every instance conceive of "the colonized," the anti-colonial agents of decolonization, or "the revolutionary" as male or masculine, nor is the "neurotic Negrophobe" incessantly envisioned as female or feminine. Critically applying revolutionary feminist and womanist hermeneutics to "The Woman of Color and the White Man" and "The Man of Color and the White Woman" exposes us to the fact that Fanon actually diagnosed both racially colonized men and women and colonizing men and women as neurotics suffering from *Negrophobia, blackaphobia,* and *Afrophobia* and, as is customary in scholarly discourse, he often quarantined his studies to specific "case studies" or significant examples to drive his psycho-existential points home to his readers, who he anticipated would not all be black, male or colonized. With regard to racially colonized subjects, both male and female, his analysis actually comes to similar conclusions: The colonized woman of color seeks to reclaim her long-denied humanity, human worth, and human dignity by averting, at all costs, her blackness and "falling back into the pit of Niggerhood." In fact, "what they must have is whiteness at any price." Fanon (1967) put it this way: "It is always essential to avoid falling back into the pit of Niggerhood, and every woman in the Antilles, whether in a casual flirtation or in a serious affair, is determined to select the least black of men," and the ultimate "least black of men" is, of course, the white man (pp. 47, 49). Fanon identified the two types of colonized women of color to which he is referring: "the Negress and the mulatto." Then, he proceeded to diagnose their situations in relation to the race, gender, and class rulers of the white and male supremacist capitalist-colonialist world: "The first [the Negress] has only one possibility and one concern: to turn white. The second [the mulatto] wants not only to turn white but also to avoid slipping back" into blackness and "Niggerhood" (p. 54). Therefore, the woman of color obstinately works to whiten herself, through what Fanon called "a kind of lactification," by obtaining white male love, the love of a white man and the white male world (p. 47).

Fanon described and criticized the colonized man of color's situation with the white woman in arguably harsher psychosexual depth and detail, declaring: "Out of the blackest part of my soul, across the zebra striping of my mind, surges this desire to be suddenly *white*" (p. 63, emphasis in original). So, even at the outset of his analysis of the colonized man of color in relation to the white woman we witness an almost identical diagnosis compared to the one he delivered to the colonized woman of color in relation to the white man: the colonized woman of color wishes to "turn white," where the colonized man of color deeply desires "to be suddenly *white*." However, Fanon went even further in his analysis of the colonized man of color in relation to the white woman by exposing his anguished inner monologue and intimate psychosexual details. Notice that the colonized man of color wants to be "loved" by a white woman, not because of the inherent value of *her* "love," but because he believes her "love" will enable him to be "loved like a white man." Sick and twisted? Yes, indeed. In no way wishing to invoke a *discourse on comparative suffering*—where sufferers sit around angrily arguing over who is *the most* oppressed and, therefore, they are distracted from the ongoing struggle to end their oppression—it could be sincerely said that Fanon's diagnosis of the colonized man of color in relation to the white woman is devastatingly damning in that the colonized man of color does not simply seek the white woman's "white love" but, if we really and truly read between the lines, his deepest desire is white male love, the love of white men and the white male supremacist capitalist-colonialist world. Here is the colonized man of color's anguished inner monologue in his irrational quest to be "loved" by a white woman in order to be "loved" "like a white man," penultimately, "loved" by white men, and, ultimately, to *become* and *be* a white man:

> I wish to be acknowledged not as *black* but as *white*. Now—and this is a form of recognition that Hegel had not envisaged—who but a white woman can do this for me? By loving me she proves that I am worthy of white love. I am loved like a white man. I am a white man. Her love takes me onto the noble road that leads to total realization . . . I marry white culture, white beauty, white whiteness. When my restless hands caress those white breasts, they grasp white civilization and dignity and make them mine. (p. 63, all emphasis in original)

What we witness in "The Woman of Color and the White Man" and "The Man of Color and the White Woman" in *Black Skin, White Masks* is precisely what Fanon meant when he stated: "White civilization and European culture have forced an existential deviation on the Negro," by which he meant both black men *and* black women (p. 14). However, here we also witness "an existential deviation" on the part of "alienated (duping and duped) whites" as well. In fact, these two chapters on interracial colonial desire are not free-standing, critical inquiries into independent issues, but actually critical inquiries into extremely interrelated and inextricable issues revolving around the racial or, rather, the racist nature of whites' colonization of

non-whites, and the ways in which the incessant internalization of racial colonialism deforms and destroys the personalities and relationships of both colonized
non-whites and colonizing whites. Fanon's feminist critics fail to see that he did not
simply address racism and colonialism in these chapters, but gender, gender identity, and sexuality as well. Far from neglecting gender, and women's life-worlds and
lived-experiences in specific, Fanon's analyses in these chapters form a unified existential phenomenology of racial, gender, and sexual pathology under the auspices
of white supremacist patriarchal colonialist capitalism. Instead of leaving women's
life-worlds and lived-experiences in the lurch, Fanon incorporated them into his
analysis, and, as with any genuinely "critical" theorist, he was intellectually audacious and not afraid to take risks. Therefore, sometimes his theories hit the mark
and, at other times, they sorely missed the mark.

Whether Fanon's feminist critics wish to acknowledge it or not, there *are* extremely gendered differences and "existential deviations" involved in racially colonized non-white people's (especially racially colonized non-white women's) always
already damaged and deformed relationships and disturbingly disingenuous interactions with whites, because these relationships and interactions are always already
taking place in a white supremacist patriarchal colonial capitalist world. Further,
these relationships and interactions, almost as if by default or automatically, take
their cues from the generic gender hierarchy, sexist social superstructure, racist re-
vulsions, colonial compulsions, capitalist constraints, religious restrictions, and linguistic laws—not to mention the myriad myths and symbols surrounding blackness
and whiteness, maleness and femaleness, and richness and poorness—on which European history, culture, and so-called "civilization" have erected their imperial white
supremacist patriarchal colonial capitalist empire. This means, then, that these relationships are not formed (or, rather, deformed), and these interactions do not take
place, in a vacuum or some backward-thinking bourgeois feminist fantasy world
where gender, and gender alone, is all that matters. Indeed, gender does matter, but
so does race and racism, and the ways in which, when combined with colonialist
and capitalist violence and exploitation, a morally repugnant and racially reductive
political economy is set up where human value, humanity, and, even more, hu-
manness is determined by how close one is in proximity to *being* or *possessing* whiteness, maleness, and richness. Gender matters, as does race and class, and all too often feminists who are not anti-racist, radical, or revolutionary willfully forget this,
especially when they approach or, rather, *reproach* Fanon's contributions to women's
decolonization and women's liberation.

Fanon's critical lexicon was shaped and shaded by the discursive and linguistic
communities of the white supremacist patriarchal colonial capitalist world in which
he was educated and miseducated, colonized and in the dogged process of attempting to decolonize. However, there *are* faint pro-feminist philosophical fissures
in *Black Skin, White Masks* that symbolize his, however inchoate, intellectual aver-
sions to, not simply white supremacy and colonialism, but patriarchy and the psychological violence that misogyny and male supremacy inflict on both black and
white women, as well as other non-white racially colonized women. Fanon developed his phenomenology of racial colonial desire and recognition in, not only an
anti-black colonial capitalist world, but also an anti-woman world. His response to
white supremacist patriarchal colonial capitalism was revolutionary decolonization,

revolutionary blackness, and revolutionary humanism, which is one of the reasons he addressed *Black Skin, White Masks*, not simply to blacks, but to whites and other non-whites as well:

> I believe that the fact of the juxtaposition of the white and black races has created a massive psychoexistential complex. I hope by analyzing it to destroy it. Many Negroes will not find themselves in what follows. This is equally true of many whites. But the fact that I feel a foreigner in the worlds of the schizophrenic or the sexual cripple in no way diminishes their reality. (p. 12)

Women were included in Fanon's phenomenology of racial colonial desire and recognition, and even though he frequently proved that he was a "foreigner" to many aspects and episodes of women's lived-experiences and lived-endurances, his texts tell us that his foreignness "in no way diminishes their reality," or the reality of any other group of suffering human souls. He knew that not all black *and* white, men *and* women would "find themselves" in *Black Skin, White Masks*, which is probably why some feminists find useful pro-feminist fragments scattered throughout the text, and his feminist critics generally do not find anything of value in his contributions to women's decolonization and women's liberation. Not finding any value in his actually existing contributions is different than acerbically arguing that he did not make any contributions to women's decolonization and women's liberation and, then, insincerely rendering them nonexistent or invisible.

In essence, "The Woman of Color and the White Man" and "The Man of Color and the White Woman" advance that the racially colonized non-white's gender is, ultimately, inconsequential, to a certain extent, in the white supremacist patriarchal colonial capitalist world because to be non-white is irrationally and automatically, by the logic of that very vulgar world, to be non-male and, therefore, non-human or, at best, subhuman. Hence, there is a terse and twisted type of transgender injustice that haunts and harries each and every interaction between the non-white colonized and the white colonizer owing to the fact that the hideous racial and gender hierarchies of the white supremacist patriarchal colonial capitalist world render non-whites, again, whether male or female, anonymous and invisible, and this anonymity and invisibility is not only racial, but also extended to gender. However, even though the white supremacist patriarchal colonial capitalist world downplayed and dismissed gender—essentially women's lived-experiences and lived-endurances—and reduced the multidimensionality of the human personality to the zero-sum game race and ethnicity, Fanon continued to accent, in his own unique way, the crucial importance of gender analysis for any authentic dialectical and critical theory of racial colonial alienation and disalienation.

In his second book, *A Dying Colonialism*, Fanon offered up what many radical and revolutionary feminists and womanists believe to be several of his definitive contributions to women's decolonization and women's liberation. In *A Dying Colonialism* Fanon critically, and more assertively than in *Black Skin, White Masks*, connected the lived-experiences and lived-endurances of the racially colonized with those of the racially *gendered* and colonized, which, to reiterate, all racially colonized people are actually clandestinely gendered, but it is the white colonizers, especially the white male colonizers of the white supremacist patriarchal colonial capitalist world who have the unmitigated and grotesque gall or, more specifically, the *white power* to gen-der or *degender*; to render the gender of non-whites and non-males absent or pres-ent, invisible or visible, androgynously-asexually ambiguous or exotically-erotically super-sexed as they wantonly wish, they, and they alone, decide and determine when, where and to whom gender does, or does not matter. Two chapters in partic-ular from *A Dying Colonialism*—"Algeria Unveiled" and "The Algerian Family"—rep-resent Fanon's (1965) turn toward a more nuanced engagement of gender and the ways in which women, and the "Algerian woman" in particular, "like her brothers, had minutely built up defense mechanisms which enable her today to play a pri-mary role in the struggle for liberation" (p. 65). Let us briefly look at the more provocatively pro-feminist of the two chapters on gender in *A Dying Colonialism*, "Al-geria Unveiled," with an eye toward the ways in which it registers Fanon's distinct contributions to women's decolonization and women's liberation.

The first chapter of Fanon's second book, *A Dying Colonialism*, is entitled "Algeria Unveiled." In the chapter Fanon imaginatively and mockingly ventriloquizes the ir-rational ethos of the white supremacist patriarchal colonial capitalist world. Here he makes women's decolonization, women's liberation, and patriarchy—the patriarchy of the white colonizers *and* the patriarchy of the non-white colonized—his main critical theoretical preoccupation. Fanon argues that the patriarchy of both the white colonizers and the non-white colonized are complicated and rendered all the more complex because it is always already much more than male supremacy on account of the fact that it is constantly being exacerbated and perpetuated in a white su-premacist patriarchal colonial capitalist world. In what ways does white supremacy and/or European imperialism shape and shade the kind of patriarchy that racially colonized women of color experience? How does the often preexisting or, rather, pre-colonial patriarchy of the racially colonized non-white nation compound and complicate all the colonized's (both men and women's) quest for decolonization and liberation? Why is it necessary to address and incorporate women's decolo-nization and women's liberation from both white supremacist patriarchal colonial-ism and non-white males' pre-colonial patriarchal colonialism at the outset and throughout the course of the process of decolonization and strongly stress that there cannot and will not be "true decolonization" or real "revolutionary decolonization" unless and until women's life-worlds and lived-experiences are decolonized and lib-erated on their own radical and revolutionary feminist and womanist terms? In "Al-geria Unveiled," Fanon amazingly offers pro-feminist and pro-womanist answers to these questions.

The Algerian woman is seen by both the white colonizing patriarchs and the non-white colonized patriarchal nationalists as, literally, the living flesh of the colonized national body, and so begins the "battle of the veil," and with deeper and deeper "Western penetration" the "forbidden" feminine mystique, the long-sequestered *hi-jab*-covered heads and *burka*-bound beautiful bodies of white supremacist patriar-chal colonial fantasy and desire are "revealed to them" and, humiliatingly, "piece by piece, the flesh of Algeria" is "laid bare" for all the white supremacist patriarchal colonial capitalist world to see, to touch and, ultimately, to "rape" (p. 36, 42). In "Algeria Unveiled," Fanon accented the ways in which racially colonized non-white women's gender is recognized by white supremacist patriarchal colonialism, not to sincerely support women's decolonization and women's liberation, but in their iniquitous efforts to further European imperialism and, more specifically, the French colonization of Algeria. "The Algerian woman," contended Fanon, "an intermediary between obscure forces and the group," between white colonizing patriarchs and non-white colonized patriarchal nationalists, "appeared in this perspective," from the perspective of the white supremacist patriarchal colonial capitalist world, "to assume a primordial importance" (p. 37).

The racially colonized non-white woman "assume[s] a primordial importance" to the white supremacist patriarchal colonial capitalist world because she is believed to be key to the continuation of colonialism if—and this is an extremely important *if*—she could be "duped" into diverting her agency and power to supporting white supremacist patriarchal colonialism and rupturing her relationship with the supposed source of racially colonized non-white nationalist men's power: their "childish" and "primitive" preoccupation with maintaining their pre-colonial male supremacy at all costs, even in light of their commitments to decolonization and liberation. Fanon exposed the irrational "logic" of the white supremacist patriarchal colonialists:

> The officials of the French administration in Algeria, committed to destroying the people's originality, and under instructions to bring about the disintegration, at whatever cost, of forms of existence likely to evoke a national reality directly or indirectly, were to concentrate their efforts on the wearing of the veil, which was looked upon at this juncture as a symbol of the status of the Algerian woman. Such a position is not the consequence of a chance intuition. It is on the basis of the analyses of sociologists and ethnologists that the specialists in so-called native affairs and the heads of the Arab Bureaus coordinated their work. At an initial stage, there was a pure and simple adoption of the well-known formula, "Let's win over the women and the rest will follow." This definition of policy merely gave a scientific coloration to the "discoveries" of the sociologists. (p. 37)

Fanon offers us several insights here. First, he demonstrates that the white supremacist patriarchal colonialists' interest in the social conditions of racially colonized non-white women is false and utterly absurd. Fanon critically comprehends the ways in which white supremacist patriarchal colonialism rearranges the gender, sexual, social, and political economy of racially colonized non-whites, constantly dividing and conquering them, thwarting any and all efforts they make to unite in the interest of toppling white supremacist patriarchal colonialism. He emphasizes the negative dialectics of white supremacist patriarchal colonialism, observing that it does not simply have a white supremacist dimension, but a male supremacist dimension as well. Hence, when and where white supremacist patriarchal colonialism is threatened or weakened by racial or cultural nationalism, when and where it cannot create "ethnic conflicts," "ethnic cleansings," and treacherous "tribalisms" between racially colonized non-whites to keep them divided and conquered, then, it pulls out its secret weapon: *white supremacist patriarchal colonial feminism*.

White supremacist patriarchal colonial feminism is a false feminism that is premised on *white supremacist patriarchal colonial pseudo-social science*. Above Fanon hints at how incredibly coordinated the white supremacist patriarchal colonial capitalist world is: from its military to its media; from its academy to its religious institutions; from its commercial industries to its entertainment industries. Nothing is sacred, and it will use anything and anyone to maintain its gruesome grip on the lives and lands of racially colonized non-whites. White supremacist patriarchal colonial feminism is actually *not* about improving the social status of racially colonized non-white women at all—which would mean morally and politically committing and contributing to women's decolonization and women's liberation—but, it is more about the continuation of racial colonialism and, even more, about unveiling the "medieval and barbaric," the "sadistic and vampirish" patriarchy of racially colonized non-white nationalist men (p. 38). In its own incredibly skewed way white supremacist patriarchal colonial feminism believed that it offered racially colonized non-white women a "choice," but racially colonized non-white women were immediately hip to the ruse: it was a fiercely false "choice" between the white supremacist patriarchal colonial capitalist world, or the pre-colonial patriarchal world dominated by narrow-minded nationalist and hypocritically hyper-religious non-white men. The racially colonized non-white women's response was loud and clear: They chose neither. They chose to simultaneously combat white supremacist patriarchal colonialism *and* "traditional" patriarchal nationalism and hyper-religious hypocrisy. They chose to create their own revolutionary alternative, one that neither the white supremacist patriarchal colonists, nor the non-white racially colonized patriarchal nationalists offered in their respective programs of colonization and decolonization.

The white supremacist patriarchal colonialists' efforts to "liberate" "oppressed" Algerian women was, therefore, nothing other than another neocolonial maneuver to re-colonize Algeria. Again, Fanon mocks the madness of the irrational "logic" of the white supremacist patriarchal colonial capitalist world: "If we want to destroy the structure of Algerian society, its capacity for resistance, we must first of all conquer the women; we must go and find them behind the veil where they hide themselves and in the houses where the men keep them out of sight" (p. 38). White supremacist patriarchal colonial feminism is a feminism that promises, promotes and is predicated on "cultural destruction," and *not* the "cultural destruction" of patriarchal culture, but the "cultural destruction" of racially colonized non-whites' precolonial and anti-colonial culture (p. 49).

In "liberating" Algerian women, by unveiling them, the white supremacist patriarchal colonial capitalist world would use its liberalism and feminism as instruments of discrimination, domination, and, ultimately, "cultural destruction." Moreover, in unveiling Algerian women the white supremacist patriarchal colonial capitalist world would also symbolically render the Algerian man naked, exposing him in the worst way, making him shamefully vulnerable before the world, and simultaneously sowing the seeds of resentment between him and the Algerian woman. After all, based on the irrational "logic" of the white supremacist patriarchal colonial capitalist world, it is the colonized Algerian patriarchal nationalists' fault that Algerian women are treated in such a "medieval and barbaric" way: "Just imagine it," white colonists, especially white women colonists contend, "they are covered from head to toe. Poor things, *meskîn*." Fanon put it this way: "Colonial society blazes up vehemently against this inferior status of the Algerian woman. Its members worry and show concern for those unfortunate women, doomed 'to produce brats,' kept behind walls," basically "banned," for all intents and purposes (p. 40). Veiled Algerian women, everywhere and always denying the white supremacist patriarchal colonialists their supposedly God-given right, again, to see, to touch and, ultimately, to "rape."

In unveiling Algerian women, and by sowing the seeds of resentment toward Algerian men, the white supremacist patriarchal colonial capitalist world hideously hoped that it could "dupe" the Algerian woman into being "an ally in the work of cultural destruction" and a two-faced white supremacist patriarchal colonial feminist double-agent, surreptitiously sowing the seeds of Algerian "cultural destruction" and European imperialism (p. 49). Fanon's words hit home: "In the colonialist program, it was the woman who was given the historic mission of shaking up the Algerian man. Converting the woman, winning her over to the foreign values, wrenching her free from her status, was at the same time achieving a real power over the man and attaining a practical, effective means of destructuring Algerian culture" (p. 39).

White supremacist women colonists joined their white supremacists patriarchal colonial men in what they were either "duped" or, based on their internalization of the irrational "logic" of the white supremacist patriarchal colonial capitalist world, dishonorably honestly believed to be the "noble" work of "liberating" Algerian women who had lived their lives under the auspices of a most "medieval and barbaric" patriarchy, which transformed them into nothing other than "an inert, demonetized, indeed dehumanized object" (p. 38). White supremacist women colonists wanted to "liberate" them and bring them into a more "modern," more "civilized" form of patriarchy, which, of course, was the more political, more sophisticated patriarchy of the white supremacist patriarchal colonial capitalist world. We see, then, that this is nothing other than the original white supremacist and European imperial "civilize and Christianize" approach to racially colonized non-white people's cultures and civilizations, and the difference is that the rules and ruses of the game have changed, placing racially colonized non-white women at the center, but, we should ask, for what purpose and in whose interest? Fanon revealed the complicity of the French feminists in the false Algerian women's liberation campaign that was initiated by white supremacists patriarchal colonial men. The French feminists, however well-meaning from their own point of view, were crucial collaborators in the continued colonization of Algeria, and Algerian women in specific. They paternalistically decided what was best for Algerian women without consulting Algerian women. This was not feminism, and certainly not radical or revolutionary feminism but, as stated above, white supremacist patriarchal colonial feminism. Fanon sliced through their hypocrisy with words (when really and critically read) that continue to cause controversy:

Mutual aid societies and societies to promote solidarity with Algerian women sprang up in great number. Lamentations were organized. "We want to make the Algerian ashamed of the fate that he metes out to women." This was a period of effervescence, of putting into application a whole technique of infiltration, in the course of which droves of social workers and women directing charitable works descended on the Arab quarters. The indigent and famished women were the first to be besieged. Every kilo of semolina distributed was accompanied by a dose of indignation against the veil and cloister. The indignation was followed up by practical advice. Algerian women were invited to play "a functional, capital role" in the transformation of their lot. They were pressed to say no to a centuries-old subjection. The immense role they were called upon to play was

described to them. The colonial administration invested great sums in this combat. After it had been posited that the woman constituted the pivot of Algerian society, all efforts were made to obtain control over her. The Algerian, it was assured, would not stir,
would resist the task of cultural destruction undertaken by the occupier, would oppose
assimilation, so long as his woman had not reversed the stream. (pp. 38–39)

Based on the irrational "logic" of the white supremacist patriarchal colonial capitalist world an inversion of sorts was now necessary to continue colonialism. Instead of directly targeting Algerian men, it would "get them" by focusing on Algerian women and indoctrinating them with a false feminism, white supremacist
patriarchal colonial feminism. Never mind that Algerian men were similarly "indigent and famished" under French colonialism, what white supremacist patriarchal
colonial feminism demanded was the aforementioned *discourse on comparative suffering*, where sufferers sit around angrily arguing over who is *the most* oppressed and,
therefore, they are distracted from the ongoing struggle to end their oppression.
White supremacist patriarchal colonial feminism would fool Algerian women into
believing that *all* of their suffering was due to the patriarchy and hyper-religious
hypocrisy of Algerian men, and not, as it actually was, partially predicated on white
supremacist patriarchal colonialism. White supremacist patriarchal colonial feminists offered French colonialism, and thereby French "civilization," as an alternative
to the patriarchy and hyper-religious hypocrisy of Algerian men, in their white supremacist patriarchal colonial feminist minds' transfiguring it, making French colonialism in Algeria a women's liberation movement.

Again, according to Fanon, Algerian women were hip to the ruse. The hidden
hypocrisy of the white supremacist patriarchal colonial feminists was quickly and
easily detected. Algerian women were well-aware that white women colonists in the
white supremacist patriarchal colonial capitalist world were always and ever, however unbeknownst to themselves, in collusion with the racial, gender, and class hierarchy of that world. From Algerian women's point of view, there was no principled
way for the white supremacist patriarchal colonial feminists to get around it; the
only viable alternative was to morally and politically commit themselves to Algerian (among other racially colonized non-white) women's decolonization and liberation. The white supremacist patriarchal colonial feminists made the major mistake
of underestimating Algerian women's pre-colonial and anti-colonial traditions of
critical thought and, however subtly as a result of the patriarchy and hyper-religious
hypocrisy of Algerian men, Algerian women's cultural criticism and social activism.
The myriads ways in which white supremacist patriarchal colonial feminists benefited from the oppression, exploitation, and violence—the "cultural destruction"
discussed above—suffered by Algerians, both female *and* male, was not lost on Algerian women and, in fact, they were extremely insulted by the white supremacist
patriarchal colonial feminists' paternalism. If this is what French women called
"feminism," if this was their version of "feminism," then, most Algerian women
wanted nothing whatsoever to do with it, and they let it be known that they rejected
French "feminism" without in any way precluding their principled commitments to
women's decolonization and women's liberation.

An amazing transformation of the Algerian woman's personality and physicality
takes place in the course of her participation in the revolution. Where she once

would have been extremely uncomfortable to appear publicly without a veil, now she disguises herself as an unveiled assimilated Algerian woman, "a woman alone in the street." This same Algerian woman warrior will, also, wear a veil when necessary, transforming herself into a "woman-arsenal," according to Fanon, using the veil as an anti-colonial camouflage to carry various essentials for the revolution (p. 58). For many female freedom fighters, then, the veil was—however temporarily—transformed from an instrument of oppression to a means of liberation. Fanon touched on the irony of unveiled and seemingly assimilated, but actually deeply-committed revolutionary Algerian women: "Carrying revolvers, grenades, hundreds of false identity cards or bombs, the unveiled Algerian woman moves like a fish in the Western waters. The soldiers, the French patrols, smile to her as she passes, compliments on her looks are heard here and there, but no one suspects that her suitcases contain the automatic pistol which will presently mow down four or five members of the patrols" (p. 58).

There is a sense in which the anti-colonial unveiled and unassimilated Algerian woman's unveiling represented both changes in her relationship with the men, the patriarchs of Algeria but, more importantly, changes within herself and with her body. Unveiling was both traumatic and triumphant for Algerian women, both intimidating and liberating, because after having been forced to wear the veil for so long and then to suddenly be without it was, for all practical purposes, to be "naked." Fanon critically engaged the dream content of recently unveiled Algerian women involved in the revolution, and his revelations were nothing short of shocking: "One must have heard the confessions of Algerian women or have analyzed the dream content of certain recently unveiled women to appreciate the importance of the veil for the body of the woman. Without the veil she has an impression of her body being cut up into bits, put adrift; the limbs seem to lengthen indefinitely" (p. 59). Having been harassed and hounded by the fear of public, familial, and personal humiliation and physical harm were they ever to have ventured out of their "homes" without their veils, now these same women were bitterly asked by the same men who veiled them, who quarantined and sequestered their bodies and souls, to unveil for the revolution, unveil to "liberate" *their* "fatherland." Is it any wonder, then, that these women felt that their bodies were being "cut up into bits" or their limbs broken and stretched beyond belief? Were they not being pulled in several different directions—psychologically, socially, politically, and religiously? And, what of the racial colonial sexual gaze of the French colonists, or the hyper-religious patriarchal gaze of Algerian men? Were these women not caught in the crossfire of a history-making and earth-shaking war where French colonists and Algerian nationalists jousted for, among many other things, the malfeasance of male supremacy, the very wrong patriarchal right to rule over Algeria, especially Algerian women, the living-flesh of Algeria, as they damn-well militaristically and misogynistically pleased?

Combating their fears or, at the least, learning to live with them and use them as a transforming and healing force, Algerian women transfigured themselves through their participation in the Algerian revolution. Wrestling with and often rejecting her feelings of "being improperly dressed," or "being naked," or her "sense of incompleteness," or "the anxious feeling that something is unfinished," the Algerian woman warrior "quickly" invents "new dimensions for her body, new means of muscular control" (p. 59). It is almost as if the veil were some sort of cocoon, and as the Algerian woman unveiled for the purposes of the revolution, she was able to overcome centuries of patriarchal hyper-religious hypocrisy and make her own distinct contribution to the Algerian revolution. She was not the "inert" and "dehumanized object" that either the colonizing French patriarchs *or* the colonized patriarchal Algerian nationalists and religious zealots imagined, but, I say again, an all together very different, and very *human* (as opposed to *subhuman*), being. Fanon drives the point home:

> She has to create for herself an attitude of unveiled-woman-outside. She must overcome all timidity, all awkwardness (for she must pass for a European), and at the same time be careful not to overdo it, not to attract notice to herself. The Algerian woman who walks stark naked into the European city relearns her body, re-establishes it in a totally revolutionary fashion. This new dialectic of the body and of the world is primary in the case of one revolutionary woman. (p. 59)

The forgoing reveals that Fanon's conception of decolonization was much broader than previously thought. He, indeed, did include women in his dialectic of decolonization and liberation. His contributions to women's decolonization and women's liberation helps to highlight the distinct differences between "true" and "false" decolonization. True decolonization, ultimately, revolves around revolutionary humanism, which is inextricable from "freedom" or, rather, real liberation. I shall conclude this chapter, therefore, with an examination of Fanon's philosophical anthropology and the ways in which it dictated and determined his revolutionary humanism and discourse on revolutionary decolonization.

## THE DEEP DESIRES OF REVOLUTIONARY DECOLONIZATION: FANON'S PHILOSOPHICAL ANTHROPOLOGY AND PHILOSOPHY OF FREEDOM

At the heart of Fanon praxis-promoting critical theory of decolonization is a philosophical anthropology which understands that human beings' fundamental nature is to be free. Emmanuel Hansen (1977) has asserted that, "Fanon regards freedom as man's supreme goal. And, the whole purpose of man's existence is to realize this supreme goal" (p. 62). Decolonization, then, is not and should not be equated with "violence for violence's sake," but, quite the converse, *violence for freedom's sake*.[17] The ultimate objective of the counter-violence of the colonized is to bring the colonial system, the colonial regime, the entire colonial world, to its knees, and then amputate both its legs so that it will never walk (on or over the corpses of the colonized) again. At the heart of Fanon's philosophy is fundamentally a philosophy of freedom, and, as Hansen noted above, it is specifically to this "supreme goal," freedom, that Fanon felt human beings entire existence revolved around and gravitated toward. In this section we will engage and explore Fanon's philosophical anthropology and the end toward which he defends and explicates the means of decolonization (and all that it elicits): his concept of freedom.

*Black Skin, White Masks*, more so than any of Fanon's other works, reveals a great deal about his philosophical anthropology, that is, his view(s) concerning the essence of human nature, without regard to race, culture, ethnicity, nationality, gender, sexual orientation, religious affiliation, social status, or class position. For Fanon, the quest for freedom is the essential element that binds one human being to another human being, one human group to another human group, and it is this principle in particular that distinguishes and defines human beings *qua* human beings. Fanon envisioned a world where human beings behaved as *humane* beings, that is, as civil and sincere, lovingkind, compassionate, and caring individuals who detested, despised, denounced, and were ultimately willing to destroy, if need be, anyone (or anything) who denied another what was most human in them: their right to self-determination and to develop to their fullest potential (Davids, 1996; Roberts, 2004; C. Wright, 1992).

*Black Skin, White Masks* was written as a rejoinder to the question "[w]hat does man want?" And, more specifically, "[w]hat does the black man [racially colonized humanity] want?" (Fanon, 1967, p. 8). By the conclusion of the book the reader has a concrete idea of what human beings want, or, at the least, from the Fanonian perspective, what they should want, and especially racially colonized humanity. Fanon declared:

> I find myself suddenly in the world and I recognize that I have one right alone: That of demanding human behavior from the other.
> One duty alone: That of not renouncing my freedom through my choices . . .
> No attempt must be made to encase man, for it is his destiny to be set free . . .
> I, the man of color, want only this: That the tool never possess the man. That the enslavement of man by man cease forever. That is, of one by another. That it be possible for me to discover and to love man, wherever he may be. (pp. 229–231)

In the event that a human being, or a human group, denies the quintessential right, that of freedom, to any other human being or human group, Fanon argued that the offended party was justified in "demanding human behavior from the other."[18] Although it took him several years to come to the precise nature the "demand" should take, ultimately revolutionary decolonization was Fanon's response to the conundrum(s) of colonialism. His philosophical anthropology supports what he conceived as "the" ultimate objective, and understood to be the "supreme goal" of human existence: total, complete, and/or absolute liberation. Any attempt to "encase" or "enslave" human beings was, for Fanon, a negation of their humanity, their being-in-the-world as free agents, and/or their ability to choose or not choose. To deny human beings their agency is to obfuscate, if not literally obliterate, their dignity and, therefore, identity. On the obfuscation and eventual obliteration of the dignity and identity of colonized peoples, Fanon, in "The So-Called Dependency Complex of Colonized Peoples," remarked:

> if at a certain stage he [the colonized] has been led to ask himself whether he is indeed a man [i.e., a human being], it is because his reality as a man has been challenged. In other words, I begin to suffer from not being a white man to the degree that the white man imposes discrimination on me, makes me a colonized native, robs me of all worth, all individuality, tells me that I am a parasite on the world, that I must bring myself as quickly as possible into step with the white world, "that I am a brute beast, that my people and I are like a walking dung-heap that disgustingly fertilizes sweet sugar cane and silky cotton, that I have no use in the world." Then I will quite simply try to make myself white: that is, I will compel the white man to acknowledge that I am human. (p. 98)[19]

Chapter 5

Colonialism, at minimum, corrodes the dignity and identity of the colonized person. It "robs" the colonized of "all worth," by which I take Fanon to mean dignity, and "all individuality," which comprehended at its most elementary level connotes those defining and distinguishing characteristics which makes one person (perhaps in a multiplicity of ways) discernible and different from another. A person's "individuality" is, in a sense, inextricable from their personality, and both of these combined, constitute a person's identity.[20] To "rob" the colonized of "all worth" and "all individuality" is to deprive them of their dignity and identity. They become dignified and distinguishable only to the extent that they bring themselves "as quickly as possible into step with the white world." This is, of course, why Fanon never grew weary of exclaiming:

> At the risk of arousing the resentment of my colored brothers, I will say that the black is not a man. . . . The black man wants to be white. . . . However painful it may be for me to accept this conclusion, I am obliged to state it: For the black man there is only one destiny. And it is [to be(come)] white. . . . The black man wants to be like the white man. For the black man there is only one destiny. And it is [to be(come)] white. (pp. 8–10, 228)

By denying the dignity and identity of the oppressed, the oppressors lump all the oppressed together. They, the oppressed, become one big black blob or mob (depending on the time and circumstance), and under such conditions the oppressors construct a world, a reality where only one particular part of humanity, the white part, is seen as human (see Gordon 1997a, pp. 69–80, 2000a, pp. 153–163). In fact, the very nature of what it means to be human becomes synonymous with the ruling race, or nation, or empire, etcetera. Hence, Fanon's reiteration: "For the black man there is only one destiny. And it is [to be(come)] white." Observe that Fanon begins and ends *Black Skin, White Masks* with this infernal epitaph. It appears in the conclusion precisely as it does in the introduction. He knew, so long as "White men consider themselves superior to black men," and, so long as "Black men want to prove to white men, at all costs, the richness of their thought, the equal value of their intellect," so long as racially colonized humanity refused to extricate themselves from their various racial colonial situations, then, for so long would the Manichean situation of the racial colonial world persist (p. 10). Whether blob or mob, the oppressed, in the world(s) the racial colonialists and racist capitalists have constructed, are denied an identity and, therefore, are perpetually perceived—by the oppressors and all too often each other—as anonymous and experience an intense and excruciating anonymity (see Blaut, 1993; Gordon, 1995b, pp. 37–66, 1997b, pp. 13–24, 2000a, pp. 153–163).

Fanon's concept of freedom rests, at bottom, on the revolutionary (re)politicization of the people, and here "the people" connotes all strata and classes of persons in a given society or social setting. He, similar to Du Bois, understood that it was possible for the State to be free and the people not to be free. Perhaps few statements capture this contradiction on the printed page better than when Fanon (1968) wrote: "Paradoxically, the national government [headed by the racially colonized bourgeoisie] in its dealing with the country people as a whole is reminiscent of certain features of the former colonial power" (p. 118). Similar to Frederick Douglass, who felt that the United States' "the fourth of July" holiday was, "from the slave's point of view," an unequivocal "sham," Fanon audaciously asserted that the fan-fare and bombast symbolizing and celebrating the inauguration of the "national government" represented nothing other than, "a fancy-dress parade and the blare of the trumpets."

This kind of "independence," if it may be referred to as "independence" at all, has little or no effect on the lives of the racially colonized people. Where Nkrumah termed it "neo-colonialism," Fanon (1968) called it "false decolonization," but whichever phrase one employs the results are the same: the continued oppression of the oppressed (p. 59). For Fanon, "true decolonization," that is to say *authentic anticolonial freedom*, is possible only when political independence is combined with personal independence, and revolutionary decolonization is the cauldron through which all must pass if human beings, both racially colonized and colonizing persons, are to achieve their "destiny," which, according to Fanon (1967), is to be "free": "No attempt must be made to encase man, for it is his destiny to be set free" (p. 230).

In order for both the colonized and the colonizers to be "set free," Fanon thought it was necessary to decolonize the whole of humanity, the colonized and the colonizers. In this sense, then, Fanon, *contra* the claims of noted African American literary theorist, Henry Louis Gates, Jr., in "Critical Fanonism," can and has been read as a global theorist and world revolutionary thinker (see Onwuanibe, 1983; Said, 1989; Turner and Alan, 1999). It is extremely important to address Gates's "anti-Fanonian" (C.J. Robinson, 1993, p. 87) assertions, because, if they are allowed to pass unchecked, then Fanon and Fanonian discourse, what Gates terms "contemporary colonial discourse theory," are reduced to nothing other than a series of diatribes and "dream[s] of decolonization" (Gates, 1999, p. 266). Further, Gates' comments on, and criticisms of, Fanon as a global theorist procures for itself a place—albeit a peculiar place—within Africana critical theoretical discourse for the precise reason that, first, Africana critical theory, by dint of harsh historical circumstances and hard intellectual labor conditions for its constituents, is, in many respects, a "trans-African" theory of global transformation (Donaldson, 1970, 1980). Second, and in agreement with Lewis Gordon, I believe, without a single reservation, that Fanon, his ideas and actions, emphatically illustrate the fact that he cannot, and must not be "made" (Gates, 1999, p. 260) to be, as Gordon (1995b, p. 197) put it, "anyone's signifying monkey." Third, if Gates and the "anti-Fanonists" are allowed to downplay or, worst (with all manner of poststructuralist and postmodernist word-wizardry), debunk the global dimensions of Fanon's dialectical thought, and especially with regard to *The Wretched of the Earth*, then a major pillar of, and contributor to Africana critical theory will have been "snuffed out," as it were, in the name of poststructuralist or postmodernist or post-Marxist or postfeminist (take your pick!) discourses' obsessive-compulsive intellectual gate-keeping and epistemological purity.

Gates (1999) quips that Edward Said, in "Representing the Colonized," "delivers Fanon as a global theorist *in vacuo*," that is, in a vacuum (p. 253; see also Said, 1989, 1993). He takes issue with the fact that Fanon seems to have been invoked by a number of theorists (almost all literary theorists or critics), on a number of occasions, as a "transcultural, transhistorical global theorist" (1999, p. 266). Fanon, according to Gates, who is closely following Albert Memmi's lead, needs to be "rehistoricized," and when and where this is done it will reveal, Gates claims, "the limits of liberation" and "the very intelligibility of his [Fanon's] dream of decolonization" (p. 266).

A *Dying Colonialism*, perhaps unbeknownst to Gates who almost exclusively limits his criticisms to the Fanon of *Black Skin, White Masks*, is Fanon's study on the Algerian revolution. It is the work in which he describes in stark detail many of the realities of the decolonization process—specifically with regard to the North African and Islamic world. However, *The Wretched of the Earth* represents the work in which Fanon said once and for all, as Jean-Paul Sartre (1968) imaginatively put it in his preface: "Natives of all underdeveloped countries, unite!" (p. 10). Sartre understood then what Gates over a quarter of a century later failed to understand, that Fanon, in *The Wretched of the Earth*, is, as Sartre said, speaking to "his brothers in Africa, Asia, and Latin America" (p. 11). These continents, the "colonies proper" according to Du Bois, house over 75 percent to 85 percent of the earth's population, which logically would give Said, and/or any other critical theorist, credence to put forward and engage Fanon as a global theorist.

Gates quite simply may have chosen the wrong historical and cultural figure or, at the least, the wrong book by the forementioned figure, to criticize. For, even though he does pull a few sentences here and there from *The Wretched of the Earth*, he surely must have overlooked or not thoroughly read the climatic conclusion of the book where Fanon (1968) stated, with literally *dying* conviction:

> Come, then, comrades; it would be as well to decide at once to change our ways. We must shake off the heavy darkness in which we were plunged, and leave it behind. The new day which is already at hand must find us firm, prudent, and resolute. . . . Leave this Europe where they are never done talking of Man, yet murder men everywhere they find them, at the corner of every one of their own streets, in all the corners of *the globe*. For centuries they have stifled almost *the whole of humanity* in the name of so-called spiritual experience. Look at them today swaying between atomic and spiritual disintegration. (p. 311, emphasis added)

It is clearly Fanon's intention here, in the last few lines of his literary life, to speak to "the globe" and to "the whole of humanity." Further, as Fanon speaks, he would ask those who would hear him, those who would join him, to "turn over a new leaf," to be "firm, prudent, and resolute" (p. 316). This is precisely where Gates is wrong, and Sartre is right; and here let us be, as Fanon admonished, "firm, prudent, and resolute" with Gates. Because Gates relegates his comments and criticism of Fanon as "a global theorist *in vacuo*" to Fanon's "first and most overtly psychoanalytic book," *Black Skin, White Masks*, he unwittingly opens himself up to a quandary that several theorists and critics of Fanon are caught in: that is, the seemingly irresolvable tension that exists between the "young" and the "mature" Fanon. Gates (1999) knows full well that Fanon wrote in a manner that was, as he himself charged, "highly porous" (p. 252). In fact, quiet as it is kept, it is exactly the "highly porous" character of Fanon's text that have enabled Gates (amongst a great gang of literary theorists and critics) to label Fanon "oppositional and postmodern" (Gates), "a global theorist" (Edward Said), "a premature poststructuralist" (Homi Bhabha), and so on and so forth. According to Gates,

> Fanon's current fascination for us [literary theorists and cultural critics we may presume] has something to do with the convergence of the problematic of colonialism with that

of subject-formation. As a psychoanalyst of culture, as a champion of the wretched of the earth, he is an almost irresistible figure for a criticism that sees itself as both oppositional and postmodern. And yet there's something Rashomon-like about his contemporary guises. It may be a matter of Judgement whether his writings are rife with contradiction or richly dialectical, polyvocal, and multivalent; they are in any event highly porous, that is, wide open to interpretation, and the readings they elicit are, as a result, of unfailing symptomatic interest: Frantz Fanon, not to put too fine a point on it, is a Rorschach blot with legs. (p. 252)

Fanon, understandably for Gates, is an "almost irresistible figure," but to whom besides himself? Gates answers: those critics who see themselves as both "oppositional and postmodern." Moving beyond the immediate read—that of Gates as both "oppositional and postmodern," that is, considering the fact that he did chose freely to write of and on Fanon—I should here like to briefly engage Gates' "*in vacuo*" claim with regard to Fanon as a global theorist. Fanon may be read as a global theorist not merely because he, in *The Wretched of the Earth*, according to Sartre, was speaking to "his brothers in Africa, Asia, and Latin America," but, because his actions and ideas have had a "global" impact, not simply on college campuses, but also in concrete cultural communities and struggles (Bulhan, 1985, p. 6; Gordon, 1995b, pp. 94–95). It could be observed initially that the very critics that Gates criticizes where born and bred in various places that span the globe. For example, Edward Said, as is well known, was Palestinian, Homi Bhabha and Gayatri Chakravorty Spivak are both Indian, Albert Memmi is Tunisian, Abdul JanMohamed is Kenyan, and Benita Parry, as we are told in the text, is a "radical South African expatriate" (Gates, 1999, p. 259). Perhaps, even on a cursory level, this goes far to illustrate Fanon's "global" irresistibility and applicability, and the very fact that each of the theorists that engaged Fanon produced (and provides us with), as Gates admits, "a usable Fanon" (p. 254). A Fanon that, according to Gates, is "highly porous," yet should be, we are told, "rehistoricized," following the theory of contemporary critical literary discourse, and condemned to the passé "colonial paradigm" (p. 266).

For, "[i]f Said made of Fanon an advocative of post-postmodern counternarratives of liberation; if JanMohamed made of Fanon a Manichean theorist of colonialism as absolute negation; and if Bhabha cloned, from Fanon's theoria, another Third World poststructuralist, [and] Parry's Fanon (which I generally find persuasive) turns out to confirm her own rather optimistic vision of literature and social action," then what, we are given liberty to query, has Gates "made" of Fanon (p. 260)? Fanon, for Gates, is "a psychoanalyst of culture," "a champion of the wretched of the earth," who by no means should be elevated "above his localities of discourse as a transcultural, transhistorical global theorist" (pp. 252, 266). However, here Gates misses Fanon's (and perhaps many critical Fanonists') point(s). In order to be, as Gates asserts, "a champion of the wretched of the earth," Fanon (1969) knew full well that he had no other recourse but to—as demonstrated in his extended essay "Racism and Culture" (in *Toward the African Revolution*)—resign himself, and risk his life, "to fight all forms of exploitation and . . . alienation of man" (p. 43). Perhaps in the end it is Gates who has flung himself into a vacuum by confining himself, as he reports, to Fanon's "first and most overtly psychoanalytic book," *Black Skin, White Masks*. In other words, Gates, not to put too fine a point on it, seems to want to overemphasize the political *particulars* without acknowledging the critical theoretical *universals* of Fanon's work and, rather oddly for such a celebrated literary theorist and critic, by limiting himself to Fanon's first book Gates grossly misinterprets Fanon and the ways in which, as Edward Said (1999, 2000) said, theory, especially critical theory, travels.

Fanon provides the workers in Africana critical theory a path down which to plod. In focusing on the international aspects of Fanon's thought it should be observed that this is precisely what makes him such an enduring figure in Africana critical theoretical and philosophical discourse. As Lou Turner and John Alan (1999), in "Frantz Fanon, World Revolutionary," have pointed out, Fanon acutely understood that the harsh realities of the colonial world were not necessarily endemic and/or inextricable to the continental African experience (p. 11; see also Turner and Alan, 1986). On the contrary, in *The Wretched of the Earth*, Fanon consistently spoke of "the colonizer" and "the colonized," "the native" and "the national bourgeoisie," "the national struggle," "national consciousness," "national culture," "the national government," and so on and so forth. That is to say that he did not specifically speak of the Algerian or North African situation, as he had done in *A Dying Colonialism*. In fact, Hussein Adam (1999) has stated that "certain ambiguities and contradictions" in Fanon may exist because "he wanted to avoid offering a rigid blueprint" of what "decolonization," "freedom," "democracy," "socialism," etcetera, might be like (pp. 135–136; see also Adam, 1974). It was indeed Fanon (1968) who said that decolonization, being "a historical process," "cannot be understood, it cannot become intelligible nor clear to itself except in the exact measure that we can discern the movements which give it historical form and content" (p. 36). Fanon knew then, as we should know now, that the agonies of Africa and its people cannot and will never follow the whims nor wishes of theoreticians, no matter how revolutionary they think they are or claim to be.

Contributing the concept of revolutionary decolonization to the discourse of Africana critical theory, Fanon provides us with the possibility and potential of being "set free." As with Du Bois, James, and the theorists of Negritude, Fanon (1967) believed, without reservation, that "what is most human in man [and woman]"— that is, in all human beings—is the incessant quest for "freedom" (p. 222). Fanon began *Black Skin, White Masks* with a series of brief, but sincere and serious, incantations:

> Toward a new humanism . . .
> Understanding among men . . .
> Our colored brothers . . .
> Mankind, I believe in you . . .
> Race Prejudice . . .
> To understand and to love . . . (p. 7)

It is here, amongst these initial remarks from his first book, that we find Fanon, as he was and as he would be until the day of his death: a philosopher of freedom. And, it should be recalled, he told us from the beginning: "I do not come with timeless truths" (p. 7). Because he knew, perhaps too well, that freedom cannot be achieved or measured by what has taken place in the past. Indeed, it was Fanon who said: "In no fashion should I undertake to prepare the world that will come later. I belong irreducibly to my time" (p. 13). The freedom which we seek today, is not the freedom

Du Bois, James, Césaire, Senghor, or Fanon fought for yesterday. Absolutely not. Du Bois did not dare broach the question of sexual orientation and its implications for our struggle, but bell hooks, Angela Davis, Audre Lorde, Essex Hemphill, Kobena Mercer, Dwight McBride, and Phillip Brian Harper have. Césaire and Senghor certainly remained silent on issues of sexual orientation and gender (Sharpley-Whiting, 2002). And, even the great Frantz Fanon is found wanting when it comes to gender theory and sexuality (Goldie, 1999; Mercer, 1999; Sharpley-Whiting, 1997). But, we must not allow these deficiencies in their thought to mar the contributions they can and must make to Africana critical theory if we are to, as Lucius Outlaw (1996a) admonished, come together "for sustained, systematic, critical reconstructions of intellectual histories that might serve as resources for our work" (p. 83).

Fanon correctly and perceptively pointed out that his words are not "timeless truths." Conversely, and in all honesty, they belong "irreducibly" to his time, and as such are words that are at once wedded to and weighted with circumstances and situations of a bygone world, a world that was. However, and we must be scrupulous here, Fanon's words do, and rightly so, carry a certain amount of weight in the neocolonial (and neocapitalist) world of the twenty-first century. Why? Because, as Emmanuel Hansen (1977) wrote:

> Fanon was not exclusively a man of study: he was a man of action. He tried to live and act in such a way as to bring the ideas in which he believed into being. In this way his life and personality were inextricably linked with ideas. (p. 12)

As I understand it, Africana Studies would do well, at all costs, to emulate Fanon in this respect. Because, it is in this way that the workers of Africana Studies can truly fulfill their mission as simultaneous intellectuals *and* activists. We must concede with the Ghanaian philosopher, Kwame Gyekye (1997), where he asserted "philosophical thought is never worked out in a cultural or historical vacuum" (p. vii). Quite the contrary, the problems that a philosopher or critical theorist addresses are always and ever colored by, and contextually situated in, specific historical, social, political, cultural, and geographical settings. These "settings" are always subjective, and it is for this reason that Gyekye contends: "Philosophers belonging to a given culture or era or tradition select those concepts or clusters of concepts that for one reason or another, matter most and that therefore are brought to the fore in their analysis" (p. 7).

For the intellectual-activists of contemporary Africana Studies, revolutionary decolonization—"the complete calling in question of the colonial situation"—should, or ought to be, one of the "concepts or clusters of concepts" "brought to the fore of their analysis." As Fanon (1968) eloquently explained, independence is not attained with "the blare of trumpets" and a "flag waving," neither is independence maintained by appeals to "superstitions" and "fanaticisms," but through a people's constant and concrete efforts to (re)create themselves, and (re)construct their own distinct critical consciousness and culture (pp. 147, 211, 233).

Fanon's concept of revolutionary decolonization acknowledges something similar to Césaire's revolutionary Negritude and Ngugi wa Thiong'o's *Decolonizing the Mind*: the fact that decolonization is not merely an anticolonial war waged for land, but an anticolonial war waged for the colonized person's way of life, their lifeworlds and lived-experiences (Osei-Nyame, 1998, 1999). Césaire (1972), it will be remembered, said "it is necessary to decolonize our minds, our inner life, at the same time that we decolonize society" (p. 78). Ngugi (1986) contends that colonialism is nothing other than a "cultural bomb" which, as he and the Gikuyu of Kenya know all too well, "annihilates a people's belief in their names, in their languages, in their environment, in their heritage of struggle, in their unity, in their capacities and ultimately in themselves" (p. 3). What these three theorists' concepts of decolonization have in common is an unfaltering belief in the necessity of decolonization, that is, an uncompromising aspiration to radically "change the world," to replace "a certain 'species'" of human beings with "another 'species'" of human beings (Ngugi, 1986, p. 3; Fanon, 1968, p. 35). As Ngugi's mid-1980s update of the concept of decolonization betrays, the need for "a complete calling in question of the colonial situation" remains one of the most pressing issues our (neo)colonial condition and (post)modern moment.

It is here, in the twilight of our (neo)colonial condition and (post)modern moment, that we must come to terms with our time and circumstances, ourselves and situations. For Fanon (1967), "[i]n no fashion," should be forced to speak for "the world that will come later" (p. 13). We, those of us who have lived to see the twenty-first century, have a responsibility to critically interpret, reflect on, and articulate a way out of the quagmire humanity appears to be arrested in. As we have seen, Fanon understood there to be "true" and "false" forms of decolonization, and Nkrumah knew as far back as 1965 that "neo-colonialism" presents and represents "imperialism in its final and perhaps its most dangerous stage." What we, the workers in Africana Studies, among others, need to keep in mind is that "[o]ld-fashioned colonialism is by no means entirely abolished" (Nkrumah, 1965, p. ix). On the contrary, and as Jurgen Habermas (1984) has perceptively pointed out, contemporary colonialism (i.e., "neo-colonialism") is just as much a threat to "developed" or advanced techno-capitalist societies as it has been and remains for "underdeveloped" societies (p. 375).

Throughout this chapter I have hinted at the ways in which Amilcar Cabral's critical theory complements Fanon's discourse on decolonization. The subsequent chapter offers an exploration of Cabral's contributions to the Africana tradition of critical theory that demonstrates his deepening of, and dialectical deviations from Fanon's philosophy. Where we have seen that Cesaire and Fanon innovatively established and extended the discourse on decolonization and revolutionary decolonization, respectively, Cabral amplified the discourse on revolutionary decolonization and dialectically augmented it with, and emphasized the concepts of "the weapon of theory," "return to the source," and, most importantly in terms of Africana critical theory, *revolutionary re-Africanization*.

## NOTES

1. Besides the biographical works cited in the text, Gendzier (1973) and Macey (2000), I have also relied on Alessandrini (1999), Bouvier (1970), Caute (1970), Cherki (2006), J. Fanon (2004), Geismar (1969, 1971), Gibson (1999a, 2003), Gordon (1995b), Gordon, Sharpley-Whiting and White (1996), E. Hansen (1977), Jinadu (1986), and Zahar (1970, 1974) to reconstruct and reinterpret Fanon's personal history and political development.

2. On Aimé Césaire, see Arnold (1981), Cismaru (1974), Hale (1974), Irele (1968), Jahn (1958), Kennedy (1968), Marteau (1961), Scharfman (1987), Sellen (1967), Tomich (1979), and Towa (1969a, 1969b), as well as the preceding chapter of the present study.

3. Madubuike (1975), Mbelelo Ya Mpiku (1976), Melone (1963), Mohome (1968), and Shelton (1964) offer solid critiques of Cesairean Negritude. In addition, the previous chapter provides critiques and comparisons of Cesaire, Senghor and Sartre's distinct articulations of Negritude.

4. With regard to the "Fanon biographers," I am thinking here particularly of Caute (1970), Geismar (1971), and Gendzier (1973). Of course, these are all "early" biographies, but it may prove prudent to note the connection that each of them establish between Césaire and Fanon. This, in a sense, has led me to comment upon the contours of continuity in Africana critical thought traditions. Please see the final section of the previous chapter for further discussion.

5. For more on *Legitime Defense*, see Kesteloot (1991, pp. 15–19).

6. The fact that Césaire sought a "political solution" to the problem of "cultural desolation" is revealing when we are reminded that Fanon would spend the rest of his short life seeking "political" and practical solutions to all manner of cultural, social, and political problems.

7. My argument here has been deeply influenced by the incomparable work of Samir Amin (1974, 1976, 1977, 1978a, 1980, 1989, 1990a, 1997, 1998a, 2003, 2004, 2006) and Walter Rodney (1963, 1967, 1970, 1972, 1976, 1981, 1990).

8. R. Collins (1998), W. Hansen (1997), Kipfer (2004), McCulloh (1983a), Melesse (1975), C.J. Robinson (1993), L. Turner (1991), Wallerstein (1979), and Worsley (1972) offer Marxist, orthodox and otherwise, interpretations and criticisms of Fanon.

9. On Marxist theory as "part and parcel of capitalism," of course, see Marx and Engels (1978), but *do* look to the work of the Frankfurt School and other so-called "Western Marxists." Rarely, if ever, do they write a single word concerning the ways in which capitalism ravages "the wretched of the earth," that is, racialized and colonized peoples. This is precisely why the analyses and theories of Du Bois, James, Césaire, Senghor, Fanon, and Amilcar Cabral are of more relevance to our present discussion. These Africana theorist-activists, among many others, attempted to grasp and grapple with not only capitalism, but also racism and colonialism. Their work is, therefore, "critical theory" in the pervasive and most profound sense of the term. If the critical theory of the Frankfurt School was, as Kellner (1989) claims, developed as a critique of the crises of both capitalism and Marxism, then one of the major characteristics of Africana critical theory is that it serves as a critique of, and response to, the crises of not only capitalism and Marxism, but also colonialism and racism (see also Rabaka, 2007a, 2008a; C.J. Robinson 2000, 2001). This is extremely important to point out, especially considering the fact the over 75 percent of the earth's population and surface has been, and, to a certain extent, remains racialized and colonized (Blaut, 1993; Said, 1979, 1993). This leads us to an extremely serious, yet simple question: Upon whose behalf were, and are, the Frankfurt school, and Frankfurt school-descended, critical theorists developing their theories? For samples of the work of the Frankfurt school, see the anthologies of Arato and Gebhardt (1997), Bronner and Kellner (1989), and Ingram and Simon-Ingram (1992). For commentary on Frankfurt school critical theory, consult Bernstein (1995), Bottomore (1984), Bronner (2002), Connerton (1980), Dubiel (1974), Friedman (1981), Guess (1981), Held (1980), Ingram (1990), Jameson (1971), Jay (1996), Kellner (1984, 1989), Marcus and Tar (1984), Rasmussen (1996), Rush (2004), Slater (1977), Therborn (1996), Wellmer (1974), and Wiggerhaus (1995). On "Western Marxism," see Gottlieb (1992), Howard (1988), Jay (1984), McLellan (1979), and *New Left Review* (1978).

10. The discourse on African socialism is still developing, and though there is no consensus on the correct conception of socialism for Africa, there does seem to be general agreement

on the fact that for socialism, or any political economic system, to really address the authentic human needs of Africa and Africans, it would have to be grounded in, and grow out of Africa's particular history and culture, Africa's multicultural and transenthic conceptions of social organization, politics, ethics, and so on. For further discussion, and some of the texts I have drawn from to development my argument here, please see, Amin (1990a), Babu (1981), Cabral (1972, 1973, 1979), Cohen and Goulbourne (1991), I. Cox (1966), Friedland (1964), Kimua (1986), Lopes (1988), Marable (1987), Mohiddin (1981), Munslow (1986), Nkrumah (1961, 1962, 1964, 1965, 1968b, 1968c, 1968d, 1968e, 1970a, 1970b, 1973a, 1973b), Nwoko (1985), Nyerere (1966, 1968, 1973), Ranuga (1996), Senghor (1959, 1962, 1964a, 1964b), and Toure (1959, 1972, 1973, 1974, 1975, 1976, 1977, 1978, 1979, 1980).

11. In "classical" Marxist theory, socialism is to serve as a transient or transitional state (or stage) between capitalism and communism. Of course, the Russian revolution of 1917 led by Lenin skipped socialism and went straight to their own "Soviet-styled" communism, which many Marxists denounced as not being an authentic communism at all. For a discussion, see Gottlieb (1992) and Kellner (1989). For a direct critique of Soviet Marxism from a major Western Marxist, see Marcuse (1958), and especially the 1985 Columbia University reprint which has an excellent introduction by Douglas Kellner that helps to situate the text in the social and political climate in which it was produced.

12. Bergner (1995, 1999), Chow (1999), Decker (1990), Dubey (1998), Faulkner (1996), Gopal (2002), Mann (2004), McClintock (1995), Sekyi-Otu (1996), Sharpley-Whiting (1997) and Vasavithasan (2004) discuss Fanon's (however contradictory) inclusion of females and male-feminism. Sharpley-Whiting (1997) is particularly noteworthy in this regard. Greater discussion is given to Fanon's contributions to womanism and feminism below.

13. For a discussion of the special uses to which Fanon employed "dramatic" language, see Kang (2004) and Sekyi-Otu (1996). And, on Fanon's uses of both the spectacular and visual in his descriptions of decolonization, see Kaplan (1999) and Kawash (1999).

14. For further discussion of Fanon's comments on, and criticisms of, "anti-democratic," among other, political trends, see Adam (1974, 1999), Gibson (1999c), E. Hansen (1974, 1977), Jinadu (1973, 1986), and Sekyi-Otu (1996).

15. My thinking along these lines has been indelibly influenced by Charles W. Mills, among others, see C.W. Mills (1997, 1998, 2001, 2003a, 2003b), as well as Fashina (1989), Ibish (2002), Maldonado-Torres (2002, 2007), McDade (1971), and Sullivan (2004), Sullivan and Tuana (2007).

16. For engagements of notions of identity and personality in Africana literature, see Drachler (1963), Hennessey (1992), Irele (1990a), Kanneh (1998), C.L. Miller (1990), Mazrui, Okpewho and Davies (1999), Wauthier (1967), and Wylie (1985).

17. In *On Violence*, Hannah Arendt (1970, p. 14, n.19) criticizes Fanon's "Concerning Violence" as a "violence for violence's sake" thesis. For a discussion of the flaws in Arendt's criticisms of Fanon, see Jinadu (1986, pp. 92–93, 231), and Bulhan (1985, pp. 145–148).

18. In this regard Fanon's thinking, in many ways, prefigures and is in line with several contemporary social and political theorists. See, for example, M. Adams (2000), Clayton and Williams (2004), Goodin and Pettit (1997), and I.M. Young (1990).

19. Fanon is, of course, here quoting from Césaire's infamous, if not a bit notorious, *Notebook of a Return to the Native Land*. See, Césaire (1983, pp. 32–85), as well as the previous chapter of the present volume.

20. On identity theory, see Appiah (1997, pp. 75–82), Bhabha (1990), and Zack (1998, pp. 67–75).

# 6

# Amilcar Cabral: Using the Weapon of Theory to Return to the Source(s) of Revolutionary Decolonization and Revolutionary Re-Africanization

Always bear in mind that the people are not fighting for ideas, for things in any-one's head. They are fighting to win material benefits, to live better and in peace, to see their lives go forward, to guarantee the future of their children. . . . [W]e do not fall back on clichés or merely harp on the struggle against imperialism and colonialism in theoretical terms, but rather we point out concrete things. . . . Hide nothing from the masses of our people. Tell no lies. Expose lies whenever they are told. Mask no difficulties, mistakes, or failures. Claim no easy victories.

—Amilcar Cabral, *Revolution in Guinea*, pp. 86, 89, 145

## CABRAL'S ADVENTURES ON THE ROCKY ROAD TO REVOLUTIONARY NATIONALISM: FROM COLONIZED BOY TO REVOLUTIONARY ANTI-COLONIAL MAN

The Cape Verdean and Guinea-Bissaun revolutionary, Amilcar Lopes Cabral, con-nects with and contributes to the discourse of Africana critical theory in several poignant, provocative, and extremely profound ways. First, it should be mentioned that "[a]lthough he did not start out or train as a philosopher," Cabral, according to the Nigerian philosopher, Olufemi Taiwo (1999a), "bequeathed to us a body of writings containing his reflections on such issues as the nature and course of social transformation, human nature, history, violence, oppression and liberation" (p. 6). Second, and as eloquently argued by the Eritrean philosopher, Tsenay Serequeber-han (1991), Cabral's ideas led to action (i.e., actual cultural, historical, social and political transformation, and ultimately revolutionary decolonization and libera-tion) and, therefore, "represents the zenith" of twentieth century Africana revolu-tionary theory and praxis (p. 20).[1] Third, and finally, his writings and reflections provide us with a series of unique contributions to critical theory, which—in the fashion of Du Bois, James, Cesaire, Senghor, and Fanon—seeks to simultaneously critique racist capitalist and racial colonialist societies.

Cabral's biography has been documented by Mario de Andrade (1980), Patrick Chabal (2003), Ronald Chilcote (1991), Mustafah Dhada (1993), Oleg Ignatiev (1975, 1990), and Jock McCulloch (1983b) and, consequently, need not be re-hearsed in its entirety here. That said, at this juncture what I am specifically inter-ested in are those aspects of his life and legacy that impacted and influenced his contributions to Africana critical theory. As Chabal (2003) observed in his pioneer-ing *Amilcar Cabral: Revolutionary Leadership and People's War*, Cabral's revolutionary theory and praxis are virtually incomprehensibly without critically engaging his gradual and often extremely interesting growth from non-violent student militant to internationally acclaimed revolutionary leader.[2]

Born of Cape Verdean parents in Bafata, Guinea-Bissau on 12 September 1924, Cabral's parents exerted an enormous influence on him. His father, Juvenal Antonio da Costa Cabral, was born on São Tiago Island, Cape Verde. The senior Cabral's fam-ily were landowners and, therefore, considered "well-to-do" by local standards. As a result, he was afforded a "proper education," as with the other members of his fam-ily (Chabal, 2003, p.29). Juvenal Cabral had early ambitions to become a priest and was summarily sent to seminary in Portugal following a glowing stint in secondary school. It is not clear whether Juvenal's studies in Portugal awakened his sense of anti-colonialism and Africanity, or whether it was the racial climate and rigid reli-gious curriculum of seminary, but what is certain is that he became a "politically conscious man who did not hesitate to speak his mind" (p. 30). For instance, on one occasion he sent a letter to the Minister of Colonies deploring what he under-stood to be the complete absence of government assistance in alleviating the cata-strophic effects of drought, going so far as to suggest several remedies. On another occasion, he wrote an article expressing his disdain with the colonial government af-ter a house collapsed in an overcrowded part of Praia, the capital of Cape Verde. He went further to criticize the inhuman conditions in which Cape Verdeans had to live because they were forced to flee the countryside and come to the already over-crowded city to find food and work.

Chabal persuasively argues that it was Cabral's father who gave him his first les-sons in political education, a point further corroborated by Dhada (1993, pp. 139–140). Juvenal Cabral also instilled in Amilcar a profound sense of the shared heritage and struggle of Guinea-Bissau and Cape Verde. He wrote poetry, polemics, and expressed an uncommon and long-lasting interest in the agricultural problems of Guinea-Bissau and Cape Verde. Juvenal, a renowned and well-respected school teacher, possessed a deep "sense of intellectual curiosity and rigor, a respect for aca-demic pursuits and for the written word," which he consistently stressed to Amilcar, among his other children (Chabal, 2003, p. 30). While it cannot be said that Juve-nal Cabral was a revolutionary nationalists by any standards, it does seem clear that he may have planted, however nascent, the seeds of nationalism in the fertile soil of his young son's heart and mind.

As it was with his father, Cabral's mother, Iva Pinhal Evora, was born on São Tiago Island, Cape Verde. However, unlike his father she was born into a poor family, which stressed hard work and piety. If Cabral's father bequeathed to him political education, a love of poetry, and an interest in agriculture, then it can be argued that his mother provided him with a very special sense of self-determination, discipline, purpose, personal ethics, and an unshakeable iron will. For a time Mrs. Cabral made good and was an entrepreneur, the proprietor of a shop and a small *pensão* (hotel). When she and Juvenal Cabral separated in 1929, things took a turn for the worst financially. She lost her business and worked as a seamstress and laborer in a fish-canning factory to support her family. Even still, her earnings were "barely sufficient to feed the family and there were days when they went without food." Chabal (2003) poignantly observers that though "Amilcar's family did not starve like so many Cape Verdeans, they were very poor" (p. 31). He went on to importantly emphasize, "Cabral never forgot the difficulties of his early years and later spoke of poverty as one of the reasons which had led him to revolt against Portuguese colonialism" (p. 31). The hardships he witnessed his mother endure and overcome caring for him and his siblings undoubtedly influenced his views on gender justice and, most especially, women as cultural workers and comrades in the national liberation struggle (Cabral, 1979, pp. 70–71, 86, 104; see also Chabal, 2003, p. 107, 118; H. Campbell, 2006; Gomes, 2006; Urdang, 1979).

In discussing Cabral's early life, and especially the influence of his parents on him, it is also important to point out that he was home-schooled until the age of twelve. Though he did not enter primary school until he was twelve, Cabral is reported to have "thrived on education and from the very beginning he was clearly an excellent student." One of his former primary school classmates, Manuel Lehman d'Almeida, recalled that Cabral was "by far the best student and that he passed his secondary school entrance exam with distinction" (Chabal, 2003, p. 31). His school records support d'Almeida's claims and lucidly illustrate that Cabral completed his studies at the *liceu* by the age of twenty, which would mean that he finished four years of primary school and seven years of secondary school in an astonishing eight years! During the last couple of years of his studies at the *liceu* Cabral became aware of the Cape Verdean literary renaissance and cultural movement commonly known as Cabo Verdianidade, which was primarily an outgrowth of the journal, *Claridade*. In many senses Cabo Verdianidade was the Cape Verdean version of the Harlem Renaissance and Negritude, both of which strongly influenced its writers.

Cabo Verdianidade was unique in that its writers for the most part broke with Eurocentric models and themes and, in a move that must be understood to be extremely bold for the time, turned their attention to Cape Verdean subjects, particularly ordinary people's life-worlds and lived-experiences: from drought to hunger, from migration to mild critiques of colonial miseducation, and from starvation to other forms of deprivation. Even so, more similar to Negritude than the Harlem Renaissance, Cabo Verdianidade was limited by its intentional aim at readers well-versed in colonial history and culture and, to make matters worse, it was essentially escapist, expressing an intense cultural alienation that did not in any way promote anti-colonial consciousness or decolonization, non-violent or otherwise. Much like the early issues of Negritude's *Présence Africaine*, then, Cabo Verdianidade's *Claridade* explored ethnic, racial and cultural politics in a vacuum, as opposed to connecting the intersections and political economy of ethnicity, race, racism, and colonialism with the machinations of modern white supremacist capitalism (Araujo, 1966; Batalha, 2004).

The first generation of Cabo Verdianidade writers established their journal, *Claridade*, in the 1930s, but by the 1940s a new cohort of Cape Verdean writers founded the journal *Certeza*. The *Certeza* writers introduced two elements into Cape Verdean consciousness that foreshadowed the future emphasis on national liberation and national culture. The first element involved their critical calling into question of Portuguese colonialism in Cape Verde and an unswerving emphasis on the necessity for political action, though not necessarily decolonization as later conceived by Cabral and his revolutionary nationalist comrades. For these writers, Marxism rather than neo-realism provided their theoretical framework and political orientation. The second element, connected in several ways to the first, revolved around this group's stress on *returning* Cape Verdeans *to the source* of their history, culture, and struggle: Africa. As we have witnessed with the writers of the Cabo Verdianidade movement, at this time most Cape Verdeans understood themselves to be Europeans, and the Cape Verdean archipelago Portugal's most prized overseas islands. The *Certeza* writers went beyond the *Claridade* collective by unequivocally emphasizing their African ancestry and longstanding connections with continental African history, culture, and struggle. Ironically Cabral had completed his studies and had left Cape Verde by the time this new movement was underway. However, he did keep track of it from abroad, and noted that it had the potential to lead to anti-colonial consciousness and an openness to nationalist ideas.

In the autumn of 1945, at the age of twenty-one, Cabral trekked to Portugal to pursue a five-year course of study at the Agronomy Institute at the Technical University of Lisbon. He attended university on a scholarship provided by the Cape Verdean branch of Casa dos Estudiantes do Império (CEI), the House of Students from the Empire, a colonial government financed social development center for students from Portugal's colonies. His scholarship remitted his tuition and supplied him with a very modest stipend of 500 escudos, which was later increased to 750 escudos. His meager stipend was, of course, not enough to live on, so Cabral tutored and took various odd jobs to supplement his income, all the while consistently maintaining the highest marks of his class. Even in light of all of this, Cabral found the time to participate in university affairs, metropolitan politics, and sundry extracurricular activities, most notably: the Radio Clube de Cabo Verde, the Radio Club of Cape Verde; Comissão Nacional para Defensa do Paz (CNDP), the National Commission for the Defense of Peace; Lisbon's Maritime Center and Africa House; the Center for African Studies (CAS); Movimento Anti-Colonialista (MAC), the Anti-Colonial Movement; and, Comité de Liberação dos Territórios Africanos Sob o Domíno Português (CLTASDP), the Committee for the Liberation of Territories Under Portuguese Domination, among others.

Indeed, Cabral was a multidimensional student-activist, though an extremely cautious one. Dhada (1993) contends that Cabral may have "stayed clear of subversive politics, largely for cautionary reasons—perhaps for fear of losing his scholarship or being hounded by the Portuguese secret police, Polícia Interncional para a Defensa do Estudo (PIDE), the International Police for the Defense of the State;" the very same secret police who would, two decades after he earned his degree in agricultural engineering, mercilessly assassinate him (p. 141). Perhaps Cabral sensed his imminent future fate but, even still, harassed and hounded by the Portuguese secret police, he managed to graduate at the top of his class on 27 March 1952. This was a real feat, especially considering the fact that he was the only student of African origin in his cohort. Out of the 220 students who began the rigorous five-year course of study with Cabral, only 22 were awarded degrees as agronomists, or agricultural engineers.

One of the students with which Cabral developed a lasting rapport was Maria Helena Rodrigues, a silviculturist who was born in Chaves, northern Portugal. One of only 20 women admitted in Cabral's initial cohort of 220 students, Rodrigues and Cabral became study partners and, after earning their degrees, husband and wife. With his studies completed and a new wife by his side, Cabral applied for a position in the Portuguese civil service and was "ranked as the best candidate, but was denied the post because he was black" (Chabal, 2003, p. 39). This insult served as a yet another reminder that Portuguese colonialism was inextricable from Portuguese racism. He then did what so many colonial subjects are forced to do when their dreams of escaping the hardships of their colonized homelands have been dashed: he returned to his native land convinced that he could make a special contribution to its development. In a word, he was doggedly determined to decolonize Cape Verde and Guinea-Bissau.

Cabral gained employment as a "grade two agronomist" with the Provincial Department of Agricultural and Forestry Services of Guinea at the Estação experimental de Pessubé, a research complex not far from Bissau. He was second in command and, from all the reports, seems to have thrown himself into a Lisbon-based Ministry for Overseas Territories-commissioned agricultural census of Guinea-Bissau. It was through this massive undertaking that Cabral become intimately familiar with the people and land in whose interest he would soon wage a protracted people's war for national liberation. He began the study in late 1953, traveling more than 60,000 kilometers, and collecting data from approximately 2,248 peasants. By December 1954 he presented he and his team's findings to the colonial authorities. The report was subsequently published in 1956 as a 200-page document. It featured statistics and analysis pertaining to Guinea-Bissau's agricultural demography, which the colonial government promised the United Nation's Food and Agricultural Organization it would use to better grapple with droughts and famine, among other issues, besetting Guinea-Bissau.

Cabral was afforded considerable expertise carrying out the agricultural census. In fact, Chabal goes so far to contend that, "[f]ew twentieth-century revolutionary and guerrilla leaders were in the enviable position of having such a specialized and detailed knowledge of the country in which they proposed to launch a people's war" (p. 53). Along with his work for the colonial government Cabral made many political contacts with both Cape Verdeans and Guinea-Bissauns. Many initially outright rejected his ideas on decolonization, but after he discursively provided examples, often empirical and irrefutable evidence (e.g., disenfranchisement, deprivation, starvation, lack of education, and violent government repression), and usually over a prolonged period of time (i.e., usually several weeks or months), they were persuaded to seriously contemplate radical political alternatives, solutions to the problem(s) of Portuguese colonialism. It is here that Cabral excelled, clandestinely making contacts with civil servants and entrepreneurs, as well as urban workers, peasants, and villagers.

Initially Cabral was open to using every available legal means of bringing about an end to Portuguese colonialism. To this end, in 1954 he formed a sports, recreational and cultural club for local youngsters with the ultimate aim of using it as a front to promote nationalism, political education and anti-colonial consciousness-raising, as had been successfully done in "British" and "French" Africa. For instance, after a game of football, Cabral and his colleagues would retire to a more private place supposedly to discuss how each player could improve their skills; what really took place were intense and eye-opening discussions about African history, culture and struggle, and the nefarious nature of Portuguese colonialism and racism. The club and its secret meetings gained considerable notoriety in and around Bissau and, as a result, were insidiously infiltrated by the Portuguese secret police's informers and swiftly terminated on government orders. Consequently, Cabral was forced to leave Guinea-Bissau and permanently banned from residing there again. He petitioned for, and was granted, annual visits to briefly see his mother and other family members.

At this point the dye was cast, and Cabral let go of any lingering hope that Cape Verde and Guinea-Bissau could be liberated using the constitutional or legal decolonization path. It was, therefore, on one of his colonial government-sanctioned visits to Guinea-Bissau on 19 September 1956 that Cabral, Luiz Cabral (his brother), Aristides Pereira, Fernando Fortes, Julio de Almeida and Eliseu Turpin founded the Partido Africano da Independência e União dos Povos da Guiné e Cabo Verde (PAIUPGC), the African Party for the Independence and Unity of Guinea-Bissau and Cape Verde. Later the name was slightly altered to Partido Africano da Independência da Guiné e Cabo Verde (PAIGC), the African Party for the Independence of Guinea-Bissau and Cape Verde. Over the next 17 years of his life, Amilcar Cabral would not only bring Portuguese colonialism to its knees and lead the people of Guinea-Bissau and Cape Verde to national liberation, but he would also reconstruct and redefine what it means to be a revolutionary nationalist *and* revolutionary humanist. Though there are many who argue that Cabral was not necessarily a theorist, and more a guerilla leader and military strategist whose work is confined to the national liberation struggle of Cape Verde and Guinea-Bissau, in what follows I challenge these assertions and illustrate several of the ways in which Cabral's intellectual life and political legacy contribute to radical politics and critical social theory, Africana and otherwise.

Under Portuguese colonialism, Cabral contended (1979), "Africans live on a sub-human standard—little or no better than serfs in their own country" (p. 17). He went further to poignantly explain:

> After the slave trade, armed conquest and colonial wars, there came the complete destruction of the economic and social structure of African society. The next phase was European occupation and ever-increasing European immigration into these territories. The lands and possessions of the Africans were looted. The Portuguese "sovereignty tax" was imposed, and so were compulsory crops for agricultural produce, forced labor, the export of African workers, and total control of the collective and individual life of Africans, either by persuasion or violence. (p. 17)

Cabral was convinced, in light of his lived-experiences and through empirical investigation, that colonial domination—chronically exacerbated by the crises of, internal to, and created by, the global imperial system—held the great majority of humanity in "sub-human" states. On these grounds, as noted above, he participated in the founding of the PAIGC and, as its undisputed leader, subsequently led the national liberation struggle in his native land(s) until he was assassinated by the Portuguese secret police on 20 January 1973.

Portuguese colonialism, contended Cabral (1972), robbed the people of Guinea-Bissau and Cape Verde of their "most elementary rights" and had created and contributed to "misery, ignorance, [and] suffering of every kind" (p. 77). Thus, on this account, colonial domination should and would be opposed by any and all available means to the colonized population. In this regard, Cabral considered the struggle of the people of Guinea-Bissau and Cape Verde a direct heir to the revolutionary histories and cultures of freedom-fighting colonized peoples the world over, stating: "Today, in taking up arms to liberate ourselves, in following the example of other peoples who have taken up arms to liberate themselves, we want to return to our history, on our own feet, by our own means and through our own sacrifices" (p. 78).

As it was with Du Bois, James and Fanon, history for Cabral was essentially a cultural compass, which provided particular groups experiencing and enduring particular and peculiar racial and colonial circumstances, with guidance and directions with respect to their decolonized destiny. Colonialism, according to Cabral (1979), is "the negation of the *historical process* of the dominated people," and the national liberation struggle symbolizes and signals the colonized peoples' conscious return to their own history (p. 141, my emphasis). This is, of course, one of the reasons Cabral consistently admonished African (among other racially colonized) people to *return to the source* (or, sources) of their own history, culture and struggle (see Cabral, 1973; and, especially the soon to be discussed "Identity and Dignity in the Context of the National Liberation Struggle" [pp. 57–69]). Similar to Cesaire's "return," Cabral's "return" is also critical and, if properly explicated, has extremely promising and profound insights and implications for an Africana (or any other) critical theory of contemporary society.

In this chapter I shall explore and explicate the thought of Amilcar Cabral for its contributions to critical theory—extremely important, albeit often-overlooked, contributions which conceptualize and earnestly attempt to think through the borderlines and boundaries between, and the dialectics at play in, various stages of "underdevelopment" and "development," tradition and modernity, and nationalism and humanism in racial colonial and racist capitalist societies. The chapter will commence with a critical engagement of Cabral's concept(s) of colonialism and emphasis on the importance of ideology and concrete philosophy. Then, it engages the unique ways in which he synthesized radical theory with revolutionary praxis (or, rather, revolutionary nationalism with guerilla warfare). Next, analysis is given to his thesis of "return to the source" and the importance and inextricability of national history and national culture in his distinctive conceptions of national liberation and *the dialectical process of revolutionary decolonization and re-Africanization.* Finally, the chapter concludes with a brief assessment and interpretation of some of the deficiencies of Cabral's contributions to the new critical theory of the twenty-first century.

## TOWARD AN AFRICANA PHILOSOPHY OF PRAXIS: CABRAL, CRITICAL THEORY, CONCRETE PHILOSOPHY, AND THE END OF (NEO)COLONIALISM

> If we do not forget the historical perspectives of the major events in the life of humanity, if while maintaining due respect for all philosophies, we do not forget that the world is the creation of man himself, then colonialism can be considered as the paralysis or deviation or even the halting of the history of one people in favor of the acceleration of the historical development of other peoples.
>
> —Amilcar Cabral, *Revolution in Guinea,* p. 76

In this single, far-seeing sentence Amilcar Cabral set down his conception of colonialism for prosperity. Although he did not present his critical theory in any discursive or systematic manner, Cabral's corpus is shot-through with critical comments on colonialism, capitalism, racism, and other forms imperial domination. Our discussion will begin by laying bare Cabral's conception of colonialism, and then we will explore and critically engage his collapse of the crude and artificial dichotomy and distinction made between colonialism and capitalism, especially when racism is factored into both. In Cabral's view, both of these "world-systems" *represent*—that is to say, they chronically present humanity again and again with—greater, more and more massive forms of imperialism. At the heart of Cabral's critical theory is an implicit "critique of domination and a theory of liberation," and this is precisely what brings his thought in line with other forms of critical theory (Kellner, 1989, p.1). However, the foci of Cabral's critical theory and concrete philosophy are not so much the dilemmas and dialectics of domination and liberation in "advanced industrial" (Marcuse, 1964), "developed" (Habermas, 1984, 1987a), and/or "techno-capitalist" (Kellner, 1989) societies, but the downtrodden, deprived, and dominated—in a word, "the wretched of the earth"—wherever they exist, whether in capitalist or colonial societies.

Cabral challenges conventional critical theory in the sense that his critical theory is not quarantined to the life-worlds and lived-experiences of white workers in capitalist societies. Much more, his thought was simultaneously revolutionary nationalist and revolutionary humanist. For instance, it was Amilcar Cabral (1972) who said in his opening address at the plenary session at the 2nd Conference of the Nationalist Organizations of the Portuguese Colonies (CONCP) held in Dar es Salaam, Tanzania, on 5 October 1965:

> Our national liberation struggle has a great significance both for Africa and for the world. We are in the process of proving that peoples such as ours—economically backward, living sometimes almost naked in the bush, not knowing how to read or write, not having even the most elementary knowledge of modern technology—are capable, by means of their sacrifices and efforts, of beating an enemy who is not only more advanced from a technological point of view but also supported by the powerful imperial forces of world imperialism. Thus before the world and before Africa we ask: were the Portuguese right when they claimed that we were uncivilized peoples, peoples without culture? We ask: what is the most striking manifestation of civilization and culture if not that shown by a people which takes up arms to defend its right to life, to progress, to work and to happiness?
>
> We, the national liberation movements joined in the CONCP, should be conscious of the fact that our armed struggle is only one aspect of the general struggle of the oppressed against imperialism, of man's struggle for dignity, freedom and progress. We should consider ourselves as soldiers, often anonymous, but soldiers of humanity in the vast front of the struggle in Africa today. (p. 79)

Based on the foregoing, it can be clearly seen that Cabral's critical theory is at its core a global theory. Where Eurocentric critical theory claims to be a global theory (Kellner, 1989)—but focuses exclusively on problems which pertain to "advanced industrial," "developed," and/or "techno-capitalist" societies—Africana critical theory, following Cabral's example, transverses the colonialist/capitalist divide and engages the world as it actually exists (p. 48). As the world actually exists, it is an imperial world, a world where one human group doggedly attempts to dominate all other human groups; where one human culture and civilization is acknowledged and exalted as the only authentic human culture and civilization; where one peoples' history is considered the "History" of humanity *in toto*.[3] Cabral's critical theory contests and combats not only global imperialism, but also Eurocentric critical theory. It emphasizes and accentuates the ways in which African and other non-European colonized people, people who more often than not have never received training in political science or political philosophy, *return to the sources of their history and culture* and simultaneously draw from and contribute to the rich resources of not only their own distinct political traditions and political cultures, but global political traditions and cultures.

Cabral's critical theory encompasses and considers both colonialism and capitalism, which is why he consistently stressed the fact that the national liberation struggle is not merely against Portuguese colonialists, or "white people," or any of their colonized African agents. More, the struggles and emancipatory efforts of colonized and alienated people, those folk who defiantly refuse "reification," must ever be against the imperial global system which promotes the destruction and degradation of human beings, their histories and heritages, their cultures and civilizations, and their lives and lands.[4] To struggle against global imperialism is to understand and believe, as Cabral (1979) asserted, in "self-determination for all peoples," and that "each people must choose their destiny, [and] take it into their own hands" (p. 63).[5]

Cabral clearly understood that the national liberation struggle of Cape Verde and Guinea-Bissau was not a struggle against the Portuguese, repeatedly reminding his comrades: "we do not confuse exploitation or exploiters with the color of men's skins; we do not want any exploitation in our countries, not even by black people" (p. 80). That is why he constantly reiterated that the ultimate question of the national liberation struggle was not only a question of revolutionary decolonization and complete liberation, but also one of genuine "progress for our people" (p. 76). Cabral's critical theory is vigilant and strives to critique and, if need be, crush anyone and anything that might harm or hinder human beings democratically developing to their highest and fullest potential. His critical theory is also a social and historical theory and, in that sense, understands that there are no boundaries or parameters that have been set once and for all, for all space and time on what can or cannot be achieved by a human group (or human being) under or enduring any type of situation or circumstance. History's pages are dotted with the dogged deeds of the dominated, rising and revolting, rescuing and reclaiming their place on the stage (and often at the center) of human history. History, as with culture, is an assertion of human agency and dignity, and this Cabral knew well, as he stressed the importance of "historical knowledge," audaciously asserting:

> Struggle is a normal condition of all living creatures in the world. All are in struggle, all struggle. . . . Everyone must struggle. . . . Our struggle is not [and cannot be] mere words but action, and we must really struggle . . . the struggle is not a debate nor verbiage, whether written or spoken. Struggle is daily action against ourselves and against the enemy, action which changes and grows each day so as to take all the necessary forms to chase the Portuguese colonialists out of our land. (pp. 31, 43, 65, 64, 65)

Observe that Cabral conceded that the (neo)colonized must "daily" or "each day" struggle "against ourselves and the enemy." This means, then, that our struggle—our assertion of our agency, dignity, culture and history—cannot and must not be merely against European and/or European American imperialists, but must also be waged against our own "internal enemies" (p. 76). That is, those "enemies" in our own countries and governments, in our local communities and schools, in our churches and mosques, and even, if truth be told, in our own heads and hearts. We must be willing each and every day to confront and combat imperialism and imperialists; to not be willing to do so is to fool ourselves, and to attempt to pray or wish away a concrete (actually existing) problem that has plagued humanity for more than five hundred years.

People of color, and especially people of African descent, have attempted to pray and/or wish away imperialism for so long that Cabral unapologetically contended: "It is not a question of wishing" (p. 48). Quite the contrary, armed with a critical consciousness, a critical theory, and an extremely concrete philosophy—a "philosophy of praxis"—Cabral waged a war, not only against Portuguese colonialism, but against imperialism in all its forms.[6] The ultimate objective of Africana critical theory, employing and applying Cabral as a major point of departure, is to chase imperialism—again, in all its forms—out of colonized lands, and perhaps more importantly, out of colonized lives.[7]

In self-reflexively acknowledging our "internal enemies," Cabral's critical theory refuses to be reduced to a biologically determined or racial essentialist position. It is not, and has never been, for Cabral or Africana critical theory, a question of biology, physiology or phenotype.[8] Cabral openly acknowledged that there were "whites" or Portuguese people who were willing, and actually did contribute (positively and progressively) to the national liberation struggle of Cape Verde and Guinea-Bissau (p. 34). Which is, of course, why he said, "we do not confuse exploitation or exploiters with the color of men's skins; we do not want any exploitation in our countries, not even by black people" (p. 80). Here he sidestepped what Cornel West (1993), in *Race Matters*, was wont to term "the pitfalls of racial reasoning" (pp. 21–32).

Cabral was in line with West's assertion that racial reasoning should be replaced by moral reasoning.[9] And, for all the issues that one could (and many *do*) have with West's essay, he makes a very good point when he writes that it is necessary "to understand the black freedom struggle not as an affair of skin pigmentation and racial phenotype but rather as a matter of ethical principles and wise politics" (p. 25).[10] Surely Cabral exemplifies "ethical principles and wise politics" when he admonished his comrades to be chronically and critically cognizant of the fact that they were participants, reluctant soldiers, if you will, in "the general struggle of the oppressed against imperialism" (1972, p. 79); when he stated that "[t]he significance of our struggle is not only in respect of colonialism, it is also in respect of ourselves" (1979, p. 33); when he chided and charged, "let us not put all the blame on the colonialists. There is also exploitation of our folk by our own folk" (1979, p. 54); and lastly, when he prefigured Cornel West's coalition politics by addressing and stressing the importance of alliances and coalitions.[11] Cabral communicated the conundrum as follows: "If we want to serve our land, our Party, our people, we must accept everyone's help. . . . no struggle can be waged without an alliance, without allies. . . . If we demand solidarity with us from other peoples, we must show solidarity with them as well" (pp. 62, 80, 81).

Many have misread Cabral. His critical theory is certainly against colonial domination, but it is also, and at certain points perhaps more so, against racial oppression and capitalist exploitation. He was well aware that he and his comrades could spend the bulk of their lives fighting against one form of colonialism only to be reinscribed and caught in the quagmires of another new form of colonialism.[12] Hence, this is precisely the reason within the realm of Cabral's critical theory that "world imperialism" is the ultimate enemy, not merely colonialism on the African continent, or capitalism in Europe or America. He somberly, but sternly stated:

[L]et us go forward, weapons in hand . . . let us prepare ourselves too, each day, and be vigilant, so as not to allow a new form of colonialism to be established in our countries, so as not to allow in our countries any form of imperialism, so as not to allow neo-colonialism, already a cancerous growth in certain parts of Africa and of the world, to reach our own countries. (Cabral, 1972, p. 85)

Cabral's critical theory is a global and historical theory insofar as it attempts to provide answers to the most pressing problems of the modern epoch; problems which continue to plague us in the twenty-first century. It seeks to offer an outline of cultural, social, and political development and the ways in which the vicissitudes of colonialism and capitalism historically have and continue currently to structure and influence world culture and civilization, and human thought and behavior. Cabral's critical theory is, ultimately, aimed at the complete destruction and revolutionary replacement of the imperial world-system(s) with new forms of government and social organizations that would perpetually promote democratic socialist global coexistence. For Cabral, the anti-colonial national liberation struggles of African people are part and parcel of global struggles against imperialism. He situated African anti-colonial struggles in a global and historical context and reminded his comrades, once again, why they were fighting:

[W]hen speaking of our struggle, we should not isolate it from the totality of the phenomena which have characterized the life of humanity, in particular Africa since the Second World War . . . we must state openly that equally if not more so, it is the concrete conditions of the life of our people—misery, ignorance, suffering of every kind, the complete negation of our most elementary rights—which have dictated our firm position against Portuguese colonialism and, consequently, against all injustice in the world. (Cabral, 1972, pp. 76–77)

Cabral's critical theory, in addition, can be considered concrete philosophy because it seeks to grasp and grapple with "the concrete conditions of the life of our people." These "concrete conditions of . . . our people," according to Cabral, have not been brought about by God, neither by natural catastrophe, nor by the people themselves, but have come from other real, live people, men and women of flesh, blood, and bones who have sought and (often) succeeded in negating the cultures and civilizations, the histories and heritages of African and other racially colonized people.[13] Moreover, Cabral's critical theory is a form of concrete philosophy in so far as it seeks to deal with the urgent issues of the existing individual and her or his current cultural, social, political, and material milieu. As concrete philosophy, Cabral's critical theory is revolutionary in the sense that it attempted to go the roots of the phenomena, place it under critical consideration for radical alteration, and then, if need be, transform it in the best interest of struggling local and global populations.

Colonialism and capitalism, comprehended as interconnected imperial world-systems, are to be opposed because they create human alienation and "reification," and unleash forces which stand against, above, and between persons; which, once present, subject all forms, feelings, views and values of "self" and "society" under their absolutely administered domination.[14] Cabral's critical theory registers as a concrete philosophy, also, insofar as it seeks simultaneously to provide critical knowledge of the existing society and become a force in its revolutionary transformation. A concrete philosophy requires a radical break with the abstractness of academic and/or "traditional" philosophy, and a dialectical deconstruction and reconstruction of philosophy towards its practical potentialities and possibilities. It seeks to eschew much of what the analytical philosophers term "philosophy," in favor of real (actually existing) problems, of real (actually existing) people, in the real (actually existing) world. It searches for the causes of human suffering, and points to and provides ways in which human suffering and social misery may be ameliorated and abolished. Concrete philosophy, further, seeks to inspire and engage actually existing individuals in the emancipatory efforts of their time and circumstances, and create a critical consciousness that places the premium on the noblest desire of any philosophy or form of knowledge: the unity of ideas and action, theory and praxis, words and deeds.

Armed with a critical theory and a concrete philosophy, Amilcar Cabral turned to the colonial world-system and humbly vowed not to rest until the last vestige of colonial violence and domination had been eradicated from his native land and the world. In order to alter a specific reality, or series of social, political, economic, and cultural conditions, Cabral contended that it was necessary to obtain an intimate knowledge of those conditions. He stated: "Anyone who leads a struggle like ours, who bears responsibility in a struggle like ours, has to understand gradually what concrete reality is . . . we need to know the reality of our land, reality in all aspects, of all kinds, so that we shall be able to guide the struggle, in general and in particular" (Cabral, 1979, pp. 58, 62). Here, Cabral best explicates why his thought can be characterized as a "concrete philosophy," because its' points of departure are consistently the "concrete conditions" (1972, pp. 77) and the "concrete reality" (1979, pp. 58) of a particular people (those of Guinea-Bissau and Cape Verde), engaged in a specific struggle against global imperialism. Cabral (1979) further corroborates these contentions with the weighted words: "So we form part of a specific reality, namely Africa struggling against imperialism, against racism and against colonialism. If we do not bear this in mind, we could make many mistakes" (p. 48).

To avoid "unnecessary efforts and sacrifices," the "many mistakes" mentioned above, Cabral was consistent in his position that the dominated always, first, "know our reality" and, second, "start out from that reality to wage the struggle" (pp. 50, 44). It is with this understanding that Cabral confronted—the specific form of imperialism that cancerously controlled his native land—colonialism. In a position paper variously titled "The Weapon of Theory" (in *Revolution in Guinea* [1972, pp.

90–111]) and "The Presuppositions and Objectives of National Liberation in Relation to Social Structure (in *Unity and Struggle* [1979, pp. 119–137]), Cabral (1979) identified two specific forms of colonialism:

1. Direct domination—by means of a political power made up of agents foreign to the dominated people (armed forces, police, administrative agents and settlers)—which is conventionally called *classical colonialism* or *colonialism*.
2. Indirect domination—by means of political power made up mainly or completely of native agents—which is conventionally called *neocolonialism*. (p. 128, emphasis in original)

According to Cabral, when and where direct domination or classical colonialism is the issue, then, the social structure of the dominated people, at whatever stage in their historical and cultural development, are more than likely to suffer the following experiences:

(a) Total destruction, generally accompanied by immediate or gradual elimination of the aboriginal population and consequent replacement by an exotic population.
(b) Partial destruction, generally accompanied by more or less intensive settlement by an exotic population.
(c) Ostensible preservation, brought about by confining the aboriginal society to areas or special reserves generally offering no means of living and accompanied by massive implantation of an exotic population. (p. 128)

Situation (a), of course, applies to the indigenous populations of the United States of America, Australia, and many islands of the Caribbean Sea. Circumstances (b) and (c) are applicable to the populations of Africa, India, Central and South America, and Canada, among other non-European peoples, cultures, and civilizations. Cabral's critical theory, in contradistinction to Eurocentric or Frankfurt School critical theory, seeks to describe, criticize, and offer alternatives to imperialism as a world-system, and not merely engage an aspect of imperialism, such as capitalism, though, his critical theory does acknowledge that capitalism is an indelible part of modern, world-historical imperialism. Colonialism and capitalism are two sides of the same coin, and the Africana critical theorists discussed in the previous chapters, among others, constantly struggled to radically alter the world, and their specific life-worlds, based upon this crucial comprehension. Africana critical theory deconstructs and deviates from European and European American critical theory in so far as European and European American critical theory are, and have consistently shown themselves to be, concerned almost exclusively with the "socio-historical transformation and the transition from one stage of capitalist development to another" (Kellner, 1989, p. 51). European and European American critical theory are purportedly "motivated by an interest in relating theory to politics and an interest in the emancipation of those who are oppressed and dominated" (p. 1), yet it does not offer a single "concrete" alternative and/or salvageable solution to what has been variously dubbed by Africana critical theorists—and Du Bois (1985a, p. 235) and Fanon (1968, p. 40) in particular—"the colonial problem."

Imperialism is the foci of Africana critical theory, and comprehended in our contemporary context it includes not merely capitalism and colonialism, but racism, sexism, and heterosexism (i.e., discrimination based upon one's sexual preferences or sexual orientation). Cabral (1979) correctly contended that "the impact of imperialism on the historical process of the dominated people is paralysis, stagnation (even in some cases, regression) in that process" (p. 128). By denying the dominated people their distinct "historical process," their right to constant (human/e) being/becoming—which every human group must be free to decide and develop in their own best interests—imperial domination violently intervenes and interrupts the culture and civilization, the history and heritage(s) of the subject/subjugated people.[15] It retards their development and has deep ramifications in both the public and the private spheres of the dominated peoples' lives, and, seemingly unbeknownst to many, imperialism, by its very nature, intensifies and increases with every passing second, minute, hour, day, month, year, etc. The colonial problem, which is nothing other than a euphemism for the global imperial problem, asphyxiates the culture and civilization of the aboriginal population. It suspends, if not outright destroys, the mode(s) of production indigenous to particular lands and particular peoples, and as a result forces the said people into accepting (whether consciously or unconsciously) the cultural concepts and categories, the social and political models and modes of existence, of imperial power(s) and populations. Cabral confirmed:

> The principal characteristic, common to every kind of imperialist domination, is the denial of the historical process of the dominated people by means of violent usurpation of the freedom of the process of development of the productive forces. Now, in a given society, the level of development of the productive forces and the system of social utilization of these forces (system of ownership) determine the *mode of production*. In our view, the mode of production, whose contradictions are manifested with more or less intensity through class struggle, is the principal factor in the history of any human whole, and the level of productive forces is the true and permanent motive force of history. (p. 141, emphasis in original)

In this sense, then, imperialism—the violent combination of capitalism and colonialism in an ever-oppressing, and on an ever-increasing global scale—is a complex series with several slants: physical and material domination, cultural and linguistic domination, political and economic domination, and the asphyxiation and/or absolute decimation of the dominated peoples' capacity for agency, and their possibilities and potentialities for making history. In arguing that the mode of production, instead of the orthodox Marxist contention of class struggle, is "the true and permanent motive force of history," Cabral distinguished his critical theory from those of Marx and his disciples. To his credit, Cabral did not simply integrate Marxist theory into his anti-imperialist critical theory; much more, he radically extended and expanded it and, in incredibly innovative ways, deconstructed and reconstructed it to speak to the special needs and struggles of Africa and its diaspora, all the while keeping in mind something that he was fond of reiterating to his European (and often extremely Eurocentric) Marxist comrades: "Marx did not write about Africa." And, it is extremely important to observe, Cabral did all of this without in anyway disqualify the progressive ways in which Marxism or Marxist-Lenin-ism had been used in other countries and contexts, and on other continents.

## CABRAL'S COUPLING OF THE WEAPON OF THEORY WITH REVOLUTIONARY PRAXIS: CRITICALLY MODIFYING (WITHOUT REPUDIATING) MARXISM, DIALECTICAL AND HISTORICAL MATERIALISM, NATIONALISM, AND HUMANISM

Marxism is not a religion . . . and Marx did not write about Africa.

—Amilcar Cabral, *Our People Are Our Mountains: Amilcar Cabral on Guinean Revolution*, pp. 21–22

[C]ertain crucial phenomena of the modern world—nationalism, racism, gender oppression, homophobia, ecological devastation—have not been adequately understood by Marxist theorists.

—Cornel West, *The Ethical Dimensions of Marxist Thought*, p. xxiii

Much has been misunderstood with regard to Cabral's radical theory and revolutionary praxis. He has often been read as a Marxist, but that interpretation betrays the fact that he consistently counseled colonized and other people struggling against racial oppression and capitalist exploitation to start from their own reality and be realists (Cabral, 1979, p. 44). He knew well that what Marx, Lenin, Mao, Minh, Guevara, and Castro may have attempted or actually accomplished in their respective times and circumstances, he was a different kind of revolutionary leader, leading a different type of revolutionary party and struggle, and enduring extremely different conditions; conditions which none of the aforementioned had ever even dared to considered for more than a mere passing moment. Patrick Chabal (1983a) relates, "Cabral consistently rejected the view that other models of development could be followed in Guinea" (p. 181). Cabral comprehended, as Cornel West (1991) would almost two decades later, "the necessity of rethinking and reinterpreting the insights of the Marxist tradition [and/or any supposed 'radical theory'] in the light of new circumstances" and situations (p. xxvi). Although Cabral was never as wedded to Marxist theory as West *was* wont to be, I believe that he, Du Bois, James, Cesaire, Senghor, Fanon, and a whole host of anti-imperialist intellectual-activists would agree with West when he writes: "certain crucial phenomena of the modern world—nationalism, racism, gender oppression, homophobia, ecological devastation—have not been adequately understood by Marxist theorists" (p. xxiii).

Cabral may be read more as a "materialist" than a "Marxist" for the exact reasons (homophobia withstanding) that West lists above.[16] Consequently, it is for these reasons that I view Cabral as a critical theorist as opposed to a Marxist, because his thought and actions explicitly and emphatically transcend the realm(s) of Marxist theory and praxis. To argue that Cabral was a Marxist, in many respects, conceptually incarcerates him and his critical theory and revolutionary praxis within the Eurocentric world of Marxism. He collapsed and contributed concepts and categories to Marxist and other purportedly radical discourses that have yet to be fully analyzed and appreciated, let alone applied. Moreover, "radicalism," it should be strongly stressed, is not synonymous—neither in the "modern" nor the supposed "post-modern" moment—with Marxism and/or Marxist-derived discourses. Cabral consistently challenged this and, in so doing, drew from those elements of Marxism, among other radical and revolutionary theory, that he understood to be most useful in the national liberation struggle of the people of Cape Verde and Guinea-Bissau.

Similar to Fanon, Cabral did not have any direct connections to the communist or socialist party. But, to a significantly greater extent than Fanon, Cabral was in a deeper critical dialogue with the Marxist tradition and openly espoused his belief in the superiority of materialist analysis; the problematics of applying the class struggle model to Africa (Cape Verde and Guinea-Bissau in specific); and, his contention that the mode of production, not class struggle, was the major determinant and the true motive force of history. Primarily employing Cabral's classic essays, "The Weapon of Theory" and "Brief Analysis of the Social Structure in Guinea," this section will accentuate his almost utterly instrumental relationship with Marxism (and Marxist-Leninism), as well as the ways in which he innovatively deconstructed and reconstructed Marxism and synthesized it with several other theoretical traditions to make several seminal contributions, not merely to Marxism (or, Marxist-Leninism) but, equally, if not more importantly, to Africana critical theory.

At first issue is Cabral's unique utilization of historical and dialectical materialism. Cabral's method may be said to be "materialist," as opposed to "idealist," in the sense that it seeks to engage and alter (through the act of revolution), the "concrete conditions" and the "concrete reality" of his social, political, historical, and cultural coordinate. As an anti-colonial and anti-racist materialist, Cabral was not concerned with adherence to, and did not feel compelled to consider, any orthodox principles or tenets—Marxist or otherwise. In fact, it is when and where he adds an anti-colonial and anti-racist dimension to his materialist analysis that Cabral's conception of critical theory betrays, perhaps more so than any other aspect, the plausibility of his theory being read as revolutionary materialism rather than mere Eurocentric Marxism.

Materialists are usually hostile to metaphysical systems, absolutism and all foundationalist theories that attempt to discover the basis for knowledge.[17] As the Frankfurt School critical theorist, Max Horkheimer (1972), correctly observed in "Materialism and Metaphysics," the views which a materialist holds at a given moment are not dictated by any unchanging metaphysical theses, but rather by

> the tasks which at any given period are to be mastered with the help of the theory. Thus, for example, criticism of a dogma of religious faith may, at a particular time and place, play a decisive role within the complex of materialist views, while under other circumstances such criticism may be unimportant. Today the knowledge of the movements and tendencies affecting society as a whole is immensely important for materialist theory, but in the eighteenth century the need for knowledge of the social totality was overshadowed by questions of epistemology, of natural science, and of politics. (pp. 20–21)[18]

Idealist views aim at *justification,* and are usually advanced by ruling race, gender, or class elites and ideologues to affirm ruling race, gender, or class interests. Whilst materialist theories aim at *explanation* with reference to (actually existing) material conditions and social constructions, which should (currently) include race, gender, class, sexuality, and other specific historical and cultural coordinates and conditions. Africana critical theory connects with Frankfurt School critical theory in the sense that both understand that: "materialism is not interested in a worldview or in the souls of men [and women]. It is concerned with changing the concrete conditions under which humans suffer and in which, of course, their souls must be stunted. This concern may be comprehended historically and psychologically; it cannot be grounded in general principles" (p. 32). Cabral's critical theory can be considered revolutionary materialist—as opposed to simply Marxist—theory because it is concerned with human suffering and with transforming the material conditions and social constructions (such as "race") that prompt and promote unprecedented human suffering and social misery.[19] The main point of revolutionary materialist analysis is to produce more humane forms of (co)existence among human beings, and human beings with nature, and a rational, democratic socialist society. It is, moreover, an analysis which assumes that "the wretchedness of our own time is connected with the structure of society; social theory therefore forms the main content of contemporary materialism" (p. 24).

Unlike much of European and European American critical theory, which maintains that "the fundamental historical role of economic relations is characteristic of the materialist position," Africana critical theory, and Cabral's contributions in particular, reject "simplistic forms of economic determinism" (Horkheimer, 1972, p. 25; Chabal, 1983a, p. 182).[20] For Cabral, as with Antonio Gramsci in the European tradition of critical theory, ideology and culture are of prime importance alongside economic issues and, as with Georg Lukács of the European tradition, Cabral (1979) admonished and asserted that none of the parts are to be privileged over the whole: "We must at all times see the part *and* the whole" (p. 47, my emphasis).[21] Africana critical theory—employing Cabral's contributions as a point of departure—moreover, refocuses, historicizes, politicizes and, dare I say, *materializes* Africana philosophy. It transcends the narrow confines of abstract, academic philosophy (in black face, or otherwise), and concedes with Lucius Outlaw (1983a) when he asserts that anything that is wont to be termed "Black," "African," "African American," or "Africana" philosophy, needs to be "grounded in the historical struggles of African peoples, in particular, and in the wider struggles of peoples for more reasonable forms of existence, in general" (p. 65; see also Outlaw, 1983b, 1983c, 1983d).

As a materialist social theory, Africana critical theory focuses on actually existing human needs and suffering, the ways in which hegemonic historical and cultural conditions produce suffering, and impede the changes necessary to eliminate human suffering and enable human liberation and social transformation. An emancipatory effort and project such as Africana critical theory requires, and is rooted in (classical and contemporary) critical social theory to the extent that the forementioned theory enables Africana critical theorists to engage and alter the cultural, economic, social and political problems of their present age. With this understanding, Africana critical theory agrees with Horkheimer (1972) when he asserted: "If materialist theory is an aspect of efforts to improve the human situation, it inevitably opposes every attempt to reduce social problems to second place" (p. 26). Diverging, however, from European and European American critical theory, Africana critical theory comprehends that it is not merely "social problems" that must be addressed, but also "social constructions," such as "race."

Africana critical theory begs to differ with Marx and Engels (1978) when they write in the opening lines of the *Communist Manifesto*: "The history of all hitherto existing society is the history of class struggles" (p. 473). Africana critical theory, deeply historicized, knows, first, that as far back as the fifteenth century *race struggles* have also played a significant and determining part in world history as well. One, perhaps, need look no further than Du Bois's *The Negro* (1915), *Black Reconstruction* (1935) and *The World and Africa* (1947); C. L. R. James's *The Black Jacobins* (1938) and *A History of Pan-African Revolt* (1938); Cesaire's *Discourse on Colonialism* (1955); Fanon's *Black Skin, White Masks* (1952) and *The Wretched of the Earth* (1961); Cedric Robinson's *Black Marxism* (2000) and *An Anthropology of Marxism* (2001); Angela Davis' *Women, Race, and Class* (1981); and, bell hooks's *Ain't I A Woman* (1981).

Secondly, Africana critical theory, unlike most Marxist discourse and contemporary European and European American critical theory, comprehends that it is not only race and class struggles that obstruct and impede the improvement of human life-worlds and lived-experiences. Surely gender and sexuality must be considered, amongst other areas and issues. If, indeed, Africana critical theory is to be a viable instrument in the arsenal of the emancipatory efforts of African people to improve human relations and situations, it inevitably must oppose every and any attempt to subvert race, gender, and sexuality (among other areas and issues) to a secondary position with respect to class struggles and economic exploitation. Moreover, Africana critical theory, at bottom a materialist social theory, must ever be marked by its staunch stance of solidarity with suffering human beings, past and present, without regard to their race, gender, class, sexual orientation or religious affiliation. Africana critical theory comprehends—again, in contradistinction to Marx, Engels, and most Marxists and Eurocentric critical theorists—that neither in the "modern" nor in the "postmodern" moment did, or do, human beings enter into "class struggles," and suffer from economic misery, in a raceless, genderless and/or sexual orientation-neutral vacuum. Quite the contrary, human beings as they actually exist may, indeed, have identity crises in connection with the fluctuations and mutations of capitalism and colonialism, but it is simultaneously unfathomable and untenable that upon the eradication of economic exploitation—if solved by some sort of socio-political panacea, say, socialism—racism, sexism, homophobia, and/or heterosexism will come to an immediate and ultimate end.[22]

Africana critical theory attempts to think through, and promote action that will eradicate, current cultural, social and political problems—and particularly, at present, racism, sexism, capitalism, colonialism, and homophobia and/or heterosexism. Africana critical theory, therefore, is not only interested in "social problems," but also, and often more so, in specific ideologies and social constructions of issues that, as exacerbated over the last five hundred years, have lead to, or caused, many of our past and present "social problems."[23] Social problems are, in many instances, the outcomes and effects of ideologies and social constructions. As they are understood in this way, Africana critical theory seeks to wrestle with the causes *and* the effects, as opposed to merely the effects—as it appears to be the case with much of European and European American critical theory (see Horkheimer, 1972, p. 26)—of our past and present "social problems." Africana critical theory, further, aims at *deracinating* social problems, going to their roots—or, *returning to the source*, as Cabral

(1973) would have it—of the phenomenon in order to critically assess and alter it.[24] As a distinct coupling of radical politics and history with philosophy and social theory, Africana critical theory spares no expense in discovering and describing past social constructions and present social problems in terms of how they were developed, how they are developing, and how they ought to be deconstructed and destroyed, and radically replaced with more multicultural, transethnic, transgender, sexuality-sensitive and democratic socialist modes of human experience and human organization. It is in this sense, then, that Africana critical theory appropriates and applies the insights and experiences of Amilcar Cabral as definitive contributions to the construction of a new multicultural, transethnic, transgender, and sexuality-sensitive critical theory of contemporary society.

Cabral, again, was no mere Marxist thinker, and Patrick Chabal (1983a), among others, has reminded us that he was "loath to commit himself to any ideology or theory" (p. 167). Therefore, it should be observed at the outset that Cabral, seemingly unbeknownst to many—if not most—of his critics "always refused to define himself in this way [i.e., as a Marxist] and on most occasions he avoided writing in such terms" (p. 167). Taking this line of thought a little further, Chabal writes:

> Cabral was primarily a man of action. His political leadership is best understood by looking at what he did rather than what he said. His writings were essentially analyses of the events in which he was involved; they were not theories about, or into, abstract social or political questions. He did not view himself as a political theorist although his writings obviously have theoretical relevance. He was loath to commit himself to any ideology or theory. The majority of his writings are party documents and they reflect the very specific purpose and audience for which they were intended. (p. 167)

One of Cabral's most famous essays, "The Weapon of Theory," lucidly reflects "the very specific purpose and audience" for which it was intended, but it also poignantly articulates his unapologetic and extremely innovative deconstruction and reconstruction of Marxist-Leninism to suit the needs of African national liberation struggles. Delivered before the Tricontinental Conference in Havana, Cuba in 1966, "The Weapon of Theory" quickly became one of Cabral's most widely cited texts, partly because in it he critically discussed the impact of imperialism on modern culture and civilization; demonstrated that in Africa colonialism is not only racial but inextricable from European and American capitalism; distinguished between colonialism and neocolonialism; noted the unique role of social classes in colonial and neocolonial societies; and, most importantly, debunked the widely held notion among European and European American Marxists that class struggle was the single and greatest determinant of historical development. With regard to this last and most pivotal point, Cabral's (1979) Marxist heresy began on a rhetorical note and quickly gave way to an audacious and intellectual history-making assertion:

> [D]oes history begin only from the *moment* of the launching of the phenomenon of class and, consequently, of class struggle? To reply in the affirmative would be to place outside of history the whole period of life of human groups from the discovery of hunting, and later of nomadic and sedentary agriculture, to cattle raising and to the private appropriation of land. It would also be to consider—and this we refuse to accept—that various human groups in Africa, Asia and Latin America were living without history or out-

side history at the moment when they were subjected to the yoke of imperialism. . . Our refusal, based as it is on detailed knowledge of the socio-economic reality of our countries and on analysis of the process of development of the phenomenon of class as we saw earlier, leads us to conclude that if class struggle is the motive force of history, it is so in a specific historical period. This means that *before* the class struggle (and, necessarily, *after* the class struggle, since in this world there is no before without an after) some factor (or several factors) was and will be the motive force of history. We have no hesitation in saying that this factor in the history of each group is the *mode of production* (the level of productive forces and the system of ownership) characteristic of that group. But, as we have seen, the definition of class and class struggle are themselves the result of the development of productive forces in conjunction with the system of ownership of the means of production. It therefore seems permissible to conclude that the level of productive forces, the essential determinant of the content and form of class struggle, is the true and permanent motive force of history. (p. 124–125, emphasis in original)

In this passage, when Cabral writes of the "productive forces" and argues that they are "the true and permanent motive force of history," he puts one of the distinct characteristics of his critical theory on display: namely, his dialectical deconstruction and reconstruction of central Marxist-Leninist concepts and categories. He borrowed the term "productive forces" from the Marxist-Leninist lexicon, but by it he meant much more than the relations and forces of production in a strictly economic sense; the very sense, or way in which most Marxist-Leninist have, of course, grossly misinterpreted him. Rather, when Cabral uses "productive forces" above he is referring to all of the cultural, political and economic resources through which the wretched of the earth (re)enter the open-ended process of their distinct historical development. Consequently, "productive forces," as it is used here, encompasses much more than economic issues. It, in a word, represents the sum total of the ways in which, and the means through which, the wretched of the earth return to the sources of their history and culture, which was rudely interrupted by European colonialism *and* capitalism, not to mention the introduction of race and racism.

Above, Cabral also lucidly lambastes the Eurocentrism of Marxist-Leninist conceptions of history, class, and class struggle, audaciously asking: "does history begin only from the moment of the launching of the phenomenon of class and, consequently, of class struggle?" From his optic, to answer this crucial question in the affirmative would be tantamount to believing one of the vilest lies of colonialism; it would be comparable to committing one of the gravest crimes against humanity; it would be the equivalent of saying that the "various human groups in Africa, Asia and Latin America were living without history or outside history at the moment when they were subjected to the yoke of imperialism" and, as he sternly stated, "this we refuse to accept." Cabral resolutely refused to give quarter to colonialism or capitalism and, even more, to the Eurocentrism of Marxism (or Marxist-Leninism). Instead of alleviating human suffering and social misery, it seemed to Cabral (as it does to contemporary Africana critical theorists), that much of Marxist-Leninism, conceptually incarcerated in its Eurocentrism, glosses over the many millions of ways in which its purportedly revolutionary and democratic socialist or communist concepts and categories historically have justified, and continues currently to give grounds for, European imperialism, and specifically the tentacles of racism, colonialism and capitalism in Africa, Asia, and the Americas.

Prior to the horrid history of class and class struggle, and that which provides both class and class struggle with, not simply its economic basis but, in addition, its ontological basis (or bases), according to Cabral, are the "productive forces" of a human group—the historical and material, cultural and economic, axiological and cosmological situation(s) of their inherited life-worlds and lived-experiences. It is, indeed, this crucial, though long-kept, historical and cultural fact of reality that substantiates and reveals itself through the formation of classes and the diabolical dynamics and, dare I say, dialectics of class struggle in the unique history and culture of a specific people. The "history of class struggle," envisaged by Marx, and therefore most Marxists, to be the definitive world-historical, history-making and history-shaping process is actually an extremely particular, if not peculiar, ontic axiom unique to European capitalist modernity (and now European capitalist postmodernity) which has been violently and ubiquitously universalized and ontologized, nauseatingly naturalized and normalized as the history of *all* humanity.[25] Marx and Engels (1978) famously declared in the opening of their *Communist Manifesto*:

> The history of all hitherto existing society is the history of class struggles. Freeman and slave, patrician and plebeian, lord and serf, guild-master and journeyman, in a word, oppressor and oppressed, stood in constant opposition to one another, carried on a uninterrupted, now hidden, now open fight, a fight that each time ended either in a revolutionary re-constitution of society at large, or in the common ruin of the contending classes.
>
> In the earlier epochs of history, we find almost everywhere a complicated arrangement of society into various orders, a manifold gradation of social rank. In ancient Rome we have patricians, knights, plebeians, slaves; in the Middle Ages, feudal lords, vassals, guild-masters, journeymen, apprentices, serfs; in almost all of these classes, again, subordinate gradations.
>
> The modern bourgeois society that has sprouted from the ruins of feudal society has not done away with class antagonisms. It has but established new classes, new conditions of oppression, new forms of struggle in place of the old ones.
>
> Our epoch, the epoch of the bourgeoisie, possesses, however, this distinctive feature: it has simplified the class antagonisms. Society as a whole is more and more splitting up into two great hostile camps, into two great classes directly facing each other: Bourgeoisie and Proletariat. (pp. 473–474)

In essence, Marx and Engels superimposed and, ultimately, universalized the history of *European* class formations and class struggles onto humanity as a whole and, in so doing, rendered the histories and cultures and, perhaps unwittingly I should add, the particular class formations and unique class struggles of non-Europeans, the very "various human groups in Africa, Asia and Latin America" that Cabral mentioned above, either "without history or outside history" until that much-bemoaned and, even more, that howlingly-hated historical "moment when they were subjected to the yoke of [European] imperialism." To be fair to Marx and Engels, they, to their credit, *did* discuss what they termed the "Asiatic mode of production," under which they subsumed the "productive forces" of Africa, Asia, and Latin America.[26] But, besides the superabundance of problems involved in lumping together the disparately unique "productive forces" which each of the aforementioned human groups created in the contexts of their own distinct histories and cultures, Marx and Engels

made a serious mistake in emphasizing the supposedly static character (when compared, of course, to European modern bourgeois society) of non-European and non-
capitalist modes of production. Many of their disciples have interpreted their various analyses of non-European societies as ultimately pointing to a dialectic of
constantly changing political empires but utterly unchanging precapitalist modes of
production, which were only belatedly altered, as the Marxist narrative goes, in light
of European capitalist colonization.

There are, indeed, fundamental tensions when and where Marxists attempt to apply
Marx's materialist concepts and categories to non-European societies and non-capitalist modes of production. The problem lies not in the concepts and categories themselves, and this is a point I should like to emphasize, but with Marxists' inability to
comprehend that though Marx employed a multiplicity of historical models and
methods, many of which indeed *did* acknowledge continuity and discontinuity in
both European and non-European modes of production, his work was particularly
aimed at altering capitalist conditions in Europe and is extremely limited when applied to precolonial, colonial, neocolonial, non-capitalist, and non-European societies. It is ironic to note that Marx himself went through great pains to qualify the concepts and categories he created, seeming to insist that his work was simultaneously
transhistorical and historically specific. A prime passage from the *Grundrisse* reads:

> Bourgeois society is the most developed and the most complex historic organization of
> production. The categories which express its relations, the comprehension of its struc-
> ture, thereby also allows insight into the structure and the relations of production of all
> the vanished social formations out of whose ruins and elements it built itself up, whose
> partly still unconquered remnants are carried along within it, whose mere nuances have
> developed explicit significance within it, etc. Human anatomy contains a key to the
> anatomy of the ape. The intimations of higher development among subordinate animal
> species, however, can be understood only after the higher development is already
> known. The bourgeois economy thus supplies the key to the ancient, etc. But not at all
> in the manner of those economists who smudge over all historical differences and see
> bourgeois relations in all forms of society. One can understand tribute, tithe, etc., if one
> is acquainted with ground rent. But one must not identify them. Further, since bour-
> geois society is itself only a contradictory form of development, relations derived from
> earlier forms will often be found within it only in an entirely stunted form, or even trav-
> estied. For example, communal property. Although it is true, therefore, that the cate-
> gories of bourgeois economics posses a truth for all other forms of society, this is to be
> taken only with a grain of salt. They can contain them in a developed, or stunted, or car-
> icatured form etc., but always with an essential difference. The so-called historical pres-
> entation of development is founded, as a rule, on the fact that the latest form regards the
> previous ones as steps leading up to itself, and, since it is only rarely and only under
> quite specific conditions able to criticize itself—leaving aside, of course, the historical
> periods which appear to themselves as times of decadence—it always conceives them
> one-sidedly. (Marx and Engels, 1978, pp. 241–242)

On the one hand, Marx felt that history was continuous enough to validate projecting an analysis that grew out of a critical interrogation of European modern capitalist societies onto all historical societies. His main contentions can be summa-
rized as follows: (1) in all societies, human beings must be creative and productive
in order to survive; (2) production is the greatest determinant of any given society;

and, consequently, (3) the materialist theory of the modes of production is relevant to an analysis of any and all societies (Marx, 1968; Marx and Engels, 1972). On the other hand, however, Marx seemed to be keenly conscious of the historical (though perhaps not the cultural) differences between various forms of "productive forces" and, what is more, was convinced that there were significant qualifications to be considered when applying materialist theory to the history of precapitalist and non-European social, political, and economic forms. The tensions mentioned above, therefore, are between diachronic and synchronic perspectives in Marx's theory; tough tensions between, first, the view that precapitalist and non-European societies are drastically different from capitalist and European societies in general and, second, tensions between efforts aimed at turning some much-needed light on the inherent flux of human history in general. This conundrum begs several questions: if capitalist and European societies are as unique historically, politically, and economically as Marx and his disciples have never wearied of saying that they are, then, how can the models and analyses developed to explain and alter these unique and historically specific societies be legitimately applied to non-capitalist and non-European societies—nay, any and all societies? Can a diachronic (continuous) historical model, in good (social scientific) conscience, be applied to synchronic (discontinuous) and very varied historical formations, especially when one considers that what Marx is referring to by the term "the Asiatic mode of production" has long constituted the "productive forces" of more than seventy-five percent of the human species? Can all human history be adequately understood from the point of view of capitalist historical development, or the history of class struggle? Can, furthermore, all human history be adequately understood by utilizing a theory that its' adherents, in one breath, openly assert is valid for any and all societies but, in the very next breath, claim is only completely applicable to European capitalist modernity?

The Marxists seem to be caught in a contradiction, one which reveals that they want it both ways: they want to claim the uniqueness of capitalist and European societies and the superiority of their theory for the critique of those societies and, at the same time, they want us to believe that their theory is also the best theory for understanding the historical development of not only "precapitalist" but non-capitalist and non-European societies, the majority of which were racially colonized by the very modern capitalist and European societies that the Marxist promise to provide the most comprehensive and revolutionary critique. Marx and many of his disciples, in point of fact, have erroneously universalized concepts and categories particular to European modernity, and Eurocentric bourgeois capitalism in particular (Abbinnett, 2006; Bartolovich and Lazarus, 2002; Freedman, 2002; Kellner, 1989). In spite of their supposedly judicious and cautious employment of their concepts and categories, Marx and the Marxists have internalized the very bourgeois, reductive and, let me painfully add, racist elements that they so doggedly claim to be working to replace with revolutionary, democratic socialist, and humanist ideals.

Though Marx did analyze the specificity of various types of production and labor, he consistently reduced all forms of human interaction and human practice to the capitalist production model; this production model, in a word, ultimately served as Marx's measure for all other production models. While he was correct in arguing that all human societies produce the means by which, and through which, they sustain and develop themselves, he was completely incorrect in over-emphasizing and projecting economic issues onto non-capitalist and non-European social, political, and cultural forms by analytically absorbing them into a mélange theory preoccupied with the "mode of production" which *a priori* allotted and strongly stressed economic relations and values. The ways in which he privileged production over and against other forms of social, political, and cultural action and interaction was, in a word, arbitrary, if not irrational from the point of view of various non-European cultures and civilizations. In many non-capitalist and non-European societies, for instance, economic issues are inextricably interrelated with a wide-range of social, political, cultural and—an area many Marxists appear woefully uninformed about—religious or spiritual factors. In fact, often the overlap between economic, social, political and cultural issues (again, including religious issues) is so substantively interwoven in non-European societies that they are, in many regards, inseparable.

What if global human history is much more localized and fragmented than Marx's historical materialism has led so many Marxists, among others, to believe? What if non-European cultures and civilizations were much more complex and complicated than Marx and his followers ever possibly imagined? What if his very valiant efforts to produce a historical materialist retrospective reading of human history from the standpoint of *his* epoch—that is, the dynamics of European bourgeois capitalist modernity and European capitalist colonization of Africa, Asia, and the Americas—have helped to not simply produce but perpetuate an imaginary or fictitious line of continuity that somehow panoramically stretches from the beginning of human history to the present, all the while purportedly demonstrating the primacy of production and class struggle, even though he is admittedly aware of historical discontinuities which simultaneously predate capitalism and were also exacerbated by the onslaught of capitalism? Marx and the admirers of his historical materialism seem to be in a serious double-bind: if historical materialism is dogmatically applied—in the totalizing fashion in which so many postmodernists and post-Marxists have criticized its application—to *all* human history, then Marx and Marxism is transformed into an ahistorical and reductive ideology (as opposed to theory, especially a critical theory) that is, in fact, not only irrational from the point of view of non-European histories and cultures but, to put it very plainly, racist or, at the least, extremely Eurocentric; if, on the contrary, Marx and the Marxists go through great pains to openly admit and present qualification after qualification concerning the limited range and reach of their theory with regard to non-European and non-capitalist societies, they will logically weaken the explanatory power of what is supposed to be one of the greatest critical, global theories of human history ever produced (Baldacchino, 1996; Barrow, 1993; Donham, 1990; Geras, 1990; Goldstein, 2005; McLennan, 1981; Mouzelis, 1990; Perry, 2002; E.O. Wright, 1992).

In light of all of this, Cabral concluded that Marxism had only a limited applicability (if certain aspects of it were applicable at all) when and where Africa, Asia, and the Americas were concerned. Africa, Asia, and the Americas' precolonial histories were not simply "the history of class struggle," or the precapitalist past leading up to European capitalist modernity and European racist capitalist colonization. Much more, they represent these human groups hard-won right to self-determination and self-definition, and this can be said while earnestly and simultaneously solemnly acknowledging the internal conflicts, ethnic feuds, infighting, political pitfalls, cultural crises, religious rivalries and, it must be admitted, forms of non-racial colonization and exploitation that existed in each and, in many instances, between each of the aforementioned human groups and their histories and societies prior to the introduction of European imperialism. According to Cabral, Marxist historical materialism is merely one of many methods that can, and in certain instances he argued *should*, be employed in efforts to critically comprehend the past, alter the present, and provide the hope for a liberated future.

Cape Verde and Guinea-Bissau, indeed, did have classes and class struggle, Cabral readily admitted, but he quickly qualified this assertion by pointing out that in the face of European racial colonialism Cape Verdean and Guinea-Bissaun class struggle, which had been paralyzed as a result of Portuguese domination, was not the motive force of history. When Marx and Engels declared, "Our epoch, the epoch of the bourgeoisie, possesses, however, this distinctive feature: it has simplified the class antagonisms. Society as a whole is more and more splitting up into two great hostile camps, into two great classes directly facing each other: Bourgeoisie and Proletariat," Cabral observed that though Cape Verde and Guinea-Bissau had non-capitalist precolonial classes and class struggles, as a consequence of European racial colonialism these long-warring classes had to, in fact, unite and fight against the European racist capitalist colonization of their homelands; a form of colonization which, if truth be told, benefited both the European bourgeoisie *and* proletariat. As Sartre (1968) succinctly put it in his preface to Fanon's *The Wretched of the Earth*: "With us [i.e., Europeans], to be a man is to be an accomplice of colonialism, since all of us without exception have profited by colonial exploitation" (p. 25). Directly discussing the "contradictions" spawned by European imperialism in a seminar he taught at the Frantz Fanon Center in Treviglio, Milan in 1964, Cabral (1972) importantly explained the ways in which Portuguese colonialism impacted the ethnic, cultural and class composition of Guinea-Bissau:

> There are contradictions which we consider secondary: you may be surprised to know that we consider the contradictions between the tribes a secondary one; we could discuss this at length, but we consider that there are many more contradictions between what you might call the economic tribes in the capitalist countries than there are between the ethnic tribes in Guinea. Our struggle for national liberation and the work done by our party have shown that this contradiction is really not so important; the Portuguese counted on it a lot but as soon as we organized the liberation struggle properly the contradiction between the tribes proved to be a feeble, secondary contradiction. This does not mean that we do not need to pay attention to this contradiction; we reject both the positions which are to be found in Africa—one which says: there are no tribes, we are all the same, we are all one people in one terrible unity, our party comprises everybody; the other saying: tribes exist, we must base parties on tribes. Our position lies between the two, but at the same time we are fully conscious that this is a problem which must constantly be kept in mind; structural, organizational and other measures must be taken to ensure that this contradiction does not explode and become a more important contradiction. (pp. 64–65)

The "contradictions" which Marx and Engels identified in European bourgeois society simply did not speak to the economic, social, political, and cultural realities of African (Cape Verdean and Guinea Bissaun) colonial society. The struggle against the capitalist colonization (and racialization) of Africa, which is to say the revolutionary decolonization struggle, lead to a process of conscious re-Africanization, which in turn gave way to a distinct revolutionary nationalism; a form of re-Africanization and revolutionary nationalism that, amazingly, seemed to rush forth from the bloodstained pages of Fanon's *The Wretched of the Earth*, especially the well-known passage where he stated: "Decolonization is the veritable creation of new men. But this creation owes nothing of its legitimacy to any supernatural power; the 'thing' which has been colonized becomes man during the same process by which it frees itself" (1968, pp. 36–37). Cabral went one step further and, as a revolutionary nationalist, contended that not only do the colonized who actively participate in revolutionary decolonization reclaim their long-denied humanity but—and this is one of the many points that distinguishes Cabral's contributions from Fanon's—he argued that they also reclaim their Africanity and, even more, in the process of revolutionary decolonization the formerly colonized forge a new national identity, consciously breaching and going far beyond precolonial or traditional "ethnic tribes," culture, politics, and social organization. Eloquently further explaining this issue to an African American audience in New York in 1972, only months before his assassination, Cabral (1973) candidly stated:

> Ten years ago [prior to the national liberation struggle], we were Fula, Mandjak, Mandinka, Balante, Pepel, and others. Now we are a nation of Guineans. Tribal divisions were one reason the Portuguese thought it would not be possible for us to fight. During these ten years we were making more and more changes, so that today we can see that there is a new man and a new woman, born with our new nation and because of our fight. This is because of our ability to fight as a nation. (pp. 78–79)

This means, then, that European capitalism in its racial colonial guise had the exact opposite effect in many parts of Africa (and we could also include Asia and the Americas) than Marx related that it did on European societies: it, indeed, did simplify "class antagonisms," but instead of it "splitting up" precolonial African classes "into two great hostile camps," in many instances, it caused them to combine into one anti-colonial *race-class* and nation-state to combat European racist capitalist colonization. European colonialism forced Africans out of their history and into European racist capitalist and colonial history. It arrested the development not only of Cape Verde and Guinea-Bissau's class formations and class struggles but, even more, it halted their "productive forces" and violently forced them to produce what Europe wanted them to produce, using the modes of production that Europe brutally demanded that they use. Cabral (1972) spoke in the most unequivocal terms on this issue in his groundbreaking essay, "Brief Analysis of the Social Structure in Guinea":

> There is a preconception held by many people, even on the left, that imperialism made us enter history at the moment when it began its adventure in our countries. This preconception must be denounced: for somebody on the left, and for Marxists in particular, history obviously means the class struggle. Our opinion is exactly the contrary. We consider that when imperialism arrived in Guinea it made us leave history—our history. We agree that history in our country is the result of class struggle, but we have our own class struggles in our own country; the moment imperialism arrived and colonialism arrived, it made us leave our history and enter another history. Obviously we agree that

the class struggle has continued, but it has continued in a very different way: our whole people is struggling against the ruling class of the imperialist countries, and this gives a completely different aspect to the historical evolution of our country. Somebody has asked which class is the "agent" of history; here a distinction must be drawn between colonial history and our history as human societies; as a dominated people we only present an ensemble vis-à-vis the oppressor. Each of our peoples or groups of peoples has been subjected to different influences by the colonizers; when there is a developed national consciousness one may ask which social stratum is the agent of history, of colonial history; which is the stratum which will be able to take power into its hands when it emerges from colonial history? Our answer is that it is all the social strata, if the people who have carried out the national revolution (i.e., the struggle against colonialism) have worked well, since unity of all the social strata is a prerequisite for the success of the national liberation struggle. As we see it, in colonial conditions no one stratum can succeed in the struggle for national liberation on its own, and therefore it is all the strata of society which are the agents of history. This brings us to what should be a void—but in fact it is not. What commands history in colonial conditions is not the class struggle. I do not mean that the class struggle in Guinea stopped completely during the colonial period; it continued, but in a muted way. In the colonial period it is the colonial state which commands history. (pp. 68–69, emphasis in original)

The harsh reality of Europe's capitalist-inspired colonization of Africa, when all is said and done, is nothing other than the violent superimposition of European history and culture on, over, and against African history and culture. It represents, in another sense, the debilitation and, ultimately, the destruction of indigenous "productive forces," which, after the initial onslaught of colonialism, are colonized and altered to suit the wishes and whims of the colonizers and their kith and kin in Europe and America. The national liberation struggle, when viewed from the perspective of the dominated people, is a struggle which has as one of its major goals the freeing of the "productive forces," which, as Cabral asserted above, would enable the colonized to rescue, reclaim, and rehabilitate their culture, thus, not only stepping back onto the stage of human history but, also, continuing their own unique contributions to human culture and civilization.

In the process of decolonization, the colonized become "new men" and "new women," as Cabral put it. This is so, partly, because they relax ethnic, local and regional distinctions in favor of a new *transethnic* and *multicultural* national identity, forged through their fight(s) as a race-class and an emerging nation-state against European capitalist colonization (and racialization). Where class (and clan) struggle may have previously been the motive force of Guinea-Bissaun history, now, in light of European racist capitalist colonization and African revolutionary decolonization and re-Africanization, it is race-class struggle, colonizer against colonized, that is the central history-making and history-shaping force. Cabral correctly "denounced" the superimposition of Eurocentric Marxist concepts and categories—such as, class struggle as the motive force of history and the proletariat as the authentic agents of historical change and the true ushers of socialism (or, communism)—onto the national liberation struggle in Guinea-Bissau and Cape Verde. He contended that there was no substitute for conceptual and categorial generation which grew out of the specific historical and cultural grounds of the African, and, more particularly, the Cape Verdean and Guinea-Bissaun revolutionary decolonization struggle.

In "Brief Analysis of the Social Structure of Guinea," Cabral developed a systematic analysis of the various ethnic groups and cultures that collectively constitute Guinea-Bissau. Early in the essay it can be easily detected that its objective is not to impose Marxist or any other (imported or indigenous) so-called "radical" or "revolutionary" concepts and categories onto the national liberation struggle and conjecture, or attempt to theoretically justify, a preconception of how their historically and culturally specific revolution should or should not develop. Instead, Cabral dug deep into Guinea-Bissaun precolonial history and culture and developed a detailed descriptive analysis that critically outlined: the class systems of the various ethnic communities; their distinct traditional social, political, economic and religious structures; the traditional and precolonial position of women in each of the societies; their relationship with the land, ancestral and otherwise; their relations with each other, noting traditional good and bad relations; their relations with the colonizers (i.e., the Portuguese); and, how this impacted each ethnic groups' way of life, political organization, and potential or concrete contributions to national liberation.

Against the generalizations of the Marxists and their Eurocentric historical materialism, Cabral emphasized "the concrete conditions of the life of our people" and the "concrete reality" of "our history" and "our own country," which, as he painstakingly demonstrated in "Brief Analysis of the Social Structure of Guinea," had its own distinct and extremely complex history and culture which Marxism did not completely or adequately address. Once he came to this conclusion, and once he was able to convince many of his more Marxist-minded colonized African comrades to accept this essential presupposition, then, he emphasized that their struggle could only be correctly comprehended as a "concrete" attempt to provide solutions to the problems peculiar to their specific history, culture and "colonial condition." His critical theory was simultaneously descriptive and explorative of the "concrete" possibilities available to the racially colonized in Cape Verde and Guinea-Bissau. It took the life-worlds and lived-experiences of the simultaneously racialized and colonized people of Cape Verde and Guinea-Bissau as its theoretical and practical points of departure, not the so-called "radical" or "revolutionary" theories that were devised and developed to liberate non-racialized and non-colonized workers in European capitalist countries.

From the foregoing analysis we can deduce several points of significance. First, and I feel as though I should say "and, for the record," Cabral was not a Marxist, orthodox or otherwise; in fact, as I have been arguing throughout this chapter, his theory and praxis seem to fall more in the realm of black radical politics and Africana critical social theory. Secondly, and as supported above by Chabal (1983a), Cabral's critical theory symbolizes a concrete philosophy (i.e., a materialist theory) insofar as it is not concerned with "theories about, or inquiries into, abstract social or political questions." Cabral, the "man of action," as Chabal put it, was "unlike many other revolutionary leaders" in that he was "never a member of a Marxist or communist party" (p. 167). Finally, what is little known, and what Chabal brings to the fore in his analysis, is the fact that "Cabral is first and foremost a nationalist. Nationalism, not communism, was his cause," by which I take Chabal to be speaking of Cabral's *revolutionary nationalism*, as his nationalism was not in any way xenophobic or jingoistic and constantly dovetailed with his *revolutionary internationalism* and his *revolutionary humanism* (p. 168; see also Chilcote, 1984; Davidson, 1984). One of the best examples of Cabral's (1972) revolutionary nationalism is revealed in his opening address to the Conference of Nationalist Organizations of Portuguese Colonies (CONCP) held in Dar es Salaam, Tanzania in 1965, where he declared:

> In Africa we are all for the complete liberation of the African continent from the colonial yoke, for we know that colonialism is an instrument of imperialism. So we want to see all manifestations of imperialism totally wiped out on the soil of Africa; in the CONCP we are fiercely opposed to neo-colonialism, whatever its form. Our struggle is not only against Portuguese colonialism; in the framework of our struggle we want to make the most effective contribution possible to the complete elimination of foreign domination in our continent. (p. 80)

Here, it must be observed that Cabral's revolutionary nationalism is tempered by an implicit and inevitable (considering his personal disposition) revolutionary humanism; a humanism that neither starts nor stops with color, culture, or continent; a humanism that unequivocally challenges what Sartre (1968) termed the "racist humanism" of Europe, "since the European has only been able to become man through creating slaves and monsters" (p. 26; see also Champigny, 1972; Gordon, 1995a).[27] Cabral's political views and values were based on ethical and moral principles, not biology (i.e., without regard to race and/or ethnicity). This is precisely why Luiz Cabral—Amilcar's biological brother and comrade in the African anti-imperialist struggle—stated that he, Amilcar Cabral, was opposed to, and driven to action against, colonial domination, and particularly Portuguese colonial domination, not only because he considered himself an African, but because of what he understood to be the demands of justice (see Chabal, 1983a, p. 168). In this sense, then, it is easy to understand why Cabral (1972) would assert:

> In Africa, we are for an African policy which seeks to defend first and foremost the interests of African peoples of each African country, but also for a policy which does not, at any time, forget the interests of the world, of all humanity. We are for a policy of peace in Africa and of fraternal collaboration with all the peoples of the world . . . we consider ourselves to be deeply committed to our people and committed to every just cause in the world. We see ourselves as part of a vast front of struggle for the good of humanity. . . . We in the CONCP are fiercely in solidarity with every just cause. (p. 81)

And, for those who would quickly label Cabral just another starry-eyed utopian democratic socialist, he goes further to identify exactly which "just causes" he and the member-movements of the CONCP stand in solidarity with; in so doing he, also, demonstrates his revolutionary internationalism. This is an important move on his part, as it concretizes his revolutionary humanism, enabling others to see precisely what is meant by "real," as opposed to "racist," as Sartre said, humanism. Cabral compassionately continued:

> That is why our hearts, in FRELIMO, in MPLA, in the PAIGC, in the CLSTP, in all the mass organizations affiliated to the CONCP, beat in unison with the hearts of our brothers in Vietnam who are giving us a shining example by facing the most shameful and unjustifiable aggression of the U.S. imperialists against the peaceful people of Vietnam.

Our hearts are equally with our brothers in the Congo who, in the bush of that vast and rich African country are seeking to resolve their problems in the face of imperialist aggression and of the maneuvers of imperialism through their puppets. . . . Our hearts are also with our brothers in Cuba, who have shown that even when surrounded by the sea, a people is capable of taking up arms and successfully defending its fundamental interests and of deciding its own destiny. We are with the Blacks of North America, we are with them in the streets of Los Angeles, and when they are deprived of all possibility of life, we suffer with them. We are with the refugees, the martyrized refugees of Palestine, who have been tricked and driven from their own homeland by the maneuvers of imperialism. We are on the side of the Palestinian refugees and we support whole-heartedly all that the sons of Palestine are doing to liberate their country, and we fully support the Arab and African countries in general in helping the Palestinian people to recover their dignity, their independence and the right to live. We are also with the peoples of Southern Arabia, of so-called "French" Somaliland, of so-called "Spanish" Guinea, and we are also most seriously and painfully with our brothers in South Africa who are facing the most barbarous racial discrimination. (pp. 81–82)

Here is Cabral's revolutionary humanism, as well as his revolutionary internationalism, in bold relief. For those who would hurriedly huddle him into this or that ideological camp, it would be prudent to bare in mind the fact that Cabral said what he said, and did what he did, with a critical self-reflexive understanding of himself and the African anti-imperialist struggle as "part of a vast front of struggle for the good of humanity." Cabral was keenly concerned about, and felt deeply connected and committed to revolutionary humanist ideals. It was "concrete conditions," "concrete reality," and actually existing, suffering human beings, much more than ideas and abstract philosophies, that stirred and moved Cabral and his comrades to action. With regard to his supposed "Marxism," it must be said that when and where socialism and/or communism did attract Amilcar Cabral, it did so not because of its theoretical, historical and/or cultural connections with Karl Marx, or any other Marxist theorist or specific school of Marxist thought, but because it promised to improve the quality and "concrete conditions" of human life, and especially continental and diasporan African life-worlds and lived-experiences.[28]

For Cabral, as it was for Du Bois, James, Cesaire, Senghor, and Fanon, Marxism was engaged as more of a methodology than an ideology. Cabral aspired to radically transform material, actually existing, "concrete conditions," and for that reason Marxism offered him one of the most dialectically sophisticated theories of social and material transformation. In regard to the "materialist" aspects of Marxism, and specifically the Frankfurt School of Marxist thought, perhaps few have captured this conception better than Horkheimer (1972) in his essay, "Metaphysics and Materialism," and especially when he wrote: "The theoretical activity of humans, like the practical, is not the independent knowledge of a fixed object, but a product of ever-changing reality" (p. 29). The problem, Cabral would contend, is not one of an "ever-changing reality"—indeed, that is understood and to be expected—but, of external imperial forces and internal enemies prompting and promoting change(s) in racially colonized peoples' reality in relation to imperial interests. Cabral and Horkheimer are, to a certain extent, at loggerheads, but perhaps not on all accounts, as we shall see.

A materialist social theory, particularly the kind that Cabral and Horkheimer subscribed to, understands that as historical and cultural conditions change, concepts and theories, perhaps even the very nature of conceptual generation and the sites and sources of radical and revolutionary knowledge production, must also change. Thus, materialist social theory, prefiguring postmodernism, among other contemporary discourse, understood as far back as Karl Marx and W. E. B. Du Bois, that there is no single, stable foundation for absolutist metaphysical views. Cabral, in particular, understood that concepts and theories are not organs of absolute knowledge, but merely instruments for achieving certain goals, which are to be developed and modified constantly in the course of lived-experience and life-struggles.[29] This is, of course, why he correctly stated:

> We cannot, from our experience, claim that Marxism-Leninism must be modified—that would be presumptuous. What we must do is to modify, to radically transform, the political, economic, social and cultural conditions of our people . . . we have to create and develop in our particular situation the solution for our country. (Cabral, 1971, p. 22)

When and where Cabral discerned Marxist theory to be applicable to his specific African (read also: human) situation, he employed it. When and where he understood it to be inapplicable or irrelevant, he augmented, amended, or—as in many cases—abandoned it; much as he, similar to Du Bois, believed outdated social scientific theories should be dispensed with. Cabral's (1972) point of departure was ever his "particular situation," but he never lost sight of the fact that his "particular situation" was "only one aspect of the general struggle of the oppressed peoples [of the world] against imperialism," and of human beings' "struggle for dignity, freedom, and progress" (p. 79). Marxist-Leninism, for Cabral, was merely a methodology, and many, critically misunderstanding this crucial point, have attempted to convert it into Cabral's "ideology." Furthermore, many may have misinterpreted Cabral's materialism as a form of Marxism, but it should be made known that Cabral (1971) remarked at a meeting in London in 1971:

> People here [in Europe] are very preoccupied with questions—are you or are you not a Marxist? Are you a Marxist-Leninist? Just ask me, please, whether we are doing well in the field. Are we really liberating our people, the human beings in our country from all forms of oppression? Ask me simply this and draw your own conclusions . . . Marx, when he created Marxism, was not a member of a tribal [read: "underdeveloped," racially colonized African] society; I think there's no necessity for us to be more Marxist than Marx or more Leninist than Lenin in the application of their theories. (pp. 22, 46)[30]

We may conclude, then, that Amilcar Cabral (1979) was not a Marxist or a Marxist-Leninist, but an African revolutionary who devoted his entire adult life to "put[ting] an end to all injustices, miseries and suffering" (p. 77).[31] As an African materialist, not a Marxist, Cabral understood that each struggling society and civilization must develop—purifying itself through the furious flames of trail and error—its own solution(s) to its own epochal issues, and in that respect—as Fanon (1967, p. 104) said of the "discoveries" of Freud—the insights and experiences of Marx, Lenin, Mao, Minh, Guevara, Castro, and their disciples "are of no use to us here." Why? Because Cabral (1979) knew that "on the political level—however fine and attractive the reality of others may be—we can only truly transform our own reality, on the basis of detailed knowledge of it and our own efforts and sacrifices" (p. 122). It is in this sense, then, that Cabral contended that "[a] very important aspect of a national liberation struggle is that those who lead the struggle must never confuse what they have in their heads with reality" (p. 45). On this point, Cabral and Horkheimer, as materialists as opposed to Marxists, connect. Echoing Cabral, Horkheimer (1972) maintained: "Materialism, unlike idealism, always understands thinking to be the thinking of particular men within a particular period of time. It challenges every claim to the autonomy of thought" (p. 32).

## CABRAL'S CRITICAL (RE)TURN TO THE SOURCE(S) AND THE NEXUSES OF NATIONAL LIBERATION, NATIONAL HISTORY, AND NATIONAL CULTURE

Cabral believed culture to be a fundamental, determining, and defining aspect of a peoples' history. He stated: "Whatever may be the ideological or idealistic characteristics of cultural expression, culture is an essential element of the history of a people" (Cabral, 1973, p. 42). In fact, for Cabral, history and culture were inextricable because history, on the one hand, "allows us to know the nature and extent of the imbalances and the conflicts (economic, political, and social) that characterize the evolution of a society" (p. 42). Culture, on the other hand, "plunges its roots into the physical [read: material] reality of the environmental humus in which it develops, and it reflects the organic nature of the society, which may be more or less influenced by external factors" (p. 42).[32] Culture, also, exposes and enables human groups to engage "the dynamic syntheses which have been developed and established by social conscience to resolve these conflicts at each stage of its evolution, in the search for survival and progress" (p. 42). It is in this special sense, then, that Cabral (1979) contended: "To speak about this [national liberation] is to speak of history but it is likewise to speak of culture" (p. 142). Hence, national liberation is simultaneously "an act of culture" (p. 141), and an act of historical reclamation and reconstruction—a "return to the source," that is, a return to our own "cultural personality" (p. 143) and "reality" (read: history)—"in the service of progress" (p. 148). In this section it is my intention to interpret and explicate Cabral's conception of national liberation and its connections to national history and national culture. I shall focus specifically on two of Cabral's more sophisticated and systematic essays in order to carry out this critical analysis: "National Liberation and Culture" (1973, pp. 39–56, 1979, pp. 138–154) and "Identity and Dignity in the Context of the National Liberation Struggle" (1973, pp. 57–74).

As observed in the preceding paragraph, Cabral's concept of culture was inextricable from his understanding of history. History, for Cabral, is the narrative of the "imbalances and conflicts (economic, political and social)" that have, and continue to shape and characterize the development of a society. And, culture is a series of "dynamic syntheses which have been developed and established" to solve and resolve social and political conflicts at each stage in the evolution of a society. Cabral (1979) emphasized the elasticity and durability of culture even in the face of colonialism:

One of the most serious mistakes, if not the most serious mistake, made by the colonial powers in Africa, may have been to ignore or underestimate the cultural strength of

African peoples. This attitude is particularly clear in the case of Portuguese colonial domination, which was not content with denying absolutely the existence of cultural values of the African and his condition as a social being, but has persisted in forbidding him any kind of political activity. (pp. 147–148)

The colonizers confused *repression* with *destruction*. To repress the colonized peoples' culture is not to destroy their culture; it is quite simply, among other things, an attempt to denounce, denude, and degrade it. But, denying something or, even more, distorting something does not destroy it, it merely means that one has chosen, perhaps, to ignore or negatively characterize an actually existing, concrete fact or form or force. However, in response to this conundrum, Cabral contended that the capacity for "cultural resistance" by African (and other racially colonized) people "was not destroyed" (p. 148). On the contrary, "African culture, though repressed, persecuted and betrayed by some social categories [or social classes] who compromised with colonialism, survived all the storms, by taking refuge in the villages, in the forests and in the spirit of generations of victims of colonialism" (p. 148). It was Cabral's distinct belief that the real potential for anti-colonial revolution, which is to say "national liberation," rested on the ironic fact that the great majority of the racially colonized people, the wretched of the earth, had only marginally been affected, if at all, by colonial culture. Deep in the forests, in the most rural and remote parts of Guinea-Bissau the semi-colonized retained and, often, recreated their cultures and reinvented ethnic identities. Cabral asserted that it was these untapped aspects of precolonial and traditional culture that should be built on in the interest of developing anti-colonial, cultural, and a new "national" transethnic consciousness.

The development of consciousness, in Cabral's conceptual universe, is inextricable from ideological development and critical conceptual generation. Cabral—in some senses similar to Antonio Gramsci, the Frankfurt School, and other European and European American critical theorists—comprehended that just as the ruling race, gender, and/or class produces ideas and theories which support their oppressing, exploiting, and alienating established (dis)order, racially colonized and dominated groups can and often *do*, as Patricia Collins (1996, p. 227, 1998, p. x) relates, produce "alternative" and "oppositional" knowledges and ideologies. For Cabral, as Carlos Lopes (1987) has pointed out,

ideology was above all knowing what one wanted in one's own particular circumstances . . . ideological strength is built by knowing what must be done in each specific situation. This does not prevent, but rather requires, a drawing on the scientific laws of historical evolution of societies. But one must always be alert to the *concrete reality of the moment*. (pp. 57–58, emphasis in original)

This is a point that has direct relevance for the discussion at hand concerning the development of Africana critical theory and Africana philosophy. First, one of the greatest challenges Cabral presents to Africana critical theory and, especially, Africana philosophy is that they constantly and self-reflexively concretize, historicize and politicize, and attempt to grasp and grapple with the world as it actually exists, that is, "the concrete reality of [their] moment." That is to say, following the best that Du Bois, James, Cesaire, Senghor, Fanon and Cabral, among others, offer to radical politics and critical social theory, contemporary Africana philosophers and Africana critical theorists must be willing and able to decidedly break with abstract academic, arbitrarily discipline-bound, epistemically insular, and often almost exclusively European- and European American-derived discourses. If, and I humbly pray *when*, this is done, it is hoped that workers in Africana philosophy and Africana critical theory will produce critical thought and texts that will prompt and promote critical consciousness-raising and radical political activity that, ultimately, leads to *revolutionary praxis* that will enable us to, not simply describe and interpret the world but, in the spirit of Cabral, positively and progressively engage and alter it in the best interests of continental and diasporan Africans and humanity as a whole.

Secondly, Cabral's concept of ideology was concrete and situation-specific. Which is, of course, why he remarked and reminded us: "Marx . . . was not a member of a tribal [read: traditional African or racially colonized African] society" and that, in point of fact, "Marxism is not a religion, and Marx did not write about Africa" (Cabral, 1971, pp. 21–22). That being said, Cabral, to an extent, acknowledged that he took Fanon's (1968) challenge very seriously when the latter asserted: "Marxist analysis should always be slightly stretched every time we have to do with the colonial problem. Everything up to and including the very nature of pre-capitalist society, so well explained by Marx must here be thought out again" (p. 40).

Cabral comprehended, as Kellner (1995) claims the Frankfurt School and other European and European American critical theorists understood, or understand, that first and foremost, "there has never been a unitary Marxian theory that has been the basis for socialist [or any other purportedly 'democratic' and/or egalitarian type of] development" (p. 6). Also, Marxist and/or any other so-called "radical" theory must, of necessity, be open to revision and reconstruction as new and novel historical, cultural, social and political situations and circumstances present themselves to local and global, national and international societies and civilizations. And, finally, Cabral understood—considering the "deficiencies" in and of Marxist theory, as discussed above with respect to "underdeveloped" and/or non-European societies— that it may very well be that our "new times" (to borrow from Stuart Hall [1996a, pp. 223–238]) require not merely revision and reconstruction of "modern" and/or "postmodern" theory, but an all together "new" critical theory to speak to the special needs of contemporary society and the world of the twenty-first century.

In advocating a "new" critical theory, I essentially have in mind a contemporary descriptive and proscriptive, dialectical and discerning, praxis-promoting social theory that does not simply chronicle and critique current crises, situations and circumstances, but acknowledges the necessity of its own internal development, self-critique, and self-correction in light of these new and novel crises, situations, and circumstances. It is an epistemically and existentially open-ended theory of contemporary society, which side-steps the intellectual insularity of much of European and European American critical theory, and attempts to engage and eradicate our current social ills; say, for instance, racism, sexism, capitalism, colonialism, homophobia/heterosexism and religious intolerance, among other issues and areas of contemporary imperialism. This "new" critical theory should build on and go beyond not solely European and European American critical theory, but must also, out of exigency and urgency, be willing and able to engage the critical theory produced by, and on behalf of, the non-European and non-white world, its radical political activists, critical social theorists and, most importantly, its working-classes and masses. In somewhat plainer English: the "new" critical theory, which our "new times" demand, should base its descriptions, prescriptions, and proscriptions on *all* available radical and revolutionary sources and, if truth be told, both European *and* non-European traditions of critical theory have much to offer.

As Stuart Hall (1996a) has correctly observed, our "new times" make it mandatory that contemporary critical theorists be conscious of changes "out there" *and* "in here" (p. 226). "[O]ut there," meaning, perhaps, "out there" in the jungles of " 'post' everything" (p. 224); or, "out there" in the world of white hegemony and (subtle) white supremacy, "ethnic absolutism" and "cultural racism" (pp. 468, 442); or, "out there" where "cultural bureaucracies" attempt to administer all aspects of public and private life, and human thought and behavior (p. 470). And, by "in here," we are wont to take Hall to mean, "in here" where political boundaries are often blurred, and some critical theorists remain undaunted and bold enough to contest and combat "cultural racism," "cultural hegemony," and "cultural bureaucracies" (pp. 468, 470); "in here" where there exists those whose critical theories represent a very real "ethnicization," "feminization," and "sexualization" of radical theory and politics; and, perhaps, "in here" where it is understood that there can be "no simple 'return' or 'recovery' of the ancestral past which is not re-experienced through categories of the present: no base for creative enunciation in a simple reproduction of traditional forms which are not transformed by the technologies and identities of the present" (p. 448).

Contemporary critical theory should, among other things, get involved in the "debate[s] about how society is changing" and "offer new descriptions and analyses of the social conditions it seeks to transcend and transform" (p. 223). Also, critical theories of contemporary society should, on the one hand, hear and heed Cabral (1979), especially when he asserts: "Experience of the struggle shows how utopian and absurd it is to seek to apply schemes developed by other peoples in the course of their liberation struggle and solutions which they found to the questions [and problems] with which they were or are confronted, without considering local reality (and especially cultural reality)" (p. 151). We must also be cognizant of Cabral's contention that anything that is wont to be labeled "critical" and "theory" needs to be an ongoing synthesis, drawing from, and hopefully contributing to, the best of contemporary radical politics and critical social theory and praxis.

On the other hand, the "new" critical theory should, to a certain extent, acknowledge and advocate with Horkheimer and Kellner that, first, critical theory must "never aim simply at an increase of knowledge as such. Its goal is man's emancipation from slavery" (Horkheimer, 1972, p. 245). And, second, with that understood, contemporary critical theory must come to accept that "classical" and orthodox Marxists and Marxism exaggerated the primacy of class and, in almost every instance, downplayed the salience of race, gender, sexuality, and other cultural and identity issues, areas, and/or arenas. In Kellner's (1995) candid words:

> Clearly, oppression takes place in many more spheres than just the economic and the workplace, so a radical politics of the future should take account of gender and race as well as class. Nonetheless, it would be wrong to ignore the centrality of class and the importance of class politics. But, a radical politics today should be more multicultural, race

and gender focused, and broad-based than the original Marxian [and Western European critical] theory. (p. 20)

Cabral contributes to Africana and European critical theory in light of the fact that his thought accents and emphasizes the ways in which national liberation—what Horkheimer above phrased "man's emancipation from slavery"—is predicated on the struggling peoples' understanding that "both in colonialism and in neocolonialism the essential characteristic of imperialist domination remains the same—denial of the historical process of the dominated people, by means of violent usurpation of the freedom of the process of development of the national productive forces" (Cabral, 1979, pp. 129–130). It is the "denial of the historical process of the dominated people," in economic, cultural, social, political, and other areas and arenas, which validates and legitimates the national liberation struggle. Because, the national liberation struggle is nothing other than the phenomena and process(es) by which a social, political, economic, and cultural group or class rejects the denial and derogation of its history and heritage. Recall, it was Cabral who audaciously asserted: "self-determination for all peoples, each people must choose their destiny, [and] take it into their own hands" (p. 63).[33] In other words, "the national liberation of a people is the regaining of the historical personality of that people, it is their return to history through the destruction of the imperialist domination to which they were subjected" (p. 130).

Deconstruction and reconstruction, as was noted in the Negritude chapter, are leitmotifs in Africana philosophical and critical theoretical discourse, and as Lucius Outlaw (1996a) has observed, considering the "European incursions into Africa" and the subsequent "enslavement and colonization" of African peoples, and the "domination by Europeans of African lands and resources," efforts to fashion an "African"—and I would add "Africana"—philosophy, "pose both deconstructive and reconstructive challenges" (pp. 52–53). In my view, Cabral's concept of national liberation puts forward such challenges because it is simultaneously an act of history and an act of culture. With regard to national liberation as a pivotal historical moment, Cabral (1979) stated: "the basis of national liberation, whatever the formulas adopted in international law, is the inalienable right of every people to have their own history; and the aim of national liberation is to regain this right usurped by imperialism, that is to free the process of development of the national productive forces" (p. 130). Concerning national liberation as an act of culture, Cabral understands that imperialist domination, by "denying . . . the dominated people their own historical process, necessarily denies their cultural process" (p. 142). This is so because "every moment of the life of a society (open or closed), culture is the result, with more or less awakened consciousness, of economic, and political activities, the more or less dynamic expression of the type of relations prevailing within that society, on the one hand, and on the other hand, among individuals, groups of individuals, social strata or classes" (p. 141).

In light of the above, it is important here to critically engage Cabral's extremely elastic concept of culture. Culture, according to Cabral, is "simultaneously the fruit of a people's history and a determinant of history, by the positive or negative influence it exerts on the evolution of relations between man and his environment and among men or human groups within a society, as well as different societies" (p.

141). Imperialism, in the form of racial colonialism, represents—to employ terms used by Cabral to describe this phenomenon—the "paralysis," "stagnation," "regression," "deviation," and "halting" of the dominated people's human agency; in a word, their capacity, ontologically speaking, to *become* and make themselves known, to each other and other human groups, on their own terms and in their own unique way (pp. 128–130).

Tsenay Serequeberhan (1994) has argued that colonialism "petrifies the subjugated culture," and the same may be said of its effect(s) on the dominated groups' history (p. 101). If, therefore, history and culture are understood as Serequeberhan— closely following Cabral's lead—comprehends them, then, history and culture can be comprehended as "the actuality of engagements, intellectual (artistic/spiritual) and material, in which a people unveils its existence" (p. 102). History and culture, then, are "always and unconditionally to be understood in the *plural*, as the various modes of being and doing of human existence" (p. 103, emphasis in original). Cabral (1979) consistently emphasized the need to, not only acknowledge but, also, challenge one-dimensional and racial essentialist interpretations of Africa's histories, cultures, and struggles:

> A profound analysis of cultural reality removes the supposition that there can be continental or racial cultures. This is because, as with history, culture develops in an uneven process, at the level of a continent, a "race" or even a society. The coordinates of culture, like those of any developing phenomenon, vary in space and time, whether they be material (physical) or human (biological and social). The fact of recognizing the existence of common and special traits in the cultures of African peoples, independently of the color of their skin, does not necessarily imply that one and only one culture exists on the continent. In the same way that from the economic and political point of view one can note the existence of various Africas, so there are also various African cultures. (p. 149)

When and where history and culture are comprehended in this way—in the *plural* and, as Serequeberhan said, as "the various modes of being and doing of human existence"—then, and perhaps only then, is Cabral's call for a "return to the source" most comprehensible. For Cabral, Africa, which is to say Africa's histories, cultures, and peoples, are much more complex, their cultures more wide-ranging and diverse than previously noted by colonial anthropologists, ethnologists, missionaries, and others, including European-educated (or, rather, miseducated) Africans and their all-encompassing theories of Africa's ancient and glorious past. This, of course, is not in any way to imply that Africa did not have an ancient and glorious past, but only to emphasize that not everything in Africa's past was paradisiacal and that contemporary Africana critical theorists should employ Cabral's unique African-centered dialectical and historical materialism when approaching Africa's histories and cultures. Additionally, Cabral argued—in some senses very similar to Fanon (1965, 1968, 1969)—that it must always be borne in mind that the national liberation struggle, or any struggle against imperialism, raises-consciousness, transforms and brings into being new traditions, and introduces new cultural elements, if not completely new African cultures and values.

One of the major dialectical dimensions of Cabral's concept of "return to the source," then, hinges on his contention that one of the strengths of a revolutionary

nationalist movement, such as that of the PAIGC, is that it preserves precolonial traditions and values but, at the same time, these traditions and values are drastically
transformed through the dialectical process of revolutionary decolonization and re-
Africanization; in other words, by the protracted struggle against the superimposition of foreign imperial cultures and values and the reconstitution and synthesis of
progressive precolonial and recently created revolutionary African traditions and
values. Therefore, according to Cabral: "The armed struggle for liberation, launched
in response to aggression by the colonialist oppressor, turns out to be a painful but
effective instrument for developing the cultural level both for the leadership strata
of the liberation movement and for the various social categories who take part in
the struggle" (pp. 151–152). Anticipating that many may misunderstand him, as
they historically have and currently continue to misunderstand and misinterpret
Fanon's concepts of revolutionary decolonization and revolutionary self-defensive
violence, Cabral further explained his conception of the national liberation struggle
as a "painful but effective instrument":

> As we know, the armed liberation struggle demands the mobilization and organization
> of a significant majority of the population, the political and moral unity of the various
> social categories, the efficient use of modern weapons and other means of warfare, the
> gradual elimination of the remnants of tribal mentality, and the rejection of social and
> religious rules and taboos contrary to the development of the struggle (gerontocracy,
> nepotism, social inferiority of women, rites and practices which are incompatible with
> the rational and national character of the struggle, etc.). The struggle brings about many
> other profound changes in the life of the populations. The armed liberation struggle im-
> plies, therefore, a veritable forced march along the road to cultural progress. (p.152)

Cabral's concept of "return to the source," therefore, is not only, as shall soon be
shown, a "return to the upwards paths of [Africans'] own culture[s]," but also "a veritable forced march along the road to cultural progress." This "return," similar to
that of Cesaire, is a critical "return" that "is not and can not in itself be an *act of struggle* against domination (colonialist and racist) and it no longer necessarily means a
return to traditions" (Cabral, 1973, p. 63, emphasis in original). Rather, the "return
to the source" that Cabral has in mind is a conscious anti-colonial and revolutionary step, however inchoate and anxiety-filled and, he asserted, "the only possible reply to the demand of concrete need, historically determined, and enforced by the
inescapable contradiction between the colonized society and the colonial power,
the mass of the people exploited and the foreign exploitive class, a contradiction in
the light of which each social stratum or indigenous class must define its position"
(p. 63). In defining their position(s) in relation to, or, better yet, *against* the colonial
and imperial powers, each member of the colonized society—individually and
collectively—*chooses*, must as a matter of life or death, *will* themselves into becoming revolutionary praxis-oriented participants, active anti-colonial agents in the dialectical process of revolutionary decolonization and revolutionary re-Africanization, the protracted process of rescuing, reclaiming, and reconstructing her or his
own humanity, history, and heritage.[34] In Cabral's candid words:

> When the "return to the source" goes beyond the individual and is expressed through
> "groups" or "movements," the contradiction is transformed into struggle (secret or

overt), and is a prelude to the pre-independence movement or of the struggle for liberation from foreign yoke. So, the "return to the source" is of no historical importance unless it brings not only real involvement in the struggle for independence, but also complete and absolute identification with the hopes of the mass of the people, who contest not only the foreign culture but also the foreign domination as a whole. Otherwise, the "return to the source" is nothing more than an attempt to find short-term benefits—knowingly or unknowingly a kind of political opportunism. (p. 63)

The "return to the source" may be said to translate into contemporary critical theory as the much touted "cultural revolution" that many have often argued proceeds and must continue throughout the national liberation struggle (see Gramsci, 1985, 2000; Lenin, 1975, 1987; Marcuse, 1964, 1968, 1972a; Nelson and Grossberg, 1988; Nkrumah, 1973a, 1973b; Nyerere, 1966, 1968, 1973). Culture, when approached from a dialectical perspective, can be reactionary or revolutionary, traditional or transformative, decadent or dynamic, and the "return," in light of this fact, must at the least be *critical* if it is to transcend and transgress futile attempts, as Serequeberhan (1994) sternly stated, "to dig out a purely African past and return to a dead tradition" (p. 107). The "return," therefore, is only partially pointed at historical recovery, socio-political transformation, and revolutionary reorganization. There is another, often over-looked aspect of Cabral's concept of "return to the source" that simultaneously and dialectically strongly stresses revolutionary cultural restoration and revolutionary cultural transformation.

Indeed, Cabral argued, it was prudent for Africans to develop critical dialogues and "real" relationships with precolonial and traditional African histories and cultures, but he also cautioned them to keep in mind the ways in which colonialism and Eurocentrism, and the struggles against colonialism and for re-Africanization, impacted and affected modern African histories and cultures, consequently creating whole new notions of "Africa," African cultures and traditions. What is more, and what is not always readily apparent, is that the dialectical process of revolutionary decolonization and revolutionary re-Africanization calls into question the very definition of what it means—ontologically, existentially, and phenomenologically speaking—to *be* "African"— that is, "African" in a world dominated by European imperialism or, to put it another way, it calls into question what is means to be "black" in a white supremacist colonial capitalist world. The dialectical process of revolutionary decolonization and revolutionary re-Africanization at its core, then, redefines "Africanity," or "blackness," if you will. It finds sustenance in Fanon's (1968) faithful words in *The Wretched of the Earth*, where he declared: "Decolonization is the veritable creation of new men," of a "new humanity," and the "'thing' which has been colonized becomes man," by which he means *becomes human, becomes African* by providing revolutionary answers to the question(s) of liberation and the question(s) of identity, "during the same process by which it frees itself" (pp. 36–37).

There is a deep, critical self-reflexive dimension to Cabral's concept of "return to the source," one which, similar to Fanon's theory of revolutionary decolonization, openly acknowledges that the colonized transforms, not simply the colonizers, but themselves through the dialectical process of revolutionary decolonization and revolutionary re-Africanization. Their theory and praxis, situated in a specific historical moment, emerges from the lived-experiences of their actually endured struggles, which in one way connects them to the past but, in another way, connects them to the *postcolonial* future. Here Horkheimer's (1972) words, once again, come into play: "The Critical Theorist's vocation is the struggle to which his thought belongs. Thought is not something independent, to be separated from this struggle" (p. 245). The "return to the source," then, should not under any circumstances be a return to tradition in its stasis or freeze-framed form, but, as Fanon (1968) has firmly stated, critical theorists—he uses terms such as "the native intellectual," "the native writer," and "the man of culture"—who wish to *think* and *act* in the best interest of the (inter)national liberation struggle "ought to use the past [read: indigenous traditions, narratives, histories, heritages, views and values] with the intention of opening the future, as an invitation to action and a basis for hope" (p. 232).

The "return," simply said, is not to the past, but to "the source"— or, as I am wont to say, *sources* (plural). The source(s) of a people's identity and dignity are, according to Cabral (1973), contained in their history and culture: "A struggle, which while being the organized political expression of a *culture* is also and necessarily a proof not only of *identity* but also of *dignity*" (p. 68, emphasis in original). A people's history and culture (and we may add language [see Fanon, 1967, pp. 17–40]) contain and carry their thought-, belief-, and value-systems and traditions; these systems and traditions are—under "normal" circumstances—ever-evolving, always contradicting, countering and overturning, as well as building on and going beyond, the ideologies and theories, and the views and values of the past. Which is why, further, the "return" is not and should not be to the past or any "dead" traditions, but to those things (spiritual and material) from our past (e.g., ideologies, theories, views, and values) which will enable us to construct a present and future that is (or would be) consistently conducive to the highest, healthiest, and most humane modes of human existence and experience.[35]

Cabral's (1979) concept of "return to the source" is doubly-distinguished in its contributions to Africana critical theory in that it enables us to critique two dominant tendencies in Africana liberation theory and praxis. The first tendency is that of the vulgar and narrow-minded nationalists who seek, or so it seems, to expunge every aspect of European culture, collapsing it almost completely with European colonization, without coming to the critical realization that: "A people who free themselves from foreign domination will not be culturally free unless, without underestimating the importance of positive contributions from the oppressor's culture and other cultures, they return to the upwards paths of their own culture" (p. 143). To "return" to the "upwards paths of [Africans'] own culture" would mean side-stepping the narrow-minded nationalists' knee-jerk reaction to everything European or non-African, and it would also mean making a critical and, even more, a dialectical distinction between white supremacy and Eurocentrism, on the one hand, and Europe and other cultures' authentic contributions to human culture and civilization that have, or could potentially, benefit the whole of humanity, on the other hand.

The second tendency that Cabral's concept of "return to the source" strongly condemns are those, usually Europeanized, petit bourgeois, alienated African's living in colonial metropoles, who seem to uncritically praise Africa's precolonial histories and cultures without coming to terms with the fact that:

Without any doubt, underestimation of the cultural values of African peoples, based upon racist feelings and the intention of perpetuating exploitation by the foreigner, has done much harm to Africa. But in the face of the vital need for progress, the following factors or behavior would be no less harmful to her: unselective praise; systematic exaltation of virtues without condemning defects; blind acceptance of the values of the culture without considering what is actually or potentially negative, reactionary or regressive; confusion between what is the expression of an objective and historical material reality and what appears to be a spiritual creation of the result of a special nature; absurd connection of artistic creations, whether valid or not, to supposed racial characteristics; and, finally, non-scientific or ascientific critical appreciation of the cultural phenomenon. (p. 150)

Cabral advocated a "critical analysis of African cultures" and, in so doing, he developed a distinct dialectical approach that Africa's wide-ranging histories, cultures, and struggles. This is extremely important to emphasize because too often Africa has been, and continues to be, engaged as though its histories, cultures, and peoples are either completely homogeneous or completely heterogeneous; as if it were impossible for the diverse and dynamic cultures of Africa to simultaneously possess commonalities *and* distinct differences. Cabral's cultural philosophy, also, includes a unique comparative dimension that recommends placing what Africans consider the "best" of their culture into critical dialogue with the contributions and advances of other, non-African cultures. This, he argued, was important in order to get a real sense of what Africa has contributed to world culture and civilization and to discover what world culture and civilization has contributed to, and currently offers Africa. In his own words:

> The important thing is not to waste time in more or less hair-splitting debates on the specificity or non-specificity of African cultural values, but to look upon these values as a conquest by a part of mankind for the common heritage of all mankind, achieved in one or several phases of its evolution. The important thing is to proceed to critical analysis of African cultures in the light of the liberation movement and the demands of progress—in the light of this new stage in the history of Africa. We may be aware of its value in the framework of universal civilization, but to compare its value with that of other cultures, not in order to decide its superiority or its inferiority, but to determine, within the general framework of the struggle for progress, what contribution African culture has made and must make and contributions it can or must receive.
>
> The liberation movement must, as we have said, base its action on thorough knowledge of the culture of the people and be able to assess the elements of this culture at their true worth, as well as the different levels it reaches in each social category. It must likewise be able to distinguish within the totality of the people's cultural values the essential and secondary, the positive and negative, the progressive and reactionary, the strengths and weaknesses. This is necessary by virtue of the demands of the struggle and in order to be able to center its action on the essential without forgetting the secondary, to instigate development of positive and progressive elements and to fight, with subtlety but strictness, negative and reactionary elements; finally so that it can make effective use of strengths and remove weaknesses, or transform them into strengths. (p. 150)

History and culture, as we see here, play a special part in national liberation, and Cabral argued that careful and critical analysis of the specificities of African cultures and ethnicities is equally, if not more important, in national liberation struggles than broad-based theories touting everything from a distinct "black soul" and African personality to a collective African mind and African communalism. Not

only were many of these theories, from Cabral's point of view, historically, culturally and sociologically inaccurate, but they were also extremely detrimental since
they often glossed over important differences and precluded historical materialist
and dialectical materialist interpretations of culture in the development of particular African societies—precolonial, colonial, or neocolonial. Moreover, from his
African historical materialist perspective, the catch-all concepts and umbrella theories about Africa had a tendency to consistently downplay the many ways in which
ethnicity, class, and religion often influenced participation, or non-participation, in
decolonization and re-Africanization efforts.

However, Cabral also did not believe that endless hours should be spent searching for minute details in efforts to distinguish one African cultural or ethnic group
from another. What was, and what remains, most important is that Africans' critically analyze and assess their own histories, cultures, and struggles, and—this
should be strongly stressed—develop a deeper comparative dimension in terms of
placing their cultures into critical dialogue, not only with each other, but with other,
non-African cultures, especially those involved in anti-racist, anti-colonialist and
anti-imperialist struggles. Above it was demonstrated that a strong humanist strain
runs through Cabral's contributions to critical theory, and here we may observe,
again, his principled stand against imperialism and for revolutionary humanism.
Even more, here we can see that in promoting a critical comparative dimension to
the national liberation struggle, Cabral connected Cape Verde and Guinea-Bissau's
national culture with global culture, their national history with world history, and,
most significantly, their national struggle with international struggles.

His conceptions of national history and national culture indelibly informed his
notion of the national liberation struggle. For instance, one would be hard-pressed
to provide an answer to Cabral's (1979, p. 75) cryptic question: "Against whom are
our people struggling?"—or, à la Cabral, Serequeberhan's (1994, p. 32) more recent
query: "[W]hat are the people of Africa trying to free themselves from and what are
they trying to establish?"—unless she or he possessed a critical cognizance of the
roots or "sources" of the particular history and culture in question; ever-willing and
able to critically inquire into *what* and *how* specific historical, cultural, social and political predicaments and impediments have been, and are *being*, transversed and
transpired. In my view, Fanon (1968) captured this conundrum best when he stated:

> A national culture is not a folklore, nor an abstract populism that believes it can dis-
> cover the people's true nature. It is not made up of inert dregs of gratuitous actions, that
> is to say actions which are less and less attached to the ever-present reality of the peo-
> ple. A national culture is the whole body of efforts made by a people in the sphere of
> thought to describe, justify, and praise the action through which that people has cre-
> ated itself and keeps itself in existence. A national culture in underdeveloped countries
> should therefore take its place at the very heart of the struggle for freedom which these
> countries are carrying on. . . . No one can truly wish for the spread of African culture if
> he [or she] does not give practical support to the creation of the conditions necessary
> to the existence of that culture; in other words, to the liberation of the whole continent.
> (pp. 233, 235)

Fanon's concept of national culture connects with Cabral's critical theory insofar
as both of their thought suggests a reliance on (or "return" to) those elements

which the subjugated population have employed, and may continue to employ, to "describe, justify, and praise the action[s] through which that people has created itself and keeps itself in existence." This means nothing less than the oppressed undergoing a process of "transvaluation of values" (Marcuse, 1989) from the existing imperialist social set-up and a "revolution in values" (Marcuse, 1973b) that totally contradicts and overturns imperial values, which are obstructions to the veritable creation of new human beings who envision and seek to bring into being a new humanity and a new society (see Fanon, 1968, p. 36). Cabral's critical return, understood as a "cultural revolution," at its core calls for—to borrow Marcuse's phrase—a "transvaluation of values." That is to say, Cabral's critical "return to the source," which unequivocally advocates cultural revolution, is a rejection of "traditional," "conventional," "established," or "accepted" imperialist values and, what is more, retrogressive precolonial or traditional African values. His "return to the source," in this sense, is more of a kind of historical and cultural critical consciousness-raising, a form of radical political education, social (re)organization, and revolutionary praxis that requests that or, rather, challenges the wretched of the earth to remain cognizant at all times of "our own situation" and "be aware of our things" (Cabral, 1979, pp. 56–57). "We must respect those things of value," contended Cabral, "which are useful for the future of our land, for the advancement of our people" (p. 57).

A "transvaluation of values," first, requires that we "be aware of our things." Meaning, we should possess an intimate knowledge of our past and present colonial and anti-colonial history and culture. Second, it necessitates that we "respect those things of value, which are useful for the future of our land, for the advancement of our people." That is, "those things of value" which will enable us to create a new, *post-imperial* society; a society without poverty and privilege; a society free from domination and exploitation; a society that utilizes science and technology as instruments of liberation as opposed to tools of domination; a society whose ultimate aim is the constant creation of those "new human beings" Fanon (1968) wrote so passionately about in *The Wretched of the Earth* (p. 36). Such a society, further, demands what Marcuse (1989) termed a "transvaluation of values" and, even more, it presupposes a new type of human being who:

> rejects the performance principles governing the established societies; a type of man who has rid himself of the aggressiveness and brutality that are inherent in the organization of established society, and in their hypocritical, puritan morality; a type of man who is biologically incapable of fighting wars and creating suffering; a type of man who has a good conscience of joy and pleasure and who works collectively and individually for a social and natural environment in which such an existence becomes possible. (p. 282)

The new human beings with new values possess a new worldview, which is the determinate negation of the presently established imperialist worldview and value-system. The connection between one's worldview and value-system should be stressed because it is precisely these things which, to a certain extent, determine a person's thought and behavior. An individual's worldview and value-system becomes their "second nature" and as such provide beliefs, norms, and aspirations which motivate them, either consciously or unconsciously, to think and act *for* or *against* the imperialist world-system (see Marcuse, 1964, 1965c, 1966, 1969a, 1970a, 1972a; Wamba-Dia-Wamba, 1991).

Cabral's contributions to critical theory offers contemporary critical theorists alternatives, not only to imperialism, but to the Eurocentrism of much of what passes currently as "critical theory." And, further, it does so without disavowing the crucial contributions that European and other non-African traditions of philosophy and critical theory provide for the Africana tradition of critical theory. Ultimately, then, for Cabral the "return to the source" is not only about the dialectical process of revolutionary decolonization and revolutionary re-Africanization, but also about revolutionary humanism and the promise of a liberated future where the "new humanity" that Fanon envisioned, and the "transvaluation of values" that Marcuse described above, is a concrete, actually existing reality.

## CRITICAL CONCERNS AND CONCLUDING COMMENTS ON THE USES AND ABUSES OF CABRAL'S CONTRIBUTIONS TO AFRICANA CRITICAL THEORY

As was stated above, Cabral presents Africana critical theory with several significant challenges, and throughout the course of this chapter I have accented and emphasized the ways in which his lifework necessitates a fundamental rethinking of critical theory in general and, more specifically, the discourse and development of Africana critical theory. As forementioned, Cabral's thought serves as a cue and calls for a concrete philosophy, an *Africana philosophy of praxis*: a historically-nuanced, culturally-grounded, and politically-charged form of critical social theory that speaks to the special needs of continental and diasporan Africans. Eschewing the scholasticism and abstract system-building of the bulk of European and European American trained philosophers of African descent, Cabral constantly developed accessible critical theories of the changing conditions of contemporary society; the prospects of Pan-African democratic socialist revolution; revolutionary decolonization; revolutionary re-Africanization; revolutionary nationalism; and, revolutionary humanism. He was ever concerned to utilize theory (philosophy) as a weapon against imperialism, and to unite it with the emancipatory aspirations and efforts of his specific struggling people, and racially colonized humanity as a whole. Cabral, also, always admonished intellectual-activists to be critically cognizant of our particular circumstances and situations, but, as revolutionary humanists, to remain open to learning what we can from the lived-experiences and experiments (e.g., social, political, and cultural experiments) of others. In his own words:

> The experience of others is highly significant for someone undergoing any experience. The reality of others is highly significant for one's reality. Many folk do not understand this, and grasp their reality with the passion that they are going to invent everything: "I do not want to do the same as others have done, nothing that others have done." This is a sign of ignorance. If we want to do something in reality, we must see who has already done the same, who has done something similar, and who has done something opposite, so that we can learn something from their experience. It is not to copy completely, because every reality has its own questions and its own answers for these questions . . . there are many things which belong to many realities jointly. It is essential that

the experience of others benefit us. We must be able to derive from everyone's experience what we can adapt to our conditions, to avoid unnecessary efforts and sacrifices. This is very important. (Cabral, 1979, pp. 49–50)

In good dialectical fashion Cabral suggested that we start with our own circumstances and situations, but maintain an *epistemic* and *experiential openness*, and be willing and able, to appropriate and adapt the advances or breakthroughs of others as they pertain to our circumstances and situations, as these advances and breakthroughs could in many instances aid us in avoiding "unnecessary efforts and sacrifices." He firmly warns us "not to copy completely," because our lived-reality, that is, our concrete conditions and unique historical happenings, are distinct from those of any people in any other age. We are to always remember that "every reality has its own questions and its own answers for these questions." Here, this caveat should also be connected to Cabral's earlier discussion of the plurality of African histories, cultures, and struggles. Indeed, Cabral and his comrades provided solutions to many problems, crucial answers to several critical questions, but contemporary critical theorists must keep cognizant of the fact that Cabral and his comrades provided solutions to the particular problems they were faced with in their specific historical moment, as they were confronting the conundrums of an extremely particular, if not peculiar, form of racial colonialism: Portuguese colonialism. Cabral (1972) critically contended:

> We, peoples of Africa, who are fighting against Portuguese colonialism, have suffered under very special conditions, because for the past forty years we have been under the domination of a fascist regime. . . . Portugal is an economically backward country, in which about 50 percent of the population is illiterate, a country which you will find at the bottom of all the statistical tables of Europe. . . . Portugal is a country in no position at all to dominate any other country. (p. 78)

This means, then, that it is equally important for contemporary critical theorists, Africana or otherwise, to critically bear in mind that however attractive Cabral's thought, no matter how fervently we believe it to speak to the special issues we are confronted with in the twenty-first century, his contributions to critical theory cannot provide us with the concrete and nuanced historical understandings necessary to develop revolutionary movements, that is, national and international liberation struggles aimed at altering the new and novel social and political problems of the present. There simply is no substitute for contemporary critical theorists practicing conceptual generation; no problem-solving proxy for their development of new theory geared toward, not only gauging but changing contemporary societies, bringing into being a new humanity, new societies and, perhaps even, a new world culture and civilization grounded in and growing out of various transethnic traditions of revolutionary decolonization, revolutionary humanism, critical multiculturalism, democratic socialism, racial justice, gender justice, women's liberation, freedom of sexual orientation, and religious tolerance, among others.

However, even in light of all the critical observations above, I continue to believe that Cabral's theoretic-strategic framework is extremely useful for those critical theorists concerned with, not merely colonialism, neocolonialism and postcolonialism, but also racism, critical race theory, revolutionary nationalism, revolutionary humanism, re-Africanization and the critique of capitalism and class struggles in contemporary society. His theoretic-strategic framework, indeed, does offer critical concepts and innovative analytical categories; it does, in fact, provide a wide-range of principles and prospects that make intelligible the constantly changing character of contemporary colonialism, capitalism, and racism. Further, it seems to prophetically prefigure and point to new, untapped types of revolutionary movement, and even goes so far to suggest several distinct directions for future radical political struggle.

Cabral's theoretic-strategic framework is distinctive in that it audaciously challenges contemporary theorists to actually, ontologically speaking, *be* simultaneously "critical" *and* "theorists," "intellectuals" *and* "activists." It explicitly asks that "critical theorists" embrace the dialectical task of transforming themselves and their societies, which, once again, are situated in specific historical moments, with concrete conditions, and particular social and political problems. Corroborating Cabral and, in a sense, updating his thesis that "every reality has its own questions and its own answers for these questions," the Ghanaian philosopher, Kwame Gyekye (1995), has stated: "Philosophers belonging to a given culture or era or tradition select those concepts or clusters of concepts that, for one reason or another, matter most and that therefore are brought to the fore in their analysis" (p. 7). These "concepts and clusters of concepts" are employed insofar as specific philosophers understand them to offer the most compelling and comprehensive means to alter contemporary societies and, even more, contemporary "souls," following the fundamental thrust of Du Bois's contributions to critical theory. Gyekye (1997) comments further:

> [I]f one were to examine the cultural and historical setting of the intellectual focus, concerns, and direction of the individual thinker, one would be convinced, beyond doubt, that philosophy is a conceptual response to the basic human problems that arise in any given society in a given epoch. Such an examination would reveal that philosophers grapple at the conceptual level with problems and issues of their times, even though this does not mean that the relevance of their ideas, insights, arguments, and conclusions is to be tethered to those times; for, more often than not, the relevance of their insights and arguments—or at least some of them—transcends the confines of their own times and cultures and, thus, can be embraced by other cultures or societies or different generational epochs. In others words, a philosophical doctrine may be historical, that is, generated originally in response to some historical events or circumstances, without our having to look on it as historicistic, without our having to confine its significance simply to those times of history when it was actually produced . . . the fact that the philosophers who produced the ideas and arguments were giving conceptual response and attention to the experiences of their times needs to be stressed and constantly borne in mind: it was the problems of the time that constituted the points of departure for their reflective analyses. (p. 19)

Cabral impels Africana critical theory to consider the concrete conditions of philosophical settings, reminding us that it may be extremely useful to acknowledge and engage the fact that, and the manner in which, philosophy is inextricable from notions of, most especially, "tradition," but also "history" and "heritage" as well. Another Ghanaian philosopher, Kwasi Wiredu (1991), has asserted that "[t]he philosophy of a people is always a tradition," and that a tradition "presupposes a certain minimum of organic relationships among (at least some of) its elements" (p. 92). He goes on to observe: "If a tradition of modern philosophy is to develop and flourish in Africa, there will have to be philosophical interaction and cross-fertilization among contemporary African workers in philosophy" (p. 92).

In as much as it is reputedly a "return" to the history and culture of African peoples, Cabral's critical return to the source(s) suggests in no uncertain terms that Africana critical theory of contemporary society concern itself with the deconstruction of European-derived continental and diasporan African philosophical discourse, and the reconstruction of a decolonized and re-Africanized critical theory and praxis tradition. The deconstruction of European-based continental and diasporan African philosophy presupposes that modern workers in Africana philosophy, and Africana Studies in general, have the conceptual and analytical skills and tools to undertake such an endeavor. Further, this endeavor, being nothing less than what has been aforementioned and outlined in the preceding paragraphs as Africana critical theory, must always and at its core—as a critical self-conscious and critical self-reflective effort—be willing and able to critique and correct its own subjective settings, concrete conditions, and insidiously inherited Eurocentric philosophical influences, as well as other imperialist intellectual influences, which in many, if not in *most* instances keeps it from *doing* what Gyekye (1997), among others, understands the fundamental tasks of philosophy to be: (1) provide people with "a fundamental system of beliefs to live by;" (2) determine "the nature of human values and how these values can be realized concretely in human societies;" (3) speculate about "the whole range of human experience" by providing "conceptual interpretations and analysis of that experience, necessarily doing so not only by responding to the basic issues and problems generated by that experience but also by suggesting new or alternative ways of thought and action;" and, (4) offer "conceptual responses to the problems posed in any given epoch for a given society or culture" (pp. 15, 23, 24, 27).

To speak of an Africana critical theory in the contemporary moment means nothing less than speaking of, and actively engaging in, the critique, appreciation, appropriation, and disruption—if need be—of hitherto "traditional" or, even more, abstract academic and Eurocentric, European-influenced forms of continental and diasporan African philosophy and conceptual generation. As Cabral's critical theory suggests, the engagement of any form or field of knowledge should always and ever be, not for scholasticism, abstract system-building, or simply nostalgia's sake, but in the interest of real, live, suffering and struggling women, men, and children; in a word, not knowledge for knowledge's sake, but *knowledge for life and liberation's sake*. Again, Gyekye offers Africana philosophers advice: "philosophical knowledge and insight should benefit the society as a whole, not [merely] the philosophers personally" (p. 18). As philosophers of African descent continue to rescue and rediscover, as well as critically engage and (re)interpret various philosophical systems and traditions, we must be vigilant, remaining consistently conscious of the fact that no matter which form or field of philosophy we feel compelled to engage, it is our solemn duty, as "philosophers," even more, as critical theorists of contemporary society, to do so—in the spirit of Du Bois, James, Cesaire, Senghor, Fanon, and Cabral—seeking solutions to the enigmatic issues of our epoch; always and ever, willing and able to criticize and offer alternatives and correctives to contemporary crises and conundrums.

## NOTES

1. Serequeberhan extends and explicates the thesis that Cabral "represents the zenith" of twentieth century continental African anti-colonial political philosophy in *The Hermeneutics of African Philosophy* (1994), and specifically chapter 4, "The Liberation Struggle: Existence and Historicity," (pp. 87–116). Cabral is also a major presence in his volume entitled, *Our Heritage* (2000), and specifically chapter 6, "The Heritage of the Idea: Violence, Counterviolence, and the Negated," (pp. 59–72). For an engagement of Serequeberhan's work that is at once critical and appreciative, consult Robert Bernasconi, "African Philosophy's Challenge to Continental Philosophy" (1997). For further discussion of continental African philosophy, see Appiah (1992), Bodunrin (1985), Coetzee and Roux (1998), English and Kalumba (1996), Eze (1997a, 1997b), Floistad (1981), D. Fraser (1974), Gbadegesin (1991a), Gyekye (1988, 1997), Hallen and Sodipo (1981, 1986), Horton (1993), Hountondji (1996), Imbo (1998), Kwame (1995), Masolo (1994), Momoh (1989), Mosley (1995a), Mudimbe (1988, 1994), Obenga (1995), Okere (1971, 1991), Ruch (1984) Serequeberhan (1991, 1994), Wiredu, (1980, 1996), and R.A. Wright (1984).

2. As I am here only concerned with Cabral insofar as his intellectual life and political legacy are understood to connect and contribute to the development an Africana theory critical of contemporary culture and society, I shall forego a detailed discussion of his biography. Readers seeking further biographical treatments of Cabral, besides the main sources listed in the text, are also asked to consult: Chabal (1980, 1983), Chaliand (1973b), Dadoo (1973), Davidson (1969, 1981), Goldfield (1973), Lopes (1987), Segal (1973), and Taiwo (1999a).

3. On this point, see Du Bois's classic statement in his 1928 essay, "Cultural Equality," where he relates that "civilization is by the definition of the term, civilization for all mankind," and it "is the rightful heritage of all and cannot be monopolized and confined to one group" (1996a, p. 397). He also states that "nobody is going to withhold applause if you make your contribution to the world" (p. 397), which is, of course, what he had been arguing and urging continental and diasporan Africans to *do* since his 1897 piece, "The Conservation of Races" (pp. 38–47). In Du Bois's view, "[a] group organization to increase and forward culture is legitimate and will bring its rewards in universal recognition and applause. But this has never been the Nordic [read: European] program" (p. 397). Quite the contrary, "[t]heir program," Du Bois thundered,

> is the subjection and rulership of the world for the benefit of the Nordics [again, read: Europeans]. They have overrun the earth and brought not simply modern civilization and technique, but with it exploitation, slavery and degradation to the majority of men. They have broken down native family life, desecrated homes of weaker peoples and spread their bastards over every corner of land and sea. They have been responsible for more intermixture of races than any other people, ancient or modern, and they have inflicted this miscegenation on helpless, unwilling slaves by force, fraud and insult; and this is the folk that today has the impudence to turn on the darker races when they demand a share of civilization, and cry: "You shall not marry our daughters!" The blunt, crude reply is: Who in the hell asked to marry your daughters? If this race problem must be reduced to a matter of sex, what we demand is the right to protect the decency of our own daughters. But the insistent demand of the Darker World is far wider and deeper than this. The black and brown and yellow men demand the right to be men. They demand the right to have the artificial barriers placed in their path torn down and destroyed; they demand a voice in their own government; the organization of industry for the benefit of colored workers and not merely for white owners and masters; they demand education on the broadest and highest lines and they demand as human beings social contact with other human beings on a basis of perfect equality. (p. 397)

In his firm insistence on the right to self-determination by all peoples, Du Bois—considered by many, including Cabral (1973, p. 91), the "father of Pan-Africanism"—concludes that if indeed "the darker races," and "the colored workers" especially, are to be held "in their place" by "white owners and masters," then this will be done only by "brute force" (Du Bois, 1996a, p. 400). However, Du Bois, as dialectician and doyen of decolonization discourse *par excellence*, forwarded a caveat to the ruling race/gender/class:

> The temptation to hold these colored people back is tremendous, because it is not merely a matter of academic wish or of wanton prejudice, but it is the kernel of the organization of modern life. You have got the colored people working for you all through the world. You have got your investments so made that they depend upon colored labor in Asia, Africa, in the southern states of the United States, and in the islands of the sea. Your income and your power depends upon that organization being kept intact. If it is overthrown, if these black laborers get higher wages, if they begin to understand what life may be, if they increase in knowledge, self-assertion and power, it means the overthrow of the whole system of exploitation which is at the bottom of modern white civilization. . . . You can sweep us off the face of the earth. You can starve us to death or make us wish we had starved in the face of your insults. But, remember, you are standing before the whole world, with hundreds of darker millions watching. No matter what happens to us, these colored people of the world are not going to take forever the kind of treatment they have been taking. They got beyond that. They have come to the place where they know what civilization is, and if you are going to keep them in their place, you are going to do it by brute force. (pp. 399–400).

Before James, Cesaire or Senghor, Fanon or Cabral, it was Du Bois who undauntedly challenged and devoted his life-work to changing the imperial world-system. Whether one wishes to speak of Pan-Africanism, Negritude, the discourse of decolonization, or contemporary Africana schools of thought and tradition-construction projects, Du Bois, as argued in the first chapter of this study, provides modern workers in continental and diasporan African schools of thought with a paradigm by which they may base and build a critical theory of contemporary society which seeks to criticize and ultimately alter the present manifold forms of imperialism; for example, racism, sexism, capitalism, and colonialism (see Rabaka 2007a, 2008a).

4. On the concept of "reification," consult Georg Lukacs, "Reification and the Consciousness of the Proletariat," in his classic text *History and Consciousness: Studies in Marxist Dialectics* (1968). For further discussion of the concept of "reification," see Bewes (2002), Gabel (1975), Rockmore (1988, 1992), and Shafai (1996).

5. As Cabral addressed the United Nations (hereafter cited as UN) General Assembly on several occasions (see Cabral 1972, pp. 24–49, 50–55, 1973, pp. 15–38), he was well aware of its "Declaration on the Granting of Independence to Colonial Countries and Peoples," General Assembly resolution 1514 (XV) of 14 December 1960, which states, in part:

1. The subjection of peoples to alien subjugation, domination and exploitation constitutes a denial of fundamental human rights, is contrary to the Charter of the United Nations and is an impediment to the promotion of world peace and co-operation.

2. All peoples have the right to self-determination; by virtue of that right they freely determine their political status and freely pursue their economic, social and cultural development.

3. Inadequacy of political, economic, social, or educational preparedness should never serve as a pretext for delaying independence.

4. All armed action or repressive measures of all kinds directed against dependent peoples shall cease in order to enable them to exercise peacefully and freely their right to complete independence, and the integrity of their national territory shall be respected.

5. Immediate steps shall be taken, in Trust and Non-Self-Governing Territories or all other territories which have not yet attained independence, to transfer all powers to the peoples of those territories, without any conditions or reservations, in accordance with their freely expressed will and desire, without any distinction as to race, creed or color, in order to enable them to enjoy complete independence and freedom.

6. Any attempt aimed at the partial or total disruption of the national unity and the territorial integrity of a country is incompatible with the purposes and principles of the Charter of the United Nations.

7. All States shall observe faithfully and strictly the provisions of the Charter of the United Nations, the Universal Declaration of Human Rights and the present Declaration on the basis of equality, non-interference in the internal affairs of all States, and respect for the sovereign rights of all peoples and their territorial integrity. (see, "Declaration on the Granting of Independence to Colonial Countries and Peoples," General Assembly resolution 1514 (XV) of 14 December 1960 in United Nations [1988, pp. 48–49])

6. I borrowed the phrase "philosophy of praxis" from the Italian Marxist philosopher, Antonio Gramsci (1971), see esp., "The Philosophy of Praxis" (pp. 321–472).

7. In "Toward a Critical Theory of Postcolonial African Identities," Eze (1997b) has made an interesting observation in this regard. He argues, as I do, that it is not in the best interest of colonized peoples to apply the prefix "post" to "colonial" until we understand and experience life- and language-worlds, and thought- and belief-systems that are not, in any way, indirectly administered by "European [and this includes the United States of America] imperial powers" (p. 341). In Eze's words: "I refer to the '(post)colonial' with the 'post' in brackets. The brackets are to be opened, but only as far as the lived actuality of the peoples and the lands formerly occupied by European imperial powers can suggest, or confirm, in some meaningful ways, the sense of that word, the 'post' of the (post)colonial . . . if we recognize that the 'post' in (post)colonial is not completely 'post' because of some pervasive and continued European and American dominations of our mind, culture, and economy, we must also be willing to recognize, as alive the 'verbeuse phraseologie anti-colonialiste'." (p. 342). In short, there is no need *yet* of speaking of the "postcolonial," as we are deeply experiencing and enduring the "neocolonialism" that Du Bois, Fanon, Nkrumah, Cabral, and Ngugi, among others, have written so bitterly, though beautifully, about and, perhaps more importantly, *against*. Eze closes his essay, stating: "Colonialism, then, is safe and sound and prospering in its *neo*-varieties, and in many places" (p. 342, emphasis in original). Contemporary critical theorists, and especially contemporary Africana critical theorists, have an historical, cultural, social and political responsibility not merely to combat capitalism, as it was with the past masters and Eurocentric Marxists, but to oppose any and all forms of imperialism; currently, for instance, this includes racism, sexism, capitalism, colonialism, homophobia, and/or heterosexism, among other areas and issues.

8. Recall, in "Africana Philosophy," Outlaw (1996a) explicitly stated: "'Africana philosophy' is meant to include, as well, the work of those persons who are neither African nor of African descent but who recognize the legitimacy and importance of issues and endeavors that constitute the philosophizing of persons African or African-descended and who contribute to discussions of their efforts, persons whose work justifies their being called 'Africanists'" (p. 76). That being understood, it is important to emphasize that Africana philosophy and Africana critical theory are not, in my view, exclusively affairs of persons of African origin and descent, but affairs of insurgent intellectual-activists who are concerned about and interested in eradicating human suffering and social misery, specifically as it pertains to continental and diasporan African life-worlds and life-struggles.

9. For a more detailed discussion of the debate on racial vs. moral reasoning, see Babbitt and Campbell (1999), and especially Lawrence Blum, "Moral Asymmetries of Racism," Marilyn Friedman, "Racism: Paradigms and Moral Appraisal (A Response to Blum)," Laurence M. Thomas, "Split-Level Equality: Mixing Love and Equality," Susan Babbitt, "Moral Risk and Darkwaters," Goldberg (1990), L. Harris (1999b), and especially Kwame Anthony Appiah, "Why There Are No Races," Gerald Torres, "Critical Race Theory: The Decline of the Universalist Ideal and the Hope of Plural Justice," David Theo Goldberg, "Racism and Rationality," McGary (1999), L.M. Thomas (1989, 1993), and Zack (1995, 1997, 1998).

10. For further discussion, consult Cowan (2003), C.S. Johnson (2003), Wood (2000), and Yancy (2001). Also of interest are Gooding-Williams (1991), Gordon (1997b), and Mc-Gary (1999).

11. On Cornel West's "coalition politics," beyond *Race Matters* (1993), see West and Lerner (1995).

12. On "new" and/or "post-independence" forms of colonialism, see Nkrumah (1965). And, on Nkrumah's influence on Cabral, see "Homage to Kwame Nkrumah," in Cabral (1979, pp. 114–119).

13. For a discussion of the negation and attempted obliteration of African culture(s), see W. E. B. Du Bois, *The Negro* (1915), *Africa, Its Geography, People and Products* (1930a), *Africa, Its Place in Modern History* (1930b), and *The World and Africa* (1965); Chancellor Williams, *The Destruction of Black Civilization* (1974); John Henrik Clarke, *Africans at the Crossroads: Notes for an African World Revolution* (1991); Walter Rodney, *How Europe Underdeveloped Africa* (1972); Joseph E. Harris, *Africans and Their History* (1987), and *Global Dimensions of the African Diaspora* (1993); Chinweizu, *The West and the Rest of Us* (1975); bell hooks, *Ain't I a Woman* (1981); Lawrence Levine, *Black Culture and Black Consciousness* (1977); John Blassingame, *The Slave Community* (1979); Vincent Harding, *There Is a River* (1983); and Sterling Stuckey, *Slave Culture* (1987).

14. For further discussion, see Herbert Marcuse, *One-Dimensional Man* (1964), "Liberation from the Affluent Society" (1989) and "A Revolution in Values" (1973b).

15. I use the term "being/becoming" in the sense that Tsenay Serequeberhan does in *The Hermeneutics of African Philosophy* (1994) where he states: "'historical being-there' (i.e., a specific person or a historical community of persons) always becomes what it is by projecting itself out of its effective past, its lived inheritance. Its 'destiny' is thus always what comes out of itself, its 'has been,' out of the prospects of its history and the possibilities of its generation. . . . It is in a constant process of self-interpretation and ongoing re-interpretation that a history, a people (and an individual within the confines of a people and a generation), constitutes itself and projects its future/destiny—the yet-to-be of its lived presence" (pp. 25–26). The being and/or becoming, literally the livelihood of a people is rooted in that people's history and culture, and the interpretation or ability to interpret their history and culture. As colonialism blocks the engagement and evolution of the history and culture of the said people, it also obstructs, and often closes off completely, the authentic autonomous desires and destiny of that people. According to Serequeberhan: "It will not do to transpose European conceptions onto the African situation since this would not allow the diverse peoples of Africa their own self-standing self-determination. Any and all pre-established frameworks will not reflect the autonomous and historical self-institution that is necessary if Africa is to be free" (p. 35). African peoples, continental and diasporan, must "be" and "become" on their own terms, just as Asian, European and Native American peoples must "be" and "become" on their own terms. We should recall here, once again, Africana critical theory's emphasis on revolutionary humanism, which always and ever extends above and beyond Africana lifeworlds and life-struggles, and sincerely seeks to aid and abet any and all human beings and human groups involved in authentic anti-imperialist struggles.

16. Homophobia and/or heterosexism "withstanding" because it is not all together clear whether Cabral would take a progressive stance on issues which pertain to contemporary sexual(ity) politics. In light of the fact that he did not speak or write explicitly on, or about, homophobia and/or heterosexism, I have opted not to be presumptuous and/or force a contemporary "controversial," and let it be said "Western," social and political issue onto a classical Africana critical theorist. Cabral, as we shall see, stands on his own terms, and he left a legacy that we can either embrace or, at our own peril, reject. Insofar as I understand Cabral to be, at his deepest level, a revolutionary humanist, I believe that he would, if he were alive today, take a positive and progressive stand on homosexual rights, because these issues are at bottom human rights issues. He abhorred any and every violation of human rights, and it is

in this sense that I have drawn my conclusions. For a series of discussions and dialogues on the contemporary homosexual experience, see Abelove, Barale and Halpern (1993), Haggerty and McGarry (2007) and Lovaas, Elia and Yep (2006), and for an anthology devoted exclusively to lesbian and gay politics, see Blasius and Phelan (1997).

17. For my conception of a materialist analysis that is (or seeks to be) couched beyond the confines of the often "one-dimensional," economy-obsessed Marxist thought, I am deeply indebted to Cornel West (1988b, 1993b, 1999).

18. Horkheimer's critical theory, particularly his early articulation, has been extremely influential here. His unique synthesis of philosophy (or theory) with social science connects his conception of, and contributions to critical theory to those of Cabral in a very special way. Their contributions to critical theory seem to have several conceptual parallels, many of which will be discussed in the subsequent sections of this chapter. For more on Horkheimer's important work, see Benhabib, Bonss, and McCole (1993), Horkheimer (1974a, 1974b, 1978, 1993), Stirk (1992), and Tar (1977).

19. At the core of constructivist arguments, specifically with regard to race, Leonard Harris (1999b), in his introduction to his edited volume, *Racism: Key Concepts in Critical Theory*, has compiled and confirmed the following:

A "constructivist"—
(a) "believes that facts about the human world are absolutely dependent on contingent cultural or social ideas";
(b) "does not believe that groups exist independent of cultural or social ideas (races are not considered natural, caused by human biologies, intrinsic to human anthropological nature, or based on inherent psychological traits, but are in some way a function of consciousness or cannot be said to exist without conceptual categorization)";
(c) "can believe that races are constructed casual agents (unnatural, without any basis in biologies, strictly contingent on self-descriptions, culturally specific, a feature of malleable social psychologies, defined by social relations of ethnic or national character, etc., and thereby cause events to occur or are strongly correlated to particular sorts of events)";
(d) "believes that the use of racial categories is never justified because they refer to objective realities; but, justified—only if they serve some special social or psychological role." (p. 19)

Harris's introduction is also extremely informative and apropos insofar as it aids in the unraveling of objectivist from constructivist racial arguments, and vice versa. He carefully lays out the differences between each area of racial discursive formation and then, by the end of the anthology, in his essay, "What, Then, Is Racism?," explicates several of the deficiencies and difficulties involved in past and present "racial thinking" (constructivist and objectivist). A few of the more noteworthy books and anthologies on race that have figured into my analysis here include: Babbitt and Campbell (1999), Goldberg (1990, 1993), Hannaford (1996), Zack (1995, 1997, 1998), and Zack, Shrage, and Sartwell (1998).

20. On "economic determinism" in the Marxist tradition, see Herbert Marcuse, "The Foundations of Historical Materialism," in *Studies in Critical Philosophy* (1973a, pp. 1–48), Callari, Cullenberg, and Biewener (1995), Magnus and Cullenberg (1995), and West (1988b, 1991).

21. I have in mind here, Antonio Gramsci's various writings on ideology and culture, as well as his distinct conception of a "philosophy of praxis." For further discussion, see Gramsci (1971, 1977, 1978, 1985, 2000). With regard to Georg Lukacs, one need look no further than his Western Marxist classic, *History and Class Consciousness: Studies in Marxist Dialectics* (1971). As Cabral (1979) asserted: "We must at all times see the part and the whole" (p. 47). Lukacs, with the original 1923 publication of *History and Class Consciousness*, a year before Amilcar Cabral (1924–1973) was born, thundered: "It is not the primacy in economic mo-

tives in historical explanation that constitutes the decisive difference between Marxism and bourgeois thought, but the point of view of totality. The category of totality, the all-pervasive supremacy of the whole over the parts is the essence of the method which Marx took over from Hegel and brilliantly transformed into the foundations of a wholly new science" (Lukacs, 1971, p. 27; see also Heller, 1983; Feenberg, 1981; Kadarkay, 1991, 1995; Lukacs, 1973; Marcus and Tarr, 1989; Parkinson, 1970). Cabral's critical theory, building on and going beyond Fanon's critical theory, seeks a comprehensive—what Lukacs would term "totalizing"—view of how even the most absurd and inharmonious aspects of the colonial world need to be interpreted and critically understood in light of the fact that the colonial world is several parts, or "compartments," as Fanon (1968, p. 37) would have it, that make up the whole. As Edward Said (1999), in "Traveling Theory Reconsidered," speculated: "Fanon seems to have read Lukacs's book [*History and Class Consciousness*] and taken from its reification chapter an understanding of how even in the most confusing and heterogeneous of situations, a rigorous analysis of one central problematic could be relied on to yield the most extensive understanding of the whole" (p. 207). Further, considering that Jock McCulloh, in his *In The Twilight of Revolution: The Political Theory of Amilcar Cabral* (1983b), and Tsenay Serequeberhan, in *The Hermeneutics of African Philosophy* (1994), have both observed levels of continuity, as well as discontinuity, in the discourses of Fanon and Cabral, it seems highly probable that Cabral, first, by critically engaging Fanon, who according to the speculations of Said (1999) translated the theory of totality and reification into the colonial world and the discourse on decolonization and, second, by acknowledging the fact that Fanon appears to have exerted a certain amount of influence on Cabral and his critical theory, may have surreptitiously been influenced by Lukacs' theory of totality and concept of reification. On "totality" as a *leitmotif* in "Western Marxist" discourse, see Martin Jay, *Marxism and Totality* (1984). It should be noted, however, that Jay *does not* include a solitary non-European/non-white Marxist in his work; nary a word concerning the life-work, theories and praxes of persons such as: W. E. B. Du Bois, C. L. R. James, George Padmore, Cyril Briggs, W.A. Domingo, Richard B. Moore, Otto Huiswood, Eloise Moore, Bonita Williams, A. Phillip Randolph, Chandler Owen, Hubert Harrison, Harry Haywood, Rev. George Washington Woodbey, Claudia Jones, Mao Tse-Tung, Ho Chi Minh, Kwame Nkrumah, Sekou Toure, Julius Nyerere, Richard Wright, Frantz Fanon, Eric Williams, Che Guevara, Fidel Castro, Amilcar Cabral, Salvador Allende, Walter Rodney, Maurice Bishop, Enrique Dussel, or Jose Carlos Mariategui, etc. Again, it should be strongly stressed, one of the major distinguishing factors of Africana critical theory is its revolutionary humanism and epistemic openness with regard to the theories and praxes of non-African radicals and revolutionaries.

22. The work of Patricia Hill Collins, among others, has been extremely influential on my thinking with regard to the necessity of including "gender" insights and issues in any authentic (especially Africana) critical social theory. Her introductory essay, "The Politics of Critical Social Theory," from her book *Fighting Words: Black Women and the Search for Justice* (1998, pp. ix–xxiii), has provided me with a paradigm and an example of *what* and *how* critical social theory *ought to* go about interpreting our life-worlds and thought- and belief-systems (ideologies) with the intention of permanently, positively, and progressively altering them. Other texts that have been influential insofar as my current position on the inclusion of "gender" insights and issues in Africana critical social theory are: A.Y. Davis (1981, 1989, 1998a), and hooks (1981, 1984, 1989, 1990, 1991). Works that figure prominently in my conception of an authentic Africana critical social theory that attempts to explicitly interpret and alter race, gender, class, and sexuality issues are, Lorde (1984, 1988, 1996, 2004), A.Y. Davis (1998a), J.A. James (1996, 1997, 1999), Johnson and Henderson (2005), and Mercer (1994).

23. For a detailed discussion of the folk philosophies, thought-formations, and social constructions that have, to a certain extent, congealed to create our current dialectics of domination and liberation and barbarity and civilization; which have collided and as a result have

had and continue to have cataclysmic effects of our life- (and language-) worlds, consult Goldberg (1993), C.W. Mills (1997), and Pateman (1988).

24. Again, according to Ashcroft, Griffiths, and Tiffin (1998), to "deracinate" means, literally, "to pluck or tear up by the roots; to eradicate or exterminate" (p. 68). Africana critical theory, then, seeks to "eradicate or exterminate" the faulty thinking of certain social constructions that lead to social problems, and it engages the social problems themselves simultaneously as it projects and provides alternative "visions of a liberated future" (see L. Neal, 1989). In this regard, Africana critical theory connects, and hopefully will contribute to the critical discourse on neo- and/or post-colonialism. For a discussion, see Ashcroft, Griffiths, and Tiffin (1989, 1995), Eze (1997b), Loomba (1998), Said (1979, 1989, 1993), and Thieme (1996).

25. For further discussion of Marxist concepts of "class," "class formation," and "class struggle," see Gibson-Graham, Resnick and Wolff (2001), Houtman (2003), Kirk (1996), and, of course, E.O. Wright (1978, 1979, 1985, 1989, 1992, 1994, 1997, 2005).

26. The Marxist discourse on the "Asiatic mode of production" is, to say the least, diverse and, quite often, heatedly debated. The major works are: Bailey and Llobera (1981), Dunn (1982), Ferenc (1979), Krader (1975), O'Leary (1989), Sawer (1977), and Schram (1969).

27. Chabal relates that Cabral (1983a) was, among other things, a humanist, and one of the "key aspects of his personality was his deep commitment to humanist ideals and his direct concern for human beings, especially the oppressed and down-trodden" (p. 168). According to Chabal: "Cabral's approach to politics in general and to revolution and socialism in particular is . . . better understood in the light of . . . more direct personal concerns than by way of his more abstract theoretical pronouncements. It becomes easier to see why his political work as a party leader and teacher emphasized the need for personal morals and decency by all and not merely political vigor and dedication on the part of the party cadre. Most of his speeches to party members stress their duty to act in accordance with principles of honesty and morality. Cabral had an almost puritanical notion of what these responsibilities implied. . . . Party members must not only seek to improve the living conditions of the population, they must also display the qualities of goodness and honesty which the revolution demanded. Cabral's view of the new society, therefore, derived largely from his view of the requirements of human virtue. Socialism was desirable because, and insofar as, it genuinely sought to create a better society, not simply a more prosperous one" (p. 179).

28. On this point, I should like to reiterate that Lewis Gordon (1997a), in the introduction to *Existence in Black: An Anthology of Black Existential Philosophy*, has asserted that: "Africana philosophy's history of Christian, Marxist, Feminist, Pragmatist, Analytical, and Phenomenological thought has . . . been a matter of what specific dimensions each had to offer the existential realities of theorizing blackness. For Marxism, for instance, it was not so much its notions of 'science' over all other forms of socialist theory, nor its promise of a world to win, that may have struck a resonating chord in the hearts of black Marxists. It was, instead, Marx and Engels famous encomium of the proletarians' having nothing to lose but their chains. Such a call has obvious affinity for a people who have been so strongly identified with chattel slavery" (p. 4). Cabral, Fanon, Du Bois, James, and the theorists of Negritude, among other Africana intectual-activists, have each critically engaged Marxist (socialist and/or communist) theory, among other traditions and schools of thought, precisely insofar as they understand them to offer viable alternatives to the human suffering and misery of their respective times and circumstances. Cesaire (1972) may very well have said it best when he stated that the necessity of "our liberation placed [and continues to place] us on the left" (p. 78). He further asserted, it need be recalled: "Marx is all right, but we need to complete Marx" (p. 70).

29. In this sense Cabral's critical theory bares startling and striking similarities to Cornel West's "prophetic pragmatism." See West, *The American Evasion of Philosophy* (1989), and es-

pecially chapter 6, "Prophetic Pragmatism: Cultural Critique and Political Engagement" (pp. 211–242), where he states that "prophetic pragmatism": (1) "closely resembles the radical democratic elements of Marxist theory, yet its flexibility shuns any dogmatic, a priori, or monistic pronouncements" (p. 214); (2) "promotes genealogical materialist modes of analysis" (p. 223); and, (3) is distinctive in the sense that its "hallmarks . . . are a universal consciousness that promotes an all-embracing democratic and libertarian moral vision, a historical consciousness that acknowledges human finitude and conditionedness, and a critical consciousness which encourages relentless critique and self-criticism for the aims of social change and personal humility" (p. 232). Although West comes to, or draws, the bulk of his conclusions from his engagement of Western European and European American (masculinist) philosophical traditions, it should be observed that he is on point on many issues, but, perhaps because he remains so closely wedded to white, Eurocentric, and masculinist philosophical traditions his work often suffers from many of the very difficulties and deficiencies that he has been wont to criticize his white/Western male colleagues' thought and texts for. West knows full well that it would be extremely absurd, and go far amiss, to purport that one was writing "a masterful text" of contemporary social theory and radical politics without considering "racial and gender subjugation" (p. 223). However, he does not appear to comprehend that observing and/or acknowledging the necessity of critically engaging racial and gender oppression (and I would add, other forms of subjugation, say, economic and heterosexist oppression, etc.) in contemporary critical social theory, does not necessarily mean that one has or is actually engaging racial and gender oppression. West, it seems to me, would have to actually engage the oppositional knowledge(s) and social theories of race and gender oppressed peoples in order to really understand and offer alternatives to the current social setting(s) that would, as he admonishes others, really and truly grapple with racial and gender oppression in positive and progressive ways. For examples of (radical) politics and (critical) social theory that does consider racial and gender (among other forms of) domination, oppression and exploitation, see A.Y. Davis (1981, 1989, 1998a), P.H. Collins (1998, 2000, 2005, 2006), hooks (1984,1991, 1995, 2000a, 2004a, 2004b), J.A. James (1996, 1997, 1999), and Rabaka (2007a, 2008a).

30. I use the term "underdeveloped" here in the sense that Walter Rodney (1972) does in *How Europe Underdeveloped Africa*, and especially in the section entitled, "What Is Underdevelopment?," when he wrote: "The question as to who, and what, is responsible for African underdevelopment can be answered at two levels. First, the answer is that the operation of the imperialist system bears major responsibility for African economic retardation by draining African wealth and by making it impossible to develop more rapidly the resources of the continent. Second, one has to deal with those who manipulate the system and those who are either agents or unwitting accomplices of the said system. The capitalists of Western Europe were the ones who actively extended their exploitation from inside Europe to cover the whole of Africa. In recent times, they were joined, and to some extent replaced, by capitalists from the United States; and for many years now even the workers of those metropolitan countries have benefited from the exploitation and underdevelopment of Africa. None of these remarks are intended to remove the ultimate responsibility for development from the shoulders of Africans. Not only are there African accomplices inside the imperial system, but every African has a responsibility to understand the system and work for its overthrow" (pp. 27–28). Rodney's work has been enormously influential on my conception of black radical politics and critical social theory. For more on Rodney, please see Rodney (1963, 1965, 1967, 1970, 1972, 1976, 1981, 1990). The noted Caribbean political scientist Rupert Lewis (1998) has provided one of the best critical commentaries on Rodney's life and legacy.

31. In *Marxism, 1844–1990: Origins, Betrayal, Rebirth*, Roger Gottlieb provides an extremely accessible yet critical interpretation of the original theories developed by Karl Marx that became, after his death, and in the hands of Fredriech Engels, Karl Kautsky, and Eduard Bern-

stein, among others, an orthodox doctrine that was to be strictly adhered to (pp. 59–71). This work is important in the sense that it lays out a one hundred and fifty year trajectory of (Western European) Marxist thought in clear and cogent language. For more technical and historicized readings of the so-called "Western Marxist" tradition (which include the Frankfurt School critical theorists), and which shed more light on the positive and progressive possibilities of Marxist thought, see *New Left Review* (1977), Jay (1984), and Howard (1988). On Marx's and Marxist influence on diasporan African intellectual-activists, see C.J. Robinson (2000). And, for a contemporary critique of the Marxist project that bids Marxism farewell, argues that "Marxism is over," and announces that "we" (read: the European and Euro-American Lefts) are "on our own," see Ronald Aronson, *After Marxism* (1995). Aronson's work eloquently explicates the overall positives and negatives of the Marxist project and does not merely question whether this or that aspect of Marxist theory is viable, but often goes against the grain of neo-Marxist literature by *not* providing another big, social blueprint that, at some remote date, is suppose to cure all social ills. Granted, Aronson's work bears striking similarities to Marcuse's *One Dimensional Man* (1964), with its bleak and at times pessimistic tone, it nonetheless does end, unlike *One Dimensional Man*, on an affirmative note; invoking not only the later "utopian" Marcuse, but also Ernst Bloch, and particularly his work, *The Principle of Hope* (1986).

32. Cabral is noted for using agronomical language in his discourse on national liberation. *Humus*, according to *Webster's Dictionary*, is a brown or black substance resulting from the partial decay of plant and animal matter, it is the organic and, often, most potent part of the soil.

33. With regard to the self-determination of all peoples, see endnote #5 above, and UN General Assembly resolutions: 523 (VI) of 12 January 1952, 626 (VII) of 21 December 1952, 1314 (XIII) of 12 December 1958, and 1803 (XVII) of 14 December 1962.

34. On this point, Ernest Wamba-Dia-Wamba (1991), in "Philosophy in Africa: Challenges of the African Philosopher," asserted: "Either philosophy unites with the popular masses, who make the authentically national history, and is thus liberating; or it is separated from them—idealizes itself—and loses its creative foundation and thus becomes oppressive. In today's Africa, to think is increasingly to think *for* or *against* imperialism. Indifference, neutrality, and even ignorance only strengthen imperialism. Any discourse on objectivism, or cognitive non-involvement as the condition of truth and science, is nothing but an imperialist form of persuasion" (p. 244, emphasis in original). As Cabral admonishes the African masses, and Wamba-Dia-Wamba African philosophers, to define their positions either *for* or *against* imperialism, I would like—considering our contemporary condition(s)—to forward a similar suggestion to contemporary Africana (and other) critical theorists. Our work must be historically rooted, socially relevant and morally responsible, and we must make every effort to relate our (concrete) philosophies and/or (critical) theories to: (1) radical political praxes that provide a foundation for and help to foster (2) revolutionary democratic socialist transformation that would ultimately lead to (3) the radical/revolutionary and rational redistribution of human and material resources—that is, the radical/revolutionary and rational redistribution of cultural capital, social wealth, and political power.

35. I am well aware that this statement, at first glance, may appear to many as fairly "utopian." However, I say to the anti-utopianists and democratic socialist skeptics precisely what Herbert Marcuse (1969b) did: "I will not be deterred by one of the most vicious ideologies of today, namely, the ideology which derogates, denounces and ridicules the most decisive concepts and images of a free society as merely 'utopian' and 'only' speculative. It may well be that precisely in those aspects of socialism which are today ridiculed as utopian, lies the decisive difference, the contrast between an authentic socialist society and the established societies, even the most advanced industrial societies" (p. 20). A certain amount of utopianism, therefore, has its place, but I contend that this type of thinking is most effective only after a (hopefully "critical") theorist has, in extremely accessible language, ex-

plicated "what is." That is to say that the theorist has engaged and interpreted the world, or a specific circumstance or situation, as it actually exists, in its concreteness. A critical theorist describes and criticizes "what is," and—perhaps herein lies the distinction of "critical" theorists and "critical" theory—projects and provides alternatives, potentialities and possibilities as to how and the ways in which we (collectively) can produce "what ought to be." It is in this light that I agree with Marcuse (1968, p. xx) when he asserted that, "freedom is only possible as the realization of what today is called utopia" (also, see Marcuse, 1970a, pp. 62–82). I take Marcuse to mean that just as human beings, history, and culture are always and ever evolving, so too should our concept(s) of what it means to be free, our concept(s) of freedom. With the present state of technology, science, communications, etc., we have the ways and the means through which we can bring into being forms of freedom (modes of human/e existence and experience) unfathomed and unimagined by any other people, in any other age or epoch. As critical theorists, it is our task, indeed, it is our solemn duty, to promote liberating, as opposed to dominating, uses of human and material resources, as well as science and technology.

# 7

# Africana Critical Theory: Overcoming the Aversion to New Theory and New Praxis in Africana Studies and Critical Social Theory

I was most interested in ways in which philosophy could serve as a basis for developing a critique of society and how that critique of society could figure into the development of practical strategies for the radical transformation of society. . . . I never saw philosophy as separate from a social critique or from social activism.

—Angela Y. Davis, *African American Philosophers: 17 Conversations*, p. 21

[T]he writings of thinkers who were engaged in very concrete struggle in their communities tend to be overlooked as philosophical or theoretical. . . . But there's a whole other part of philosophy and theory that is not professionalized and that, for me, is the exciting part.

—Joy A. James, *African American Philosophers: 17 Conversations*, pp. 255–256

Practice without thought is blind; thought without practice is empty. . . . Social revolution must therefore have, standing firmly behind it, an intellectual revolution, a revolution in which our thinking and philosophy are directed towards the redemption of our society. Our philosophy must find its weapons in the environment and living conditions of the African people. It is from those conditions that the intellectual content of our philosophy must be created.

—Kwame Nkrumah, *Consciencism: Philosophy and Ideology for Decolonization*, p. 78

If it is true that a revolution can fail, even though it be nurtured on perfectly conceived theories, nobody has yet successfully practiced Revolution without a revolutionary theory.

—Amilcar Cabral, *Unity and Struggle: Speeches and Writings of Amilcar Cabral*, p. 123

## RECONSTRUCTING AND REPOLITICIZING CRITICAL SOCIAL THEORY: SYNTHESIZING CRITICAL RACE THEORY, BLACK MARXISM, BLACK FEMINISM, WOMANISM, REVOLUTIONARY DECOLONIZATION, AND REVOLUTIONARY RE-AFRICANIZATION

We may conclude in light of the foregoing chapters that the relationship between theory and praxis has always been a core concern within the classical Africana tradition of critical theory, and remains relevant for contemporary Africana critical theorists. In terms of Du Bois's inauguration and contributions to classical Africana critical theory, we have witnessed that it not only promoted and provides a paradigm for an ongoing transdisciplinary synthesis of philosophy with history, sociology, psychology, political science and economics, among other disciplines, but that from its inception Africana critical theory distinguished itself from Eurocentric and Marxist class conflict-focused critical theory by strongly stressing the importance of race, racism, and white supremacy; gender, sexism, and patriarchy; colonialism, racial colonialism, and capitalist colonialism, as well as its unique race-centered and racism-conscious critique of capitalism and promotion of radical and, at times, revolutionary democratic socialism. For example, though Du Bois's early work undoubtedly falls within the realm of black bourgeois intellectualism, his middle period and later work ultimately gave way to what can only properly be called *praxis-promoting theory*, or *theory with practical intent*, which he conceived to be the critical theoretical arm of radical, and later, revolutionary social and political struggles and movements. With regard to Fanon's contributions to Africana critical theory, he consistently linked theory to revolutionary decolonization, calling on the wretched of the earth to shake free from the physical *and* psychological shackles that have long bound them and arrested their development. For Cabral, theory is employed as a weapon in the war against imperialism. It is not the exclusive domain of petit bourgeois intellectuals, colonial administrators, or anti-colonial party or movement leaders, but can be utilized and put into action by anyone who is willing to think critically about the colonial world and its connections to capitalism, racism, and sexism.

Even with the intense emphasis on the production of praxis-promoting theory, theory with practical intent, and theory grounding in and growing out of radical and revolutionary continental and diasporan movements, very few contemporary Africana intellectual-activists, with very few exceptions, have explored the practical dimensions of Africana Studies in general, and Africana theory in specific (Aldridge and Young, 2000; Aldridge and James, 2007; Asante and Karenga, 2006; Bobo and Michel, 2000; Bobo, Hudley and Michel, 2004; Gordon and Gordon, 2006a, 2006b; Hudson-Weems, 2007; Marable, 2000, 2005). Consequently, the Africana tradition of critical theory has suffered as serious deficit and scarcely any Africana Studies scholars, including Africana philosophers, have consciously contributed to the discourse and development of an Africana critical theory of contemporary culture and society. While several contemporary Africana Studies scholars have produced detailed and often comprehensive works in cultural criticism, social theory, philosophy, liberation theology and literary theory, their contributions to "concrete philosophy," "philosophy of praxis," "theory with practical intent," and radical politics are more than modest in view of the innovativeness and enormity of the classical contributions to the Africana tradition of critical theory. The classical contributions have been chronicled and often apolitically analyzed, usually from disciplinary perspectives other than those of Africana Studies, throughout the twentieth century, but their radical and, even more, their revolutionary promise has sadly remained unrealized, and this is all the more bewildering considering the resurgence of issues at the dawn of the twenty-first century which plagued continental and diasporan Africans, as well as humanity as a whole, in the twentieth century. This book offers the first extended examination of the Africana tradition of critical theory and demonstrates why this tradition remains relevant to, not simply Africana Studies and Africana intellectual-activists, but to struggling continental and diasporan Africans, "the black masses," if you will, who are the authentic architects, tireless teachers, and the singular subjects of Africana Studies. This book, also, has implications for non-African cultural critics, social theorists, postcolonial theorists, critical race theorists, revolutionary nationalists, and revolutionary humanists, among others, who understand the increasing importance of critical comparative cultural studies, revolutionary multiculturalism, and transethnic insurgent intellectual-activism.

The Africana tradition of critical theory has several serious challenges before it; challenges which if not adequately addressed could potentially signal setbacks in its continued conceptual generation and much-needed discursive development or, worst, setbacks that ultimately symbolize Africana critical theory's intellectual epitaph. One of the many major challenges Africana critical theory must immediately engage involves developing a deeper dialogue with the discourse(s) of Africana Women's Studies, which includes both black feminist and womanist theory (Dove, 1998a; Guy-Sheftall, 1995, Hudson-Weems, 1995, 2004; James and Sharpley-Whiting, 2000; Nnaemeka, 1998; Sharpley-Whiting, 2002). Another major conceptual hurdle that Africana critical theory must urgently address is simultaneously deepening and developing its relationship with black radical politics in general, and the discourse of black Marxism in particular.

There is a tendency in Africana Studies where black feminists seem to dialogue more deeply and more frequently with white feminists than with the womanists diligently working in their own field—womanists who have been and currently continue to work on a wide-range of often-identical issues employing transdisciplinary research methods and cross-cultural critical perspectives that are much more compatible with black feminism than those of the majority of white feminists (Allan, 1995; K.G. Cannon, 1988, 1995; P.H. Collins, 1995; Dove, 1998a, 1998b; Floyd-Thomas, 2006a, 2006b; Houston and Idriss, 2002; Hudson-Weems, 1995, 1997, 1998a, 1998b, 1998c, 2000, 2001a, 2001b, 2004, 2007; L. Phillips, 2006; Riggs, 1994; Townes, 1993a, 1993b, 1995, 2006; S. Williams, 1990). This is due, in part, to the controversy surrounding nomenclature, not simply in Africana Women's Studies, but in Africana Studies in general (Aldridge and Young, 2000; Asante and Karenga, 2006; Gordon and Gordon, 2006a, 2006b; Hudson-Weems, 2007). Many women of African descent are fine with being labeled "black feminists," while others prefer to "self-name," "self-describe," and "self-define" themselves and their work as "womanists" and "womanism," respectively. Though continuing to call herself a black feminist, Patricia Hill Collins (2000) has argued that "[r]ather than developing definitions and arguing over naming practices—for example, whether this thought [or, thought-tradition] should be called black feminism, womanism,

Afrocentric feminism, Africana womanism, and the like—a more useful approach lies in revisiting the reasons why black feminist thought exists at all" (p. 22). According to Collins, black feminist thought exists as a consequence of the "dialectical relationship linking African American women's oppression and activism." She continues, "[a]s long as black women's subordination within intersecting oppressions of race, class, gender, sexuality, and nation persists, black feminism as an activist response to that oppression will remain needed" (p. 22). This means, then, that no matter how women of African descent define, describe, and identify themselves and their classical and contemporary thought-tradition(s), what is of paramount importance is that Africana critical theorists *recognize* and *utilize* their theories and praxes, along with the work of others (e.g., authentic anti-racist white feminists, as well as Native American, Chicana/Latina, and Asian radical/revolutionary feminists and womanists), in their efforts to critically engage the interlocking, intersecting, and overlapping nature of race, gender, class, and sexuality oppression in continental and diasporan African life-worlds and life-struggles (see also, P.H. Collins, 1986a, 1986b, 1998, 2003, 2005, 2006).

We witness a similar situation when we come to the work of the black Marxists. They, too, it seems to me, exhibit a propensity to dialogue more deeply and more frequently with white Marxists and the Eurocentric Marxist tradition in general than they tend to dialogue with and critically develop the black radical tradition, which, if truth be told, pre-dates the Eurocentric Marxist tradition, and offers a wealth of critical social and critical racial theories that speak more directly to the special issues confronting continental and diasporan Africans (Bogues, 2003; C.W. Mills, 1987, 2003). This is not in any way to say that the black Marxists and the black feminists should not critically dialogue with white Marxists and white feminists, but only to remind them that their dialogues with the Eurocentric theorists working in their respective areas of interest usually either exhibit an intense intellectual inferiority complex, or are stuck in a deconstructive mode where there is merciless criticism of every aspect of Marxism or feminism that may even seem to be Eurocentric or patriarchal without, and this is the real problem, contributing to efforts aimed at reconstructing the black radical tradition—which has always included radical black women, many of whom pre-date the black feminism versus womanism debate— and creating new critical theories of race, gender and (neo)colonialism, as well as incorporating conventional critical theory's critique of capitalism and bourgeois culture.[1] In other words, there is a predisposition on the part of many black Marxists and black feminists to contribute to the critique and deconstruction of Eurocentric and patriarchal theory, but no real conscious efforts aimed at the critical reconstruction of the black radical tradition, of which black feminism and black Marxism are merely two of myriad trends, and, even more, there seems to be very little emphasis on conceptual generation: that is, the creation of new critical theory that not only transgresses Eurocentric and patriarchal theory, but transcends the black radical tradition, simultaneously strongly stressing the black radical tradition's need to constantly and self-reflexively identify and rid itself of its obsolete aspects, and its need to maintain an epistemic openness, not only to new theories emerging from Africana Studies, but new theoretical developments in the discourses of Marxism, feminism, and humanism, among others areas, as well (Rabaka, 2007a, 2008a).

Here, then, let us critically examine some of the major movements in contemporary critical social theory and, particularly, cutting-edge work on the radical socialist-feminist scene. This will aid us in our endeavor to distinguish the Africana tradition of critical theory from the insights and advances of those working in the Frankfurt School tradition of critical theory. Moreover, by engaging the work of those theorists operating from a simultaneously Marxist and feminist perspective we will be able to further identify and deepen our understanding of the issues that conceptually confront and pose pivotal conceptual pitfalls for the future development of Africana critical theory, and specifically its ongoing efforts to emphasize the importance of race and racism, as well as other issues, with regard to any theory that claims to be a theory "critical" of the established (dis)order's ideologies, domination, oppression, and exploitation. A brief but critical examination of Frankfurt School-based feminism will, therefore, provide us with an opportunity to take a serious look at one of the most provocative theoretical productions in recent radical thought history: Nancy Fraser's (1989) articulation of a "feminist critical theory" of contemporary society.

## THE SUBTLETIES OF WHITE SUPREMACY: THE RACE(IST) POLITICS OF MARXIST CRITICAL THEORY AND EUROCENTRIC FEMINIST THEORY

In "What's Critical About Critical Theory?: The Case of Habermas and Gender," the noted feminist and critical theorist Nancy Fraser (1991) asserts that "a critical social theory of capitalist societies needs gender-sensitive categories," which is to say that critical theory should move away from the "usual androcentric understanding" and ordering of things commonplace in orthodox Marxian theory (p. 371). It should, contrary to the critical theories of many members of the Frankfurt School (and their discursive descendants), seriously engage the particularities of, and differences between, female and male domination and discrimination. For instance, as Jürgen Habermas says "virtually nothing about gender" in *Theory of Communicative Action*, his much-touted magnum opus, Fraser finds his critical theory seriously deficient (p. 358). By conducting a "gender-sensitive reading" of his social theory, Fraser reveals that "there are some major lacunae in Habermas's otherwise powerful and sophisticated model of the relations between public and private institutions in classical capitalism" (p. 370). For Fraser, when Habermas writes of the worker-citizen-soldier in his critique of the public and private spheres under capitalism, he lays bear some of the major weaknesses of his—and, in my opinion, many of the other members of the Frankfurt School's—critical theory: his failure to come to critical terms with "the gender subtext of the relations and arrangements he describes," and the fact that "feminine and masculine identity run like pink and blue threads through the areas of paid work, state administration and citizenship as well as through the domain of familial and sexual relations. This is to say that gender identity is lived out in all arenas of life" (pp. 367, 370).[2]

In agreement with Fraser, I believe that "gender-sensitive readings" of, and radical changes in, "the very concepts of citizenship, childrearing and unpaid work," as well as "changes in the relationships among the domestic, official-economic, state and political-public spheres" are necessary (p. 371). However, my conception of critical theory also takes into consideration the *racial subtext(s)* and argues for *race-sensitive readings* of power relations in the modern and "postmodern" moments. I am very excited about the prospects of developing "feminist," "gender sensitive" and/or, as I prefer, *critical women's liberation theory*. Which, in other words, is to say that I am deeply devoted to developing critical social theory and cultural analysis that acknowledges, in Fraser's words, that: "We are, therefore, struggling for women's autonomy in the following special sense: a measure of collective control over the means of interpretation and communication sufficient to permit us to participate on par with men in all types of social interaction, including political deliberation and decision-making" (p. 378).

What bothers me about Fraser's articulation of a feminist critical theory, however, is the limited scope of her social-theoretical framework. While she correctly takes Habermas—and, in many senses, the whole of the Frankfurt School tradition of critical theory—to task for the "gender-blindness" or, what I am wont to call, the *gender insensitivity* of his social-theoretical framework, like Habermas, Fraser fails to theorize some of the ways in which racism adds a different, perhaps deeper dimension to domination and discrimination in contemporary culture and society. Put another way, I am highly perplexed by the *racial myopia*, that is, the racial blindness of a sophisticated feminist social theorist such as Fraser who, perhaps utilizing the Frankfurt School critical-theoretical framework and philosophically following many of its male members, treats race, racism, anti-racist struggle and critical race theory as incidental and, more to the point, tertiary to the critique of sexism (and particularly patriarchy) and capitalism.[3]

Many theorists have explored sexism, and many theorists have explored racism, and a multitude of theorists (especially Marxists!) have critiqued capitalism. But, racism *and* sexism *and* capitalism (*and* colonialism, I might add), treated in a critical conjunctive manner—perhaps of the sort advocated by the "black lesbian feminist socialist mother of two, including one boy," Audre Lorde (1984, p. 114), and the kind of analysis that the black feminist sociologist Deborah King (1995) writes of in her classic essay, "Multiple Jeopardy, Multiple Consciousness: The Context of Black Feminist Ideology"—calls for a critical engagement of the Africana tradition of critical theory and its distinct contributions to radical politics and critical social theory.

What do we find when we turn to the Africana tradition of critical theory?

In this often-overlooked critical thought-tradition we are undoubtedly, and perhaps unexpectedly for some, exposed to an arsenal of criticisms, a wide-range of theoretical weapons, which challenge and seek to provide solutions to several of the major social and political problems of the nineteenth, twentieth and, I should like to be one of the first to add, twenty-first centuries. This assertion is all the more evident when we critically engage Du Bois's contributions to critical theory. Though his thought covers a wide-range of intellectual terrain and ducks and dips into and out of various academic disciplines (history, sociology, philosophy, political science, economics, religion, education, and literature, among others), Du Bois, it can be said at this point with little or no fan-fare, laid a foundation and provides a critical theoretical framework for the systematic study of the four key forms of domination and discrimination that have shaped the modern world for several centuries: racism, sexism, colonialism, and capitalism. All of his work, whether we turn to his novels, volumes of poetry, plays, autobiographies, cultural criticisms, histories, social studies, political treatises or economic analyses, emanate from the critique of the four aforementioned forms of oppression. Further, when Du Bois's thought is placed into critical dialogue with the work of other classical contributors to Africana critical theory, such as those examined in this study, and contemporary contributors to Africana critical theory—such as, Angela Davis (1981, 1989, 1998a), Lucius Outlaw (1996a, 2005), Cornel West (1982, 1988a, 1989, 1991, 1993a, 1999, 2004), bell hooks (1984, 1995, 2000a), Audre Lorde (1984, 1996, 2004), Manning Marable (1983, 1985a, 1987, 1993, 1996), Patricia Hill Collins (1998, 2000, 2005), Cedric Robinson (2000, 2001), Lewis Gordon (1995b, 1997b, 2000a, 2006a, 2008), and Joy James (1996a, 1997, 1999), among others—a distinguishable Africana tradition of critical theory emerges as not simply a deconstructive critique of Eurocentric Marxist and feminist critical theory, but also a reconstructive challenge to all contemporary or "new" critical theorists.

Returning to Fraser and feminist critical theory, again, I feel compelled to reiterate that I utterly agree with her project when and where she argues that the worker-citizen-soldier in classical and contemporary Marxian traditions (of which Frankfurt School critical theory is a provocative and extremely important twentieth century strand) is not androgynous or gender neutral but, in fact, dreadfully gendered, and malevolently masculinist and male-centered at that. Fraser's radical socialist-feminist theory resonates deeply with my articulation of an Africana critical theory of contemporary society when she accents some of the ways in which basic Marxian categories, such as "worker," "wage," "consumer," and "citizen,"—in her own words:

> are not, in fact, strictly economic concepts. Rather, they have an implicit gender subtext and thus are "gender-economic" concepts. Likewise, the relevant concept of citizenship is not strictly a political concept; it has an implicit gender subtext and so, rather, is a "gender-political" concept. Thus, this analysis reveals the inadequacy of those critical theories that treat gender as incidental to politics and political economy. It highlights the need for a critical-theoretical categorical framework in which gender, politics and political economy are internally integrated. (Fraser, 1991, p. 371)

For Fraser, there are few, if any, gender-neutral concepts in Marxian theory. In fact, much of Marxism, as she avers above, is rather gender-specific and often only speaks to male struggles against economic exploitation; which is to say that Marxism, as it was originally conceived and propagated from Karl Marx through to Herbert Marcuse and the Western or Hegelian Marxist tradition, is one long theorization of working-class men's experience of, and class struggles against, the evils of capitalism (P. Anderson, 1976; Gottlieb, 1992; Kolakowski, 1978a, 1978b, 1978c; Jay, 1984). The trick, though, and one that has not gone unnoticed by Marxist feminists and socialist feminists, is that for a very long time many Marxists (and, many female Marxists notwithstanding) did not realize or critically take into consideration the simple fact that when they wrote or spoke of "workers," "wages," "citizens," and the like, their ideas and arguments were premised on a false gender neutrality that more often than not signified males and their gender-specific sociopolitical wishes and whims (see M. Barrett, 1980; Boxer and Quartaert, 1978; Braun, 1987; M.J. Buhle,

1981; Di Stephano, 1991, 2008; Eisenstein, 1979; A. Ferguson, 1986, 1998; K.E. Ferguson, 1980; Guettel, 1974; Hansen and Philipson, 1990; Hennessey and Ingraham, 1997; Holmstrom, 2002; Meulenbelt, 1984; Roberts and Mizuta, 1993; Rowbotham, 1973, 1979; Sargent, 1981; Slaughter and Kern, 1981). In a patriarchal society, it is "normal," utterly "universal" for theorizing men to exclude the plight of women from their so-called "radical social theory," "theories of social change," and/or their dialectical discourses on domination and liberation (see Benhabib and Cornell, 1987; Essed, Goldberg and Kobayashi, 2005). For male theorists to identify themselves and their discourses as patriarchal, male-supremacist or masculinist, or to make mention of gender at all, is—from their vantage point—superfluous because of the super-structural and supra-structural dynamics of patriarchy and the ways it plays itself out in the said society. Fraser is, indeed, on point when she suggests that what is needed is a closer, more critical "gender-sensitive reading" of classical and contemporary radical thought and praxis in order to develop a critical theory of contemporary society.

Africana critical theory of contemporary society, however, parts company with Fraser's feminist critical theory when it calls for "a critical-theoretical categorical framework in which gender, politics and political economy are internally integrated" without so much as mentioning, let alone seriously engaging, the socio-historical fact that race and racism as well have shaped the modern world and, therefore, should be included in any authentic critical theory of *contemporary* society. Contemporary society, as several self-described "feminists" and "womanists" of African descent have argued, is simultaneously sexist, racist, and economically exploitive—one need not think long about the various vicissitudes of contemporary capitalism and colonialism. The task, then, of contemporary critical theory is to seek solutions to these four fundamental social and political problems, among others as they arise.

In the classical Marxist tradition, and in most of the contemporary Marxist tradition, when Marxists theorize the plight of the "worker," they are not only writing about gender-specific workers, *male workers*, but also racially-specific workers, *white workers*. The terms that the Marxists use are neither gender nor race neutral terms. For instance, just as males are normative in a patriarchal society, so too are whites in a socio-historically white supremacist society. Again, it is superfluous to make mention of such matters as race and gender in a white and male supremacist society, because the white male worldview is always and ever thought and taught to be "neutral" and "universal." To put it plainly: In a white *and* male supremacist society, all are indoctrinated with the dominant ideology, which is inherently a hegemonic white male worldview. Moreover, the appeal of purportedly gender and race neutral terms—such as, *worker, consumer,* and *citizen*—is that they often silently signify white males without actually overtly saying so. What this means, then, is that there are actually invisible pre-reflexive parenthetical adjectives clandestinely attached to these supposedly gender and race neutral terms: (white male) *worker*, (white male) *consumer*, and (white male) *citizen*.[4]

Hence, had Fraser turned to the Africana tradition of critical theory, and especially the work of Angela Davis (1981, 1989, 1998a), Audre Lorde (1984, 1988, 1996, 2004), bell hooks (1981, 1984, 1991, 1995, 2000a, 2004a, 2004b), and Patricia Hill Collins (1998, 2000, 2005, 2006), she would have found not only a critical and analytical engagement of capitalism and sexism, but also some of the most sustained and sophisticated theorizations of race and racism, and the ways in which racism, sexism and capitalism overlap, interlock and intersect, in recent human history. She would, further, have been able to observe not simply the gendered subtext(s) of the Marxian tradition, but also its racial (and, oft times, racist) subtext(s), ultimately positing, as I intend to, the need for Marxists to critically note that their basic concepts and categories are race and gender specific (and supremacist), as well as political and economic. In other words, I am arguing, following the Eritrean philosopher, Tsenay Serequeberhan (1994), that "political 'neutrality' in philosophy, as in most other things, is at best a 'harmless' naiveté, and at worst a pernicious subterfuge for hidden agendas" (p. 4). It is not enough, from the Africana critical theoretical perspective, for Fraser to highlight gender's import for radical political and economic analysis without, in the spirit of the Africana tradition of critical theory, stretching it to encompass the study of race, racism, critical race theory, and contemporary anti-racist struggle. Finally, in the Africana tradition of critical theory, had Fraser turned to it, she would have also found an anti-colonial theory and discourse on revolutionary decolonization that could have possibly helped her extend and expand her concepts of the "inner colonization of the life-world," which she borrowed from Habermas, and "decolonization," which she—similar to almost the entire Frankfurt School tradition of critical theory—limits to life-worlds and lived-experiences in capitalist countries (Fraser, 1989, pp. 129-143, 161-187).[5]

Capitalism, it should be stated outright, does marginalize, exploit, and oppress women in ways markedly different from men, and especially in patriarchal capitalist societies. However, and equally important, capitalism also perpetuates and exacerbates racial domination and discrimination. This is a socio-historical fact that many Marxist feminists and socialist feminists have long neglected, and also a fact to which the Africana tradition of critical theory, and especially Africana women's liberation theorists, have devoted a great deal of time and intellectual energy. Though there is much more in Fraser's theory and the feminist critiques of Frankfurt School critical theory that I find philosophically fascinating, for the purposes of the discussion at hand I have accentuated those aspects of Fraser's arguments that help to highlight the distinctive features of Africana critical theory of contemporary society.

## (RE)CONSTRUCTING THE AFRICANA TRADITION OF CRITICAL THEORY: PLACING A GREATER EMPHASIS ON, AND INCORPORATING THE INSIGHTS OF, AFRICANA WOMEN'S STUDIES

It is not my intention here to (re)interpret and (re)inscribe the Africana male critical theorists examined in the previous chapters as super anti-sexist social theorists. They, quite candidly, were not. However, some of their work does provide contemporary critical theorists, Africana and otherwise, with paradigms that might be extremely useful in the reconstruction and, even more, the creation of new critical theories that speak to the special needs and new problems of the twenty-first century. What I am advocating here, then, is a critical and dialectical, simultaneously womanist *and* black feminist approach to the contributions to the Africana tradition of critical theory explored in this study.[6]

I am well aware of the ways that an anti-sexist male perspective in a male supremacist society is not as suspect as an anti-sexist female perspective—though I would respectfully concede that an anti-sexist male perspective *is* suspect to a certain degree and that gender progressive males are marginalized and ostracized in such a social world, though they have never been marginalized and ostracized to the extent to which (anti-sexist) women have historically been in the said social world. However, and in all intellectual honesty, an anti-sexist male (with the most minute amount of academic credentials and/or institutional affiliation) can quickly become, in the minds of the ruling race/gender/class and their media machines in a male supremacist social world, an authoritative anti-sexist "voice of reason." This, of course, is similar in many senses to the ways that white "race traitors" and white anti-racists are exalted as the definitive voices of anti-racist reason and radical anti-racist political practice in white supremacist society. Africana critical theory must decidedly destabilize and resist efforts to position it as a racialist *or* anti-racist, Marxist *or* Pan-Africanist, black feminist *or* womanist, continental *or* diasporan, or black nationalist *or* revolutionary humanist discourse, because—as stated above—it must continuously critically and dialectically deepen and develop the basic concepts and categories of its socio-theoretical framework and synthesize disparate discourses into its own original *anti-racist, anti-sexist, anti-capitalist, anti-colonialist, and sexual orientation-sensitive critical theory of contemporary society.*

To read Du Bois's *The Souls of Black Folk* and *Darkwater*, or Fanon's *Black Skin, White Masks* and *The Wretched of the Earth*, it is to read not merely studies in race and racism, but also studies in class and caste. To read Du Bois's *Black Reconstruction* and *Color and Democracy*, or C. L. R. James's *The Black Jacobins* and *A History of Pan-African Revolt*, it is not simply to read studies in race, caste and class, but also studies in Pan-Africanism and anti-colonialism. And, finally, when Du Bois's "The Damnation of Women," Angela Davis's *Women, Race, and Class* and *Women, Culture, and Politics*, or bell hooks's *Ain't I A Woman* and *Feminist Theory* are read, what one is reading are not merely studies in race and class theory, but also critical analyses of gender domination and discrimination, and especially as these overlapping, interlocking, and intersecting systems of oppression and exploitation effect the life-worlds and lived-experiences of black women. It is the multidimensionality and transdisciplinary nature of the Africana tradition of critical theory that makes it difficult for opportunistic interpreters to appropriate and (re)articulate this radical thought-tradition in a monodimensional and monodisciplinary manner. Moreover, it is this same multidimensionality and transdisciplinarity of the contributions to the Africana tradition of critical theory explored in the present study that provides paradigmatic examples of some of the ways contemporary male anti-sexist social theorists can simultaneously avoid being appropriated as "the" authoritative and most rational voices of gender justice, and connect critiques of serious sexism with those of racism and classism.

If male anti-sexist social theorists openly and honestly dialogue with, document and disseminate the community and campus work of female anti-sexist social theorists, then, it will be very difficult for male supremacist media machines to project the gender progressive male voice as the definitive voice of gender justice. Critically engaging women's liberation theory and praxis by actively participating in the said theory and praxis, male anti-sexist social theorists can and should expand the range and use(s) of women's liberation theory and other anti-sexist social theory to include the work of both women *and* men who sought and are seeking gender justice. Male anti-sexist social theorists must simultaneously (re)claim and (re)construct male anti-sexist, gender justice, and women's liberation theory and praxis traditions, and share the knowledge they discover and create with gender justice-seeking women and men. In fact, one of the special tasks of anti-sexist men is to encourage our brother-friends to critically examine the ways in which they embrace patriarchy and perpetuate and exacerbate sexism and female domination and discrimination. Male anti-sexist social theorists and activists are long overdue in articulating to sexist men the violent psychological and physical consequences of male supremacist thought and behavior, and how, as quiet as it is kept, this thought and behavior not only robs women of their human and civil rights, but also often causes serious life-threatening conflicts and contradictions among men.[7]

What I am calling for here is for anti-sexist men to unflinchingly encourage sexist men to self-consciously confront and correct their sexist socialization and sexist thought and behavior. Anti-sexist men must embrace the revolutionary responsibility of providing new paradigms for modern masculinity. We must repentantly show the world, and especially women, our sister-friends, that patriarchal, phallocentric, militaristic and misogynistic masculinity are not definitive practices or modes of masculinity but deformations and destructions of masculinity. Masculinity, henceforth and forevermore, must be predicated on moral practice. What it means to be a "man" must begin to be bound up with males' embrace of the ethical obligation to end female domination and discrimination and their promotion of women's decolonization, women's liberation, and radical anti-sexist sociopolitical reorganization.

Africana male anti-sexist social theorists and radical political activists must be bold enough and brave enough to take our cue from our anti-sexist forefathers, men ("father figures") like Charles Lenox Remond, Frederick Douglass, W. E. B. Du Bois, and Frantz Fanon, among others, who—as I have endeavored to illustrate throughout this study—possessed problematic but nonetheless progressive stances on gender justice and, specifically, Africana women's decolonization and liberation. However, and even more than turning to the anti-sexist thought and practice traditions of our forefathers, anti-sexist men of African descent must learn the many lessons our freedom fighting foremothers' legacies of liberation thought and practice have to teach. This impulse to learn radical life-saving and life-enhancing lessons from our foremothers must also extend to the thought, texts and practices of anti-sexist Africana women in our present age. A common characteristic of both black feminist and womanist discourse is the notion that theory and practice must simultaneously speak to the special needs of women of African descent and the emancipatory aspirations of *all* continental and diasporan Africans, which, of course, includes men of African descent. This means, then, that (most) modern black feminists and womanists do not adhere to the constraints of Eurocentric constructions of gender and/or sex roles. The only "role" women and men of African descent have is that of black revolutionaries: radical anti-racist, anti-sexist, and anti-imperialist rebels and renegades. Here, then, lies one of the greatest and, I should say, gravest challenges to the development of critical theory in general, and the Africana tradition of critical theory in specific.

## WAGING WAR WITH THE WEAPON OF AFRICANA CRITICAL THEORY: INTELLECTUAL HISTORICAL AMNESIA, THEORETICAL INHERITANCE, AND ONGOING EPISTEMIC OPENNESS

As an ongoing social praxis-promoting theory and intellectual archaeology project, African critical theory stands very little chance of realization if one of the major problematics of Africana Studies is not critically and consciously overcome—and that is, its seeming hostility toward or, at the least, reluctance to produce new theory to guide new praxis. All too often in Africana Studies and, ironically, even in Africana philosophy, theory is opposed to praxis, to radical politics, to the life-worlds, lived-experiences and life-struggles of continental and diasporan Africans, as though it is something intrinsically outside of Africana revolutionary praxis, and, even more, as though critical thought is somehow absent when and where black revolutionaries and black radical praxis are present. A similar observation could be made of the obverse: All too often black radical praxis is exalted as an end in itself and, very rarely, is it critically and reflexively examined for its contribution to black radical politics and Africana critical theory. It is astonishing that Africana Studies, which prides itself on its intellectual-activist inception and growth out of radical grassroots movements (e.g., the Black Power, Black Arts, Black Women's Liberation, Black Liberation Theology, Black Anti-War, among other, movements), seems to regularly reject or lamely label "Eurocentric" new theories produced by Africana Studies scholars who critically dialogue with a wide-range of anti-racist, anti-sexist, anti-capitalist, anti-colonialist, and sexual orientation-sensitive theory produced by non-Africana Studies scholars, be it critical race theory, feminist theory, Marxist theory, postcolonial theory or queer theory, among others. Narrow-minded notions such as these not only display the *epistemic exclusiveness* and *intellectual insularity* that Africana critical theory on principle challenges and wants nothing whatsoever to do with, but it also demonstrates that this one-dimensional conception of Africana Studies is not in any way revolutionary and, actually, is retrogressive, since it seeks to deform and collapse the traditionally transdisciplinary discipline of Africana Studies into a monstrously mangled monodisciplinary discipline which studies continental and diasporan Africans from some supposed pristine and perfect "African" or "black" racial, ethno-cultural and, this should be emphasized, *essentialist* perspective.

It is all the more interesting that these tendencies to downplay the relationship between, or dislodge the unity of, theory and praxis by many contemporary black *academics* (as opposed to Africana *intellectual-activists*) should be so strong in a field, Africana Studies, which, if truth be told, evolved out of grassroots efforts to consciously connect theory to praxis, and praxis to theory; a field which from its inauguration was amazingly transdisciplinary, transnational, transethnic, transgender, and transgenerational, simultaneously seeking to transgress and transcend the boundaries of both white supremacy and narrow-minded black nationalism; a field which currently has unprecedented access to intellectual and political resources, perhaps, unfathomed by the architects and founders of the field (see Anderson and Stewart, 2007; Blassingame, 1973; Croutchett, 1971; P.T.K. Daniels, 1981; Ford, 1973; P.A. Hall, 1999; Hare, 1972; Harris, Hine and McKay, 1990; Kershaw, 2003; Kilson, 1973, 2000a; Marable, 2000, 2005; Nelson, 2001; Rojas, 2007; Rooks, 2006;

J.B. Stewart, 1996b, 2004; J. Turner, 1984). This seeming *aversion to new theory and new praxis* is, indeed, yet another bewildering, if not cruel, irony in contemporary Africana Studies. The often forgotten fact that theory was never alien to, or outside of—indeed, it was integral to, and inextricable from—every great black radical and black revolutionary movement in the modern moment, and especially throughout the twentieth century, has never been concretely comprehended, deeply internalized, or fully appreciated by contemporary Africana Studies scholars and students. Historically "theory" in Africana Studies, as is so often the contemporary case, has long been associated with the esoterica, obscurantism, and dilettantism of black academic elites or ebony-ivory tower intellectualism, the twentieth and twenty-first century "Talented Tenth," if you will, or, worst, it has been clumsily connected to Eurocentric intellectualism, and specifically European and European American philosophy and science. However, theory in Africana Studies has very rarely been interpreted as we witnessed Cabral advocated it should be, as a "weapon," as a guide to revolutionary praxis, indeed, as an essential instrument in efforts aimed at initiating or continuing the protracted dialectical process of revolutionary decolonization and revolutionary re-Africanization.[8]

Those contemporary Africana Studies scholars who spurn theory and conceptual generation in favor of praxis and concrete activities, not only do a great disservice to the original Africana Studies conception of the unity of theory and praxis, but they inevitably ultimately avoid the key complicated issues, complex dilemmas, and crucial questions that must be resolved if Africana Studies and, even more, continental and diasporan Africans are to really progress, as opposed to regress, and rescue, reclaim and rehabilitate their histories and cultures, as well as continue to make their unique contributions to human culture and civilization. Viewed from an Africana critical theoretical perspective, then, theory is nothing other than the cognitive dimension of revolution which, in other words, means that *Africana critical theory* is nothing other than *serious and systematic, critical and dialectical thinking about the goals, methods, strategies and tactics of continental and diasporan African revolutionary self and social transformation*; what has been referred to as *the dialectical process of revolutionary decolonization and revolutionary re-Africanization*. A wide-range of insurgent intellectual and radical political activities can and do contribute to Africana critical theory, but always emphasis is placed on connecting theory to praxis and praxis to theory, as it was when Africana Studies was established. In the Africana tradition of critical theory, ideas and action, words and deeds, theory and praxis are understood to be inextricable, each deeply implicating and dialectically guiding and informing the other, not separated, or one thought to be more important than the other. In fact, Africana critical theory maintains that the traditional white supremacist social scientific one-sided embrace of *either* theory *or* praxis reduces both of them to uncritical, undialectical, and extremely empty bourgeois abstractions, and this is especially the case when and where past, present, and future continental and diasporan African revolutions are concerned.

More specifically, it is important to observe here that many black radicals and Africana Studies scholars' obsession with immediate practical solutions, with quick concrete choices, with "hurrying up and getting things done" (an idea which, Cornel West asserted in *The American Evasion of Philosophy* [1989], may actually owe a lot more to American pragmatism and anti-intellectualism than revolutionary black nationalism and Pan-Africanism), is actually in line with the way the white supremacist, patriarchal, capitalist-colonial world views black radical politics and revolutionary social movements. Black anti-intellectualism and the over-emphasis on, often antiquated, black radical praxis, no matter how soul-satisfying, mind-boggling and militant, may indeed *temporarily* challenge and transgress white supremacy, patriarchy, capitalism and colonialism, but it historically has not *permanently* solved these pressing problems. Therefore, Africana critical theory argues that *anti-theory action-oriented black radical politics often unwittingly aids imperialism because it does not provide its practitioners with the weapon(s) of theory, which they will need to chart the changes of, and wage war against, the new forms of racism, sexism, capitalism, and colonialism.* In the final analysis, then, the anti-theory thesis or, at the least, the over-emphasis on praxis thesis put forward by many black radicals is actually an a sign of their own intense internalization of Eurocentrism and imperialism, and specifically *the diabolical dialectic of white intellectual superiority and black intellectual inferiority.* What the anti-theory black radicals fail to understand is that the rationale for, and the role of, Africana critical theory is to aid in efforts to create the critical consciousness, the weapons of black revolutionary theory and black revolutionary praxis through which the white supremacist, patriarchal, and capitalist-colonial world is permanently negated and transcended and, even more, the long-hoped for revolutionary anti-racist, critical multicultural, democratic socialist, sexual orientation-sensitive, and liberated women's world is finally established. A further failure of the anti-theory approach to black radical politics and revolutionary social movements is that it seeks to side-step the historical fact that most continental and diasporan Africans have, in one way or another, been racially colonized and that some sort of reflexive theory, dialectical thought, and/or critical thinking is needed to raise an awareness and create a critical consciousness of, not simply their continued racial colonization, oppression and exploitation, but classical and contemporary efforts aimed at revolutionary decolonization and revolutionary re-Africanization.

At the same time, it must be honestly admitted that much more than "theory" in the traditional sense is needed to incite and influence black radical praxis and revolutionary social movements in the modern moment. Again, theory is indispensable to any liberation project but, as we have witnessed with the anti-theorists who over-emphasize what seems to border on anarchic political action, theory is not and should never be made to appear to be an end in itself. Africana critical theory simultaneously intellectually and politically historicizes and epistemically opens up entirely new conceptions and approaches to praxis and revolution, all the while introducing new conceptions and approaches to critical theory, unprecedentedly emphasizing its unique and integral role in the dialectical process of revolutionary decolonization and revolutionary re-Africanization. From the Africana critical theoretical perspective, all human beings are theorists in light of the fact that all human beings think, have the capacity to create, and are essentially social beings who readily participate in, and contribute to, ongoing *shared human projects* and the construction of *shared human products* which constitute the world-historical process of creating new human cultures and civilizations. As this is the case, and to the extent that all human beings have ideas, beliefs, feelings, and aesthetics as they participate in their respective evolving socio-political and cultural orders, and, further, to the extent that all human beings exert some influence on their respective environments, then, all human beings are potentially, if not actually, theorists, though admittedly not "critical" theorists. An additional assertion could be made concerning all human beings as bearers of consciousness, though admittedly not bearers of "critical" consciousness.

Of course, many other critical questions remain: What about the nature and level of consciousness? In what ways do the overlapping, interlocking, and intersecting combined effects of racism, sexism, capitalism, and colonialism impact and affect the creation of critical consciousness amongst continental and diasporan Africans? What forms of consciousness-raising are most promising in the present? Africana critical theory endeavors to resolve the longstanding dichotomy between "the intellectuals" and "the masses," "the experts" and "the laypersons," and "the leaders" and "the followers." It openly challenges Du Bois's original "Talented Tenth" theory and encourages its practitioners to turn to his theory of the "Guiding Hundredth." Where his Talented Tenth thesis has been criticized for being bourgeois, elitist, and unconcerned with the black masses, Du Bois's doctrine of the Guiding Hundredth was almost the complete opposite: revolutionary, collectively led by radical workers and activist-intellectuals, and utterly concerned with the black masses. His additional emphasis on human rights and civil rights ultimately gave way to a discussion of character and service. It was no longer enough for the Talented Tenth to be talented, quipped Du Bois, they also had to be willing and able to struggle, sacrifice, and serve in the best interests of the black masses and humanity as a whole. Du Bois (1996c), then, charged the new Talented Tenth, his Guiding Hundredth, with the task of providing "self-sacrificing," "unselfish, farseeing" leadership through its "honesty of character and purity of motive" (p. 173). He brazenly criticized his 1903 articulation of the Talented Tenth thesis, observing that it "put in control and power, a group of selfish, self-indulgent, well-to-do men, whose basic interest in solving the Negro Problem was [purely] personal" (p. 162).[9]

Africana critical theory compels its practitioners to critically comprehend that the distinctions made between black intellectual elites and the black masses, the "Talented Tenth" and the allegedly "Untalented Ninetieth," if you will, are not simply counter-revolutionary, but also a trend that is central to the social and political division of labor in white supremacist patriarchal bourgeois society. Therefore, Africana critical theory argues that "theory," in the revolutionary sense, should not be disconnected from praxis, but should always be linked to the ongoing process of revolutionary decolonization and revolutionary re-Africanization. There, quite simply, is no room in the Africana tradition of critical theory for black exceptionalism, black intellectual elitism or black vanguardism, à la Du Bois's initial articulation of the Talented Tenth. Africana intellectual-activists must, indeed, continue to practice conceptual generation, but with a deeper and more critical dialogue with the black masses who, in the final analysis, are the true creators and wielders of the weapon of Africana critical theory.

The Africana tradition of critical theory has been often overlooked in annuals of Africana intellectual history, and when on rare occasions it has been engaged it has been seen as the exclusive domain of a very small cohort of big word-wielding and super-sophisticated theorists; many of whom maintain that their work represents an historically-necessary stage in the development of black radical politics and critical social theory. Africana critical theory acknowledges that "theory" in Africana Studies has often been manipulated for elitist and extremely opportunistic purposes which, consequently, explains why so many contemporary Africana Studies scholars and black radicals seem to have a revulsion against or, at the least, an aversion to new theory and new praxis, and often uncritically advocate "returning" to classical black radical political theories and revolutionary praxes. Employing Cabral as one of its primary points of departure, Africana critical theory, indeed, does advocate "returning to the sources" of classical black radical politics and revolutionary praxis, but it importantly distinguishes itself from the theses of the anti-theory or anti-new theory advocates through its emphasis on ongoing epistemic openness and synthesis of classical theory with contemporary theory, Africana and otherwise, in the interest of creating critical theories and revolutionary praxes that address the new and novel issues of the twenty-first century. Africana critical theory argues that it will never be enough for black academics to write sophisticated philosophical treatise and elaborate analyses of racism, sexism, capitalism, and colonialism; though, it does acknowledge that work such as this is undoubtedly indispensable and a significant contribution to the Africana tradition of critical theory. What is more crucial in the long run for Africana critical theory is the popularization and diffusion of the weapon of theory, which is an indispensable aid in, not only critically understanding, but consciously transgressing, transcending and—I dare say—transfiguring white supremacy, patriarchy, capitalism, colonialism, and heterosexism, among other aspects of modern imperialism, in the interest of bringing into being a new, post-imperialist humanity, society, and world. I shall end the way I humbly began, softly saying, singing this solemn, sacred prayer: *Nkosi Sikelel' iAfrika. . . .*

## NOTES

1. As we witnessed in chapter 4 of the present study, Lucius Outlaw (1996a) has provided, perhaps, the best programmatic exposition of the *over-emphasis* on deconstructing Eurocentrism and the *under-emphasis* on the reconstruction of Africana thought-traditions in his classic essay, "African 'Philosophy'?: Deconstructive and Reconstructive Challenges" (pp. 51–74). It would be virtually impossible to overstate the influence of this essay, as well as Outlaw's equally important essay, "Africana Philosophy," on my general argument in this section and throughout the remainder of this conclusion (pp. 75–96). Professor Outlaw, as is well-known, served on my doctoral dissertation committee and was, in many ways, a sort of philosophical "midwife," if you will, who assisted in my conception of Africana critical theory. His thought and texts continue to contribute to my conceptions of black radical politics and critical social theory. It is my humble hope that my work will be seen as an extension and expansion of his conception of "critical theory in the interests of black folk," which he was developing long before I was born (Outlaw, 2005). I, once again, say *asante sana* (thank you a thousand times) to Professor Outlaw for his kind counsel and continued encouragement. He is, without one single doubt, a rare and beautiful human being, and one of the most principled and provocative philosophers critically theorizing at present.

2. With regard to Frankfurt School critical theory, Erich Fromm and Herbert Marcuse incorporated aspects of what could loosely be termed "feminist theory" into their articulations of a critical theory of contemporary society. However, neither theorist was consistent nor ever fully developed a feminist and/or anti-sexist dimension of their respective theories of social change. Though Fromm's inchoate socialist-feminist thinking by far surpasses that of Marcuse prior to the 1960s, it is important to observe Marcuse's efforts in the last decade of his life to

take a "feminist turn," if you will, and to merge Marxism with feminism, among other elements of 1960's radical social thought and political practice. See, for example, Fromm's "The Theory of Mother Right and its Relevance for Social Psychology," "Sex and Character," "Man-Woman," and "The Significance of Mother Right for Today," and Marcuse's "Dear Angela," *Counterrevolution and Revolt*, and "Marxism and Feminism" (Fromm, 1947, 1955, 1970a; Marcuse, 1971, 1972a, 1974). For critical commentary on these thinkers' pro-feminist thought, see Funk (1982), Kellner (1984, 1989, 1992), and P. Mills (1987). And, for further feminist critiques of classical and contemporary Frankfurt School-based critical theory, see Benhabib (1986, 1992), Fraser (1989, 1991), Heberle (2006), and Meehan (1995). More than any other major Frankfurt School critical theorist—Theodor Adorno, Walter Benjamin, Max Horkheimer, and Jürgen Habermas—my conception of critical theory has been indelibly influenced by Herbert Marcuse, whose critical theory increasingly incorporated and openly exhibited the influence of Africana liberation theory (Martin Luther King, Jr., Malcolm X, Frantz Fanon and the Black Panthers), Latin American liberation theory (Che Guevara and Fidel Castro), and women's liberation theory (Rosa Luxemburg and Angela Davis) (see Marcuse, 1969a, pp. 7, 46–47, 79–91, 1970a, pp. 82–108, 1972a). Though Marcuse never dialogued with Africana, Latin American, and women's liberation theory with the depth and detail which he did European and European American (male) theory, and considering the fact that his approach to the life-worlds and lived-experiences of non-Europeans/non-whites was thoroughly shot-through with the accoutrements of Eurocentrism—Marcuse (1972a, pp. 9, 29) employed labels and language such as, "backward capitalist countries" and "barbarian civilization[s]"—there may, yet and still, be much in his social thought that could be of use to Africana and other non-European/non-white critical theorists (see Marcuse, 1964, 1965c, 1969a, 1970a, 1970b, 1972a, 1972b, 1973, 1978a, 1997a, 2001, 2004, 2007a, 2007b). In fact, and in all intellectual honesty, my own deep respect for, and interest in, Marcuse and Marcusean critical theory has been indelibly influenced by the critically acclaimed African American feminist philosopher and radical political activist Angela Davis (2005b), who was one of his students in the late 1960s and who recently remarked at a conference held in honor of the centennial of his birth:

> It seems to me that the overarching themes of Marcuse's thought are as relevant today on the cusp of the twenty-first century as they were when his scholarship and political interventions were most widely celebrated. . . . I am not suggesting that Marcuse should be revived as the preeminent theorist of the twenty-first century. He, more than anyone, insisted on the deeply historical character of theory. It would certainly militate against the spirit of his ideas to argue that his work contains the solution to the many dilemmas facing us as scholars, organizers, advocates, artists, and, I would add, as marginalized communities, whose members are increasingly treated as detritus and relegated to prisons, which, in turn, generate astronomical profits for a growing global prison industry. An uncritical and nostalgic version of Marcuse, which, for example, fails to acknowledge the limits of an aesthetic theory that maintains a rigid distinction between high and low art, one that is not willing to engage seriously with popular culture and all its contradictions, would not be helpful to those who are seeking to forge radical political vocabularies today. But if we abandon our Marcuse nostalgia and attempt to incorporate his ideas into a historical memory that draws upon the useful aspects of the past in order to put them to work in the present, we will be able to hold on to Marcuse's legacies as we explore terrains that he himself could never have imagined. (pp. xi, xiii–xiv)

3. Once again the work of Lucius Outlaw (2005) weighs in. Here and throughout the remainder of this section his work in philosophy of race and critical race theory are juxtaposed with Fraser's feminist philosophy and feminist critical theory. In particular, Outlaw's essays, "Toward a Critical Theory of Race," "Critical Theory in a Period of Radical Transformation," and "Critical Social Thought in the Interests of Black Folk," have been employed as deconstructive and reconstructive paradigms. Where I find Fraser's conception of critical theory weak in terms of grasping and grappling with race and racism, I believe that one of the

major weaknesses of Outlaw's conception of critical theory is that it, in most instances, either does not adequately acknowledge gender, sexism, or patriarchy, or it inadequately engages them when and where it does. My conception of critical theory, Africana critical theory, seeks to salvage and synthesize the most radical, if not revolutionary, aspects of Fraser and Outlaw's conceptions of critical theory, along with a wide-range of new critical theory, to create and contribute a simultaneously anti-racist, anti-sexist, anti-capitalist, anti-colonialist, and sexual orientation-sensitive critical theory of contemporary society (see Rabaka, 2003b, 2004, 2006a, 2007a, 2008a, 2008b).

4. In terms of my argument here, the influence of the Caribbean philosopher, Charles Mills (1997, 1998, 2003a), simply cannot be overstated, and specifically his book *Blackness Visible: Essays on Philosophy and Race* (1998) where he innovatively asserted:

> Suppose we place race at the center rather than in the wings of theory. The idea is to follow the example of those feminist of the 1970s once characterized as radical (as against liberal or Marxist), who, inspired by the U.S. black liberation movement, decided to put gender at the center of their theorizing and appropriated the term *patriarchy* to describe a system of male domination. So rather than starting with some other theory and then smuggling in gender, one begins with the fact of gender subordination. . . . The important point—as "race men" [and "race women"] have always appreciated—is that a racial perspective on society can provide insights to be found in neither a white liberalism nor a white Marxism [nor a white feminism], and when suitably modified and reconstructed, such a perspective need not imply biological generalizations about whites or commit the obvious moral error of holding people responsible for something (genealogy, phenotype) they cannot help. (pp. 98, 104, emphasis in original)

Deeply indebted to Mills's work, Africana critical theory advocates a *conjunctive* approach to critical theory; an approach which places race *and* gender *and* class *and* sexuality at the center of, not only critical analyses of contemporary society, but of the creation and reconstruction of the radical theories and revolutionary praxes aimed at transforming contemporary society. Africana critical theory, therefore, does not argue that race and racism are the most pressing social and political problems confronting the critical theorists of the twenty-first century, and it does not claim that class should be replaced with race or gender as the central problematic of critical theory. However, it does audaciously assert that critical theory stands in need of radical reconstruction, and that critical race theory, philosophy of race, sociology of race, feminism, womanism, and postcolonialism, among other theoretical perspectives, should be critically utilized to *supplement* conventional critical theory's critiques of capitalist class struggle and political economy. The main idea here is to correct the methodological omissions and strengthen the epistemic weaknesses of classical and contemporary critical theory, not prescribe yet another intellectually insular and myopic methodology.

5. I think it most fitting to conclude here by noting that since she published "What's Critical About Critical Theory?: The Case of Habermas and Gender" (which was originally published in 1985), Fraser (1998) has critically engaged the discourse of critical race theory, especially in her breath-takingly brilliant essay, "Another Pragmatism: Alain Locke, Critical 'Race' Theory, and the Politics of Culture." Therefore, I want to make it clear that my criticisms of her conception of critical theory are specific to this particular essay and are not in anyway indicative of my, otherwise, profound intellectual admiration for and affinity to her work. Truth be told, she, too, has made her own unique contribution to my conception of Africana critical theory. Here, then, I have only raised my concerns about how her omission of critical race theory and the Africana tradition of critical theory weakened her otherwise extremely erudite and astute articulation of a new critical theory of contemporary society.

6. Here, it should be observed, that Africana critical theory openly draws from bell hooks (1981), Patricia Hill Collins (1998, 2000), Deborah Gray White (1999), Joy James (1996a, 1997, 1999), and Kimberly Springer (2005), among others', critically acclaimed studies that document and clearly demonstrate Africana women's contributions to black radicalism. This

book not only employs their work as critical paradigms and points of departure but it seeks to humbly offer new, male-feminist and male-womanist, among other, interpretations of Africana men's contributions to black radicalism. The male theorists discussed in this volume—Du Bois probably representing an extremely problematic exception (see Rabaka, 2003b, 2003d, 2004, 2007a)—were neither "male-feminist" nor "male-womanist," and certainly not in the sense that these terms are being employed in contemporary Africana Studies, and Africana Women's Studies in specific, but their ideas and actions may yet and still make a special contribution to new critical theory, to a reconstructed black radicalism, just as the work of the womanists and black feminists mentioned above has, indeed, contributed to the deconstruction and reconstruction of the black radical tradition (see also Awkward, 2000; Byrd and Guy-Sheftall, 2001; Carbado, 1999; Lemons, 1997).

7. My argument here and throughout this section has benefited from a wide-range of work in women's, men's, and gender studies, as well as male-feminism and male-womanism. For example: Adams and Savran (2002), Awkward (1995), Brod (1987), Brod and Kaufman (1994), Buchbinder (1994), Byrd and Guy-Sheftall, (2001), Carbado (1999), H. Christian (1994), P.H. Collins (2000, 2005), Cornwall and Lindisfarne (1994), Digby (1998), Dench (1996), Gardiner (2002), Gilmore (1990), Goldrick-Jones (2002), hooks (2004a, 2004b), Jardine and Smith (1987), Kiberd (1985), Kimmel (1987, 1995, 1996, 2004a, 2004b, 2006), Kimmel and Aronson (2004), Kimmel, Hearn and Connell (2005), Kimmel and Mosmiller (1992), May, Strikwerda and Hopkins (1996), Murphy (2004), M.A. Neal (2005), Porter (1992), Schacht and Ewing (1998), Seidler (1991), Spender (1981), Stoltenberg (1993), and Whitehead and Barrett (2001).

8. The black radical feminist philosopher, Joy James (1998), perceptively pointed to the historical relationship between theory and praxis in Africana Studies and black freedom movements in answering the question, "So, what is African American philosophy?" Her response, in part, was:

> Well . . . there is no monolithic African American thought. There have been ways in which our theory and philosophy have served in our liberation project and there have been ways in which it's resonated with particular aspects of culture, American culture and Black American or African American culture. I see it though now splintering in a lot of ways. *Transcending the Talented Tenth: Black Leaders and American Intellectuals* takes a look at this construction of the Black intellectual, which has been debated quite a bit in recent years. So, there is a lot of this questioning of—and I'm not sure if people would use this term "philosophers" anymore as they would intellectuals—who we are as Black intellectuals, what are our responsibilities, what are our intellectual abilities. I think that there is an incredible amount of insecurity running through a lot this discourse right now that reflects the levels of performance and the lack of substance. There seems to be almost an ungroundedness in political thought and the ability to critique structure. And in this ungroundedness, there is a false performance. There is a type of vanity, the projection of the self as this Black intellectual self and a Black critical thinker, even though apparently the Emperor and Empress have lost some of their garments. This splintering of African American critical thought (I do think there is a difference between philosophy and theory) has to do a lot with our low expectations and even lower levels of political courage. (pp. 252–253; see also J.A. James, 1997)

James not only speaks to the intense interconnectedness of theory and praxis in Africana Studies, but she also critiques the intellectual inferiority, intellectual timidity, pseudo-substance, propensity to perform, and lack of radical political courage on the part of many, if not most, contemporary black academics. Like Lucius Outlaw, she self-reflexively critiques nomenclature, such as "philosopher," that might be misinterpreted, or place what could be perceived as even greater distance between black intellectuals and the black masses. Outlaw (1998) hit the issue on its head when he said, "once you get into the business of talking about Black, African American or Africana philosophy, you are already working against certain elitist and otherwise restrictive notions of philosophy. For philosophizing had been defined literally as reserved for a certain elite class of civilized people—white people—and among them the most civilized and capable of strenuous rational activity" (p. 315). Following James and Outlaw's lead, my articulation of Africana critical theory seeks to "return to the sources" of the Africana tradition of critical theory and black radical praxis by steering clear of hierarchical thought and verbose language which could potentially alienate the black masses from black intellectuals, or black intellectuals from the black masses. In fact, Africana critical theory goes a step further and endeavors to destabilize the artificial and, therefore, arbitrary dichotomy between the "black intellectuals" and the "black masses" by reminding contemporary Africana Studies scholars and students, which includes Africana philosophers, that it was always, and that it remains, humble, struggling continental and diasporan Africans, the "black masses," if you must, who are the authentic architects, tireless teachers, and the singular subjects of Africana Studies.

9. For further critical discussion of Du Bois's "Talented Tenth" and "Guiding Hundredth" theories, please see my "The Du Bois-Washington Debate: Social Leadership, Intellectual Legacy, and the Lingering Problematics of African American Politics," in *Du Bois's Dialectics: Black Radical Politics and the Reconstruction of Critical Social Theory*, where I contend:

> When he took the podium to deliver the "Talented Tenth Memorial Address," on August 12, 1948, Du Bois, then an octogenarian, critically returned to his early leadership thought, and physically returned to the site where he began his academic career, Wilberforce University. At Wilberforce, he would simultaneously eulogize the old, war-worn Talented Tenth thesis and conceptually christen the more democratic "doctrine of the Guiding Hundredth." Before an audience, who heretofore would have been ideal candidates for his erstwhile Talented Tenth cadre of race leaders, Du Bois criticized his elite leadership model, permanently disassociating himself and his discourse from the Talented Tenth. In his address, Du Bois advocated the radical democratization and internationalization of black leadership and the black liberation struggle. Though he had intimated it previously, or so he thought, he now wanted to strongly stress that black leaders and the black liberation struggle must be preoccupied with more than merely the "race question" and achieving racial justice. With the work that many consider his magnum opus, *Black Reconstruction* (1935), Du Bois began an intense study of the political economy of race and racism, employing Marxist methodology and coupling it with the ever-evolving philosophy of race (and critical race theory) he had been developing for over half a century. From the start of his Marxist studies, orthodox (or, rather, white) Marxists attacked his interpretation and application of Marxism to black America and later Pan-Africa, charging him with "revisionism" and dubbing Du Bois (as they did C. L. R. James),—as Anthony Bogues has so perceptively put it—a "black heretic." He was not dismayed, and after more than a decade of deeply dialoguing with Marxism and incorporating it into his political philosophy and social program(s), Du Bois, utilizing the Marxian dialectical method, deconstructed and reconstructed his leadership and liberation thought. (Rabaka, 2008a, pp. 104–105)

Du Bois's discourse on the Guiding Hundredth distinctly demonstrates many of the lessons he had learned from, not only black America's betrayal at the hands of his Talented Tenth, but also the lessons he learned from half a century of participating in the Pan-African movement; toppling Booker T. Washington's Tuskegee Machine; bitterly battling Marcus Garvey and his Back to Africa movement; witnessing two World Wars; observing the rise of Russian communism; and, intensely studying Marxism for over a quarter of a century. One of the many reasons Du Bois was consistently attacked by white Marxists during the latter years of his intellectual and political life was because his "revisionism" moved beyond Karl Marx and Marxists' most privileged agents of revolution: the *white* working class, or the "proletariat," in Marxian vernacular. Du Bois charged, not merely the white working class and labor unions with white supremacy, but he also asserted that most white Marxists' and their party politics suffered from white supremacy. As a result, he argued, white Marxists could not be counted as "comrades" (to borrow once again from Marxian vernacular) in African American and Pan-African liberation struggles.

In radically and anti-racistly calling into question traditional Marxian concepts of the proletariat as the privileged agent of revolution and the predestined revolutionary subjects, Du Bois endeavored to demonstrate that the Marxian model simply could not be grafted onto a white supremacist capitalist society with multi-racial workers. Race and racism, central social issues that Marxists have historically neglected, and of which Du Bois is considered to have pioneered the critical and systematic study, makes Marxism, as Cornel West (1993a) once put it, "indispensable" as a methodological orientation critical of capitalism and class struggle, but "ultimately inadequate" in grasping the distinctive features of anti-black racism and global white supremacy (p. 259). Du Bois, therefore, contributed a critical theory of race to Marxian discourse, laying a foundation for many of the first race-class concepts and opening it to anti-racist categories of critical analysis, and, in so doing, he simultaneously broadened the base of both Marxism and the Africana tradition of critical theory. The Guiding Hundredth, following in the footsteps of the widely-read, well-traveled, and world-historical eighty year-old W. E. B. Du Bois, was awesomely envisioned by its conceptual creator and discursive doyen, Du Bois himself, as simultaneously and multidimensionally: internationalist, revolutionary humanist, critical multiculturalist, pacifist, Pan-Africanist, democratic socialist, anti-colonialist, anti-capitalist, anti-racist, and, though he does not adequately emphasize it in this specific address, anti-sexist. Even more than his theory of the Talented Tenth or his concept of double-consciousness, it is clear that Du Bois intended his "doctrine of the Guiding Hundredth" to be both a concrete contribution to African American and Pan-African leadership and liberation thought, and, however subtly, a late-life conceptual creation by which his intellectual trajectory could be properly charted and critically characterized.

# Bibliography

Abanuka, Bartholomew. (2003). *Two Enquiries in African Philosophy*. Onitsha, Nigeria: Spiritan Publications.

———. (2004). *Philosophy and the Igbo World*. Onitsha, Nigeria: Spiritan Publications.

Abbinnett, Ross. (2006). *Marxism After Modernity: Politics, Technology, and Social Transformation*. New York: Palgrave.

Abdel-Malek, Anouar. (1981). *Social Dialectics*. London: Macmillan.

Abelove, Henry, Barale, Michele Aina, and Halperin, David M. (Eds.). (1993). *The Lesbian and Gay Studies Reader*. New York: Routledge.

Abu-Lughod, Janet L. (1991). *Before European Hegemony: The World-System A.D. 1250–1350*. New York: Oxford University Press.

Abromeit, John, and Cobb, W. Mark. (Eds.). (2005). *Herbert Marcuse: A Critical Reader*. New York: Routledge.

Ackah, William. (1999). *Pan-Africanism: Exploring the Contradictions, Politics, Identity, and Development in Africa and the African Diaspora*. Brookfield, VT: Ashgate.

Adam, Hussein. (1974). "The Social and Political Thought of Frantz Fanon." Ph.D. dissertation, Harvard University.

———. (1999). "Fanon as Democratic Theorist." In Nigel C. Gibson (Ed.), *Rethinking Fanon: The Continuing Dialogue* (pp. 119–140). Amherst, NY: Humanity Books.

Adams, Julia, Clemens, Elisabeth S., and Orloff, Ann S. (Eds.). (2005). *Remaking Modernity: Politics, History, and Sociology*. Durham: Duke University Press.

Adams, Maurianne. (Eds.). (2000). *Readings for Diversity and Social Justice*. New York: Routledge.

Adams, Paul. (1970). "The Social Psychiatry of Frantz Fanon." *American Journal of Psychiatry* 127, 109–114.

Adams, Rachel, and Savran, David. (Eds.). (2002). *The Masculinity Studies Reader*. Malden, MA: Blackwell.

Adi, Hakim. (2003). *Pan-African History: Political Figures from Africa and the Diaspora*. New York: Routledge.

Adorno, Theodor W. (1967). *Prisms*. London: Neville Spearman.

———. (1973a). *Negative Dialectics*. New York: Continuum.

———. (1973b). *Jargon of Authenticity*. Evanston: Northwestern University Press.

———. (1974). *Minima Moralia: Reflections on a Damaged Life*. London: New Left Books.

——. (1982). *Against Epistemology, A Metacritique: Studies in Husserl and the Phenomenological Antinomies.* Cambridge: MIT Press.

——. (1983). *Prisms.* Cambridge, MA: MIT Press.

——. (1989). *Kierkegaard: Construction of the Aesthetic* (Robert Hullot-Kentor, Ed.). Minneapolis: University of Minnesota Press.

——. (1991). *The Culture Industry: Selected Essays on Mass Culture* (Jay M. Bernstien, Ed.). New York: Routledge.

——. (1992). *Notes to Literature* (Rolf Tiedmann, Ed.). New York: Columbia University Press.

——. (1993). *Hegel: Three Studies.* Cambridge, MA: MIT Press.

——. (1994). *Adorno: The Stars Down to Earth and Other Essays on the Irrational in Culture* (Stephen Crook, Ed.). New York: Routledge.

——. (1997). *Aesthetic Theory.* Minneapolis: University of Minnesota Press.

——. (1998). *Critical Models: Interventions and Catchwords.* New York: Columbia University Press.

——. (1999). *The Complete Correspondence, 1928–1940* (Henry Lonitz, Ed.). Cambridge, MA: Harvard University Press.

——. (2000a). *The Adorno Reader* (Brain O'Connor, Ed.). Malden, MA: Blackwell.

——. (2000b). *Metaphysics: Concepts and Problems* (Rolf Tiedemann, Ed.). Stanford: Stanford University Press.

——. (2000c). *Problems of Moral Philosophy* (Thomas Schroder, Ed.). Stanford: Stanford University Press.

——. (2000d). *Introduction to Sociology* (Christoph Godde, Ed.). Stanford: Stanford University Press.

——. (2003). *Can One Live After Auschwitz?: A Philosophical Reader* (Rolf Tiedemann, Ed.). Stanford: Stanford University Press.

——. (2006). *History and Freedom: Lectures, 1964-1965.* Cambridge: Polity.

——. (2007). *Dream Notes* (Christoph Godde and Henri Lonitz, Ed.). Cambridge: Polity.

Adu-Poku, S. (2001). "Envisioning (Black) Male Feminism: A Cross-Cultural Perspective." *Journal of Gender Studies* 10, 157–167.

Agger, Ben. (1992a). *The Discourse of Domination: From the Frankfurt School to Postmodernism.* Evanston, IL: Northwestern University Press.

——. (1992b). *Cultural Studies as Critical Theory.* Washington, DC: Falmer Press.

——. (1993). *Gender, Culture, and Power: Toward a Feminist Postmodern Critical Theory.* Westport, CT: Praeger.

——. (1998). *Critical Social Theory.* Boulder, CO: Westview.

——. (2006). *Critical Social Theories: An Introduction.* Boulder: Paradigm Publishers.

Ajayi, Omofolabo. (1997). "Negritude, Feminism, and the Quest for Identity." *Women's Studies Quarterly* 25 (3/4), 35–53.

Ako, Edward Oben. (1982). "The Harlem Renaissance and the Negritude Movement: Literary Relations and Influences." Ph.D. dissertation, University of Illinois at Urbana-Champaign.

Albritton, Robert. (1999). *Dialectics and Deconstruction in Political Economy.* New York: St. Martin's Press.

Albritton, Robert, and Simoulidis, John. (Eds.). (2003). *New Dialectics and Political Economy.* New York: Palgrave Macmillan.

Aldridge, Delores. (Ed.). (1988). *New Perspectives on Black Studies.* Special Issue, *Phylon* 49, (1).

Aldridge, Delores, and Young, Carlene. (Eds.). (2000). *Out of the Revolution: An Africana Studies Anthology.* Lanham, MD: Lexington Books.

Aldridge, Delores P., and James, E. Lincoln. (Eds.). (2007). *Africana Studies: Philosophical Perspectives and Theoretical Paradigms.* Pullman, WA: Washington State University Press.

Alessandrini, Anthony C. (Ed.). (1999). *Frantz Fanon: Critical Perspectives.* New York: Routledge.

Alexander, Elizabeth. (1995). "We Must Be About Our Father's Business: Anna Julia Cooper and the In-Corporation of the Nineteenth Century African American Woman Intellectual." *Signs* 20, (2), 336–356.

Alexander, Jeffrey C. (1982). *Theoretical Logic in Sociology* (4 Volumes). Berkeley, CA: University of California Press.

———. (Ed.). (2001). *Mainstream and Critical Social Theory: Classical, Modern, and Contemporary* (8 Volumes). Thousand Oaks, CA: Sage.

———. (2003). *The Meanings of Social Life: A Cultural Sociology.* Oxford: Oxford University Press.

Alexander, Jeffrey, Boudon, Raymond, and Cherkaoui, Mohamed. (Eds.). (1997). *The Classical Tradition in Sociology: The American Tradition* (4 Volumes). Thousand Oaks, CA: Sage.

Alkalimat, Abdul. (1986). *Introduction to Afro-American Studies: A People's College Primer.* Chicago: Twenty-First Century Books and Publications.

———. (Ed.). (1990). *Paradigms in Black Studies: Intellectual History, Cultural Meaning, and Political Ideology.* Chicago: Twenty-First Century Books and Publications.

Alkebulan, Paul. (2007). *Survival Pending Revolution: The History of the Black Panther Party.* Tuscaloosa: University of Alabama.

Allan, Tuzyline Jita. (1995). *Womanist and Feminist Aesthetics: A Comparative Review.* Athens: Ohio University Press.

Allen, Robert I. (1968). *Dialectics of Black Power.* New York: Weekly Guardian Associates.

———. (1974). "The Politics of the Attack on Black Studies." *Black Scholar* 6 (1), 1–7.

Alridge, Derrick P. (1997). "The Social, Economic, and Political Thought of W. E. B. Du Bois during the 1930s: Implications for Contemporary African American Education." Ph.D. dissertation, Pennsylvania State University.

———. (1999a). "Conceptualizing a Du Boisian Philosophy of Education: Toward a Model for African American Education." *Educational Theory* 49 (3), 359–379.

———. (1999b). "Guiding Philosophical Principles for a Du Boisian-Based African American Educational Model." *Journal of Negro Education* 68 (2), 182–199.

———. (2003). "W. E. B. Du Bois: Race Man, Teacher, and Scholar." In Sherry Field and Michael Bergson (Eds.), *They Led by Teaching: Influential Educators* (pp. 102–114). Indianapolis, IN: Phi Delta Pi Publications.

———. (2008). *The Educational Thought of W. E. B. Du Bois: An Intellectual History.* New York: Teachers College Press.

Alva, J.J.K. de. (1995). "The Postcolonization of the (Latin) American Experience, A Reconsideration of 'Colonialism,' 'Postcolonialism' and 'Mestizaje'." In Gyan Prakash (Ed.), *After Colonialism: Imperial Histories and Postcolonial Displacements* (pp. 241–275). Princeton, NJ: Princeton University Press.

Amin, Samir. (1973). *Neo-Colonialism in West Africa.* New York: Monthly Review.

———. (1974). *Accumulation on a World Scale: A Critique of the Theory of Underdevelopment.* New York: Monthly Review Press.

———. (1976). *Unequal Development: An Essay on the Social Formation of Peripheral Capitalism.* New York: Monthly Review.

———. (1977). *Imperialism and Unequal Development.* New York: Monthly Review.

———. (1978a). *Law of Value and Historical Materialism.* New York: Monthly Review.

———. (1978b). *Arab Nation.* New York: Zed Books.

———. (1980). *Class and Nation: Historically and in the Current Crisis.* New York: Monthly Review.

———. (1982). *Arab Economy Today.* London: Zed Books.

———. (1989). *Eurocentrism.* New York: Monthly Review.

———. (1990a). *Future of Socialism.* Harare, Zimbabwe: SAPES Trust.

———. (1990b). *Delinking: Towards a Polycentric World.* New York: Zed Books.

———. (1994). *Re-Reading the Postwar Period: An Intellectual Itinerary.* New York: Monthly Review.

———. (1997). *Capitalism in the Age of Globalization: The Management of Contemporary Society.* New York: Zed Books.

———. (1998a). *Spectres of Capitalism: A Critique of Current Intellectual Fashions.* New York: Monthly Review.

———. (1998b). *Africa and the Challenge of Development: Essays* (Chris O. Uroh, Ed.). Ibadan, Nigeria: Hope Publications.

———. (2003). *Obsolescent Capitalism: Contemporary Politics and Global Disorder.* New York: Zed Books.

———. (2004). *Liberal Virus: Permanent War and the Americanization of the World.* New York: Monthly Review.

———. (2005). *Europe and the Arab World: Patterns and Prospects for the New Relationship.* New York: Zed Books.

———. (2006). *Life Looking Forward: Memoirs of an Independent Marxist.* New York: Zed Books.

Amin, Samir, and Cohen, Robin. (Eds.). (1977). *Classes and Class Struggle in Africa.* Lagos, Nigeria: Afrografika Publishers.

Amott, Teresa, and Matthaei, Julie. (1999). *Race, Gender, and Work: A Multicultural History of Women in the United States.* Boston: South End.

Anderson, Elijah, and Zuberi, Tukufu. (Eds.). (2000). *The Study of African American Problems: W. E. B. Du Bois's Agenda, Then and Now.* Thousand Oaks, CA: Sage.

Anderson, Perry. (1976). *Considerations on Western Marxism.* London: New Left Books.

Anderson, Talmadge. (Ed.). (1990). *Black Studies: Theory, Method and Cultural Perspective.* Pullman, WA: Washington State University Press.

Anderson, Talmadge, and Stewart, James B. (2007). *Introduction to African American Studies: Transdisciplinary Approaches and Implications.* Balitmore, MD: Black Classic Press.

Andrade, Mario de. (1980). *Amilcar Cabral: Essai de Biographie Politique.* Paris: Maspero.

Andrews, William L. (Ed.). (1985). *Critical Essays on W. E. B. Du Bois.* Boston: G.K. Hall.

Andrews, William L., Foster, Frances Smith, and Harris, Trudier. (Eds.). (1997). *The Oxford Companion to African American Literature.* New York: Oxford University Press.

Anise, Ladun. (1974). "The African Redefined: The Problems of Collective Black Identity." *Issue: A Journal of Opinion* 4 (4), 26–32.

Anived, Sheo N.S. (2003). *Deconstructing the Hegemony of the State: Dialectics of Domination and Resistance.* New Delhi: Nehru Memorial Museum and Library.

Appadurai, Arjun. (1996). *Modernity at Large: Cultural Dimensions of Globalization.* Minneapolis, MN: University of Minnesota Press.

Appiah, Kwame Anthony. (1985). "The Uncompleted Argument: Du Bois and the Illusion of Race." *Critical Inquiry* 12 (1), 21–37.

———. (1990). "Racisms." In David Theo Goldberg (Ed.), *Anatomy of Racism* (pp. 3–17). Minneapolis: University of Minnesota Press.

———. (1992). *In My Father's House: Africa in the Philosophy of Culture.* New York: Oxford University Press.

———. (1995). "The Uncompleted Argument: Du Bois and the Illusion of Race." In Albert G. Mosley (Ed.), *African Philosophy: Selected Readings* (pp. 199–215). Englewood Cliffs, NJ: Prentice Hall.

———. (1994). "Identity, Authenticity, Survival: Multicultural Societies and Social Reproduction." In Amy Gutmann (Ed.), *Multiculturalism* (pp. 149–165). Princeton: Princeton University Press.

———. (1996). "Race, Culture, Identity." In Kwame Anthony Appiah and Amy Gutman, *Color Conscious: The Political Morality of Race* (pp. 3–75). Princeton: Princeton University Press.

———. (1997). " 'But Would That Still Be Me?': Notes on Gender, 'Race,' Ethnicity as a Source of Identity." In Naomi Zack (Ed.), *Race/Sex: Their Sameness, Difference, and Interplay* (pp. 75–82). New York: Routledge.

———. (2003). *Thinking It Through: An Introduction to Contemporary Philosophy.* New York: Oxford University Press.

———. (2005). *The Ethics of Identity.* Princeton, NJ: Princeton University Press.

———. (2006). *Cosmopolitanism: Ethics in a World of Strangers.* New York: Norton.

———. (2008). *Experiments in Ethics.* Camrbidge, MA: Harvard University Press.

Appiah, Kwame Anthony, and Gates, Henry Louis, Jr. (Eds.). (1999). *Africana: The Encyclopedia of the African and African American Experience.* New York: Basic/Civitas Books.

Appleby, Joyce, Covington, Elizabeth, Hoyt, David, Latham, Michael, and Snieder, Allison. (Eds.). (1996). *Knowledge and Postmodernism in Historical Perspective.* New York: Routledge.

Aptheker, Bettina. (1975). "W. E. B. Du Bois and the Struggle for Women's Rights: 1910-1920." *San Jose Studies* 1 (2), 7–16.

Aptheker, Herbert. (1948). "W. E. B. Du Bois: The First Eighty Years." *Phylon* 9, 58–69.

———. (1949). "The Washington-Du Bois Conference of 1904." *Science and Society* 13, 344-351.

———. (1961). "Dr. Du Bois and Communism." *Political Affairs* 40, 13–20.

———. (1963). "To Dr. Du Bois—With Love." *Political Affairs* 42, 35–42.

———. (1964). "Du Bois on Douglass: 1895." *Journal of Negro History* 49, 264–268.

———. (1965). "Some Unpublished Writings of W. E. B. Du Bois." *Freedom* 5, 103–128.

———. (1966). "W. E. B. Du Bois: The Final Years." *Journal of Human Relations* 14, 149–155.

———. (1971). "*The Souls of Black Folk*: A Comparison of the 1903 and 1952 Editions." *Negro History Bulletin* 34.

———. (Ed.). (1973). *An Annotated Bibliography of the Published Writings of W. E. B. Du Bois.* Millwood, New York: Kraus-Thompson.

———. (1980). "Introduction to *Prayers for Dark People*." In W. E. B. Du Bois, *Prayers for Dark People* (pp. iv–xi). Amherst, MA: University of Massachusetts.

———. (1981). "W. E. B. Du Bois and Africa." *Political Affairs* 60.

———. (1982). "W. E. B. Du Bois and Religion: A Brief Reassessment." *Journal of Religious Thought* 59, 5–11.

———. (1983). *W. E. B. Du Bois and the Struggle Against Racism.* New York: United Nations Center Against Apartheid.

———. (1985). "Introduction to Du Bois's Creative Writings." In Herbert Aptheker (Ed.), *Creative Writings by W. E. B. Du Bois: A Pageant, Poems, Short Stories, and Playlets* (pp. ix–xii). White Plains, NY: Kraus International.

———. (1989). *The Literary Legacy of W. E. B. Du Bois.* White Plains, NY: Kraus International.

———. (1990). "W. E. B. Du Bois: Struggle Not Despair." *Clinical Sociology Review* 8, 58–68.

———. (1997). "Personal Recollections: Woodson, Wesley, Robeson, and Du Bois." *Black Scholar* 27 (2), 42.

Arato, Andrew. (1993). *From Neo-Marxism to Democratic Theory: Essays on the Critical Theory of Soviet-Type Societies.* Armonk, NY: M.E. Sharpe.

Arato, Andrew, and Gebhardt, Eike. (Eds.). (1997). *The Essential Frankfurt School Reader.* New York: Continuum.

Araujo, Norman. (1966). *A Study of Cape Verdean Literature.* Chestnut Hill, MA: Boston College.

Archer-Straw, Petrine. (2000). *Negrophilia: Avante-Garde Paris and Black Culture in the 1920s.* New York: Thames and Hudson.

Arendt, Hannah. (1969). *On Violence.* New York: Harcourt Brace & Jovanovitch.

Arisaka, Yoko. (2001). "Women Carrying Water: At the Crossroads of Technology and Critical Theory." In William S. Wilkerson and Jeffrey Paris (Eds.), *New Critical Theory: Essays on Liberation* (pp. 155–174). Lanham, MD: Rowman and Littlefield Publishers.

Arnold, James A. (1981). *Modernism and Negritude: The Poetry of Aime Cesaire.* Cambridge: Harvard University Press.

Arnold, N. Scott. (1990). *Marx's Radical Critique of Capitalist Society.* New York: Oxford University Press.

Aronowitz, Stanley. (1988)."The Production of Scientific Knowledge: Science, Ideology, and Marxism." In Cary Nelson and Lawrence Grossberg (Eds.), *Marxism and the Interpretation of Culture* (pp. 519–542). Chicago: University of Illinois Press.

Aronson, Ronald. (1995). *After Marxism.* New York: Guilford.

Asante, Molefi Kete. (1969). *The Rhetoric of Black Revolution.* Boston: Allyn and Bacon.

———. (1972). *Language, Communication, and Rhetoric in Black America.* New York: Harper and Row.

———. (1973). *Transracial Communication.* Englewood Cliffs, NJ: Prentice-Hall.

———. (1987). *The Afrocentric Idea.* Philadelphia: Temple University Press.

———. (1988). *Afrocentricity.* Trenton: Africa World Press.

———. (1990). *Kemet, Afrocentricity, and Knowledge.* Trenton: Africa World Press.

———. (1993). *Malcolm X as Cultural Hero and Other Afrocentric Essays.* Trenton: Africa World Press.

———. (1998). *The Afrocentric Idea.* Philadelphia: Temple University Press.

———. (1999). *The Painful Demise of Eurocentrism.* Trenton: Africa World Press.

———. (2000). *The Egyptian Philosophers: Ancient African Voices from Imhotep to Akhenaten.* Chicago: African American Images.

———. (2001). *African American History: A Journey of Liberation.* Saddle Brook, NJ: Peoples Publishing Group.

———. (2002). *Culture and Customs of Egypt.* Westport, CT: Greenwood Press.

———. (2003a). *Afrocentricity: Theory of Social Change.* Chicago: African American Images.

———. (2003b). *Erasing Racism: The Survival of the American Nation.* Amherst, NY: Promethues Books.

———. (2005a). *Race, Rhetoric, and Identity: The Architecton of Soul.* Amherst, NY: Humanity Books.

———. (2005b). *Ebonics: An Introduction to African American Language.* Chicago: American American Images.

———. (2005c). *Cheikh Anta Diop: An Intellectual Portrait.* Chicago: Third World Press.

———. (2007a). *An Afrocentric Manifesto.* Oxford, UK: Polity Press.

———. (2007b). *The History of Africa: The Quest for Eternal Harmony.* New York: Routledge.

Asante, Molefi K., and Asante, Kariamu Welsh. (Eds.). (1985). *African Culture: The Rhythms of Unity.* Westport, CT: Greenwood.

Asante, Molefi K., and Abarry, Abu S. (Eds.). (1996). *The African Intellectual Heritage.* Philadelphia: Temple University.

Asante, Molefi K., and Gudykunst, William. (Eds.). (1989). *Handbook of Intercultural and International Communication.* Thousand Oaks, CA: Sage.

Asante, Molefi K., and Karenga, Maulana. (Eds.). (2006). *The Handbook of Black Studies.* Thousand Oaks, CA: Sage.

Asante, Molefi K., and Rich, Andrea. (Eds.). (1970). *The Rhetoric of Revolution.* Durham, NC: Moore Publishing.

Asante, Molefi K., and Robb, Steve. (Eds.). (1971). *The Voice of Black Rhetoric.* Boston: Allyn and Bacon.

Asante, Molefi K., and Vandi, Abdulai S. (Eds.). (1980). *Contemporary Black Thought: Alternative Analyses in Social and Behavioral Science.* Beverly Hills, CA: Sage.

Asante-Darko, Kwaku. (2000). "The Co-centrality of Racial Conciliation in Negritude Literature." *Research in African Literature* 31 (2), 151–163.

Ashcroft, Bill, Griffiths, Gareth, and Tiffin, Helen. (1989). *The Empire Writes Back: Theory and Practice in Postcolonial Literatures.* New York: Routledge.

——. (Eds.). (1995). *The Post-Colonial Studies Reader.* New York: Routledge.

——. (Eds.). (1998). *Key Concepts in Postcolonial Studies.* New York: Routledge.

Asouzu, Innocent. (2004). *The Method and Principles of Complementary Reflection in and Beyond African Philosophy.* Calabar, Nigeria: University of Calabar Press.

Assimeng, J.M. (1990). *The Influence of Neo-Marxism on the Social Systems of West African States.* Pretoria: Express Copy.

Awkward, Michael. (1995). *Negotiating Difference: Race, Gender, and the Politics of Positionality.* Chicago: University of Chicago.

——. (2000). "A Black Man's Place in Black Feminist Criticism." In Joy A. James and T. Denean Sharpley-Whiting (Eds.), *The Black Feminist Reader* (pp. 88-108). Malden, MA: Blackwell.

Axelsen, Diana E. (1984). "Philosophical Justifications for Contemporary African Social and Political Values and Strategies." In Richard A. Wright (Ed.), *African Philosophy: An Introduction, Third Edition* (pp. 227–244). Lanham, MD: University of America Press.

Azenabor, G.E. (1998). *Understanding the Problems of African Philosophy.* Lagos, Nigeria: First Academic Publishers.

Azevedo, Mario. (Ed.). (2005). *Africana Studies: A Survey of Africa and the African Diaspora.* Durham: Carolina Academic Press.

Ba, Sylvia Washington. (1973). *The Concept of Negritude in the Poetry of Leopold Sedar Senghor.* Princeton: Princeton University Press.

Ba Nikongo, Nikongo. (Ed.). (1997). *Leading Issues in African American Studies.* Durham: Carolina Academic Press.

Babbitt, Susan E., and Campbell, Sue. (Eds.). (1999). *Racism and Philosophy.* Ithaca, NY: Cornell University Press.

Babu, Abdul R.M. (1981). *African Socialism, or Socialist Africa?* London: Zed Books.

Bailey, Anne M., and Llobera, Joseph R. (Eds.). (1981). *The Asiatic Mode of Production: Science and Politics.* New York: Routledge and Kegan Paul.

Bailey, Marianne Wichmann. (1992). *The Ritual Theater of Aime Cesaire: Mythic Structures of Dramatic Imagination.* Tubingen: Narr Publishers.

Bailey, Ronald. (1970). "Why Black Studies?" *The Education Digest* 35 (9), 46–48.

Baker, Houston A., Jr., Diawara, Manthia, and Lindeborg, Ruth H. (Eds.). (1996). *Black British Cultural Studies: A Reader.* Chicago: University of Chicago Press.

Baker, Lee D. (1998). *From Savage to Negro: Anthropology and the Construction of Race, 1896–1954.* Berkeley, CA: University of California Press.

Baker-Fletcher, Karen. (1991). "A 'Singing Something': The Literature of Anna Julia Cooper as a Resource for a Theological Anthropology of Voice." Ph.D. dissertation, Harvard University.

——. (1994). *A Singing Something: Womanist Reflections on Anna Julia Cooper.* New York: Crossroads.

Baldacchino, John. (1996). *Post-Marxist Marxism: Questioning the Answer—Difference and Realism After Lukacs and Adorno.* Brookfield, VT: Averbury.

Bambara, Toni Cade. (Ed.). (1970). *The Black Woman: An Anthology.* New York: Signet.

Bamikunle, Aderemi James. (1982). "The Harlem Renaissance and Negritude Poetry: The Development of Black Written Literature." Ph.D. dissertation, University of Wisconsin at Madison.

Bannerji, Himani. (1995). *Thinking Through: Essays on Feminism, Marxism, and Anti-Racism.* Toronto: Women's Educational Press.

——. (2001). *Inventing Subjects: Studies in Hegemony, Patriarchy, and Colonialism.* New Delhi: Tulika.

Baraka, Amiri. (1966). *Home: Social Essays.* New York: Morrow.

——. (1970). *It's Nation Time!* Chicago: Third World Press.

——. (1971). *Raise, Race, Rays, Raze: Essays Since 1965.* New York: Random House.

——. (Ed.). (1972). *African Congress: A Documentary of the First Modern Pan-African Congress.* New York: Morrow.

——. (1984). *Daggers and Javelins: Essays, 1974-1979.* New York: Morrow.

——. (1994). *Conversations with Amiri Baraka* (Charles Reilly, Ed.). Jackson: University Press of Mississippi.

——. (1995). *Wise, Why's, Y's: Social and Political Essays.* Chicago: Third World Press.

——. (1997). *The Autobiography of LeRoi Jones/Amiri Baraka.* Chicago: Lawrence Hill.

——. (2000). *LeRoi Jone/Amiri Baraka Reader* (William J. Harris, Ed.). New York: Thunder's Mouth Press.

Baraka, Amiri, and Neal, Larry. (Eds.). (1968). *Black Fire: An Anthology of Afro-American Writing.* New York: Morrow.

Baraka, Amiri, and Fundi. (1970). *In Our Terribleness: Some Elements and Meaning in Black Style.* Indianapolis: Bobbs-Merrill.

Baraka, Amiri, and Baraka, Amina. (Eds.). (1983). *Confirmation: An Anthology of African American Women.* New York: Quill.

Barnes, James B. (1982). "Alain Locke and the Sense of the African Legacy." In Russell J. Linnemann (Ed.), *Alain Locke: Reflections on a Modern Renaissance Man* (pp. 100–108). Baton Rouge, LA: Louisiana State University.

Barrett, Margaret Dwight, and Carey, Phillip. (Eds.). (2003). *The Diaspora: Introduction to Africana Studies.* Kendall/Hunt Publishing.

Barrett, Michele. (1980). *Women's Oppression Today: Problems in Marxist Feminist Analysis.* London: Verso.

Barrington, Lowell W. (Ed.). (2006). *After Independence: Making and Protecting the Nation in Postcolonial and Postcommunist States.* Ann Arbor: University of Michigan Press.

Barrow, Clyde W. (1993). *Critical Theories of the State: Marxist, Neo-Marxist, Post- Marxist.* Madison, WI: University of Wisconsin Press.

Bartok, Philip J. (2003). "Sexism and Phenomenological Method in Sartre's Analysis of Bad Faith." Paper presented at the Pacific Division of the American Philosophical Association. Available online at: http://pbartok.com/pdf/SartreSexism.pdf [Accessed 21 June 2005].

Bartolovich, Crystal. (2000). "Global Capital and Transnationalism." In Henry Schwarz and Sangeeta Ray (Eds.), *A Companion to Postcolonial Studies* (pp. 126–161). Malden, MA: Blackwell.

Bartolovich, Crystal, and Lazarus, Neil. (Eds.). (2002). *Marxism, Modernity, and Postcolonial Studies.* Cambridge: Cambridge University Press.

Bassett, John Earl. (1992). *Harlem in Review: Critical Reactions to Black American Writers, 1917–1939.* Selinsgrove: Susquehanna University Press.

Bastide, Roger. (1961). "Variations on Negritude." *Presence Africaine* 8 (36), 83–91.

Batalha, Luis. (2004). *The Cape Verdean Diaspora in Portugal: Colonial Subjects in a Postcolonial World.* Lanham, MD: Lexington Books.

Bates, Robert H., Mudimbe, V.Y., and O'Barr, Jean. (Eds.). (1993). *Africa and the Disciplines: The Contributions of Research in Africa to the Social Sciences and Humanities.* Chicago: University of Chicago Press.

Baulding, Lisa. (Producer). (1992). *W. E. B. Du Bois of Great Barrington.* [Documentary]. WGBY-TV Springfield, MA: PBS Video.

Bauman, Zygmunt. (1973). *Culture as Praxis.* Boston: Routledge & K. Paul.

——. (1976a). *Towards a Critical Sociology: An Essay on Common Sense and Emancipation.* Boston: Routledge & K. Paul.

———. (1978). *Hermeneutics and Social Science*. New York: Columbia University Press.

———. (1982). *Memories of Class: The Pre-History and After-Life of Class*. Boston: Routledge & K. Paul.

———. (1987). *Legislators and Interpreters: On Modernity, Post-Modernity, and Intellectuals*. Cambridge: Polity.

———. (1988). *Freedom*. Milton Keynes, England: Open University Press.

———. (1989). *Modernity and Holocaust*. Ithaca, NY: Cornell University Press.

———. (1990). *Thinking Sociologically*. Cambridge, MA: Blackwell.

———. (1991). *Modernity and Ambivalence*. Ithaca, NY: Cornell University Press.

———. (1992a). *Intimations of Postmodernity*. New York: Routledge.

———. (1992b). *Mortality, Immortality and Other Life Strategies*. Stanford, CA: Stanford University Press.

———. (1995). *Life in Fragments: Essays on Morality*. Cambridge, MA: Blackwell.

———. (1997). *Postmodernity and Its Discontents*. New York: New York University Press.

———. (1998a). *Globalization: The Human Consequences*. New York: Columbia University Press.

———. (1998b). *Work, Consumerism and the New Poor*. Buckingham: Open University Press.

———. (1999). *In Search of Politics*. Stanford, CA: Stanford University Press.

———. (2000). *Liquid Modernity*. Cambridge: Polity.

———. (2004a). *Wasted Lives: Modernity and Its Outcasts*. Oxford: Polity.

———. (2004b). *Europe: An Unfinished Adventure*. Cambridge: Polity.

———. (2005). *Liquid Life*. Cambridge: Polity.

———. (2006). *Liquid Fear*. Cambridge: Polity.

———. (2007a). *Liquid Times: Living in an Age of Uncertainty*. Cambridge: Polity.

———. (2007b). *Consuming Life*. Cambridge: Polity.

———. (2008). *Does Ethics Have a Chance in a World of Consumers?* Cambridge, MA: Harvard University Press.

Bay, Mia. (1998). "'The World Was Thinking Wrong About Race': *The Philadelphia Negro* and Nineteenth-Century Science." In Michael B. Katz and Thomas J. Sugrue (Eds.), *W. E. B. Du Bois, Race, and the City: The Philadelphia Negro and Its Legacy* (pp. 41–60). Philadelphia: University of Pennsylvania Press.

Beale, Frances. (1995). "Double Jeopardy: To Be Black and Female." In Beverly Guy-Sheftall (Ed.), *Words of Fire: An Anthology of African American Feminist Thought* (pp. 146–156). New York: Free Press.

Beavers, Herman. (2000). "Romancing the Body Politic: Du Bois's Propaganda of the Dark World." *Annals of the American Academy of Political and Social Science* 568 (March), 250–264.

Beck, Hamilton. (1996). "W. E. B. Du Bois as a Study Abroad Student in Germany, 1892–1894." *Frontiers: The Interdisciplinary Journal of Study Abroad* 2 (1), 45–63.

Beier, Ulli. (1959). "The Theme of the Ancestors in Senghor's Poetry." *Black Orpheus* 5, 15–17.

———. (Ed.). (1967). *Introduction to African Literature: An Anthology of Critical Writings from "Black Orpheus."* Evanston, IL: Northwestern University Press.

Bell, Linda A., and David Blumenfeld (Eds.). (1995). *Overcoming Racism and Sexism* Lanham, MD: Rowman and Littlefield.

Bell, Richard H. (2002). *Understanding African Philosophy: A Cross-Cultural Approach to Classical and Contemporary Issues in Africa*. New York: Routledge.

Belles, A. Gilbert. (1982). "The Politics of Alain Locke." In Russell J. Linnemann (Ed.), *Alain Locke: Reflections on a Modern Renaissance Man* (pp. 50–62). Baton Rouge, LA: Louisiana State University.

Benhabib, Seyla. (1986). *Critique, Norm, and Utopia*. New York: Columbia University Press.

———. (1992). *Situating the Self: Gender, Community, and Postmodernism in Contemporary Ethics*. New York: Routledge.

Benhabib, Seyla, and Cornell, Drucilla. (1987). *Feminism as Critique: Essays on the Politics of Gender in Late-Capitalist Societies.* London: Polity Press.

Benhabib, Seyla, Bonss, Wolfgang, and McCole, John. (Eds.). (1993). *On Max Horkheimer: New Perspectives.* Cambridge, MA: MIT Press.

Benjamin, Walter. (1969). *Illuminations: Essays and Reflections* (Hannah Arendt, Ed.). New York: Schocken.

———. (1973). *Charles Baudelaire: A Lyric Poet in the Ear of High Capitalism.* London: New Left Books.

———. (1977). *The Origin of German Tragic Drama.* London: New Left Books.

———. (1979). *One-Way Street and Other Writings.* London: New Left Books.

———. (1985). *Moscow Diary* (Gary Smith, Ed.). Cambridge, MA: Harvard University Press.

———. (1986). *Reflections: Essays, Aphorisms, Autobiographical Writings.* (Peter Demetz, Ed.). New York: Schocken.

———. (1989). *The Correspondence of Walter Benjamin and Gershom Scholem, 1932–1940* (Gershom Scholem, Ed.). New York: Schocken.

———. (1994). *The Correspondence of Walter Benjamin, 1910–1940* (Gershom Scholem and Theodor W. Adorno, Ed.). Chicago: University of Chicago Press.

———. (1996). *Walter Benjamin: Selected Writings, Volume 1, 1913–1926* (Marcus Bullock and Michael W. Jennings, Ed.). Cambridge, MA: Harvard University Press.

———. (1999a). *The Arcades Project.* Cambridge, MA: Harvard University Press.

———. (1999b). *Walter Benjamin: Selected Writings, Volume 2, 1927–1934* (Michael W. Jennings, Howard Eiland, and Gary Smith, Ed.). Cambridge, MA: Harvard University Press.

———. (1999c). *The Complete Correspondence of Theodor W. Adorno and Walter Benjamin, 1928–1940* (Henri Lonitz, Ed.). Cambridge, MA: Harvard University Press.

———. (2002). *Walter Benjamin: Selected Writings, Volume 3, 1935–1938* (Howard Eiland and Michael W. Jennings, Ed.). Cambridge, MA: Harvard University Press.

———. (2003). *Walter Benjamin: Selected Writings, Volume 4, 1938–1940* (Howard Eiland and Michael W. Jennings, Ed.). Cambridge, MA: Harvard University Press.

———. (2006a). *The Writer of Modern Life: Essays on Charles Baudelaire* (Michael W. Jennings, Ed.). Cambridge, MA: Harvard University Press.

———. (2006b). *On Hashish* (Marcus Boon, Ed.). Cambridge, MA: Harvard University Press.

———. (2006c). *Berlin Childhood Around 1900.* Cambridge, MA: Harvard University Press.

———. (2007). *Walter Benjamin's Archive: Images, Texts, Signs* (Ursula Marx, Gudrun Schwarz, Michael Schwarz, and Erdmut Wizisla, Ed.). New York: Verso.

———. (2008). *The Work of Art in the Age of Its Technological Reproducibility, and Other Writings on Media* (Michael W. Jennings, Brigid Doherty and Thomas Y. Levin, Ed.). Cambridge, MA: Harvard University Press.

Benner, Eric. (1995). *Really Existing Nationalisms: A Post-Communist View from Marx and Engels.* New York: Oxford University Press.

Bennett, Judith M. (2006). *History Matters: Patriarchy and the Challenge of Feminism.* Philadelphia: University of Pennsylvania Press.

Bennetta, Jules-Rosette. (2007). "Jean-Paul Sartre and the Philosophy of Negritude: Race, Self, and Society." *Theory & Society* 36 (3), 265–285.

Bergner, Gwen. (1995). "Who Is That Masked Woman?, Or the Role of Gender in Fanon's *Black Skin, White Masks.*" *PMLA* 110 (1), 75–88.

———. (1999). "Politics and Pathologies: On the Subject of Race in Psychoanalysis." In Anthony C. Alessandrini (Ed.), *Frantz Fanon: Critical Perspectives* (pp. 219–234). New York: Routledge.

Berlowitz, Marvin J., Jackson, Erich R., and Long, Nathan A. (Eds.). (2003). *Reflections of African American Peace Leaders: A Documentary History, 1898–1967.* Lewiston, NY: Edwin Mellen Press.

Berman, Russell A. (1989). *Modern Culture and Critical Theory: Art, Politics, and the Legacy of the Frankfurt School.* Madison, WI: University of Wisconsin Press.

———. (1997). "Du Bois and Wagner: Race, Nation, and Culture Between the United States and Germany." *German Quarterly* 70 (2), 123–135.

Bernasconi, Robert. (1996). "Casting the Slough: Fanon's New Humanism for a New Humanity." In Lewis R. Gordon, T. Denean Sharpley-Whiting, and Renee T. White (Eds.), *Fanon: A Critical Reader* (pp. 113–121). Cambridge: Blackwell.

———. (1997). "African Philosophy's Challenge to Continental Philosophy." In Emmanuel Eze (Ed.), *(Post) Colonial African Philosophy: A Critical Reader* (pp. 183–196). Malden, MA: Blackwell.

———. (Ed.). (2001). *Race.* Malden, MA: Blackwell.

———. (2002). "The Assumption of Negritude: Aime Cesaire, Frantz Fanon, and the Vicious Circle of Racial Politics." *Parallax* 8 (2), 69–83.

———. (Ed.). (2003). *Race and Racism in Continental Philosophy.* Bloomington: Indiana University Press.

———. (Ed.). (2004). *Race and Anthropology.* Bristol: Thoemmes.

———. (Ed.). (2005). *Race, Hybridity, and Miscegenation.* Bristol: Thoemmes.

Bernasconi, Robert, and Lott, Tommy L. (2000). (Ed.). *The Idea of Race.* Hackett Publishing.

Bernstein, Jay M. (Ed.). (1995). *The Frankfurt School: Critical Assessments.* London: Routledge.

Berrian, Albert, and Long, Richard. (Eds.). (1967). *Negritude: Essays and Studies.* Hampton, VA: Hampton Institute Press.

Best, Steven. (1995). *The Politics of Historical Vision: Marx, Foucault, Habermas.* New York: Guilford.

Best, Steven and Kellner, Douglas. (1991). *Postmodern Theory: Critical Interrogations.* New York: Guilford.

———. (1997). *The Postmodern Turn.* New York: Guilford.

———. (2001). *The Postmodern Adventure.* New York: Guilford.

Bewes, Timothy. (2002). *Reification, or, The Anxiety of Late Capitalism.* New York: Verso.

Bhabha, Homi. (1990). "Interrogating Identity: Frantz Fanon and the Postcolonial Prerogative." In David Theo Goldberg (Ed.), *The Anatomy of Racism* (pp. 183–209). Minneapolis: University of Minnesota Press.

———. (1996). "Day by Day...with Frantz Fanon." In Alan Read (Ed.), *The Fact of Blackness: Frantz Fanon and Visual Representation* (pp. 186–205). Seattle: Bay Press.

———. (1999). "Remembering Fanon: Self, Psyche, and the Colonial Condition." In Nigel C. Gibson (Ed.), *Rethinking Fanon: The Continuing Dialogue* (pp. 179–196). Amherst, NY: Humanity Books.

Biakolo, Emevwo. (1998). "Categories of Cross-Cultural Cognition and the African Condition." In Pieter H. Coetzee and Abraham P.J. Roux (Eds.), *The African Philosophy Reader* (pp. 1–14). New York: Routledge.

Bienen, Henry. (1977). "State and Revolution: The Work of Amilcar Cabral." *Journal of Modern African Studies* 15 (4), 555–568.

Birbalsingh, Frank M. (1984). "The Literary Achievement of C. L. R. James." *Journal of Commonwealth Literature* 19 (1) 108–121.

Birt, Robert E. (Ed.). (2002). *The Quest for Community and Identity: Critical Essays in Africana Social Philosophy.* Lanham, MD: Rowman and Littlefield.

Black, Edwin. (2004). *War Against the Weak: Eugenics and America's Campaign to Create a Master Race.* New York: Thunder's Mouth Press.

Blackburn, Robin. (1972). *Ideology in Social Science: Readings in Critical Social Theory.* New York: Pantheon.

———. (1995). "*The Black Jacobins* and New World Slavery." In Selwyn Cudjoe and William E. Cain (Eds.), *C. L. R. James: His Intellectual Legacies* (pp. 81–97). Amherst: University of Massachusetts Press.

Blackey, Robert. (1974). "Fanon and Cabral: A Contrast in Theories of Revolution for Africa." *Journal of Modern African Studies* 12 (2), 191–209.

Blair, Dorothy S. (1961a). "Negritude I." *Contrast* (Capetown) 1 (2), 38–48.

———. (1961b). "Negritude II." *Contrast* 1 (3), 38–49.

———. (1966). "Whither Negritude?" *The Classic* (Johannesburg) 2 (2), 5–10.

———. (1971). *Negritude, Whence and Whither?: Some Aspects of Creative Writing in French from "Black Africa."* Johannesburg, South Africa: Institute for the Study of Man.

Blair, Karen. (1980). *The Clubwoman as Feminist: True Womanhood Redefined, 1868–1914.* New York: Holmes & Meier.

Blasius, Mark, and Phelan, Shane. (Eds.). (1997). *We Are Everywhere: A Historical Sourcebook of Gay and Lesbian Politics.* New York: Routldge.

Blassingame, John. (Ed). (1973). *New Perspectives on Black Studies.* Chicago: University of Illinois Press.

———. (1979). *The Slave Community: Plantation Life in the Antebellum South.* New York: Oxford University Press.

Blaut, James M. (1987). *The Colonial Question: Decolonizing the Theory of Nationalism.* London: Zed Books.

———. (1993). *The Colonizer's Model of the World: Geographical Diffusionism and Eurocentric History.* New York: Guilford Press.

———. (2000). *Eight Eurocentric Historians.* New York: Guilford Press.

Blee, Kathleen M. (1991). *Women of the Klan: Racism and Gender in the 1920s.* Berkeley, CA: University of California Press.

———. (2002). *Inside Organized Racism: Women in the Hate Movement.* Berkeley, CA: University of California Press.

Bloch, Ernst. (1986). *The Principle of Hope.* Camrbidge, MA: MIT Press.

Bloom, Harold. (2001). *W. E. B. Du Bois.* Broomall: Chelsea House Publishers.

Blum, Edward J. (2004). "The Soul of W. E. B. Du Bois." *Philosophia Africana* 7 (2), 1– 16.

———. (2005a). "Religion and the Sociological Imagination of W. E. B. Du Bois." *Sociation Today* 3 (1). Online at: http://www.ncsociology.org/sociationtoday/v31/blum.htm [Accessed 23 February 2005].

———. (2005b). "There Won't Be Any Rich People in Heaven': The Black Christ, White Hypocrisy, and the Gospel According to W. E. B. Du Bois." *Journal of African American History* 90 (4), 368–386.

———. (2007). *W. E. B. Du Bois: American Prophet.* Philadelphia, PA: University of Pennsylvannia Press.

Boateng, Charles Adom. (2003). *The Political Legacy of Kwame Nkrumah of Ghana.* Lewiston, NY: Edwin Mellen Press.

Bobo, Jacqueline. (1995). *Black Women as Cultural Readers.* New York: Columbia University.

———. (Ed.). (2001). *Black Feminist Cultural Criticism.* Malden, MA: Blackwell.

Bobo, Jacqueline, and Michel, Claudine. (Eds.). (2000). *Black Studies: Current Issues, Enduring Questions.* Dubuque, IA: Kendall/Hunt.

Bobo, Jacqueline, Hudley, Cynthia, and Michel, Claudine. (Eds.). (2004). *The Black Studies Reader.* New York: Routledge.

Bobo, Lawrence D. (2000). "Reclaiming a Du Boisian Perspective on Racial Attitudes." *Annals of the American Academy of Political and Social Science* 568, 186–202.

Bodunrin, Peter O. (1984). "The Question of African Philosophy." In Richard A. Wright (Ed.), *African Philosophy: An Introduction* (Third Edition, pp. 1–24). Lanham, MD: University of America Press.

———. (1975). " 'Theoretical Identities' and Scientific Explanation: The Horton-Skorupski Debate." *Second Order* 4 (1), 56–65.

———. (Ed.). (1985). *Philosophy in Africa: Trends and Perspectives*. Ile-Ife, Nigeria: University of Ife Press.

———. (1991)."The Question of African Philosophy." In Tsenay Serequeberhan (Ed.), *African Philosophy: The Essential Readings* (pp. 63–86). New York: Paragon House.

———. (1995). "Magic, Witchcraft, ESP: A Defense of Scientific and Philosophical Skepticism." In Albert G. Mosley (Ed.), *African Philosophy: Selected Readings* (pp. 371–386). Englewood Cliffs, NJ: Prentice Hall.

Boggs, Carl. (1982). *The Impasse of European Communism*. Boulder, CO: Westview Press.

———. (1986). *Social Movements and Political Power: Emerging Forms of Radicalism in the West*. Philadelphia: Temple University Press.

———. (1993). *Intellectuals and the Crisis of Modernity*. Albany, NY: State University of New York Press.

———. (1995). *The Socialist Tradition: From Crisis to Decline*. New York: Routledge.

Boggs, Grace Lee. (1993). "Thinking and Acting Dialectically: C. L. R. James, The American Years." *Monthly Review* 45 (5), 38–46.

———. (1995). "C. L. R. James: Organizing in the USA, 1938-1953." In Selwyn Cudjoe and William E. Cain (Eds.), *C. L. R. James: His Intellectual Legacies* (pp. 163–172). Amherst: University of Massachusetts Press.

Bogues, Anthony. (Ed.). (1983). *Marxism and Black Liberation*. Cleveland: Hera Press.

———. (1997). *Caliban's Freedom: The Early Political Thought of C. L. R. James*. London: Pluto Press.

———. (1998). "Investigating the Radical Caribbean Intellectual Tradition." *Small Axe* 4, 29–45.

———. (2002). "Politics, Nation, and PostColony: Caribbean Inflections." *Small Axe* 11 (6, 1), 1–30.

———. (2003). *Black Heretics, Black Prophets: Radical Political Intellectuals*. New York: Routledge.

———. (2004). "Teaching Radical Africana Political Thought and Intellectual History." *Radical History Review* 78, 146–155.

———. (2005). "Working Outside Criticisms: Thinking Beyond Limits." *Boundary 2* 32 (1), 71–93.

———. (2008). "Writing Caribbean Intellectual History." *Small Axe* 26 (12, 2), 168–178

Bologh, Roslyn W. (1990). *Love or Greatness: Max Weber and Masculine Thinking, A Feminist Inquiry*. Boston: Unwin Hayman.

Bongmba, Elias K. (2006). *The Dialectics of Transformation in Africa*. New York: Palgrave Macmillan.

Bonilla-Silva, Eduardo. (2001). *White Supremacy and Racism in the Post-Civil Rights Era*. Boulder, CO: Lynne Rienner.

———. (2003). *Racism Without Racists: Color-Blind Racism and the Persistence of Racial Inequality in the United States*. Lanham, MD: Rowman and Littlefield.

Bonilla-Silva, Eduardo, and Doane, Ashley. (Eds.). (2003). *White Out: The Continuing Significance of Racism*. New York: Routledge.

Bonilla-Silva, Eduardo, and Zuberi, Tukufu. (Eds.). (2008). *White Logic, White Methods: Racism and Methodology*. Lanham, MD: Rowman and Littlefield.

Boodhoo, Ken I. (Ed.). (1986). *Eric Williams, the Man and the Leader*. Lanham, MD: University Press of America.

———. (2001). *The Elusive Eric Williams*. Port of Spain, Trinidad and Tobago: Prospect Press.

Bose, Christine, Feldberg, Roslyn, and Sokoloff, Natalie. (Eds.). (1987). *Hidden Aspects of Women's Work*. New York: Praeger.

Bottomore, Tom. (1984). *The Frankfurt School*. New York: Tavistock.

———. (2002). *The Frankfurt School and Its Critics*. New York: Routledge.

Botwe-Asamoah, Kwame. (2005). *Kwame Nkrumah's Politico-Cultural Thought and Policies: An African-Centered Paradigm for the Second Phase of the African Revolution.* New York: Routledge.

Boudon, Raymond, Cherkaoui, Mohamed, and Alexander, Jeffrey. (Eds.). (1997). *The Classical Tradition in Sociology: The European Tradition* (4 Volumes). Thousand Oaks, CA: Sage.

Bouvier, Pierre. (1971). *Fanon.* Paris: Editions Universitaires.

Boxer, Marilyn J., and Quataert, Jean H. (Eds.). (1978). *Socialist Women: European Socialist Feminism in the Nineteenth and Early-Twentieth Centuries.* New York: Elsevier North-Hollad.

Boxill, Bernard. (1977-78). "Du Bois and Fanon on Culture." *Philosophical Forum* 9 (2- 3), 326–38.

———. (1992). *Blacks and Social Justice.* Lanham, MD: Rowman and Littlefield.

———. (1996). "Du Bois on Cultural Pluralism." In In Bernard W. Bell, Emily R. Grosholz, and James B. Stewart (Eds.), *W. E. B. Du Bois: On Race and Culture* (pp. 57–86). New York: Routledge.

———. (1997a). "Washington, Du Bois and Plessy vs. Ferguson." *Law & Philosophy* 16 (3), 299–330.

———. (1997b). "Two Traditions in African American Political Philosophy." In John P. Pittman (Ed.), *African American Perspectives and Philosophical Traditions* (pp. 119–135). New York: Routledge.

———. (1997c). "Populism and Elitism in African American Political Thought." *Journal of Ethics* 1 (3), 209–238.

Boyd, Melba Joyce. (1994). *Discarded Legacy: Politics and Poetics in the Life of Frances E. W. Harper.* Detroit, MI: Wayne State University.

Braley, Mark Steven. (1994). "The Circle Unbroken: W. E. B. Du Bois and the Encyclopedic Narrative." Ph.D. dissertation, Princeton University.

Braun, Lily. (1987). *Selected Writings on Feminism and Socialism.* Bloomington, IN: Indiana University Press.

Bronner, Stephen E. (2002). *Of Critical Theory and Its Theorists.* New York: Routledge.

Bronner, Stephen E., and Kellner, Douglas. (Eds.). (1989). *Critical Theory and Society: A Reader.* New York: Routledge.

Brockway, Fenner. (1963). *African Socialism.* Chester Springs, PA: Dufour Editions.

Brod, Harry. (Ed.). (1987). *The Making of Masculinities: The New Men's Studies.* Boston: Allen and Unwin.

Brod, Harry, and Kaufman, Michael. (Eds.). (1994). *Theorizing Masculinities.* Thousand Oaks, CA: Sage Publications.

Broderick, Francis L. (1955). "W. E. B. Du Bois: The Trail of His Ideas." Ph.D. dissertation, Harvard University.

———. (1958a). "The Academic Training of W. E. B. Du Bois." *Journal of Negro Education* 27, 10-16.

———. (1958b). "German Influence on the Scholarship of W. E. B. Du Bois." *Phylon* 19, 367–371.

———. (1958c). "The Tragedy of W. E. B. Du Bois." *Progressive* 22, 29–32.

———. (1959). *W. E. B. Du Bois: Negro Leader in a Time of Crisis.* Palo Alto, CA: Stanford University Press.

———. (1974). "W. E. B. Du Bois: History of an Intellectual." In James E. Blackwell and Morris Janowitz (Eds.), *Black Sociologists: Historical and Contemporary Perspectives* (pp. 3–24). Chicago: University of Chicago Press.

Brown, Lee M. (Ed.). (2004). *African Philosophy: New and Traditional Perspectives.* New York: Oxford University Press.

Bruce, Dickson D., Jr. (1992). "W. E. B. Du Bois and the Idea of Double Consciousness." *American Literature* 64, 299–309.

——. (1995). "W. E. B. Du Bois and the Dilemma of Race." *American Literary History* 7 (2), 334–343.

Brundage, William F. (2005). *The Southern Past: A Clash of Race and Memory.* Cambridge, MA: Belknap/Harvard University Press.

Bubner, Rudiger. (1988). *Essays in Hermeneutics and Critical Theory.* New York: Columbia University Press.

Buchbinder, David. (1994). *Masculinities and Identities.* Carlton: Melbourne University Press.

Buck, Christopher. (2005). *Alain Locke: Faith and Philosophy.* Los Angeles: Kalimat.

Buhle, Mari Jo. (1981). *Women and American Socialism, 1870–1920.* Urbana: University of Illinois Press.

Buhle, Mari Jo, Buhle, Paul, and Georgakas, Dan, (Eds.). (1992). *The Encyclopedia of the American Left.* Chicago: University of Illinois Press.

Buhle, Paul. (Ed.). (1986a). *C. L. R. James: His Life and Work.* New York: Allison and Busby.

——. (1986b). "The Politic Styles of C. L. R. James." In Paul Buhle (Ed.), *C. L. R. James His Life and Work* (pp. 22-29). New York: Allison and Busby.

——. (1986c). "Marxism in the USA." In Paul Buhle (Ed.), *C. L. R. James His Life and Work* (pp. 81–104). New York: Allison and Busby.

——. (1988). *C. L. R. James: The Artist as Revolutionary.* London: Verso.

——. (1991). *Marxism in the United States.* London: Verso.

——. (1994). "Marxism in the USA." In Scott McLemee and Paul Le Blanc (Eds.), *C. L. R. James and Revolutionary Marxism: Selected Writings of C. L. R. James, 1939–1949* (pp. 55–76). Atlantic Highlands, NJ: Humanities Press.

——. (1995). "From a Boigrapher's Notebook: The Field of C. L. R. James Scholarship." In Selwyn Cudjoe and William E. Cain (Eds.), *C. L. R. James: His Intellectual Legacies* (pp. 435–453). Amherst: University of Massachusetts Press.

Bulhan, Hussein A. (1980a). "Frantz Fanon: Revolutionary Psychiartrist." *Race & Class* 21 (3), 251–271.

——. (1980b). "The Revolutionary Psychology of Frantz Fanon and Notes on His Theory of Violence." *Fanon Center Journal* 1 (1), 34–47.

——. (1985). *Frantz Fanon and the Psychology of Oppression.* New York: Plenum Press.

Bulmer, Martin. (1991). "W. E. B. Du Bois as a Social Investigator: *The Philadelphia Negro,* 1899." In Martin Bulmer and Kevin Bales (Eds.), *The Social Survey in Historical Perspective, 1880–1940.* Cambridge: Cambridge University Press.

——. (1995). "The Challenge of African American Leadership in an Ambiguous World: W. E. B. Du Bois, Cater G. Woodson, Ralph Bunche and Thurgood Marshall in Historical Perspective." *Ethnic & Racial Studies* 18 (3), 629–647.

Bulmer, Martin, and Solomos, John. (Eds.). (1999a). *Racism.* Oxford: Oxford University Press.

Bulmer, Martin, and Solomos, John. (Eds.). (1999b). *Ethnic and Racial Studies Today.* London: Routledge.

Bulmer, Martin, and Solomos, John. (Eds.). (2004). *Researching Race and Racism:* New York: Routledge.

Burbridge, Lynn C. (1999). "W. E. B. Du Bois as Economic Analyst: Reflections on the 100th Anniversary of *The Philadelphia Negro.*" *Review of Black Political Economy* 26 (3), 13–31.

Busby, Margaret. (Ed.). (1992). *Daughters of Africa: An International Anthology of Words and Writings by Women of African Descent from Ancient Egyptian to the Present.* New York: Pantheon.

Bush, Roderick D. (1999). *We Are Not What We Seem: Black Nationalism and the Class Struggle in the American Century.* New York: New York University Press.

Butler, Johnnella E. (1981). *Black Studies—Pedagogy and Revolution: A Study of Afro-American Studies and the Liberal Arts Tradition Through the Discipline of Afro- American Literature.* Lanham, MD: University Press of America.

———. (2000). "African American Studies and the 'Warring Ideals': The Color Line Meets the Borderlands." In Manning Marable (Ed.), *Dispatches from the Ebony Tower: Intellectuals Confront the African American Experience* (pp. 141–152). New York: Columbia University Press.

———. (Ed.). (2001). *Color-Line to Borderlands: The Matrix of American Ethnic Studies.* Seattle, WA: University of Washington Press.

Butler, Johnnella E., and Walter, John C. (Eds.). (1991). *Transforming the Curriculum: Ethnic Studies and Women's Studies.* Albany, NY: State University of New York Press.

Byerman, Keith E. (1978). "Two Warring Ideals: The Dialectical Thought of W. E. B. Du Bois." Ph.D. dissertation, Purdue University.

———. (1981). "Hearts of Darkness: Narrative Voices in *The Souls of Black Folk.*" *American Literary Realism* 14, 43–51.

———. (1994). *Seizing the Word: History, Art, and Self in the Work of W. E. B. Du Bois.* Athens: University of Georgia Press.

Byrd, Rudolph P., and Guy-Sheftall, Beverly. (Eds.). (2001). *Traps: African American Men on Gender and Sexuality.* Indianapolis: Indiana University Press.

Cabral, Amilcar. (1971). *Our People Are Our Mountains: Amilcar Cabral on Guinean Revolution.* London: Committee for Freedom in Mozambique, Angola and Guinea.

———. (1972). *Revolution in Guinea: Selected Texts.* New York: Monthly Review Press.

———. (1973). *Return to the Source: Selected Speeches of Amilcar Cabral.* New York: Monthly Review Press.

———. (1974). *Textos Politicos de Amilcar Cabral: Declaracoes Sobre o Assassinato.* Lisboa: Livraria Ler.

———. (1975). *La Descolonizacion del Africa Portuguesa: Guinea-Bissau.* Buenos Aires: Ediciones Periferia.

———. (1979). *Unity and Struggle: Speeches and Writings of Amilcar Cabral.* New York: Monthly Review Press.

Cain, William E. (1990a). "W. E. B. Du Bois's *Autobiography* and the Politics of Literature." *Black American Literature Forum* 24, 299–313.

———. (1990b). "Violence, Revolution, and the Cost of Freedom: John Brown and W. E. B. Du Bois." *Boundary* 2 (17), 305–330.

———. (1993). "From Liberalism to Communism: The Political Thought of W. E. B. Du Bois." In Amy Kaplan and Donald E. Pease (Eds.), *Culture of United States Imperialism* (pp. 456–473). Durham: Duke University Press.

Calhoun, Craig. (1995). *Critical Social Theory: Culture, History, and the Challenge of Difference.* Malden, MA: Blackwell.

———. (Ed.). (2002). *Classical Sociological Theory.* Malden, MA: Blackwell.

Callari, Antonio, Cullenberg, Stephen, and Biewener, Carole. (Eds.). (1995). *Marxism in the Postmodern Age: Confronting the New World Order.* New York: Guilford.

Camara, Babacar. (2008). *Marxist Theory, Black/African Specificities, and Racism.* Lanham, MD: Lexington Books.

Camara, Sana. (2002). "Birago Diop's Poetic Contributions to the Ideology of Negritude." *Research in African Literatures* 33 (4), 101–124.

Campbell, Horace. (2006). "Revisiting the Theories and Practices of Amilcar Cabral in the Context of the Exhaustion of the Patriarchal Model of African Liberation." In John Fobanjong and Thomas Ranuga (Eds.), *The Life, Thought and Legacy of Cape Verde's Freedom Fighter Amilcar Cabral (1924–1973): Essays on His Liberation Philosophy* (pp. 79–102). Lewiston, NY: Mellen Press.

Cannon, Bob. (2001). *Rethinking the Normative Content of Critical Theory: Marx, Habermas and Beyond.* New York: Palgrave Macmillan.

Cannon, Katie G. (1988). *Black Womanist Ethics.* Atlanta: Scholars Press.

———. (1995). *Katie's Canon: Womanism and the Soul of the Black Community.* New York: Continuum.

Caraway, Nancie. (1991). *Segregated Sisterhood: Racism and the Politics of American Feminism.* Knoxville: University of Tennessee.

Carbado, Devon W. (Ed.). (1999). *Black Men on Race, Gender, and Sexuality: A Critical Reader.* New York: New York University Press.

Carby, Hazel V. (1987). *Reconstructing Womanhood: The Emergence of the Afro- American Woman Novelist.* New York: Oxford University Press.

———. (1998). *Race Men: The W. E. B. Du Bois Lectures.* Cambridge: Harvard University Press.

Carr, Edward H. (1966). *The Bolshevik Revolution* (3 Volumes). London: Pelican.

Carroll, Anne Elizabeth. (2005). *Word, Image, and the New Negro: Representation and Identity in the Harlem Renaissance.* Bloomington: Indiana University Press.

Carver, Terrell. (1982). *Marx's Social Theory.* Oxford: Oxford University Press.

———. (Ed.). (1991). *The Cambridge Companion to Marx.* New York: Cambridge University Press.

———. (1998). *The Postmodern Marx.* University Park, PA: Penn State University Press.

Cash, Floris Loretta. (1986). "Womanhood and Protest: The Club Movement Among Black Women, 1892–1922." Ph.D. dissertation, State University of New York, Stony Brook.

———. (2001). *African American Women and Social Action: The Clubwomen and Volunteerism from Jim Crow to the New Deal, 1896–1936.* Westport, CT: Greenwood Press.

Castoriadis, Cornelius. (1988a). *Political and Social Writings, Volume1, 1946–1955: From the Critique of Bureaucracy to the Positive Content of Socialism* (David Ames, Ed.). Minneapolis, MN: University of Minnesota Press.

———. (1988b). *Political and Social Writings, Volume 2, 1955–1960: From the Worker's Struggle Against Bureaucracy to Revolution in the Age of Modern Capitalism* (David Ames, Ed.). Minneapolis, MN: University of Minnesota Press.

———. (1991). *Philosophy, Politics, Autonomy* (David Ames, Ed.). New York: Oxford University Press.

———. (1993). *Political and Social Writings, Volume 3, 1961–1979: Recommencing the Revolution–From Socialism to the Autonomous Society* (David Ames, Ed.). Minneapolis, MN: University of Minnesota Press.

———. (1995). "C. L. R. James and the Fate of Marxism." In Selwyn Cudjoe and William E. Cain (Eds.), *C. L. R. James: His Intellectual Legacies* (pp. 277–297). Amherst: University of Massachusetts Press.

———. (1997). *The Castoriadis Reader* (David Ames, Ed.). Malden, MA: Blackwell.

Cateau, Heather, and Carrington, S.H.H. (Eds.). (2000). *Capitalism and Slavery, Fifty Years Later: Eric Eustace Williams—A Reassessment of the Man and His Work.* New York: Peter Lang.

Caute, David. (1970). *Frantz Fanon.* New York: Viking Press.

Cazenave, Odile. (2005). *Afrique sur Seine: A New Generation of African Writes in Paris.* Lanham, MD: Lexington Books.

Cesaire, Aime. (1958). *Discours sur le Colonialisme.* Paris: Presence Africaine.

———. (1967a). *Une Saison au Congo.* Paris: Editions du Seuil.

———. (1967b). *Aime Cesarie: Ecrivain Martiniquais.* Paris: F. Nathan.

———. (1972). *Discourse on Colonialism.* New York: Monthly Review Press.

———. (1981). *Toussaint L'Ouverture: La Revolution Francaise et le Probleme Colonial.* Paris: Presence Africaine.

———. (1983). *Aimé Césaire: The Collected Poetry* (Clayton Eshelman and Annette Smith, Eds.). Berkeley: University of California Press.

———. (1984). *Non-Vicious Circle: Twenty Poems.* Stanford, CA: Stanford University Press.

———. (1986). *Lost Body.* New York: Braziller.

——. (1990). *Lyric and Dramatic Poetry, 1946–1982* (Clayton Eshelman and Annette Smith, Eds.). Charlottesville: University Press of Virginia.

——. (1995). *Aime Cesaire: Pour Aujourd'hui et pour Demain.* Saint-Maur: Sepia.

——. (1996). *Anthologie Poetique.* Paris: Nationale Editions.

——. (2005). *Negre je Suis, Negre je Resteral.* Paris: Albin Michel.

Chabal, Patrick. (1980). "Amilcar Cabral as Revolutionary Leader." Ph.D. dissertation, Trinity College, University of Cambridge.

——. (1981a). "The Social and Political Thought of Amilcar Cabral: A Reassessment." *Journal of Modern African Studies* 19 (1), 31–56.

——. (1981b). National Liberation in Portuguese Guinea, 1956–1974." *African Affairs* 80, 75–99.

——. (1983a). *Amilcar Cabral: Revolutionary Leadership and People's War.* Cambridge: Cambridge University Press.

——. (1983b). "Party, State and Socialism in Guinea-Bissau." *Canadian Journal of African Studies* 17 (2), 189–210.

——. (2003). *Amilcar Cabral: Revolutionary Leadership and People's War.* Trenton, NJ: Africa World Press.

Chaffee, Mary Law. (1956). "W. E. B. Du Bois's Concept of the Racial Problem in the United States." *Journal of Negro History* 41, 241–258.

Cha-Jua, Sundiata K. (1998). "C. L. R. James, Blackness, and the Making of a Neo- Marxist Diasporan Historiography." *Nature, Society & Thought* 11, 53–89.

——. (2000). "Black Studies in the New Millennium: Resurrecting Ghosts of the Past." *Souls: A Critical Journal of Black Politics, Culture and Society* 2, 43–49.

——. (2001). "Racial Formation and Transformation: Toward a Theory of Black Racial Oppression." *Souls: A Critical Journal of Black Politics, Culture and Society* 3, 25–60.

Chaliand, Gerard. (1969). *Armed Struggle in Africa.* New York: Monthly Review Press.

——. (1973a). "The PAIGC without Cabral." *Ufahamu* 3 (3), 87–95.

——. (1973b). "The Legacy of Amilcar Cabral." *Ramparts*, 17–20.

Chambers, Iain, and Curti, Lidia. (Eds.). (1996). *The Post-Colonial Question: Common Skies, Divided Horizons.* New York: Routledge.

Champigny, Robert. (1972). *Humanism and Human Racism: A Critical Study of Essays by Sartre and Camus.* The Hague: Mouton.

Chandler, Nahum Dimitri. (1997). "The Problem of Purity: A Study in the Early Work of W. E. B. Du Bois." Ph.D. dissertation, University of Chicago.

Chappelle, Yvonne Reed. (1974/75). "The Negritude Process." *Black World* 24, 72–76.

Chatterjee, Partha. (1993). *The Nations and Its Fragments: Colonial and Postcolonial Histories.* Princeton: Princeton University Press.

Cherki, Alice. (2006). *Frantz Fanon: A Portrait.* Ithaca, NY: Cornell University Press.

Cherni, Nabil. (Ed.). (2004). *Visions of the Wretched: Homage to Frantz Fanon.* Manouba, Tunisia: Manouba Faculty of Letters, Arts, and Humanities.

Chikwendu, E.E. (1977). "The Relevance of Negritude to Senegalese Development." *Umoja: A Scholarly Journal of Black Studies* 1 (3), 43–58.

Chilcote, Ronald H. (1967). "Nationalist Documents on Portuguese Guinea, the Cape Verde Islands and Mozambique." *African Studies Bulletin* 10, 22–42.

——. (1968). "The Political Thought of Amilcar Cabral." *Journal of Modern African Studies* 6 (3), 373–388.

——. (1972). *Emerging Nationalism in Portuguese Africa: Documents.* Stanford: Hoover Institution Press.

——. (1974). "Amilcar Cabral: A Bibliography of His Life and Thought, 1925–1973." *Africana Library Journal* 5 (4), 289–307.

——. (1977). "Guinea-Bissau's Struggle: Past and Present." *Africa Today* 24, 1.

———. (1984). "The Theory and Practice of Amilcar Cabral: Revolutionary Implications for the Third World." *Latin American Perspectives* 11 (2), 3–14.

———. (1991). *Amilcar Cabral's Revolutionary Theory and Practice.* Boulder, CO: Lynne Rienner.

Childs, Peter, and Williams, R.J. Patrick. (1997). *An Introduction to Postcolonial Theory.* New York: Prentice-Hall.

Chinweizu. (1975). *The West and the Rest of Us: White Predators, Black Slavers and the African Elite.* New York: Random House.

———. (1983). *Toward the Decolonization of African Literature.* Washington, DC: Howard University Press.

———. (1987). *Decolonizing the African Mind.* Lagos, Nigeria: Pero Press.

———. (Ed.). (1988). *Voices from Twentieth-Century Africa: Griots and Towncriers.* London: Faber and Faber.

Chow, Rey. (1999). "The Politics of Admittance: Female Sexual Agency, Miscegenation, and the Formation of Community in Frantz Fanon." In Anthony C. Alessandrini (Ed.), *Frantz Fanon: Critical Perspectives* (pp. 34–56). New York: Routledge.

Chukwu, Cletus N. (2002). *Introduction to Philosophy in an African Perspective.* Eldoret, Kenya: Zapf Chancery.

Chrisman, Laura. (2003). *Postcolonial Contraventions: Cultural Readings of Race, Imperialism, and Transnationalism.* New York: Manchester University Press.

Christian, Harry. (1994). *The Making of Anti-Sexist Men.* New York: Routledge.

Christian, Barbara. (1985). *Black Feminist Criticism, Perspectives on Black Women Writers.* New York: Pergamon.

———. (1989). "But Who Do You Really Belong To—Black Studies or Women's Studies?" *Women's Studies* 17 (1–2), 17–23.

———. (1994). "Diminishing Returns: Can Black Feminism(s) Survive the Academy?" In David Theo Goldberg (Ed.), *Multicultarism: A Critical Reader* (pp. 168–179). Cambridge, MA: Blackwell.

Christian, Mark (2002). "An African Centered Perspective on White Supremacy." *Journal of Black Studies* 33 (2), 179–198.

———. (2006). "Philosophy and Practice for Black Studies: The Case of Researching White Supremacy." In Molefi K. Asante and Maulana Karenga (Eds.), *The Handbook of Black Studies* (pp. 76–88). Thousand Oaks, CA: Sage.

Cismaru, Alfred. (1974). "Negritude in Selected Works of Aime Cesaire." *Renascence* 26, 105–111.

Clarke, John Henrik. (1991). *Africans at the Crossroads: Notes for an African Revolution.* Trenton, NJ: Africa World Press.

———. (1993). *African People in World History.* Baltimore, MD: Black Classic Press.

Clarke, John Henrik, Jackson, Esther, Kaiser, Ernest, and O'Dell, J.H. (Eds.). (1970). *Black Titan: W. E. B. Du Bois.* Boston: Beacon.

Clayton, Matthew, and Williams, Andrew. (Eds.). (2004). *Social Justice: Black Readings in Philosophy.* Malden, MA: Blackwell.

Clifford, James. (1988). *The Predicament of Culture: Twentieth Century Ethnography, Literature, and Art.* Cambridge: Harvard University Press.

Climo, Martha Louise. (1976). "Leopold Sedar Senghor's Imagery: An Expression of His Negritude." In *Hommage à Léopold Sédar Senghor: Homme de Culture* (pp. 241–277). Paris: Presence Africaine.

Coetzee, Pieter H., and Roux, Abraham P.J. (Eds.). (1998). *The African Philosophy Reader.* New York: Routledge.

Cohen, Jean. (1987). *Class and Civil Society: The Limits of Marxian Critical Theory.* Amherst: University of Massachusetts Press.

Cohen, Jean, and Arato, Andrew. (1992). *Civil Society and Political Theory.* Cambridge: MA: MIT Press.

Cohen, Robin, and Goulbourne, Harry. (Eds.). (1991). *Democracy and Socialism in Africa*. Boulder, Co: Westview.

Cole, George D.H. (1953). *History of Socialist Thought: The Forerunners* (Volume1). New York: MacMillan.

———. (1955). *History of Socialist Thought: Marxism and Anarchism* (Volume 2). New York: MacMillan.

———. (1957). *History of Socialist Thought: The Second International, 1889–1914* (Volume 3). New York: MacMillan.

———. (1959). *History of Socialist Thought: Communism and Social Democracy, 1914–1931* (Volume 4). New York: MacMillan.

———. (1960). *History of Socialist Thought: Socialism and Fascism, 1931–1939* (Volume 5). New York: MacMillan.

Collier-Thomas, Bettye. (1980). *NCNW: National Council of Negro Women*. Washington, DC: National Council of Negro Women.

———. (1993). "National Council of Negro Women." In Darlene Clark Hine, Elsa Barkley Brown, and Rosalyn Teborg-Penn (Eds.), *Black Women in America: An Historical Encyclopedia*, 2 volumes (pp. 853–864). Brooklyn: Carlson.

———. (1997). "Frances Ellen Watkins Harper: Abolitionist and Feminist Reformer, 1825–1911." In Ann D. Gordon and Bettye Collier-Thomas (Eds.), *Afro-American Women and the Vote, 1837–1965*, Amherst, MA: University of Massachusetts Press.

Collins, Patricia Hill. (1986a). "The Emerging Theory and Pedagogy of Black Women's Studies." *Feminist Issues* 6 (1), 3–17.

———. (1986b). "Learning from the Outsider Within: The Sociological Significance of Black Feminist Thought." *Social Problems* 33 (6), 14–32.

———. (1990). *Black Feminist Thought: Knowledge, Consciousness, and the Politics of Empowerment*. New York: Routledge.

———. (1993). "Black Feminism in the Twentieth Century." In Darlene Clark Hine, Elsa Barkley Brown, and Rosalyn Teborg-Penn (Eds.), *Black Women in America: An Historical Encyclopedia*, 2 volumes (pp. 418–425). Brooklyn: Carlson.

———. (1995). "What's in a Name: Womanism, Black Feminism, and Beyond." *Black Scholar* 26 (1), 9–17.

———. (1996). "The Social Construction of Black Feminist Thought." In Ann Garry and Marilyn Pearsall (Eds.), *Women, Knowledge, and Reality: Explorations in Feminist Philosophy* (pp. 222–248). New York: Routledge.

———. (1998). *Fighting Words: Black Women and the Search for Social Justice*. Minneapolis: University of Minnesota Press.

———. (2000). *Black Feminist Thought: Knowledge, Consciousness, and the Politics of Empowerment* (Second Edition). New York: Routledge.

———. (2003). "Some Group Matters: Intersectionality, Situated Standpoints, and Black Feminist Thought." In Tommy L. Lott and John P. Pittman (Eds.), *A Companion to African American Philosophy* (pp. 205–230). Malden: Blackwell.

———. (2005). *Black Sexual Politics: African Americans, Gender, and the New Racism*. New York: Routledge.

———. (2006). *From Black Power to Hip Hop: Racism, Nationalism, and Feminism*. Philadelphia: Temple University Press.

Collins, Randall. (2000). *The Sociology of Philosophies: A Global Theory of Intellectual Change*. Cambridge: Harvard University Press.

Collins, Roger. (1998). "What Does Anarchism Offer the Wretched of the Earth?: An Appreciation of Frantz Fanon and Karl Marx." *Seeing Red* 1 (2). Available online at: http://www.seeingred.com/Copy/fanon.html [Accessed on 19 June 2001].

Connerton, Paul. (1980). *The Tragedy of Enlightenment: An Essay of the Frankfurt School*. Cambridge: Cambridge University Press.

Conrad, Joseph. (1984). *The Nigger of the "Narissus": A Tale of the Sea.* Oxford: Oxford University Press.

——. (2006). *Heart of Darkness: Authoritative Text, Backgrounds, and Contexts.* New York: W.W. Norton.

——. (2007). *The Portable Conrad* (Michael Conrad, Ed.). New York: Penguin.

Contee, Clarence G. (1969a). "W. E. B. Du Bois and African Nationalism, 1914–1945." Ph.D. dissertation, American University, Washington, D.C.

——. (1969b). "The Emergence of Du Bois as an African Nationalist." *Journal of Negro History* 54, 48–63.

——. (1970). "W. E. B. Du Bois and *Encyclopedia Africana.*" *Crisis* 77, 375–379.

——. (1971). "A Crucial Friendship Begins: Du Bois and Nkrumah, 1935–1945." *Crisis* 78, 181–185.

——. (1972). "Du Bois, the NAACP, and the Pan-African Congress of 1919." *Journal of Negro History* 57, 13–28.

Conyers, James L. (Ed.). (2003). *Afrocentricity and the Academy: Essays on Theory and Practice.* Jefferson, NC: McFarland & Co.

——. (Ed.). (2005). *Africana Studies: A Disciplinary Quest for Both Theory and Method.* Jefferson, NC: McFarland & Co.

Cook, Mercer, and Henderson, Stephen E. (Eds.). (1969). *The Militant Black Writer in Africa and the United States.* Madison: University of Wisconsin Press.

Cooper, Anna Julia. (1998). *The Voice of Anna Julia Cooper: Including* A Voice From the South *and Other Important Essays, Papers, and Letters* (Charles Lemert and Esme Bhan, Eds.). Lanham, MD: Rowman and Littlefield.

Cooper, David. (Ed.). (1968). *The Dialectics of Liberation.* Harmondsworth: Penguin.

Cooper, Wayne F. (1982). *Stranger and Pilgrim: The Life of Claude McKay, 1890–1948.* New Brunswick, NJ: Rutgers University Press.

——. (1987). *Claude McKay: Rebel Sojourner in the Harlem Renaissance.* Baton Rouge: Louisiana State University Press.

Cooppan, Vilashini. (1996). "Inner Territories: Postcoloniality and the Legacies of Psychoanalysis (Severo Sarduy, Joseph Conrad, Frantz Fanon, W. E. B. Du Bois)." Ph.D. dissertation, Stanford University.

Cortada, Rafael. (1974). *Black Studies in Urban and Comparative Curriculum.* Lexington, MA: Xerox College Publishing.

Cornell, Drucilla. (1992). *The Philosophy of the Limit.* New York: Routledge.

——. (1993). *Transformation: Recollective Imagination and Sexual Difference.* New York: Routledge.

——. (1995). *The Imaginary Domain: Abortion, Pornography and Sexual Harassment.* New York: Routledge.

——. (1998). *At the Heart of Freedom: Feminism, Sex, and Equality.* Princeton: Princeton University Press.

——. (1999). *Beyond Accommodation: Ethical Feminism, Deconstruction, and the Law.* Lanham, MD: Rowman and Littlefield.

——. (2002). *Between Women and Generations: Legacies of Dignity.* New York: Palgrave.

——. (2004). *Defending Ideals: War, Democracy, and Political Struggles.* New York: Routledge.

——. (2008). *Moral Images of Freedom: A Future for Critical Theory.* Lanham, MD: Rowman and Littlefield.

Cornwall, Andrea, and Lindisfarne, Nancy. (Eds.). (1994). *Dislocating Masculinity: Comparative Ethnographies.* New York: Routledge.

Cowan, Roaemary. (2003). *Cornel West: The Politics of Redemption.* Cambridge, UK: Polity.

Cox, Idris. (1966). *Socialist Ideas in Africa.* London: Lawrence & Wishart.

Cox, Oliver C. (1948). *Caste, Class, and Race: A Study in Social Dynamics.* New York: Monthly Review Press.

——. (1950a). "The New Crisis in Leadership Among Negroes." *Journal of Negro Education* 19, 459–465.

——. (1950b). "Leadership Among Negroes in the United States." In Alvin W. Gouldner (Ed.), *Studies in Leadership* (pp. 79–96). New York: Harper.

——. (1951). "The Leadership of Booker T. Washington." *Social Forces* 30, 91–97.

——. (1959). *The Foundations of Capitalism*. New York: Philosophical Library.

——. (1962). *Capitalism and American Leadership*. New York: Philosophical Library.

——. (1964). *Capitalism as a System*. New York: Monthly Review Press.

——. (1976). *Race Relations: Elements of Social Dynamics*. Detroit: Wayne State University Press.

——. (1987). *Race, Class, and the World System* (Herbert M. Hunter and Sameer Y. Abraham, Eds.). New York: Monthly Review Press.

——. (2000). *Race: A Study in Social Dynamics*. New York: Monthly Review Press.

Crenshaw, Kimberle, Gotanda, Neil, Peller, Gary, and Thomas, Kendall. (Eds.). (1995). *Critical Race Theory: The Key Writings That Formed the Movement*. New York: New Press.

Crossley, Nick. (Ed.). (2005). *Key Concepts in Critical Social Theory*. Thousand Oaks, CA: Sage.

Crouch, Stanley, and Benjamin, Playthell. (2002). *Reconsidering The Souls of Black Folk: Thoughts on the Groundbreaking Classic Work of W. E. B. Du Bois*. Philadelphia: Running Press.

Croutchett, Larry. (1971). "Early Black Studies Movements." *Journal of Black Studies* 2, 189–200.

Cruse, Harold. (1965). *Marxism and the Negro Struggle*. New York: Pioneer Publishers.

——. (1967). *The Crisis of the Negro Intellectual: A Historical Analysis of the Failure of Black Leadership*. New York: Quill.

——. (1969). *Rebellion or Revolution?* New York: Morrow.

——. (2002). *The Essential Harold Cruse: A Reader* (William J. Cobb, Ed.). New York: Palgrave.

Cudjoe, Selwyn, and Cain, William E. (Eds.). (1995). *C. L. R. James: His Intellectual Legacies*. Amherst: University of Massachusetts Press.

Cureau, Rebecca T. (1982). "Toward an Aesthetic of Black Folk Expression." In Russell J. Linnemann (Ed.), *Alain Locke: Reflections on a Modern Renaissance Man* (pp. 77–90). Baton Rouge, LA: Louisiana State University.

Dacy, Elo. (Ed.). (1986). *L'Actualite de Frantz Fanon: Actes du Colloque de Brazzaville*. Paris: Editions Karthala.

Dadoo, Yusuf. (1973). "Amilcar Cabral: Outstanding Leader of Africa's Liberation Movements." *African Communist* 53, 38–43.

D'Amato, Paul. (2006). *The Meaning of Marxism*. Chicago: Haymarket Books.

Daniels, Jessie. (1997). *White Lies: Race, Class, Gender and Sexuality in White Supremacist Discourse*. New York: Routledge.

Daniels, Phillip T.K. (1980). "Black Studies: Discipline or Field of Study?" *Western Journal of Black Studies* 4 (3), 195–199.

——. (1981). "Theory Building in Black Studies." *Black Scholar* 12 (3), 29–36.

Dant, Tim. (2003). *Critical Social Theory: Culture, Society, and Critique*. Thousand Oaks, CA: Sage.

Dash, Michael. (1973). "Marvelous Realism: The Way Out of Negritude." *Caribbean Studies* 13 (4), 57–70.

Davids, Michael. (1996). "Frantz Fanon: The Struggle for Inner Freedom." *Free Associations* 6 (2), 205–234.

Davidson, Basil. (1969). *Liberation of Guinea*. Baltimore: Penguin.

——. (1981). *No Fist Is Big Enough to Hide the Sky: The Liberation of Guinea and Cape Verde: Aspects of an African Revolution*. London: Zed.

——. (1984). "On Revolutionary Nationalism: The Legacy of Cabral." *Latin American Perspectives*, 11 (2), 15–42.

Davies, Carole Boyce. (1994). *Black Women, Writing, and Identity: Migrations of the Subject.* New York: Routledge.

———. (2007). *Left of Karl Marx: The Political Life of Black Communist Claudia Jones.* Durham, NC: Duke University Press.

Davies, Carole Boyce, and Fido, Elaine Savory. (Eds.). (1990). *Out of the Kumbla: Caribbean Women and Literature.* Trenton, NJ: African World Press.

Davies, Carole Boyce, Gadsby, Meredith, Peterson, Charles, and Williams, Henrietta. (Eds.). (2003). *Decolonizing the Academy: African Diaspora Studies.* Trenton, NJ: Africa World Press.

Davies, Carole Boyce, and Graves, Anne A. (Eds.). (1986). *Ngambika: Studies of Women in African Literature.* Trenton, NJ: African World Press.

Davies, Carole Boyce, and Ogundipe-Leslie, Molara. (Eds.). (1995). *Moving Beyond Boundaries* (2 Volumes). New York: New York University Press.

Davies, Gregson. (1997). *Aime Cesaire.* Cambridge: Cambridge University Press.

Davis, Angela Y. (1971a). *If They Come in the Morning: Voices of Resistance.* New York: Third Press.

———. (1971b). *Angela Davis Speaks* [Compact Disc]. Washington, DC: Smithsonian Folkways Records.

———. (1972). *Frame-Up: The Opening Defense Statement Made by Angela Y. Davis.* San Francisco, CA: National Committee to Free Angela Y. Davis.

———. (1974a). *Angela Davis: An Autobiography.* New York: Random House.

———. (1974b). *Angela Davis Case Collection.* Dobbs Ferry, NY: Trans-Media Publishing.

———. (1981). *Women, Race and Class.* New York: Vintage.

———. (1985). *Violence Against Women and the Ongoing Challenge to Racism.* Latham, NY: Kitchen Table.

———. (1989). *Women, Culture, and Politics.* New York: Vintage.

———. (1995). "Reflections on the Black Woman's Role in the Community of Slaves." In Beverly Guy-Sheftall (Ed.), *Words of Fire: An Anthology of African American Feminist Thought* (pp. 200–218). New York: Free Press.

———. (1998a). *The Angela Y. Davis Reader* (Joy A. James, Ed.). Malden, MA: Blackwell.

———. (1998b). "Angela Y. Davis: An Interview." In George Yancy (Ed.), *African American Philosophers: 17 Conversations* (pp. 13–31). New York: Routledge.

———. (1998c). *Blues Legacies and Black Feminism: Gertrude "Ma" Rainey, Bessie Smith and Billie Holiday,* New York: Vintage.

———. (1999). *The Prison Industrial Complex* [Compact Disc]. San Francisco, CA: AK Press Audio.

———. (2003). *Are Prisons Obsolete?* New York: Seven Stories Press.

———. (2005a). *Abolition Democracy: Beyond Empire, Prisons, and Torture.* New York: Seven Stories Press.

———. (2005b). "Marcuses's Legacies." In John Abromeit and W. Mark Cobb (Eds.), *Herbert Marcuse: A Critical Reader* (pp. 43–50). New York: Routledge.

Davis, Elizabeth L. (1996). *Lifting As They Climb: The National Association of Colored Women.* New York: G.K. Hall.

Davis, William Allison. (1974). *Du Bois and the Problem of the Black Masses.* Atlanta: Atlanta University Press.

Dawson, Michael C. (1994). *Behind the Mule: Race, Class and African American Politics.* Princeton: Princeton University Press.

———. (2001). *Black Visions: The Roots of Contemporary African American Political Ideologies.* Chicago: University of Chicago Press.

Dawahare, Anthony. (2003). *Nationalism, Marxism, and African American Literature Between the Wars: A New Pandora's Box.* Jackson, MS: University Press of Mississippi.

Deegan, Mary Jo. (1988). "W. E. B. Du Bois and the Women of Hull House, 1895–1899." *American Sociologist* 19 (4), 301–311.

———. (2001). "American Pragmatism and Liberation Sociology: The Theory and Praxis of Jane Addams, W. E. B. Du Bois, G.H. Mead, and Joe Feagin." Paper presented at the annual meeting of the *Society for the Study of Social Problems.*

Decker, Jeffrey L. (1990). "Terrorism (Un)Veiled: Frantz Fanon and the Women of Algiers." *Cultural Critique* 17, 177–186.

DeGrood, David H. (1978). *Dialectics and Revolution*. Amsterdam: Gruner.

Delgado, Richard. (Ed.). (1995). *Critical Race Theory: The Cutting Edge*. Philadelphia: Temple University Press.

Delgado, Richard, and Stefancic, Jean. (Eds.). (1997). *Critical White Studies: Looking Behind the Mirror*. Philadelphia: Temple University Press.

Delgado, Richard, and Stefancic, Jean. (2001). *Critical Race Theory: An Introduction*. New York: New York University Press.

DeMarco, Joseph P. (1974). "The Rationale and Foundation of Du Bois's Theory of Economic Cooperation." *Phylon* 35, 5–15.

———. (1983). *The Social Thought of W. E. B. Du Bois*. Lanham, MD: University Press of America.

Dench, Geoff. (1996). *Transforming Men: Changing Patterns of Dependency and Dominance in Gender Relations*. New Brunswick: Transaction Publishers.

Dennis, Rutledge M. (1972). "W. E. B. Du Bois as Sociologist." *Journal of African American Studies* 2, 62–79.

———. (1975). "The Sociology of W. E. B. Du Bois." Ph.D. dissertation, Washington State University.

———. (1977). "Du Bois and the Role of the Educated Elite." *Journal of Negro Education* 46 (4), 388–402.

———. (1996a). "Continuities and Discontinuities in the Social and Political Thought of W. E. B. Du Bois." *Research in Race & Ethnic Relations* 9, 3–23.

———. (1996b). "Du Bois's Concept of Double Consciousness: Myth and Reality." *Research in Race & Ethnic Relations* 9, 69–90.

———. (1997). "Introduction: W. E. B. Du Bois and the Tradition of Radical Intellectual Thought." *Research in Race & Ethnic Relations* 10, xi–xxiv.

Denyer, Nicholas. (1991). *Language, Thought, and Falsehood in Ancient Greek Philosophy*. New York: Routledge.

Deosaran, Ramesh. (1981). *Eric Williams the Man, His Ideas, and His Politics: A Study of Political Power*. Port of Spain, Trinidad and Tobago: Signum Publishing.

Depestre, René. (1986). "Critique of Negritude." In Lou Turner and John Alan (Eds.), *Frantz Fanon, Soweto, and American Black Thought* (pp. 70–73). Chicago: News and Letters.

Derrida, Jacques. (1994). *Specters of Marx: The State of Debt, the Work of Mourning, and the New International*. New York: Routledge.

Devenney, Mark. (2004). *Ethics and Politics in Contemporary Theory: Between Critical Theory and Post-Marxism*. New York: Routledge.

Dews, Peter. (1987). *Logics of Disintegration: Post-Structuralist Thought and the Claims of Critical Theory*. New York: Verso.

Dhada, Mustafah. (1993). *Warriors at Work: How Guinea was Really Set Free*. Niwot, CO: University Press of Colorado.

Dhondy, Farrukh. (2001). *C. L. R. James*. London: Weidenfeld and Nicolson.

Di Stephano, Christine. (1991). "Masculine Marx." In Mary Lyndon Shanley and Carole Pateman (Eds.), *Feminist Interpretations and Political Theory* (pp. 146–164). University Park, PA: Penn State University Press.

———. (Ed.). (2008). *Feminist Interpretations of Karl Marx*. University Park, PA: Pennsylvania State University Press.

Diawara, Manthia. (2000). *In Search of Africa*. Cambridge, MA: Harvard University Press.

Dickson, Lynda Faye. (1982). "The Early Club Movement Among Black Women in Denver: 1890–1925." Ph.D. dissertation, University of Colorado at Boulder.

Digby, Tom. (Ed.). (1998). *Men Doing Feminism*. New York: Routledge.

Dill, Bonnie Thornton. (1979). "The Dialectics of Black Womanhood: Towards a New Model of American Femininity." *Signs: A Journal of Women and Culture in Society* 4 (3), 543–555.

——. (1983). "Race, Class, and Gender: Prospects for an All-Inclusive Sisterhood." *Feminist Studies* 9 (1), 131–150.

Diop, Alioune. (1962). "Remarks on African Personality and Negritude." In the American Society of African Culture (Ed.), *Pan-Africanism Reconsidered* (pp. 337–357). Berkeley: University of California Press.

Diop, Cheikh Anta. (1974). *The African Origin of Civilization: Myth or Reality.* Chicago: Lawrence Hill Books.

——. (1978a). *The Cultural Unity of Black Africa.* Chicago: Third World Press.

——. (1978b). *Black Africa: The Economic and Cultural Basis for a Federated State.* Chicago: Lawrence Hill Books.

——. (1987). *Precolonial Black Africa.* Chicago: Lawrence Hill Books.

——. (1991). *Civilization or Barbarism: An Authentic Anthropology.* Chicago: Lawrence Hill Books.

——. (1996). *Towards the African Renaissance: Essays in Culture and Development.* London: Karnak House.

Dirilik, Arif. (1994). "The Postcolonial Aura: Third World Criticism in the Age of Global Capitalism." *Critical Inquiry* 20 (2), 328–356.

——. (1997). *The Postcolonial Aura: Third World Criticism in the Age of Global Capitalism.* Boulder: Westview.

Dixson, Adrienne D., and Rousseau, Celia K. (Eds.). (2006). *Critical Race Theory in Education: All God's Children Got a Song.* New York: Routledge.

Doane, Mary Ann. (1991). *Femmes Fatales: Feminism, Film Theory, Psychoanalysis.* New York.

Dobratz, Betty A., and Shanks-Melie, Stephanie L. (1997). *"White Power, White Pride!": The White Separatist Movement in the United States.* New York: Twayne.

Docherty, Thomas. (1999). *Criticism and Modernity: Aesthetics, Literature, and Nations in Europe and Its Academies.* New York: Oxford University Press.

Doherty, Thomas P. (2003). *Cold War, Cool Medium: Television, McCarthyism, and American Culture.* New York: Columbia University Press.

Donaldson, Jeff. (1970). "Ten in Search of a Nation." *Black World* 19, 80–89.

——. (1980). "Trans-African Art." *The Black Collegian* 11, 90–101.

Donaldson, Laura E. (1993). *Decolonizing Feminisms.* New York: Routledge.

Donham, Donald L. (1990). *History, Power, Ideology: Central Issues in Marxism and Anthropology.* Cambridge: Cambridge University Press.

Douglass, Frederick. (1950-1975). *The Life and Writings of Frederick Douglass* (5 Volumes, Philip S. Foner, Ed.). New York: International.

——. (1992). *Frederick Douglass on Women's Rights* (Philip S. Foner, Ed.). New York: Da Capo Press.

——. (1994). *Autobiographies: Narrative of the Life, My Bondage and My Freedom, Life and Times.* New York: Library of America.

——. (1996). *The Oxford Frederick Douglass Reader* (Williams L. Andrews, Ed.). New York: Oxford University Press.

——. (1999). *Frederick Douglass: Speeches and Selected Writings* (Philip S. Foner, Ed., abridged and adapted by Yuval Taylor). New York: Library of America.

Dove, Nah. (1998a). *Afrikan Mothers: Bearers of Culture, Makers of Social Change.* Albany: State University of New York Press.

——. (1998b). "Africana Womanism: An Afrocentric Theory." *Journal of Black Studies* 28 (5), 515–539.

Diggins, John Patrick. (1992). *The Rise and Fall of the American Left.* New York: Norton.

Dirlik, Arif. (1994). "The Postcolonial Aura: Third World Criticism in the Age of Global Capitalism." *Critical Inquiry* 20 (2), 328–356.

——. (1997). *The Postcolonial Aura: Third World Criticism in the Age of Global Capitalism.* Boulder: Westview.

——. (2000). *Postmodernity's Histories: The Past as Legacy and Project.* Lanham, MD: Rowman and Littlefield.

——. (2005). *Marxism and the Chinese Revolution.* Lanham, MD: Rowman and Littefield.

——. (2007). *Global Modernity: Modernity in the Age of Global Capitalism.* Boulder: Paradigm Publishers.

Drachler, Jacob. (Ed.). (1963). *African Heritage: An Anthology of Black African Personality and Culture.* London and New York: Collier and Macmillan.

Drake, St. Clair. (1986–87). "Dr. W. E. B. Du Bois: A Life Lived Experimentally and Self-Documented." *Contributions in Black Studies* 8, 111–134.

Drake, William Avon. (1985). "From Reform to Communism: The Intellectual Development of W. E. B. Du Bois." Ph.D. dissertation, Cornell University, Ithaca, NY.

Drummer, Raydora Susan. (1995). "Transformational Leadership in the Life of W. E. B. Du Bois: 1900–1930." Ph.D. dissertation, Michigan State University.

Duara, Prasenjit. (2003). *Decolonization: Perspectives from Now and Then.* New York: Routledge.

Dubey, Madhu. (1998). "The 'True Lie' of the Nation: Fanon and Feminism." *Differences: A Journal of Feminist Cultural Studies* 10 (2), 1–29.

Dubiel, Helmut. (1985). *Theory and Politics: Studies in the Development of Critical Theory.* Cambridge: MIT Press.

Du Bois, W. E. B. (1898). "The Study of Negro Problems." *Annals of the American Academy of Political and the Social Science* 11 (January), 1–23.

——. (1906). *The Health and Physique of the Negro American.* Atlanta: Atlanta University Press.

——. (1911a). *The Quest of the Silver Fleece: A Novel.* Chicago: McClurg.

——. (1911b). "Writers." *Crisis* 1 (6), 20–21.

——. (1928). *Dark Princess: A Romance.* New York: Harcourt, Brace & Co.

——. (1930a). *Africa, Its Geography, People, and Products.* Girard, Kansas: Haldeman- Julius.

——. (1930b). *Africa, Its Place in Modern History.* Girard, Kansas: Haldemen-Julius.

——. (1938). *A Pageant in Seven Decades, 1868–1938.* Atlanta: Atlanta University Press.

——. (1939). *Black Folk Then and Now: An Essay in the History and Sociology of the Negro Race.* New York: Henry Holt.

——. (1945). *Color and Democracy: Colonies and Peace.* New York: Hartcourt Brace.

——. (1952). *In Battle for Peace: The Story of My 83rd Birthday.* New York: Masses & Mainstream.

——. (1957). *The Ordeal of Mansart.* New York: Mainstream.

——. (1958). *Pan-Africa, 1919–1958.* Accra, Ghana: Bureau of African Affairs.

——. (1959). *Mansart Builds a School.* New York: Mainstream.

——. (1960a). *W. E. B. Du Bois: A Recorded Autobiography* [Compact Disc]. Washington, DC: Folkways.

——. (1960b). *W. E. B. Du Bois: Socialism and the American Negro* [Compact Disc]. Washington, D.C.: Folkways.

——. (1960c). *Africa in Battle Against Colonialism, Racism, and Imperialism.* Chicago: Afro-American Heritage Association.

——. (1961a). *Africa: An Essay Toward a History of the Continent of Africa and Its Inhabitants.* Moscow: Soviet Institute of African Studies.

——. (1961b). *Worlds of Color.* New York: Mainstream.

——. (1962). *John Brown.* New York: International Publishers.

——. (1963). *Colonial and Colored Unity: A Program of Action* (George Padmore, Ed.). London: Hammersmith.

——. (1964). *The Selected Poems of W. E. B. Du Bois.* Accra, Ghana: University of Ghana Press.

——. (1965). *The World and Africa: An Inquiry into the Part which Africa Has Played in World History.* New York: International Publishers.

———. (1968a). *The Autobiography of W. E. B. Du Bois: A Soliloquy on Viewing My Life from the Last Decade of Its First Century*. New York: International Publishers.

———. (1968b). *Dusk of Dawn: An Essay Toward an Autobiography of a Race Concept*. New York: Schocken.

———. (1969a). *Darkwater: Voices from Within the Veil*. New York: Schocken.

———. (1969b). *The Souls of Black Folk*. New York: New American Library.

———. (1969c). *An ABC of Color: Selections from over a Half Century of the Writings of W. E. B. Du Bois*. New York: International Publishers.

———. (Ed.). (1969d). *Atlanta University Publications, 1896–1916*, Nos. 1–20 (2 Volumes). New York: Arno Press.

———. (1970a). *The Negro*. New York: Oxford University Press.

———. (1970b). *The Gift of Black Folk: The Negro in the Making of America*. New York: Simon & Schuster.

———. (1970c). *W. E. B. Du Bois: A Reader* (Meyer Weinberg, Ed.). New York: Harper and Row.

———. (1970d). *W. E. B. Du Bois Speaks: Speeches and Addresses, 1899–1963*, 2 volumes (Philip S. Foner, Ed.). New York: Pathfinder Press.

———. (1970e). *The Selected Writings of W. E. B. Du Bois* (Walter Wilson, Ed.). New York: Mentor Books.

———. (1971a). *The Seventh Son: The Thought and Writings of W. E. B. Du Bois*, volume 1 (Julius Lester, Ed.). New York: Vintage Books.

———. (1971b). *The Seventh Son: The Thought and Writings of W. E. B. Du Bois*, volume 2 (Julius Lester, Ed.). New York: Vintage Books.

———. (1971c). *W. E. B. Du Bois: A Reader* (Andrew Paschal, Ed.). New York: Collier Books.

———. (1972a). *The Emerging Thought of W. E. B. Du Bois* (Henry Lee Moon, Ed.). New York: Simon & Schuster.

———. (1972b). *W. E. B. Du Bois: The Crisis Writings* (Daniel Walden, Ed.). Greenwich, CT: Fawcett.

———. (1972c). *The Reminiscences of W. E. B. Du Bois: An Oral History*. New York: Columbia University Libraries.

———. (1973). *The Education of Black People: Ten Critiques, 1906–1960* (Herbert Aptheker, Ed.). New York: Monthly Review Press.

———. (1977). *Book Reviews by W. E. B. Du Bois* (Herbert Aptheker, Ed.). Millwood, NY: Kraus-Thomson.

———. (1978). *W. E. B. Du Bois on Sociology and the Black Community* (Dan S. Green and Edwin D. Driver, Eds.). Chicago: University of Chicago Press.

———. (1980a). *Contributions of W. E. B. Du Bois in Government Publications and Proceedings* (Herbert Aptheker, Ed.). Millwood, NY: Kraus-Thomson.

———. (1980b). *Selection from Phylon* (Herbert Aptheker, Ed.). Millwood, NY: Kraus-Thomson.

———. (1980c). *Prayers for Dark People* (Herbert Aptheker, Ed.). Amherst: University of Massachusetts Press.

———. (1980d). *Selections from the Brownies Book* (Herbert Aptheker, Ed.). Millwood, NY: Kraus-Thomson.

———. (1980e). *The Papers of W. E. B. Du Bois, 1877–1963* (89 reels of microfilm; Herbert Aptheker, Ed.). Sanford, NC: Microfilming Corporation of America.

———. (1982a). *Writings in Periodicals Edited by Others*, vol. 1 (Herbert Aptheker, Ed.). Millwood, NY: Kraus-Thomson.

———. (1982b). *Writings in Periodicals Edited by Others*, vol. 2 (Herbert Aptheker, Ed.). Millwood, NY: Kraus-Thomson.

———. (1982c). *Writings in Periodicals Edited by Others*, vol. 3 (Herbert Aptheker, Ed.). Millwood, NY: Kraus-Thomson.

——. (1982d). *Writings in Periodicals Edited by Others*, vol. 4 (Herbert Aptheker, Ed.). Mill-wood, NY: Kraus-Thomson.

——. (1982e). *Writings in Non-Periodical Literature Edited by Others* (Herbert Aptheker, Ed.). Millwood, NY: Kraus-Thomson.

——. (1983a). *Selections from the Crisis*, vol. 1 (Herbert Aptheker, Ed.). Millwood, NY: Kraus-Thomson.

——. (1983b). *Selections from the Crisis*, vol. 2. (Herbert Aptheker, Ed.). Millwood, NY: Kraus-Thomson.

——. (1985a). *Against Racism: Unpublished Essays, Papers, Addresses, 1887–1961* (Herbert Aptheker, Ed.). Amherst, MA: University of Massachusetts Press.

——. (1985b). *Creative Writings by W. E. B. Du Bois: A Pageant, Poems, Short Stories and Playlets* (Herbert Aptheker, Ed.). Millwood, NY: Kraus-Thomson.

——. (1985c). *Selections from Horizon* (Herbert Aptheker, Ed.). White Plains, NY: Kraus-Thomson.

——. (1986a). *Du Bois: Writings* (Nathan Irvin Huggins, Ed.). New York: Library of America Press.

——. (1986b). *Pamphlets and Leaflets* (Herbert Aptheker, Ed.). New York: Kraus- Thomson.

——. (1986c). *Newspaper Columns by W. E. B. Du Bois*, vol. 1 (Herbert Aptheker, Ed.). White Plains, NY: Kraus-Thomson.

——. (1986d). *Newspaper Columns by W. E. B. Du Bois*, vol. 2 (Herbert Aptheker, Ed.). White Plains, NY: Kraus-Thomson.

——. (1989). *The Souls of Black Folk*. New York: Bantam-Doubleday.

——. (1992). *The World of W. E. B. Du Bois* (Meyer Weinberg, Ed.). Westport, CT: Green-wood.

——. (1995a). *W. E. B. Du Bois Reader* (David Levering Lewis, Ed.). New York: Henry Holt.

——. (1995b). *Black Reconstruction in America, 1860–1880*. New York: Touchstone.

——. (1996a). *The Oxford W. E. B. Du Bois Reader* (Eric Sundquist, Ed.). New York: Oxford University Press.

——. (1996b). *The Philadelphia Negro: A Social Study*. Philadelphia: University of Pennsylvania Press.

——. (1996c). "The Talented Tenth Memorial Address." In Henry Louis Gates, Jr. and Cornel West, *The Future of the Race* (pp. 159–179). New York: Alfred A. Knopf.

——. (1997a). *The Souls of Black Folk* (Robert Gooding-Williams and David W. Blight, Eds.). Boston: Bedford Books.

——. (1997b). *The Correspondence of W. E. B. Du Bois: Volume I— Selections, 1877–1934* (Herbert Aptheker, Ed.). Amherst, MA: University of Massachusetts Press.

——. (1997c). *The Correspondence of W. E. B. Du Bois: Volume II—Selections, 1934–1944* (Herbert Aptheker, Ed.). Amherst, MA: University of Massachusetts Press.

——. (1997d). *The Correspondence of W. E. B. Du Bois: Volume III— Selections, 1944–1963.* (Herbert Aptheker, Ed.). Amherst, MA: University of Massachusetts Press.

——. (1998a). "The Socialism of the German Socialists." *Central European History* 31 (3), 189–225 [Special Issue on "W. E. B. Du Bois and the Kaiserreich Articles"].

——. (1998b). "The Present Condition of German Politics—1893." *Central European History* 31 (3), 171–189 [Special Issue on "W. E. B. Du Bois and the Kaiserreich Articles"].

——. (1999). *Darkwater: Voices from within the Veil*. Mineola, NY: Dover.

——. (2000a). "The Salvation of the American Negro Lies in Socialism." In Manning Marable and Leith Mullings (Eds.), *Let Nobody Turn Us Around: Voices of Resistance, Reform, and Renewal, An African American Anthology* (pp. 409–419). Lanham, MD: Rowman and Littlefield.

——. (2000b). *Du Bois on Religion* (Phil Zuckerman, Ed.). Walnut Creek: Altamira.

——. (2000c). *W. E. B. Du Bois's Historic Lecture: "The Sufferings of Black Americans, Socialism, and the Arrogance of U.S. Capitalism"* [Compact Disc]. Durham, NC: Black Historic CD Series.

——. (2001). *The Negro*. Mineola, NY: Dover.

——. (2002). *Du Bois on Education* (Eugene F. Provenzo, Jr., Ed.). Walnut Creek: Altamira.

——. (2004). *The Social Theory of W. E. B. Du Bois* (Phil Zuckerman, Ed.). Thousand Oaks: Sage.

——. (2005a). *W. E. B., Du Bois on Asia: Crossing the World Color Line* (Bill Mullen and Cathryn Watson, Eds.). Jackson, MS: University Press of Mississippi.

——. (2005b). *Du Bois on Reform: Periodical-Based Leadership for African Americans* (Brian Johnson, Ed.). Lanham, MD: AltaMira Press.

——. (2005c). *The Illustrated Souls of Black Folk* (Eugene F. Provenzo, Jr., Ed.). Boulder, CO: Paradigm Publishers.

Du Bois, W. E. B. and Washington, Booker T. (1970). *The Negro in the South*. New York: University Books.

du Cille, Ann. (1994). "The Occult of True Black Womanhood: Critical Demeanor and Black Feminist Studies." *Signs* 19 (3), 591–629.

Duffield, Mark R. (1988). *Black Radicalism and the Politics of De-Industrialization: The Hidden History of Indian Foundry Workers*. Brookfield, VT: Avebury.

Dunayevskaya, Raya. (1996). *Women's Liberation and the Dialectics of Revolution: Reaching for the Future*. Detroit: Wayne State University Press.

Dunn, Stephen. (1982). *The Fall and Rise of the Asiatic Mode of Production*. New York: Routledge and Kegan Paul.

Dupuy, Alex. (1995). "Toussaint L'Ouverture and the Haitian Revolution: A Reassessment of C. L. R. James's Interpretation." In Selwyn Cudjoe and William E. Cain (Eds.), *C. L. R. James: His Intellectual Legacies* (pp. 106–117). Amherst: University of Massachusetts Press.

Duran, Jane, and Stewart, Earl L. (1999). "Alain Locke, Essentialism, and the Notion of a Black Aesthetic." In Leonard Harris (Ed.), *The Critical Pragmatism of Alain Locke: A Reader on Value, Theory, Aesthetics, Community, Culture, Race, and Education* (pp. 111–126). Lanham, MD: Rowman and Littlefield.

During, Simon. (1987). "Postmodernism or Postcolonialism Today," *Textual Practice* 1 (1), 32–47.

Durr, Marlese. (Ed.). (2001). *The New Politics of Race: From Du Bois to the 21st Century*. Westport, CT: Greenwood.

Dussel, Enrique. (1985). *Philosophy of Liberation*. Maryknoll, NY: Orbis.

——. (1988). *Ethics and Community*. Mayknoll, NY: Orbis.

——. (1995). *The Invention of the Americas: Eclipse of the "Other" and the Myth of Modernity*. New York: Continuum.

——. (1996). *The Underside of Modernity: Apel, Ricoeur, Rorty, Taylor, and the Philosophy of Liberation* (Eduardo Mendieta, Ed.). New York: Prometheus.

——. (2001). *Towards an Unknown Marx: A Commentary on the Manuscripts of 1861–1863*. New York: Routledge.

——. (2003). *Beyond Philosophy: Ethics, History, Marxism, and Liberation Theology*. Lanham, MD: Rowman and Littefield.

Echero, Michael J. (1993). "Negritude and History: Senghor's Argument with Frobenius." *Research in African Literatures* 24, 1–13.

Edelin, Ramona Hoage. (1981). "The Philsophical Foundations and Implications of William Edward Burghardt Du Bois's Social Ethic." Ph.D. dissertation, Boston University Graduate School.

Edwards, Barrington Steven. (2001). "W. E. B. Du Bois: Empirical Social Research and the Challenge to Race, 1868–1910." Ph.D. dissertation, Harvard University.

Edwards, Brent Hayes. (2005). "Aime Cesaire and the Syntax of Influence." *Research in African Literature* 36 (2), 1–18.

Efrat, Edgar S. (1967). "Incipient Pan-Africanism: W. E. B. Du Bois and the Early Days." *Australian Journal of Politics & History* 13 (3), 382–393.

Egbuna, Obi B. (1986). "The Dialectic Process in Modern African Literature: A Study in the Epistemology of Decolonization." Ph.D. dissertation, Howard University.

Eisenstein, Zillah. (Ed.). (1979). *Capitalist Patriarchy and the Case for Socialist Feminism.* New York: Monthly Review Press.

Ekei, J. Chukwuemeka. (2001). *Justice in Communalism: A Foundation of Ethics in African Philosophy.* Lagos, Nigeria: Realm Communications.

Ellington, Duke. (1973). *Music Is My Mistress.* New York: Da Capo Press.

Elliott, Anthony. (2003). *Critical Vision: New Directions in Social Theory.* Lanham, MD: Rowman and Littlefield.

Ellison, Ralph. (1980). *Invisible Man.* New York: Vintage Books.

Engels, Friedrich. (1972). *The Origin of the Family, Private Property, and the State.* New York: International Publishers.

English, Parker. (1996). "On Senghor's Theory of Negritude." In Parker English and Kibujjo M. Kalumba (Eds.). *African Philosophy: A Classical Approach* (pp. 57–65). Upper Saddle River, NJ: Prentice Hall.

English, Parker, and Kalumba, Kibujjo M. (Eds.). (1996). *African Philosophy: A Classical Approach.* Upper Saddle River, NJ: Prentice Hall.

Erickson, Glenn W. (1990). *Negative Dialectics and the End of Philosophy.* Wolfeboro, NH: Longwood Academic Press.

Esedebe, P. Olisanwuche. (1994). *Pan-Africanism: The Idea and Movement, 1776–1991.* Washington, DC: Howard University Press.

Eshelman, Clayton, and Smith, Annette. (1983). "Introduction." In Clayton Eshelman and Annette Smith (Eds.), *Aimé Césaire: The Collected Poetry* (pp. 1–31). Berkeley: University of California Press.

Essed, Philomena, and Goldberg, David Theo. (Eds.). (2001). *Race Critical Theories: Texts and Contexts.* Malden: Blackwell.

Essed, Philomena, Goldberg, David Theo, and Kobayashi, Audrey. (Eds.). (2005). *Companion to Gender Studies.* Malden, MA: Blackwell.

Etuk, Emma S. (1989). *Destiny Is Not a Matter of Chance: Essays in Reflection and Contemplation on the Destiny of Blacks.* New York: Peter Lang.

Everage, James H. (1979). "W. E. B. Du Bois, A Pioneer in American Sociology: *The Philadelphia Negro* Revisited." *Southern Sociological Society.*

Eze, Emmanuel Chukwudi. (Ed.). (1997a). *African Philosophy: An Anthology.* Malden, MA: Blackwell.

———. (Ed.). (1997b). *(Post)Colonial African Philosophy: A Critical Reader.* Malden, MA: Blackwell.

———. (Ed.). (1997c). *Race and the Enlightenment: A Reader.* Malden, MA: Blackwell.

———. (2001). *Achieving Our Humanity: The Idea of the Post-Racial Future.* New York: Routledge.

———. (2008). *On Reason: Rationality for a World of Cultural Conflict and Racism.* Durham: Duke University Press.

Fabre, Michel. (1975). "Rene Maran, the New Negro and Negritude." *Phylon* 36 (3), 340–351.

———. (1993) *From Harlem to Paris: Black Writers in France, 1840–1980.* Chicago: University of Illinois Press.

Fabre, Michel, and Eburne, Jonathan P. (2005). "Rene, Louis, and Leopold: Senghorian Negritude as a Black Humanism." *Modern Fiction Studies* 51 (4), 921–935.

Fanon, Frantz. (1965). *A Dying Colonialism* New York: Grove.

———. (1967). *Black Skin, White Masks.* New York: Grove.

———. (1968). *The Wretched of the Earth.* New York: Grove.

———. (1969). *Toward the African Revolution.* New York: Grove.

———. (2001). "The Lived Experience of the Black." In Robert Bernasconi (Ed.), *Race* (pp. 184–202). Malden, MA: Blackwell.

Fanon, Joby. (2004). *Frantz Fanon: De La Martinique àl 'Algerie et a l'Afrique.* Paris: Hartmattan.

Farber, Stephen. (1981). "Violence and Material Class Interests: Fanon and Gandhi." *Journal of Asian and African Studies* 16, 196–211.

Farred, Grant. (Ed.). (1996). *Rethinking C. L. R. James.* Cambridge, MA: Blackwell.

Fashina, O. (1989). "Frantz Fanon and the Ethical Justification of Anti-Colonial Violence." *Social Theory and Practice* 15, 179–212.

Fatton, Robert. (1986). *Black Consciousness in South Africa: The Dialectics of Ideological Resistance to White Supremacy.* Albany, NY: State University of New York Press.

Faulkner, Rita A. (1996). "Women, Veils, and Land: Assia Djebar and Frantz Fanon." *World Literature Today* 70 (4), 847–856.

Favor, J. Martin. (1999). *Authentic Blackness: The Folk in the New Negro Renaissance.* Durham, NC: Duke University Press.

Feathersome, Simon. (2005). *Postcolonial Cultures.* Jackson: University Press of Mississippi.

Feenberg, Andrew. (1981). *Lukacs, Marx, and the Sources of Critical Theory.* Totowa, NJ: Rowman and Littlefield.

Ferber, Abby L. (1998). *White Man Falling: Race, Gender, and White Supremacy.* Lanham, MD: Rowman and Littlefield.

———. (Ed.). 2004. *Home-Grown Hate: Gender and Organized Racism.* New York: Routledge.

Ferenc, Tokei. (1979). *Essays on the Asiatic Mode of Production.* Budapest: Akadamiai Kiado.

Ferguson, Ann. (1986). "Motherhood and Sexuality: Some Feminist Questions." *Hypatia* 1 (2), 87-102.

———. (1998). "Socialism." In Alison M. Jaggar and Iris Marion Young (Eds.), *A Companion to Feminist Philosophy* (pp. 520–540). Malden, MA: Blackwell.

Ferrarotti, Franco. (2003). *An Invitation to Classical Sociology: Meditations on Some Great Social Thinkers.* Lanham, MD: Lexington Books.

Feuser, Willfried. (1966). "Negritude—The Third Phase." *The New African* 5 (3), 63–64.

———. (1976). "Afro-American Literature and Negritude." *Comparative Literature* 28, 289–308.

Fierce, Milfred C. (1991). *Africana Studies Outside the United States: Africa, Brazil, and the Caribbean.* Ithaca, NY: Cornell University Press.

Fischer, Sibylle. (2004). *Modernity Disavowed: Haiti and the Cultures of Slavery in the Age of Revolution.* Durham: Duke University Press.

Finn, Julio. (1988). *Voices of Negritude.* New York: Quartet Books.

Fitzpatrick, Sheila. (2001). *The Russian Revolution, 1917–1932.* New York: Oxford University Press.

Flather, Newell. (1966). "Negritude: Words and Deeds—Impressions of the Dakar Festival." *Africa Report* 11 (5), 57–60.

Floistad, Guttorm. (Ed.). (1981). *Contemporary Philosophy: A New Survey* (10 Volumes). Boston: Kluwer.

Floyd-Thomas, Stacey M. (2006a). *Mining the Motherlode: Methods in Womanist Ethics.* Cleveland, Ohio: Pilgrim Press.

———. (Eds.). (2006b). *Deeper Shades of Purple: Womanism in Religion and Society.* New York: New York University Press.

Fobanjong, John, and Ranuga, Thomas. (Eds.). (2006). *The Life, Thought and Legacy of Cape Verde's Freedom Fighter Amilcar Cabral (1924–1973): Essays on His Liberation Philosophy.* Lewiston, NY: Mellen Press.

Foley, Barbara. (2003). *Spectres of 1919: Class and Nation in the Making of the New Negro.* Urbana: University of Illinois Press.

Foner, Philip S. (1976). *Organized Labor and the Black Worker, 1619–1973.* New York: International Publishers.

———. (1977). *American Socialism and Black Americans: From the Age of Jackson to World War II.* Westport: Greenwood Press.

Foner, Philip S., and Allen, James S. (Eds.). (1987). *American Communism and Black Americans: A Documentary History, 1919–1929.* Philadelphia: Temple University Press.

Foner, Philip S., and Lewis, Ronald L. (Eds.). (1989). *Black Workers: A Documentary History from Colonial Times to the Present.* Philadelphia: Temple University Press.

Foner, Philip S., and Shapiro, Herbert. (Eds.). (1991). *American Communism and Black Americans: A Documentary History, 1930–1934.* Philadelphia: Temple University Press.

Fontenot, Chester J. (1975). "Frantz Fanon: *Black Skin, White Masks* and *The Wretched of the Earth* as Visionary Apprehensions of Reality." Ph.D. dissertation, University of California, Irvine.

——. (1979). *Frantz Fanon: Language as the God Gone Astray in the Flesh.* Lincoln: University of Nebraska Press.

——. (Ed.). (2001). *W. E. B. Du Bois & Race: Essays Celebrating the Centennial Publication of The Souls of Black Folk.* Macon: Mercer University.

Fontenot, Chester J., Jr., and Keller, Mary. (Eds.). (2007). *Re-Cognizing W. E. B. Du Bois in the Twenty-First Century: Essay on W. E. B. Du Bois.* Macon, GA: Mercer University Press.

Ford, Nick Aaron. (1973). *Black Studies: Threat or Challenge.* New York: Kennikat.

Fossett, Judith Jackson, and Tucker, Jeffrey A. (Eds.). (1997). *Race Consciousness: African American Studies for the New Century.* New York: New York University Press.

Foster, Frances Smith. (1993). "Frances Ellen Watkins Harper." In Darlene Clark Hine, Elsa Barkley Brown, and Rosalyn Teborg-Penn (Eds.), *Black Women in America: An Historical Encyclopedia,* 2 volumes (pp. 532–536). Brooklyn: Carlson.

Foucault, Michel. (1977a). *Language, Counter-Memory, Practice: Selected Essays and Interviews by Michel Foucault* (Donald F. Bouchard, Ed.). Ithaca: Cornell University Press.

——. (1977b). *Power/Knowledge: Selected Interviews and Other Writings, 1972–1977* (Colin Gordon, Ed.). New York: Pantheon.

——. (1984). *The Foucault Reader* (Paul Rabinow, Ed.). New York: Pantheon.

——. (1988). *Politics, Philosophy, Culture: Interviews and Other Writings, 1977–1984* (Lawrence D. Kritzman, Ed.). New York: Routledge.

——. (1997). *The Essential Works of Michel Foucault, 1954–1984, volume 1—Ethics: Subjectivity and Truth* (Paul Rabinow, Ed.). New York: New Press.

——. (1998). *The Essential Works of Michel Foucault, 1954–1984, volume 2—Aesthetics, Method, and Epistemology* (Paul Rabinow, Ed.). New York: New Press.

——. (2000). *The Essential Works of Michel Foucault, 1954–1984, volume 3—Power* (Paul Rabinow, Ed.). New York: New Press.

Fox, Bonnie. (Ed.). (1980). *Hidden in the Household: Women's Domestic Labor Under Capitalism.* Toronto: Women Educational Press.

Franklin, V.P. (1995). "The Autobiographical Legacy of W. E. B. Du Bois." In V.P. Franklin, *Living Our Stories, Telling Our Truths: Autobiography and the Making of the African American Intellectual Tradition.* New York: Scribner.

Fraser, Douglas. (1974). *African Art as Philosophy.* New York: Interbook.

Fraser, Nancy. (1989). *Unruly Practices: Power, Discourse and Gender in Contemporary Social Theory.* Minneapolis: University of Minnesota Press.

——. (1991). "What's Critical About Critical Theory?: The Case of Habermas and Gender." In David Ingram and Julia Simon-Ingram (Eds.), *Critical Theory: The Essential Readings* (pp. 357–387). New York: Paragon House.

——. (1997). *Justice Interruptions: Critical Reflections on the "Postsocialist" Condition.* New York: Routledge.

——. (1998). "Another Pragmatism: Alain Locke, Critical 'Race' Theory, and the Politics of Culture." In Morris Dickstein (Ed.), *The Revival of Pragmatism: New Essays on Social Thought, Law, and Culture* (pp. 157–175). Durham: Duke University Press.

Fraser, Richard S. (2004). *Revolutionary Integration: A Marxist Analysis of African American Liberation.* Seattle, WA: Red Letter Press.

Freedman, Carl H. (2002). *The Incomplete Projects: Marxism, Modernity, and the Politics of Culture.* Middletown, CT: Wesleyan University Press.

Freundlieb, Dieter, Hudson, Wayne, and Rundell, John F. (Eds.). (2004). *Crtical Theory After Habermas.* Boston: Brill.

Frey, Raymond G., and Wellman, Christopher H. (Eds.). (2003). *A Companion to Applied Ethics.* Malden: Blackwell.

Fried, Albert. (1997). *McCarthyism: The Greatest American Red Scare, A Documentary History.* New York: Oxford University Press.

Friedland, William H. (1964). *African Socialism.* Stanford: Stanford University Press.

Friedman, George. (1981). *The Political Philosophy of the Frankfurt School.* Ithaca: Cornell University Press.

Fromm, Erich. (1941). *Escape from Freedom.* New York: Holt, Rhinehart and Winston.

———. (1947). *Man for Himself: An Inquiry into the Psychology of Ethics.* New York: Rhinehart.

———. (1950). *Psychoanalysis and Religion.* New Haven: Yale University Press.

———. (1951). *The Gorgotten Language: An Introduction to the Understanding of Dreams, Fairy Tales, and Myths.* New York: Rhinehart.

———. (1955). *The Sane Society.* New York: Rhinehart.

———. (1956). *The Art of Loving.* New York: Harper.

———. (1959). *Sigmund Freud's Mission: An Analysis of His Personality and Influence.* New York: Harper.

———. (1960a). *Zen Buddhism & Psychoanalysis.* New York: Harper.

———. (1960b). *Let Man Prevail: A Socialist Manifesto and Program.* New York: Call Association.

———. (1961a). *Marx's Concept of Man.* New York: Ungar.

———. (1961b). *May Man Prevail?" An Inquiry into the Facts and Fictions of Foreign Policy.* Garden City, NY: Doubleday.

———. (1962). *Beyond the Chains of Illusion: My Encoutner with Marx and Freud.* New York: Simon and Schuster.

———. (1963). *The Dogma of Christ, and Other Essays on Religion, Psychology, and Culture.* London: Routledge & Kegan Paul.

———. (1964). *The Heart of Man, Its Genius for Good and Evil.* New York: Harper and Row.

———. (Ed.). (1965). *Socialist Humanism: An International Symposium.* Garden City, NY: Doubleday.

———. (1966). *You Shall Be as Gods: A Radical Interpretation of the Old Testament and Its Tradition.* New York: Holt, Rhinehart and Winston.

———. (1968a). *The Revolution of Hope: Toward a Humanized Technology.* New York: Harper and Row.

———. (1968b). *The Nature of Man: Readings.* New York: Macmillan.

———. (1970a). *The Crisis of Psychoanalysis.* New York: Holt, Rhinehart and Winston.

———. (1970b). *Social Character in a Mexican Village: A Sociopsychoanalytic Study.* Englewood Cliffs, NJ: Prentice-Hall.

———. (1973). *The Anatomy of Human Destructiveness.* New York: Holt, Rhinehart and Winston.

———. (1976). *To Have or To Be?* New York: Harper and Row.

———. (1980). *Greatness and Limitations of Freud's Thought.* New York: Harper and Row.

———. (1981). *On Disobedience and Other Essays.* New York: Seabury Press.

———. (1984). *The Working-Class in Weimar Germany: A Psychological and Sociological Study.* Cambridge, MA: Harvard University Press.

———. (1985). *For the Love of Life.* New York: Free Press.

———. (1989). *The Art of Loving.* New York: Harper and Row.

———. (1992). *The Art of Being.* New York: Continuum.

———. (1993). *The Revision of Psychoanalysis.* Boulder, CO: Westview.

———. (1994a). *The Art of Listening.* New York: Continuum.

———. (1994b). *On Being Human.* New York: Continuum.

———. (1995). *The Essential Fromm: Life Between Having and Being.* New York: Continuum.

———. (1997). *Love, Sexuality, and Matriarchy: About Gender.* New York: Fromm International Publishing.

Frutkin, Susan. (1973). *Aime Cesaire: Black Between Worlds.* Miami, FL: University of Miami.

Frye, Charles A. (1978). *Towards a Philosophy of Black Studies.* San Francisco: R & E Research Associates.

———. (Ed.). (1980). *Values in Conflict: Blacks and the American Ambivalence Toward Violence.* Washington, D.C.: University Press of America.

———. (1988). *From Egypt to Don Juan: The Anatomy of Black Philosophy.* Lanham, MD: University of America Press.

Funk, Rainer. (1982). *Erich Fromm: The Courage to Be Human.* New York: Continuum.

Fuss, Diana. (1995). *Identification Papers: Readings on Psychoanalysis, Sexuality, and Culture.* New York: Routledge.

Gabbidon, Shaun L. (1996). "The Criminological Writings of W. E. B. Du Bois: A Historical Analysis." Ph.D. dissertation, Indiana University of Pennsylvania.

———. (2000). "An Early American Crime Poll by W. E. B. Du Bois." *Western Journal of Black Studies* 24 (3), 167–174.

———. (2001). "W. E. B. Du Bois: Pioneering American Criminologist." *Journal of Black Studies* 31 (5), 581–599.

Gabel, Joseph. (1975). *False Consciousness: An Essay on Reification.* Oxford: Blackwell.

Gabel, Leona C. (1982). *From Slavery to the Sorbonne and Beyond: The Life and Writings of Anna Julia Cooper.* Northampton, MA: Smith College Studies in History.

Gaines, Kevin K. (1996). *Uplifting the Race: Black Leadership, Politics, and Culture in the Twentieth Century.* Chapel Hill: University of North Carolina Press.

Gaines, Stanley O., Jr. (1996). "Perspectives of Du Bois and Fanon on the Psychology of Oppression." In Lewis R. Gordon, T. Denean Sharley-Whiting, and Renee T. White (Eds.), *Fanon: A Critical Reader* (pp. 24–34). Cambridge, MA: Blackwell.

Gaines, Stanley O., Jr., and Reed, Edward S. (1994). "Two Social Psychologies of Prejudice: Gordon W. Allport, W. E. B. Du Bois, and the Legacy of Booker T. Washington." *Journal of Black Psychology* 20 (1), 8–28.

Gair, Christopher. (Ed.). (2006). *Beyond Boundaries: C. L. R. James and Postnational Studies.* London: Pluto Press.

Gardiner, Judith K. (Ed.). (2002). *Masculinity Studies and Feminist Theory.* New York: Columbia University Press.

Gatens, Moira. (1991). *Feminism and Philosophy: Perspectives on Difference and Equality.* Indianapolis: Indiana University Press.

Gates, Henry Louis, Jr. (Ed.). (1990). *Reading Black/Reading Feminist: A Critical Anthology.* New York: Meridian.

———. (1996). "W. E. B. Du Bois and 'The Talented Tenth'." In Henry Louis Gates, Jr., and Cornel West, *The Future of the Race* (pp. 115–132). New York: Alfred A. Knopf.

———. (1999). "Critical Fanonism." In Nigel C. Gibson (Ed.), *Rethinking Fanon: The Continuing Dialogue* (pp. 251–270). Amherst, NY: Humanity Books.

———. (2000). "W. E. B. Du Bois and the Encyclopedia Africana, 1909–1963." *Annals of the American Academy of Political and Social Science* 568 (March), 203–219.

Gates, Henry Louis, Jr., and West, Cornel. (1996). *The Future of the Race.* New York: Alfred A. Knopf.

Gatewood, William B. (1994). "W. E. B. Du Bois: Elitist as Racial Radical." *Georgia Historical Quarterly* 78 (2), 306–327.

Gayle, Addison. (1972). *Claude McKay: The Black Poet at War.* Detroit: Broadside Press.

Gbadegesin, Segun. (1991a). *African Philosophy: Traditional Yoruba Philosophy and Contemporary African Realities.* New York: Peter Lang.

———. (1991b). "Negritude and Its Contribution to the Civilization of the Universal: Leopold Senghor and Question of Ultimate Reality and Meaning," *Ultimate Reality and Meaning* 14 (1), 67–92.

———. (1996). "Kinship of the Dispossessed: Du Bois, Nkrumah, and the Foundations of Pan-Africanism." In Bernard W. Bell, Emily R. Grosholz, and James B. Stewart (Eds.), *W. E. B. Du Bois: On Race and Culture: Philosophy, Politics, and Poetics* (pp. 219–242). New York: Routledge.

Geggus, David P. (2002). *Haitian Revolutionary Studies.* Bloomington: Indiana University Press.

Geismar, Peter. (1969). "Frantz Fanon: Evolution of a Revolutionary." *Monthly Review* 21, 22–30.

———. (1971). *Frantz Fanon.* New York: Dial Press.

Geiss, Imanuel. (1974). *The Pan-African Movement: A History of Pan-Africanism in America, Europe, and Africa.* New York: Holmes & Meier.

Gelderen, Charles van. (1994). "C. L. R. James: Thinker, Writer, Revolutionary." In Scott McLemee and Paul Le Blanc (Eds.), *C. L. R. James and Revolutionary Marxism: Selected Writings of C. L. R. James, 1939–1949* (pp. 41–44). Atlantic Highlands, NJ: Humanities Press.

Gendzier, Irene. (1973). *Frantz Fanon: A Critical Study.* New York: Pantheon.

Genova, James Eskridge. (2004). *Colonial Ambivalence, Cultural Authenticity, and the Limitations of Mimicry in French-Ruled West Africa, 1914–1956.* New York: Peter Lang.

Gerard, Albert. (1962). "Humanism and Negritude: Notes on the Contemporary Afro-American Novel." *Diogenes* 10 (37), 115–133.

———. (1964). "Historical Origins and Literary Destiny of Negritude." *Diogenes* 48, 14–38.

———. (1970). "An Introduction to the Poetry of Aime Cesaire." *Negro Digest* 19 (3), 64–65.

———. (1971). *Black Africa.* Jamaica, NY: St. John's University Press.

———. (1972). *Four African Literatures: Xhosa, Sotho, Zulu, Amharic.* Berkeley: University of Califonia Press.

———. (1981). *African Language Literatures: An Introduction to the Literary History of Sub-Saharan Africa.* Washington, DC: Three Continents Press.

———. (Ed.). (1986). *European-Language Writing in Sub-Saharn African* (2 Volumes). Budapest: Akademiai Kiado.

———. (1990). *Contents of African Literature.* Amsterdam: Rodopi.

———. (Ed.). (1992). *Comparative Literature and African Literature.* Goodwood: Viva Afrika Press.

Geras, Norman. (1990). *Discourses of Extremity: Radical Ethics and Post-Marxist Extravagances.* New York: Verso.

Gershoni, Yekutiel. (1995). "Contributions of W. E. B. Du Bois to Pan-Africanism." *Journal of Third World Studies* 12 (2), 440–443.

Gerson, Lloyd P. (1990). *God and Greek Philosophy: Studies in the Early History of Natural Theology.* New York: Routledge.

Geuss, Raymond. (1981). *The Idea of Critical Theory: Habermas and the Frankfurt School.* Cambridge: Cambridge University Press.

Gibson, Nigel C. (1994). "Fanon's Humanism and the Second Independence in Africa." In Eileen McCarthy-Arnolds, David R. Penna, and Debra Joy Cruz Sobrepena (Eds.), *Africa, Human Rights, and the Global System.* Westport, CT: Greenwood Press.

———. (1995). "Post-Colonial Ideological Battles." *Africa Today* 42 (3), 73–82.

———. (1996a). "Jammin' the Airwaves and Tuning into the Revolution: The Dialectics of the Radio in *L' An V de la Revolution Algerienne.*" In Lewis R. Gordon, T. Denean Sharley-Whiting, and Renee T. White (Eds.), *Fanon: A Critical Reader* (pp. 273–282). Cambridge, MA: Blackwell.

——. (1996b). "Thoughts About Doing Fanonism in the 1990s." *College Literature* 26 (2), 96–118.

——. (1997). "Beyond Manicheanism: A Critical Study of Frantz Fanon's Dialectic of Liberation." Ph.D. dissertation, Political Science Department, Columbia University, New York.

——. (Ed.). (1999a). *Rethinking Fanon: The Continuing Dialogue.* Amherst, NY: Humanity Books.

——. (1999b). "Introduction to *Rethinking Fanon: The Continuing Dialogue.*" In Nigel C. Gibson (Eds.), *Rethinking Fanon: The Continuing Dialogue* (pp. 9–48). Amherst, NY: Humanity Books.

——. (1999c). "Radical Mutations: Fanon's Untidy Dialectic of History." In Nigel C. Gibson (Eds.), *Rethinking Fanon: The Continuing Dialogue* (pp. 408–446). Amherst, NY: Humanity Books.

——. (1999d). "Fanon and the Pitfalls of Cultural Studies." In Anthony C. Alessandrini (Ed.), *Frantz Fanon: Critical Perspectives* (pp. 99–125). New York: Routledge.

——. (1999e). "Beyond Manicheanism: Dialectics in the Thought of Frantz Fanon." *Journal of Political Ideologies* 4 (3), 337–365.

——. (2001). "The Oxygen of Revolution: Gendered Gaps and Radical Mutations in Frantz Fanon's *A Dying Colonialism.*" *Philosophia Africana* 4 (2), 47–62.

——. (2002). "Dialectical Impasses: Turning the Table on Hegel and the Black." *Parallax* 8 (2), 30–45.

——. (2003). *Fanon: The Postcolonial Imagination.* Cambridge: Polity.

——. (2005). "The Limits of Black Political Empowerment: Fanon, Marx, 'the Poors" and the 'New Reality of the Nation' in South Africa." *Theoria* 107, 89–118.

Gibson-Graham, J.K., Resnick, Stephen, and Wolff, Richard D. (Eds.). (2001). *Re/Presenting Class: Essays in Postmodern Marxism.* Durham, NC: Duke University Press.

Giddens, Anthony. (1971). *Capitalism and Modern Social Theory: An Analysis of the Writings of Marx, Durkheim and Max Weber.* Cambridge: Cambridge University Press.

——. (1976). *New Rules of Sociological Method: A Positive Critique of Interpretative Sociologies.* New York: Basic Books.

——. (1977). *Studies in Social and Political Theory.* New York: Basic Books.

——. (1979). *Central Problems in Social Theory: Action, Structure, and Contradiction in Social Analysis.* Berkeley, CA: University of California Press.

——. (1981). *A Contemporary Critique of Historical Materialism.* Berkeley, CA: University of California Press.

——. (1984). *The Constitution of Society: Introduction of the Thoery of Structuration.* Berkeley, CA: University of California Press.

——. (1987a). *Social Theory Today.* Stanford, CA: Stanford University Press.

——. (1987b). *Social Theory and Modern Sociology.* Stanford, CA: Stanford University Press.

——. (1991). *The Consequences of Modernity.* Cambridge, UK: Polity Press.

——. (1995). *Politics, Sociology and Social Theory: Encounters with Classical and Contemporary Social Thought.* Standford, CA: Stanford University Press.

Giddings, Paula. (1984). *When and Where I Enter: The Impact of Black Women on Race and Sex in America.* New York: Quill.

Giles, James R. (1976). *Claude McKay.* Boston: Twayne.

Gilkes, Cheryl Townsend. (1996). "The Margin as the Center of a Theory of History: African American Women, Social Change, and the Sociology of W. E. B. Du Bois." In Bernard W. Bell, Emily R. Grosholz, and James B. Stewart (Eds.), *W. E. B. Du Bois: On Race and Culture* (pp. 111–141). New York: Routledge.

——. (2001). *If It Wasn't for the Women: Black Women's Experience and Womanist Culture in Church and Community.* Maryknoll, NY: Orbis.

Gillman, Susan, and Weinbaum, Alys E. (Eds.). (2007). *Next to the Color-Line: Gender, Sexuality, and W. E. B. Du Bois.* Minneapolis, MN: University of Minnesota Press.

Gilmore, David D. (1990). *Manhood in the Making: Cultural Concepts of Masculinity.* New Haven: Yale University Press.

Gilroy, Paul. (1987). *There Ain't No Black in the Union Jack.* New York: Routledge.

——. (1993a). *The Black Atlantic: Modernity and Double Consciousness.* Cambridge: Harvard University Press.

——. (1993b). *Small Acts: Thoughts on the Politics of Black Cultures.* New York: Serpent's Tail.

——. (2000). *Against Race: Imagining Political Culture Beyond the Color Line.* Cambridge: Harvard University Press.

Gines, Kathryn T. (2003). "From Political Space to Political Agency: Arendt, Sartre, and Fanon on Race and Revolutionary Violence." Ph.D. dissertation, University of Memphis.

Giroux, Henry A. (1992). *Border Crossings: Cultural Workers and the Politics of Education.* New York: Routledge.

Glaberman, Martin. (1966). "C. L. R. James: The Man and His Works." *Flambeau* 6, 22–23.

——. (1990). "C. L. R. James—A Recollection." *New Politics* 2 (2), 78–84.

——. (1995). "The Marxism of C. L. R. James." In Selwyn Cudjoe and William E. Cain (Eds.), *C. L. R. James: His Intellectual Legacies* (pp. 304–316). Amherst: University of Massachusetts Press.

——. (1999). "Introduction to *Marxsism For Our Times: C. L. R. James on Revolutionary Organization.*" In Martin Glaberman (Ed.), *Marxism for Our Times: C. L. R. James on Revolutionary Organization* (pp. xi–xxvii). Jackson, MS: University of Mississippi Press.

Glaude, Eddie S., Jr. (2000). *Exodus!: Religion, Race, and Nation in Early Nineteenth-Century Black America.* Chicago: University of Chicago Press.

——. (Ed). (2002). *Is It Nation Time?: Contemporary Essays on Black Power and Black Nationalism.* Chicago: University of Chicago Press.

——. (2007). *In a Shade of Blue: Pragmatism and the Politics of Black America.* Chicago: University of Chicago Press.

Goldberg, David Theo. (1987). "Raking the Field of the Discourse of Racism." *Journal of Black Studies* 18, 58–71.

——. (Ed.). (1990). *Anatomy of Racism.* Minneapolis: University of Minnesota Press.

——. (1993). *Racist Culture: Philosophy and the Politics of Meaning.* Cambridge: Blackwell.

——. (Ed.). (1994). *Multiculturalism: A Critical Reader.* Cambridge: Blackwell.

——. (1997). *Racial Subjects: Writing on Race in America.* New York: Routledge.

——. (2000). "Heterogeneity and Hybridity: Colonial Legacy, Postcolonial Heresy." In Henry Schwarz and Sangeeta Ray (Eds.), *A Companion to Postcolonial Studies* (pp. 72–86). Malden, MA: Blackwell.

——. (2001). *The Racial State.* Malden, MA: Blackwell.

Goldberg, David Theo, Musheno, Michael, and Bower, Lisa. (Eds.). (2001). *Between Law and Culture: Relocating Legal Studies.* Minneapolis: University of Minnesota Press.

Goldberg, David Theo, and Quayson, Ato. (Eds.). (1999). *Relocating Postcolonialism: A Critical Reader.* Malden, MA: Blackwell.

Goldberg, David Theo, and Solomos, John. (Eds.). (2002). *A Companion to Racial and Ethnic Studies.* Malden: Blackwell.

Golden, L. Hanga, and Milikan, Ov. (1966). "William E.B. Du Bois: Scientist and Public Figure." *Journal of Human Relations* 14, 156–168.

Goldfield, Steve. (1973). "Amilcar Cabral and the Liberation Struggle in Portuguese Guinea." *Socialist Revolution* 13/14, 127–30.

Goldie, Terry. (1999). "Saint Fanon and 'Homosexual Territory'." In Anthony C. Alessandrini (Ed.), *Frantz Fanon: Critical Perspectives* (pp. 75–86). New York: Routledge.

Goldrick-Jones, Amanda. (2002). *Men Who Believe in Feminism.* Westport, CT: Praeger.

Goldstein, Philip. (2005). *Post-Marxist Theory: An Introduction.* Albany, NY: State University of New York Press.

Gomes, Crispina. (2006). "The Women of Guinea-Bissau and Cape Verde in the Struggle for National Independence." In John Fobanjong and Thomas Ranuga (Eds.), *The Life, Thought and Legacy of Cape Verde's Freedom Fighter Amilcar Cabral (1924–1973): Essays on His Liberation Philosophy* (pp. 69–78). Lewiston, NY: Mellen Press.

Gonzales-Cruz, Luis F. (1979). "Nature and the Black Reality in Three Caribbean Poets: A New Look at the Concept of Negritude." *Perspectives on Contemporary Literature* 5, 138–145.

Goodin, Patrick. (2002). "Du Bois and Appiah: The Politics of Race and Racial Identity." In Robert E. Birt (Ed.), *The Quest for Community and Identity: Critical Essays in Africana Social Philosophy* (pp. 73–83). Lanham, MD: Rowman & Littlefield.

Goodin, Robert E., and Pettit, Philip. (Eds.). (1993). *A Companion to Contemporary Political Philosophy*. Malden, MA: Blackwell.

Goodin, Robert E., and Pettit, Philip. (Eds.) (1997). *Contemporary Political Philosophy: An Anthology*. Cambridge: Blackwell.

Gooding-Williams, Robert. (1987). "Philosophy of History and Social Critique in *The Souls of Black Folk.*" *Social Science Information* 26, 99–114.

———. (1991). "Evading Narrative Myth, Evading Prophetic Pragmatism: A Review of Cornel West's *The American Evasion of Philosophy.*" *American Philosophical Association Newsletter of the Black Experience* 90 (3), 12–16.

———. (1991–92). "Evading Narrative Myth, Evading Prophetic Pragmatism: Cornel West's *The American Evasion of Philosophy.*" *Massachusetts Review* 32 , 517–542.

———. (1994). "Du Bois's Counter-Sublime." *Massachusetts Review* 35, 203–224.

———. (1996). "Outlaw, Appiah, and Du Bois's 'The Conservation of Races'." In Bernard W. Bell, Emily R. Grosholz, and James B. Stewart (Eds.), *W. E. B. Du Bois: On Race and Culture* (pp. 39–56). New York: Routledge.

———. (2005). *Look, a Negro!: Philosophical Essays on Race, Culture and Politics*. New York: Routledge.

Goody, Jack. (2004). *Capitalism and Modernity: The Great Debate*. Cambridge, UK: Polity.

Gopal, P. (2002). "Frantz Fanon, Feminism, and the Question of Relativism." *New Formations* 47, 38–42.

Gordon, Lewis R. (1993). "Racism as a Form of Bad Faith." *APA Newsletter on Philosophy and the Black Experience* 92 (2), 6–8.

———. (1995a). *Bad Faith and Anti-Black Racism*. Atlantic Highlands, NJ: Humanities Press.

———. (1995b). *Fanon and the Crisis of the European Man: An Essay on Philosophy and the Human Sciences*. New York: Routledge.

———. (1995c). "Sartrean Bad Faith and Anti-black Racism." In Steven Crowell (Ed.), *The Prism of the Self: Essays in Honor of Maurice Natanson* (pp. 107–129). Dordrecht, the Netherlands: Kluwer Academic Publishers.

———. (1996a). "The Black Body and the Body Politic: Fanon's Existential Phenomenological Critique of Psychoanalysis." In Lewis R. Gordon, T. Denean Sharpley-Whiting, and Renee T. White, T. (Eds.), *Fanon: A Critical Reader* (pp. 74–84). Cambridge, MA: Blackwell.

———. (1996b). "Fanon's Tragic Revolutionary Violence." In Lewis R. Gordon, T. Denean Sharpley-Whiting, and Renee T. White, T. (Eds.), *Fanon: A Critical Reader* (pp. 297–308). Cambridge, MA: Blackwell.

———. (Ed.). (1997a). *Existence in Black: An Anthology of Black Existential Philosophy*. New York: Routledge.

———. (1997b). *Her Majesty's Other Children: Sketches of Racism from a Neocolonial Age*. Lanham, MD: Rowman and Littlefield.

———. (1998a). "African American Philosophy: Theory, Politics, and Pedagogy." *Philosophy of Education Yearbook: 1998* [On-line article]. Available at: http://www.ed.uiuc.edu/EPS/PES-Yearbook/1998/gordon.htm [17 October 2001].

———. (1998b). "Contracting White Normativity." *Small Axe: A Caribbean Journal of Criticism* 4, 166–175.

———. (1998c). "Lewis R. Gordon: An Interview." In George Yancy (Ed.), *African American Philosophers: 17 Conversations* (pp. 95–119). New York: Routledge.

———. (1998d). "The Problem of Autobiography in Theoretical Engagements with Black Intellectual Production." *Small Axe: A Caribbean Journal of Criticism* 4, 47–64.

———. (1999). "A Short History of the 'Critical' in Critical Race Theory." *APA Newsletter on Philosophy and the Black Experience* 98 (2), 23–26.

———. (2000a). *Existentia Africana: Understanding Africana Existential Thought*. New York: Routledge.

———. (2000b). "What Does It Mean to Be a Problem?: W. E. B. Du Bois on the Study of Black Folk." In Lewis R. Gordon, *Existentia Africana: Understanding Africana Existential Thought* (pp. 62–95). New York: Routledge.

———. (2000c). "Du Bois's Humanistic Philosophy of Human Sciences." *Annals of the American Academy of Political and Social Science* 568, 265–280.

———. (2001). "The Unacknowledged Fourth Tradition: An Essay on Nihilism, Decadence, and the Black Intellectual Tradition in the Existential Pragmatic Thought of Cornel West." In George Yancy (Ed.), *Cornest West: A Critical Reader* (pp. 38–58). Malden, MA: Blackwell.

———. (2002). "Sartrean Bad Faith and Anti-Black Racism." In Julie K. Ward and Tommy L. Lott (Eds), *Philosophers on Race: Critical Essays* (pp. 241–259). Malden, MA: Blackwell.

———. (2003). "African American Existential Philosophy." In Tommy L. Lott and John P. Pittman (Eds.), *A Companion to African American Philosophy* (pp. 33–47). Malden, MA: Blackwell.

———. (2004a). "Fanon and Development: A Philosophical Look." *African Development/ Afrique Development* 29 (1), 65–88.

———. (2004b). "Critical Reflections on Three Popular Tropes in the Study of Whiteness." In George Yancy (Ed.), *What White Lokks Like: African American Philosophers on the Whiteness Question* (pp. 173–193). New York: Routledge.

———. (2004c). "Philosophical Anthropology, Race, and the Political Economy of Disenfranchisement." *The Columbian Human Rights Law Review* 36 (1), 145–172.

———. (2005a). "Through the Zone of Nonbeing: A Reading of *Black Skin, White Masks* in Celebration of Fanon's Eightieth Birthday." *C. L. R. James Journal* 11 (1), 1–43.

———. (2005b). "Black Latin@s and Blacks in Latin America: Some Philosophical Considerations." In Ramon Grosfoguel, Nelson Maldonad-Torres, and Jose D. Saldivar (Eds.), *Latin@s in the World-System: Towards the Decolonization of U.S. Empire in the 21st Century* (pp. 89–103). Boulder, CO: Paradigm Publishers.

———. (2006a). *Disciplinary Decadence: Living Thought in Trying Times*. Boulder, CO: Paradigm Publishers.

———. (2006b). "African American Philosophy, Race, and the Geography of Reason." In Lewis R. Gordon and Jane Anna Gordon (Eds.), *Not Only the Master's Tools: African American Studies in Theory and Practice* (pp. 3–50). Boulder, CO: Paradigm.

———. (2006c). "Is the Human a Teleological Suspension of Man?: A Phenomenological Exploration of Sylvia Wynter's Fanonian and Biodicean Reflections." In Anthony Bogues (Ed.), *African Man, Towards the Human: Critical Essays on the Thought of Sylvia Wynter* (pp. 237–257). Kingston, JA: Ian Randle.

———. (2006d). "Cultural Studies and Invention in Recent African Philosophy." In P. Tiyambe Zeleza (Ed.), *The Study of Africa: Disciplinary and Interdisciplinary Encounters* (pp. 418–443). Dakar: CODESRIA.

———. (2006e). "Of Tragedy and the Blues in an Age of Decadence: Thoughts on Nietzsche and African America." In Jcqueline R. Scott and Todd Franklin (Eds.), *Critical Affinites: Nietzsche and the African American Experience* (pp.75–97). Albany, NY: Stante University of New York Press.

———. (2006f). "Theorizing Race and Racism in an Age of Disciplinary Decadence." *Shibboleths: Journal of Comparative Theory* 1 (1), 20–36.

———. (2006g). "Fanon and Philosophy of Liberation." *Edicion en CD-ROM de las Memorias del XIII Congreso de Filosofia.*

———. (2006h). "Through the Hellish Zone of Nonbeing: Thinking Through Fanon, Disaster, and the Damned of the Earth." *Human Architecture: Journal of the Sociology of Self-Knowledge* 5 (3&4), 5–12.

———. (2007a). "Problematic People and Epistemic Decolonization: Toward the Postcolonial in Africana Political Thought." In Nalini Persram (Ed.), *Postcolonialism and Political Theory* (pp. 121–141). Lanham, MD: Lexington Books.

———. (2007b). "What Is Afro-Caribbean Philosophy?" In George Yancy (Ed.), *Philosophy in Multiple Voices* (pp. 145–175). Lanhma, MD: Rowman and Littlefield.

———. (2008). *An Introduction to Africana Philosophy.* Cambridge: Cambridge University Press.

Gordon, Lewis R., and Gordon, Jane Anna. (Eds). (2006a). *A Companion to African American Studies.* Malden, MA: Blackwell.

Gordon, Lewis R., and Gordon, Jane Anna. (Eds.). (2006b). *Not Only the Master's Tools: African American Studies in Theory and Practice.* Boulder, CO: Paradigm.

Gordon, Lewis R., Sharpley-Whiting, T. Denean, and White, Renee T. (Eds.). (1996). *Fanon: A Critical Reader.* Cambridge. MA: Blackwell.

Gosciak, Josh. (2006). *The Shadowed Country: Claude McKay and the Romance of the Victorians.* New Brunswick, NJ: Rutgers University Press.

Gossett, Thomas F. (1953). "The Idea of Anglo-Saxon Superiority in American Thought, 1865–1915." Ph.D. dissertation, University of Minnesota, Twin Cities.

———. (1997). *Race: The History of an Idea in America.* New York: Oxford University Press.

Gottlieb, Roger S. (1992). *Marxism, 1844–1990: Origins, Betrayal, Rebirth.* New York: Routledge.

———. (Ed.). (1989). *An Anthology of Western Marxism: From Lukács and Gramsci to Socialist-Feminism.* New York: Oxford University Press.

Gould, Carol. (1973). "The Women Question: Philosophy of Liberation and the Liberation of Philosophy." *Philosophical Forum* 5, 5–44.

———. (1984). *Beyond Domination: New Perspectives on Women and Philosophy.* Totowa, NJ: Rowman and Allanheld.

Gould, Carol, and Wartofsky, Margaret. (Eds.). (1976). *Women and Philosophy: Toward a Theory of Liberation.* New York: Putman.

Gouldner, Alvin W. (1980). *The Two Marxisms: Contradictions and Anomalies in the Development of Theory.* New York: Seabury.

Graham, Maryemma. (1973). "The Threefold Cord: Blackness, Womanness and Art: A Study of the Life and Works of Frances Ellen Watkins Harper." M.A. thesis, Cornell University.

———. (1986). "Frances Ellen Watkins Harper." In Trudier Harris and Thadious M. Davis (Eds.), *Afro-American Writers Before the Harlem Renaissance.* Detroit: Gale.

Gramsci, Antonio. (1967). *The Modern Prince and Other Writings* (Louis Marks, Ed.). New York: International.

———. (1971). *Selections from the Prison Notebooks of Antonio Gramsci* (Quintin Hoare and Geoffrey Nowell-Smith, Eds.). New York: International.

———. (1975). *History, Philosophy, and Culture in the Young Gramsci* (Pedro Cavalcanti and Paul Piccone, Eds.). St. Louis: Telos Press.

———. (1977). *Selections from the Political Writings, 1910–1920* (Quintin Hoare, Ed.). New York: International.

———. (1978). *Selections from the Political Writings, 1921–1926* (Quintin Hoare, Ed.). New York: International.

———. (1985). *Selections from the Cultural Writings.* (David Forgacs and Geoffrey Nowell-Smith, Eds.). Cambridge: Harvard University Press.

———. (1992). *Prison Notebooks*, volume 1 (Joseph A. Buttigieg, Ed.). New York: Columbia University Press.

———. (1994a). *Antonio Gramsci: Pre-Prison Writings* (Richard Bellamy, Ed). New York: Cambridge University Press.

———. (1994b). *Letters from Prison*, 2 volumes (Frank Rosengarten, Ed.). New York: Columbia University Press.

———. (1995a). *Antonio Gramsci: Further Selections from the Prison Notebooks* (Derek Boothman, Ed). Minneapolis: University of Minnesota Press.

———. (1995b). *The Southern Question* (Pasquale Vericchio, Ed.). West Lafayette, IN: Bordighera.

———. (1996). *Prison Notebooks*, volume 2 (Joseph A. Buttigieg, Ed.). New York: Columbia University Press.

———. (2000). *The Antonio Gramsci Reader: Selected Writings, 1916–1935* (David, Forgacs, Ed.). New York: New York University Press.

Gran, Peter. (1996). *Beyond Eurocentrism: A New View of Modern World History.* Syracuse: Syracuse University Press.

Graves, Joseph L. (2001). *The Emperor's New Clothes: Biological Theories of Race at the Millennium.* New Brunswick, NJ: Rutgers University Press.

———. (2004). *The Race Myth: Why We Pretend Race Exists in America.* New York: Dutton.

Greco, Rose Dorothy. (1984). "The Educational Views of Booker T. Washington and W. E. B. Du Bois: A Critical Comparison." Ph.D. dissertation, Loyola University of Chicago.

Green Dan S. (1973). "The Truth Shall Make Ye Free: The Sociology of W. E. B. Du Bois." Ph.D. dissertation, University of Massachusetts.

———. (1977). "W. E. B. Du Bois's Talented Tenth: A Strategy for Racial Advancement." *Journal of Negro Education* 46 (3), 358–366.

Green, Dan S. and Driver, Edwin D. (1976). "W. E. B. Du Bois: A Case in the Sociology of Sociological Negation." *Phylon* 37 (4), 308–333.

Green, Dan S., and Smith, Earl. (1983). "W. E. B. Du Bois and the Concepts of Race and Class." *Phylon* 44, 262–272.

Green, Judith M. (1999). "Alain Locke's Multicultural Philosophy of Value: A Transformative Guide for the Twenty-First Century." In Leonard Harris (Ed.), *The Critical Pragmatism of Alain Locke: A Reader on Value, Theory, Aesthetics, Community, Culture, Race, and Education* (pp. 85–96). Lanham, MD: Rowman and Littlefield.

Greer, Beatrice Tatum. (1952). "A Study of the Life and Works of Mrs. Frances Ellen Watkins Harper." M.A. thesis, Hampton Institute.

Gregg, Robert. (1998). "Giant Steps: W. E. B. Du Bois and the Historical Enterprise." In Michael B. Katz and Thomas J. Sugrue (Eds.), *W. E. B. Du Bois, Race, and the City: The Philadelphia Negro and Its Legacy* (pp. 77–100). Philadelphia: University of Pennsylvania Press.

Gregory, Steven, and Sanjek, Roger. (Eds.). (1994). *Race.* New Brunswick, NJ: Rutgers University Press.

Griffin, Farah Jasmine. (2000). "Black Feminists and W. E. B. Du Bois: Respectability, Protection, and Beyond." *Annals of the American Academy of Political and Social Science* 568 (March), 28–40.

Grigsby, Daryl R. (1987). *For the People: Black Socialists in the United States, Africa, and the Caribbean.* San Diego: Asante Publications.

Grimshaw, Jean. (1986). *Philosophy and Feminist Thinking.* Minneapolis: University of Minnesota Press.

Grosholz, Emily R. (1996). "Nature and Culture in *The Souls of Black Folk* and *Quest of the Silver Fleece.*" In Bernard W. Bell, Emily R. Grosholz, and James B. Stewart (Eds.), *W. E. B. Du Bois: On Race and Culture* (pp. 177–192). New York: Routledge.

Gueddi, Slimane. (1991). "The Problematic of Violence in Frantz Fanon's Work, *The Wretched of the Earth* and *Black Skin, White Masks*: Humanism, Colonialism, Postcolonialism." Ph.D. dissertation, University of California, San Diego.

Guettel, Charnie. (1974). *Marxism and Feminism*. Toronto: Women's Educational Press.

Guevara, Ernesto "Che." (1968). *Venceremos!: The Speeches and Writings of Che Guevara* (John Gerassi, Ed.). New York: Macmillan.

Gugelberger, George M. (Ed.). (1985). *Marxism and African Literature*. London: James Currey.

Gunaratnam, Yasmin. (2003). *Researching Race and Ethnicity: Methods, Knowledge, and Power*. Thousand Oaks, CA: Sage.

Gunderson, Morley. (1994). *Comparable Worth and Gender Discrimination: An International Perspective*. Geneva: International Labor Office.

Guzman, Jessie P. (1961). "W. E. B. Du Bois—The Historian." *Journal of Negro Education* 30, 377–385.

Guy-Sheftall, Beverly. (1990). *Daughters of Sorrow: Attitudes Toward Black Women, 1880–1920*. Brooklyn, NY: Carlson.

——. (Ed.). (1995). *Words of Fire: An Anthology of African American Feminist Thought*. New York: The Free Press.

Gyekye, Kwame. (1988). *The Unexamined Life: Philosophy and the African Experience*. Accra, Ghana: University of Ghana Press.

——. (1995). *An Essay on African Philosophical Thought: The Akan Conceptual Scheme*. Philadelphia: Temple University Press.

——. (1996). *African Cultural Values: An Introduction*. Elkins Park, PA: Sankofa Publishing.

——. (1997). *Tradition and Modernity: Philosophical Reflections on the African Experience*. New York: Oxford University Press.

Habermas, Jurgen. (1975). *Legitimation Crisis*. Boston: Beacon.

——. (1979) *Communication and the Evolution of Society*. Boston: Beacon.

——. (1983). *Philosophical-Political Profiles*. Cambridge: MIT Press.

——. (1984). *Theory of Communicative Action*, volume 1. Boston: Beacon.

——. (1986a). *Theory and Practice*. Cambridge: Polity Press.

——. (1986b). *Knowledge and Human Interests*. Cambridge: Polity Press.

——. (1986c). *Toward a Rational Society*. Cambridge: Polity Press.

——. (1987a). *Theory of Communicative Action*, volume 2. Boston: Beacon.

——. (1987b). *The Philosophical Discourse on Modernity*. Cambridge: MIT Press.

——. (1988). *On the Logic of the Social Sciences*. Cambridge: MIT Press.

——. (1989a). *The Structural Transformation of the Public Sphere: An Inquiry into a Category of Bourgeois Society*. Cambridge: MIT Press.

——. (1989b.) *On Society and Politics: A Reader* (Steven Seidman, Ed.). Boston: Beacon.

——. (1989c). *The New Conservatism: Cultural Criticism and the Historians' Debate*. Cambridge: MIT Press.

——. (1990). *Moral Consciousness and Communicative Action*. Cambridge: MIT Press.

——. (1992a). *Autonomy and Solidarity: Interviews with Jurgen Habermas* (Peter Dews, Ed.). London: Verso.

——. (1992b). *Postmetaphysical Thinking: Philosophical Essays*. Cambridge: Polity Press.

——. (1993). *Justification and Application: Remarks on Discourse Ethics*. Cambridge: Polity Press.

——. (1994). *The Past as Future*. Lincoln: University of Nebraska Press.

——. (1995). *Between Facts and Norms: Contributions to a Discourse Theory of Law and Democracy*. Cambridge: MIT Press.

——. (1998a). *On the Pragmatics of Communication* (Maeve Cooke, Ed.). Cambridge: MIT Press.

——. (1998b). *The Inclusion of the Other: Studies in Political Theory*. Cambridge: MIT Press.

——. (2000). *On the Pragmatics of Social Interaction: Preliminary Studies in the Theory of Communicative Action*. Cambridge: MIT Press.

——. (2001a).*The Postnational Constellation: Political Essays*. Cambridge: MIT Press.

——. (2001b). *The Liberating Power of Symbols: Philosophical Essays*. Cambridge: MIT Press.

———. (2002). *Religion and Rationality: Essays on Reason, God, and Modernity*. Cambridge: MIT Press.

———. (2003a). *Truth and Justification*. Cambridge: MIT Press.

———. (2003b). *The Future of Human Nature*. Cambridge: Polity.

———. (2006a). *The Divided West*. Cambridge: Polity.

———. (2006b). *Time of Transition*. Cambridge: Polity.

Haddour, Azzedine. (2005). "Sartre and Fanon: On Negritude and Political Participation." *Sartre Studies International* 11 (1–2), 286–301.

Haggerty, George E., and McGarry, Molly. (Eds.). (2007). *A Companion to Lesbian, Gay, Bisexual, Transgender, and Queer Studies*. Malden, MA: Blackwell.

Haines, Herbert M. (1988). *Black Radicals and the Civil Rights Mainstream, 1954–1970*. Knoxville: University of Tennessee Press.

Hale, Thomas A. (1974). "Aime Cesaire: His Literary and Political Writings, with a Bio-Bibliography." Ph.D. dissertation, University of Rochester.

Hall, George. (1982). "Alain Locke and the Honest Propaganda of Truth and Beauty." In Russell J. Linnemann (Ed.), *Alain Locke: Reflections on a Modern Renaissance Man* (pp. 91–99). Baton Rouge, LA: Louisiana State University.

Hall, Perry A. (1999). *In the Vineyard: Working in African American Studies*. Knoxville: University of Tennessee Press.

Hall, Stuart. (1992). "C. L. R. James: A Portriat." In Paget Henry and Paul Buhle (Eds.), *C. L. R. James's Caribbean* (pp. 3–16). Durham: Duke University Press.

———. (1996a). *Stuart Hall: Critical Dialogues in Cultural Studies* (David Morley and Kuan-Hsing Chen, Eds.). New York: Routledge.

———. (1996b). "The After-life of Frantz Fanon: Why Fanon? Why Now? Why *Black Skins, White Masks*?" In Alan Read (Ed.), *The Fact of Blackness: Frantz Fanon and Visual Representation* (pp. 13–38). Seattle: Bay Press.

———. (1996c). "A Conversation with C. L. R. James." In Grant Farred (Ed.), *Rethinking C. L. R. James* (pp. 15–44). Cambridge, MA: Blackwell.

Hallen, Barry. (2002). *A Short History of African Philosophy*. Bloomington: Indiana University Press.

———. (2006). *African Philosophy: The Analytic Approach*. Trenton, NJ: Africa World Press.

Hallen, Barry, and J.O. Sodipo. (1981). *An African Epistemology: The Knowledge-Belief Distinction*. Ife, Nigeria: University of Ife.

———. (1986). *Knowledge, Belief, and Witchcraft*. Stanford: Stanford University Press.

Hames-Garcia, Michael. (2001). "Can Queer Theory Be Critical Theory." In William S. Wilkerson and Jeffrey Paris (Eds.), *New Critical Theory: Essays on Liberation* (pp. 201–222). Lanham, MD: Rowman and Littlefield Publishers.

Hamilton, Cynthia. (1992). "A Way of Seeing: Cultures as Political Expression in the Works of C. L. R. James." *Journal of Black Studies* 22 (3), 429–443.

Hamminga, Bert. (Ed.). (2005). *Knowledge Cultures: Comparative Western and African Epistemology*. Amsterdam: Rodopi.

Hammond, Evelynn M. (1997). "Toward A Genealogy of Black Female Sexuality: The Problematic of Silence." In M. Jacqui Alexander and Chandra Talpade Mohanty (Eds.), *Feminist Genealogies, Colonial Legacies, Democratic Futures*. (pp. 170–181). New York: Routledge.

Hanley, David. (1976). "Frantz Fanon: Revolutionary Nationalist?" *Political Studies* 24 (2), 120–131.

Hannaford, Ivan. (1996). *Race: The History of an Idea in the West*. Baltimore, MD: Johns Hopkins University Press.

Hansberry, William Leo. (1970). "W. E. B. Du Bois's Influence on African History." In John Henrik Clarke, Esther Jackson, Ernest Kaiser, and J.H. O'Dell (Eds.), *Black Titan: W. E. B. Du Bois* (pp. 98–114). Boston: Beacon.

Hansen, Emmanuel. (1974). "Frantz Fanon: Social and Political Thought." Ph.D. dissertation, Indiana University.

——. (1977). *Frantz Fanon: Social and Political Thought.* Columbus, OH: Ohio State University Press.

Hansen, Karen V., and Philipson, Ilene J. (Ed.). (1990). *Women, Class, and the Feminist Imagination: A Socialist-Feminist Reader.* Philadelphia: Temple University Press.

Hansen, William. (1997). "Another Side of Frantz Fanon: Reflections on Socialism and Democracy." *New Political Science* 40, 89–111.

Harding, Sandra. (Ed.). (2004). *The Feminist Standpoint Theory Reader: Intellectual and Political Controversies.* New York: Routledge.

Harding, Vincent. (1970). "W. E. B. Du Bois and the Black Messianic Vision." In John Henrik Clarke, Esther Jackson, Ernest Kaiser, and J.H. O'Dell (Eds.), *Black Titan: W. E. B. Du Bois* (pp. 52–68). Boston: Beacon.

———. (1981). *There Is a River: The Black Struggle for Freedom in America.* New York: Harcourt Brace Jovanovich.

Hare, Nathan. (1969). "W.E. Burghardt Du Bois: An Appreciation." In W. E. B. Du Bois, *The Souls of Black Folk.* New York: New American Library.

——. (1972). "The Battle of Black Studies." *Black Scholar* 3 (9), 32–37.

——. (1998). "The Challenge of a Black Scholar." In Joyce A. Ladner (Ed.), *The Death of White Sociology: Essays on Race and Culture* (pp. 67–80). Baltimore: Black Classic Press.

Harley, Sharon, and Terborg-Penn, Rosalyn. (Eds.). (1978). *The Afro-American Woman: Struggle and Images.* Port Washington, NY: Kennikat Press.

Harper, Frances Ellen Watkins. (1988). *The Complete Poems of Frances E.W. Harper* (Maryemma Graham, Ed.). New York: Oxford University Press.

——. (1990). *A Brighter Coming Day: A Frances Ellen Watkins Harper Reader* (Frances Smith Foster, Ed.). New York: The Feminist Press at CUNY.

——. (1994). *Minnies Sacrifice; Sowing and Reaping; Trial and Triumph: Three Rediscovered Novels.* Boston: Beacon.

——. (1995). "Woman's Political Future." In Beverly Guy-Sheftall (Ed.), *Words of Fire: An Anthology of African American Feminist Thought* (pp. 40–42). New York: The Free Press.

——. (2007). *The Collected Works of Frances Ellen Watkins Harper.* Charleston, SC: BiblioBazaar.

Harris, Cheryl I. (1995). "Whiteness as Property." In Kimberle Crenshaw, Neil Gotanda, Gary Peller, and Kendall Thomas (Eds.), *Critical Race Theory: The Key Writings That Formed the Movement* (pp. 276–291). New York: New Press.

Harris, Joseph E. (1987). *Africans and Their History.* New York: Mentor.

——. (Ed). (1993). *Global Dimensions of the African Diaspora.* Washington, DC: Howard University Press.

Harris, Leonard. (Ed.). (1983). *Philosophy Born of Struggle: An Anthology of Afro-American Philosophy from 1917.* Dubuque, IA: Kendall/Hunt.

——. (Ed.). (1989). *The Philosophy of Alain Locke: Harlem Renaissance and Beyond.* Philadelphia: Temple University Press.

——. (Ed.). (1999a). *The Critical Pragmatism of Alain Locke: A Reader on Value, Theory, Aesthetics, Community, Culture, Race, and Education.* Lanham, MD: Rowman and Littlefield.

——. (Ed.). (1999b). *Racism: Key Concepts in Critical Theory.* Amherst, NY: Humanity Books.

Harris, Robert, Hine Darlene Clark, and McKay, Nellie. (Eds.). (1990). *Black Studies in the Academy.* New York: The Ford Foundation.

Harrison, Faye V. (1992). "The Du Boisian Legacy in Anthropology." *Critique of Anthropology* 12 (3), 239–260.

Hartmann, Heidi I. (1981). "The Unhappy Marriage of Marxism and Feminism: Towards A More Progressive Union." In Lydia Sargent (Ed.), *Women and Revolution: A Discussion of the Unhappy Marriage of Marxism and Feminism* (pp. 1–41). Boston: South End.

Hartsock, Nancy C.M. (1998). *The Feminist Standpoint Revisited and Other Essays.* Boulder, CO: Westview Press.

Hattery, Angela J., and Smith, Earl. (2005). "William Edward Burghardt Du Bois and the Concepts of Race, Class, and Gender." *Sociation Today* 3 (1). Online at: http://www.ncsociology .org/sociationtoday/v31/smith.htm [Accessed on 23 February 2005].

Harvey, William B. (1982). "The Philosophical Anthropology of Alain Locke." In Russell J. Linnemann (Ed.), *Alain Locke: Reflections on a Modern Renaissance Man* (pp. 17–28). Baton Rouge, LA: Louisiana State University.

Hayes, Floyd W. (Ed.). (2000). *A Turbulent Voyage: Readings in African American Studies.* Lanham, MD: Rowman and Littlefield Publishers.

Haywood, Harry. (1934). *The Road Negro Liberation.* New York: Workers' Library Publishing.

——. (1948). *Negro Liberation.* New York: International Publishers.

——. (1978). *Black Bolshevik: Autobiography of an Afro-American Communist.* Chicago: Lake View Press.

Heberle, Renee J. (Ed.). (2006). *Feminist Interpretations of Theodor Adorno.* University Park, PA: Pennsylvania State University Press.

Hekman, Susan. (Ed.). (1996). *Feminist Interpretations of Michel Foucault.* University Park, PA: Penn State University Press.

Helbling, Mark I. (1999). *The Harlem Renaissance: The One and the Many.* Westport, CT: Greenwood Press.

Held, David. (1980). *Introduction to Critical Theory: Horkheimer to Habermas.* Berkeley: University of California Press.

Held, David, Hubert, Don, Thompson, Kenneth, and Hall, Stuart. (Eds.). (1996). *Modernity: An Introduction to Modern Societies.* Malden, MA: Blackwell.

Heller, Agnes. (Ed.). (1983). *Lukacs Reappraised.* NewYork: Columbia University Press.

Hendricks, Wanda A. (1998). *Gender, Race, and Politics in the Midwest: Black Clubwomen in Illinois.* Bloomington, IN: Indiana University Press.

Hennessey, Alistair. (Ed.). (1992). *Intellectuals in the Twentieth-Century Caribbean* (2 Volumes). London: Macmillan.

Hennessey, Rosemary, and Ingraham, Chrys. (Eds.). (1997). *Materialist Feminism: A Reader in Class, Difference, and Women's Lives.* New York: Routledge.

Henderson, Lenneal J., Jr. (1970). "W. E. B. Du Bois, Black Scholar, and Prophet." *Black Scholar* 1, 48–57.

Henderson, Vivian W. (1974). *Race, Economics, and Public Policy: With Reflection on W. E. B. Du Bois.* Atlanta: Atlanta University Press.

——. (1976). "Race, Economics, and Public Policy with Reflections on W. E. B. Du Bois." *Phylon* 37 (1), 1–11.

Hennessey, Alistair. (Ed.). (1992). *Intellectuals in the Twentieth-Century Caribbean* (2 Volumes). London: Macmillan, Caribbean.

Hennessey, Rosemary, and Ingraham, Chrys. (Eds.). (1997). *Materialist Feminism: A Reader in Class, Difference, and Women's Lives.* New York: Routledge.

Henry, Charles P. (1990). *Culture and African American Politics,* Bloomington: Indiana University Press.

——. (Ed.). *Foreign Policy and the Black (Inter)national Interest.* Albany, NY: State University of New York Press.

——. (2007). *Long Overdue: The Politics of Racial Reparations.* New York: New York University Press.

Henry, Paget. (1992a). "C. L. R. James and the Caribbean Economic Tradition." In Paget Henry and Paul Buhle (Eds.), *C. L. R. James's Caribbean* (pp. 145–173). Durham: Duke University Press.

——. (1992b). "C. L. R. James and the Antiguan Left." In Paget Henry and Paul Buhle (Eds.), *C. L. R. James's Caribbean* (pp. 225–262). Durham: Duke University Press.

——. (1996). "Fanon, African and Afro-Caribbean Philosophy." In Lewis R. Gordon, Tracey D. Sharpley-Whiting, and Renée T. White (Eds.), *Fanon: A Critical Reader* (pp. 220–243). Malden, MA: Blackwell.

——. (1997). "African and Afro-Caribbean Existential Philosophy." In Lewis R. Gordon (Ed.), *Existence in Black: An Anthology of Black Existential Philosophy* (pp. 11– 36). New York: Routledge.

——. (2000). *Caliban's Reason: Introducing Afro-Caribbean Philosophy.* New York: Routledge.

——. (2003). "African American Philosophy: A Caribbean Perspective." In Tommy L. Lott and John P. Pittman (Eds.), *A Companion to African American Philosophy* (pp. 48–66). Malden, MA: Blackwell.

Henry, Paget, and Buhle, Paul. (Eds.). (1992). *C. L. R. James's Caribbean.* Durham: Duke University Press.

Hibbert, Christopher. (1984). *Africa Explored: Europeans in the Dark Continent, 1769–1889.* New York: Penguin.

Higbee, Mark David. (1993). "W. E. B. Du Bois, F.B. Ransom, the Madam Walker Company, and Black Business Leadership in the 1930s." *Indiana Magazine of History* 89, 101–124.

——. (1995a). "W. E. B. Du Bois and the Problems of the Twentieth Century: Race, History, and Literature in Du Bois's Political Thought, 1903–1940." Ph.D. dissertation, Columbia University.

——. (1995b). "Du Bois: The First Half Century." *Science & Society* 59 (1), 82–87.

Higginbotham, Evelyn Brooks. (1989). "Beyond the Sound of Silence: Afro-American Women in History." *Gender & History* 1 (1), 50–67.

——. (1993). *Righteous Discontent: The Women's Movement in the Black Baptist Church, 1880–1920.* Cambridge: Harvard University Press.

Higginbotham, A. Leon, Jr. (1978). *In the Matter of Color: Race and the American Legal Process—The Colonial Period.* New York: Oxford University Press.

——. (1996). *Shades of Freedom: Racial Politics and Presumptions of the American Legal Process.* New York: Oxford University Press.

Hill Patricia L. (1978). "American Popular Response to W. E. B. Du Bois's *The Souls of Black Folk.*" *Western Journal of Black Studies* 2 (1), 54–59.

Hill, Patricia Liggins. (1982). "Alain Locke on Black Folk Music." In Russell J. Linnemann (Ed.), *Alain Locke: Reflections on a Modern Renaissance Man* (pp. 122–132). Baton Rouge, LA: Louisiana State University.

Hill, Robert A. (1986). "In England, 1932–1938." In Paul Buhle (Ed.), *C. L. R. James His Life and Work* (pp. 61–70). New York: Allison and Busby.

Himmelfarb, Gertrude. (2004). *The Roads to Modernity: The British, French and American Enlightenments.* New York: Knopf.

Hindess, Barry. (1993). "Marxism." In Robert E. Goodin and Philip Pettit (Eds.), *A Companion to Contemporary Political Philosophy* (pp. 312–333). Malden, MA: Blackwell.

Hine, Darlene Clark. (Ed.). (1990). *Black Women in the United States 1619–1989* (16 Volumes). Brooklyn: Carlson.

——. (1994a). *Hine Sight: Black Women and the Re-Construction of American History.* Bloomington: Indiana University Press.

——. (1994b). *Culture, Consciousness, and Community: The Making of an African American Women's History.* Greenville, NC: East Carolina University Press.

Hine, Darlene Clark, Brown, Elsa Barkley, and Teborg-Penn, Rosalyn. (Eds.). (1993). *Black Women in America: An Historical Encyclopedia* (2 Volumes). Brooklyn: Carlson.

Hine, Darlene Clark, and Gaspar, David B. (Eds.). (2004). *Beyond Bondage: Free Women of Color in the Americas.* Urbana: University of Illinois Press.

——. (Eds). *More Than Chattel: Black Women and Slavery in the Americas.* Bloomington: Indiana University Press.

Hine, Darlene Clark, King, Wilma, and Reed, Linda. (Eds.). (1995). *We Specialize in the Wholly Impossible: A Reader in Black Women's History.* Brooklyn: Carlson.

Hine, Darlene Clark, and Thompson, Kathleen. (1998). *A Shining Thread of Hope: The History of Black Women in America.* New York: Broadway Books.

Hine, Darlene Clark, and Jenkins, Earnestine. (Ed.). (1999). *A Question of Manhood: A Reader in U.S. Black Men's History and Masculinity* (Volume 1). Bloomington: Indiana University Press.

Hine, Darlene Clark, and Jenkins, Earnestine. (Ed.). (2001). *A Question of Manhood: A Reader in U.S. Black Men's History and Masculinity* (Volume 2). Bloomington: Indiana University Press.

Hine, Darlene Clark, Hine, William C., and Harrold, Stanley. (2002). *The African American Odyssey* (2nd Edition). Upper Saddle River, NJ: Prentice Hall.

Holcomb, Gary E. (2007). *Claude McKay, Code Name Sasha: Queer Black Marxism and the Harlem Renaissance.* Gainesville, FL: University of Florida.

Holland, Nancy, and Huntingdon, Patricia. (Eds.). (2001). *Feminist Interpretations of Martin Heidegger.* University Park, PA: Penn State University Press.

Holloway, Jonathan S., and Keppel, Ben. (Eds.). (2007). *Black Scholars on the Line: Race, Social Science, and American Thought in the Twentieth Century.* Notre Dame, IN: University of Notre Dame Press.

Holloway, Joseph E. (Ed.). (1991). *Africanisms in American Culture.* Bloomington: Indiana University Press.

Holmes, Eugene C. (1970). "W. E. B. Du Bois: Philosopher." In John Henrik Clarke, Esther Jackson, Ernest Kaiser, and J.H. O'Dell (Eds.), *Black Titan: W. E. B. Du Bois* (pp. 76–81). Boston: Beacon.

Holmstrom, Nancy C.L. (2002). *The Socialist Feminist Project: A Contemporary Reader in Theory and Politics.* New York: Monthly Review.

Holt, Thomas C. (1982). "The Lonely Warrior: Ida B. Wells-Barnett and the Struggle for Black Leadership." In John Hope Franklin and August Meier (Eds.), *Black Leaders of the Twentieth Century* (pp. 39–62). Chicago: University of Illinois Press.

———. (1990). "The Political Uses of Alienation: W. E. B. Du Bois on Politics, Race, and Culture, 1903–1940." *American Quarterly* 42 (2), 301–323.

———. (1998). "W. E. B. Du Bois's Archaeology of Race: Re-Reading "The Conservation of Races." In Michael B. Katz and Thomas J. Sugrue (Eds.), *W. E. B. Du Bois, Race, and the City: The Philadelphia Negro and Its Legacy* (pp. 61–76). Philadelphia: University of Pennsylvania Press.

———. (2002). *The Problem of Race in the 21st Century.* Cambridge: Harvard University Press.

Honneth, Axel. (1991). *The Critique of Power: Reflective Stages in a Critical Social Theory.* Cambridge, MA: MIT Press.

———. (1995). *The Fragmented World of the Social: Essays in Social and Political Philosophy.* Albany, NY: State University of New York Press.

hooks, bell. (1981). *Ain't I a Woman: Black Women and Feminism.* Boston: South End.

———. (1984). *Feminist Theory: From Margin to Center.* Boston: South End.

———. (1989). *Talking Back: Thinking Feminist, Thinking Black.* Boston: South End.

———. (1990). *Yearning: Race, Gender, and Cultural Politics.* Boston: South End.

———. (1991). *Black Looks: Race and Representation.* Boston: South End.

———. (1992). *Sisters of the Yam: Black Women and Self-Recovery.* Boston: South End.

———. (1994a). *Teaching to Transgress: Education as the Practice of Freedom.* Boston: South End.

———. (1994b). *Outlaw Culture: Resisting Representation.* New York: Routledge.

———. (1995). *Killing Rage: Ending Racism.* New York: Henry Holt.

———. (1996). *Reel to Real: Race, Sex, and Class at the Movies.* New York: Routldge.

———. (2000a). *Where We Stand: Class Matters.* New York: Routledge.

———. (2000b). *Feminism Is for Everybody: Passionate Politics.* New York: Routledge.

——. (2003a). *Teaching Community: A Pedagogy of Hope.* New York: Routledge.

——. (2003b). *Rock My Soul: Black People and Self-Esteem.* New York: Atria.

——. (2004a). *The Will to Change: Men, Masculinity, and Love.* New York: Atria.

——. (2004b). *We Real Cool: Black Men and Masculinity.* New York: Routledge.

——. (2006). *Homegrown: Engaged Cultural Criticism.* Cambridge, MA: South End.

——. (2008). *Belonging: A Culture of Place.* New York: Routledge.

Hopton, John. (1995). "The Application of the Ideas of Frantz Fanon to the Practice of Mental Health Nursing." *Journal of Advanced Nursing* 21 (4), 723–728.

Hord, Fred Lee. (Ed.). (2005). *Black Culture Centers: Politics for Survival and Identity.* Chicago: Third World Press.

Hord, Fred Lee, and Lee, Johnathan Scott. (Eds.). (1995). *I Am Because We Are: Readings in Black Philosophy.* Amherst: University of Massachusetts Press.

Horkheimer, Max. (1972). *Critical Theory: Selected Essays.* New York: Continuum.

——. (1974a). *Eclipse of Reason.* New York: Continuum.

——. (1974b). *Critique of Instrumental Reason: Lectures and Essays Since the End of World War II.* New York: Continuum.

——. (1978). *Dawn and Decline: Notes, 1926–1931 and 1950–1969.* New York: Continuum.

——. (1993). *Between Philosophy and Social Science: Selected Early Writings.* Cambridge: MIT Press.

——. (2007). *A Life in Letters: Selected Correspondence* (Manfred R. Jacobson and Evelyn M. Jacobson, Ed.). Lincoln: University of Nebraska.

Horkheimer, Max, and Adorno, Theodor W. (1995). *Dialectic of Enlightenment.* New York: Continuum.

Horne, Gerald. (1986). *Black and Red: W. E. B. Du Bois and the Afro-American Response to the Cold War, 1944–1963.* Albany: State University of New York Press.

——. (2000). *Race Woman: The Lives of Shirley Graham Du Bois.* New York: New York University Press.

Hornsman, Reginald. (1986). *Race and Manifest Destiny: Origins of American Racial Anglo-Saxonism.* Cambridge, MA: Harvard University Press.

Horton, Robin. (1973). *Modes of Thought: Essays on Thinking in Western and Non- Western Societies.* London: Faber.

——. (1993). *Patterns of Thought in Africa and the West: Essays on Magic, Religion, and Science.* Cambridge: Cambridge University Press.

Hountondji, Paulin J. (1996). *African Philosophy: Myth and Reality.* Indianapolis: Indiana University Press.

Houtman, Dick. (2003). *Class and Politics in Contemporary Social Science: "Marxism Lite" and Its Blind Spot for Culture.* New York: Aldine de Gruyter.

Houston, Marsha, and Idriss, Olga D. (Eds.). (2002). *Centering Ourselves: African American Feminist and Womanist Studies of Discourse.* Cresskill, NJ: Hampton Press.

How, Alan. (2003). *Critical Theory.* New York: Palgrave Macmillan.

Howard, Dick. (1972). *The Development of the Marxian Dialectic.* Carbondale and Edwardsville, IL: Southern Illinois University Press.

——. (1988). *The Marxian Legacy.* Minneapolis: University of Minnesota Press.

Howard, Dick, and Klare, Karl E. (Eds.). (1972). *The Unknown Dimension: European Marxism Since Lenin.* New York: Basic Books.

Howells, Christina. (Ed.). (1992). *The Cambridge Companion to Sartre.* Cambridge: Cambridge University Press.

Hudson-Weems, Clenora. (1989). "Cultural and Agenda Conflicts in Academia: Critical Issues for Africana Women's Studies." *Western Journal of Black Studies* 13 (4), 185–189.

——. (1992). "Africana Womanism." *Voice: The Caribbean International Magazine* 37–38, 46.

———. (1995). *Africana Womanism: Reclaiming Ourselves.* Boston: Bedford.

———. (1997). "Africana Womanism and the Critical Need for Africana Theory and Thought." *Western Journal of Black Studies* 21 (2), 79–84.

———. (1998a). "Africana Womanism: An Historical, Global Perspective for Women of African Descent." In Patricia Liggins Hill (Ed.), *Call and Response: The Riverside Anthology of the African American Literary Tradition* (pp. 1811–1815). Boston: Houghton Mifflin.

———. (1998b). "Africana Womanism, Black Feminism, African Feminism, Womanism." In Obioma Nnaemeka (Ed.), *Sisterhood, Feminisms, and Power: From Africa to the Diaspora* (pp. 149–162). Trenton, NJ: Africa World Press.

———. (1998c). "Self-Naming and Self-Defining: An Agenda for Survival." In Obioma Nnaemeka (Ed.), *Sisterhood, Feminisms, and Power: From Africa to the Diaspora* (pp. 449–452). Trenton, NJ: Africa World Press.

———. (2000). "Africana Womanism: An Overview." In Delores Aldridge and Carlene Young (Eds.), *Out of the Revolution: The Development of Africana Studies* (pp. 205–217). Lanham, MD: Lexington Books.

———. (2001a). "Africana Womanism, Black Feminism, African Feminism, Womanism." In William Nelson, Jr., (Ed.), *Black Studies: From the Pyramids to Pan-Africanism and Beyond.* New York: McGraw-Hill.

———. (2001b). "Africana Womanism: Entering the New Millennium." In Jemadari Kamara and T. Menelik Van Der Meer (Eds.), *State of the Race, Creating Our 21st Century: Where Do We Go From Here.* Amherst: University of Massachusetts Press.

———. (2004). *Africana Womanist Literary Theory.* Trenton, NJ: Africa World Press.

———. (Ed). (2007). *Contemporary Africana Theory, Thought, and Action: A Guide to Africana Studies.* Trenton, NJ: Africa World Press.

Huggins, Nathan I. (1971). *The Harlem Renaissance.* New York: Oxford University Press.

———. (Ed.). (1995). *Voices from the Harlem Renaissance.* New York: Oxford University Press.

Huggins, Nathan I., Kilson, Martin, and Fox, Daniel M. (Eds.). (1971). *Key Issues in the Afro-American Experience.* New York: Harcourt Brace Jovanovich.

Hughes, John A., Sharrock, Wes W., and Martin, Peter J. (2003). *Understanding Classical Sociology: Marx, Weber Durkheim.* Thousand Oaks, CA: Sage.

Hull, Gloria T., Scott, Patricia Bell, and Smith, Barbara. (Eds.). (1982). *All the Women Are White, All the Blacks Are Men, But Some of Us Are Brave: Black Women's Studies.* New York: The Feminist Press at CUNY.

Huntington, Patricia. (2001). "Challenging the Colonial Contract: The Zapatistas' Insurgent Imagination." In William S. Wilkerson and Jeffrey Paris (Eds.), *New Critical Theory: Essays on Liberation* (pp. 105–134). Lanham, MD: Rowman and Littlefield Publishers.

Hutchinson, Earl Ofari. (1995). *Blacks and Reds: Race and Class in Conflict, 1919–1990.* East Lansing: Michigan State University Press.

Hutchinson, George. (1995). *Harlem Renaissance in Black and White.* Cambridge, MA: Harvard University Press.

———. (Ed.). (2007). *The Companion to the Harlem Renaissance.* New York: Cambridge University Press.

Hutchinson, Louise D. (1981). *Anna Julia Cooper: A Voice from the South.* Washington, DC: Anacostia Neighborhood Museum and Smithsonian Press.

———. (1993). "Anna Julia Haywood Cooper." In Darlene Clark Hine, Elsa Barkley Brown, and Rosalyn Teborg-Penn (Eds.), *Black Women in America: An Historical Encyclopedia* (Volume 1, pp. 275–280). Brooklyn: Carlson.

Hwang, Hae-Sung. (1988). "Booker T. Washington and W. E. B. Du Bois: A Study in Race Leadership, 1895–1915." Ph.D. dissertation, University of Hawaii.

Hyman, Jacques. (1971). *Leopold Sedar Senghor: An Intellectual Biography.* Edinburgh: University of Edinburgh Press.

Ibish, Hussein Y. (2002). "Nationalism as an Ethical Problem for Postcolonial Theory (Edward Said, Homi Bhaba, Frantz Fanon)." Ph.D. dissertation, University of Massachusetts, Amherst.

Idahosa, Paul. (1995). "James and Fanon and the Problem of the Intelligentsia in Popular Organizations." In Selwyn Cudjoe and William E. Cain (Eds.), *C. L. R. James: His Intellectual Legacies* (pp. 388–404). Amherst: University of Massachusetts Press.

Ignatiev, Oleg K. (1975). *Amilkar Kabral: Syn Afriki.* Moskva: Izd-vo Polit Litry.

——. (1990). *Amilcar Cabral.* Muscova: Edicoes da Agencia de Imprensa Novosti.

Ijere, Martin O. (1974). "W. E. B. Du Bois and Marcus Garvey as Pan-Africanists: A Study in Contrasts." *Presence Africaine* 79, 188–206.

Imbo, Samuel O. (1998). *An Introduction to African Philosophy.* Lanham, MD: Rowman and Littlefield.

——. (2002). *Oral Traditions as Philosophy: Okot p'Bitek's Legacy for African Philosophy.* Lanham, MD: Rowman and Littlefield.

Ingram, David. (1990). *Critical Theory and Philosophy.* New York: Paragon House.

Ingram, David, and Simon-Ingram, Julia. (Eds.). (1992). *Critical Theory: The Essential Readings.* New York: Paragon House.

Irele, Abiola. (1964). "A Defense of Negritude: A Propos of *Black Orpheus* by Jean-Paul Sartre." *Transition* 3 (13), 9–11.

——. (1965a). "Negritude: Literature and Ideology." *Journal of Modern African Studies* 3 (4), 499–526.

——. (1965b). "Negritude or Black Cultural Nationalism," *Journal of Modern African Studies* 3 (3), 321–48.

——. (1968). "Postcolonial Negritude: The Political Plays of Aimé Césaire." *West Africa* 27, 100–101.

——. (Ed.). (1969). *Lectures Africaines: A Prose Anthology of African Writing in French.* London: Heinemann.

——. (1970). "The Theory of Negritude." In *Proceedings of the Seminar on Political Theory and Ideology in African Society.* Edinburgh: University of Edinburgh Press.

——. (1971). "Negritude Revisited." *Odu* 5, 3–26.

——. (1977). "Negritude: Philosophy of African Being." *Nigeria Magazine* 122/123, 1–13.

——. (1983). "Introduction to *African Philosophy: Myth and Reality.*" In Paulin J. Hountondji, *African Philosophy: Myth and Reality* (pp. 7–32). Indianapolis: Indiana University Press.

——. (1986). "The Negritude Debate." In *European-Language Writing in Sub-Saharan Africa* 1 (pp. 43–72). Budapest: Akademia Kiado.

——. (1990a). *The African Experience in Literature and Ideology.* Indianapolis: Indiana University Press.

——. (1990b). "The African Imagination." *Research in African Literatures* 21, 49–67.

——. (1992). "In Praise of Alienation." In V.Y. Mudimber (Ed.), *The Surreptitious Speech: Présence Africaine and the Politics of Otherness, 1947–1987* (pp. 201–226). Chicago: University of Chicago Press.

——. (1993). "Narrative, History, and the African Imagination." *Narrative* 1 (2), 64–73.

——. (1995). "Contemporary Thought in French Speaking Africa." In Albert Mosley (Ed.), *African Philosophy: Selected Readings* (pp. 263–296). Englewood Cliffs, NJ: Prentice Hall.

——. (1999a). "Hountondji." In Robert L. Arrington (Ed.), *A Companion to the Philosophers* (pp. 27–29). Malden: Blackwell.

——. (1999b). "Senghor." In Robert L. Arrington (Ed.), *A Companion to the Philosophers* (pp. 30–32). Malden: Blackwell.

——. (2001). *The African Imagination: Literature in Africa and the Black Diaspora.* Oxford: Oxford University Press.

———. (2004). "The Harlem Renaissance and the Negritude Movement." In Abiola Irele and Simon Gikanda (Eds.), *The Cambridge History of African and Caribbean Literature* (pp. 759–784). Cambridge: Cambridge University Press.

Irele, Abiola, and Gikanda, Simon. (Eds.). (2004). *The Cambridge History of African and Caribbean Literature*. Cambridge: Cambridge University Press.

Isbister, John. (2001). *Promises Not Kept: The Betrayal of Social Change in the Third World*. Bloomfield, CT: Kumarian Press.

Jack, Belinda Elizabeth. (1996). *Negritude and Literary Criticism: The History and Theory of "Negro-African" Literature in French*. Westport, CT: Greenwood Press.

Jackson, Stevi. (Ed.). (1993). *Women's Studies: Essential Readings*. New York: New York University Press.

Jacoby, Russell. (1981). *Dialectic of Defeat: Contours of Western Marxism*. Cambridge: Cambridge University Press.

Jafri, Naqi Husain. (2004). *Critical Theory: Perspectives from Asia*. New Delhi: Jamia Millia Islamia University Press.

Jahn, Janheinz. (1958). "Aimé Césaire." Black Orpheus 2, 32–36.

———. (1961). *Muntu: African Culture and the Western World*. New York: Grove Press.

———. (1962). *Through African Doors: Experience and Encounters in West Africa*. New York: Grove Press.

———. (1968). *Neo-African Literature: A History of Black Writing*. New York: Grove Press.

Jaggar, Alison M. (1983). *Feminist Politics and Human Nature*. Totowa, NJ: Rowman and Allanheld.

Jaggar, Alison M., and Young, Iris Marion. (Eds.). (1998). *A Companion to Feminist Philosophy*. Malden, MA: Blackwell.

Jain, Jasbir. (Eds.). (2005). *Women in Patriarchy: Cross-Cultural Readings*. Jaipur: Rawat Publications.

James, C. L. R. (1933). *The Case for West Indian Self-Government*. London: Hogarth Press.

———. (1960). *Modern Politics: A Series of Lectures on the Subject*. Trinidad: Political Information Committee.

———. (1962). *Party Politics in the West Indies: PNM Go Forward!* San Juan, Trinidad: Velic Enterprises.

———. (1963). *The Black Jacobins: Toussaint L'Ouverture and the San Domingo Revolution*. New York: Vintage Books.

———. (1965). *Wilson Harris: A Philosophical Approach*. St. Augustine, Trinidad: Busby's Printerie.

———. (1969). *State Capitalism and World Revolution*. Detroit: Facing Reality.

———. (1970). "The Black Scholar Interviews C. L. R. James." *Black Scholar* 2 (1), 35–43.

———. (1971a). *Minty Alley*. London: New Beacon Books.

———. (1971b). "C. L. R. James and Pan-Africanism: An Interview." *Black World* 21 (1), 3–17.

———. (1972). *The Invading Socialist Society*. Detroit: Bewick Publishing.

———. (1977a). *The Future in the Present: Selected Writings*. London: Allison and Busby.

———. (1977b). *Nkrumah and the Ghana Revolution*. London: Allison and Busby.

———. (1980a). *Spheres of Existence: Selected Writings*. London: Allison and Busby.

———. (1980b). *Notes on Dialectics: Hegel, Marx, Lenin*. London: Allison and Busby.

———. (1980c). *Fighting Racism in World War II*. New York: Pathfinder Press.

———. (1983). *Walter Rodney and the Question of Power*. London: Race Today.

———. (1984). *At the Rendezvous of Victory: Selected Writings*. London: Allison and Busby.

———. (1985). *Mariners, Renegades, and Castaways: The Story of Herman Melville and the World We Live In*. London: Allison and Busby.

———. (1986). *Cricket*. London: Allison and Busby.

———. (1992). *The C. L. R. James Reader* (Anna Grimshaw, Ed.). Cambridge: Blackwell.

———. (1993a). *American Civilization* (Anna Grimshaw and Keith Hart, Eds.). Cambridge: Blackwell.

———. (1993b). *Beyond A Boundary.* Durham: Duke University Press.

———. (1993c). *World Revolution, 1917–1936: The Rise and Fall of the Communist International.* Atlantic Highlands, NJ: Humanities Press.

———. (1994). *C. L. R. James and Revolutionary Marxism: Selected Writings of C. L. R. James, 1939–1949* (Scott McLemee and Paul Le Blanc, Eds.). Atlantic Highlands, NJ: Humanities Press.

———. (1995). *A History of Pan-African Revolt.* Chicago: Charles H. Kerr Publishing.

———. (1996a). *C. L. R. James on the "Negro Question"* (Scott McLemee, Ed.). Jackson, MS: University of Mississippi Press.

———. (1996b). *Special Delivery: The Letters of C. L. R. James to Constance Webb, 1939–1948* (Anna Grimshaw, Ed.). Cambridge: Blackwell.

———. (1999). *Marxism for Our Times: C. L. R. James on Revolutionary Organization* (Martin Glaberman, Ed.). Jackson, MS: University of Mississippi Press.

———. (2003). *Letters from London: Seven Essays by C. L. R. James.* Port of Spain, Trinidad: Prospect Press.

James, Joy A. (1996a). *Resisting State Violence: Radicalism, Gender, and Race in U.S. Culture.* Minneapolis: University of Minnesota Press.

———. (1996b). "The Profeminist Politics of W. E. B. Du Bois, with Respects to Anna Julia Cooper and Ida B. Wells Barnett." In Bernard W. Bell, Emily R. Grosholz, and James B. Stewart (Eds.), *W. E. B. Du Bois: On Race and Culture: Philosophy, Politics, and Poetics* (pp. 141–161). New York: Routledge.

———. (1997). *Transcending the Talented Tenth: Black Leaders and American Intellectuals.* New York: Routledge.

———. (1998). "Joy A. James: An Interview." In George Yancy (Ed.), *African American Philosophers: 17 Conversations* (pp. 245–262). New York: Routledge.

———. (1999). *Shadow Boxing: Representations of Black Feminist Politics.* New York: St. Martin's Press.

———. (2000). "The Future of Black Studies: Political Communities and the 'Talented Tenth'." In Manning Marable (Ed.), *Dispatches from the Ebony Tower: Intellectuals Confront the African American Experience* (pp. 153–157). New York: Columbia University Press.

James, Joy A., and Sharpley-Whiting, T. Denean. (Eds.). (2000). *The Black Feminist Reader.* Malden, MA: Blackwell.

James, Stanlie, and Busia, Abena. (Eds.). (1993). *Theorizing Black Feminism: The Visionary Pragmatism of Black Women.* New York: Routledge.

James, Winston. (1998). *Holding Aloft the Banner of Ethiopia: Caribbean Radicalism in Early Twentieth-Century America.* New York: Verso.

———. (2000). *A Fierce Hatred of Injustice: Claude McKay's Jamaica and His Poetry of Rebellion.* New York: Verso.

———. (2003). "Becoming the People's Poet: Claude McKay's Jamaican Years, 1889–1912." *Small Axe 7* (13), 17–45.

Jameson, Fredric. (1971). *Marxism and Form: Twentieth-Century Dialectical Theories of Literature.* Princeton, NJ: Princeton University Press.

———. (1975). "Notes Toward a Marxist Cultural Politics." *Minnesota Review* 5, 35–39.

———. (1979a). "Marxism and Historicism." *New Literary History* 11, 41–73.

———. (1979b). "Marxism and Teaching." *New Political Science* 2/3, 31–36.

———. (1979c). "Reification and Utopia in Mass Culture." *Social Text* 1, 130–148.

———. (1990). *Late Marxism: Adorno, or, The Persistence of the Dialectic.* London: Verso.

———. (1991). *Postmodernism, or, The Cultural Logic of Late Capitalism.* Durham: Duke University Press.

JanMohamed, Abdul R. (1984). "Humanism and Minority Literature: Toward a Definition of Counter-Hegemonic Discourse." *Boundary 2* 12/13 (3/1), 281–299.

———. (1985). "The Economy of Manichean Allegory: The Function of Racial Difference in Colonialist Literature." *Critical Inquiry* 12, 59–87.

———. (1988). *Aesthetics: The Politics of Literature in Colonial Africa* (2nd Edition). Amherst, MA: University of Massachusetts Press.

———. (2005). *The Death-Bound-Subject: Richard Wright's Archaeology of Death*. Durham, NC: Duke University Press.

JanMohamed, Abdul R., and Lloyd, David. (Eds.). (1990). *The Nature and Context of Minority Discourse*. New York: Oxford University Press.

Jardine, Alice, and Smith, Paul. (Eds.). (1987). *Men in Feminism*. New York: Methuen.

Jay, Martin. (1984). *Marxism and Totality: The Adventures of a Concept from Lukács to Habermas*. Berkeley: University of California Press.

———. (1985a). *Adorno*. Cambridge, MA: Harvard University Press.

———. (1985b). *Permanent Exiles: Essays on the Intellectual Migration from Germany to America*. New York: Columbia University Press.

———. (1988). *Fin-De-Siecle Socialism and Other Essays*. New York: Routledge.

———. (1993a). *Force Fields: Between Intellectual History and Cultural Critique*. New York: Routledge.

———. (1993b). *Downcast Eyes and the Denigration of Vision in Twentieth-Century French Thought*. Berkeley: University of California Press.

———. (1996). *The Dialectical Imagination: A History of the Frankfurt School and the Institute of Social Research, 1923–1950*. Berkeley: University of California Press.

———. (1998). *Cultural Semantics*. Amherst: University of Massachusetts Press.

———. (2003). *Refractions of Violence*. New York: Routledge.

———. (2005). *Songs of Experience: Modern American and European Variations on a Universal Theme*. Berkeley: University of California Press.

Jeanpierre, W.A. (1961). "Negritude, Its Development and Significance." *Presence Africaine* 11 (39), 32–49.

Jefferson, Paul. (1996). "Present at the Creation: Rethinking Du Bois's "Practice Theory." *Research in Race & Ethnic Relations* 9, 127–169.

Jinadu, Liasu Adele. (1973). "The Political Ideas of Frantz Fanon: An Essay in Interpretation and Criticism." Ph.D. dissertation, University of Minnesota.

———. (1978). "Some African Theorists of Culture and Modernization: Fanon, Cabral and Some Others." *African Studies Review* 21 (1), 121–138.

———. (1986). *Fanon: In Search of the African Revolution*. London: KPI/Routledge and Kegan Paul.

Johnson, Arthur L. (1949). "The Social Theories of W. E. B. Du Bois." M.A. thesis, Atlanta University, Atlanta, GA.

Johnson, Brain L. (2008). *W. E. B. Du Bois: Toward Agnosticism, 1868–1934*. Lanham, MD: Rowman and Littlefield.

Johnson, Cedric. (2007). *Revolutionaries to Race Leaders: Black Power and the Making of African American Politics*. Minneapolis: University of Minnesota Press.

Johnson, Clarence S. (2003). *Cornel West and Philosophy: The Quest for Social Justice*. New York: Routledge.

Johnson, Eloise E. (1997). *Rediscovering the Harlem Renaissance: The Politics of Exclusion*. New York: Garland.

Johnson, Karen A. (2000). *Uplifting the Women and the Race: The Educational Philosophies and Social Activism of Anna Julia Cooper and Nannie Helen Burroughs*. New York: Garland.

Johnson, E. Patrick, and Henderson, Mae G. (Eds.). (2005). *Black Queer Studies: A Critical Anthology*. Durham, NC: Duke University Press.

Johnson, Vernon, and Lyne, Bill. (Eds.). (2002). *Walkin' the Talk: An Anthology of African American Studies*. Prentice Hall.

Johnson-Feelings, Dianne. (Ed.). (1996). *The Best of the Brownies Book*. New York: Oxford University Press.

Jones, Atlas Jack. (1976). "The Sociology of W. E. B. Du Bois." *Black Sociologists* 6 (1), 4–15.

Jones, Edward A. (Ed.). (1971). *Voices of Negritude*. Valley Forge, PA: Judson Press.

Jones, Gail. (1997). "W. E. B. Du Bois and the Language of the Color-Line." In Judith Jackson Fossett and Jeffrey A. Tucker (Eds.), *Race Consciousness: African American Studies for the New Century* (pp. 19–35). New York: New York University Press.

Jones, Jacqueline. (1985). *Labor of Love, Labor of Sorrow: Black Women, Work and the Family from Slavery to the Present*. New York: Basic Books.

——. (1998). " 'Lifework' and Its Limits: The Problem of Labor in *The Philadelphia Negro*." In Michael B. Katz and Thomas J. Sugrue (Eds.), *W. E. B. Du Bois, Race, and the City: The Philadelphia Negro and Its Legacy* (pp. 103–126). Philadelphia: University of Pennsylvania Press.

Jordan, Winthrop D. (1968). *White Over Black: American Attitudes Toward the Negro, 1550–1812*. Chapel Hill, NC: University of North Carolina Press.

Joseph, Clara A.B., and Wilson, Janet. (Eds.). (2006). *Global Fissures: Postcolonial Fusions*. Amsterdam: Rodopi.

Joseph, Peniel E. (2006a). *Waiting 'Til the Midnight Hour: A Narrative History of Black Power in America*. New York: Henry Holt.

——. (Ed.). (2006b). *Black Power Movement: Rethinking the Civil Rights-Black Power Era*. New York: Routledge.

Judy, Ronald T. (1994). "The New Black Aesthetic and W. E. B. Du Bois, or Hephaestus Limping." *Massachusetts Review* 35 (2), 249–282.

——. (Eds.). (2000a). *Sociologically Hesitant: Thinking with W. E. B. Du Bois*. Durham, NC: Duke University Press.

——. (2000b). "Introduction: On W. E. B. Du Bois and Hyperbolic Thinking." *Boundary 2* 27 (3), 1–35.

Juguo, Zhang. (2001). *W. E. B. Du Bois: Quest for the Abolition of the Color Line*. New York: Routledge.

Jules-Rosette, Bennetta. (1998). *Black Paris: The African Writers' Landscape*. Urbana: University of Illinois Press.

Kadarkay, Arpad. (1991). *Georg Lukacs: Life, Thought, and Politics*. Cambridge, MA: Blackwell.

Kaiser, Ernest. (1970). "Cultural Contributions of Dr. Du Bois." In John Henrik Clarke, Esther Jackson, Ernest Kaiser, and J.H. O'Dell (Eds.), *Black Titan: W. E. B. Du Bois* (pp. 69–75). Boston: Beacon.

Kang, Hyeong-Min. (2004). "The Politics of Violence in Colonization and Decolonization: A Fanonian Study of Selected Postcolonial Drama." Ph.D. dissertation, Indiana University of Pennsylvannia.

Kanneh, Kadiatu. (1998). *African Identities: Race, Nation, and Culture in Ethnography, Pan-Africanism and Black Literatures*. New York: Routledge.

Kaphagawani, Didier N. (1998a). "What Is African Philosophy?" In Pieter H. Coetzee and Abraham P.J. Roux (Eds.), *The African Philosophy Reader* (pp. 86–98). New York: Routledge.

——. (1998b). "African Conceptions of Personhood and Intellectual Identities." In Pieter H. Coetzee and Abraham P.J. Roux (Eds.), *The African Philosophy Reader* (pp. 169–176). New York: Routledge.

Kaplan, E. Ann. (1999). "Fanon, Trauma, and Cinema." In Anthony C. Alessandrini (Ed.), *Frantz Fanon: Critical Perspectives* (pp. 146–158). New York: Routledge.

Kaplan, Jeffrey, and Bjorgo, Tore. (Eds.). (1998). *Nation and Race: The Developing Euro-American Racist Subculture*. Boston: Northeastern University Press.

Karenga, Maulana. (1988). "Black Studies and the Problematic of Paradigm: The Philosophical Dimension," *Journal of Black Studies* 18 (4), 395–414.

———. (Ed.). (1989). *Selections from the Husia: Sacred Wisdom of Ancient Egypt.* Los Angeles, CA: University of Sankore Press.

———. (Ed.). (1990). *The Book of Coming Forth by Day: The Ehics of the Declarations of Innocence.* Los Angeles: University of Sankore Press.

———. (1996). *Reconstructing Kemetic Culture.* Los Angeles: University of Sankore Press.

———. (1997). "African Culture and the Ongoing Quest for Excellence: Dialogue, Principles, Practice." *The Black Collegian,* 160–163.

———. (1999). *Odu Ifa: The Ethical Teachings.* Los Angeles: University of Sankore Press.

———. (2001). "Mission, Meaning and Methodology in Africana Studies: Critical Reflections from a Kawaida Framework." *Black Studies Journal* 3, 54–74.

———. (2002). *Introduction to Black Studies* (Third Edition). Los Angeles: University of Sankore Press.

———. (2003). "Du Bois and the Question of the Color Line: Race and Class in the Age of Globalization." *Socialism and Democracy* 17, 1 (33), 141–160. Available online at: http://www.sdonline.org/33/maulana_karenga.htm [Accessed on 23 February 2003].

———. (2004). *Maat, The Moral Ideal in Ancient Egypt: A Study in Classical African Ethics.* New York: Routledge.

———. (2005). *Kawaida Theory: An African Communitarian Philosophy.* Los Angeles: University of Sankore Press.

———. (2008). *Kawaida and Questions of Life and Struggle: African American, Pan-African, and Global Issues.* Los Angeles: University of Sankore of Press.

Karp, Ivan, and Bird, Charles S. (Eds.). (1980). *Explorations in African Systems of Thought.* Bloomington: Indiana University Press.

Karp, Ivan, and Masolo, Dismas A. (Eds.). (2000). *African Philosophy as Cultural Inquiry.* Bloomington: Indiana University Press.

Katz, Michael B. (2000). "Race, Poverty, and Welfare: Du Bois's Legacy for Policy." *Annals of the American Academy of Political and Social Science* 568, 111–127.

Katz, Michael B., and Sugrue, Thomas J. (Eds.). (1998). *W. E. B. Du Bois, Race, and the City: The Philadelphia Negro and Its Legacy.* Philadelphia: University of Pennsylvania Press.

Katz, Stephen. (1980). *Marxism, Africa, and Social Class: A Critique of Relevant Theories.* Montreal: Center for Developing-Area Studies, McGill University.

Katznelson, Ira. (1999). "Du Bois's Century." *Social Science History* 23 (4), 459–474.

Kauffman, Linda S. (Ed.). (1993). *American Feminist Thought at Century's End.* Cambridge, MA: Blackwell.

Kawash, Samira. (1999). "Terrorists and Vampires: Fanon's Spectral Violence of Decolonization." In Anthony C. Alessandrini (Ed.), *Frantz Fanon: Critical Perspectives* (pp. 235–257). New York: Routledge.

Kebede, Messay. (1999). *Survival and Modernization—Ethiopia's Enigmatic Present: A Philosophical Discourse.* Lawrenceville, NJ: Red Sea Press.

———. (2001). "The Rehabilitation of Violence and the Violence of Rehabilitation." *Journal of Black Studies* 31 (5), 539–553.

———. (2004). *Africa's Quest for a Philosophy of Decolonization.* Amsterdam: Rodopi.

Keene, Jennifer D. (2001). "W. E. B. Du Bois and the Wounded World: Seeking Meaning in the First World War for African Americans." *Peace & Change* 26 (2), 135–152.

Keita, Lansana. (1991). "Contemporary African Philosophy: The Search for a Method." In Tsenay Serequeberhan (Ed.), *African Philosophy: The Essential Readings* (pp. 132–155). New York: Paragon House.

Keita, Maghan. (2000). *Race and the Writing of History: Riddle of the Sphinx.* New York: Oxford University Press.

Keller, Edmond J., and Rothchild, Donald. (Eds.). (1987). *Afro-Marxist Regimes: Ideology and Public Policy*. Boulder, CO: Lynne Rienner Publisher.

Kelley, Robin D.G. (1990). *Hammer and Hoe: Alabama Communists During the Great Depression*. Chapel Hill, NC: University of North Carolina Press.

———. (1994). *Race Rebels: Culture, Politics, and the Black Working Class*. New York: Free Press.

———. (1995). "Introduction to C. L. R. James's *A History of Pan-African Revolt*." In C. L. R. James, *A History of Pan-African Revolt* (pp. 1–35). Chicago: Charles H. Kerr.

———. (1996). "The World the Diaspora Made: C. L. R. James and the Politics of History." In Grant Farred (Ed.), *Rethinking C. L. R. James* (pp. 103–130). Cambridge, MA: Blackwell.

———. (1997a). *Yo' Mama's Disfunktional: Fighting the Culture Wars in Urban America*. Boston: Beacon.

———. (1997b). "Looking B(L)ackward: African American Studies in the Age of Identity Politics." In Judith Jackson Fossett and Jeffrey A. Tucker (Eds.), *Race Consciousness: African American Studies for the New Century* (pp. 1–17). New York: New York University Press.

———. (2002). *Freedom Dreams: The Black Radical Imagination*. Boston: Beacon.

Kellner, Douglas. (1984). *Herbert Marcuse and the Crisis of Marxism*. Berkeley: University of California Press.

———. (1989). *Critical Theory, Marxism, and Modernity*. Baltimore: Johns Hopkins University Press.

———. (1990a). "The Postmodern Turn in Social Theory: Positions, Problems, and Prospects." In George Ritzer (Ed.), *The Frontiers of Social Theory: The New Syntheses* (pp. 255–286). New York: Columbia University Press.

———. (1990b). "Critical Theory and Ideology Critique." In Ronald Roblin (Ed.), *Critical Theory and Aesthetics* (pp. 85–123). Lewistown: Edwin Mellen Press.

———. (1990c). "Critical Theory and the Crisis of Social Theory." *Sociological Perspectives* 33 (1), 11–33.

———. (1992). "Erich Fromm, Feminism, and the Frankfurt School." In Michael Kessler and Rainer Funk (Eds.), *Erich Fromm und die Frankfurter Schule* (pp. 111–130). Tubingen: Francke Verlag.

———. (1993). "Critical Theory and Social Theory: Current Debates and Challenges." *Theory, Culture, and Society* 10 (2), 43–61.

———. (1995). "The Obsolescence of Marxism?" Bernard Magnus and Stephen Cullenberg (Eds.), *Whither Marxism?: Global Crises in International Perspective* (pp. 3–30). New York: Routledge.

———. (1996). *Media Culture: Cultural Studies, Identity, and Politics Between the Modern and the Postmodern*. New York: Routledge.

———. (2003). *Media Spectacle*. New York: Routledge.

Kelly, Michael. (1982). *Modern French Marxism*. Baltimore: John Hopkins University Press.

———. (Ed.). (1990). *Hermeneutics and Critical Theory in Ethic and Politics*. Cambridge: MIT Press.

Kennedy, Ellen Conroy. (1968). "Aime Cesaire: Interview with an Architect of Negritude." *Negro Digest* 17, 53–61.

———. (1972). "Leon Damas: *Pigments* and the Colonized Personality." *Black World* 21 (3), 4–12.

———. (1988). "Cesaire and Senghor: When Parallel Lives Converged." *Delos* 4, 14–23.

———. (Ed.). (1990). *The Negritude Poets*. New York: Thunder's Mouth.

Kennedy, Ellen, and Trout, Paulette J. (1966). "The Roots of Negritude." *African Report* 2 (5), 61–62.

Kershaw, Terry. (1989). "The Emerging Paradigm in Black Studies." *Western Journal of Black Studies* 13 (1), 45–51.

———. (1992). "Toward A Black Studies Paradigm: An Assessment and Some Directions." *Journal of Black Studies* 22 (4), 477–493.

———. (2003). "The Black Studies Paradigm: The Making of Scholar-Activists." In James L. Conyers (Ed.), *Afrocentricity and the Academy* (pp. 27–36). Jefferson, NC: McFarland & Co.

Kesteloot, Lilyan. (1972). *Intellectual Origins of the African Revolution*. Washington, DC: Black Orpheus Press.

———. (1990). "Senghor, Negritude and Francophonie on the Threshold of the Twenty-first Century." *Research in African Literatures* 21 (3), 51–57.

———. (1991). *Black Writers in French: A Literary History of Negritude*. Washington, DC: Howard University Press.

———. (1992). "Myth, Epic, and African History." In V.Y. Mudimber (Ed.), *The Surreptitious Speech: Présence Afraine and the Politics of Otherness, 1947–1987* (pp. 136–146). Chicago: University of Chicago Press.

———. (1995). "Cesaire: The Poet and the Politician." *Research in African Literatures* 26 (2), 169–174.

Kesteloot, Lilyan, and Ellen C. Kennedy. (1974). "Negritude and Its American Sources." *Boston University Journal* 22 (11), 54–56.

Kiberd, Declan. (1985). *Men and Feminism in Modern Literature*. New York: St. Martin's Press.

Kilson, Martin. (1973). "Reflections on Structure and Content in Black Studies." *Journal of Black Studies* 1 (3), 197–214.

———. (2000a). "Black Studies Revisited." In Manning Marable (Ed.), *Dispatches from the Ebony Tower: Intellectuals Confront the African American Experience* (pp. 171– 176). New York: Columbia University Press.

———. (2000b). "The Washington and Du Bois Leadership Paradigms Reconsidered." *Annals of the American Academy of Political and Social Science* 568, 298–313.

Kimbrough, Marvin Gordon. (1974). "W. E. B. Du Bois as Editor of *The Crisis*." Ph.D. dissertation, University of Texas, Austin.

Kimmel, Michael S. (Ed.). (1987). *Changing Men: New Directions in Research on Men and Masculinity*. Newbury Park, CA: Sage Publications.

———. (Ed). (1995). *The Politics of Manhood: Profeminist Men Respond to the Mythopoetic Men's Movement (and Mythopoetic Leaders Answer)*. Philadelphia: Temple University Press.

———. (1996). *Manhood in America: A Cultural History*. New York: Free Press.

———. (2004a). *The Gendered Society*. New York: Oxford University Press.

———. (Ed.). (2004b). *The Gender Society Reader*. New York: Oxford University Press.

———. (2006). *Manhood in America: A Cultural History*. New York: Oxford University Press.

Kimmel, Michael S., and Aronson, Amy. (Eds.). (2004). *Men and Masculinities: A Social, Cultural, and Historical Encyclopedia*. Santa Barbara, CA: ABC-CLIO.

Kimmel, Michael S., and Mosmiller, Thomas E. (Ed.). (1992). *Against the Tide: Pro-Feminist Men in the United States, 1776–1990: A Documentary History*. Boston: Beacon.

Kimmel, Michael S., Hearn, Jeff, and Connell, R.W. (Eds.). (2005). *Handbook of Studies on Men and Masculinity*. Thousand Oaks, CA: Sage Publications.

Kimua, Tegakimwa H. (1986). *Let Socialism Come of Itself: A Message to the Black African Continent*. Nairobi, Kenya: Gifeon S. Were Press.

King, Deborah K. (1995). "Multiple Jeopardy, Multiple Consciousness: The Contest of Black Feminist Ideology." In Beverly Guy-Sheftall (Ed.), *Words of Fire: An Anthology of African American Feminist Thought* (pp. 294–318). New York: Free Press.

King, Martin Luther, Jr. (1970). "Honoring Dr. Du Bois." In Philip S. Foner (Ed.), *W. E. B. Du Bois Speaks: Speeches and Addresses, 1890–1919* (pp. 20–29). New York: Pathfinder.

King, Nicole. (2001). *C. L. R. James and Creolization: Circles of Influence*. Jackson: University Press of Mississippi.

Kipfer, Stefan. (2004). "Urbanization, Difference and Everyday Life: Lefebvre, Gramsci, Fanon, and the Problematic of Hegemony." Ph.D. dissertation, York University, Canada.

Kirk, Neville. (Ed.). (1996). *Social Class and Marxism: Defenses and Challenges*. Brookfield, VT: Ashgate.

Kiros, Teodros. (1992). *Moral Philosophy and Development: The Human Condition in Africa.* Athens, OH: University of Ohio Press.

——. (1994). *The Meditations of Zara Yaquob: A 17th Century Ethiopian Philosopher.* Boston: Boston University Press.

——. (2001). *Explorations in African Political Thought: Identity, Community, and Ethics.* New York: Routledge.

——. (2004). "Frantz Fanon (1925–1961)." In Kwasi Wiredu (Ed.), *A Companion to African Philosophy* (pp. 216–224). Malden: Blackwell.

——. (2005). *Zara Yacob: Rationality of the Human Heart.* Lawrenceville, NJ: Red Sea Press.

Kluback, Williams. (1997). *Leopold Sedar Senghor: From Politics to Poetry.* New York: Peter Lang.

Knight, Vere W. (1974). "Negritude and the Isms." *Black Images* 3 (1), 3–20.

Knipp, Thomas R. (1974). "Negritude and Negation." *Books Abroad* 48, 511–514.

Knupfer, Anne Meis. (1996). *Toward a Tender Humanity and a Nobler Womanhood: African American Women's Clubs in Turn-of-the-Century Chicago.* New York: New York University Press.

Kohn, Hans, and Sokolsky, Wallace. (Eds.). (1965). *African Nationalism in the Twentieth Century.* New York: Van Nostrand.

Kolakowski, Leszek. (1978a). *Main Currents of Marxism: I. The Founders.* New York: Oxford University Press.

——. (1978b). *Main Currents of Marxism: II. The Golden Age.* New York: Oxford University Press.

——. (1978c). *Main Currents of Marxism: III. The Breakdown.* New York: Oxford University Press.

Kohlenbach, Margarete, and Geuss, Raymond. (Eds.). (2005). *The Early Frankfurt School and Religion.* New York: Palgrave Macmillan.

Konadu, Kwasi. (2005). *Truth Crushed to the Earth Will Rise Again!: The East Organization and the Principles and Practice of Black Nationalist Development.* Trenton, NJ: African World Press.

Kopano, Baruti N., and Williams, Yohuru R. (Eds.). (2004). *Treading Our Ways: Selected Topics in Africana Studies.* Kendall/Hunt Publishing.

Kornweibel, Theodore. (1998). *Seeing Red: Federal Campaigns Against Black Militancy.* Bloomington: Indiana University Press.

——. (2002). *"Investigate Everything": Federal Efforts to Compel Black Loyalty During World War I.* Bloomington: Indiana University Press.

Kosik, Karel. (1976). *Dialectics of the Concrete.* Boston: Reidel Publishers.

——. (1995). *The Crisis of Modernity: Essays and Observations from the 1968 Era.* Lanham, MD: Rowman and Littlefield.

Kostelanetz, Richard. (1985). "Fictions for a Negro Politics: The Neglected Novels of W. E. B. Du Bois." In William L. Andrews (Ed.), *Critical Essays on W. E. B. Du Bois* (pp. 173–193). Boston: G.K. Hall.

——. (1991). *Politics of the African American Novel: James Weldon Johnson, W. E. B. Du Bois, Richard Wright, and Ralph Ellison.* Westport, CT: Greenwood.

Kosukhin, Nikolai. (1985). *Revolutionary Democracy in Africa: Its Ideology and Policy.* Moscow: Progress Press.

Kourany, Janet A., Sterba, James P., and Tong, Rosemarie. (Eds.). (1999). *Feminist Philosophies: Problems, Theories, and Applications* (2nd Edition). Englewood, NJ: Prentice Hall.

Krader, Lawrence. (1975). *The Asiatic Mode of Production: Sources, Development, and Critique in the Writings of Karl Marx.* Assen: Van Gorcum.

Kramer, Victor A., and Russ, Robert A. (Eds.). (1997). *The Harlem Renaissance Re-Examined.* Troy, NY: Whitson Publishing.

Krell, David Farrell. (2000). "The Bodies of Black Folk: From Kant and Hegel to Du Bois and Baldwin." *Boundary 2* 27 (3), 103–134.

Krishnaswamy, Revathi, and Hawley, John C. (Eds.). (2008). *The Postcolonial and the Global.* Minneapolis: University of Minnesota Press.

Kubayanda, Josaphat Bekunuru. (1990). *The Poet's Africa: Africanness in the Poetry of Nicolas Guillen and Aime Cesaire.* New York: Greenwood Press.

Kuhn, Annette, and Wolpe, Ann Marie. (Eds.). (1978). *Feminism and Marxism: Women and Modes of Production.* Boston: Routledge & Kegan.

Kwame, Safro. (Ed.). (1995). *Readings in African Philosophy: An Akan Collection.* New York: University Press of America.

Laclau, Ernesto, and Mouffe, Chantal. (1985). *Hegemony and Socialist Strategy: Toward a Radical Democratic Politics.* New York: Verso.

Laclau, Ernesto, and Mouffe, Chantal. (1987). "Post-Marxism Without Apologies." *New Left Review* 166, 79–106.

Lacy, Leslie Alexander. (1970). *Cheer the Lonesome Traveler: The Life of W. E. B. Du Bois.* New York: Dial.

Ladner, Joyce A. (Ed.). (1998). *The Death of White Sociology: Essays on Race and Culture.* Baltimore: Black Classic Press.

Lafollette, Hugh. (Ed.). (1999). *Blackwell Guide to Ethical Theory.* Malden: Blackwell.

———. (Ed.). (2003). *Oxford Handbook of Practical Ethics.* New York: Oxford University Press.

Lagneau, L. Kesteloot. (1961). "The Negritude of Leopold Sedar Senghor." *Presence Africaine* 11 (39), 124–139.

Lai, Walton Look. (1992). "C. L. R. James and Trinidadian Nationalism." In Paget Henry and Paul Buhle (Eds.), *C. L. R. James's Caribbean* (pp. 174–209). Durham: Duke University Press.

Lane, Anne J. (1976). "Women in Society: A Critique of Friedrich Engels." In Bernice A. Carroll (Ed.), *Liberating Women's History* (pp. 4–26). Champaign: University of Illinois Press.

Lang, Jesse Michael. (1992). *Anticipations of the Booker T. Washington–W. E. B. Du Bois Dialectic in the Writings of Frances E.W. Harper, Ida B. Wells, and Anna Julia Cooper.* MA thesis, Georgetown University.

Langley, J. Ayodele. (1973). *Pan-Africanism and Nationalism in West Africa, 1900–1945: A Study in Ideology and Social Classes.* New York: Oxford University Press.

———. (1979). *Ideologies of Liberation in Black Africa, 1856–1970.* London: Collings Publishing Group.

Laroussi, Farid, and Miller, Christopher L. (2003). *French and Francophone: The Challenge of Expanding Horizons.* New Haven, CT: Yale University Press.

Larsen, Neil. (1996). "Negativities of the Popular: C. L. R. James and the Limits of 'Cultural Studies'." In Grant Farred (Ed.), *Rethinking C. L. R. James* (pp. 85–102). Cambridge, MA: Blackwell.

Larue, H.C. (1971). "W. E. B. Du Bois and the Pragmatic Method of Truth." *Journal of Human Relations* 19, 76–83.

Lash, John S. (1957). "Thought, Research, Action: Dr. Du Bois and History." *Phylon* 18, 184–185.

Lawson, Bill E. (Ed.). (1992). *The Underclass Question.* Philadelphia: Temple University Press.

Lazarus, Neil. (1990). *Resistance in Postcolonial African Fiction.* New Haven: Yale University Press.

———. (1992). "Cricket and National Culture in the Writings of C. L. R. James." In Paget Henry and Paul Buhle (Eds.), *C. L. R. James's Caribbean* (pp. 92–110). Durham: Duke University Press.

———. (1999). "Disavowing Decolonization: Fanon, Nationalism, and the Question of Representation in Postcolonial Theory." In Anthony C. Alessandrini (Ed.), *Frantz Fanon: Critical Perspectives* (pp. 161–194). New York: Routledge.

———. (2000). *Nationalism and Cultural Practice in the Postcolonial World.* Cambridge: Cambridge University Press.

——. (Ed.). (2004). *The Cambridge Companion to Postcolonial Literary Studies*. Cambridge, UK: Cambridge University Press.

Lazerow, Jama, and Williams, Yohuru. (Eds.). (2006). *In Search of the Black Panther Party: New Perspectives on a Revolutionary Movement*. Durham, NC: Duke University Press.

Le Blanc, Paul. (1994). "Introduction: C. L. R. James and Revolutionary Marxism." In Scott McLemee and Paul Le Blanc (Eds.), *C. L. R. James and Revolutionary Marxism: Selected Writings of C. L. R. James, 1939–1949* (pp. 1–37). Atlantic Highlands, NJ: Humanities Press.

Le Vine, Victor T. (2004). *Politics in Francophone Africa*. Boulder, CO: Lynne Rienner Publishers.

Lee, Jayne Chong–Soon. (1995). "Navigating the Topology of Race." In Kimberle Crenshaw, Neil Gotanda, Gary Peller, and Kendall Thomas (Eds.), *Critical Race Theory: The Key Writings That Formed the Movement* (pp. 441–448). New York: New Press.

Lee, Lenetta Raysha. (2000). "Whose Images: An Africological Study of the *Brownies Book* Series." Ph.D. dissertation, Temple University, Philadelphia.

Lee, Maurice. (1999). "Du Bois the Novelist: White Influence, Black Spirit, and *The Quest of the Silver Fleece*." *African American Review* 33 (3), 389–400.

Legum, Colin. (1962). *Pan-Africanism: A Short Political Guide*. New York: Praeger.

Lehmann, Jennifer M. (1994). *Durkheim and Women*. Lincoln: Unversity of Nebraska.

Lemelle, Sidney, and Kelley, Robin D.G. (Eds.). (1994). *Imagining Home: Class, Culture, Nationalism in the African Diaspora*. London: Verso.

Lemert, Charles C. (1994). "A Classic from the Veil: Du Bois's *Souls of Black Folk*." *Sociological Quarterly* 35 (3), 383–396.

——. (1998). "Anna Julia Cooper: The Colored Woman's Office." In Anna Julia Cooper, *The Voice of Anna Julia Cooper: Including* A Voice From the South *and Other Important Essays, Papers, and Letters* (Charles Lemert and Esme Bhan, Eds.) (pp. 1–51). Lanham: Rowman and Littlefield.

——. (2000a). "The Race of Time: Du Bois and Reconstruction." *Boundary 2* 27 (3), 215–248.

——. (2000b). "W. E. B. Du Bois." In George Ritzer (Ed.), *The Blackwell Companion to Major Social Theorists* (pp. 345–367). Malden: Blackwell.

Lemons, Gary L. (1997). "To Be Black, Male and 'Feminist'—Making Womanist Space for Black Men." *International Journal of Sociology and Social Policy* 17, 37–53.

——. (2001). "'When and Where [We] Enter': In Search of a Feminist Forefather—Reclaiming the Womanist Legacy of W. E. B. Du Bois." In Rudolph P. Byrd and Beverly Guy-Sheftall (Eds.), *Traps: African American Men on Gender and Sexuality* (pp. 71–89). Indianapolis: Indiana University Press.

Lengermann, Patricia M., and Niebrugge-Brantley, Jil. (Eds.). (2007). *The Women Founders: Sociology and Social Theory, 1830–1930: A Text/Reader*. Long Grove, IL: Waveland Press.

Lenin, Vladimir I. (1960a). *Lenin on Imperialism: The Eve of the Proletarian Social Revolution*. Peking: Foreign Language Press.

——. (1960b). *Lenin on War and Peace*. Peking: Foreign Language Press.

——. (1960c). *Lenin on the Revolutionary Proletarian Party of a New Type*. Peking: Foreign Language Press.

——. (1960d). *Lenin on Proletarian Revolution and Proletarian Dictatorship*. Peking: Foreign Language Press.

——. (1965a). *Imperialism, The Highest Stage of Capitalism: A Popular Outline*. Peking: Foreign Language Press.

——. (1965b). *The Land Question and the Fight for Freedom*. Peking: Foreign Language Press.

——. (1965c). *The State and Revolution: Marxist Teachings on the State and the Tasks of the Proletariat in the Revolution*. Peking: Foreign Language Press.

——. (1967). *Lenin on the National and Colonial Questions: Three Articles*. Peking: Foreign Language Press.

———. (1968). *Critical Remarks on the National Question: The Right of Nations to Self-Determination.* Moscow: Progress Publishers.

———. (1972). *Materialism and Empirio-Criticism.* Peking: Foreign Language Press.

———. (1973). *What Is to Be Done?: Burning Questions of Our Movement.* Peking: Foreign Language Press.

———. (1975). *The Lenin Anthology* (Robert C. Tucker, Ed.). New York: Norton.

———. (1987). *The Essential Works of Lenin: "What Is to Be Done?" and Other Writings.* Mineola, NY: Dover.

Leonhard, Wolfgang. (1971). *Three Faces of Marxism.* New York: Holt, Rinehart & Winston.

Lerner, Gerda. (Ed.). (1972). *Black Women in White America: A Documentary History.* New York: Vintage.

Lester, Julius. (1971). "Introduction to *The Seventh Son.*" In Julius Lester (Ed.), *The Seventh Son: The Thought and Writings of W. E. B. Du Bois* (Volume 1, pp. 1–153). New York: Vintage Books.

Levi, Darrell E. (1991). "C. L. R. James: A Radical West Indian Vision of American Studies." *American Studies Quarterly* 43 (3), 486–501.

Levine, Lawrence. (1977). *Black Culture and Black Consciousness: Afro-American Folk Thought from Slavery to Freedom.* New York: Oxford University Press.

Lewis, David Levering. (1989). *When Harlem Was in Vogue.* New York: Oxford University Press.

———. (1993). *W. E. B. Du Bois: Biography of a Race, 1868–1919.* New York: Henry Holt.

———. (Ed). (1994). *The Portable Harlem Renaissance Reader.* New York: Viking.

———. (2000). *W. E. B. Du Bois: The Fight for Equality and the American Century, 1919–1963.* New York: Henry Holt.

———. (2008). *W. E. B. Du Bois: A Biography.* New York: Henry Holt.

Lewis, Rupert. (1998). *Walter Rodney's Intellectual and Political Thought.* Detroit: Wayne State University Press.

Lewis, Shireen K. (2006). *Race, Culture, and Identity: Francophone West African and Caribbean Literature and Theory, from Negritude to Creolite.* Lanham, MD: Lexington Books.

Lewis, W. Arthur. (Ed.). (1994). *The Face of Man: Perspectives on the Economic, Social, Cultural and Political Development of the Caribbean (The Dr. Eric E. Williams Memorial Lectures).* Port of Spain, Trinidad and Tobago: Central Bank of Trinidad and Tobago Publishing.

Lichtheim, George. (1965). *Marxism.* New York: Praeger.

Lichtman, Richard. (1993). *Essays in Critical Social Theory: Toward a Marxist Critique of Liberal Ideology.* New York: Peter Lang.

Lindfors, Bernth. (1970). "Anti-Negritude in Algiers." *Africa Today* 17 (1), 5–7.

———. (1980). "Negritude and After: Responses to Colonialism and Independence in African Literatures." *Problems in National Literary Identity and the Writer as Social Critic* (pp. 29–37). Whitestone, NY: Council on National Literatures.

Linnemann, Russell J. (Ed.). (1982). *Alain Locke: Reflections on a Modern Renaissance Man.* Baton Rouge, LA: Louisiana State University.

Liss, Julia. (1998). "Diasporic Identities: The Science and Politics of Race in the Work of Franz Boas and W. E. B. Du Bois, 1894–1919." *Cultural Anthropology: Journal of the Society for Cultural Anthropology* 13 (2), 127–166.

Litwack, Leon. (1961). *North of Slavery: The Negro in the Free States, 1790–1860.* Chicago: University of Chicago Press.

———. (1979). *Been in the Storm So Long: The Aftermath of Slavery.* New York: Knopf.

———. (1998). *Trouble in Mind: Black Southerners in the Age of Jim Crow.* New York: Knopf.

Litwack, Leon, and Meier, August. (Eds.). (1988). *Black Leaders of the Nineteenth Century.* Chicago: University of Illinois Press.

Lloyd, David. (2003). "Rethinking National Marxism." *International Journal of Postcolonial Studies* 5 (3), 345–370.

Lloyd, Genevieve. (1984). *The Man of Reason: "Male" and "Female" in Western Philosophy.* Minneapolis: University of Minnesota.

Locke, Alain L. (1933). *The Negro in America.* Chicago: American Library Association.

———. (1936a). *Negro Art: Past and Present.* Washington, DC: Howard University Press.

———. (1936b). *The Negro and His Music.* New York: Arno Press.

———. (1940). *The Negro in Art: A Pictorial Record on the Negro Artists and of the Negro Theme in Art.* New York: Hacker Art Books.

———. (1949). *When Peoples Meet: A Study in Race and Culture.* New York: Hinds, Hayden, and Eldredge.

———. (Ed.). (1968). *The New Negro.* New York: Antheneum.

———. (1983). *The Critical Temper of Alain Locke: A Selection of His Essay on Art and Culture* (Jeffrey C. Stewart, Ed.). New York: Garland Publishing.

———. (1989). *The Philosophy of Alain Locke: Harlem Renaissance and Beyond* (Leonard Harris, Ed.). Philadelphia: Temple University Press.

———. (1992). *Race Contacts and Interracial Relations: Lectures on the Theory and Practice of Race* (Jeffrey C. Stewart, Ed.). Washington, DC: Howard University Press.

Loewberg, Bert James, and Bogin, Ruth. (Eds.). (1976). *Black Women in Nineteenth Century American Life: Their Words, Their Thoughts, Their Feelings.* University Park, PA: Pennsylvania State University Press.

Logan, Paul E. (1978). "Leo Frobenius and Negritude." *Negro Historical Bulletin* 41, 794–796.

Logan, Rayford W. (1940). *The Attitude of the Southern White Press Toward Negro Suffrage, 1932–1940.* Washington, DC: Howard University Press.

———. (Ed.). (1944). *What the Negro Wants.* Chapel Hill, NC: University of North Carolina Press.

———. (1954). *The Negro in American Life and Thought: The Nadir, 1877–1901.* New York: Dail Press.

———. (1967). *The American Negro: Old World Background and New World Experience.* Boston: Houghton-Mifflin.

———. (1965). *The Betrayal of the Negro: From Rutherord B. Hayes to Woodrow Wilson.* New York: Collier.

———. (Ed.). (1971). *W. E. B. Du Bois: A Profile.* New York: Hill & Wang.

Long, A.A. (Ed.). (1999). *The Cambridge Companion to Early Greak Philosophy.* Cambridge, UK: Cambridge University Press.

Long, Richard. (1969). "Negritude." *Negro Digest* 18 (7), 11–15, 57–59.

Loomba, Ania. (1998). *Colonialism/Postcolonialism.* New York: Routledge.

———. (Eds.). (2005). *Postcolonial Studies and Beyond.* Durham: Duke University Press.

Lopes, Carlos. (1987). *Guinea-Bissua: From Liberation Struggle to Independent Statehood.* Boulder, CO: Westview.

———. (1988). *The Socialist Ideal in Africa: A Debate.* Uppsala: Scandinavian Institute of African Studies.

Lopez, Ian F.H. (1995). "The Social Construction of Race." In Richard Delgado (Ed.), *Critical Race Theory* (pp. 191–203). Philadelphia: Temple University Press.

———. (1996). *White by Law: The Legal Construction of Race.* New York: New York University Press.

Lorde, Audre. (1984). *Sister Outsider: Essays and Speeches by Audre Lorde.* Freedom, CA: The Crossing Press Feminist Series.

———. (1988). *A Burst of Light: Essays by Audre Lorde.* Ithaca, NY: Firebrand.

———. (1996). *The Audre Lorde Compendium: Essays, Speeches, and Journals.* London: Pandora.

———. (2004). *Conversations with Audre Lorde* (Joan Wylie Hall, Ed.). Jackson: University Press of Mississippi.

Lott, Tommy L. (1997). "Du Bois on the Invention of Race." In John P. Pittman (Ed.), *African American Perspectives and Philosophical Traditions* (pp. 166–187). New York: Routledge.

———. (Ed.). (1998). *Subjugation and Bondage: Critical Essays on Slavery and Social Philosophy.* Lanham, MD: Rowman and Littlefield.

———. (1999). *The Invention of Race: Black Culture and the Politics of Representation.* Malden, MA: Blackwell.

———. (2000). "Du Bois and Locke on the Scientific Study of the Negro." *Boundary 2* 27 (3), 135–152.

———. (2001). "Du Bois's Anthropological Notion of Race." In Robert Bernasconi (Ed.), *Race* (pp. 59–83). Malden, MA: Blackwell.

———. (Ed). (2002). *African American Philosophy: Selected Readings.* Upper Saddle River, NJ: Prentice Hall.

Lott, Tommy L., and Pittman, John P. (Eds.). (2003). *A Companion to African American Philosophy.* Malden, MA: Blackwell.

Lovaas, Karen E., Elia, John P., and Yep, Gust A. (Eds.). (2006). *LGBT Studies and Queer Theory: New Conflicts, Collaborations, and Contested Terrains.* New York: Harrington Park Press.

Lucal, Betsy. (1996). "Race, Class, and Gender in the Work of W. E. B. Du Bois: An Exploratory Study." *Research in Race & Ethnic Relations* 9, 191–210.

Lukacs, Georg. (1971). *History and Class Consciousness.* Cambridge: MIT Press.

———. (1971c). *Lenin: A Study on the Unity of His Thought.* Cambridge: MIT Press.

———. (1972). *Tactics and Ethics: Political Essays, 1919–1929* (Rodney Livingstone, Ed.). New York: Harper and Row.

———. (1973). *Marxism and Human Liberation: Essays on History, Culture and Revolution.* New York: Dell.

———. (1976). *The Young Hegel.* Cambridge: MIT Press.

———. (1981a). *Essays on Realism.* (Rodney Livingstone, Ed.). Cambridge: MIT Press.

———. (1981b). *The Destruction of Reason.* Atlantic Highlands, NJ: Humanities Press.

———. (1986). *Georg Lukács: Selected Correspondence 1902–1929.* New York: Columbia University Press.

Luvai, A.I. (1974). "Negritude: A Redefinition." *Busara* 6 (11), 79–90.

Macey, David. (1999). "The Recall of the Real: Frantz Fanon and Psychoanalysis." *Constellations* 6 (1), 97–107.

———. (2000). *Frantz Fanon: A Biography.* New York: Picador.

———. (2004). "Frantz Fanon, or the Difficulty of Being Martinican." *History Workshop Journal* 58, 211–223.

Madubuike, Ihechukwu. (1975). "What Negritude Is Not: A Comment." *Renaissance* 2, (4), 27–29.

Magnus, Bernard, and Cullenberg, Stephen, (Eds.). (1995). *Whither Marxism?: Global Crises in International Perspective.* New York: Routledge.

Magubane, Bernard, and Ntalaja, Nzongola. (Eds.). (1983). *Proletarianization and Class Struggle in Africa.* San Francisco: Synthesis Publications.

Makang, Jean-Marie. (1993). "The Problem of Democratic Inclusion in the Light of the Racial Question: W. E. B. Du Bois and the Emancipation of Democracy." Ph.D. dissertation, Boston College.

Makuru, Simon J. (2005). "Violence and Liberation: Fanon's Political Philosophy of Humanization in the Historical Context of Racism and Colonialism." Ph.D. dissertation, Boston College.

Maldonado-Torres, Nelson. (2002). "Thinking from the Limits of Being: Levinas, Fanon, Dussel and Cry of Ethical Revolt." Ph.D. dissertation, Brown University.

———. (2005a). "Frantz Fanon and C. L. R. James on Intellectualism and Enlightened Rationality." *Caribbean Studies* 33 (2), 149–194.

———. (2005b). "Decolonization and the New Identitarian Logics After September 11: Eurocentricism and Americanism Against the New Barbarian Threats." *Radical Philosophy Review* 8 (1), 35–67.

———. (2006). "Cesaire's Gift and Decolonial Turn." *Radical Philosophy Review* 9 (2), 111–138.

———. (2007). "On the Coloniality of Being." *Cultural Studies* 21 (2/3), 240–270.

Malos, Ellen. (Ed.). (1980). *The Politics of Housework*. London: Allison & Busby.

Malpas, Simon, and Wake, Paul. (Eds.). (2006). *Routledge Companion to Critical Theory*. Routledge: New York.

Mann, Anika M. (2004). "Ethics from the Standpoint of Race and Gender: Sartre, Fanon and Feminist Standpoint Theory (Jean-Paul Sartre, Frantz Fanon, Maurice Merleau-Ponty, Simone de Beauvoir, Sandra Harding, Anna Julia Cooper)." Ph.D. dissertation, University of Memphis.

Manning, Patrick. (1998). *Francophone Sub-Saharan Africa, 1880–1995*. New York: Cambridge University Press.

Marable, Manning. (1982). "Alain Locke, W. E. B. Du Bois, and the Crisis of Black Education During the Great Depression." In Russell J. Linnemann (Ed.), *Alain Locke: Reflections on a Modern Renaissance Man* (pp. 63–76). Baton Rouge, LA: Louisiana State University.

———. (1983). *How Capitalism Underdeveloped Black America*. Boston: South End.

———. (1983/84). "Peace and Black Liberation: The Contributions of W. E. B. Du Bois." *Science & Society* 47, 385–405.

———. (1985a). *Black American Politics: From the Washington Marches to Jesse Jackson*. London: Verso.

———. (1985b). "The Black Faith of W. E. B. Du Bois: Sociocultural and Political Dimensions of Black Religion." *Southern Quarterly* 23, 15–33.

———. (1985c). "W. E. B. Du Bois and the Struggle Against Racism." *Black Scholar* 16 (May-June), 43–44, 46–47.

———. (1986). *W. E. B. Du Bois: Black Radical Democrat*. Boston: Twayne.

———. (1987). *African and Carribean Politics: From Kwame Nkrumah to Maurice Bishop*. New York: Verso.

———. (1991). *Race, Reform, and Rebellion: The Second Reconstruction in Black America, 1945–1990*. Jackson, MS: University Press of Mississippi.

———. (1992). *The Crisis of Color and Democracy: Essays on Race, Class and Power*. Monroe, MA: Common Courage Press.

———. (1993). *Blackwater: Historical Studies in Race, Class Consciousness, and Revolution*. Niwot, CO: University Press of Colorado.

———. (1995). *Beyond Black and White: Transforming African American Politics*. New York and London: Verso.

———. (1996). *Speaking Truth to Power: Essays on Race, Resistance, and Radicalism*. Boulder, CO: Westview.

———. (1997). *Black Liberation in Conservative America*. Boston: South End.

———. (1998). *Black Leadership*. New York: Columbia University Press.

———. (Ed.). (2000). *Dispatches from the Ebony Towers: Intellectuals Confront the African American Experience*. New York: Columbia University Press.

———. (2002). *The Great Wells of Democracy: The Meaning of Race in American Life*. New York: Basic/Civitas.

———. (Ed). (2005). *The New Black Renaissance: The Souls Anthology of Critical African American Studies*. Boulder, CO: Paradigm Publishers.

———. (2006). *Living Black History: How Re-Imagining the African American Past Can Remake America's Racial Future*. New York: Basic/Civitas.

Marable, Manning and Mullings, Leith. (Eds.). (2000). *Let Nobody Turn Us Around: Voices of Resistance, Reform, and Renewal—An African American Anthology*. Lanham, MD: Rowman and Littlefield.

Marable, Manning, Ness, Immanuel, and Wilson, Joseph. (Eds.). (2006). *Race and Labor Matters in the New U.S. Economy*. Lanham, MD: Rowman and Littlefield.

Marcano, Donna-Dale. (2003). "Sartre and the Social Construction of Race." In Robert Bernasconi (Ed.), *Race and Racism in Continental Philosophy* (pp. 214–226). Bloomington: Indiana University Press.

Marcus, Judith, and Tar, Zoltan. (Eds.). (1984). *The Foundations of the Frankfurt School of Social Research*. New York: Transaction Books.

Marcuse, Herbert. (1958). *Soviet Marxism*. New York: Columbia University Press.

———. (1960). *Reason and Revolution*. Boston: Beacon.

———. (1964). *One-Dimensional Man: Studies in the Ideology of Advanced Industrial Society*. Boston: Beacon.

———. (1965a). "Socialism in the Developed Countries." *International Socialist Journal* 2 (8), 139–151.

———. (1965b). "Socialist Humanism?" In Erich Fromm (Ed.), *Socialist Humanism* (pp. 107–117). New York: Doubleday.

———. (1965c). "Repressive Tolerance." In Robert Paul Wolff, Barrington Moore, Jr., and Herbert Marcuse, *A Critique of Pure Tolerance* (pp. 81–118). Boston: Beacon.

———. (1966). *Eros and Civilization*. Boston: Beacon.

———. (1967). "The Obsolescence of Marxism." In Nikolaus Lobkowicz (Ed.), *Marxism in the Western World* (pp. 409–417). Notre Dame: University of Notre Dame Press.

———. (1968). *Negations: Essays in Critical Theory*. Boston: Beacon.

———. (1969a). *An Essay on Liberation*. Boston: Beacon.

———. (1969b). "The Realm of Freedom and the Realm of Necessity: A Reconsideration." *Praxis* 5 (1/2), 20–25.

———. (1970a). *Five Lectures: Psychoanalysis, Politics, and Utopia*. Boston: Beacon.

———. (1970b). "Marxism and the New Humanity: An Unfinished Revolution." In John C. Raines and Thomas Dean (Eds.), *Marxism and Radical Religion: Essays Toward a Revolutionary Humanism* (pp. 3–10). Philadelphia: Temple University Press.

———. (1971). "Dear Angela." *Ramparts* 9, 22.

———. (1972a). *Counter-Revolution and Revolt*. Boston: Beacon.

———. (1972b). *From Luther to Popper*. London: Verso.

———. (1973). *Studies in Critical Philosophy*. Boston: Beacon.

———. (1974). "Marxism and Feminism." *Women's Studies* 2 (3), 279–288.

———. (1976a). "On the Problem of the Dialectic" (Part 1). *Telos* 27, 12–24.

———. (1976b). "On the Problem of the Dialectic" (Part 2). *Telos* 27, 12–39.

———. (1976c). *Revolution or Reform?: A Confrontation*. Chicago: New University Press.

———. (1978a). *The Aesthetic Dimension: Toward a Critique of Marxist Aesthetics*. Beacon: Boston.

———. (1978b). "BBC Interview: Marcuse and the Frankfurt School." In Bryan Magee (Ed.), *Man of Ideas* (pp. 62–73). London: BBC Publishing.

———. (1978c). "Theory and Politics: A Discussion." *Telos* 38, 124–153.

———. (1979a). "The Reification of the Proletariat." *Canadian Journal of Philosophy and Social Theory* 3 (1), 20–23.

———. (1979b). "The Failure of the New Left?" *New German Critique* 18, 3–11.

———. (1989). "Liberation from the Affluent Society." In Stephen E. Bronner and Douglas Kellner (Eds.), *Critical Theory and Society: A Reader* (pp. 276–287). New York: Routledge.

———. (1997a). *Technology, War and Fascism: The Collected Papers of Herbert Marcuse*, volume 1 (Douglas Kellner, Ed.). New York: Routledge.

———. (1997b). "A Note on Dialectic." In Andrew Arato and Eike Gebhardt (Eds.), *The Essential Frankfurt School Reader* (pp. 444–451). New York: Continuum.

———. (2001). *Towards a Critical Theory of Society: The Collected Papers of Herbert Marcuse*, volume 2 (Douglas Kellner, Ed.). New York: Routledge.

———. (2004). *The New Left and the 1960s: The Collected Papers of Herbert Marcuse*, volume 3 (Douglass Kellner, Ed.). New York: Routledge.

———. (2005). *Heideggerian Marxism.* (Richard Wolin and John Abromeit, Eds.). Lincoln: University of Nebraska Press.

———. (2007a). *Art and Liberation: The Collected Papers of Herbert Marcuse,* volume 4 (Douglass Kellner, Ed.). New York: Routledge.

———. (2007b). *The Essential Marcuse: Selected Writings of Philosopher and Social Critic Herbert Marcuse* (Andrew Feenberg and William Leiss, Eds.). Boston: Beacon.

Markovitz, Irving Leonard. (1967). "Leopold Sedar Senghor: A Case Study of Senegalese Ideology." Ph.D. dissertation, University of California at Berkeley.

———. (1969). *Leopold Sedar Senghor and the Politics of Negritude.* New York: Atheneum.

Marsh, James L. (1995). *Critique, Action, and Liberation.* Albany: SUNY Press.

———. (1998). *Post-Cartesian Meditations.* New York: Fordham University Press.

———. (1999). *Process, Praxis, and Transcendence.* Albany: SUNY Press.

———. (2001). "Toward a New Critical Theory." In William S. Wilkerson and Jeffrey Paris (Eds.), *New Critical Theory: Essays on Liberation* (pp. 49–64). Lanham, MD: Rowman and Littlefield.

Marsh-Lockett, Carol P. (1997). "Womanism." In William L. Andrews, Frances Smith Foster, and Trudier Harris (Eds.), *The Oxford Companion to African American Literature* (pp. 784–785). New York: Oxford University Press.

Marshall, Jessica. (1994). " 'Counsels of Despair': W. E. B. Du Bois, Robert E. Park, and the Establishment of American Race Sociology." Ph.D. dissertation, Harvard University.

Marteau, Pierre. (1961). "Aime Cesaire's 'Cadastre'." *Presence Africaine* 9 (37), 45–55.

Martin, Michael, and Yeakey, Lamont. (1982). "Pan-African and Asian Solidarity: A Central Theme in W. E. B. Du Bois's Conception of Racial Stratification and Struggle on a World Scale." *Phylon* 43, 202–217.

Martin, Tony. (Ed.). (1991). *African Fundamentalism: A Literary and Cultural Anthology of Garvey's Harlem Renaissance.* Dover, MA: Majority Press.

———. (1999). "Rescuing Fanon from the Critics." In Nigel C. Gibson (Ed.), *Rethinking Fanon: The Continuing Dialogue* (pp. 83–102). Amherst, NY: Humanity Books.

Martin, Waldo E., Jr. (1984). *The Mind of Frederick Douglass.* Chapell Hill, NC: University of North Carolina Press.

———. (1990). "Images of Frederick Douglass in the Afro-American Mind: The Recent Black Freedom Struggle." In Eric J. Sundquist (Ed.), *Frederick Douglass: New Literary and Historical Essays* (pp. 271–286). New York: Cambridge University Press.

———. (2005). *No Coward Soldiers: Black Cultural Politics in Post-War America.* Cambridge, MA: Harvard University Press.

Marx, Karl. (1964). *Early Writings* (Tom B. Bottomore, Ed.). New York: McGraw-Hill.

———. (1968). *Karl Marx on Colonialism and Modernization: His Dispatches and Other Writings on China, India, Mexico, the Middle East and North Africa* (Shlomo Avineri, Ed.). Garden City, NY: Doubleday.

———. (1971). *Early Texts* (David McLellan, Ed.). New York: Barnes & Nobles.

———. (1974). *Karl Marx on Religion* (Saul Padover, Ed.). New York: McGraw-Hill.

———. (1975). *Karl Marx: Texts on Method* (Terrell Carver, Ed.). New York: Barnes & Nobles.

———. (1976a). *Political Writings, Volume 1: The Revolution of 1848* (David Fernbach, Ed.). New York: Random House.

———. (1976b). *Political Writings, Volume 2: Surveys from Exile* (David Fernbach, Ed.). New York: Random House.

———. (1976c). *Political Writings, Volume 3: The First International and After* (David Fernbach, Ed.). New York: Random House.

———. (1983). *The German Ideology.* New York: International Publishers.

———. (1984). *Karl Marx: Selected Writings in Sociology and Social Philosophy* (Tom Bottomore and Maximilien Rubel, Eds.). New York: McGraw-Hill.

————. (1994). *Marx: Early Political Writings* (Joseph O'Malley, Ed.). New York: Cambridge University Press.

————. (1996). *Marx: Later Political Writings* (Terrell Carver, Ed.). New York: Cambridge University Press.

————. (2002). *Marx on Religion* (John Raines, Ed.). Philadelphia: Temple University Press.

Marx, Karl, and Engels, Friedrich. (1964). *On Religion*. New York: Schocken.

Marx, Karl, and Engels, Friedrich. (1972). *On Colonialism*. New York: International.

Marx, Karl, and Engels, Friedrich. (1978). *The Marx-Engels Reader* (2nd Edition, Robert C. Tucker, Ed.). New York: Norton.

Marx, Karl, and Engels, Friedrich. (1989). *Marx & Engels: The Basic Writings on Politics and Philosophy* (Lewis S. Feuer, Ed.). New York: Anchor.

Marx, Karl, and Engels, Friedrich. (2008). *Karl Marx and Friedrich Engels on Religion*. Mineola, NY: Dover.

Masilela, Ntongela. (1994). "Pan-Africanism or Classical African Marxism?" In Sidney Lemelle and Robin D.G. Kelley (Eds.), *Imagining Home: Class, Culture, and Nationalism in the African Diaspora* (pp. 308–331). New York: Verso.

Massey, Douglas S., and Denton, Nancy A. (1993). *American Apartheid: Segregation and the Making of the Underclass*. Cambridge: Harvard University Press.

Massiah, Louis. (Director). (1995). *W. E. B. Du Bois: A Biography in Four Voices* [Documentary]. San Francisco: California Newsreel.

Masolo, Dismas A. (1994). *African Philosophy in Search of Identity*. Indianapolis: Indiana University Press.

————. (1998). "Sartre Fifty Years Later: A Review of Lewis R. Gordon's *Fanon and the Crisis of the European Man.*" *APA Newsletter on Philosophy and the Black Experience* 97 (2). Available online at: http://www.apa.udel.edu/apa/archive/newsletters/v97n2/black/sartre.asp [Accessed 21 June 2005].

Mason, Ernest D. (1982). "Alain Locke's Philosophy of Value." In Russell J. Linnemann (Ed.), *Alain Locke: Reflections on a Modern Renaissance Man* (pp. 1–16). Baton Rouge, LA: Louisiana State University.

Matsuda, Mari J. (Ed.). (1993). *Words That Wound: Critical Race Theory, Assaultive Speech, and the First Amendment*. Boulder, CO: Westview.

Matustik, Martin B. (1998). *Specters of Liberation: Great Refusals in the New World Order*. Albany: SUNY Press.

Maxwell, William J. (1999). *New Negro, Old Left: African American Writing and Communism Between the Wars*. New York: Columbia University Press.

May, Larry, Strikwerda, Robert, and Hopkins, Patrick D. (Eds.). (1996). *Rethinking Masculinity: Philosophical Explorations in Light of Feminism*. Lanham, MD: Rowman and Littlefield.

May, Vivian M. (2007). *Anna Julia Cooper, Visionary Black Feminist: A Critical Introduction*. New York: Routledge.

Mazrui, Ali A. (1967). *Towards a Pax Africana: A Study of Ideology and Ambition*. Chicago: University of Chicago Press.

————. (1974). *World Culture and the Black Experience*. Seattle: University of Washington Press.

————. (1975). *The Political Sociology of the English Language: An African Perspective*. The Hague: Mouton.

————. (1976). "Negritude, the Talmudic Tradition and the Intellectual Performance of Blacks and Jews." *Hommage à Léopold Sédar Senghor* (pp. 300–326). Paris: Presence Africaine.

————. (1978). *Political Values and the Educated Class in Africa*. Berkeley: University of California Press.

————. (1980). *The African Condition: A Political Diagnosis*. New York: Cambridge University Press.

————. (1986). *The Africans: A Triple Heritage*. Boston: Little Brown.

——. (1993). *Africa since 1935*. Berkeley: University of California Press.

——. (1998). *The Power of Babel: Language and Governance in the African Experience*. Chicago: University of Chicago Press.

——. (2002a). *Black Reparations in the Era of Globalization*: Binghamton, NY: Institute of Global Culture Publications, Binghamton University.

——. (2002b). *Africa and Other Civilizations: Conquest and Counter-Conquest*. Trenton, NJ: Africa World Press.

——. (2002c). *Africanity Re-defined*. Trenton, NJ: Africa World Press.

——. (2004). *Power, Politics, and the African Condition*. Trenton, NJ: Africa World Press.

Mazrui, Ali A., Okpewho, Isidore, and Davies, Carole Boyce. (Eds.). (1999). *The African Diaspora: African Origins and New World Identites*. Bloomington: Indiana University Press.

Mazrui, Ali A. (1976). "Negritude, the Talmudic Tradition and the Intellectual Performance of Blacks and Jews." *Hommage à Léopold Sédar Senghor* (pp. 300–326). Paris: Presence Africaine.

Mbelelo Ya Mpiku, J. (1971). "From One Mystification to Another: 'Negritude' and 'Negraille' in 'Le Devoir de Violence'." *Review of National Literatures* 2 (2), 124–147.

Mburu, James Ndungu. (2003). *Thematic Issues in African Philosophy*. Nairobi, Kenya: Acacia Publishers.

McAuley, Christopher. (2004). *The Mind of Oliver C. Cox*. Notre Dame: University of Notre Dame Press.

McCarthy, Michael. (1983). *Dark Continent: Africa As Seen By Americans*. Westport: Greenwood.

McCarthy, Thomas. (1991). *Ideal and Illusion: On Reconstruction and Deconstruction in Contemporary Critical Theory*. Cambridge: MIT Press.

McCarthy, Thomas, and Hoy, David. (1994). *Critical Theory*. Cambridge: Blackwell.

McClendon, John H. (2005). *C. L. R. James's Notes on Dialectics: Left Hegelianism or Marxist-Humanism*. Lanham, MD: Lexington Books.

McClennen, Sophia A. (2004). *The Dialectics of Exile: Nation, Time, Language, and Space in Hispanic Literatures*. West Lafayette: Purdue University Press.

McClintock, Anne. (1992). "The Angel of Progress: Pitfalls of the Term 'Post-Colonialism'." *Social Text* 10 (31–32), 84–98.

——. (1995). *Imperial Leather: Race, Gender, and Sexuality in the Colonial Conquest*. New York: Routledge.

McClintock, Anne, Mufti, Aamir, and Shobat, Ella. (Eds.). (1997). *Dangerous Liaisons: Gender, Nation, and Postcolonial Perspectives*. Minneapolis: University of Minnesota Press.

McCollester, Charles. (1973). "The Political Thought of Amilcar Cabral." *Monthly Review* (March), 10–21.

McCulloch, Jock. (1983a). *Black Soul, White Artifact: Fanon's Clinical Psychology and Social Theory*. Cambridge: Cambridge University Press.

——. (1983b). *In the Twilight of Revolution: The Political Theory of Amilcar Cabral*. London and Boston: Routledge and Kegan Paul.

McDade, Jesse N. (1971). "Frantz Fanon: The Ethical Justification of Revolution." Ph.D. dissertation, Boston University.

McDaniel, Antonio. (1998). "*The Philadelphia Negro*, Then and Now: Implications for Empirical Research." In Michael B. Katz and Thomas J. Sugrue (Eds.), *W. E. B. Du Bois, Race, and the City: The Philadelphia Negro and Its Legacy* (pp. 155–194). Philadelphia: University of Pennsylvania Press.

McGary, Howard. (1974). "Reparations and Inverse Discrimination." *Dialogue* 17 (1), 4–17.

——. (1977–1978). "Justice and Reparations." *Philosophical Forum* 9 (2–3), 250–263.

——. (1984). "Reparations, Self-Respect, and Public Policy." *The Journal* 1, 15–26.

——. (1986). "Morality and Collective Liability." *Journal of Value Inquiry* 20, 157–165.

——. (1999). *Race and Social Justice*. Malden, MA: Blackwell.

McGary, Howard, and Bill Lawson. (1992). *Between Slavery and Freedom: Philosophy and American Slavery*. Indianapolis: Indiana University Press.

McGee, B.R. (1998). "Speaking About the Other: W. E. B. Du Bois Responds to the Klan." *Communications Abstracts* 21, 6.

McGill, Ralph. (1965). "W. E. B. Du Bois." *Atlantic Monthly* (November), 78–81.

McKay, Claude. (1953). *The Selected Poems of Claude McKay*. New York: Harcourt, Brace & World.

———. (1968). *Harlem, Negro Metropolis*. New York: Harcourt, Brace & Jovanovich.

———. (1970). *A Long Way from Home*. New York: Harcourt, Brace & Jovanovich.

———. (1973). *The Passion of Claude McKay: Selected Poetry and Prose*. New York: Schocken.

———. (1998). *Harlem Glory: A Fragment of Aframerican Life*. Chicago: Charles H. Kerr Publishing.

———. (2004). *The Complete Poems of Claude McKay* (William J. Maxwell, Ed.). Urbana: University of Illinois Press.

McKay, Nellie Y. (1985). "W. E. B. Du Bois: The Black Woman in His Writings—Selected Fictional and Autobiographical Portraits." In William L. Andrews (Ed.), *Critical Essays on W. E. B. Du Bois* (pp. 230–252). Boston: G.K. Hall.

———. (1990). "The Souls of Black Women Folk in the Writings of W. E. B. Du Bois." In Henry Louis Gates, Jr. (Ed.), *Reading Black/Reading Feminist: A Critical Anthology* (pp. 227–243). New York: Meridian.

McKee, James B. (1993). *Sociology and the Race Problem: The Failure of a Perspective*. Urbana: University of Illinois Press.

McLaren, Peter. (1997). *Revolutionary Multiculturalism: Pedagogies of Dissent for the New Millennium*. Boulder, CO: Westview.

McLellan, David. (1970). *Marx Before Marxism*. New York: Harper & Row.

———. (1971). *The Thought of Karl Marx: An Introduction*. New York: Harper Torchbooks.

———. (1973). *Karl Marx: His Life and Thought*. New York: Harper & Row.

———. (1978). *Friedrich Engels*. New York: Penguin.

———. (1979). *Marxism After Marx*. Boston: Houghton Mifflin.

———. (Ed.). (1981). *Karl Marx: Interviews and Recollections*. Totwa, NJ: Barnes and Noble Books.

———. (1983a). *Karl Marx: The Legacy*. London: BBC Books.

———. (Ed.). (1983b). *Marx: The First Hundred Years*. London: Fontana Books.

———. (2006). *Karl Marx: A Biography*. New York: Palgrave.

McLemee, Scott. (1994). "Afterword—American Civilization and World Revolution: C. L. R. James in the United States, 1938–1953 and Beyond." In Scott McLemee and Paul Le Blanc (Eds.), *C. L. R. James and Revolutionary Marxism: Selected Writings of C. L. R. James, 1939–1949* (pp. 209–283). Atlantic Highlands, NJ: Humanities Press.

———. (1996). "Introduction: The Egnima of Arrival." In Scott McLemee (Ed.), *C. L. R. James on the "Negro Question"* (pp. xi–xxxvii). Jackson: University of Mississippi Press.

McLennan, Gregor. (1981). *Marxism and the Methodologies of History*. New York: Verso.

McLeod, Alan L. (Ed.). (1992). *Claude McKay: Centennial Studies*. New Delhi: Sterling Publishers.

McLeod, John. (Ed.). (2007). *The Routledge Companion to Postcolonial Studies*. New York: Routledge.

McMurry, Linda O. (1998). *To Keep the Waters Troubled: The Life of Ida B. Wells*. New York: Oxford University Press.

McNann, Carole, and Kim, Seung-Kyung. (Eds.). (2002). *Feminist Theory Reader: Local and Global Perspectives*. New York: Routledge.

Meade, Homer Lee, II. (1987). "W. E. B. Du Bois and His Place in the Discussion of Racism." Ph.D. dissertation, University of Massachusetts.

Meehan, Johanna. (Ed.). (1995). *Feminists Read Habermas: Gendering the Subject of Discourse.* New York: Routledge.

Meeks, Brian. (1993). *Caribbean Revolutions and Revolutionary Theory: An Assessment of Cuba, Nicaragua, and Grenada.* London: Macmillan.

——. (1996). *Radical Caribbean: From Black Power to Abu Bakar.* Kingston, Jamaica: University of West Indies Press.

——. (2000). *Narratives of Resistances: Jamaica, Trinidad and the Caribbean.* Kingston, Jamaica: University of West Indies Press.

Meeks, Brian, and Lindahl, Folke. (Eds.). (2001). *New Caribbean Thought: A Reader.* Kingston, Jamaica: University of West Indies Press.

Meier, August. (1954). "Booker T. Washington and the Rise of the NAACP." *Crisis* 60.

——. (1959). "From 'Conservative' to 'Radical': The Ideological Development of W. E. B. Du Bois, 1885–1905." *Crisis* 75, 527–536.

——. (1963). *Negro Thought in America, 1880–1915: Racial Ideologies in the Age of Booker T. Washington.* Ann Arbor: University of Michigan Press.

——. (1969). *The Making of Black America: Essays in Negro Life and History.* New York: Atheneum.

——. (1976). *From Plantation to Ghetto: An Interpretive History of American Negroes.* New York: Hill and Wang.

Meier, August, and Bracey, John H. (1993). "The NAACP as a Reform Movement, 1909–1965: 'To Reach the Conscience of America.'" *Journal of Southern History* 59 (1), 3–30.

Meier, August, and Rudwick, Elliott. (1976). *Along the Color-Line: Explorations in the Black Experience.* Urbana: University of Illinois Press.

Meier, August, and Rudwick, Elliott. (Eds.). (1986). *Black History and the Historical Profession, 1915–1980.* Urbana: University of Illinois Press.

Melady, Margaret Badum. (1971). *Leopold Sedar Senghor: Rhythm and Reconciliation.* South Orange, NJ: Seton Hall University Press.

Melesse, Ayalew. (1975). "The Problem of Revolution in the Third World: Frantz Fanon and Marxism." Ph.D. dissertation, Columbia University.

Melone, Thomas. (1963). "The Theme of Negritude and Its Literary Problems." *Presence Africaine* 20 (48), 166–181.

Memmi, Albert. (1967). *The Colonizer and the Colonized.* Boston: Beacon.

——. (1969). *Dominated Man: Notes Toward a Portrait.* Boston: Beacon.

——. (1984). *Dependence: A Sketch for a Portrait of the Dependent.* Boston: Beacon.

——. (2000). *Racism.* Minneapolis, MN: University of Minnesota Press.

——. (2006). *Decolonization and the Decolonized.* Minneapolis, MN: University of Minnesota Press.

Mendieta, Eduardo. (2007). *Global Fragments: Critical Theory, Latin America, and Globalization.* Albany, NY: SUNY Press.

Mercer, Kobena. (1994). *Welcome to the Jungle: New Positions in Black Cultural Studies.* New York: Routledge.

Meulenbelt, Anja. (Ed.). (1984). *A Creative Tension: Explorations in Socialist Feminism.* London: Pluto Press.

Meyer, Arthur S. (1999). "W. E. B. Du Bois and the Open Forum: Human Relations in a 'Difficult Industrial District'." *Journal of Negro History* 84 (2), 192–212.

Mezu, S. Okechukwu. (1965). *The Philosophy of Pan-Africanism: A Collection of Papers on the Theory and Practice of the African Unity Movement.* Washington, DC: Georgetown University Press.

——. (1973). *The Poetry of Leopold Sedar Senghor.* London: Heinemann.

Mignolo, Walter. (2005). *The Idea of Latin America.* Malden, MA: Blackwell.

——. (2003). *The Darker Side of the Renaissance: Literacy, Territoriality, and Colonization.* Ann Arbor: University of Michigan Press.

——. (2000). *Local Histories/Global Designs: Coloniality, Subaltern Knowledges, and Border Thinking.* Princeton: Princeton University Press.

Miller, Christopher L. (1985). *Blank Darkness: Africanist Discourse in French.* Chicago: University of Chicago Press.

——. (1990). *Theories of Africans: Francophone Literature and Anthropology of Africa.* Chicago: University of Chicago Press.

——. (1998). *Nationalists and Nomads: Essays on Francophone African Literature and Culture.* Chicago: University Chicago Press.

Miller, Khadijah Olivia Turner. (2001). "Everyday Victories: The Pennsylvania State Federation of Negro Women's Clubs, Inc., 1900-1930." Ph.D. dissertation, Temple University.

Miller, Pavla. (1998). *Transformations of Patriarchy in the West, 1500-1900.* Bloomington: Indiana University Press.

Miller, Toby. (Ed.). (2001). *Companion to Cultural Studies.* Malden, MA: Blackwell.

Millette, James. (1995). "C. L. R. James and the Politics of Trinidad and Tobago, 1938-1970." In Selwyn Cudjoe and William E. Cain (Eds.), *C. L. R. James: His Intellectual Legacies* (pp. 328-347). Amherst: University of Massachusetts Press.

Milligan, Nancy Muller. (1985). "W. E. B. Du Bois's American Pragmatism." *Journal of American Culture* 8 (2), 31-37.

Mills, Charles W. (1987). "Race and Class: Conflicting or Reconcilable Paradigms?" *Social and Economic Studies* 36 (2), 69-108.

——. (1997). *The Racial Contract.* Ithaca: Cornell University Press.

——. (1998). *Blackness Visible: Essays on Philosophy and Race.* Ithaca: Cornell University Press.

——. (1999). "The Racial Polity." In Susan E. Babbitt and Susan Campbell (Eds.), *Racism and Philosophy* (pp. 13-31, [endnotes] 255-257). Ithaca: Cornel University Press.

——. (2000). "Race and the Social Contract Tradition." *Social Identities: A Journal for the Study of Race, Nation and Culture* 6 (4), 441-462.

——. (2001). "White Supremacy and Racial Justice." In James Sterba (Ed.), *Social and Political Philosophy: Contemporary Perspectives* (pp. 321-337). New York: Routledge.

——. (2003a). *From Class to Race: Essays in White Marxism and Black Radicalism.* Lanham, MD: Rowman and Littlefield.

——. (2003b). "White Supremacy." In Tommy L. Lott and John P. Pittman (Eds.), *A Companion to African American Philosophy* (pp. 269-284). Malden, MA: Blackwell.

Mills, Patricia. (1987). *Women, Nature and Psyche.* New Haven: Yale University Press.

Mills, Patricia J. (Eds). (1996). *Feminist Interpretations of G.W.F. Hegel.* University Park, PA: Penn State University Press.

Mishra, V. and Hodge, B. (1991). "What Is Post(-)Colonialism?" *Textual Practice* 5 (3), 399-415.

Mitchell, Ella Pearson. (1993). "Du Bois's Dilemma and African American Adaptiveness." In Gerald Early (Ed.), *Lure and Loathing: Essays on Race, Identity, and the Ambivalence of Assimilation* (pp. 264-273). New York: Viking/Penguin.

Mizruchi, Susan. (1996). "Neighbors, Strangers, and Corpses: Death and Sympathy in the Early Writings of W. E. B. Du Bois." In Robert Newman (Ed.), *Centuries' Ends, Narrative Means.* Stanford: Stanford University Press.

Mkabela, N.Q. (1997). *Towards an African Philosophy of Education.* Pretoria, South Africa: Kagiso Publishers.

Mohanty, Chandra Talpade. (1991). *Third World Women and the Politics of Feminism.* Bloomington, IN: Indiana University Press.

——. (2003). *Feminism Without Borders: Decolonizing Theory, Praticing Solidarity.* Durham, NC: Duke University Press.

Mohiddin, Ahmed. (1981). *African Socialism in Two Countries.* London: Croom Helm.

Mohome, Paulus M. (1968). "Negritude: Evaluation and Elaboration." *Presence Africaine* 68, 122-140.

Moitt, Bernard. (1995). "Transcending Linguistic and Cultural Frontiers in Caribbean Historiography: C. L. R. James, French Sources, and Slavery in San Domingo." In Selwyn Cudjoe and William E. Cain (Eds.), *C. L. R. James: His Intellectual Legacies* (pp. 136–162). Amherst: University of Massachusetts Press.

Momoh, Campbell S. (1985). "African Philosophy: Does It Exist?" *Diognes* 130, 73–104.

———. (1989). *Substance of African Philosophy*. Auchi: Nigeria African Philosophical Project.

———. (1991). *Philosophy of a New Past and an Old Future*. Auchi: Nigeria African Philosophical Projects.

Monteiro, Anthony. (1994). "The Scientific and Revolutionary Legacy of W. E. B. Du Bois." *Political Affairs* 73 (2), 1–19.

———. (2000). "Being an African in the World: The Du Boisian Epistemology." *Annals of the American Academy of Political and Social Science* 568 (March), 220–234.

Montmarquet, James, and Hardy, William. (Eds.). (2000). *Reflections: An Anthology of African American Philosophy*. San Francisco: Wadsworth.

Moon, Henry Lee. (1968). "The Leadership of W. E. B. Du Bois." *Crisis* 75, 51–57.

Moore, Jack B. (1981). *W. E. B. Du Bois*. Boston: Twayne.

Moore, Jacqueline M. (2003). *Booker T. Washington, W. E. B. Du Bois, and the Struggle for Racial Uplift*. Wilmington, DE: Scholarly Resources.

Moore, Percy L. (1996). "W. E. B. Du Bois: A Critical Study of His Philosophy of Education and Its Relevance for Three Contemporary Issues in Education of Significance to African Americans." Ph.D. dissertation, Wayne State University.

Moore, Richard B. (1970). "Du Bois and Pan-Africa." In John Henrik Clarke, Esther Jackson, Ernest Kaiser, and J.H. O'Dell (Eds.), *Black Titan: W. E. B. Du Bois* (pp. 187–212). Boston: Beacon.

Moore, T. Owens. (2005). "A Fanonian Perspective on Double-Consciousness." *Journal of Black Studies* 35 (6), 751–762.

Moore-Gilbert, Bart. (1997). *Postcolonial Theory: Contexts, Practices, Politics*. London: Verso.

Moreira, Americo M. (1989). "The Role of Marxism in the Anti-Colonial Revolution in Black Africa." Ph.D. dissertation, Boston College.

Morgan, Ted. (2003). *Reds: McCarthyism in Twentieth-Century America*. New York: Random House.

Morrison, Hugh James. (2000). "The Evolution of a Reform Plan: W. E. B. Du Bois's Sociological Research, 1896–1910." Ph.D. dissertation, Queen's University at Kingston, Canada.

Morrison, Toni. (1990). *Playing in the Dark: Whiteness and the Literary Imagination*. Cambridge: Harvard University Press.

Morrow, Raymond A. (1994). *Critical Theory and Methodology* (with David D. Brown). Thousands Oaks, CA: Sage.

Morton, Patricia. (1991). *Disfigured Images: The Historical Assault on Afro-American Women*. New York: Praeger.

Moscovici, Claudia. (2002). *Double Dialectics: Between Universalism and Relativism in Enlightenment and Postmodern Thought*. Lanham, MD: Rowman and Littlefield.

Moses, Wilson Jeremiah. (1975). "The Poetic of Ethiopianism: W. E. B. Du Bois and Literary Black Nationalism." *American Literature* 47, 411–427.

———. (1978). *The Golden Age of Black Nationalism, 1850–1925*. New York: Oxford University Press.

———. (1990). "Sexual Anxieties of the Black Bourgeoisie in Victorian America: The Cultural Context of W. E. B. Du Bois's First Novel." In Wilson Jeremiah Moses, *The Wings of Ethiopia: Studies in African American Life and Letters*. Ames, IA: Iowa State University Press.

———. (1993a). "W. E. B. Du Bois's 'The Conservation of Races' and Its Context: Idealism, Conservatism, and Hero Worship." *Massachusetts Review* 34, 275–294.

———. (1993b). "Du Bois's *Dark Princess* and the Heroic Uncle Tom." In Wilson Jeremiah Moses, *Black Messiahs and Uncle Toms: Social and Literary Manipulations of a Religious Myth.* University Park, PA: Pennsylvania State University Press.

———. (1996). "Culture, Civilization, and the Decline of the West: The Afrocentricism of W. E. B. Du Bois." In Bernard W. Bell, Emily R. Grosholz, and James B. Stewart (Eds.), *W. E. B. Du Bois: On Race and Culture* (pp. 243–260). New York: Routledge.

———. (1998). "W. E. B. Du Bois and Antimodernism." In Wilson Jeremiah Moses, *Afrotopia: The Roots of African American Popular History* (pp. 136–168). New York: Cambridge University Press.

———. (2004). *Creative Conflict in African American Thought: Frederick Douglass, Alexander Crummell, Booker T. Washington, W. E. B. Du Bois, and Marcus Garvey.* New York: Cambridge University Press.

Mosley, Albert G. (1983). "Negritude, Magic, and the Arts: A Pragmatic Perspective." In Leonard Harris (Ed.), *Philosophy Born of Struggle: An Anthology of Afro-American Philosophy from 1917* (pp. 272–282). Dubuque, IA: Kendall/Hunt.

———. (Ed.). (1995a). *African Philosophy: Selected Readings.* Englewood Cliffs, NJ: Prentice Hall.

———. (1995b). "Negritude, Nationalism, and Nativism: Racists or Racialists?" In Albert G. Mosley (Ed.), *African Philosophy: Selected Readings* (pp. 216–235). Englewood Cliffs, NJ: Prentice Hall.

Moss, Alfred A. (1981). *The American Negro Academy: Voice of the Talented Tenth.* Baton Rouge, LA: Louisiana State University Press.

Moss, Richard Lawrence. (1975). "Ethnographic Perspectives and Literary Strategies in the Early Writings of W. E. B. Du Bois." Ph.D. dissertation, State University of New York, Buffalo.

Mostern, Kenneth. (1996). "Three Theories of the Race of W. E. B. Du Bois." *Cultural Critique* 34, 27–63.

———. (2000). "Postcolonialism after W. E. B. Du Bois." *Rethinking Marxism* 12 (2), 61–80.

Moten, Fred. (2003). *In the Break: The Aesthetics of the Black Radical Tradition.* Minneapolis: University of Minnesota Press.

Moulard-Leonard, Valentine. (2005). "Revolutionary Becomings: Negritude's Anti-Humanist Humanism." *Human Studies* 28 (3), 231–249.

Mouzelis, Nicos P. (1990). *Post-Marxist Alternatives: The Construction of Social Orders.* London: Macmillan.

Mudimbe, Valentin Y. (1983). "African Philosophy as an Ideological Practice: The Case of French Speaking Africa." *African Studies Review* 26 (3/4), 133–154.

———. (1985). "African Gnosis, Philosophy, and the Order of Knowledge: An Introduction." *African Studies Review* 28 (2/3), 140–233.

———. (1986). "African Art as a Question Mark." *African Studies Review* 29 (1), 3–4.

———. (1988). *The Invention of Africa: Gnosis, Philosophy, and the Order of Knowledge.* Indianapolis: Indiana University Press.

———. (1991). *Parables and Fables: Exegesis, Textuality, and Politics in Central Africa.* Madison: University of Wisconsin Press.

———. (Ed.). (1992). *The Surreptitious Speech: Présence Africaine and the Politics of Otherness, 1947–1987.* Chicago: University of Chicago Press.

———. (1994). *The Idea of Africa.* Indianapolis: Indiana University Press.

Mullaney, Marie Marmo. (1983). *Revolutionary Women: Gender and the Socialist Revolutionary Role.* New York: Praeger.

Mullen, Bill V. (Ed.). (1995). *Revolutionary Tales: African American Women's Short Stories, from the Frist Story to the Present.* New York: Laurel.

——. (1999). *Popular Fronts: Chicago and African American Cultural Politics.* Urbana: University of Illinois Press.

——. (2001). "Breaking the Signifying Chain: A New Blueprint for African American Literary Studies." *Modern Fiction Studies* 47 (1), 145–163.

——. (2002). "Notes on Black Marxism." *Cultural Logic* 4 (2). Available online at: http://clogic.eserver.org/4-2/mullen.html [Accessed on 20 July, 2002].

——. (2003). "Du Bois, *Dark Princess*, and the Afro-Asian International." *Positions* 11 (1), 217–239.

——. (2004). *Afro-Orientalism.* Minneapolis: University of Minnesota Press.

Mullen, Bill V., and Ho, Fred. (Eds.). (2008). *Afro-Asia: Revolutionary Political and Cultural Connections Between African Americans and Aisan Americans.* Durham: Duke University Pres.

Mullen, Bill V., and Linkon, Sherry L. (Eds.). (1996). *Radial Revisions: Rereading 1930s Culture.* Urbana: University of Illinois Press.

Mullen, Bill V., and Smethurst, James. (Eds.). (2003). *Left of the Color-Line: Race, Radicalism, and Twentieth Century Literature of the United States.* Chapel Hill: University of North Carolina Press.

Munro, Martin. (2000). *Sharing and Reshaping the Caribbean: The Work of Aime Cesaire and Rene Depastre.* Leeds: Maney Publishers for the Modern Humanities Research Association.

——. (2004). "Can't Stand Up for Falling Down: Haiti, Its Revolutions, and Twentieth Century Negritude." *Research in African Literatures* 35 (2), 1–17.

Munslow, Barry (Ed.). (1986). *Africa: Problems on the Transition to Socialism.* London: Zed Books.

Murphy, Julien S. (Ed.). (1999). *Feminist Interpretations of Jean-Paul Sartre.* University Park, PA: Pennsylvania state University Press.

——. (2002). "Sartre on American Racism." In Julie K. Ward and Tommy L. Lott (Eds.), *Philosophers on Race: Critical Essays* (pp. 222–240). Malden, MA: Blackwell.

Murphy, Peter F. (Ed.). (2004). *Feminism and Masculinities.* New York: Oxford University Press.

Murray, Hugh. (1987). "Du Bois and the Cold War." *Journal of Ethnic Studies* 15 (3), 115–124.

Nagl-Docekal, Herta. (1998). "Modern Moral and Political Philosophy." In Alison M. Jaggar and Iris Marion Young (Eds.), *A Companion to Feminist Philosophy* (pp. 58–65). Malden, MA: Blackwell.

Naison, Mark. (1983). *Communists in Harlem During the Depression.* Urbana: University of Illinois Press.

Namasaka, Boaz Nalika. (1971). "William E. B. Du Bois and ThorsteinVeblen: Intellectual Activists of Progressivism, A Comparative Study, 1900–1930." Ph.D. dissertation, Claremont Graduate School and University Center, Claremont, CA.

Ndongo, Donato. (2007). *Shadows of Your Black Memory.* New York: Swan Isle Press.

Ndubuisi, F.N. (2005). *Reflections on Epistemology and Scientific Orientations in African Philosophy.* Lagos, Nigeria: Foresight Press.

Neal, Larry. (1989). *Visions of a Liberated Future: Black Arts Movements Writings.* New York: Thunder's Mouth Press.

Neal, Mark Anthony. (2005). *New Black Man.* New York: Routledge.

Neal, Terry Ray. (1984). "W. E. B. Du Bois's Contributions to the Sociology of Education." Ph.D. dissertation, University of Cincinnati.

Nealon, Jeffrey T., and Irr, Caren. (Eds.). (2002). *Rethinking the Frankfurt School: Alternative Legacies of Cultural Critique.* Albany, NY: State University of New York Press.

Nelson, Cary, and Grossberg, Lawrence. (Eds.). (1988). *Marxism and the Interpretation of Culture.* Chicago: University of Illinois Press.

Nelson, William, Jr. (Ed.). (2001). *Black Studies: From the Pyramids to Pan-Africanism and Beyond.* New York: McGraw-Hill.

Nelson, Truman. (1958). "W. E. B. Du Bois: Prophet in Limbo." *Nation* (January 25), 76–79.

———. (1970). "W. E. B. Du Bois as a Prophet." In John Henrik Clarke, Esther Jackson, Ernest Kaiser, and J.H. O'Dell (Eds.), *Black Titan: W. E. B. Du Bois* (pp. 138–151). Boston: Beacon.

Nesbitt, Francis Njubi. (2004). *Race for Sanctions: African Americans Against Apartheid, 1946–1994.* Bloomington: Indiana University Press.

Nesbitt, Nick. (2000). "Antinomies of Double-Consciousness in Aime Cesaire's *Cahier d'un retour au pays natal." Mosaic: A Journal for the Interdisciplinary Study of Literature* 33 (3), 107–129.

*New Left Review.* (1978). *Western Marxism: A Critical Reader.* London: Verso.

Newman, Louise M. (1999). *White Women's Rights: The Racial Origins of Feminism in the United States.* New York: Oxford University Press.

Newsome, Elaine Mitchell. (1971). "W. E. B. Du Bois's 'Figure in the Carpet': A Cyclical Pattern in the Belletristic Prose." Ph.D. dissertation, University of North Carolina, Chapel Hill.

Neyland, James. (1992). *W. E. B. Du Bois.* Los Angeles, CA: Melrose Square Publishing.

Nicholson, Linda J. (Ed.). (1990). *Feminism/Postmodernism.* New York: Routledge.

Nielsen, Aldon L. (1995). "Reading James Reading." In Selwyn Cudjoe and William E. Cain (Eds.), *C. L. R. James: His Intellectual Legacies* (pp. 348–358). Amherst: University of Massachusetts Press.

———. (1997). *C. L. R. James: A Critical Introduction.* Jackson: University of Mississippi Press.

Nightingale, Andrea W. (2004). *Spectacles of Truth in Classical Greek Philosophy: Theoria in Its Cultural Context.* Cambridge: Cambridge University Press.

Nikopoulos, Konstantina H. (2003). "W. E. B. Du Bois, Martin Luther King, Jr., and the FBI's Historic Abuse of the Civil Rights of Two Leaders of the Civil Rights Movement." M.A. thesis, University of Houston, Clear Lake.

Ngúgí wa Thiong'o. (1972). *Homecoming: Essays on African and Caribbean Literature, Culture, and Politics.* New York: Lawrence Hill.

———. (1983). *Barrel of a Pen: Resistance to Repression in Neocolonial Kenya.* Trenton, NJ: Africa World Press.

———. (1986). *Decolonizing the Mind: The Politics of Language in African Literature.* Portsmouth, NH: James Currey/ Heinemann.

———. (1993). *Moving the Center: The Struggle for Cultural Freedoms.* Portsmouth, NH: James Currey/Heinemann.

———. (1997). *Writers in Politics: A Re-Engagement with Issues of Literature and Society.* Portsmouth, NH: James Currey/EAEP/Heinemann.

Nkrumah, Kwame. (1961). *I Speak of Freedom: A Statement of African Ideology.* London: Heinemann.

———. (1962). *Towards Colonial Freedom.* London: Panaf Books.

———. (1964). *Consciencism: Philosophy and Ideology for Decolonization.* New York: Monthly Review Press.

———. (1965). *Neo-Colonialism: The Last Stage of Imperialism.* London: Panaf Books.

———. (1967a). *Challenge of the Congo.* New York: International.

———. (1967b). *Voice from Conarky.* London: Panaf Books.

———. (1968a). *The Handbook of Revolutionary Warfare.* New York: International.

———. (1968b). *The Big Lie.* London: Panaf Books.

———. (1968c). *The Spectre of Black Power.* London: Panaf Books.

———. (1968d). *Two Myths.* London: Panaf Books.

———. (1968e). *The Way Out: Statements to the People of Ghana.* London: Panaf Books.

———. (1969). *Axioms of Kwame Nkrumah.* London: Panaf Books.

———. (1970a). *Africa Must Unite.* New York: International.

———. (1970b). *Class Struggle in Africa.* New York: International.

———. (1973a). *Revolutionary Path.* London: Panaf Books.

——. (1973b). *The Struggle Continues*. London: Panaf Books.

——. (1973c). *Ghana: The Autobiography of Kwame Nkrumah*. London: Panaf Books.

——. (1976). *The Rhodesia File*. London: Panaf Books.

——. (1990). *Kwame Nkrumah: The Conakry Years, His Life and Letters*. London: Panaf Books.

——. (1997). *Kwame Nkrumah: Selected Speeches*. Accra, Ghana: Afram Publications.

Nnaemeka, Obioma. (Ed.). (1998). *Sisterhood, Feminisms, and Power: From Africa to the Diaspora*. Trenton, NJ: Africa World Press.

Noble, Jeanne. (1978). *Beautiful, Also, Are the Souls of My Black Sisters: A History of the Black Woman in America*. Englewood Cliffs, NJ: Prentice-Hall.

Nolen, Claude H. (1967). *The Negro's Image in the South: The Anatomy of White Supremacy*. Lexington, KY: University of Kentucky Press.

Nonini, Donald. (1992). "Du Bois and Radical Theory and Practice." *Critique of Anthropology* 12 (3), 292–318.

Norment, Nathaniel, Jr. (2007a). *An Introduction to African American Studies: The Discipline and Its Dimensions*. Durham, NC: Carolina Academic Press.

——. (Ed.). (2007b). *The African American Studies Reader*. Durham, NC: Carolina Academic Press.

Nove, Alec. (1986). *Marxism and "Really Existing Socialism."* New York: Harwood Academic Publishing.

Novick, Michael. (1995). *White Lies, White Power: The Fight Against White Supremacy and Reactionary Violence*. Monroe, ME: Common Courage Press.

Nuckolls, Charles W. (1996). *The Cultural Dialectics of Knowledge and Desire*. Madison: University of Wisconsin Press.

Nwankwo, Henry C. (1989). "The Educational Philosophy of W. E. B. Du Bois: A Nigerian Interpretation." Ph.D. dissertation, East Texas State University.

Nwigwe, Boniface E. (2004). *Emergent and Contentious Issues in African Philosophy: The Debated Revisited*. Port Harcourt, Nigeria: University Port Harcourt Press.

Nwoko, Matthew I. (1985). *The Rationality of African Socialism*. Roma: Nwoko.

Nye, Andrea. (1988). *Feminist Theory and the Philosophies of Man*. New York: Croom Helm.

Nyerere, Julius Kambarage. (1966). *Freedom and Unity/Uhura na Umoja: A Selection From Writings and Speeches, 1952–1965*. New York: Oxford University Press.

——. (1968). *Freedom and Socialism/Uhuru na Ujamaa: A Selection from Writings and Speeches, 1965–1967*. New York: Oxford University Press.

——. (1969). *Nyerere on Socialism*. New York: Oxford University Press.

——. (1970). *Ujamaa: Essays on African Socialism*. New York: Oxford University Press.

——. (1973). *Freedom and Development/Uhuru na Maendeleo: A Selection from Writings and Speeches, 1968–1973*. New York: Oxford University Press.

——. (1974). *Man and Development/Binadamu na Maendeleo*. New York: Oxford University Press.

——. (1977). *The Arusha Declaration Ten Years After*. Dar es Salaam, Tanzania: Government Printing Press.

——. (1978). *Crusade for Liberation*. New York: Oxford University Press.

——. (2004). *Nyerere on Education: Selected Essays and Speeches, 1954–1998*. Dar es Salaam, Tanzania: HakiElimu.

Nzegwu, Nkiru. (2006). *Family Matters: Feminist Concepts in African Philosophy of Culture*. Albany, NY: State University of New York Press.

Oatts, Terry O'Neal. (2003). "W. E. B. Du Bois and Critical Race Theory: Toward a Du Boisian Philosophy of Education." Ed.D. dissertation, Georgia Southern University.

——. (2006). *W. E. B. Du Bois and Critical Race Theory: Toward a Du Boisian Philosophy of Education*. Sydney: Exceptional Publications.

Obenga, Theophile. (1990). *Origine Commune de L'Egyptien Ancien, Du Copte et des Langues Negro-Africaines Modernes: Introduction a la Linguistique Historique Africaine.* Paris: LHarmattan.

———. (1992). *Ancient Egypt and Black Africa: A Handbook for the Study of Ancient Egypt in Philosophy, Linguistics and Gender Relations* (Amon Saba Saakana, Ed.). London: Karnak House.

———. (1993). *La Philosophie Africaine de la Periode Pharaonique, 2780–330 Avant Notre Ere.* Paris: L'Harmattan.

———. (1995). *A Lost Tradition: African Philosophy in World History.* Philadelphia, PA: Source Editions.

———. (1996). *Icons of Maat.* Philadelphia, PA: Source Editions.

———. (2004). *African Philosophy: The Pharaonic Period, 2780–330 B.C.* Popenguine, Senegal: Per Ankh Publishing.

O'Dell, Jack H. (1970). "Du Bois and 'The Social Evolution of the Black South'." In John Henrik Clarke, Esther Jackson, Ernest Kaiser, and J.H. O'Dell (Eds.), *Black Titan: W. E. B. Du Bois* (pp. 152–163). Boston: Beacon.

Ofari, Earl. (1970). "W. E. B. Du Bois and Black Power." *Black World* 19 (August), 26–28.

Ofuatey-Kudjoe, W. (Ed.). (1986). *Pan-Africanism: New Directions in Strategy.* Lanham, MD: University of America Press.

Ogbar, Jeffrey O.G. (2004). *Black Power: Radical Politics and African American Identity.* Baltimore: Johns Hopkins University Press.

Ogunmodede, Francis I. (2001). *Of History and Historiography in African Philosophy.* Ibadan, Nigeria: Hope Publications.

———. (Ed.). (2004). *African Philosophy Down the Ages: 10,000 B.C. to the Present.* Ibadan, Nigeria: Hope Publications.

Okere, Theophilus. (1971). "Can There Be an African Philosophy?: A Heremeneutical Investigation with Special Reference to Igbo Culture." Ph.D. dissertation, Louvain University.

———. (1991). *African Philosophy: A Historico-Hermeneutical Investigation of the Conditions of Its Possibility.* Lanham, MD: University of America Press.

———. (2005). *Philosophy, Culture, and Society in Africa: Essays.* Nsukka, Nigeria: Afro-Orbis Publications.

Okin, Susan Moller. (1992). *Women in Western Political Thought.* Princeton, NJ: Princeton University Press.

Okolo, Chukwudum B. (1985). *Philosophy and Nigerian Politics.* Urowulu, Obosi, Nigeria: Pacific College Press.

———. (1987). *What Is African Philosophy?: A Short Introduction.* Enugu, Nigeria: Freemans Press.

———. (1990a). *Okolo on African Philosophy and African Theology: Silver Jubilee Essays.* Engugu, Nigeria: CECTA.

———. (1990b). *Problems of African Philsophy and One other Essay.* Engugu, Nigeria: CECTA.

———. (1993a). *African Philosophy: A Short Introduction.* Enugu, Nigeria: CECTA.

———. (1993b). *African Social and Political Philosophy: Selected Essays.* Nsukka, Nigeria: Fulladu Publishing.

———. (1993c). *What Is It to Be African?: An Essay on African Identity.* Enugu, Nigeria: CECTA.

———. (1994a). *The African Synod: Hope for the Continent's Liberation.* Eldoret, Kenya: AMECEA Gaba Publications.

———. (1994b). *Squandermania Mentality: Reflections on Nigerian Culture: Educational Philosophy for Nigerians.* Nsukka, Nigeria: University of Nigeria Press.

———. (1996). *The African Condition: Any Way Out?* Enugu, Nigeria: Laurel Nigeria Enterprise.

Okolo, Okondo. (1991). "Tradition and Destiny: Horizons of an African Philosophical Hermeneutics." In Tsenay Serequeberhan (Ed.), *African Philosophy: The Essential Readings* (pp. 201–211). New York: Paragon House.

Okoro, Martin Umachi. (1982). "W. E. B. Du Bois's Ideas on Education: Implications for Nigerian Education." Ph.D. dissertation, Loyola University of Chicago.

Okrah, K. Asafo-Agyei. (2003). *Nyansapo (The Wisdom Knot): Toward an African Philosophy of Education*. New York: Routledge.

Oladipo, Olusegun. (1992). *The Idea of African Philosophy*. Ibadan, Nigeria: Molecular Publishers.

——. (1996). *Philosophy and the African Experience: The Contributions of Kwasi Wiredu*. Ibadan, Nigeria: Hope Publications.

——. (1998a). *The Idea of African Philosophy: A Critical Study of the Major Orientations in Contemporary African Philosophy*. Ibadan, Nigeria: Hope Publications.

——. (Ed.). (1998b). *Remaking Africa: Challenges of the Twenty-First Century*. Ibadan, Nigeria: Hope Publications.

——. (Ed.). (2002). *The Third Way in African Philosophy: Essays in Honor of Kwasi Wiredu*. Ibadan, Nigeria: Hope Publications.

——. (2004). *Philosophy and the African Protest: Selected Essays*. Idadan, Nigeria: Hope Publications.

——. (Ed.). (2006). *Core Issues in African Philosophy*. Ibadan, Nigeria: Hope Publication.

Olaniyan, Tejumola. (1992). "Narrativing Postcoloniality: Responsibilities." *Public Culture* 5 (1), 47–55.

——. (1995). *Scars of Conquest/Masks of Resistance: The Invention of Cultural Identity in African, African American, and Caribbean Drama*. New York: Oxford University Press.

——. (2000). "Africa: Varied Colonial Legacies." In Henry Schwarz and Sangeeta Ray (Eds.), *A Companion to Postcolonial Studies* (pp. 269–281). Malden, MA: Blackwell.

O'Leary, Brendan. (1989). *The Asiatic Mode of Production: Despotism, Historical Materialism and Indian History*. New York: Blackwell.

Oliver, Kelly, and Pearsall, Marilyn. (Eds.). (1998). *Feminist Interpretations of Friedrich Nietzsche*. University Park, PA: Penn State University Press.

Omi, Michael, and Winant, Howard. (1994). *Racial Formation in United States: From the 1960s to the 1990s*. New York: Routledge.

O'Neill, John. (Ed.). (1976). *On Critical Theory*. New York: Seabury Press.

Onwuanibe, Richard C. (1983). *A Critique of Revolutionary Humanism: Frantz Fanon*. St. Louis: Warren H. Green.

Onyewuenyi, Innocent C. (1993). *The African Origin of Greek Philosophy: An Exercise in Afrocentricism*. Nsukka, Nigeria: University of Nigeria Press.

Oruka, H. Odera. (1990a). *Trends in Contemporary African Philosophy*. Nairobi, Kenya: Shirikon.

——. (Ed.). (1990b). *Sage Philosophy: Indigenous Thinkers and Modern Debate on African Philosophy*. New York: E.J. Brill.

Osei-Nyame, Kwadwo. (1998). "Love and Nation: Fanon's African Revolution and Ayi Kwei Armah's *The Beautyful Ones Are Not Yet Born*." *Journal of Commonwealth Literature* 33 (2), 97–107.

——. (1999). "Ngugi wa Thiongo'o's *Matigari* and the Politics of Decolonization." *ARIEL: A Review of International English Literature* 30, 3:127–140.

——. (2002). "On Revolutionary Humanism: The Existentialist Legacy of Frantz Fanon." *New Formations: A Journal of Culture/Theory/Politics* 47, 27–31.

Otite, Olewu. (Ed.). (1978). *Themes in African Social and Political Thought*. London: Forth Dimension Publishers.

Ottaway, David. (1986). *Afro-Communism*. New York: Africana Publishing Company.

Outlaw, Lucius T., Jr. (1974). "Language and Consciousness: Foundations for a Hermeneutics of Black Culture." *Cultural Hermeneutics* 1, 403–413.

———. (1983a). "Philosophy, Hermeneutics, Social-Political Theory: Critical Thought in the Interest of African American." In Leonard Harris (Ed.), *Philosophy Born of Struggle: An Anthology of Afro-American Philosophy from 1917* (pp. 60–88). Dubuque, IA: Kendall/Hunt.

———. (1983b). "Race and Class in the Theory and Practice of Emancipatory Social Transformation." In Leonard Harris (Ed.), *Philosophy Born of Struggle: An Anthology of Afro-American Philosophy from 1917* (pp. 117–129). Dubuque, IA: Kendall/Hunt.

———. (1983c). "Philosophy and Culture: Critical Hermeneutics and Social Transformation." In *Philosophy and Cultures: Proceedings of the 2nd Afro-Asian Philosophy Conference* (pp. 26–31). Nairobi, Kenya: Bookwise Limited.

———. (1983d). "Critical Theory in a Period of Radical Transformation." *Praxis International* 3 (2), 138–46.

———. (1987)."On Race and Class, or, On the Prospects of 'Rainbow Socialism'." In Marable, Manning, Mike Davis, Fred Pfeil, and Michael Sprinker, (Eds.), *The Year Left 2: Toward a Rainbow Socialism—Essays on Race, Ethnicity, Class and Gender* (pp. 73–90). London: Verso.

———. (1990). "Toward a Critical Theory of 'Race'." In David Theo Goldberg (Ed.), *Anatomy of Racism* (pp. 58–82). Minneapolis: University of Minnesota Press.

———. (1992). "The Thought of W. E. B. Du Bois." *African Philosophy* 4 (1), 13–28.

———. (1995). "On W. E. B. Du Bois's 'The Conservation of Races'." In Linda A. Bell and David Blumenfeld (Eds.), *Overcoming Racism and Sexism* (pp. 79–102). Lanham, MD: Rowman and Littlefield.

———. (1996a). *On Race and Philosophy.* New York: Routledge.

———. (1996b). "'Conserve' Races?: In Defense of W. E. B. Du Bois." In Bernard W. Bell, Emily R. Grosholz, and James B. Stewart (Eds.), *W. E. B. Du Bois: On Race and Culture* (pp. 15–38). New York: Routledge.

———. (1997a). "African, African American, Africana Philosophy." In John P. Pittman (Ed.), *African American Perspectives and Philosophical Traditions* (pp. 63–93). New York: Routledge.

———. (1997b). "Is There a Distinctive African American Philosophy?" *Academic Questions* 10 (2), 29–46.

———. (1998). "Lucius T. Outlaw, Jr.: An Interview." In George Yancy (Ed.), *African American Philosophers: 17 Conversations* (pp. 307–327). New York: Routledge.

———. (2000). "W. E. B. Du Bois on the Study of Social Problems." *Annals of the American Academy of Political and Social Science* 568, 281–297.

———. (2001). "On Cornel West on W. E. B. Du Bois." In George Yancy (Ed.), *Cornel West: A Critical Reader* (pp. 261–279). Malden, MA: Blackwell.

———. (2005). *Critical Social Theory in the Interests of Black Folk.* Lanham, MD: Rowman and Littlefield.

Owomoyela, Oyekan. (1996). *African Difference: Discourses on Africanity and the Relativity of Cultures.* New York: Peter Lang.

Padmore, George. (1931). *The Life and Struggles of Negro Toilers.* London: R.I.L.U. Magazine.

———. (1936). *How Britain Rules Africa.* London: Wishart Books.

———. (1942). *The White Man's Duty: An Analysis of the Colonial Question in Light of the Atlantic Charter.* London: W.H. Allen.

———. (1945). *The Voice of Colored Labor.* Manchester: Panaf.

———. (1946). *How Russia Transformed Her Colonial Empire: A Challenge to the Imperialist Powers.* London: Dennis Dobson.

———. (1949). *Africa: Britain's Third Empire.* London: Dennis Dobson.

———. (1953). *The Gold Coast Revolution: The Struggle of an African People from Slavery to Freedom.* London: Dennis Dobson.

———. (1956). *Pan-Africanism or Communism?: The Coming Struggle for Africa.* London: Dennis Dobson.

———. (1972). *Africa and World Peace*. London: Cass.

Painter, Nell Irvin. (1993). "Sojourner Truth." In Darlene Clark Hine, Elsa Barkley Brown, and Rosalyn Teborg-Penn (Eds.), *Black Women in America: An Historical Encyclopedia* (Volume 2, pp. 1172–1176). Brooklyn: Carlson.

———. (1996). *Sojourner Truth: A Life, A Symbol*. New York: Norton.

Pallister, Janis L. (1991). *Aime Cesaire*. New York: Twayne Publishers.

Palmer, Colin A. (1976). *Slaves of the White God: Blacks in Mexico, 1570–1650*. Cambridge, MA: Harvard University Press.

———. (1981). *Human Cargoes: The British Slave Trade to Spainish America, 1700–1739*. Urbana: University of Illinois Press.

———. (1994). *The First Passage: Blacks in the Americas, 1502–1617*. New York: Oxford University Press.

———. (1996). *The Worlds of Unfree Labor: From Undentured Servitude to Slavery*. Mona, Jamaica: University of West Indies Press.

———. (1998). *Passageways: An Interpretive History of Black America*. Fort Worth, TX: Harcourt Brace College Publishers.

———. (2006). *Eric Williams and the Making of the Modern Caribbean*. Chapel Hill, NC: University of North Carolina Press.

Palmer, Colin A., and Knight, Franklin W. (Eds.). (1989). *The Modern Caribbean*. Chapel Hill, NC: University of North Carolina.

Parascandola, Louis J. (Ed.). (2005). *Look For Me All Around You: Anglophone Caribbean Immigrants in the Harlem Renaissance*. Detroit: Wayne State University.

Parker, Laurence, Deyhle, Donna, and Villenas, Sofia. (Eds.). (1999). *Race Is—Race Isn't: Critical Race Theory and Qualitative Studies in Education*. Boulder, CO: Westview.

Parkinson, G.H.R. (Ed.). (1970). *Georg Lukacs: The Man, His Work, and His Ideas*. New York: Random House.

Parry, Benita. (1987). "Problems in Current Theories of Colonial Discourse." *Oxford Literary Review* 9 (1), 2–12.

———. (2004). *Postcolonial Studies: A Materialist Critique*. New York: Routledge.

Paschal, Andrew G. (1971). "The Spirit of W. E. B. Du Bois." *Black Scholar* 20, 38–50.

Pateman, Carole. (1988). *The Sexual Contract*. Stanford: Stanford University Press.

———. (1989). *The Disorder of Women: Democracy, Feminism, and Political Theory*. Stanford: Stanford University Press.

Pauley, Garth E. (2000). "W. E. B. Du Bois on Woman Suffrage: A Critical Analysis of His Crisis Writings." *Journal of Black Studies* 30 (3), 383–410.

Payne, Charles M., and Green, Adam. (Eds.). (2003). *Time Longer Than Rope: A Century of African American Activism, 1850–1950*. New York: New York University Press.

Paynter, Robert. (1992). "W. E. B. Du Bois and the Material World of African Americans in Great Barrington, Massachusetts." *Critique of Anthropology* 12 (3), 277–291.

Pearsall, Marilyn. (Ed.). (1986). *Women and Values: Readings in Recent Feminist Philosophy*. Belmont, CA: Wadsworth.

Peebles-Wilkins, Wilma, and Aracelis, Fran. (1990). "Two Outstanding Women in Social Welfare History: Mary Church Terrell and Ida B. Wells." *Affilia* 5, 87–95.

Peeks, Edward. (1971). *The Long Struggle for Black Power*. New York: Scribner.

Peller, Gary. (1995). "Race-Consciousness." In Kimberle Crenshaw, Neil Gotanda, Gary Peller, and Kendall Thomas (Eds.), *Critical Race Theory: The Key Writings That Formed the Movement* (pp. 127–158). New York: New Press.

Pensky, Max. (Ed.). (2005). *Globalizing Critical Theory*. Lanham, MD: Rowman and Littlefield.

Perkins, Linda M. (1981). "Black Women and Racial 'Uplift' Prior to Emancipation." In Filomina Chioma Steady (Ed.), *The Black Woman Cross-Culturally* (pp. 314–317). Cambridge: Schenkman.

———. (1997). "Women's Clubs." In William L. Andrews, Frances Smith Foster, and Trudier Harris (Eds.), *The Oxford Companion to African American Literature* (pp. 787–788). New York: Oxford University Press.

Perry, Matt. (2002). *Marxism and History.* New York: Palgrave.

Persram, Nalini. (Ed.). (2007). *Postcolonialism and Political Theory* (pp. 121–141). Lanham, MD: Lexington Books.

Peters, Erskine. (1982). *Developing the Inner: Meditations Based Upon African Wisdom.* Oakland, CA: Warren Press.

Peters, Michael, Olssen, Mark, and Lankshear, Colin. (Eds.). (2003). *Futures of Critical Theory: Dreams of Difference.* Lanham, MD: Rowman and Littlefield.

Peters, Michael, Lankshear, Colin, and Olssen, Mark. (Eds.). (2003). *Critical Theory and the Human Condition.* New York: Peter Lang,

Peterson, Charles F. (2000). "Du Bois, Fanon, and Cabral and the Margins of Colonized Elite Leadership." Ph.D. dissertation, Binghamton University.

———. (2007). *Du Bois, Fanon, Cabral: The Margins of Elite Anti-Colonial Leadership.* Lanham, MD: Lexington Books.

Peterson, Dale. (1994). "Notes from the Underworld: Dostoyevsky, Du Bois and the Discovery of Ethnic Soul." *Massachusetts Review* 35, 225–247.

Phillips. Layli. (Ed.). (2006). *The Womanist Reader.* New York: Routledge.

Phillips, L.W. (1995). "W. E. B. Du Bois and Soviet Communism: *The Black Flame* as Social Realism." *South Atlantic Quarterly* 94 (3), 837–863.

Pieterse, Jan Nederveen. (1992). *White on Black: Images of Africa and Blacks in Western Popular Culture.* New Haven, CT: Yale University Press.

Pinkney, Alphonso. (1976). *Red, Black, and Green: Black Nationalism in the United States.* Cambridge: Cambridge University Press.

Pinn, Anthony B. (Ed.). (2001). *By These Hands: A Documentary History of African American Humanism.* New York: New York University.

Pitcaithley, Dwight T. (2003). *Memory in Black and White: Race, Commemoration, and the Post-Bellum Landscape.* Landham, MD: AltaMira.

Pithouse, Richard. (2003). " 'That the Tool Never Possess the Man': Taking Fanon's Humanism Seriously." *Politikon: South African Journal of Political Studies* 30 (2), 107–131.

Pittman, John P. (Ed.). (1992–1993). "African American Perspectives and Philosophical Traditions." (Special Triple Issue). *The Philosophical Forum* 24, 1–3.

———. (Ed.). (1997). *African American Perspectives and Philosophical Traditions.* New York: Routledge.

Pobi-Asamani, Kwadwo O. (1993). *W. E. B. Du Bois: An Exploration of His Contributions to Pan-Africanism.* San Bernardino, CA: Borgo Press.

Poddar, Prem, and Johnson, David. (Eds.). (2005). *A Historical Companion to Postcolonial Thought in English.* New York: Columbia University.

Poe, Daryl Zizwe. (2003). *Kwame Nkrumah's Contributions to Pan-Africanism: An Afrocentric Analysis.* New York: Routledge.

Pohlman, Marcus. (2003). *African American Political Thought* (6 Volumes). New York: Routledge.

Pollard, Alton B. (1993). "The Last Great Battle of the West: W. E. B. Du Bois and the Struggle for African America's Soul." In Gerald Early (Ed.), *Lure and Loathing: Essays on Race, Identity, and the Ambivalence of Assimilation* (pp. 41–54). New York: Viking/Penguin.

Popeau, Jean Baptiste. (2003). *Dialogues of Negritude: An Analysis of the Cultural Context of Black Writing.* Durham, NC: Carolina Academic Press.

Porter, David. (Ed.). (1992). *Between Men and Feminism.* New York: Routledge.

Posnock, Ross. (1995). "The Distinction of Du Bois: Aesthetics, Pragmatism, Politics." *American Literary History* 7 (3), 500–524.

———. (1997). "How Does it Feel to Be a Problem?: Du Bois, Fanon, and the 'Impossible Life' of the Black Intellectual." *Critical Inquiry* 23 (2), 323–349.

———. (1998). *Color and Culture: Black Writers and the Making of the Modern Intellectual*. Cambridge: Harvard University Press.

Praeg, Leonhard. (2000). *African Philosophy and the Quest for Autonomy: A Philosophical Investigation*. Amsterdam: Rodopi.

Prakash, Gyan. (Ed.). (1995). *After Colonialism: Imperial Histories and Postcolonial Displacements*. Princeton, NJ: Princeton University Press.

Prashad, Vijay. (2000). *The Karma of Brown Folk*. Minneapolis: University of Minnesota.

———. (2001). *Everybody Was Kung Fu Fighting: Afro-Asian Connections and the Myth of Cultural Purity*. Boston: Beacon Press.

Pulido, Laura. (2006). *Black, Brown, Yellow, and Left: Radical Activism in Los Angeles*. Berkeley: University of California Press.

Pulitano, Elvira. (2003). *Toward a Native American Critical Theory*. Lincoln: University of Nebraska Press.

Puri, Shalini. (2004). *The Caribbean Postcolonial: Social Equality, Post-Nationalism, and Cultural Hybridity*. New York: Palgrave Macmillan.

Pyne-Timothy, Helen. (1995). "Identity, Society, and Meaning: A Study of the Early Stories of C. L. R. James." In Selwyn Cudjoe and William E. Cain (Eds.), *C. L. R. James: His Intellectual Legacies* (pp. 51–60). Amherst: University of Massachusetts Press.

Quainoo, Vanessa Wynder. (1993). "*The Souls of Black Folk*: In Consideration of W. E. B. Du Bois and the Exigency of an African American Philosophy of Rhetoric." Ph.D. dissertation, University of Massachusetts.

Quayson, Ato. (2000a). *Postcolonialism: Theory, Practice or Process?* Malden: Polity.

———. (2000b). "Postcolonialism and Postmodernism." In Henry Schwarz and Sangeeta Ray (Eds.), *A Companion to Postcolonial Studies* (pp. 87–111). Malden: Blackwell.

Quaynor, Thoma Addo. (1966). The Politicization of Negritude. Ph.D. dissertation, Southern Illinois University.

Rabaka, Reiland. (2002). "Malcolm X and/as Critical Theory: Philosophy, Radical Politics, and the African American Search for Social Justice." *Journal of Black Studies* 33 (2), 145–165.

———. (2003a). "W. E. B. Du Bois's Evolving Africana Philosophy of Education." *Journal of Black Studies* 33 (4), 399–449.

———. (2003b). "W. E. B. Du Bois and 'The Damnation of Women': An Essay on Africana Anti-Sexist Critical Social Theory." *Journal of African American Studies* 7 (2), 39–62.

———. (2003c). "'Deliberately Using the Word *Colonial* in a Much Broader Sense': W. E. B. Du Bois's Concept of 'Semi-Colonialism' as Critique of and Contribution to Postcolonialism." *Jouvert: A Journal of Postcolonial Studies* 7, (2), 1–32. Available online at: http://social.chass.ncsu.edu/jouvert/index.htm [Accessed on 23 February 2003].

———. (2003d). "W. E. B. Du Bois and/as Africana Critical Theory: Pan-Africanism, Critical Marxism, and Male-Feminism." In James L. Conyers (Ed.), *Afrocentricity and the Academy* (pp. 67–112). Jefferson, NC: McFarland & Co.

———. (2004). "The Souls of Black Female Folk: W. E. B. Du Bois and Africana Anti-Sexist Critical Social Theory." *Africalogical Perspectives* 1 (2), 100–141.

———. (2005a). W. E. B. Du Bois and Decolonization: Pan-Africanism, Postcolonialism, and Radical Politics. In James L. Conyers (Ed.), *W. E. B. Du Bois, Marcus Garvey, and Pan-Africanism* (pp. 123–154). Lewistown, NY: Mellen Press.

———. (2005b). "W. E. B. Du Bois's Theory of the Talented Tenth." In Molefi K. Asante and Ama Mazama (Eds.), *The Encyclopedia of Black Studies* (pp. 443–445). Thousand Oaks, CA: Sage.

———. (2005c). "Booker T. Washington's Philosophy of Accommodationism." In Molefi K. Asante and Ama Mazama (Eds.), *The Encyclopedia of Black Studies* (pp. 1–3). Thousand Oaks, CA: Sage.

———. (2005d). "African Worldview." In Molefi K. Asante and Ama Mazama (Eds.), *The Encyclopedia of Black Studies* (pp. 56–57). Thousand Oaks, CA: Sage.

———. (2006a). "Africana Critical Theory of Contemporary Society: Ruminations on Radical Politics, Social Theory, and Africana Philosophy." In Molefi K. Asante and Maulana Karenga (Eds.), *The Handbook of Black Studies* (pp. 130–152). Thousand Oaks, CA: Sage.

———. (2006b). "The Souls of Black Radical Folk: W. E. B. Du Bois, Critical Social Theory, and the State of Africana Studies." *Journal of Black Studies* 36 (5), 732–763.

———. (2006c). "W. E. B. Du Bois's "The Comet" and Contributions to Critical Race Theory: An Essay on Black Radical Politics and Anti-Racist Social Ethics." *Ethnic Studies Review: Journal of the National Association of Ethnic Studies* 29 (1), 34–57.

———. (2006d). "The Souls of White Folk: W. E. B. Du Bois's Critique of White Supremacy and Contributions to Critical White Studies (Part I)." *Ethnic Studies Review: Journal of the National Association for Ethnic Studies* 29 (2), 1–19.

———. (2007a). *W. E. B. Du Bois and the Problems of the Twenty-First Century: An Essay on Africana Critical Theory.* Lanham, MD: Lexington Books.

———. (2007b). "The Souls of White Folk: W. E. B. Du Bois's Critique of White Supremacy and Contributions to Critical White Studies (Part II)." *Journal of African American Studies* 11 (1), 1–15.

———. (2008a). *Du Bois's Dialectics: Black Radical Politics and the Reconstruction of Critical Social Theory.* Lanham, MD: Lexington Books.

———. (2008b). "Malcolm X and Africana Critical Theory: Rethinking Revolutionary Black Nationalism, Black Radicalism, and Black Marxism." In James L. Conyers and Andrew P. Smallwood (Eds.), *Malcolm X: A Historical Reader* (pp. 281–298). Durham, NC: Carolina Academic Press.

———. (2008c). "The Prophet of Problems: W. E. B. Du Bois, Philosophy of Religion, Sociology of Religion, and Black Liberation Theology—A Critical Review of Edward J. Blum's *W. E. B. Du Bois: American Prophet.*" *Journal of Southern Religion.*

———. (2008d). "Critical Reparations Theory: W. E. B. Du Bois, Black Radicalism, Revolutionary Humanism, and Critical Racce Theory." *Africana Studies Annual Review* 2 (1).

Rabbitt, Kara M. (1995). "C. L. R. James's Figuring of Toussaint Le'Ouverture: *The Black Jacobins* and the Literary Hero." In Selwyn Cudjoe and William E. Cain (Eds.), *C. L. R. James: His Intellectual Legacies* (pp. 118–135). Amherst: University of Massachusetts Press.

Rajan, Rajeswari. (1993). *Real and Imagined Women: Gender, Culture and Postcolonialism.* New York: Routledge.

Rajan, Gita, and Mohanran, Radhika. (Eds.). (1995). *Postcolonial Discourse and Changing Cultural Context: Theory and Criticism.* Westport, CT: Greenwood.

Ramesh, Kotti S. (2006). *Claude McKay: The Literary Identity from Jamaica to Harlem and Beyond.* Jefferson, NC: McFarland.

Ramose, Mogobe B. (1999). *African Philosophy Through Ubuntu.* Harare, Zimbabwe: Mond Books.

Rampersad, Arnold. (1989). "Slavery and the Literary Imagination: Du Bois's *The Souls of Black Folk.*" In Deborah E. McDowell and Arnold Rampersad (Eds.), *Slavery and the Literary Imagination: Selected Papers from the English Institute, 1987.* Baltimore: Johns Hopkins University Press.

———. (1990). *The Art and Imagination of W. E. B. Du Bois.* New York: Schocken.

———. (1996a). "Du Bois's Passage to India—*Dark Princess.*" In Bernard W. Bell, Emily R. Grosholz, and James B. Stewart (Eds.), *W. E. B. Du Bois: On Race and Culture* (pp. 161–176). New York: Routledge.

———. (1996b). "W. E. B. Du Bois, Race, and the Making of American Studies." In Bernard W. Bell, Emily R. Grosholz, and James B. Stewart (Eds.), *W. E. B. Du Bois: On Race and Culture* (pp. 289–305). New York: Routledge.

Randolph, A. Philip, and Owen, Chandler. (1971). "Du Bois Fails as a Theorist." In August Meier, Elliott Rudwick, and Francis L. Broderick (Eds.), *Black Protest Thought in the Twentieth Century* (pp. 91–94). New York: MacMillan.

Randolph, A. Philip, and Owen, Chandler. (1973). "Du Bois on Revolution: A Reply." In Theodore G. Vincent (Ed.), *Voices of a Black Nation: Political Journalism in the Harlem Renaissance* (pp. 88–92). Trenton, NJ: Africa World Press.

Ranuga, Thomas K. (1996). *New South Africa and the Socialist Vision: Positions and Perspectives Toward a Post-Apartheid Society.* Atlantic Highlands, NJ: Humanities Press.

Rasmussen, David M. (Ed.). (1996). *The Handbook of Critical Theory.* Malden, MA: Blackwell.

Rasmussen, David M., and Swindal, James. (Eds.). (2004). *Critical Theory* (4 Volumes). Thousand Oaks, CA: Sage.

Rath, Richard Cullen. (1997). "Echo and Narcissus: The Afrocentric Pragmatism of W. E. B. Du Bois." *Journal of American History* 84 (2), 461–495.

Rattansi, Ali. (1997). "Postcolonialism and Its Discontents." *Economy and Society* 26 (4), 480–500.

Rawls, Anne Warfield. (2000). "'Race' as an Interaction Order Phenomenon: W. E. B. Du Bois's 'Double-Consciousness' Thesis Revisited." *Sociological Theory* 18 (2), 241–274.

Rawls, John. (1971). *A Theory of Justice.* Cambridge: Harvard University Press.

———. (1997). "Justice as Fairness." In Robert E. Goodin and Philip Pettit (Eds.), *Contemporary Political Philosophy: An Anthology* (pp. 187–202). Cambridge: Blackwell.

Ray, Larry J. (1993). *Rethinking Critical Theory: Emancipation in the Age of Global Social Movements.* Thousand Oaks, CA: Sage.

———. (1999). *Theorizing Classical Sociology.* Philadelphia, PA: Open University Press.

Razanajao, C., Postel, J., and Allen, D.F. (1996). "The Life and Psychiatric Work of Frantz Fanon." *History of Psychiatry* 7 (28), 499–524.

Recht, J.J. (1971). "From W. E. B. Du Bois to Marcus Garvey: Shadows and Lights." *Revue Francaise d'Etudes Politiques Africaines* 62, 40–59.

Redding, J. Saunders. (1949). "Portrait of W. E. B. Du Bois." *American Scholar* 18, 93–96.

———. (1970). "*The Souls of Black Folk*: Du Bois's Masterpiece Lives On." In John Henrik Clarke, Esther Jackson, Ernest Kaiser, and J.H. O'Dell (Eds.), *Black Titan: W. E. B. Du Bois* (pp. 47–51). Boston: Beacon.

———. (1979). "The Correspondence of W. E. B. Du Bois: A Review Article." *Phylon* 40, 119–122.

Reed, Adolph L., Jr. (1975). "The Political Philosophy of Pan-Africanism: A Study of the Writings of Du Bois, Garvey, Nkrumah, and Padmore and Their Legacy." M.A. thesis, Atlanta University, Atlanta, GA.

———. (1985). "W. E. B. Du Bois: A Perspective on the Bases of His Political Thought." *Political Theory* 13, 431–456.

———. (1986). "Pan-Africanism as Black Liberation: Du Bois and Garvey." In W. Ofuatey-Kudjoe (Ed.), *Pan-Africanism: New Directions in Strategy.* Lanham, MD: University of America Press.

———. (1992). "Du Bois's 'Double-Consciousness': Race and Gender in Progressive Era American Thought." *Studies in American Political Development* 6, 132–137.

———. (1997). *W. E. B. Du Bois and American Political Thought: Fabianism and the Color Line.* New York: Oxford University Press.

———. (2000). "The Case Against Reparations." *Progressive* 64, 15–17.

Reiss, Edward. (1997). *Marx: A Clear Guide.* London: Pluto Press.

Reiss, Timothy J. (2002). *Against Autonomy: Global Dialectics of Cultural Exchange.* Palo Alto: Stanford University Press.

Renton, Dave. (2007). *C. L. R. James: Cricket's Philosopher King.* London: Haus Books.

Rescher, Nicholas. (1977). *Dialectics: A Controversy-Oriented Approach to the Theory of Knowledge.* Albany, NY: State University of New York Press.

——. (2006). *Philosophical Dialectics: An Essay on Metaphilosophy.* Albany, NY: State University of New York Press.

Rhoads, John K. (1991). *Critical Issues in Social Theory.* University Park, PA: Pennsylvania State University.

Richards, Glen. (1995). "C. L. R. James on Black Self-Determination in the United States and the Caribbean." In Selwyn Cudjoe and William E. Cain (Eds.), *C. L. R. James: His Intellectual Legacies* (pp. 317–327). Amherst: University of Massachusetts Press.

Richards, Paul. (1970). "W. E. B. Du Bois and American Social History: Evolution of a Marxist." *Radical America* 5, 43–87.

Riggs, Marcia Y. (1994). *Awake, Arise, and Act: A Womanist Call for Black Liberation.* Cleveland, OH: Pilgrim Press.

Rigsby, Gregory. (1968). Negritude: A Critical Analysis. Ph.D. dissertation, Howard University.

Roberts, Marie M., and Mizuta, Tamae. (Eds.). (1993). *The Reformers: Socialist Feminism.* New York: Routledge.

Roberts, Neil. (2004). "Fanon, Sartre, Violence, and Freedom." *Sartre Studies International* 10 (2), 139–160.

Robinson, Armstead, Foster, Craig C., and Ogilvie, Donald L. (Eds.). (1969). *Black Studies in the University: A Symposium.* New York: Bantam.

Robinson, Cedric J. (1977). "A Critique of W. E. B. Du Bois's *Black Reconstruction.*" *Black Scholar* 8 (7), 44–50.

——. (1990). "Du Bois and Black Sovereignty: The Case of Liberia." *Race & Class* 32 (2), 39–50.

——. (1993). "The Appropriation of Frantz Fanon." *Race & Class* 35 (1), 79–91.

——. (1994). "W. E. B. Du Bois and Black Sovereignty." In Sidney Lemelle and Robin D.G. Kelley (Eds.), *Imagining Home: Class, Culture, and Nationalism in the African Diaspora* (pp. 145–158). New York: Verso.

——. (1995). "C. L. R. James and the World-System." In Selwyn Cudjoe and William E. Cain (Eds.), *C. L. R. James: His Intellectual Legacies* (pp. 244–259). Amherst: University of Massachusetts Press.

——. (1997). *Black Movements in America.* New York: Routledge.

——. (2000). *Black Marxism: The Making of the Black Radical Tradition.* Chapel Hill: University of North Carolina.

——. (2001). *An Anthropology of Marxism.* Aldershot, UK: Ashgate.

Rockmore, Tom. (Eds.). (1988). *Lukacs Today: Essays in Marxist Philosophy.* Boston: Kluwer Academic Publishers.

——. (1992). *Irrationalism: Lukacs and the Marxist View of Reason.* Philadelphia: Temple University Press.

Roche de Coppens, Peter. (1976). *Ideal Man in Classical Sociology: The Views of Comte, Durkheim, Pareto, and Weber.* University Park, PA: Pennsylvania State University Press.

Roderick, Rick. (1995). "C. L. R. James: Further Adventures of the Dialectic." In Selwyn Cudjoe and William E. Cain (Eds.), *C. L. R. James: His Intellectual Legacies* (pp. 205–214). Amherst: University of Massachusetts Press.

Rodgers-Rose, La Frances. (Ed.). (1980). *The Black Woman.* Beverly Hills: Sage.

Rodney, Walter. (1963). "The Role of the Historian in the Developing West Indies." *The Social Scientist* (December 18), 13–14, 16.

——. (1965). "Portuguese attempts at monopoly on the Upper Guinea Coast." *Journal of African History* 6 (3), 307–322.

——. (1966). "A History of the Upper Guinea Coast, 1545–1800." Ph.D. dissertation, University of London.

——. (1967). *West Africa and the Atlantic Slave-Trade*. Nairobi: East African Publishing House.

——. (1970). *A History of the Upper Guinea Coast, 1545–1800*. New York and London: Monthly Press Review.

——. (1972). *How Europe Underdeveloped Africa*. Washington, D.C.: Howard University Press.

——. (1976). "Guyana's Socialism." *Race & Class* 18 (2), 109–128.

——. (1981). *Marx in the Liberation of Africa*. Georgetown, Guyana: People's Progressive Party Press.

——. (1990). *Walter Rodney Speaks*. Trenton, NJ: Africa World Press.

Roediger, David R. (1994). *Towards the Abolition of Whiteness: Essays on Race, Politics, and Working Class History*. New York: Verso.

——. (1999). *The Wages of Whiteness: Race and the Making of the American Working Class*. New York: Verso.

Rogers, Ben F. (1955). "W. E. B. Du Bois, Marcus Garvey, and Pan-Africa." *Journal of Negro History* 40, 154–165.

Rojas, Fabio. (2007). *From Black Power to Black Studies: How a Radical Social Movement Became an Academic Discipline*. Baltimore: Johns Hopkins University Press.

Romero, Patricia W. (1976). "W. E. B. Du Bois, Pan-Africanists, and Africa, 1963–1973." *Journal of Black Studies* 6 (4), 321–336.

Rooks, Noliwe M. (2006). *White Money/Black Power: The Surprising History of African American Studies and the Crisis of Race in Higher Education*. Boston: Beacon Press.

Rorty, Richard. (1979). *Philosophy and the Mirror of Nature*. Princeton: Princeton University Press.

——. (1982). *Consequences of Pragmatism: Essays, 1972–1980*. Minneapolis: University of Minnesota Press.

——. (1998). *Achieving Our Country: Leftist Thought in Twentieth Century America*. Cambridge, MA: Harvard University Press.

——. (1999). *Philosophy and Social Hope*. New York: Penguin.

——. (2007). *Philosophy as Cultural Politics*. Cambridge: Cambridge University Press.

Rosenberg, Jonathan. (2000). "The Global Editor: Du Bois and *The Crisis*." *The New Crisis* 107 (4), 15.

Rosengarten, Frank. (2008). *Urbane Revolutionary: C. L. R. James and the Struggle for a New Society*. Jackson: University Press of Mississippi.

Ross, Andrew. (1996). "Civilization in One Country?: The American James." In Grant Farred (Ed.), *Rethinking C. L. R. James* (pp. 75–84). Cambridge, MA: Blackwell.

Ross, R. (Ed.). (1982). *Racism and Colonialism*. Leyden: Martinus Nijhoff.

Roth, Benita. (2003). *Separate Roads to Feminism: Black, Chicana and White Feminist Movements in America's Second Wave*. New York: Cambridge University Press.

Rothberg, Robert, and Mazrui, Ali. (Eds.). (1970). *Protest and Power in Black Africa*. New York: Oxford University Press.

Rowbotham, Sheila. (1973). *Woman's Consciousness, Man's World*. Harmondsworth: Penguin.

——. (1979). *Beyond the Fragments: Feminism and the Making of Socialism*. London: Merlin.

Royster, Jacqueline Jones. (1997). *Southern Horrors and Other Writings: The Anti-Lynching Campaign of Ida B. Wells, 1892–1930*. Boston: Bedford.

Ruch, E.A. (1984). *African Philosophy: An Introduction to Main Philosophical Trends in Contemporary Africa*. Rome: Catholic Book Agency.

Rucker, Walter. (2002). "'A Negro Nation Within the Nation': W. E. B. Du Bois and the Creation of a Revolutionary Pan-Africanist Tradition, 1903–1947." *Black Scholar* 32 (3/4), 37–46.

Ruddick, Sara. (1999). "Maternal Thinking as a Feminist Standpoint." In Janet A. Kourany, James P. Sterba, and Rosemarie Tong (Eds.), *Feminist Philosophies: Problems, Theories, and Applications* (2nd Edition, pp. 404–414). Englewood, NJ: Prentice Hall.

Rudwick, Elliot M. (1956). "W. E. B. Du Bois: A Study in Minority Group Leadership." Ph.D. dissertation, University of Pennsylvania.

——. (1957a). "The Niagara Movement." *Journal of Negro History* 42, 177–200.

——. (1957b). "The National Negro Committee Conference of 1909." *Phylon* 18 (4), 413–419.

——. (1957c). "W. E. B. Du Bois and the Atlanta University Studies on the Negro." *Journal of Negro Education* 26 (4), 466–476.

——. (1958a). "W. E. B. Du Bois: In the Role of *Crisis* Editor." *Journal of Negro History* 18, 214–240.

——. (1958b). "Du Bois's Last Year as *Crisis* Editor." *Journal of Negro Education* 27 (4), 426–433.

——. (1959a). "Du Bois versus Garvey: Race Propagandists at War." *Journal of Negro Education* 28, 421–429.

——. (1959b). "W. E. B. Du Bois and the Universal Races Congress of 1911." *Phylon* 20 (4), 372–378.

——. (1960a). *W. E. B. Du Bois: A Study in Minority Group Leadership.* Philadelphia: University of Pennsylvania.

——. (1960b). "Booker T. Washington's Relations with the National Association for the Advancement of Colored People." *Journal of Negro Education* 29 (2), 134–144.

——. (1968). *W. E. B. Du Bois: Propagandists of the Negro Protest.* New York: Antheneum.

——. (1969). "Notes on a Forgotten Black Sociologists: W. E. B. Du Bois and the Sociological Profession." *American Sociologist* 4 (4), 303–336.

——. (1974). "W. E. B. Du Bois as Sociologists." In James E. Blackwell and Morris Janowitz (Eds.), *Black Sociologists: Historical and Contemporary Perspectives.* (pp. 25–55). Chicago: University of Chicago Press.

——. (1982a). *W. E. B. Du Bois: Voice of the Black Movement.* Urbana: University of Illinois Press.

——. (1982b). "W. E. B. Du Bois: Protagonist of the Afro-American Protest." In John Hope Franklin and August Meier (Eds.), *Black Leaders of the Twentieth Century* (pp. 63–84). Chicago: University of Illinois Press.

Rush, Fred. (Ed.). (2004). *The Cambridge Companion to Critical Theory.* Cambridge: Cambridge University Press.

Sabbagh, Suha. (1982). "Going Against the West from Within: The Emergence of the West as an Other in Frantz Fanon's Work." Ph.D. dissertation, University of Wisconsin.

Sadar, Ziauddin. (1998). *Postmodernism and the Other: The New Imperialism of Western Culture.* London: Pluto Press.

Said, Edward W. (1979). *Orientalism.* New York: Vintage.

——. (1989). "Representing the Colonized: Anthropology's Interlocutors." *Critical Inquiry* 15 (2), 205–227.

——. (1993). *Culture and Imperialism.* New York: Knopf.

——. (1994). *Representations of the Intellectual.* New York: Vintage.

——. (1999). "Traveling Theory Reconsidered." In Nigel C. Gibson (Ed.), *Rethinking Fanon* (pp. 197–214). Amherst, NY: Humanity Books.

——. (2000). "Traveling Theory." In Moustafa Bayoumi and Andrew Rubin (Eds.), *The Edward Said Reader* (pp. 195–217). New York: Vintage.

——. (2001). *Power, Politics, and Culture: Interviews with Edward W. Said.* New York: Pantheon.

——. (2003). *Culture and Resistance: Conversations with Edward Said.* Cambridge, MA: South End Press.

——. (2004). *Humanism and Democratic Criticism.* New York: Columbia University Press.

Saldivar, Jose D. (1991). *The Dialectics of Our America: Genealogy, Cultural Critique, and Literary History.* Durham: Duke University Press.

Saldivar, Ramon. (1990). *Chicano Narrative: The Dialectics of Difference.* Madison: University of Wisconsin Press.

Sadar, Ziauddin. (1998). *Postmodernism and the Other: The New Imperialism of Western Culture.* London: Pluto Press.

Sales, Brian P. (1993). "The Dialectical Political Philosophy of W. E. B. Du Bois: Nationalism, Liberalism, Pan-Africanism and Socialism." Ph.D. dissertation, Cornell University.

Samoiloff, Louise C. (1997). *C. L. R. James: Memories and Commentaries.* New York: Cornwall Books.

San Juan, E., Jr. (1988). *Ruptures, Schisms, Interventions: Cultural Revolution in the Third World.* Manila, Philippines: De La Salle University Press.

——. (1992). *Racial Formations/Critical Transformations.* Atlantic Highlands, NJ: Humanities Press.

——. (1998). *Beyond Postcolonial Studies.* Durham: Duke University Press.

——. (1999). ""Fanon: An Intervention into Cultural Studies." In Anthony C. Alessandrini (Ed.), *Frantz Fanon: Critical Perspectives* (pp. 126–146). New York: Routledge.

——. (2002). *Racism and Cultural Studies: Critiques of Multiculturalist Ideology and the Politics of Difference.* Durham: Duke University Press.

——. (2003). "Marxism and the Race/Class Problematic: A Re-Articulation." *Cultural Logic* 6. Avialable online at: http://clogic.eserver.org/2003/sanjuan.html [Accessed on 23 February 2003].

——. (2004). *Working Through Contradictions: From Cultural Theory to Critical Practice.* Lewisburg, PA: Bucknell University Press.

Sanchez, Lisa. (1991). "W. E. B. Du Bois: Clinical Sociologist." *Sociological Practice Association/ISA Working Group in Clinical Sociology.*

Sandoval, Chela. (2000). *Methodology of the Oppressed.* Minneapolis: University of Minnesota Press.

Sargent, Lydia. (Ed.). (1981). *Women and Revolution: A Discussion of the Unhappy Marriage of Marxism and Feminism.* Boston: South End.

Sartre, Jean-Paul. (1948). "Orphée Noir." In Leopold Senghor (Ed), *Anthology de la Nouvelle Poésie Nègre et Malgache de Langue Francaise* (pp. ix–xliv). Paris: Presses Universitaires de France.

——. (1963). *Search for a Method.* New York: Knopf.

——. (1965). *Anti-Semite and Jew.* New York: Schocken.

——. (1968). "Preface." In Frantz Fanon, *The Wretched of the Earth* (pp. 7–35). New York: Grove Press.

——. (1973). *Existentialism and Humanism.* London: Methuen.

——. (1974). *Between Existentialism and Marxism: Sartre on Philosophy, Politics, Psychology, and the Arts.* New York: Pantheon.

——. (1975). *The Writings of Jean-Paul Sartre* (2 Volumes; Michel Contat and Michel Rybalka, Eds.). Evanston, IL: Northwestern University Press.

——. (1976). *Critique of Dialectical Reason, Volume I: Theory of Ensembles* (Jonathan Ree, Ed.). London: Verso.

——. (1992). *Notebooks for an Ethics.* Chicago: University of Chicago Press.

——. (1995). *Colonialism and Neocolonialism* (Azzedine Haddour, Ed.). New York: Routledge.

——. (1997). "Return from the United States: What I Learned about the Black Problem." In Lewis R. Gordon (Ed.), *Existence in Black: An Anthology of Black Existential Philosophy* (pp. 81–91). New York: Routledge.

——. (2001). "Black Orpheus." In Robert Bernasconi (Ed.), *Race* (pp. 115–143). Malden, MA: Blackwell.

——. (2002). *Jean-Paul Sartre: Basic Writings* (Stephen Priest, Ed.). New York: Routledge.

——. (2005). *Conversations with Jean-Paul Sartre* (Perry Anderson, Ed.). New York: Seagull Books.

——. (2006). *Critique of Dialectical Reason, Volume II: Unfinished.* (Arlette Elkaïm- Sartre, Ed.). London: Verso.

——. (2007). *Existentialism Is a Humanism.* New Haven: Yale University Press.

Savage, Barbara Dianne. (2000). "W. E. B. Du Bois and 'The Negro Church'." *Annals of the American Academy of Political and Social Science* 568 (March), 253–249.

Sawer, Marian. (1977). *Marxism and the Question of the Asiatic Mode of Production.* The Hague: Nijhoff.

Schacht, Steven P., and Ewing, Doris W. (Eds.). (1998). *Feminism and Men: Reconstructing Gender Relations.* New York: New York University Press.

Schafer, Alex R. (2001). "W. E. B. Du Bois, German Social Thought, and the Racial Divide in American Progressivism, 1892–1909." *Journal of American History* 88 (3), 925–949.

Schall, John V. (1975). "Defining What Is African: Problems in African Political Philosophy." *Worldview* 18 (9), 6–13.

Scharfman, Ronnie Leah. (1987). *Engagements and the Language of the Subject in the Poetry of Aime Cesaire.* Gainesville: University of Florida Press.

Schechter, Patricia A. (2001). *Ida B. Wells-Barnett and American Reform, 1880–1930.* Chapel Hill, NC: University of North Carolina Press.

Schindler, Jeremiah Ronald. (1998). *The Frankfurt School Critique of Capitalist Culture: A Critical Theory for Post-Democratic Society and Its Re-Education.* Brookfield, VT: Ashgate.

Schloesser, Pauline E. (2002). *The Fair Sex: White Women and Racial Patriarchy in the Early American Republic.* New York: New York University Press.

Schneider, Paul Ryan. (1998). "Inventing the Public Intellectual: Ralph Waldo Emerson, W. E. B. Du Bois, and the Cultural Politics of Representing Men." Ph.D. dissertation, Duke University.

Scholz, Sally J. (1999). "Values and Language: Toward a Theory of Translation for Alain Locke." In Leonard Harris (Ed.), *The Critical Pragmatism of Alain Locke: A Reader on Value, Theory, Aesthetics, Community, Culture, Race, and Education* (pp. 39–52). Lanham, MD: Rowman and Littlefield.

Schor, Joel. (1977). *Henry Highland Garnet: A Voice of Black Radicalism in the Nineteenth Century.* Westport: Greenwood Press.

Schott, Robin. (Ed.). (1997). *Feminist Interpretations of Immanuel Kant.* University Park, PA: Penn State University Press.

Schrager, Cynthia D. (1996). "Both Sides of the Veil: Race, Science, and Mysticism in W. E. B. Du Bois." *American Quarterly* 48 (4), 551–619.

Schram, Stuart R. (1969). *Marxism and Asia: An Introduction with Readings.* London: Allen Lane.

Schrecker, Ellen. (1998). *Many Are the Crimes: McCarthyism in America.* Boston: Little Brown.

——. (2002). *The Age of McCarthyism: A Brief History with Documents.* Boston: Bedford/St. Martin's.

Schroyer, Trent. (1975). *The Critique of Domination: The Origins and Development of Critical Theory.* Boston: Beacon.

Schwarz, Henry and Ray, Sangeeta. (Eds.). (2000). *A Companion to Postcolonial Studies.* Malden, MA: Blackwell.

Scott, David. (2004). *Conscripts of Modernity: The Tragedy of Colonial Enlightenment.* Durham: Duke University Press.

Scott, Jacqueline, and Franklin, A. Todd. (Eds.). (2006). *Critical Affinities: Nietzsche and African American Thought.* Albany, NY: State University of New York.

Scriven, Darryl. (2007). *A Dealer of Old Clothes: Philosophical Conversations with David Walker.* Lanham, MD: Lexington Books.

Sedley, David. (Ed.). (2003). *The Cambridge Companion to Greek and Roman Philosophy.* Cambridge: Cambridge University Press.

Seidler, Victor J. (1991). *Recreating Sexual Politics: Men, Feminism, and Politics.* New York: Routledge.

Segal, Aaron. (1973). "Amilcar Cabral: In Memoriam." *Third World* 2 (4), 7–8.

Sekyi-Otu, Ato. (1975). "Form and Metaphor in Fanon's Critique of Racial and Colonial Domination." In Alkis Kontos (Ed.), *Domination* (pp. 133–161). Toronto: University of Toronto Press.

——. (1977). "Frantz Fanon's Critique of the Colonial Experience." Ph.D. dissertation, University of Toronto, Toronto.

——. (1989). "The African Context of the Battle of Azania: National Liberation as Social Revolution?" In Simeon W. Chilungu and Sada Niang (Eds.), *African Communities/ L'Héritage Africaine* (pp. 53–67). Toronto: Terebi.

——. (1996). *Fanon's Dialectic of Experience.* Cambridge: Harvard University Press.

——. (2003). "Fanon and the Possibility of Postcolonial Critical Imagination." Paper preared for and presented at the *Codesria Symposium on Canonical Works and Continuing Innovations in African Arts and Humanities,* University of Ghana, Legon, September 17–19, 2003 [Available online at: http://www.codesria.org/Links/conferences/accra/Sekyi_Otu.pdf (Accessed on 19 June 2005)].

Self, Peter. (1993). "Socialism." In Robert E. Goodin and Philip Pettit (Eds.), *A Companion to Contemporary Political Philosophy* (pp. 333–365). Malden, MA: Blackwell.

Sellen, Eric. (1967). "Aime Cesaire and the Legacy of Surrealism." *Kentucky Romance Quarterly,* Supplement 13, 71–79.

Senghor, Leopold Sedar. (1956). "The Spirit of Civilization, or the Laws of African Negro Culture." *Presence Africaine* 8–10, 51–67.

——. (1959). *African Socialism: A Report to the Constitutive Congress of the Party of African Federation.* New York: American Society of African Culture.

——. (1961). *Nation et Voie Africaine du Socialisme.* Paris: Presence Africaine.

——. (1962). *Negrohood and the African Road to Socialism.* Paris: Presence Africaine.

——. (1964a). *On African Socialism.* New York: Praeger.

——. (1964b). *Liberte* (5 Volumes). Paris: Editions du Seuil.

——. (1964c). *Selected Poems.* New York: Antheneum.

——. (1964d). "Latinity and Negritude." *Presence Africaine* 24 (52), 9–22.

——. (1965). *Prose and Poetry* (John Reed and Clive Wake, Eds.). New York: Oxford University Press.

——. (1966). *The Mission of the Poet.* Port of Spain, Trinidad: University of the West Indies Press.

——. (1968). *Los Racismos Politicos.* Barcelona: Editorial Nova Terra.

——. (1970). *Theorie et Pratique du Socialisme Senegalais.* Dakar, Senegal: G.I.A. Publications.

——. (1971). *The Foundations of "Africanité" or "Negritude" and "Arabite."* Paris: Presence Africaine.

——. (1991). *Leopold Sedar Senghor: The Collected Poetry* (Melvin Dixon, Trans.) Charlottesville: University Press of Virginia.

——. (1995a). "On Negrohood: Psychology of the African Negro." In Albert Mosley (Ed.), *African Philosophy: Selected Readings* (pp. 116–127). Englewood Cliffs, NJ: Prentice Hall.

——. (1995b). "Negritude: A Humanism of the Twentieth Century." In Fred Lee Hord and Jonathan Scott Lee (Eds.), *I Am Because We Are: Readings in Black Philosophy* (pp. 45–54). Amherst: University of Massachusetts Press.

———. (1996). "On African Homelands and Nation-States, Negritude, Assimilation, and African Socialism." In Parker English and Kibujjo M. Kalumba (Eds.), *African Philosophy: A Classical Approach* (pp. 40–56). Upper Saddle River, NJ: Prentice Hall.

———. (1998). "Negritude and African Socialism." In Pieter H. Coetzee and Abraham P.J. Roux (Eds.), *The African Philosophy Reader* (pp. 438–448). New York: Routledge.

———. (1999). *Listen to Africa: A Call from L.S. Senghor.* Pretoria: University of South Africa Press.

Serequeberhan, Tsenay. (1988). "The Possibility of African Freedom: A Philosophical Exploration." Ph.D. dissertation, Boston College.

———. (1990). "Karl Marx and African Emancipatory Thought: A Critique of Marx's Euro-Centric Metaphysics." *Praxis International* 10 (1/2), 161–181.

———. (Ed.). (1991). *African Philosophy: The Essential Readings.* New York: Paragon House.

———. (1994). *The Hermeneutics of African Philosophy: Horizon and Discourse.* New York: Routledge.

———. (1996). "Fanon and the Contemporary Discourse of African Philosophy." In Lewis R. Gordon, Tracey D. Sharpley-Whiting, and Renée T. White (Eds.), *Fanon: A Critical Reader* (pp. 244–254). Malden, MA: Blackwell.

———. (1997). "The Critique of Eurocentrism and the Practice of African Philosophy." In Emmanuel C. Eze (Ed.), *(Post)Colonial African Philosophy: A Critical Reader* (pp. 141–161). Malden, MA: Blackwell.

———. (1998). "Africanity at the End of the Twentieth Century," *African Philosophy* 11 (1), 13–21.

———. (2000). *Our Heritage: The Past in the Present of African American and African Existence.* Lanham, MD: Rowman and Littlefield.

———. (2003). "The African Anti-Colonial Struggle: An Effort at Reclaiming History." *Philosophia Africana* 6 (1), 47–58.

———. (2006). "Amilcar Cabral and the Practice of Theory." In John Fobanjong and Thomas Ranuga (Eds.), *The Life, Thought and Legacy of Cape Verde's Freedom Fighter Amilcar Cabral (1924–1973: Essays on His Liberation Philosophy.* (pp. 17–38). Lewiston, NY: Mellen Press.

———. (2007). *Contested Memory: The Icon of the Occidental Tradition.* Trenton, NJ: Africa World Press.

Service, Robert. (1999). *The Russian Revolution, 1900–1927.* New York: St. Martin's Press.

———. (2007). *Comrades!: A History of World Communism.* Cambridge: Harvard University Press.

Seshadri-Crooks, Kalpana. (2002). "I Am a Master: Terrorism, Masculinity, and Political Violence in Frantz Fanon." *Parallax* 8 (2), 84–98.

Sevitch, Benjamin. (2002). "W. E. B. Du Bois and Jews: A Lifetime of Opposing Anti-Semitism." *Journal of African American History* 87, 323–338.

Shafai, Fariborz. (1996). *The Ontology of George Lukacs: Studies in Materialist Dialectics.* Aldershot: Avebury.

Shapiro, Herbert. (1988). *White Violence and Black Response: From Reconstruction to Montgomery.* Amherst: University of Massachusetts Press.

Shapiro, Norman R. (Ed.). (1970). *Negritude: Black Poetry from Africa and the Caribbean.* New York: October House.

Sharpley-Whiting, T. Denean. (1996). "Anti-Black Femininity and Mixed-Race Identity: Engaging Fanon to Reread Capécia." In Lewis R. Gordon, Tracey D. Sharpley-Whiting, and Renée T. White (Eds.), *Fanon: A Critical Reader* (pp. 155–162). Malden, MA: Blackwell.

———. (1997). *Frantz Fanon: Conflicts and Feminisms.* Lanham, MD: Rowman and Littlefield.

———. (1999). "Fanon and Capécia." In Anthony C. Alessandrini (Ed.), *Frantz Fanon: Critical Perspectives* (pp. 57–74). New York: Routledge.

———. (2002). *Negritude Women*. Minneapolis: University of Minnesota Press.

Shaw, Stephanie J. (1991). "Black Club Women and the Creation of the National Association of Colored Women." *Journal of Women's History* 3 (2), 1–25.

Shaw, Timothy M. (1985). *Towards a Political Economy for Africa: The Dialectics of Dependence*. London: Macmillan.

Shawki, Ahmed. (2006). *Black Liberation and Socialism*. Chicago: Haymarket Books.

Shelby, Tommie. (2005). *We Who Are Dark: The Philosophical Foundations of Black Solidarity*. Cambridge, MA: Harvard University Press.

Shelton, Austin J. (1964). "The Black Mystique: Reactionary Extremes in 'Negritude'." *African Affairs* 63 (251), 115–28.

———. (Ed.). (1968). *The African Assertion: A Critical Anthology of African Literature*. New York: Odyssey Press.

Shiach, Morag. (Ed.). (1999). *Feminism and Cultural Studies*. New York: Oxford University Press.

Shohat, Ella. (1993). "Notes on the 'Post-Colonial'." *Social Text* 10 (31/32), 99–113.

———. (Ed.). (1998). *Talking Visions: Multicultural Feminism in Transnational Age*. Cambridge, MA: MIT Press.

Shohat, Ella, and Stam, Robert. (1994). *Unthinking Eurocentrism: Multiculturalism and the Media*. New York: Routledge.

Shuford, John. (2001). "Four Du Boisian Contributions to Critical Race Theory." *Transactions of the Charles S. Peirce Society* 37 (3), 301–337.

Shumaker, Wayne. (1964). *Elements of Critical Theory*. Berkeley: University of California Press.

Shusterman, Richard. (2002). *Surface and Depth: Dialectics of Criticism and Culture*. Ithaca: Cornell University Press.

Shutte, Augustine. (1995). *Philosophy for Africa*. Milwaukee, WI: Marquette University Press.

———. (1998). "African and European Philosophizings: Senghor's Civilization of the Universal'." In Pieter H. Coetzee and Abraham P.J. Roux (Eds.), *The African Philosophy Reader* (pp. 428–437). New York: Routledge.

Shuttlesworth-Davidson, Carolyn Elizabeth. (1980). Literary Collectives of the New Negro Renaissance and the Negritude Movement. Ph.D. dissertation, University of Michigan.

Sica, Alan. (Ed.). (1998). *What Is Social Theory?: The Philosophical Debates*. Malden, MA: Blackwell.

Siemerling, Winfried. (2001). "W. E. B. Du Bois, Hegel, and the Staging of Alterity." *Callaloo* 24, (1), 325–333.

Simon, Erica. (1963). "Negritude and Cultural Problems of Contemporary Africa." *Presence Africaine* 19 (47), 122–146.

Simpson, Lorenzo C. (2003). "Critical Theory, Aesthetics, and Black Modernity." In Tommy L. Lott and John P. Pitman (Eds.), *A Companion to African American Philosophy* (pp. 386–398). Malden, MA: Blackwell Publishers.

Singer, Peter. (Ed.). (1993). *A Companion to Ethics*. Malden: Blackwell.

Sinha, Manisha, and Von Eschen, Penny. (Eds.). (2007). *Contested Democracy: Freedom, Race, and Power in America History*. New York: Columbia University Press.

Singh, Amritjit, and Schimdt, Peter. (Eds.). (2000). *Postcolonial Theory and the United States: Race, Ethnicity and Literature*. Jackson: University Press of Mississippi.

Singh, Nikhil P. (2004). *Black Is a Country: Race and the Unfinished Struggle for Democracy*. Cambridge: Havard Univerity Press.

Singham, A.W. (1970). "C. L. R. James on the Black Jacobin Revolution in San Domingo—Notes Toward a Theory of Black Politics." *Savacou* 1 (1), 82–96.

Sivanandan, Ambalavaner. (1990). *Communities of Resistance: Writings on Black Struggles for Socialism*. New York: Verso.

Slater, Phillip. (1977). *Origin and Significance of the Frankfurt School*. London: Routledge.

Slaughter, Jane, and Kern, Robert. (Eds.). (1981). *European Women on the Left: Socialism, Feminism, and the Problems Faced by Political Women, 1880 to the Present.* Westport, CT: Greenwood.

Sloan, Ella Faye. (2003). "W. E. B. Du Bois's 'Talented Tenth': A Pioneering Conception of Transformational Leadership." Ed.D. dissertation, University of San Diego.

Smedley, Audrey. (2007). *Race in North America: Origin and Evolution of a Worldview.* Boulder, CO: Westview Press.

Smethurst, James Edward. (1999). *The New Red Negro: The Literary Left and African American Poetry, 1930–1946.* New York: Oxford University Press.

Smith, Andrea. (2005). *Conquest: Sexual Violence and American Indian Genocide.* Boston: South End.

Smith, Barbara. (Ed.). (1983). *Home Girls: A Black Feminist Anthology.* New York: Kitchen Table Press.

——. (1998). *The Truth That Never Hurts: Writings on Race, Gender, and Freedom.* New Brunswick, NJ: Rutgers University Press.

Smith, Linda Tuhiwai. (1999). *Decolonizing Methodologies: Research and Indigenous Peoples.* Dunedin: University of Otago Press.

Smith, Tony. (1993). *Dialectical Social Theory and Its Critics: From Hegel to Analytical Marxism and Postmodernism.* Albany, NY: State University of New York Press.

Smith, Valerie. (1987). *Self-Discovery and Authority in Afro-American Narrative.* Cambridge: Harvard University Press.

——. (Ed.). (1997). *Representing Blackness: Issues in Film and Video.* New Brunswick, NJ: Rutgers University Press.

——. (1998). *Not Just Race, Not Just Gender: Black Feminist Readings.* New York: Routledge.

Snedeker, George. (2004). *The Politics of Critical Theory.* Lanham, MD: University Press of America.

Snyder, Emile. (1963). "The Problem of Negritude in Modern French Poetry." *Comparative Literature Studies* 1, 101–113.

Sodipo, J.O. (2004). *Philosophy and the African Prospect: Selected Essays.* Ibadan, Nigeria: Hope Publications.

Sogolo, Godwin. (1993). *Foundations of African Philosophy: A Definitive Analysis of Conceptual Issues in African Thought.* Ibadan, Nigeria: Ibadan University Press.

——. (1998a). "The Concept of Cause in African Thought." In Pieter H. Coetzee and Abraham P.J. Roux (Eds.), *The African Philosophy Reader* (pp. 177–185). New York: Routledge.

——. (1998b). "Logic and Rationality." In Pieter H. Coetzee and Abraham P.J. Roux (Eds.), *The African Philosophy Reader* (pp. 217–233). New York: Routledge.

Solomon, Esther A. (1976). *Indian Dialectics: Methods of Philosophical Discussion.* Ahmedabad: B.J. Institute of Learning and Research.

Solomos, John. (1988). *Black Youth, Racism, and the State: The Politics of Ideology and Policy.* Cambridge: Cambridge University Press.

——. (1995). *Race, Politics, and Social Change.* London: Routledge.

——. (1996). *Racism and Society.* New York: St. Martin's Press.

Solomos, John, and Les Back. (Eds.). (2000). *Theories of Race and Racism: A Reader.* London: Routledge.

Solomos, John, and Murji, Karim. (Eds.). (2005). *Racialization: Studies in Theory and Practice.* Oxford: Oxford University Press.

Solomos, John, and Jenkins, Richard. (Eds.). (1987). *Racism and Equal Opportunity Policies in the 1980s.* Canbridge: Cambridge University Press.

Solow, Barbara L., and Engerman, Stanley L. (Eds.). (1987). *British Capitalism and Caribbean Slavery: The Legacy of Eric E. Williams.* Cambridge: Cambridge University Press.

Soyinka, Wole. (1976). *Myth, Literature, and the African World*. Cambridge: Cambridge University Press.

———. (1990). "The African World and the Ethnocultural Debate." In Molefi K. Asante and Kariamu Welsh Asante (Eds.), *African Culture: The Rhythms of Unity* (pp. 13–38). Westport, CT: Greenwood.

———. (1993). *Art, Dialogue, and Outrage: Essays on Literature and Culture*. New York: Pantheon.

Soto, Michael. (2006). "The Negritude Renaissance." *Twentieth Century Literature* 52 (1), 92–95.

Speck, Beatrice F. (1974). "W. E. B. Du Bois: A Historiographical Study." Ph.D. dissertation, Texas Christian University.

Spender, Dale. (Ed.). (1981). *Men's Studies Modified: The Impact of Feminism on the Academic Discipline*. New York: Pergamon Press.

Spleth, Janice S. (1985). *Leopold Sedar Senghor*. Boston: Twayne Publishers.

———. (Ed.). (1993). *Critical Perspectives on Leopold Sedar Senghor*. Washington, D.C.: Three Continents Press.

Springer, Kimberly. (Ed.). (1999). *Still Lifting, Still Climbing: Contemporary African American Women's Activism*. New York: New York University Press.

———. (2005). *Living for the Revolution: Black Feminist Organizations, 1968–1980*. Durham, NC: Duke University Press.

St. Louis, Brett. (2007). *Rethinking Race, Politics, and Poetics: C. L. R. James's Critique of Modernity*. New York: Routledge.

Staniland, Martin. (1968). *Frantz Fanon and the African Political Class*. Brighton: University of Sussex.

Stanley, Henry M. (1899). *Through the Dark Continent, or, The Sources of the Nile Around the Great Lakes of Equatorial Africa and Down the Livingstone River to the Atlantic Ocean*. Mineola, NY: Dover.

Stannard, David E. (1992). *American Holocaust: Columbus and the Conquest of the New World*. New York: Oxford University Press.

Steady, Filomina Chioma. (Ed.). (1981). *The Black Woman Cross-Culturally*. Cambridge: Schenkman.

———. (1987). "African Feminism: A Worldwide Perspective." In Rosalyn Terborg-Penn, Sharon Harley, and Andrea Benton Rushing (Eds.), *Women in Africa and the African Diaspora* (pp. 3–24). Washington, DC: Howard University Press.

Stein, Judith. (2001). "The Difficult Doctor Du Bois." *Reviews in American History* 29 (2), 247–254.

Stephan, Nancy Leys. (1982). *The Idea of Race in Science: Great Britain, 1800–1960*. New York: MacMillan.

———. (1990). "Race and Gender: The Role of Analogy in Science." In David Theo Goldberg (Ed.), *Anatomy of Racism* (pp. 38–57). Minneapolis: University of Minnesota Press.

Stephens, Ronald J. (2003). "Narrating Acts of Reisistance: Explorations of Untold Heroic and Horrific Battle Stories Surrounding Robert Franklin Williams' Residance in Lake County, Michigan." *Journal of Black Studies* 33 (5), 675–703.

———. (2004). "Garveryism in Idlewild, Michigan, 1927–1936." *Journal of Black Studies* 34 (4), 462–488.

Stephanson, Anders. (1996). *Manifest Destiny: American Expansion and the Empire of Right*. New York: Hill and Wang.

Stepto, Robert B. (1985). "The Quest of the Weary Traveler: W. E. B. Du Bois's *The Souls of Black Folk*." In William L. Andrews (Ed.), *Critical Essays on W. E. B. Du Bois* (pp. 139–172). Boston: G.K. Hall.

Sterba, James P. (Ed.). (1998). *Ethics*. Malden: Blackwell.

———. (Ed.). (1999). *Feminism and Its Critics.* Lanham: Rowman and Littlefield.

———. (Ed.). (2000). *Controversies in Feminism.* Lanham: Rowman and Littlefield.

Sterling, Dorothy. (1965). *Lift Every Voice: The Lives of Booker T. Washington, W. E. B. Du Bois, Mary Church Terrell, and James Weldon Johnson.* Garden City, NY: Doubleday.

———. (1979). *Black Foremothers: Three Lives.* Old Westbury, NY: Feminist Press.

———. (Ed.). (1984). *We Are Your Sisters: Black Women in the Nineteenth Century.* New York: Norton.

Stewart, James B. (1976). "Black Studies and Black People in the Future." *Black Books Bulletin* 4 (2), 20–25.

———. (1979). "Introducing Black Studies: A Critical Examination of Some Textual Materials." *Umoja* 3 (1), 5–17.

———. (1981). "Alternative Models of Black Studies." *Umoja* 5 (3), 17–39.

———. (1983). "The Psychic Duality of Afro-Americans in the Novels of W. E. B. Du Bois." *Phylon* 44 (2), 93–107.

———. (1984). "The Legacy of W. E. B. Du Bois for Contemporary Black Studies." *Journal of Negro Education* 53, 296–311.

———. (1992). "Reaching for Higher Ground: Toward an Understanding of Black/Africana Studies." *The Afrocentric Scholar* 1 (1), 1–63.

———. (1996a). "In Search of a Theory of Human History: W. E. B. Du Bois's Theory of Social and Cultural Dynamics." In Bernard W. Bell, Emily R. Grosholz, and James B. Stewart (Eds.), *W. E. B. Du Bois: On Race and Culture* (pp. 261–288). New York: Routledge.

———. (1996b). "Africana Studies: New Directions for the Twenty-First Century." *International Journal of Black Studies* 4 (1&2), 1–21.

———. (1999). "Deciphering the Thought of W. E. B. Du Bois: A Thematic Approach." In James L. Conyers (Ed.), *Black American Intellectualism and Culture: A Social Study of African American Social and Political Thought* (pp. 57–84). Stamford, CT: JAI Press.

———. (2004). *Flight: In Search of Vision.* Trenton, NJ: Africa World Press.

Stewart, James, Hare, Bruce, Young, Alfred, and Aldridge, Delores. (2003). "The State of Africana Studies." *International Journal of Africana Studies* 8 (1), 1–26.

Stewart, Maria W. (1987). *Maria W. Stewart, America's First Black Woman Political Writer: Essays and Speeches* (Marilyn Richardson, Ed.). Indianapolis: Indiana University Press.

Stewart-Cain, Karen LaVerne. (2003). "W. E. B. DuBois: The Neglected American Sociologist. A Study in Race-Biased Exclusion from the Academy." Ph.D. dissertation, Union Institute and University.

Stirk, Peter M.R. (1992). *Max Horkheimer: A New Interpretation.* Hemel Hempstead, UK: Harvester Wheatsheaf.

———. (2000). *Critical Theory, Politics, and Society.* London: Pinter Press.

Stoltenberg, John. (1993). *The End Manhood: A Book for Men of Conscience.* New York: Dutton.

Stuckey, Sterling. (1987). *Slave Culture: Nationalist Theory and the Foundations of Black America.* New York: Oxford University Press.

———. (1994). *Going Through the Storm: The Influence of African American Art in History.* New York: Oxford University Press.

Sullivan, Shannon. (2004). "Ethical Slippages, Shattered Horizons, and the Zebra Stripping of the Unconscious: Fanon on Social, Bodily, and Psychical Space." *Philosophy and Geography* 7 (1), 9–24.

Sullivan, Shannon, and Tuana, Nancy. (Eds.). (2007). *Race and Epistemologies of Ignorance.* Albany, NY: State University of New York Press.

Sumner, Claude. (1962). *Eight Types of Ethical Theory.* Addis Ababa, Ethiopia: Addis Ababa University Press.

———. (1970). *Sonata to the Universe.* Addis Ababa, Ethiopia: Addis Ababa University Press.

———. (1974). *Ethiopian Philosophy.* Addis Ababa, Ethiopia: Addis Ababa University Press.

——. (1985). *Classical Ethiopian Philosophy.* Addis Ababa, Ethiopia: Addis Ababa University Press.

——. (1986). *The Source of African Philosophy: The Ethiopian Philosophy of Man.* Stuttgart, Germany: F. Steiner Verlag Wiesbaden.

——. (1999). *Living Springs of Wisdom and Philosophy.* Addis Ababa, Ethiopia: Addis Ababa University Press.

Sumner, Claude, and Wolde, Samuel. (Eds). (2002). *Perspectives in African Philosophy: An Anthology on the Problematics of an African Philosophy.* Addis Ababa: Addis Ababa University Press.

Sumpter, Richard David. (1973). "A Critical Study of the Educational Thought of W. E. B. Du Bois." Ph.D. dissertation, Peabody College for Teacher of Vanderbilt University.

——. (2000). "W. E. B. Du Bois on Education: Its Socialistic Foundation." *Journal of Thought* 35 (1), 61–87.

——. (2001). "W. E. B. Du Bois: Reflections on Democracy." *Journal of Thought* 36 (2), 25–32.

Sundquist, Eric J. (Ed.). (1990). *Frederick Douglass: New Literary and Historical Essays.* New York: Cambridge University Press.

——. (1993). *To Wake the Nations: Race in the Making of American Literature.* Cambridge: Harvard University Press.

——. (1996). "W. E. B. Du Bois and the Autobiography of Race." In W. E. B. Du Bois, *The Oxford W. E. B. Du Bois Reader* (Eric Sundquist, Ed., pp. 3–36). New York: Oxford University Press.

Surber, Jere Paul. (1998). *Culture and Critique: An Introduction to the Critical Discourses of Cultural Studies.* Boulder, CO: Westview Press.

Syrotinski, Michael. (2007). *Deconstruction and the Postcolonial: At the Limits of Theory.* Liverpool: Liverpool University Press.

Tar, Zoltan. (1977). *The Frankfurt School: The Critical Theories of Max Horkheimer and Theodor W. Adorno.* New York: Wiley.

Tarver, Australia, and Barnes, Paula C. (Eds.). (2006). *New Voices on the Harlem Renaissance: Essays on Race, Gender, and Literary Discourse.* Madison, NJ: Fairleigh Dickinson University Press.

Taiwo, Olufemi. (1999a). "Cabral." In Robert L. Arrington (Ed.), *A Companion to the Philosophers* (pp. 5–12). Malden: Blackwell.

——. (1999b). "Fanon." In Robert L. Arrington (Ed.), *A Companion to the Philosophers* (pp. 13–19). Malden: Blackwell.

Taylor, Carl McDonald. (1971). "W. E. B. Du Bois: The Rhetoric of Redefinition." Ph.D. dissertation, University of Oregon.

Taylor, Carol M. (1981). "W. E. B. Du Bois's Challenge to Scientific Racism." *Journal of Black Studies* 11, 449–60.

Taylor, Paul C. (2000). "Appiah's Uncompleted Argument: W. E. B. Du Bois and the Reality of Race." *Social Theory and Practice* 26 (1), 103–128.

——. (2004). *Race: A Philosophical Introduction.* Malden, MA: Blackwell.

Taylor, Ula Y. (2002). *The Veiled Garvey: The Life and Times of Amy Jacques Garvey.* Chapel Hill, NC: University of North Carolina Press.

Tedla, Elleni. (1995). *Sankofa: African Thought and Education.* New York: Peter Lang.

Teffo, Lesiba J., and Abraham P.J. Roux. (1998). "Metaphysical Thinking in Africa." In Pieter H. Coetzee and Abraham P.J. Roux (Eds.), *The African Philosophy Reader* (pp. 134–148). New York: Routledge.

Temple, Christel N. (2005). *Literary Pan-Africanism: History, Contexts, and Criticism.* Durham, NC: Carolina Academic Press.

————. (Ed.). (2007). *Literary Spaces: Introduction to Comparative Black Literature*. Durham, NC: Carolina Academic Press.

Terborg-Penn, Rosalyn. (1998). *African American Women in the Struggle for the Vote, 1850–1920*. Bloomington: Indiana University Press.

Terborg-Penn, Rosalyn, Harley, Sharon, and Rushing, Andrea Benton. (Eds.). (1987). *Women in Africa and the African Diaspora*. Washington, D.C.: Howard University Press.

Tester, Keith. (1992). *The Two Sovereigns: Social Contradictions of European Modernity*. New York: Routledge.

Tewari, Shruti Bhawana. (2002). "A Revolution of the Colored Races: Merging of African and Indian Thought in the Novels of W. E. B. Du Bois." M.A. thesis, Michigan State University.

Theoharis, Athan G. (2002). *Chasing Spies: How the FBI Failed in Counterintelligence But Promoted the Politics of McCarthyism in the Cold War Years*. Chicago: Ivan R. Dee.

Theoharis, Jeanna F., and Woodard, Komozi. (Eds.). (2003). *Freedom North: Black Freedom Struggles Outside the South, 1940–1980*. New York: Palgrave Macmillan.

Theoharis, Jeanna F., and Woodard, Komozi. (Eds.). (2005). *Groundwork: Local Black Freedom Movements in America*. New York: New York University Press.

Therborn, Goran. (1996). "Critical Theory and the Legacy of Twentieth-Century Marxism." In Barry S. Turner (Ed.), *The Blackwell Companion to Social Theory* (pp. 53–82). Malden, MA: Blackwell.

Thiam, Awa. (1978). *Black Sister, Speak Out: Feminism and Oppression in Black Africa*. London: Pluto Press.

Thieme, John. (1996). *The Arnold Anthology of Postcolonial Literatures in English*. New York: Arnold.

Thomas, Dominic R. D. (2002). *Nation-Building, Propaganda, and Literature in Francophone Africa*. Bloomington: Indiana University Press.

Thomas, Gregory A. (1999). "Re-Reading Frantz Fanon and E. Franklin Frazier on the Erotic Politics of Racist Assimilation by Class." *Presence Africaine* 159, 71–87.

Thomas, Laurence M. (1989). *Living Morally: A Psychology of Moral Character*. Philadelphia: Temple University Press.

————. (1993). *Vessels of Evil: American Slavery and the Holocaust*. Philadelphia: Temple University Press.

Thomas, Louis Vincent. (1965). "Senghor and Negritude." *Presence Africaine* 26 (54), 102–133.

Thomas, Tony. (1974). *Black Liberation and Socialism*. New York: Pathfinder.

Thompson, John B. (1990). *Ideology and Modern Culture: Critical Social Theory in the Era of Mass Communication*. Palo Alto, CA: Stanford University Press.

Thompson, Peter S. (2002). "Negritude and a New Africa: An Update." *Research in African Literatures* 33 (4), 143–154.

Thompson, Vincent Bakpetu. (1969). *Africa and Unity: The Evolution of Pan-Africanism* London: Longman.

————. (1987). *The Making of the African Diaspora*. New York: Longman.

————. (2000). *Africans of the Diaspora: The Evolution of African Consciousness and Leadership in the Americas, from Slavery to the 1920s*. Trenton, NJ: Africa World Press.

Tiffin, Helen. (1988). "Post-colonialism, Post-modernism and the Rehabilitation of Post-colonial History." *Journal of Commonwealth Literatures* 23 (1), 169–181.

Tillery, Tyrone. (1992). *Claude McKay: A Black Poet's Struggle for Identity*. Amherst: University of Massachusetts.

Tomich, Dale. (1979). "The Dialectic of Colonialism and Culture: The Origins of the Negritude of Aime Cesaire." *Review of National Literatures* 2 (3), 351–385.

Tomisawa, Rieko. (2003). "The Crisis of Democracy in a Pluralistic Society: A Genealogy of W. E. B. Du Bois's Double Consciousness." Ph.D. dissertation, Michigan State University.

Tong, Rosemarie. (1989). *Feminist Thought: A Comprehensive Introduction*. Boulder, CO: West-view Press.

Toure, Ahmed Sekou. (1959). *Toward Full Re-Africanization: Policy and Principles of the Guinea Democratic Party*. Paris: Présence Africaine.

——. (1972). *Africa and the Revolution*. London: Panaf Books.

——. (1973). *Africa and Imperialism*. Newark, NJ: Jihad Publishing.

——. (1974). *Defending the Revolution*. London: Panaf Books.

——. (1975). *The People's Power*. London: Panaf Books.

——. (1976). *Revolution, Culture, Pan-Africanisme*. Conakry, Republique de Guinee: Bureau de Presse de la Presidence de la Republique.

——. (1977). *Cultural Revolution*. London: Panaf Books.

——. (1978). *The Technique of Revolution*. London: Panaf Books.

——. (1979). *Africa on the Move*. London: Panaf Books.

——. (1980). *For a People's Revolutionary Economy*. London: Panaf Books.

Towa, Marcien. (1969a). "Aime Cesaire: Prophete de la Revolution des Peuples Noir." *Abbia* 21, 49–57.

——. (1969b). " 'Les pur-sang': Negritude Cesairienne et Surrealisme." *Abbia* 23, 71–82.

——. (1971). *Leopold Sedar Senghor: Negritude or Servitude?* Yaounde, Cameroon: Editions C.L.E.

——. (1972). *Philosophy in Contemporary Africa*. Rockville, MD: Black Orpheus.

——. (1973). "Consciencism." *Presence Africaine* 85, 148–177.

——. (1991). "Conditions for the Affirmation of a Modern African Philosophical Thought." In Tsenay Serequeberhan (Ed.), *African Philosophy: The Essential Readings* (pp. 187–200). New York: Paragon House.

Townes, Emilie M. (1993a). *Womanist Justice, Womanist Hope*. Atlanta: Scholars Press.

——. (Ed.). (1993b). *A Troubling in My Soul: Womanist Perspectives on Evil and Suffering*. Mary-knoll, NY: Orbis Books.

——. (1995). *In a Blaze of Glory: Womanist Spirituality as Social Witness*. Nashville, TN: Abing-don.

——. (Eds.). (1997). *Embracing the Spirit: Womanist Perspectives on Hope, Salvation, and Trans-formation*. Maryknoll, NY: Orbis Books.

——. (2006). *Womanist Ethics and the Cultural Production of Evil*. New York: Palgrave Macmil-lan.

Towns, Saundra. (1974). "The Black Woman as Whore: Genesis of the Myth." *The Black Posi-tion* 3, 39–59.

Travis, Toni Michelle C. (1996). "Double Consciousness and the Politics of the Elite." *Re-search in Race and Ethnic Relations* 9, 91–123.

Trout, Paulette, and Ellen Kennedy. (1968). "David Diop: Negritude's Angry Young Man." *Journal of the New African Literature and the Arts* 5/6, 76–78.

Tuana, Nancy. (1992). *Woman and the History of Philosophy*. New York: Paragon House.

Tuana, Nancy, and Tong, Rosemarie. (Eds.). (1995). *Feminism & Philosophy: Essential Readings in Theory, Reinterpretation, and Application*. Boulder, CO: Westview.

Tucker, Kenneth H. (2002). *Classical Social Theory: A Contemporary Appraoch*. Malden, MA: Blackwell.

Tucker, Mark. (Ed). (1993). *The Duke Ellington Reader*. New York: Oxford University Press.

Turner, Barry S. (Ed.). (1996). *The Blackwell Companion to Social Theory*. Malden, MA: Black-well.

Turner, Bryan S. (1999). *Classical Sociology*. Thousand Oaks, CA: Sage.

Turner, James. (Ed.). (1984). *The Next Decade: Theoretical and Research Issues in Africana Stud-ies*. Ithaca, NY: Africana Studies and Research Center, Cornell University.

Turner, James, and McGann, Charles S. (1980). "Black Studies as an Integral Tradition in African American Intellectual History." *Journal of Negro Education* 49, 52–59.

Turner, Joyce Moore. (2005). *Caribbean Crusaders and the Harlem Renaissance*. Urbana: University of Illinois Press.

Turner, Lou. (1989). "Frantz Fanon's Journey into Hegel's 'Night of the Absolute'." *Quarterly Joumral of Ideology* 13 (4), 47–63.

———. (1991). "Marxist Humanist Legacy of Frantz Fanon." *News & Letters* 38, 10.

———. (1995). "Epistemology, Absolutes, and the Party: A Critical Examination of Philosophic Divergences within the Johnson-Forest Tendency, 1948–1953." In Selwyn Cudjoe and William E. Cain (Eds.), *C. L. R. James: His Intellectual Legacies* (pp. 193–204). Amherst: University of Massachusetts Press.

———. (1996). "On the Difference Between the Hegelian and Fanonian Dialectic of Lordship and Bondage." In Lewis R. Gordon, T. Denean Sharpley-Whiting, and Renee T. White, (Eds.), *Fanon: A Critical Reader* (pp. 134–154). Cambridge: Blackwell.

———. (1999). "Fanon and the FLN: Dialectics of Organization and the Algerian Revolution." In Nigel C. Gibson (Ed.), *Rethinking Fanon: The Continuing Dialogue* (pp. 369–407). Amherst, NY: Humanity Books.

Turner, Lou, and Alan, John. (1986). *Frantz Fanon, Soweto and American Black Thought*. Chicago: News and Letters.

———. (1999). "Frantz Fanon, World Revolutionary." In Nigel C. Gibson (Ed.), *Rethinking Fanon: The Continuing Dialogue* (pp. 103–118). Amherst, NY: Humanity Books.

Tushnet, Mark. (1987). "The Politics of Equality in Constitutional Law: The Equal Protection Clause, Dr. Du Bois, and Charles Hamilton Houston." *Journal of American History* 74 (3), 884–903.

Tuttle, William M. (Ed.). (1957). *W. E. B. Du Bois*. Boston: Beacon.

———. (Ed.). (1973). *W. E. B. Du Bois: Essays and Explorations*. Englewood Cliffs, NJ: Prentice-Hall.

———. (1974). "W. E. B. Du Bois's Confrontation with White Liberalism During the Progressive Era." *Phylon* 35 (3), 241–258.

Twine, Frances W., and Blee, Kathleen M. (Eds.). (2001). *Feminism and Anti-Racism: International Struggles for Justice*. New York: New York University Press.

Tyler, Bruce Michael. (1992). *From Harlem to Hollywood: The Struggle for Racial and Cultural Democracy, 1920–1943*. New York: Garland.

Tyner, James. (2006). *Geography of Malcolm X: Black Radicalism and the Remaking of American Space*. New York: Routledge.

Tyner, Jarvis. (1997). "From the Talented Tenth to the Communist Party: The Evolution of W. E. B. Du Bois." *Political Affairs* 76 (2), 5–9.

Ucelli, Juliet. (2001). "Frantz Fanon and Revolutionary Anti-colonial Psychology." *Freedom Road Socialist Organization* [Available Online at: http://www.freedomroad.org/content/view/299/55/lang,en/ [Accessed on 20 July 2002].

Unah, Jim. (1995). *Essays in Philosophy*. Lagos, Nigeria: Panaf Press.

———. (Ed.). (1996). *Metaphysics, Phenomenology, and African Philosophy*. Ibadan, Nigeria: Hope Publications.

———. (1999). *African Philosophy: Trends and Projections in Six Essays*. Lagos, Nigeria: Concept Publications.

———. (2002). *Essays on Applied Phenomenology: Crisis Management, Gender Crisis, Controversy Surrounding African Philosophy, Existential Ontology, Postmodernism and the Legitimation Crisis*. Lagos, Nigeria: Foresight Press.

United Nations. (1988). *Human Rights: A Compilation of International Instruments*. Geneva and New York: Center for Human Rights, United Nations Publications.

Urdang, Stephenie. (1979). *Fighting Two Colonialisms: Women in Guinea-Bissau*. New York: Monthly Review.

Vaillant, Janet G. (1990). *Black, French, and African: A Life of Leopold Sedar Senghor*. Cambridge: Harvard University Press.

Valdes, Francisco, Culp, Jerome M., and Harris, Angela P. (Eds.). (2002). *Crossroads, Directions, and A New Critical Theory of Race.* Philadelphia: Temple University Press.

Valls, Andrew. (Ed.). (2005). *Race and Racism in Modern Philosophy.* Ithaca, NY: Cornell University Press.

Van Deburg, William. (1992). *New Day in Babylon: The Black Power Movement and American Culture, 1965–1975.* Chicago: University of Chicago Press.

———. (1997a). *Black Camelot: African American Culture Heroes in Their Times, 1960–1980.* Chicago: University of Chicago Press.

———. (Ed.). (1997b). *Modern Black Nationalism: From Marcus Garvey to Louis Farrakhan.* New York: New York University Press.

Van Niekerk, Marlene. (1998). "Understanding Trends in 'African Thinking'—A Critical Discussion." In Pieter H. Coetzee and Abraham P.J. Roux (Eds.), *The African Philosophy Reader* (pp. 52–85). New York: Routledge.

Van Staden, Christo. (1996). "Claiming the African Mind: Postcoloniality and Cultural Studies." *Communication* 22 (2), 71–76.

———. (1998). "Using Culture in African Contexts." In Pieter H. Coetzee and Abraham P.J. Roux (Eds.), *The African Philosophy Reader* (pp. 15–25). New York: Routledge.

Vasavithasan, Rathika. (2004). "Feminism(s), Nationalism(s), and Frantz Fanon." M.A. thesis, University of Toronto, Canada.

Vaz, Kim Marie. (Ed.). (1995). *Black Women in America.* Thousand Oaks, CA: Sage.

Velikova, R. (2000). "W. E. B. Du Bois vs. 'the Sons of the Fathers': A Reading of *The Souls of Black Folk* in the Context of American Nationalism." *African American Review* 34 (3), 431–442.

Venn, Couze. (2006). *The Postcolonial Challenge: Towards Alternative Worlds.* Thousand Oaks, CA: Sage.

Vincent, Theodore G. (1973). *Voices of a Black Nation: Political Journalism in the Harlem Renaissance.* Trenton, NJ: Africa World Press.

Vivian, John Donald. (1997). "The Making of a Radical: W. E. B. Du Bois's Turn to the Left." M.A. thesis, Florida Atlantic University.

Vlastos, Gregory. (1995). *Studies in Greek Philosophy.* Princeton: Princeton University Press.

Vogel, Lise. (1983). *Marxism and the Oppression of Women: Towards a Unitary Theory.* New Brunswick: Rutgers University Press.

———. (1995). *Woman Questions: Essays for a Materialist Feminism.* New York: Routledge.

Vogeler, Ingolf, and de Souza, Anthony R. (Eds.). (1980). *Dialectics of Third World Development.* Montclair, NJ: Allanheld and Osmun.

Von Eschen, Penny. (1997). *Race Against Empire: Black American and Anti-Colonialism, 1937–1957.* Ithaca, NY: Cornell University Press.

———. (2004). *Satchmo Blows Up the World: Jazz Ambassadors Play the Cold War.* Cambridge: Harvard University Press.

Wade, Rex A. (1969). *The Russian Search for Peace, February to October 1917.* Stanford: Stanford University Press.

———. (1984). *Red Guards and Workers' Militias in the Russian Revolution.* Stanford: Stanford University Press.

———. (2001). *The Bolshevik Revolution and Russian Civil War.* Westport, CT: Greenwood Press.

———. (2005). *The Russian Revolution, 1917.* New York: Cambridge University Press.

Wake, Clive. (1963). "Cultural Conflict in the Writings of Leopold Senghor and Mongo Beti." *Books Abroad* 37, 156–169.

Walby, Sylvia. (1990). *Theorizing Patriarchy.* Oxford: Basil Blackwell.

Walden, Daniel. (1963a). "NAACP Mourns the Passing of Dr. Du Bois, A Founder." *Crisis* 70 (October).

———. (1963b). "W. E. B. Du Bois: Pioneer Reconstruction Historian." *Negro History Bulletin* 26, 159–160, 164.

———. (1966). "W. E. B. Du Bois's Essential Years: The Link from Douglass to the Present." *Journal of Human Relations* 14, 28–41.

———. (1977). "W. E. B. Du Bois: A Renaissance Man in the Harlem Renaissance." *Minority Voices* 2 (1), 11–20.

Walker, S. Jay. (1975). "Du Bois's Uses of History: On Nat Turner and John Brown." *Black World* 24, 4–11.

Wallace, Michele. (1990a). *Black Macho and the Myth of the Superwoman.* New York: Verso.

———. (1990b). *Invisibility Blues: From Pop to Theory.* New York: Verso.

Wallerstein, Immanuel M. (1974). *The Modern World-System.* New York: Academic Press.

———. (1979). *The Capitalist World-Economy: Essays.* Cambridge: Cambridge University Press.

———. (1980a). *Processes of the World-System.* Beverly Hills, CA: Sage.

———. (1980b). *The Modern World-System II: Mercantilism and the Consolidation of the European World Economy, 1600–1750.* New York: Academic Press.

———. (1981). *Patterns and Prospectives of the Capitalist World-Economy.* Tokyo: United Nations University.

———. (1983). *Historical Capitalism.* London: Verso.

———. (1984). *The Politics of the World-Economy: The States, The Movements, and the Civilizations.* Cambridge: Cambridge Uniersity Press.

———. (1989). *The Second Era of Great Expansion of the Capitalist World-Economy, 1730–1840s.* San Diego: Academic Press.

———. (1991a). *Geopolitics and Geoculture: Essays on the Changing World-System.* Cambridge: Cambridge University Press.

———. (1991b). *Unthinking Social Science: The Limits of Nineteenth Century Paradigms.* Cambridge, MA: Polity Press.

———. (1995). *After Liberalism.* New York: New Press.

———. (1999). *The End of the World as We Know It: Social Science for the Twenty-First Century.* Minneapolis: University of Minnesota Press.

———. (2000). *The Essential Wallerstein.* New York: New Press.

———. (2003). *The Decline of American Power: The U.S. in a Chaotic World.* New York: New Press.

———. (2004a). *World-Systems Analysis: An Introduction.* Durham: Duke University Press.

———. (2004b). *The Uncertainties of Knowledge.* Philadelphia: Temple University Press.

———. (2004c). *Alternatives: The United States Confronts the World.* Boulder, CO: Paradigm Publishers.

———. (2006). *European Universalism: The Rhetoric of Power.* New York: New Press.

Walters, Ronald W. (1993). *Pan-Africanism in the African Diaspora: An Analysis of Modern Afrocentric Political Movement.* Detroit: Wayne State University Press.

Walton, Sidney. (1969). *The Black Curriculum: Developing Programs in Afro-American Studies.* East Palo Alto: Black Liberation Publishers.

Walraven, Klaas van. (1999). *Dreams of Power: The Role of the Organization of African Unity on the Politics of Africa, 1963–1993.* Aldershot: Ashgate.

Wamba-Dia-Wamba, Ernest. (1991). "Philosophy in Africa: Challenges of the African Philosopher." In Tsenay Serequeberhan (Ed.), *African Philosophy: The Essential Readings* (pp. 211–246). New York: Paragon House.

Wanja, Chris L. (1974). "African Response to Negritude and Pan-Africanism." *Busara* 6 (1), 39–42.

Ward, Julie K., and Lott, Tommy L. (Eds.). (2002). *Philosophers on Race: Critical Essays.* Malden, MA: Blackwell.

Ware, Vron. (1992). *Beyond the Pale: White Women, Racism, and History.* New York: Verso.

Warren, Kenneth W. (2000). "An Inevitable Drift?: Oligarchy, Du Bois, and the Politics of Race between the Wars." *Boundary 2* 27 (3), 153–169.

Warren, Nagueyalti. (1984). "The Contributions of W. E. B. Du Bois to Afro-American Studies in Higher Education." Ph.D. dissertation, University of Mississippi.

Washington, Johnny. (1986). *Alain Locke and Philosophy: A Quest for Cultural Pluralism*. New York: Greenwood Press.

———. (1994). *A Journey Into the Philosophy of Alain Locke*. New York: Greenwood Press.

Washington, Mary Helen. (Ed.). (1987). *Invented Lives: Narratives of Black Women, 1860–1960*. Garden City, NY: Anchor.

Washington, Robert E. (2001). *The Ideologies of African American Literature: From the Harlem Renaissance to the Black Nationalist Revolt*. Lanham, MD: Rowman and Littlefield.

Waters, Kristin, and Conaway, Carol B. (Eds.). (2007). *Black Women's Intellectual Traditions: Speaking Their Minds*. Burlington, VT: University of Vermont Press.

Watson, Steven. (1995). *The Harlem Renaissance: Hub of African American Culture, 1920–1930*. New York: Pantheon.

Watts, Jerry G. (2001). *Amiri Baraka: The Politics and Art of a Black Intellectual*. New York: New York University Press.

Wauthier, Claude. (1967). *The Literature and Thought of Modern Africa*. New York: Praeger.

Weate, Jeremy. (2001). "Fanon, Merleau-Ponty and the Difference of Phenomenology." In Robert Bernasconi (Ed.), *Race* (pp. 169–183). Malden, MA: Blackwell.

Weinbaum, Alys Eve. (2001). "Reproducing Racial Globality: W. E. B. Du Bois and the Sexual Politics of Black Internationalism." *Social Text* 19 (2), 15–41.

Weinbaum, Batya. (1978). *The Curious Courtship of Women's Liberation and Socialism*. Boston: South End.

Wellmer, Albrecht. (1974). *The Critical Theory of Society*. New York: Seabury.

Wells, Diana. (Ed.). (1993). *We Have a Dream: African American Visions of Freedom*. New York: Carroll and Graf.

Wells, Ida B. (1969). *On Lynchings*. New York: Arno Press.

———. (1970). *Crusade for Justice: The Autobiography of Ida B. Wells* (Alfreda Duster, Ed.). Chicago: University of Chicago Press.

———. (1991). *The Selected Works of Ida B. Wells-Barnett* (Trudier Harris, Ed.). New York: Oxford University Press.

———. (1993). *A Red Record: Lynchings in the U.S.* Salem, NH: Ayer & Co.

———. (1995). *The Memphis Dairy of Ida B. Wells* (Miriam Decosta-Willis, Ed.). Boston: Beacon.

Werbner, Richard P. (Ed.). (2002). *Postcolonial Subjectivities in Africa*. London: Zed.

Wesley, Charles H. (1965). "W. E. B. Du Bois: Historian." *Freedomways* 5, 59–72.

———. (1984). *The History of the National Association of Colored Women's Clubs: A Legacy of Service*. Washington, DC: National Association of Colored Women.

West, Cornel. (1982). *Prophesy Deliverance!: An Afro-American Revolutionary Christianity*. Philadelphia: Westminister.

———. (1988a). *Prophetic Fragments*. Grand Rapids: Eerdmans.

———. (1988b). "Marxist Theory and the Specificity of Afro-American Oppression." In Cary Nelson and Lawrence Grossberg (Eds.), *Marxism and the Interpretation of Culture* (pp. 17–34). Chicago: University of Illinois Press.

———. (1989). "W. E. B. Du Bois: The Jamesian Organic Intellectual." In *The American Evasion of Philosophy: A Genealogy of Pragmatism* (pp. 138–150). Madison, WI: University of Wisconsin Press.

———. (1991). *The Ethical Dimensions of Marxist Thought*. New York: Monthly Review.

———. (1993a). *Keeping Faith: Philosophy and Race in America*. New York: Routledge.

———. (1993b). *Race Matters*. New York: Random House.

———. (1993c). *Beyond Eurocentrism and Multiculturalism, Volume One: Prophetic Thought in Postmodern Times*. Monroe, ME: Common Courage.

———. (1993d). *Beyond Eurocentricism and Multiculturalism, Volume Two: Prophetic Reflections: Notes on Race and Power in America.* Monroe, ME: Common Courage.

———. (1996). "Black Strivings in a Twilight Civilization." In Henry Louis Gates, Jr. and Cornel West, *The Future of the Race* (pp. 53–114). New York: Alfred A. Knopf.

———. (1998). "Cornel West: An Interveiw." In George Yancy (Ed.), *African American Philosophers: 17 Conversations* (pp. 31–49). New York: Routledge.

———. (Ed.). (1999). *The Cornel West Reader.* New York: Civitas.

———. (2004). *Democracy Matters: Winning the Fight Against Imperialism.* New York: Penguin.

West, Cornel, and Lerner, Michael. (1995). *Jews and Blacks: Let the Healing Begin.* New York: Grossett/ Putnam.

Wexler, Philip. (1991). *Critical Theory Now.* New York: Routledge.

White, Deborah Gray. (1999). *Too Heavy A Load: Black Women in Defense of Themselves, 1894–1994.* New York: Norton.

White, E. Frances. (1984). "Listening to the Voices of Black Feminism." *Radical America* 18 (2–3), 7–25.

———. (1995). "Africa On My Mind: Gender, Counter Discourse and African American Nationalism." In Beverly Guy-Sheftall (Ed.), *Words of Fire: An Anthology of African American Feminist Thought* (pp. 504–524). New York: The Free Press.

Whitehead, Stephen M., and Barrett, Frank J. (Eds.). (2001). *The Masculinities Reader.* Cambridge, UK: Polity.

Whitten, Norman E., Jr., and Torres, Arlene. (Eds.). (1998). *Blackness in Latin America and the Caribbean: Social Dynamics and Cultural Transformations* (2 Volumes). Indianapolis: Indiana University Press.

Wiatrowski-Phillips, Lily. (1995). "W. E. B. Du Bois and Soviet Communism: *The Black Flame* as Socialist Realism." *Southern Atlantic Quarterly* 94 (3), 837–875.

Widmer, Kingsley. (1988). *Counterings: Utopian Dialectics in Contemporary Contexts.* Ann Arbor: UMI Research Press.

Wiggerhaus, Rolf. (1995). *The Frankfurt School: Its History, Theories, and Political Significance.* Cambridge: MIT Press.

Wilder, Craig S. (2001). *In the Company of Black Men: The African Influence on African American Culture in New York City.* New York: New York University.

Wilder, Gary. (2003a). "Colonial Ethnology and Political Rationality in French West Africa." *Radical History Review* 90, 31–38.

———. (2003b). "Pan-Africanism and the Republican Political Sphere." In Tyler Stovall and Sue Peabody (Eds.), *The Color of Liberty: Histories of Race in France.* (pp. 237–258). Durham: Duke University Press.

———. (2003c). "Unthinking French History: Colonial Studies Beyond National Identity." In Antoinette Burton (Ed.), *After the Imperial turn: Critical Approaches to 'National' Histories and Literatures* (pp. 125–143). Durham: Duke University Press.

———. (2004). "Race, Reason, Impasse: Cesaire, Fanon, and the Legacy of Emancipation." *Radical History Review* 90, 31–61.

———. (2005). *The French Imperial Nation-State: Negritude and Colonial Humanism Between the Two World Wars.* Chicago: University of Chicago Press.

Wilkerson, William S., and Paris, Jeffrey. (Eds.). (2001). *New Critical Theory: Essays on Liberation.* Lanham, MD: Rowman and Littlefield.

Willet, Cynthia. (2001). "The Mother Wit of Justice: Eros and Hubris in the African American Context." In William S. Wilkerson and Jeffrey Paris (Eds.), *New Critical Theory: Essays on Liberation* (pp. 223–248). Lanham, MD: Rowman and Littlefield Publishers.

Williams, Chancellor. (1974). *The Destruction of Black Civilization: Great Issues of a Race from 4500 B.C. to 2000 A.D.* Chicago: Third World Press.

Williams, Eric E. (1942). *The Negro in the Caribbean.* New York: Haskell House.

———. (1955). *The Case for Party Politics in Trinidad and Tobago.* Port of Spain: People's National Movement Publishing.

———. (1961). *Massa Day Done: A Masterpiece of Political and Sociological Analysis.* Port of Spain: People's National Movement Publishing.

———. (1962). *History of the People of Trinidad and Tobago.* Port of Spain: People's National Movement Publishing.

———. (1963). *Documents of West Indian History.* Port of Spain: People's National Movement Publishing.

———. (1964). *British Historians and the West Indies.* Port of Spain: People's National Movement Publishing.

———. (1965). *Reflections on the Caribbean Economic Community: A Series of Seven Articles.* Port of Spain: People's National Movement Publishing.

———. (1966). *Capitalism and Slavery.* New York: Capricorn Books.

———. (1969). *Britain and the West Indies.* London: University of Essex Press.

———. (1970). *From Columbus to Castro: The History of the Caribbean, 1492–1969.* London: Deutsch.

———. (1993). *Eric E. Williams Speaks: Essays on Colonialism and Independence.* Wellesley, MA: University of Massachusetts Press.

Williams, Patrick, and Chrisman, Laura. (Eds.). (1994). *Colonial Discourse and Postcolonial Theory: A Reader.* London: Harvester Wheatsheaf.

Williams, Randall. (2001). *W. E. B. Du Bois: A Scholar's Courageous Life.* Montgomery: New South.

Williams, Robert C. (1983). "W. E. B. Du Bois: Afro-American Philosopher of Social Reality." In Leonard Harris (Ed.), *Philosophy Born of Struggle: An Anthology of Afro-American Philosophy from 1917* (pp. 11–20). Dubuque, IA: Kendall/Hunt.

Williams, Shirley. (1990). "Some Implications of Womanist Theory." In Henry Louis Gates, Jr., (Ed.), *Reading Black/Reading Feminist: A Critical Anthology* (pp. 6875). New York: Meridian.

Wilmore, Gayraud S. (1998). *Black Religion and Black Radicalism: An Interpretation of the Religious History of African Americans.* Maryknoll, NY: Orbis.

Wilson, Kathleen. (Ed) (2004). *A New Imperial History: Culture, Identity, and Modernity in Britain and the Empire, 1660–1840.* Cambridge: Cambridge University Press.

Wilson, Kirt H. (1999). "Toward a Discursive Theory of Racial Identity: The Souls of Black Folk as a Response to Nineteenth-Century Biological Determinism." *Western Journal of Communication* 63 (2), 193–216.

Winant, Howard. (2001). *Racial Conditions: Politics, Theory, Comparisons.* Minneapolis, MN: University of Minnesota Press.

Wing, Adrien Katherine. (Ed.). (1997). *Critical Race Feminism: A Reader.* New York: New York University Press.

———. (Ed). (2000). *Global Critical Race Feminism: An International Reader.* New York: New York University Press.

Winks, Robin W., and Neuberger, Joan. (2005). *Europe and the Making of Modernity, 1815–1914.* New York: Oxford University Press.

Wintz, Cary D. (1996a). *African American Political Thought, 1890–1930: Washington, Du Bois, Garvey, and Randolph.* Armonk: M.E. Sharpe.

———. (Ed.). (1996b). *The Politics and Aesthetics of "New Negro" Literature.* New York: Garland.

Wiredu, Kwasi. (1980). *Philosophy and an African Culture.* New York: Cambridge University Press.

———. (1991). "On Defining African Philosophy." In Tsenay Serequeberhan (Ed.), *African Philosophy: The Essential Readings* (pp. 87–110). New York: Paragon House.

———. (1995). *Conceptual Decolonization in African Philosophy: Four Essays*. Ibadan, Nigeria: Hope Publications.

———. (1996). *Cultural Universals and Particulars: An African Perspective*. Indianapolis: Indiana University Press.

———. (Ed.). (2004). *A Companion to African Philosophy*. Malden, MA: Blackwell.

Wohlforth, Tim. (1969). *Black Nationalism and Marxist Theory*. New York: Labor Publications.

Wolin, Richard. (1992). *The Terms of Cultural Criticism: The Frankfurt School, Existentialism, Postructuralism*. New York: Columbia University Press.

———. (1994). *Walter Benjamin: An Aesthetic of Redemption*. Berkeley: University of California Press.

———. (1995). *Labyrinths: Explorations on the Critical History of Ideas*. Amherst, MA: University of Massachusetts Press.

———. (2006). *The Frankfurt School Revisited: And Other Essays on Politics and Society*. New York: Routledge.

Wolter, Udo. (2001). *Das Obskure Subjekt der Begierde: Frantz Fanon und die Fallstricke des Subjekts der Befreiung*. Munster: Unrast.

Wolters, Raymond. (2001). *Du Bois and His Rivals*. Columbia: University of Missouri Press.

Woodard, Frederic. (1976). "W. E. B. Du Bois: The Native Impulse—Notes toward an Ideological Biography, 1868–1897." Ph.D. dissertation, University of Iowa.

Woodard, Komozi. (1999). *A Nation Within a Nation: Amiri Baraka (LeRoi Jones) and Black Power Politics*. Chapel Hill: University of North Carolina Press.

———. (2000). *The Black Power Movement: Amiri Baraka—From Blacks Arts to Black Radicalism*. Bethesda, MD: University Publications of America.

Wood, David. (2000). *Cornel West and the Politics of Prophetic Pragmatism*. Urbana: University of Illinios Press.

Woods, Jeff. (2004). *Black Struggle, Red Scare: Segregation and Anti-Communism in the South, 1948–1968*. Baton Rouge: Louisiana State University Press.

Worcester, Kent. (1984). *C. L. R. James and the American Century: 1938–1953*. Puerto-Rico: Inter-American University of Puerto-Rico. CISCLA Working Paper no. 12.

———. (1985). *West Indian Politics and Cricket: C. L. R. James and Trinidad, 1958–1963*. Puerto-Rico: Inter-American University of Puerto-Rico. CISCLA Working Paper no. 20.

———. (1991). "C. L. R. James, Marxism, and America." *Research and Society* 4.

———. (1992a). "The Question of the Canon: C. L. R. James and *Modern Politics*." In Paget Henry and Paul Buhle (Eds.), *C. L. R. James's Caribbean*. (pp. 210–224). Durham: Duke University Press.

———. (1992b). "C. L. R. James and the Gospel of American Modernity." *Socialism and Democracy* 16/17.

———. (1995). "C. L. R. James and the American Century." In Selwyn Cudjoe and William E. Cain (Eds.), *C. L. R. James: His Intellectual Legacies* (pp. 173–192). Amherst: University of Massachusetts Press.

———. (1996). *C. L. R. James: A Political Biography*. Albany, NY: State University of New York Press.

Worsley, Peter. (1969). "Frantz Fanon: Evolution of a Revolutionary—Revolutionary Theories." *Monthly Review* 21, 30–49.

———. (1972). "Frantz Fanon and the 'Lumpenproletariat'." *Socialist Register*. New York: Monthly Review Press.

Wortham, John M. (1997). "The Economic Ideologies of Booker T. Washington and W. E. B. Du Bois: 1895–1915." Ph.D. dissertation, Boston University.

Wortham, Robert A. (2005a). "The Early Sociological Legacy of W. E. B. Du Bois." In Anthony J. Blasi (Ed.), *Diverse Histories of American Sociology*. Boston: Brill.

———. (2005b). "Introduction to the Sociology of W. E. B. Du Bois." *Sociation Today* 3 (1). On-line at: http://www.ncsociology.org/sociationtoday/v31/atlanta.htm [Accessed on 23 February 2005]

Wright, Claudia. (1992). "National Liberation, Consciousness, Freedom and Frantz Fanon." *History of European Ideas* 15 (1–3), 427–436.

Wright, Earl. (2001). "The Atlanta Sociological Laboratory: America's First Model of Urban Sociological Research." *Southern Sociological Society.*

Wright, Erik O. (1978). *Class, Crisis, and the State.* London: NewLeft Books.

———. (1979). *Varieties of Marxist Conceptions of Class Structure.* Madison: University of Wisconsin Press.

———. (1980). *Class Structure and Income Determination.* New York: Academic Press.

———. (1985). *Classes.* New York: Verso.

———. (1989). *The Debate on Classes.* New York: Verso.

———. (1992). *Reconstructing Marxism: Essays on Explanation and the Theory of History.* New York: Verso.

————. (1994). *Interrogating Inequality: Essays on Class Analysis, Socialism, and Marxism.* New York: Verso.

———. (1997). *Class Counts: Comparative Studies in Class Analysis.* Cambridge: Cambridge University Press.

———. (2003). *Deepening Democracy: Institutional Innovations in Empowered Participatory Governance.* New York: Verso.

———. (Ed.). (2005). *Approaches to Class Analysis.* Cambridge: Cambridge University Press.

Wright, Richard A. (Ed.). (1984). *African Philosophy: An Introduction, Third Edition* Lanham, MD: University of America Press.

Wright, William. (1978). "Du Bois's Theory of Political Democracy." *Crisis* 85, 85–89.

Wright, William D. (1985). "The Socialist Analysis of W. E. B. Du Bois." Ph.D. dissertation, State University of New York, Buffalo.

Wylie, Hal. (1985). "Negritude and Beyond: The Quest for Identity and Meaning." Kofi Anyodoho (Ed.), *Interdisciplinary Dimensions of African Literature* (pp. 47–65). Washington, D.C.: Three Continents Press.

Wynter, Sylvia. (1982). *Beyond Liberal and Marxist-Leninist Feminisms: Towards an Autonomous Frame of Reference.* San Francisco: Institute for Research on Women and Gender.

———. (1986). "In Quest of Mathew Bondman: Some Cultural Notes on the Jamesian Journey." In Paul Buhle (Ed.), *C. L. R. James His Life and Work* (pp. 131–145). New York: Allison and Busby.

———. (1992). "Beyond Categories of the Master Conception: The Counter-Doctrine of the Jamesian Poiesis." In Paget Henry and Paul Buhle (Eds.), *C. L. R. James's Caribbean* (pp. 63–91). Durham: Duke University Press.

Yancy, George. (Ed.). (1998). *African American Philosophers: 17 Conversations.* New York: Routledge.

———. (Ed.). (2001). *Cornel West: A Critical Reader.* Malden, MA: Blackwell.

———. (Ed.). (2002). *The Philosophical I: Personal Reflections on Life in Philosophy.* Lanham, MD: Rowman and Littlefield.

———. (Ed.). (2004). *What White Looks Like: African American Philosophers on the Whiteness Question.* New York: Routledge.

———. (Ed.). (2005). *White on White/Black on Black.* Lanham, MD: Rowman and Littlefield.

———. (Ed.). (2007). *Philosophy in Multiple Voices.* Lanham, MD: Rowman and Littlefield.

———. (2008). *Black Bodies, White Gazes.* Lanham, MD: Rowman and Littlefield.

Yee, Shirley J. (1992). *Black Women Abolitionists: A Study in Activism, 1828–1860.* Knoxville: University of Tennessee Press.

Yellin, Jean Fagan. (1973). "Du Bois's Crisis and Woman's Suffrage." *Massachusetts Review* 14 (2), 365–375.

Young, Iris Marion. (1990). *Justice and the Politics of Difference*. Princeton: Princeton University Press.

Young, Robert Alexander. (1996). *The Ethiopian Manifesto*. In Wilson Jeremiah Moses (Ed.), *Classical Black Nationalism: From the American Revolution to Marcus Garvey*. New York: New York University Press.

Young, Robert J. (1995). *Colonial Desire: Hybridity in Theory, Culture and Race*. New York: Routledge.

———. (1999). *Postcolonialism: An Historical Introduction*. Malden, MA: Blackwell.

———. (2003). *Postcolonialism: A Very Short Introduction*. New York: Oxford University Press.

Youssef, Hanafy A., and Fadl, Salah A. (1996). "Frantz Fanon and Political Psychiatry." *History of Psychiatry* 7 (28), 525–532.

Ysern-Borras, Eduardo. (1985). "The Colonized Personality: Frantz Fanon's Concept of the Psychology of People Living Under Socio-Political Conditions of Colonialism." Ph.D. dissertation, Wright Institute.

Yuan, Ji. (1998). "W. E. B. Du Bois and His Socialist Thought." Ph.D. dissertation, Temple University, Philadelphia.

———. (2000). *W. E. B. Du Bois and His Socialist Thought*. Lawrenceville, NJ: Africa World Press.

Zack, Naomi. (1993). *Race and Mixed Race*. Philadelphia: Temple University Press.

———. (Ed.). (1995). *American Mixed Race: The Culture of Microdiversity*. Lanham, MD: Rowman and Littlefield.

———. (1996). *Bachelors of Science: Seventeenth Century Identity, Then and Now*. Philadelphia: Temple University Press.

———. (Ed.). (1997). *Race/Sex: Their Sameness, Difference, and Interplay*. New York: Routledge.

———. (1998). *Thinking About Race*. Albany, NY: Wadsworth.

———. (Ed.). (2000). *Women of Color and Philosophy: A Critical Reader*. Malden, MA: Blackwell.

Zack, Naomi, Shrage, Laurie, and Sartwell, Crispin. (Eds.). (1998). *Race, Class, Gender, and Sexuality: The Big Questions*. Cambridge: Blackwell.

Zahar, Renate. (1970). *L'Oeuvre de Frantz Fanon*. Paris: Maspero.

———. (1974). *Frantz Fanon: Colonialism and Alienation, Concerning Frantz Fanon's Political Theory*. New York: Monthly Review Press.

Zamir, Shamoon. (1994). "'The Sorrow Songs'/'Song of Myself': Du Bois, the Crisis of Leadership, and Prophetic Imagination." In Werner Sollors and Maria Diedrich (Eds.), *The Black Columbiad: Defining Moments in African American Literature and Culture* (pp. 145–166). Cambridge, MA: Harvard University Press.

———. (1995). *Dark Voices: W. E. B. Du Bois and American Thought, 1888–1903*. Chicago: University of Chicago Press.

———. (Ed). (2008). *The Cambridge Companion to W. E. B. Du Bois*. Cambridge: Cambridge University Press.

Zegeye, Abebe, Harris, Leonard, and Maxted, Julia. (Eds.). (1991). *Exploitation and Exclusion: Race and Class in Contemporary US Society*. London: Hans Zell.

Zinn, Maxine Baca, and Dill, Bonnie Thornton. (Eds.). (1994). *Women of Color in U.S. Society*. Philadelphia: Temple University Press.

Zinn, Maxine Baca, Cannon, Lynn Weber, Higginbotham, Elizabeth, and Dill, Bonnie Thornton. (1986). "The Cost of Exclusionary Practices in Women's Studies." *Signs* 11 (2), 290–303.

Zuberi, Tukufu. (1995). *Swing Low, Sweet Chariot: The Mortality Cost of Colonizing Liberia in the Nineteenth Century*. Chicago: University of Chicago Press.

———. (2001). *Thicker Than Blood: How Racial Statistics Lie*. Minneapolis: University of Minnesota Press.

Zuckerman, Phil. (2002). "The Sociology of Religion of W. E. B. Du Bois." *Sociology of Religion* 63 (2), 239–253.

———. (2004). "Introduction to the Social Theory of W. E. B. Du Bois". In Phil Zuckerman (Ed.), *The Social Theory of W. E. B. Du Bois* (pp. 1–17). Thousand Oaks: Sage.

Zuckerman, Phil, Barnes, Sandra L., and Cady, Daniel. (2003). "*The Negro Church*: An Introduction." In W. E. B. Du Bois (Ed.), *The Negro Church* (pp.vii–xxvi). Walnut Creek: AltaMira.

# Index

abolitionism, 59, 70, 174

Achille, Louis, 150

Adorno, Theodor, ix, 17, 300–301n2. *See also* Frankfurt School

Africa/Africans, *passim*, but esp., 43–50, 94–100, 127–145, 151–161, 186–199, 209–224, 227–273

African holocaust, 3–4, 38, 112, 130, 133

African philosophy, 34–35n10, 119–121, 127–131, 139, 153–161, 158, 273–274, 282n34

African Studies. *See* Africana Studies

African Americans, 3, 18–19, 25, 38, 56, 59–61, 63–66, 69–70, 77, 90, 102–107, 146, 148–152, 163n20, 243, 252, 288

African American philosophy, 18–19, 34–35n10, 39–43, 50–63, 79n3, 153–161, 163n20, 303–304n8

African American Studies. *See* Africana Studies

Africana critical theory, *passim*, but esp., xi–xiv, 5–10, 16–28, 31–32n3, 285–300; African philosophy, dialectical rapport and critical relationship with, 34–35n10, 119–121, 127–131, 139, 153–161, 158, 273–274, 282n34; African American philosophy, dialectical rapport and critical relationship with, 18–19, 34–35n10, 39–43, 50–63, 79n3, 153–161, 163n20, 303–304n8; Africana hermeneutics/Africana philosophy of interpretation, appropriation and

synthesis of, 21, 35n11, 195–196, 277n15; Africana philosophy, dialectical rapport and critical relationship with, 8–9, 18–21, 25, 34–35n10, 152–61, 163n20, 233–41, 259–60, 270–73, 274n1, 276n8, 280n28, 296, 300n1, 303–304n8; Africana Studies, as paradigm and point of departure for, ix-xii, 2–3, 5–10, 18, 20–30, 30–31n2, 33n8, 44–45, 77, 85–86n29, 113, 156–161, 223–224, 285–300, 304–305n9; Africana Women's Studies, intense emphasis on and promotion of, 27, 293–296; anti-black racism, conception and critique of, 2–3, 36n14, 64, 83–84n23, 84n24, 95–96, 118–119, 125–126, 131–132, 138–139, 208–209; black existentialism/Africana philosophy of existence, appropriation and synthesis of, 25–26, 36n14, 40, 96, 124, 140, 204, 206–209, 265; black feminist theory/black feminism, appropriation and synthesis of, 63–78, 84n27, 86n31, 87n33, 199–216, 286–290, 293–295, 302–303n6; black invisibility and Africana anonymity, conception and critique of, 3, 9, 16, 26, 36n14, 40, 42, 200–201, 204, 209–210; black Marxism, dialectical rapport and critical relationship with, 4, 10–16, 25, 27, 33n7, 38, 50–63, 81n16, 104, 286–289; black radicalism/the black radical

415

tradition, appropriation and synthesis of, xi-xii, 2-10, 12-19, 24-25, 30n1, 33n7, 52-63, 117-119, 143-45, 168, 174, 182, 287; and Cabral, Amilcar, appropriation and synthesis of his conception of "the weapon theory," theory of "return to the source," discourse on revolutionary decolonization, ruminations on revolutionary re-Africanization, and principled promotion of revolutionary humanism (*see* Cabral, Amilcar); capitalism (racial capitalism), conception and critique of, 3-4, 10-16, 32-33n6, 33-34n9, 50-63, 89-110, 112-118, 122, 126, 141-144, 173, 175-186, 190-193, 198-199, 225n9, 226n11, 229, 234, 237-240, 244-246, 249-250, 252, 260, 272, 286-293; Caribbean philosophy, dialectical rapport and critical relationship with, 12, 18-9, 25, 34-35n10, 53, 81n16, 89-109, 119-131, 165-224; and Collins, Patricia Hill, appropriation and synthesis of her conceptions of black feminist sociology, sociology of race and sociology of knowledge, 1, 66, 70, 86n30, 259, 279n22, 287-88, 291-92; colonialism (racial colonialism), conception and critique of, 14-18, 43-50, 94-100, 119-145, 151-156, 169-174, 186-199, 233-241, 258-270; cosmetic multiculturalism, conception and critique of, xiii, 188; critical race theory, conception of and conceptual connections to, ix, 2-3, 10, 13-15, 25, 31-32n3, 36n13, 39-43, 50-63, 271-272, 276n9, 286-289; and Davis, Angela Y., appropriation and synthesis of her black feminist philosophy, insurgent intellectualism, radical political activism and conception of critical social theory, 1, 8, 12, 86n32, 87n37, 185, 291-292, 300-301n2; deconstruction and reconstruction, dialectics of and discourse on, ix, xi-xiv, 3-5, 16, 30n1, 31-32n3, 38, 42, 51, 62, 71, 107-109, 120-121, 144, 156-161, 176, 240-242, 245-246, 262, 273, 288, 291, 300n1, 304-305n9; democratic socialism (radical and revolutionary democratic socialism), conception and synthesis of, 53-54, 58, 60-62, 81-82n18, 142, 189, 200, 271, 286; dialectics, discourse on, 5, 16, 23, 35-36n12, 67, 139, 189-190, 211, 234, 247, 279-280n23; domination and discrimination, conception and critique of, xiii, 5, 14-18, 20-23, 26-27, 33-34n9, 42-49, 63-70, 74, 76-78, 93, 104-105, 110n1, 126-129, 142-144, 167, 172, 177, 185, 187, 201-203, 212, 232-235, 238-240, 255, 258-259, 262-266, 269, 271, 275-276n5, 290-295; and, Du Bois, W. E. B., appropriation and synthesis of his philosophy of race, sociology of race, critical race theory, contributions to critical white studies, Pan-Africanism, concept of "semi-colonialism," discourse on decolonization, race-centered and racism-conscious critique of capitalism and Marxism, discourse on democratic socialism, contributions to black feminism and womanism, and contributions to women's decolonization and women's liberation (*see* Du Bois, W. E. B.); epistemic exclusiveness, conception and critique of, 4, 12, 20, 23-28; epistemic openness, intense emphasis on and promotion of, 13, 16, 20-23, 25, 288, 296-300; Eurocentrism, conception and critique of, x-xii, 3-9, 11-14, 18-20, 23, 25-29, 50, 55, 58, 61-62, 68, 80n13, 92-93, 106, 108, 114, 116, 120, 124, 128, 130, 134, 137-138, 141-145, 149, 152, 157-158, 178, 181-185, 190, 195, 197, 201, 234-235, 246, 250, 253-254, 265-266, 270, 273, 286-293; existential phenomenology, conception and critique of, 114, 117-118, 121, 141, 145; existentialism/Eurocentric existentialism, conception and critique of, 3, 25, 36n14, 69-70, 86n32, 96, 100, 112, 114-115, 117-118, 121-122, 124-125, 138, 140-143, 145-146, 183, 186, 192, 194, 199, 204, 206-209, 265, 280n28; and Fanon, Frantz, appropriation and synthesis of his discourse on revolutionary decolonization, views on revolutionary violence and ruminations on revolutionary humanism (*see* Fanon, Frantz); and the Frankfurt School, conception and critique of, ix, xii, 1, 6–9, 14, 17, 25, 31–32n3, 37, 64, 68, 143, 225n9, 239, 243, 256, 259–260, 289–291, 293, 300–301n2; and Fraser, Nancy, appropriation and synthesis of her conception of feminist critical theory and critique of Jurgen Habermas's inattention to gender oppression and women's liberation, 289–293, 301–302n3, 302–303n5; and Gordon, Lewis R., appropriation and synthesis of his articulation of Africana philosophy and black existentialism/Africana philosophy of existence, 25–26, 36n14, 91, 280n28, 291; and Gramsci, Antonio, appropriation and synthesis of his philosophy of praxis and concepts of "cultural hegemony," "ideological hegemony," "organic intellectuals," "historical bloc," "war of position," "war of maneuver," and "ensemble of ideas and social relations," xii, 24, 36n13, 93, 146, 243, 259, 276n6, 278–279n21; and the Harlem Renaissance, 9, 28–29, 111–113, 144, 146, 148–152, 154, 161n1, 162n17, 163n19; and hooks, bell, appropriation and synthesis of her black feminist theory and cultural criticism, 69, 86n32, 202–203, 206, 291–292, 302–303n6; humanism (Eurocentric and/or "racist" humanism), conception and critique of, 14, 40, 113–114, 134, 140, 157–161, 191, 216–224, 241–258; human liberation and social transformation, discourse on and theory of, xii–xiii, 3–5, 12–20, 22–25, 31–32n3, 94–100, 132–133, 175, 180, 186–194, 199–224, 258–270, 292–293, 296–300; as intellectual archaeology project, xii, 31–32n3, 92, 109, 179–180, 201–202, 296–300; intellectual historical amnesia, conception and critique of, 6, 8, 296–300; intellectual insularity, conception and critique of, xiii, 4, 12, 23–28, 206, 260, 296–300; and James, C. L. R., appropriation and synthesis of his pioneering Pan-African Marxism, black radicalism, assertion of Africans as historical and cultural agents/actors (as opposed to spectators), and race-

centered and racism-conscious critique of capitalism and Marxism (*see* James, C. L. R.); and James, Joy A., appropriation and synthesis of her articulation of Africana/African American philosophy, insurgent intellectual-activism, and ruminations on black radical feminist theory, 63, 67, 73, 75, 84n27, 86n32, 87n37, 201–202, 303–304n8; male-feminism, appropriation and synthesis of, 38, 63–78, 84n27, 84–85n28, 85–86n29, 86n30, 199–216, 226n12, 286–289, 293–295, 302–303n6; male-womanism, appropriation and synthesis of, 63–78, 84–85n28, 199–216, 226n12, 286–289, 293–295, 302–303n6; and Marcuse, Herbert, critique, appropriation and synthesis of his conception of critical theory, xiii, 16–17, 32–33n6, 33–34n9, 46, 129–130, 269–270, 277n14, 278n20, 282–283n35; Marxism (white/Eurocentric Marxism), conception and critique of, xii–xiv, 10–16, 24–28, 31–32n3, 33n7, 50–63, 80n14, 80n15, 81n18, 81–82n19, 82n21, 83n22, 89–110, 115–119, 121–127, 141–145, 175–186, 241–258, 270–273, 278–297n21, 281–282n31, 282–283n35, 286–293; and methods (research methods and modes of analysis), xiii, 5–9, 15, 17–18, 20–21, 23, 25, 33n8, 84n25, 98–99, 256, 302n4, 304–305n9; and, Mills, Charles W., appropriation and synthesis of his conception of critical race theory, critique of white supremacy, and contributions to black Marxism, 12–15, 104, 110n1, 226n15, 302n4; modernity/European modernity, conception and critique of, 3–5, 14, 19, 24, 42–43, 143, 197–198, 247–250; new critical theory (contemporary critical theory), conception of and conceptual connections to, x–xiv, 10–16, 31–32n3, 32n4, 33–34n9, 92, 109, 286–289, 296–300; and Outlaw, Lucius, appropriation and synthesis of his articulation of Africana philosophy, ruminations on radical politics, and conception(s) of critical social theory "in the interests of black folk," 1, 18–19,

34–35n10, 156–158, 223, 243, 262, 276n8, 300n1, 301–302n3, 303–304n8; Pan-Africanism, conception of and conceptual connections to, 25, 27, 30–31n2, 38, 43, 45, 47, 49–52, 73–74, 76–77, 80n11, 82n21, 90–100–109, 112, 116–117, 121, 133–135, 141–148, 167–168, 174, 181, 183, 194, 270, 294, 298; postcolonialism, conception and critique of, xi, 10, 25, 43–50, 79n6, 187–194, 258–270; postmodernism, conception and critique of, x-xi, 3–5, 11–12, 16–17, 20, 22, 24–25, 31–32n3, 35–36n11, 47–50, 68, 80n13, 181, 193–194, 219–221, 244, 250, 257, 260, 290; as praxis-promoting theory or theory with practical intent, 7, 13, 18, 23, 286; radical politics, conception and promotion of, xii–xiv, 10–16, 30n1, 50–63, 91–93, 99, 108–109, 112, 131, 144–145, 157, 161n2, 194, 232–233, 244–245, 259–262, 286–289, 296–300; prophetic pragmatism, conception, critique, appropriation and synthesis of, 25, 280–281n29; "return to Marx" thesis, conception and critique of the, x-xiv, 2–4, 10–16, 23–28, 31–32n3, 32–33n6, 33n7, 33–34n9, 50–63, 81n18, 81–82n19, 82n21, 83n22, 83–84n23; revolutionary decolonization and revolutionary re-Africanization, dialectics of and discourse on, 4, 7–9, 121–127, 168, 173, 175, 186–194, 208–210, 216, 219, 22–223, 233, 235, 252–253, 264–265, 268–271, 286–289; revolutionary humanism, intense emphasis on and principled promotion of, 5, 29, 40, 117, 160–161, 163n28, 168, 191, 208–209, 216–224, 241–258, 268–272, 277n15, 278–279n21; as revolutionary theory, 23–24; and Robinson, Cedric J., appropriation and synthesis of his discourse on black Marxism and "racial capitalism," 12, 38, 62, 91, 104, 108, 291; and Said, Edward, appropriation and synthesis of his conception of "traveling theory," 13–14, 22, 222, 279; and Sartre, Jean-Paul, critique, appropriation and synthesis of his conception of Negritude, role of the black revolutionary, philosophy of race,

"anti-racist racism," contributions to critical race theory and critical white studies, "black-being-in-the-world," existential phenomenology, and ruminations on Europe's "racist humanism," 111–121, 125–126, 132–145, 158–161, 161n3, 162n11, 173, 185, 220–221, 225n3, 251, 255; as self-reflexive social theory, 5, 23–28, 187, 235–236, 256, 259–260, 265–266, 288; and Serequeberhan, Tsenay, appropriation and synthesis of his conception of Africana hermeneutics/Africana philosophy of interpretation, 21, 35–36n11, 46, 124, 173, 183, 195, 198–199, 263, 265, 268, 274n1, 277n15, 278–279n21, 293; standpoint theory, appropriation and synthesis of, 65–66, 86n30, 204, 250; on textual tokenism, xiii; on textual masculinism, 200–201; theoretical eclecticism, conception and critique of, 27–28; theoretical myopia, conception and critique of, xiii, 21–24, 302n4; transdisciplinarity, intense emphasis on and promotion of, xiii, 2, 5, 18–21, 30–31n2, 91, 286–287, 294–296; and West, Cornel, critique, appropriation and synthesis of his conceptions of Afro-American critical thought, "prophetic pragmatism," theory of the "pitfalls of racial reasoning," and concept of "coalition politics," 3, 19–20, 236, 277n11, 280–281n29, 297; white superiority and black inferiority, critique of the dialectics of and discourse on, xiv, 6–7, 39–43, 168–174, 267, 296–300; white supremacy, conception and critique of, 2–8, 12–18, 22–23, 26, 33n8, 34–35n10, 39–43, 49–50, 52, 55, 57, 59–61, 64, 75–76, 83–84n23, 95, 100–107, 114–118, 125–127, 131–132, 134, 137–141, 143–144, 159, 173–174, 182–188, 199, 208–216, 229, 261, 265–266, 289–293, 296–300; womanist theory/womanism, appropriation and synthesis of, 4, 25, 36n13, 65, 74–77, 84n27, 85–86n29, 86n31, 199–216, 286–295, 302n4; women's decolonization and women's liberation, intense emphasis on and principled promotion of, 63–77, 199–216, 289–296

Africana hermeneutics/Africana philosophy of interpretation, 21, 35n11, 195–196, 277n15

Africana philosophy, *passim*, but esp., 7–9, 18–19, 21, 25, 34–35n10, 35–36n11, 146, 152–161, 233–241, 259–260, 270–273, 276n8, 280n28, 296–300

Africana philosophy of existence. *See* black existentialism

Africana Studies, *passim*, but esp., ix–xii, 2–3, 5–10, 18, 20–30, 30–31n2, 33n8, 44–45, 77, 85–86n29, 113, 156–161, 223–224, 285–300, 304–305n9; Africana Women's Studies, need for greater emphasis on and the principled promotion of, 27, 293–295; research methods and modes of analysis, xiii, 5–6, 8–9, 16–18, 20–23, 25, 30–31n2, 33n8, 34–35n10, 38–39, 53–55, 57–58, 286–287, 297, 302n4; as transdisciplinary discipline, x–xiii, 2, 5, 18–21, 30–31n2, 41–43, 51, 90–94, 286–300

Africana tradition of critical theory. *See* Africana critical theory

Africana Women's Studies, 293–295. *See also* black feminist theory and womanist theory

Africanity, 132–145

Afro-Americans. *See* African Americans

Afro-American Studies. *See* Africana Studies

Afro-Asian Studies. *See* Africana Studies

Afro-Latino Studies. *See* Africana Studies

Afro-Native American Studies. *See* Africana Studies

Alan, John, 222

Algeria/Algerians, 123–124, 126, 145–148, 209–216, 222

Algerian Revolution, 209–216

Algerian women, 209–216

American apartheid, xii, 93, 104, 109

American Revolution, 4, 107

Amin, Samir, 176, 185, 225n7

Andrade, Mario de, 228

anti-black racism, 2–3, 36n14, 64, 83–84n23, 84n24, 95–96, 118–119, 125–126, 131–132, 138–139, 208–209. *See also* Eurocentrism and white supremacy

Appiah, Kwame Anthony, 39, 45, 79n3, 276n9

Arabia/Arabs, 123, 126, 135, 256

Arabism, 135

Arabité, 135

the "Asiatic mode of production," 247–249, 280n26. *See also* Marxism and Leninism

Ayalew, Melesse, 183

Baker, Ella, xi

Bakunin, Mikhail, 192

Baraka, Amiri, 185

Bartolovich, Crystal, 48

Benjamin, Walter, ix, 17, 129–130, 300–301n2

Bergner, Gwen, 200

Bethune, Mary McLeod, 70

Bhabha, Homi, 220–221

Birbalsingh, Frank, 91

black Americans. *See* African Americans

black existentialism (Africana philosophy of existence), 25–26, 36n14, 40, 96, 124, 140, 204, 206–209, 265

black feminist theory (black feminism), 63–78, 84n27, 86n31, 87n33, 199–216, 286–290, 293–295, 302–303n6

black Marxism, 4, 10–16, 25, 27, 33n7, 38, 50–63, 81n16, 104, 286–289

black nationalism, 4, 25, 51, 56, 90, 97–98, 102, 116–117, 134–135, 296

"Black Orpheus" (Sartre), 111, 113–115, 118–120, 125, 134, 139

Black Power Movement, xi, 9, 83–84n23, 296

black radicalism (the black radical tradition), x–xiv, 1–20, 24–25, 27–30, 30n1, 33n7, 52–63, 111–119, 143–45, 168, 174, 182, 254–258, 286–289, 296–300

black radical politics. *See* black radicalism

Blaut, James, 190

Boggs, Paul, 91

Bogues, Anthony, 2, 9, 12, 14, 89, 91, 93, 95–99, 304–305n9

Breton, André, 112, 120

Briggs, Cyril, 148, 279

Broderick, Francis, 50–51

Brown, John, 59

Brown, Sterling, 148

Buhle, Paul, 89, 91

Cabo Verdianidade, 229–230

Cabral, Amilcar: and Africana philosophy, 233–241, 259–262, 270–273; and the Africana tradition of critical theory/Africana critical theory, 227–283; as agronomist, 250–251, 282n32; on anti-black racism, 229–232, 234, 238, 246, 260–261, 271–273; anti-colonialism of, 233–241, 258–270; anti-racism of, 229–232, 234, 236–238, 246, 260–261, 271–273; on armed struggle, 234–235, 264–265; and the "Asiatic mode of production," 247–249, 280n26; banned from Guinea-Bissau, 232; black radicalism/black radical politics of, 231–233, 241–245, 254, 256–257; and Cabo Verdianidade, 229–230; on capitalism, 234, 237–240, 244–246, 250, 252, 260, 271–273; childhood poverty of, 229; on class, 240–242, 243–254, 259, 261–262, 264; on class struggle, 240, 242, 244–247, 249–253, 271–273; on colonialism, 233–241, 258–270; on communism, 242, 246, 254–256; on consciousness (African and/or critical consciousness), 229–231, 236, 238, 253, 259–260, 262–263; on culture, 229–230, 232–237, 240, 243, 245–247, 250, 252–255, 258–259, 262–269, 271–273; data collection procedures of, 231; on decolonization, 230–231, 235, 251–253, 264–265, 268, 270–273; on development, 231, 233, 237, 239–241, 245–246, 248–249, 252, 258–260, 262, 264, 267–268, 281n30; on dignity, 233–236, 255–258, 266–267; education of, 228–231; expelled from Guinea-Bissau, 232; on gender justice, 229; on guerilla warfare, 234–235, 264–265; on history, 232–233, 235–236, 240, 242, 244–254, 258, 262–264, 266–269, 272–273; humanism of, 241–258, 270–273; on imperialism, 227, 232, 234–241, 245–247, 250–253, 255–257, 262–265, 268–270, 281n30, 282n34; on internal enemies, 235–236, 256; on identity, 233, 244, 252–253, 258, 261, 265–267; and Marxism (dialectical rapport and critical relationship with white/Eurocentric Marxism), 240–258; as materialist social theorist, 241–258,
263, 268; on the mode of production, 240–242, 245–250, 280n26; on the motive force of history, 240–242, 245–247, 251–256; on national culture, 229–230, 233, 258–270; on national history, 232–233, 235–236, 240, 242, 244–254, 258, 262–264, 266–269, 272–273; on national liberation, 229–239, 242, 245, 251–254, 258–270; nationalism of, 227–233, 241–258; Pan-Africanism of, 234–235, 241–270; and the Partido Africano da Independência da Guiné e Cabo Verde (PAIGC), 232; and the Partido Africano da Independência e União dos Povos da Guiné e Cabo Verde (PAIUPGC), 232; philosophy of praxis of, 233–241, 270; and the Policía Interncional para a Defensa do Estudo (PIDE), 230; on Portuguese colonialism, 229, 231–232, 236–237, 251–252, 254–255, 271–273; on pre-capitalist Africa, 230, 232–258; on pre-colonial Africa, 232–258; on productive forces, 240, 245–249, 252–253; on racial capitalism, 234, 237–240, 244–246, 250, 252, 260, 271–273; on racial colonialism, 233–241, 239, 258–270; radicalism/radical politics of, 231–233, 241–273; "return to the source," critical theory of, 233, 235, 258, 263–266, 270–273; on revolutionary re-Africanization, 233, 251–253, 263–265, 268, 270–273; on revolutionary decolonization, 230–231, 235, 251–253, 264–265, 268, 270–273; revolutionary humanism of, 234–235, 241–258, 270–273; revolutionary nationalism of, 227–235, 241–258; on revolutionary violence, 233–241, 263–264; on self-determination, 228, 235, 250, 262, 274–275n3, 275–276n5, 282n32; on socialism, 241–258; on solidarity, 236–237, 244, 255–256; on struggle, 227, 232–241, 251–258, 261–271; as student-activist, 230; on violence, 232, 238, 263–264; on the "weapon of theory," 237–238, 241–258, 270; on women's liberation, 229

Cabral, Iva Pinhal Evora, 228–229

Cabral, Juvenal Antonio da Costa, 228–229

Cabral, Luiz, 232, 255
Cabral, Maria Helena Rodrigues, 231
Capecia, Mayotte, 200, 204
capitalism, 3–4, 10–16, 32–33n6, 33–34n9,
  50–63, 89–110, 112–118, 122, 126,
  141–144, 173, 175–186, 190–193,
  198–199, 225n9, 226n11, 229, 234,
  237–240, 244–246, 249–250, 252, 260,
  272, 286–293
Caribbean, xii, 12, 14, 18, 25, 45, 53,
  81n16, 90, 93, 97, 106, 108–109, 120,
  125, 148, 151, 162n6, 166–168, 170,
  239, 281n30
Caribbean philosophy, 12, 18–19, 25,
  34–35n10, 53, 81n16, 89–109,
  119–131, 165–224. *See also* Africana
  philosophy
Caribbean Studies. *See* Africana Studies
Castoriadis, Cornelius, 91
Catt, Carrie Chapman, 64
Caute, David, 169–171
*Certeza*, 229–230
Cesaire, Aime: on Africa, 119–121,
  127–131; and the Africana tradition of
  critical theory/Africana critical theory,
  x–xii, 12, 28, 44, 93, 104, 109, 112–131,
  157, 161; on alienation (on black or
  racial alienation), 122, 128, 139–140; on
  anti-black racism, 119–127; anti-
  capitalism of, 119–129; anti-colonialism
  of, 119–127; anti-racism of, 119–127;
  assimilation, critique of, 115–116, 121,
  125, 130–131; on black civilizations
  (ancient Africa), 127–129, 151; on black
  identity, 121, 124, 128; black
  radicalism/black radical politics of,
  121–127; on black solidarity, 113, 121,
  128; "boomerang effect of colonization,"
  critical theory of the, 124–126; on
  cannibalism, 130–131; on capitalism,
  119–127; on colonialism, 119–127; on
  communism, 119–127; on
  consciousness (black and/or critical
  consciousness), 120–121, 125–126, 128,
  147, 151; on cultural desolation, 170;
  decolonization (discursive development
  of and conceptual contributions to),
  119–128; and *Discourse on Colonialism*,
  44, 119, 122, 125, 147, 171–173; on
  European decadence, 122–123; on
  European civilization, 122–123; and

Fanon, Frantz, 119–121, 169–174; on
  the Haitian Revolution, 129; on Hitler,
  Adolph, 125–126, 171–172; humanism
  of, 122; on language, 121, 125–126; on
  L'Ouverture, Toussaint, 129–130; on
  madness, 130–131; on memory (esp.,
  blood memory), 127–128, 131; on
  Marxism, 119–127, 143–145; on
  Nazism, 125–126; on negation (esp., on
  European civilization as "the negation of
  civilization"), 119–122; on pre-colonial
  Africa, 119–121, 127–131; on racial
  capitalism, 119–127; on racial
  colonialism, 119–127; on remembering,
  129–131; "return," conception and
  critical theory of, 119–121, 127–131;
  revolutionary humanism of, 117, 122,
  125–127; and revolutionary Negritude
  (discursive development of and
  conceptual contributions to), 119–127;
  on socialism, 119–127; on values (on
  the values of Negritude and Africa), 121,
  128–129; on violence (on racial,
  colonial, capitalist, and anti-imperialist
  violence), 124–127, 147, 153
Chabal, Patrick, 228–229, 231, 245, 254,
  274n2, 280n27
Chilcote, Ronald, 228
China, 62
Christophe, Henri, 129
Civil Rights Movement, xi, 9, 83–84n23
Civil War (U.S.), 107
*Clarindade*, 229–230
Clifford, James, 112
Collins, Patricia Hill, 1, 66, 70, 86n30, 259,
  279n22, 287–88, 291–292. *See also* black
  feminist theory
colonialism, 14–18, 43–50, 94–100,
  119–145, 151–156, 169–174, 186–199,
  233–241, 258–270. *See also* racial
  colonialism
Conrad, Joseph, 131
contemporary critical theory. *See* Africana
  critical theory and new critical theory
Cooper, Anna Julia, 70, 72–75, 87n37
cosmetic multiculturalism, xiii
Cox, Oliver C., 43, 52
Critical Legal Studies Movement, 13
critical race theory, ix, 2–3, 10, 13–15, 25,
  31–32n3, 36n13, 39–43, 50–63,
  271–272, 276n9, 286–289

critical social theory. *See* critical theory
critical theory, *passim,* but esp., ix–xiv,
     10–28, 31–32n3, 32n4, 32n5, 33–34n9,
     36n13, 286–293, 296–300, 300–301n2,
     301–302n3, 302n4, 302n5. *See also*
     Africana critical theory; the Frankfurt
     School; and new critical theory
Crummell, Alexander, 38
Cuffe, Paul, 59
Cullen, Countee, 148, 151

d'Almeida, Manuel Lehman, 229
Damas, Leon, 151, 171
Davis, Angela Y., 8, 12, 86n32, 87n37, 185,
     223, 244, 291–292, 294, 300–301n2. *See
     also* black feminist theory
de Chardin, Teilhard, 131, 133, 137–138,
     145, 160
decolonization, 43–50, 119, 121–128, 141,
     143–144, 160–161, 169–174, 186–194,
     216–224, 235–236, 251–253, 264–265,
     268–270, 286–289; women's
     decolonization, 63–77, 199–216,
     289–296
de-Frenchifize/de-Frenchifization (Sartre),
     115, 125. *See also* decolonization and
     Sartre, Jean-Paul
democratic socialism (radical and
     revolutionary democratic socialism),
     53–54, 58, 60–62, 81–82n18, 142, 189,
     200, 271, 286
Depestre, René, 151
deracination, 120–121, 126, 139, 189, 197,
     180n24. *See also* postcolonialism
Dhada, Mustafah, 228, 230
Dhondy, Farrukh, 91
dialectics, discourse on, 5, 16, 23,
     35–36n12, 67, 139, 189–190, 211, 234,
     247, 279–280n23
Dirlik, Arif, 48
Divine, Father, 102
Domingo, W.A., 148, 279
Douglass, Frederick, 38, 59, 64–65, 77, 218,
     295
Du Bois, W. E. B.: and the Africana tradition
     of critical theory/Africana critical theory,
     37–87; anti-colonialism of, 43–50; anti-
     racism of, 39–43; as anti-sexist critical
     social theorist, 63–78; Appiah, Kwame
     Anthony, critique of, 39, 79n3; black
     feminism, contributions to, 63–78; and

black Marxism (discursive development
     of and conceptual contributions to the
     black Marxist tradition), 49–63; on black
     mothers/motherhood, 66–68, 74, 76–77;
     black nationalism of, 56–63, 81–82n19;
     on black women, 63–78; on black
     women as revolutionaries, 69–78; on
     black workers, 49–63; on capitalism
     (esp., racial capitalism), 49–63; on class,
     50–63; on class struggle (class conflict),
     50–63; as classical critical race theorist,
     13–14, 41–43; on colonialism, 43–50;
     on colonial racism, 43–50; on
     communism, 50–63; and Cooper, Anna
     Julia, 72–76; critical race theory of,
     14–15, 39–43; critical social theory of,
     37–87; as critical sociologist, 65–70;
     critical theory of, 37–87; and critical
     white studies (discursive development of
     and conceptual contributions to critical
     white studies), 41–42; on decolonization,
     43–50; democratic socialism of, 49–63;
     and Douglass, Frederick, 38, 59, 64–65,
     77; feminism, contributions to, 63–78,
     84n27, 85–86n29; on gender justice,
     63–78; gender-sensitive critical
     conception of race and racism of, 42;
     Gender Studies, contributions to, 63–78;
     gift theory of, 17; and Harper, Frances
     Ellen Watkins, 70–72; humanism of,
     40–41, 61–62; on labor unions (white
     labor unions), 59–61; male-feminism of,
     63–78, 84n27, 84–85n28; on male
     supremacy, 64–70, 74–78; male-
     womanism of, 63–78; and Marxism
     (dialectical rapport and critical
     relationship with white/Eurocentric
     Marxism), 49–63; on McKay, Claude,
     56–59; on neocolonialism, 43–50; Pan-
     Africanism of, 43–50; on patriarchy,
     64–70, 74–78; as paradigm and point of
     departure for Africana critical theory, 2–3,
     6–7, 9, 38–39; on peasants, 67–68;
     philosophy of race of, 39–43; and
     postcolonialism, 43–50; on the
     proletariat (on the racialization and
     colonization of the proletariat), 49–63;
     on race, 39–43; as race/class theorist,
     42–43; on racial capitalism, 49–63; on
     racial colonialism, 43–50; on racism,
     39–43; radicalism/radical politics of,

37–87; radical/revolutionary humanism of, 40–41, 61–62; on Reconstruction (U.S.), 58–59; on the Russian Revolution, 51–54, 56–59; on self-defensive violence, 61, 79–80n9, 83–84n23, 87n37; on sexism, 63–78; sexism-critical conception of race and racism of, 42; on semi-colonialism, 44–45; socialism of, 50–63; on the Socialist Party U.S.A., 60–63; and sociology, 69–70; and sociology of race (discursive development of and conceptual contributions to sociology of race), 39–43; on violence, 50–52, 60–62, 73; on the white women's suffrage movement, 64; on whiteness, 41–42; on white supremacy, 41–42; on white workers, 49–63; womanism, contributions to, 63–78; on women (esp., black women) and American democracy, 67–69; on women's liberation, 63–78; on women's rights, 63–78; on women's right to vote, 63–65; Women's Studies, contributions to, 63–78; on the women's suffrage movement, 64

Dublé, Marie-Joseph (Josie Fanon), 166

Durkheim, Emile, 69

Ellington, Duke, ix, xvii

Egypt. *See* Kemet

Engels, Friedrich, 25, 52, 61, 97, 123–124, 139, 162n8, 175, 225n9, 244, 247, 251, 280n28, 281–282n31. *See also* Marx, Karl, and Marxism

epistemic exclusiveness, 4, 12, 20, 23–28

epistemic openness, 13, 16, 20–23, 25, 288, 296–300

ethnophilosophy, 146, 153, 163n23

etiquette of anti-ethics, 195

Eurocentrism, x–xii, 3–9, 11–14, 18–20, 23, 25–29, 50, 55, 58, 61–62, 68, 80n13, 92–93, 106, 108, 114, 116, 120, 124, 128, 130, 134, 137–138, 141–145, 149, 152, 157–158, 178, 181–185, 190, 195, 197, 201, 234–235, 246, 250, 253–254, 265–266, 270, 273, 286–293. *See also* anti-black racism and white supremacy

experiential openness, 271

existence, xiv, 1, 33–34n9, 35n11, 95–96, 108, 114–115, 124, 127, 136–137, 156, 158–159, 195, 197–199, 211, 216–217, 240, 243, 258–259, 263, 266, 268–269

existential phenomenology, 114, 117–118, 121, 141, 145. *See also* Sartre, Jean-Paul, and Gordon, Lewis R.

existentialism, 3, 25, 112, 122, 125, 143, 161, 162n7, 183, 194. *See also* Sartre, Jean-Paul, and Gordon, Lewis R.

Eze, Emmanuel, 45, 276n7

Fanon, Elénore Médélice, 166

Fanon, Félix Casimir, 166

Fanon, Frantz: and the Africana tradition of critical theory/Africana critical theory, 165–226; on Algerian muslimas, 210–216; and the Algerian Revolution, 166–167, 199–216; on Algerian women, 210–216; on alienation, 173–174, 178, 183, 193, 202, 207–209, 221; anti-colonialism of, 186–199, 216–224; anti-racism of, 195–197, 183, 198–199, 200–201, 209, 216–217, 222–223; as anti-sexist critical social theorist, 210–216; black feminism, contributions to, 210–216; and black Marxism (discursive development of and conceptual contributions to the black Marxist tradition), 175–186; black radicalism/black radical politics of, 175–199, 216–224; on the bourgeoisie (on the European capitalist and African racially colonized bourgeoisies), 171, 182, 185, 187–191, 195, 197, 206, 208, 222; on bourgeois decolonization, 190–191; on Capecia, Mayotte, 200, 204; on capitalism (esp., racial capitalism), 172–185, 187–191, 193, 198–199, 209–214; and Cesaire, Aime, 169–175; on class, 172–185, 187–191, 193, 198–199; on class struggle (class conflict), 172–185, 187–191, 193, 198–199, 209–214; on colonialism, 186–199, 216–224; on colonial racism, 186–199, 216–224; critical social theory of, 165–226; critical theory of, 165–226; de-Africanization, critique of, 182; death of, 168; on decolonization, 186–194; democratic socialism of, 175–186; on disalienation, 204, 207, 209, 221; education of, 166; Eurocentrism, conception and critique of, 178–179,

181–182; on "false" decolonization, 186–194; feminism, contributions to, 210–216; on French colonialism, 166, 209–216; and the Front de Libération Nationale (the FLN), 166–167; on gender justice, 210–216; Gender Studies, contributions to, 210–216; and the Gouvernement Provisoire de la République Algérienne (the GPRA), 167–168; humanism of, 168, 205, 208–209, 216–224; on intellectuals (esp., anti-colonial and racially colonized intellectuals), 177–182, 184, 190–191; on "lactification," 206–207; on love (on the racialization and colonization of love), 206–207, 217, 222; on the lumpenproletariat (esp., the African lumpenproletariat), 171, 197–198; male-feminism of, 210–216; on male supremacy, 210–216; male-womanism of, 210–216; on Manicheism (Manichaeism), 177, 199, 218, 221; and Marxism (dialectical rapport and critical relationship with white/Eurocentric Marxism), 175–186; masculinism of, 200–207; medical training of, 166; on the "mulatto," 206–207; nationalism of (Algerian and African nationalism of), 167–169, 174, 181, 183–184, 194, 216; on the "Negress," 206–207; on neocolonialism, 178–182, 187–188, 190, 193, 212; on "Niggerhood," 206–207; Pan-Africanism of, 167–168, 174, 181, 183, 194; patriarchal nationalism, critique of, 210–212, 214–216; on patriarchy, 210–216; on peasants, 171–172, 192; philosophical anthropology of, 216–224; on political education, 127, 170, 192–193; on the proletariat (esp., on the racialization and colonization of the proletariat), 171, 175–176, 179, 181, 185; as psychiatrist, 166–167; on racial capitalism, 172–185, 187–191, 193, 198–199, 209–214; on racial colonialism, 186–199, 216–224; on racism,167–168, 173, 177–179, 182–185, 190–191, 207–208, 221, 225n9; radicalism/radical politics of, 175–199, 216–224; on re-Africanization, 182, 189–191; radical/revolutionary humanism of, 168, 205, 208–209,

216–224; on revolutionary decolonization, 175–199, 216–224; on revolutionary violence, 173–174, 194–199; on sexism, 210–216; socialism of, 175–186; as soldier (in the French Army), 166; on the "Third World," 168, 184–185; on "true" decolonization, 186–194; on violence, 167–168, 173–174, 194–199, 216; on the white proletariat, 174, 181–182; on white supremacy, 206–216; on white workers, 174, 181–182; womanism, contributions to, 210–216; women's decolonization and women's liberation, contributions to, 210–216; Women's Studies, contributions to, 210–216
Fanon, Joby, 170–171, 173
Fanon, Josie, 166
First Congress of Negro-African Writers and Artists, 135
Foucault, Michel, 21, 31–32n3, 153
Frankfurt School, ix, xii, 1, 6–9, 14, 17, 25, 31–32n3, 37, 64, 68, 143, 225n9, 239, 243, 256, 259–260, 289–291, 293, 300–301n2. *See also* Adorno, Theodor; Benjamin, Walter; Fromm, Erich; Habermas, Jurgen; Horkheimer, Max; and Marcuse, Herbert
France, 125,133–134, 138, 140–141, 144–145, 149–150, 162n6, 166, 170, 178
Fraser, Nancy, 289–293, 301–302n3, 302–303n5
French Revolution (of 1789), 4, 97, 176
French colonialism, 125, 140–141, 144–145, 162n6, 166, 214
French National Assembly, 150
Freud, Sigmund, 17, 26, 200, 257
Fromm, Erich, ix, 17, 300–301n2

Garvey, Amy Ashwood, 99, 103
Garvey, Amy Jacques, 148
Garvey, Marcus, xi, 57, 148–149, 183, 304
Garveyism/Garvey Movement, 102
Gates, Henry Louis, 219–222
Geismar, Peter, 170
Gendzier, Irene, 113, 224n1, 225n4
Ghana, 45, 82, 90, 127, 167, 169, 180, 193, 223, 272
Gibson, Nigel, 132, 165, 175, 177, 181
Giddens, Anthony, 69

Gilkes, Cheryl Townsend, 38, 42, 65, 67–70
Glaberman, Martin, 91
Goethe, Johann Wolfgang von, 15, 123
Gordon, Lewis R., 2, 25–26, 36n14, 91, 177, 183, 193, 219, 280n28, 291
Gottlieb, Roger, 52, 281–282n31
Gramsci, Antonio, xii, 24, 36n13, 93, 146, 243, 259, 276n6, 278–279n21
Great Depression (U.S.), 59, 111
"Greco-European Rational Man" (Outlaw), 157–158
Greece/Greeks, 7
Griaule, Marcel, 133
Guevara, Che, 46, 241, 257, 278–279n21, 300–301n2
Guy-Sheftall, Beverly, 38, 64, 84n27
Gyekye, Kwame, 36n14, 154–155, 233, 272–273

Habermas, Jurgen, 11, 17, 31–32n3, 224, 234, 289–290, 293, 300–301n2
Haitian Revolution, 90, 97, 129
Hall, Stuart, xi, 91, 260–261
Hamer, Fannie Lou, xi
Hansen, Emmanuel, 168–169, 173, 183, 216, 223
Harlem Renaissance, 9, 28–29, 111–113, 144, 146, 148–152, 154, 161n1, 162n17, 163n19
Harper, Frances Ellen Watkins, 70–72, 74, 87n35, 87n37
Harper, Phillip Brian, 223
Harris, Leonard, 17, 278n19
Harrison, Hubert, 148, 279
Haywood, Harry, 279
Hegel, Georg Wilhelm Friedrich/Hegelianism, 17, 115–116, 139, 158–160, 162n12, 176, 200, 207–208, 279, 291
Hemphill, Essex, 223
Hobbes, Thomas, 71
Holden, Roberto, 167
hooks, bell, 69, 86n32, 185, 202–203, 205–206, 223, 244, 277n13, 291–292, 294, 302–303n6. *See also* black feminist theory
Horkheimer, Max, ix, 1, 6, 17, 242–244, 256, 258, 261–262, 266, 278n18, 300–301n2
Hountondji, Paulin, 36n14, 132–134, 138, 153

House Committee on Un-American Activities, 52
Huggins, Nathan, 146, 148–151
Hughes, Langston, 148, 151
humanism (Eurocentric and/or "racist" humanism), 14, 40, 113–114, 134, 140, 157–161, 191, 216–224, 241–258. *See also* revolutionary humanism

Idahosa, Paul, 91
Ignatiev, Oleg, 228
India/Indians (East Indians), 122–124, 126, 166, 221, 239
*International African Opinion*, 99
International African Service Bureau (IASB), 103
Irele, Abiola, 111–112

Jahn, Janheinz, 111, 146–147, 150, 162n11
James, C. L. R.: and the Africana tradition of critical theory/Africana critical theory, 89–110; on Africans as historical and cultural agents/actors, 90–94, 107; on African Americans, 93, 100–107; on African Americans as "potentially the most revolutionary section of the [U.S.] population," 100–107; on the American Revolution, 107; on anti-black racism, 95, 99–107; anti-colonialism of, 94–100; anti-racism of, 100–108; and black Marxism (discursive development of and conceptual contributions to the black Marxist tradition), 89–109; black nationalism of, 97–98, 102, 108; black radicalism/black radical politics of, 91–94, 100–108; on capitalism, 90, 93, 99–109; on the Civil War (U.S.), 101; on colonialism, 93, 95, 99, 104–109; on communism, 100–107; on the Communist Party, 101–107; critical race theory of, 100–109; on Du Bois, W. E. B., 53, 58; on economic exploitation, 100–101; Eurocentricism of, 92–93, 104, 109; on the Haitian Revolution, 90, 97–99; on imperialism, 92, 95–99, 105; on the "independent Negro movement" (on autonomous African American social and political movements), 102–103, 107; and the *International African Opinion*, 99; and the International African Service Bureau (IASB), 99–100;

on the Italian invasion of Ethiopia, 95, 99; on Leninism, 90, 93, 97–99; on L'Ouverture, Toussaint, 90, 97–99; and Marxism (dialectical rapport and critical relationship with white/Eurocentric Marxism), 89–110; and Marxist-Leninism, 90, 97–99; Pan-Africanism of, 91–92, 94–100, 102–104, 106–109, 110n3; and Pan-African Marxism (discursive development of and conceptual contributions to), 90–100; on the proletariat, 98–107; on racial capitalism, 90, 93, 99–109; on racial colonialism, 93, 95, 99, 104–109; on racism, 95, 99–100, 100–107; on revolution, 94–100; on socialism, 100–107; on the Socialist Party, 101–107; transdisciplinarity of, 91–92; and Trotskyism (Leon Trotsky), 93, 97–99; on white leaders, 101–102; on white organizations, 101–102
James, Joy, 38, 42, 63, 67, 73, 75, 84n27, 86n32, 185, 200–202, 291, 302–303n6, 303–304n8
JanMohamed, Abdul, 221
Jews, 60, 31n3
Jewish holocaust, 15, 126
Jinadu, L. Adele, 183
Jones, Claudia, xi, 148, 279

Kagame, Alexis, 133
Kant, Immanuel, 71, 200
Kearney, Belle, 64
Kelley, Robin D.G., 90–93, 96, 98, 185
Kellner, Douglas, 10–12, 31–32n3, 225n9, 226n11, 260–261
Kemet, 6
Kenyatta, Jomo, 99, 103
Kesteloot, Lilyan, 121, 149–151
King, Deborah, 69
King, Nicole, 91
Kiros, Teodros, 168

Lai, Walton Look, 91
Lazarus, Neil, 91, 187
Le Blanc, Paul, 91–92, 96
Lemert, Charles, 73
Lemons, Gary, 65, 84n27, 85–86n29
Lenin, Vladimir Ilyich, 57, 97–99, 105, 110n4, 175, 183, 226n11

Leninism, 62, 90, 93, 97, 110n4, 175, 193, 226n11, 240–242, 245–246, 257
Lewis, David Levering, 38, 58, 78n1
Locke, Alain, 152, 163n20, 302
Locke, John, 71
Loomba, Ania, 47–48
Lopes, Carlos, 259
Lorde, Audre, 174, 223, 290–292. *See also* black feminist theory
Lukacs, Georg, 243, 275, 278–279n21
Lumumba, Patrice, 167

Macey, David, 167
Makonnen, Ras, 99
Manicheism (Manicheanism), 137, 160, 177, 199, 218, 221
Marable, Manning, 55–56, 64, 81–82n19, 87n37, 143, 185, 291
Marcuse, Herbert, ix, xiii, 8, 32–33n6, 33–34n9, 46, 92, 129–130, 234, 269–270, 277n14, 278n20, 281–282n31, 282–283n35, 300–301n2
Marsh, James, 11
Martin, Tony, 174–176, 183–184
Martinique/Martiniquans, 120, 125, 128, 150, 166, 168, 169–171, 200
Marx, Karl, 14, 52, 60–61, 69, 81n18, 82n21, 98, 110n5, 122, 175–176, 183–184, 198, 256–257, 281–282n31, 291, 304–305n9
Marxism (white/Eurocentric Marxism), xii–xiv, 10–16, 24–28, 31–32n3, 33n7, 50–63, 80n14, 80n15, 81n18, 81–82n19, 82n21, 83n22, 89–110, 115–119, 121–127, 141–145, 175–186, 241–258, 270–273, 278–297n21, 281–282n31, 282–283n35, 286–293. *See also* Marx, Karl
Marxist-Leninism, 35–36n12, 62, 90, 97–98, 193, 241–242, 245–246, 257
Masolo, Dismas, 113–114, 128, 148–149, 163n26
Mbiti, John, 133
M'Boya, Tom, 167
McBride, Dwight, 223
McCarthy, Joseph, 52
McClendon, John, 35–36n12, 91
McCulloch, Jock, 228
McKay, Claude, 56–57, 82n20, 83–84n23, 148, 151
McKay, Nellie, 38, 64–65, 85–86n29

McLemee, Scott, 53, 91, 102
Melville, Herman, 90
Memmi, Albert, 219, 221
Mercer, Kobena, 223
Millette, James, 91
Mills, Charles W., 12–15, 104, 110n1, 226n15, 302n4
Moore, Richard B., 148, 279
Moses, Wilson Jeremiah, 54, 81–82n19
Mudimbe, Valentin Y., 155–156

Nardal, Paulette, 150
National American Woman Suffrage Association, 64
National Association of Colored Women (NACW), ix
National Association for the Advancement of Colored People (NAACP), 55
National Council of Negro Women (NCNW), ix
National Urban League, 102
Negritude: and African identity, 162n10; on "African reality," 162n18; and African philosophy, 111, 119–121, 127–131, 139, 151–161; and Africana philosophy, 121, 133, 146, 149, 152–161, 160, 163n20; and the Africana tradition of critical theory/Africana critical theory, 111–163; anti-black racism, conception and critique of, 111–121, 125–126, 131–134, 137–139, 143, 160–161, 163n28; anti-racism of, 111–121, 125–126, 131–134, 137–139, 143, 160–161, 163n28; as anti-racist racism, 115–119; anti-colonialism of,112, 116, 119–127, 134–135, 143, 145; and the black aesthetic, 112, 146; as black militant Marxism, 111–119; black radicalism/black radical politics of, 113, 117, 119, 121, 124, 130, 143, 145, 147–148, 150, 152, 157; and Breton, André, 112, 120; capitalism, conception and critique of, 111–112, 115–118, 122–123, 125–126, 128, 132, 134, 141–144, 161; colonialism, conception and critique of, 112–114, 116–127, 129, 131–135, 137–148, 150–151, 153–157, 160–161; and communism, 118, 125, 142; decolonization, discourse on, 119, 121, 126–128, 141, 143–144, 160–161;

and ethnophilosophy, 114, 127–146, 153, 163n23; and existentialism/existential phenomenology, 111–119, 122, 125, 143–144; and feminism, 159, 163n27; and French colonialism, conception and critique of, 162n6; guerilla intellectuals, Negritude theorists as, 112; and the Harlem Renaissance, 111–113, 144, 146, 148–152, 154, 161n1, 162n17; and humanism, 159–160, 163n28; and Locke, Alain, 151–152, 163n20; and Marxism, 111–119, 122, 124, 134, 139, 141–146, 160–162n7; and negation, 161n4; and "objective Negritude," 113–115; Pan-Africanism of, 112, 116–117, 134–135, 145–149; pre-colonial African traditions, intense emphasis on and promotion of, 120–131, 142, 150–156; racial capitalism, 112, 116–118, 122, 126, 132, 141–145; racial colonialism, 112, 114, 116–120, 122–127, 132–141, 143–147, 150–157, 160–161; racism, conception and critique of, 111–121, 125–126, 131–134, 137–139, 143, 160–161, 163n28; and radicalism (appropriation and synthesis of black and white radicalism), 112–113, 161n2; revolutionary Negritude, 116, 119–127, 162n7; and Sartre, Jean-Paul, 111–121, 125–126, 132–145, 158–161, 161n3, 162n11; and Sartrean Negritude, 111–121, 125–126, 132–145, 158–161, 161n3, 162n11; and socialism, 112, 124–125, 131–132, 141–146, 162n14; and "subjective Negritude," 113–115; and surrealism, 112, 115, 121–122, 125–126, 134, 143–144, 161; values of, 113, 121, 128–129, 132–133, 135, 137–138, 140–144, 149–154, 156–160; white supremacy, conception and critique of, 116, 118, 126, 130–131, 141, 143–144
New Negro Movement, 148, 151
new critical theory, x–xiv, 10–16, 31–32n3, 32n4, 33–34n9, 92, 109, 286–289, 296–300
Nielsen, Aldon, 91
Ngugi (Ngugi wa Thiongo), 172, 177, 223–224, 276n7

Nkrumah, Kwame, 46, 48, 80n10, 82n21, 90, 104, 142, 144, 167, 176, 179, 184–186, 193, 219, 224, 276n7, 227n12, 278–279n21, 285
Nyerere, Julius, 82, 104, 142, 144, 185

Olaniyan, Tejumola, 43, 79n7
"Orphée Noir" (Sartre), 111, 113–115, 118–120, 125, 134, 139
Outlaw, Lucius, 1, 7, 18–19, 34–35n10, 79n3, 156–158, 223, 243, 262, 276n8, 291, 300n1, 301–302n3, 303–304n8

Padmore, George, 12, 89, 99, 103, 279
Pan-Africanism, 25, 27, 30–31n2, 38, 43, 45, 47, 49–52, 73–74, 76–77, 80n11, 82n21, 90–109, 110n3, 112, 116–117, 121, 133–135, 141–148, 167–168, 174, 181, 183, 194, 270, 294, 298
Paris, Jeffrey, 10
Parry, Benita, 221
patriarchy, 4, 10, 16–17, 27–29, 42–44, 63–77, 159, 168, 182, 191, 199–216, 289–295
phenomenology, 3, 25, 114, 117–118, 121, 125, 138, 141, 145, 183, 194, 208–209, 265, 280n28. *See also* Sartre, Jean-Paul, and Gordon, Lewis R.
postcolonialism, xi, 10, 25, 43–50, 79n6, 187–194, 258–270
postmodernism, x–xi, 3–5, 11–12, 16–17, 20, 22, 24–25, 31–32n3, 35–36n11, 47–50, 68, 80n13, 181, 193–194, 219–221, 244, 250, 257, 260, 290
prophetic pragmatism, 25, 280–281n29. *See also* West, Cornel
Pyne-Timothy, Helen, 91

Rabbitt, Kara, 91
racial capitalism. *See* capitalism
racial colonialism, 15, 43–50, 95, 135, 143, 173, 176, 182, 187–188, 191, 194–199, 212, 251–252, 262–263, 270–272. *See also* colonialism
racism. *See* anti-black racism and white supremacy
radicalism. *See* radical politics
radical politics, xii–xiv, 10–16, 30n1, 50–63, 91–93, 99, 108–109, 112, 131, 144–145, 157, 161n2, 194, 232–233, 244–245, 259–262, 286–289, 296–300

Reed, Adolph L., 37, 50
Remond, Charles Lenox, 38, 77, 295
revolutionary humanism, 5, 29, 40, 117, 160–161, 163n28, 168, 191, 208–209, 216–224, 241–258, 268–272, 277n15, 278–279n21
Richards, Glen, 91
Robeson, Paul, 90
Robinson, Cedric, 12–13, 38, 62, 91, 104, 108, 185, 244, 291
Roderick, Rick, 91
Rodney, Walter, 143, 225n7, 277n13, 278–279n21, 281n30
Rorty, Richard, 130
Rosengarten, Frank, 91
Ross, Andrew, 91
Rousseau, Jean-Jacques, 71
Ruffin, Josephine St. Pierre, 70
Russia, 56–57, 60, 62, 81n18
Russian Revolution (of 1917), 51–52, 54, 56–57, 90, 97–98, 192, 226n11
Rustin, Bayard, xi, 83–84n23

Said, Edward, 13–14, 22, 219–220, 222, 279
Sartre, Jean Paul, 111–121, 125–126, 132–145, 158–161, 161n3, 162n11, 173, 185, 220–221, 225n3, 251, 255
Sartrean Negritude, 111–121, 125–126, 132–145, 158–161, 161n3, 162n11
Schoelcher, Victor, 119
Second International of the Labor Party, 142
Sekyi-Out, Ato, 113, 156, 165, 169, 183
Senghor, Leopold: on Africa, 132–141; on "the African," 136–137; on African epistemology, 134–138; on the African holocaust, 141; on African mysticism, 136; on African socialism ("the African mode of socialism"), 141–145; and the Africana tradition of critical theory/Africana critical theory, 132–145; Africanity, discursive development of and conceptual contributions to, 132–145; anti-African and anti-socialist socialism of, 145; on anti-black racism, 132–134, 137–138, 143, 160–161; anti-capitalism of, 141–145; anti-colonialism of, 132–145; anti-racism of, 132–145; on Arabism, 135; on Arabité, 135; on assimilation, 132–141; black radicalism/black radical politics of,

132–145; on "the backwardness of black Africa," 141, 145; on capitalism, 141–145; on the "Civilization of the Universal," 131, 135, 137, 141–142, 160, 162n16; on colonialism, 132–145; on communism, 141–145; "cultural mulattoism" of, 139–140; on cultural synthesis, 131, 139, 141, 145, 160; and de Chardin, Teilhard, 131, 133, 137–138, 145, 160; on decolonization, 141, 143–144, 160–161; and ethnophilosophy, 133, 138, 146, 153, 163n23; on "the European," 135–139; on European epistemology, 134–137; on France, 133–134, 138, 140–141, 144–145; on French colonialism, 140–141, 144–145; on French culture, 133–134, 138, 140; on the French language, 133–134, 140–141; on the Harlem Renaissance, 144, 146–152, 154, 161n1; on Marxism, 134, 139, 142–146; on negation (on Negritude as negation), 141, 158, 161n4; on "the Negro," 135–136, 139; on "Negro-African values," 135; Pan-Africanism of, 134–135, 141–145; on pre-colonial Africa, 132–141; on racial capitalism, 141–145; on racial colonialism, 132–145; racial essentialism of, 138–139, 141–143; and the recolonization (of Senegal/Africa), 141, 145; revised Negritude of, 142–144, 160–161; and Sartre, Jean-Paul, 132–141; on Senegal, 134, 140–141, 144; on socialism, 141–145; on symbiosis, 135–136, 141; on synthesis (cultural synthesis), 131, 139, 141, 145, 160; on values (on the values of Negritude and Africa/Africans), 132–133, 135, 137–138, 140–144, 149–154, 156–160
on white reason, 136–137
Serequeberhan, Tsenay, 21, 35–36n11, 46, 124, 173, 183, 195, 198–199, 263, 265, 268, 274n1, 277n15, 278–279n21, 293
sexism. *See* patriarchy
Shakespeare, William, 90
Sharpley-Whiting, Tracy Denean, 163n27, 202, 205, 226n12
Soviet Union, 62, 95. *See also* Russia
Soyinka, Wole, 155–156

Spivak, Gayatri Chakravorty, 221
Spleth, Janice, 134
St. Louis, Brett, 91
Stalin, Joseph, 95, 98
Stalinism, 105
standpoint theory, 65–66, 86n30, 204, 250
Stanley, Henry, 131
Stewart, Maria, 70–71
surrealism, 112, 115, 121–122, 125–126, 134, 143–144, 161

Taiwo, Olufemi, 227
Tempels, Placide, 133, 138, 146, 153–154
Terrell, Mary Church, 70
textual tokenism, xiii
Toomer, Jean, 148, 151
Toure, Sekou, 82, 104, 142, 144, 184–185, 278–279n21
transdisciplinary/transdisciplinarity, x-xiii, 2, 5, 18–21, 30–31n2, 41–43, 51, 90–94, 286–300. *See also* Africana critical theory and Africana Studies
traveling theory. *See* Edward Said
Truth, Sojourner, 70
Tubman, Harriet, 59
Turner, Lou, 222
Turner, Nat, 59

Underground Railroad, 59

Vaillant, Janet, 150–151
Vesey, Denmark, 59

Washington, Booker T., ix, 38, 59, 87n35, 304n9
Weber, Max, 17, 69
Wells, Ida B., 70, 87n36
West, Cornel, 3, 19–20, 185, 236, 241, 277n11, 278n17, 280–281n29, 297, 204–205n9
white supremacy, 2–8, 12–18, 22–23, 26, 33n8, 34–35n10, 39–43, 49–50, 52, 55, 57, 59–61, 64, 75–76, 83–84n23, 95, 100–107, 114–118, 125–127, 131–132, 134, 137–141, 143–144, 159, 173–174, 182–188, 199, 208–216, 229, 261, 265–266, 289–293, 296–300. *See also* anti-black racism
West Indies/West Indians. *See* Caribbean
Wilkerson, William, 10

Williams, Eric E., 14, 52, 89, 108, 143,
    278–279n21
Wiredu, Kwasi, 36n14, 82n21, 153–155,
    163n26, 180–181, 184, 272–273
women's decolonization. *See* women's
    liberation
women's liberation, 63–77, 199–216,
    289–296
Worcester, Kent, 91
World War I, 51, 83, 107, 304–305n9

World War II, 15, 93, 107, 134, 142, 237,
    304–305n9
Wright, Richard, 12, 90, 105,
    278–279n21
Wynter, Sylvia, 91

X, Malcolm (El-Hajj Malik El-Shabazz), xi,
    xviii, 83, 126, 185, 194, 301

Zahar, Renate, 183, 193

# About the Author

REILAND RABAKA is an Associate Professor of Africana Studies in the Department of Ethnic Studies at the University of Colorado at Boulder, where he is also an Affiliate Professor of Women and Gender Studies and a Research Fellow at the Center for Studies of Ethnicity and Race in America (CSERA). His ongoing research interests include Africana philosophy, critical race theory, feminist theory, womanist theory, postcolonial theory, radical politics, critical social theory, critical pedagogy, and liberation theology. Included among his regular teaching topics are Black Abolitionism, the Black Women's Club Movement, the New Negro Movement, the Harlem Renaissance, Pan-Africanism, Negritude, Black Nationalism, Black Marxism, the Civil Rights Movement, the Black Power Movement, the Black Women's Liberation Movement, Black Liberation Theology, and Hip Hop Studies. Employing a critical pedagogical perspective, his courses intensely emphasize and encourage students to become active agents in emancipatory education and radical social transformation, as well as conscious and committed participants in the dialectical deconstruction, reconstruction, and dissemination of classical and contemporary schools of thought and systems of knowledge. His research has been published in *Journal of African American Studies*, *Journal of Black Studies*, *Western Journal of Black Studies*, *Africana Studies Annual Review*, *Africalogical Perspectives*, *Handbook of Black Studies*, *Ethnic Studies Review*, *Jouvert: A Journal of Postcolonial Studies*, and *The Malcolm X Critical Reader*, among others. Professor Rabaka is the author of *W. E. B. Du Bois and the Problems of the Twenty-First Century* and *Du Bois's Dialectics: Black Radical Politics and the Reconstruction of Critical Social Theory*, both published by Lexington Books. His first book, *Du Bois and the Problems of the Twenty-First Century*, won the W. E. B. Du Bois-Anna Julia Cooper Award, which was conferred by the National Council for Black Studies (NCBS), the premier professional organization for Africana Studies scholars. He has delivered lectures nationally and internationally, and has been the recipient of numerous community service citations, teaching awards, and research fellowships.

Printed in the USA
CPSIA information can be obtained
at www.ICGtesting.com
CBHW081024230824
13615CB00006BA/235

9 780739 128862